The Cosmopolitanism Reader

The Cosmopolitanism Reader

Edited by
Garrett Wallace Brown and David Held

polity

First published in 2010 by Polity Press
Reprinted 2012, 2013, 2014, 2015 (twice), 2017

Polity Press
65 Bridge Street
Cambridge CB2 1UR, UK

Polity Press
350 Main Street
Malden, MA 02148, USA

ISBN-13: 978-0-7456-4871-2
ISBN-13: 978-0-7456-4872-9(pb)

A catalogue record for this book is available from the British Library.

Typeset in 10 on 12 pt Swift
by Toppan Best-set Premedia Limited
Printed and bound by CPI Group (UK) Ltd, Croydon, CR0 4YY

The publisher has used its best endeavours to ensure that the URLs for external websites referred to in this book are correct and active at the time of going to press. However, the publisher has no responsibility for the websites and can make no guarantee that a site will remain live or that the content is or will remain appropriate.

For further information on Polity, visit our website: www.politybooks.com

Contents

Acknowledgements

Trying to cover the broad scope and application of cosmopolitan thought in one volume is not easy. This is because cosmopolitanism, like any political theory, has many interdisciplinary facets and sophisticated idiosyncrasies. To help us in our endeavor to provide the most comprehensive Reader possible, we have sought the advice and expertise of several colleagues, friends and fellow cosmopolitans. Because of their help, we owe considerable appreciation to Daniele Archibugi, Mathias Koenig-Archibugi, Gideon Baker, Richard Beardsworth, Ali Bohm, James Brassett, John Charvet, Luis Cabrera, Robert Fine, Antonio Franceschet, Patrick Hayden, Megan Kime, Raffaele Marchetti, David Miller, Martha Nussbaum, Angie Pepper, Richard Shapcott and William Smith for their useful comments and suggestions. In addition, we are extremely grateful to Ryan Wilber who went above and beyond the call of duty in organizing the material for editing this volume and to Rachel Naish for her work on the project. Lastly, we would like to thank Sarah Lambert and the editorial, marketing and production team at Polity Press for their exceptional help and patience throughout.

We are grateful to the following for permission to reproduce copyright material:
    Cambridge University Press and Professor Reiss, for material from "Idea of a Universal History with a Cosmopolitan Purpose" by Immanuel Kant in *Kant's Political Writings*, by Hans Reiss, 1970, published by Cambridge University Press reproduced with permission; The MIT Press for 27 page extract from "Kant and Cosmopolitanism" by Martha Nussbaum published in *Perpetual Peace: Essays on Kant's Cosmopolitan Ideal* edited by James Bohman and Matthias Lutz-Bachmann, pp. 25–51, plus references, copyright © 1997, Massachusetts Institute of Technology, by permission of The MIT Press, and Martha Nussbaum; Edinburgh University Press for material from *Grounding Cosmopolitanism: From Kant to the idea of a Cosmopolitan Constitution* by Garrett Wallace Brown, 2009, copyright © Edinburgh University Press, www.euppublishing.com; Polity Press and Stanford University Press for material from "A Kantian Approach to Transnational Justice" by Onora O'Neill from *Political Theory Today* by David Held copyright © 1991 David Held, by permission of Polity Press, Onora O'Neill and Stanford University; Wiley-Blackwell for material abridged from "Justice and International Relations" by Charles Beitz published in *Philosophy and Public Affairs Journal*, Vol 4(4), Summer 1975, pp. 360–389, copyright © 1975 Wiley-Blackwell; Princeton University Press for material abridged from "International Society from A Cosmopolitan Perspective" by Brian Barry in *International Society: Diverse Ethical Perspectives* edited by

David Mapel and Terry Nardin, 1998, pp. 144–161, copyright © 1998 Princeton University Press. Reprinted by permission of Princeton University Press; University of Chicago Press for material abridged from "Cosmopolitanism and Sovereignty," by Thomas W. Pogge from *Ethics* 103(1) 1992, pp. 48–75, copyright © 1992, The University of Chicago Press, reproduced with permission of University of Chicago Press and Thomas Pogge; Wiley-Blackwell for material abridged from "International Distributive Justice: A Review" by Simon Caney, published in *Political Studies Journal*, Vol 49, 2001, pp. 974–989, copyright © 2001 Wiley-Blackwell; Beacon Press for material from "Patriotism and Cosmopolitanism", published in *For Love of Country* by Martha C. Nussbaum, copyright © 1996 Martha C. Nussbaum and Joshua Cohen. Reprinted by permission of Beacon Press, Boston and Martha C. Nussbaum; Wiley-Blackwell for material abridged from "What is Cosmopolitan?" by Jeremy Waldron, published in *Journal of Political Philosophy*, Vol 8(2), 1999, pp. 227–243, copyright © 1999 Wiley-Blackwell; Cambridge University Press for material from "Nationalism and Cosmopolitanism" in *Justice without Borders: Cosmopolitanism, Nationalism, and Patriotism* by Kok-Chor Tan, copyright © Kok-Chor Tan, 2004, published by Cambridge University Press reproduced with permission of Cambridge University Press and Kok-Chor Tan; Wiley-Blackwell for material abridged from "Distributive Justice and the State" by Simon Caney, published in *Political Studies Journal*, Vol 56(3), 2008, pp. 487–514, copyright © 2008 Wiley-Blackwell; Polity Press for material abridged from "The Cosmopolitan Manifesto" in *World Risk Society* by Ulrich Beck, 1999, pp. 1–18. Reproduced by permission of Polity Press; Cambridge University Press for material from "Principles of Cosmopolitan Order" in *The Political Philosophy of Cosmopolitanism* by David Held, edited by G. Brock and H. Brighouse, copyright © G. Brock and H. Brighouse 2005, published by Cambridge University Press and reproduced with permission; Wiley-Blackwell for material abridged from "Moving Cosmopolitan Legal Theory to Legal Practice: Models of Cosmopolitan Law" by Garrett Wallace Brown, published in *Legal Studies Journal*, Vol 28(3), 2008, pp. 430–451 copyright © 2008 Garrett Wallace Brown; Polity Press for material abridged from "A Political Constitution for the Pluralist World Society" in *Between Naturalism & Religion: Philosophical Essays* by Jurgen Habermas, 2008, pp. 312–352. Reproduced by permission of Polity Press; Polity Press for material abridged from "Reframing Global Governance: Apocalypse soon or reform!" in *Globalization Theory: Approaches and Controversies* by David Held and A. McGrew, 2007, pp. 240–257. Reproduced by permission of Polity Press; Princeton University Press for material abridged from 'The Architecture of Cosmopolitan Democracy' in *The Global Commonwealth of Citizens: Toward Cosmopolitan Democracy* by Daniele Archibugi, 2008, pp. 86–122, copyright © 2008 Princeton University Press. Reprinted by permission of Princeton University Press; Polity Press and Stanford University Press for material from *New and Old Wars: Organized Violence in a Global Era*, 2/ed by Mary Kaldor, copyright © 1991, 2006 Mary Kaldor, reproduced with permission from Polity Press and Stanford University Press; Ashgate Publishing Ltd for material abridged from "The Environment, Global Justice and World Environment Citizenship" published in *Cosmopolitan Global Politics: The Pursuit of a Humane World Order* by Patrick Hayden, copyright © 2005 Ashgate; Oxford University Press for material abridged from "Cosmopolitanism" in *National Responsibilities and Global Justice* by David Miller, 2007, pp. 23–50 copyright © Oxford University Press; Wiley-Blackwell for material abridged from "The Problem of Global Justice" by Thomas Nagel published in *Philosophy and Public Affairs Journal*, Vol 33(2), 2005, pp. 114–147, copyright © 2005 Wiley-Blackwell; Cengage and Editions Galilée for material from *On Cosmopolitanism and Forgiveness* by Jacques Derrida 2001, copyright ©

Cengage, reproduced with permission from Cengage and Editions Galilée; Cambridge University Press for material from "Can International Institutions be Democratic? A Skeptic's View" by Robert Dahl, copyright © Cambridge University Press, 1999, reproduced with permission of Cambridge University Press and Robert Dahl; and Cambridge University Press for material from "Citizenship in an Era of Globalization" by Will Kymlicka in *Democracy's Edges (Contemporary Political Theory)* edited by I. Shapiro and C. Hacker-Cordon, copyright © Cambridge University Press, 1999, reproduced with permission of Cambridge University Press and Will Kymlicka.

Every effort has been made to trace all copyright holders, but if any have been inadvertently overlooked the publisher will be pleased to include any necessary credits in any subsequent reprint or edition.

Editors' Introduction
Garrett Wallace Brown and David Held

We often hear the saying that "the world is getting smaller" or that "it's a small world." These phrases evoke the idea that events, peoples, climates, economic systems, and cultural lifeworlds in one part of the world have bearing, meaning, and impact on places and people in other parts of the world. In addition, these sayings are often used to add emphasis to global interconnections and to denote a limited degree of separation between the peoples of the world. In many ways, these common sayings represent aspects usually associated with the term *globalization*, for they capture a growing perception that the world has become increasingly interconnected (in both positive and negative ways) and that there are shrinking distances between most facets of human coexistence.

Although there remains debate regarding the scope, meaning, and importance of globalization, recent events such as the global financial meltdown, the spread of infectious diseases, and the threats of climate change highlight the fact that events in one part of the world have significant widespread impact. Because of the growing empirical reality that "the world is getting smaller," it is now common for politicians, academics, and ordinary people to engage in discussions about what this increasing interconnection means to our everyday lives, as well as to the lives of others. Because of this, we have started to ask ourselves about what normative principles should be adopted to help guide future cohabitation on our planet. It is because of this increased human interconnection and the moral questions that this enjoins that cosmopolitanism as a global political theory has found renewed enthusiasm as well as reinvigorated practical relevance.

In its most basic form, cosmopolitanism maintains that there are moral obligations owed to all human beings based solely on our humanity alone, without reference to race, gender, nationality, ethnicity, culture, religion, political affiliation, state citizenship, or other communal particularities. In contrast to traditional paradigms in International Relations, which have usually focused on states, the maximization of state interest, nationality, or securing power balances between states, cosmopolitanism, as a political theory, is based on "the acknowledgement of some notion of common humanity that translates ethically into an idea of shared or common moral duties toward others by virtue of this humanity."[1] From this basic ethical orientation, cosmopolitanism as a political theory generally posits three corresponding moral and normative commitments. First, cosmopolitans believe that the primary units of moral concern are individual human beings, not states or other forms of communitarian or political association. Although this does not rule out localized obligations, or render states "meaningless," cosmopolitanism does insist that there are universal commitments to respect the moral worth of individuals everywhere. Second, cosmopolitans maintain that this moral concern for individuals should be equally applied, where "the status of ultimate concern attaches to every living human equally."[2] As many of the chapters in this Reader argue, a cosmopolitan commitment to the individual translates into an impartial commitment that can respect all human beings equally, despite where one is born and regardless of what communal association that person happens to be placed in. Third, as the etymology of the word suggests, cosmopolitanism is universal in its scope, maintaining that all humans are equal in their moral standing and that this moral standing applies to everyone everywhere, *as if we are* all citizens of the world. As is developed in Thomas Pogge's chapter "Cosmopolitanism and Sovereignty," what distinguishes a cosmopolitan position from traditional state-centric models is that it advocates the liberal moral features of individualism, egalitarianism, and universalism beyond the borders of the state *while also* insisting that these moral features should act as key regulative principles in reforming global institutional structures.

In this regard, cosmopolitanism is both a moral and a political project and we can understand that it contains two adjoined, yet unique, elements when examining questions of universal human worth, global cohabitation, and what duties we have to those beyond our borders. As Pogge's typology suggests, the first element pertains largely to examining what moral principles underwrite a cosmopolitan condition. In this respect, most cosmopolitan thinking, if not all, has a distinctive moral and normative component, which explores and defends the cosmopolitan idea that "every human being has a global stature as the ultimate unit of moral concern."[3] As several chapters in this Reader highlight, *moral cosmopolitanism* often translates into corresponding duties of global justice, the protection of universal human rights, and reforming unjust international systems so that they are in line with cosmopolitan moral principles. This moral dimension can be related to, but can also be distinct from, what Charles Beitz has described as *institutional cosmopolitanism*, which focuses primarily on examining what institutional designs might best implement the normative considerations of its moral counterpart. As Beitz suggests, institutional cosmopolitanism "holds that the world's political structure should be reshaped so that states and other political units are brought under the authority of supranational agencies of some kind."[4] In most cases, an institutional focus is occupied with questions about how cosmopolitan principles can be structured in practice or with how current global systems are failing the ethical concerns of moral cosmopolitanism.

Although it is hard to imagine institutional arguments devoid of any moral cosmopolitan foundation, the reasoning for establishing supranational institutions can have both a moral dimension (it is the right thing to do) and a practical dimension (a response to a pressing global collective action problem), and it is possible to draw some separation between them. As Brian Barry points out in his chapter "International Society from a Cosmopolitan Perspective," "there is no automatic move from ethical premises to any particular conclusion about the ideal world constitution" and it is tenable to hold a moral position without also knowing exactly how it could be implemented institutionally.[5] This division between what we morally *ought to do* and *how we might do it* is important to note, for one critique of cosmopolitanism is that it is empirically unfeasible. As will be presented in Section VI, most cosmopolitan sceptics believe cosmopolitanism to be institutionally unfeasible (see Nagel) and politically impractical (see Dahl), as well as damaging to a plurality of cultural values (see Miller and Kymlicka).

It is for this reason that a distinction between moral and institutional cosmopolitanism becomes important, for most cosmopolitans would suggest that just because something is difficult and improbable under current circumstances does not also mean that it is impossible, or, more importantly, that it is not something we ought morally to do. Furthermore, as many of the chapters in Sections IV and V of this Reader argue, there exists compelling evidence to suggest that the world has already become and is slowly becoming more cosmopolitan, in both moral and institutional terms.

As was suggested at the beginning, it is because cosmopolitanism operates at the global level, both morally and institutionally, beyond traditional state-centric models, that it has enjoyed renewed enthusiasm and applied relevance. This is due to the fact there is now growing empirical evidence that the "world is getting smaller" and that the forces of globalization have increasing impact upon our *shared* human existence. As is argued in David Held's "Reframing Global Governance: Apocalypse Soon or Reform!," the forces of globalization have made our lives inextricably interconnected and the world is increasingly faced with pressing collective action problems such as climate change, disease, abject poverty, terrorism, genocide, nuclear proliferation, and financial crisis, to name but a few. As Ulrich Beck suggests in his chapter "The Cosmopolitan Manifesto," an awareness of these common global risks helps to cultivate a universal belief in a globally shared collective future and that this growing perception of a "world risk society" not only makes a cosmopolitan future possible, but also makes it politically and sociologically necessary. As a result, where it was once reasonable to see the earth as made up of fairly isolated communities 100 years ago, it is becoming increasingly impossible to hold such a view. For as everyday events often indicate, humans are now increasingly locked into "overlapping communities of fate" whereby events in one part of the world can have profound impact on the lives of those everywhere.[6] Whereas a retreat into self-determined Westphalian sovereignty was an option for people and states in the past, cosmopolitans argue that this is no longer an option for the future and that globalization in some form will continue to be an active force in our collective lives. It is because of this empirical condition that most cosmopolitan thought, if not all, is premised on the idea that the world is an interconnected and interdependent community and that our moral responsibility is therefore, correspondingly, a globalized and universal concern – a concern "whose primary allegiance is to the community of human beings in the entire world."[7]

The origins of contemporary cosmopolitan thought

Despite the fact that the forces of globalization have given contemporary relevance to cosmopolitanism, the idea that we have universal duties to all human beings is not a particularly new way of thinking. Although the first section of this Reader begins with Immanuel Kant and three additional chapters discussing his impact and continued relevance in contemporary cosmopolitan thinking, as Martha Nussbaum's chapter on Kant and the Stoic tradition clearly illustrates, Kant was not the first scholar to champion cosmopolitan ideas. This is because cosmopolitanism enjoys a long history and we can locate various approximations of cosmopolitan thought in early monotheistic thinking, such as those espoused by the Egyptian Anhnaton (1526 BC). It is Anhnaton who may have first asserted that all human beings have moral duties to one another beyond their immediate communal spheres.[8] Furthermore, we can locate various iterations of cosmopolitan thought in the varied and often incomplete ancient works of several Phaeacians, Hebrews, Chinese, Ethiopians, Assyrians, and Persians.[9] Nevertheless, most contemporary cosmopolitans have assigned the origins of cosmopolitan thought to ancient Greece and to the statements of the Cynic Diogenes of Sinope (400–323 BC). This is because Diogenes is reputed for claiming that he was a "citizen of the world" when responding to questions regarding his place of origin.[10] By insisting that he was a universal citizen (*kosmopolites*), Diogenes was suggesting that "the morally good are all friends," that we are all part of a fraternity of mankind and that as a member of the *cosmos* he could not be defined merely by his city-state affiliation.[11] As a consequence, Diogenes held that all human beings are owed certain positive duties of hospitality and brotherly love, *as if they were* common citizens.[12]

It is from Diogenes and the philosophy of the Cynics that many early philosophers found cosmopolitan inspiration. These thinkers include Crate of Thebes (365–285 BC), Chrysippus (280–207 BC), and, most importantly, the founder of Stoicism, Zeno of Citium (334–262 BC). As is often claimed, the Cynics were a great influence on Zeno (he was a student of Crate, for example) and Zeno in return can be seen to have had significant influence on the cosmopolitan thought of many Roman Stoics.[13] Although there is considerable disagreement as to the exact meaning of Zeno's prescription for a universal "city under one law,"[14] it is not unreasonable to argue that Zeno's thought represents a more positive version of Diogenes' universal citizenship. Certainly, he has been interpreted in this fashion by many influential Roman Stoics. As is often related, Zeno held that "we should regard all men as fellow-citizens and local residents, and there should be one way of life and order, like that of a herd grazing together and nurtured by a common law."[15] From this quote and others like it, we can see Zeno's metaphorical insistence on establishing a humanist brotherhood of all mankind. In addition, we can see Zeno's insistence on maintaining a social ethic that can be universally applied and that is in line with common laws of nature. Lastly, and as many Roman Stoics were inspired to believe, one could interpret Zeno as calling for a cosmopolitan utopia that reached beyond the confines of traditional political association – that is, a cosmopolitan utopia that required not only a new sense of cosmopolitan citizenship and common brotherly love, but a world-wide political order that could embrace all of humanity under a form of universal law.

The cosmopolitan legacy of Zeno and the Greek Cynics becomes more enunciated in the works of Marcus Cicero (106–43 BC), Seneca (4 BC – AD 65) and Marcus Aurelius (AD 121–80). Although a more detailed discussion of Stoic cosmopolitanism and its influence on Kant is provided in Nussbaum's chapter "Kant and Cosmopolitanism," it is beneficial to outline briefly some general Stoic themes. This is because it is useful to have a sense of chronological development as well as to highlight key philosophical themes found throughout classical cosmopolitanism. However, before doing so, it is important to recognize that there is no easy way of generalizing Stoicism and the various nuances involved with its influence on cosmopolitan thought. This is because the Greco-Roman Stoic tradition spans almost half a millennium, contains sophisticated theoretical distinctions between its thinkers, and presents us with several challenging links and disconnects in the history of political thought. With this in mind, and for the purpose of efficient summarization, we will posit Stoic cosmopolitanism as maintaining roughly three general and interrelated themes.

First, many Stoics believed that human beings share a similar capacity for reason and that this universal trait bestowed a moral worth upon any individual who wished to exercise it. In addition, this common capacity for reason establishes a basic foundation for human fraternity and universal community. As with Zeno, many Stoics believed that human reason separated man from beast, and from this common trait a sense of brotherly love and universal commitment could be generated. As exemplified by Cicero, the "bond of connection is reason and speech, which . . . associate men together and unite them into a sort of natural fraternity."[16] Because of this natural fraternity and the rational bond between human beings, we share a similar fate and thus also share the potential for a common political community. As Aurelius wrote:

> If the intellectual capacity is common to us all, common too is the reason, which makes us rational creatures. If so, that reason is common which tells us to do or not to do. If so, law is common. If so, we are citizens. If so, we are fellow members of an organized community. If so, the universe is as it were a state – of what other single polity can the whole race of mankind be said to be fellow members? And from it, this common state, we get the intellectual, the rational, and the legal instinct, or whence do we get them?[17]

As this quote illustrates, for the Stoics, human reason and our shared capacity for reason tie the human race together as members of the same species, and from this it generates an interrelated moral and political community. As a result of this belief, many Stoics shared a second theme. Influenced largely by the Cynics, most Stoics believed that all humans inhabit two communities, one that is local and determined by place of birth and one that represents a community of humankind. As Seneca suggests, the community of humankind is "truly great and truly common," and because of this we should "measure the boundaries of our nation by the sun."[18] Despite a common accusation made against cosmopolitanism that it ignores the value of local obligation and community (see Miller and Kymlicka), this accusation is simply not reflective of most cosmopolitan arguments or of the sentiments expressed here by Seneca. Similar to Seneca, many contemporary cosmopolitans argue that local communities can have profound importance in our lives and should be understood as being meaningful sources for our personal and communal identities (see Waldron). Nevertheless, where cosmopolitanism differs from a communitarian approach, and where the thoughts of Seneca can be seen to underwrite contemporary cosmopolitanism, is in the recognition that these local communities are not the only important communities in which human beings belong (see Held, "Principles"). As many cosmopolitans suggest, where one is born is an event of happenstance and because of this fact, from a moral point of view, there is no reason why one particular community has more intrinsic moral value than another (see Caney, "Global Distributive Justice and the State"). In other words, and as Seneca points out, we may be born into a society by "accident of birth" and we will inevitably feel a sense of communal bond with that society.[19] However, we are also born into the human species, and because we share common moral and political traits as a species, we also share duties and obligations to other human beings as co-members of an earthly *cosmos*.

From this, a third theme can be found within the Stoic tradition, and it relates to ideas about natural law, teleological purpose, and the belief that human reason should be in harmony with natural universal law. As is often noted, many Stoics maintained that there are discoverable laws of nature and that, through human reason, we can locate and comply with these laws. The implication is that if there are universal laws of nature and if we can understand these axioms through the universal capacity for reason, then it is also possible to generate universal human laws that are in harmony with these natural laws. As Cicero developed in *De republica*: "True law is right reason in agreement with nature; it is of universal application, unchanging and everlasting; it summons to duty by its commands, and adverts wrongdoing by its prohibitions . . . We cannot be freed from its obligations by senate or people, and we need not look outside ourselves for an expounder or interpreter of it."[20]

Cicero further expands the need for harmonious balance in the political realm by suggesting that human laws "should be valid for all subjects" and, if properly constituted, these laws of reason can "make way for the law of the world society."[21] In this regard, and in connection to other Stoic themes, we can understand Stoic cosmopolitanism as embodying a philosophical outlook that sought to unify individuals in a moral and political community that encompasses all of humanity.

Although the Christianization of the Roman Empire may have marked an end to the Stoic tradition, Stoic influence did not disappear in the philosophical writings of Christianity. This is because we are able to see strong traces of Stoic cosmopolitanism throughout Judeo-Christian thought. This is especially the case in the philosophies of St. Augustine (354–430), Thomas Aquinas (1225–74), and Martin Luther (1483–1546), who adapted and fused aspects of Stoic philosophical language into their own seminal texts. In particular, we can see in these Christian thinkers similar themes about universal human dignity, peaceful human coexistence, and natural law. Nevertheless, arguably the most influential cosmopolitan texts during the period between the late Stoa and the Enlightenment were the works associated with the School of Salamanca and the cosmopolitan theories generated by the Neo-Thomist thinkers of Bartolome de las Casas (1484–1566), Francisco de Vitoria (1492–1546), and Francisco Suarez (1548–1617). In direct response to the "civilizing missions" of empire and the discovery of the New World, these scholars sought to expand Judeo-Christian arguments of natural law to include the Native Americans and to create legal and religious duties to respect them as having equal natural rights. In a similar language to the Stoics, las Casas argues that "all the peoples of the world are human and there is only one definition of all humans and of each one, that is that they are rational . . . and thus all the races of humankind are one."[22] This statement, along with many similar others, was in response to what many Neo-Thomist thinkers saw as the "wholesale slaughter" of the American Indians, which, for them, amounted to the violation of a universal natural right bestowed upon all humans by God.[23] For las Casas, as well as for other scholars of the School of Salamanca, any human law that permits the violation of natural right is in violation of universal natural law and thus represents a contravention of the will of God. As las Casas claims, the native Indians are not only "men like us," but also endowed with basic natural rights as "God's rational creatures."[24] In this manner, these scholars were making bold cosmopolitan claims: that natural rights are held by every human being regardless of religious belief or place of birth, and that these basic natural rights were equal to those of the "civilized people" of Europe and thus required universal respect.

Although the foundations for these natural rights were religiously inspired, there are obvious traces of traditional Stoic cosmopolitanism in the works of las Casas and other Neo-Thomist scholars. Like the Stoics before him, las Casas is advocating a universal respect for all human beings beyond one's immediate communal and religious borders, and in turn insisting that there are corresponding moral and legal obligations. We can see this idea further expressed in terms of international legal obligation by Vitoria. For it is Vitoria who, in a fashion similar to Cicero, claimed that "the whole world, which in a sense is a commonwealth, has the power to enact laws which are just and convenient to all men: and these make up the law of nations . . . [and] no kingdom may choose to ignore this law of nations, because it has the sanction of the whole world."[25] As with the Stoics, this statement reflects several foundational features found in classical cosmopolitan thought. First, humans are all rational creatures with the capacity for reason, and through this reason we can discover the universal laws of nature. Second, the legitimacy of human law depends on its consanguinity with the axioms of these universal laws. Third, as a result of our universal capacity for reason, humans are all members of the same species, and all individuals and nations share a similar human fate. Fourth, it is from this similar fate as rational beings that we can establish a political community that is bound by universal laws of reason that are "convenient to all men." As is disclosed in Neo-Thomist thought, and specifically in Vitoria, this seems to translate into a demand for a sense of universal justice beyond borders and a demand that "international law must be a consistent whole based on principles and reasoning that can be shared by all involved parties."[26] Consequently, it is important to highlight the stress placed upon universal right and mutual consensus within this vein of classical cosmopolitanism, for, as will become evident throughout the works contained in this volume, the establishment of cosmopolitan justice is still very much a preoccupying topic in contemporary cosmopolitan thought.

Furthermore, it is important to highlight these themes of universal right and mutual consensus because they illustrate crucial transitions from classical cosmopolitanism to the more modern works of the Enlightenment. As is widely recognized, Stoic and Thomist cosmopolitanism were sources of considerable inspiration for several key Enlightenment philosophers, such as Hugo Grotius (1583–1645), John Locke (1632–1704), F. M. A. Voltaire (1694–1778), Denis Diderot (1713–84), Immanuel Kant (1724–1804), Thomas Paine (1734–1809), and Thomas Jefferson (1743–1826). In addition, the Stoic and Thomist ideas of universal human reason, equal human worth, and the demands of universal justice can be seen as playing pivotal roles in the development of cosmopolitan thought during the Enlightenment.[27] For example, the absorption of classical cosmopolitan ideas can be evidenced in the writings of Locke, who claimed "the state of nature has a law of nature to govern it, which obliges everyone: and reason, which is that law, teaches all mankind, who will but consult it, that being all equal and independent, no one ought to harm another in his life, health, liberty and possessions."[28] Moreover, this basic cosmopolitan sentiment is expressed as a foundation of enlightened emancipation and revolution in the thought of Paine, who wrote that the "rights of man" required a "great nation . . . which extends and promotes the principles of universal society; whose mind rises above the atmosphere of local thoughts, and considers mankind, of whatever nation or profession they may be, as the work of one creator."[29] Finally, other expressions of cosmopolitanism can be found in Diderot's Stoic-inspired insistence that he was a member of "the great city of the world,"[30] and in Voltaire's musings about a cosmopolitan republic of mankind.[31] In this regard, like the cosmopolitans before them, these Enlightenment thinkers sought to further a cosmopolitan ethic in which all human beings are treated as if they are common citizens of the world.

However, the Enlightenment's strongest link to contemporary cosmopolitanism comes arguably from the political philosophy of Immanuel Kant. This is because Kant offered a more sophisticated and practically oriented form of cosmopolitanism, which reached far beyond the basic ethical, religious, and legal ideas of his cosmopolitan predecessors. In its most basic form, Kant's cosmopolitanism is concerned with delineating the moral, legal, and political conditions required to establish a condition of cosmopolitan justice. In a similar fashion to most contemporary cosmopolitans, Kant believed that the world had become increasingly interconnected, to the point where human contact is unavoidable, and to such an extent that "a violation of rights in one part of the world is felt everywhere."[32] Because of the profound empirical and moral consequences of global interdependency, and the problems this condition creates for securing mutual *public right*, Kant proposed that "the greatest problem for the human species . . . is that of attaining a civil society, which can administer justice universally."[33] Although there were contemporaneous arguments which suggested that the Treaty of Westphalia (1648) solidified a peaceful system of independent sovereign nation-states, Kant firmly believed that, without an overarching commitment to cosmopolitan legal principles, every sovereign state (and its citizens) would continue to face external threats and that this condition was unable to secure public right.[34] It is in response to this challenge that Kant famously suggests that "a constitution allowing the greatest possible human freedom in accordance with laws which ensure that the freedom of each can coexist with the freedom of all the others . . . is at all events a necessary idea which must be made the basis of not only the first outline of a political constitution but of all laws as well."[35] As Kant further explains, what is needed are mutually consistent international and cosmopolitan principles "which may eventually be regulated by public laws, thus bringing the human race nearer and nearer to a cosmopolitan constitution."[36]

It is due to Kant's significance and continued influence on cosmopolitan thought that this volume begins with his seminal essay "Idea for a Universal History with a Cosmopolitan Purpose." Furthermore, because of his impact and continued relevance, the entire first section of this Reader is dedicated exclusively to an exploration of Kant's cosmopolitanism and his relationship to contemporary debates about universal human worth (see Nussbaum, "Kant and Cosmopolitanism"), the practical need to establish cosmopolitan law (see Brown, "Kant's Cosmopolitanism"), and global justice (see O'Neill). Nevertheless, and before moving forward, it is necessary to point out that the history of cosmopolitan thought does not go dormant after Kant only to be reinvigorated in recent history by contemporary cosmopolitans. This is because the ideas of Kant and other cosmopolitans before him have shaped and inspired many global movements in the recent past. As the chapters in this Reader will illustrate, we can see various cosmopolitan principles involved with many modern political and ethical movements. For example, we can witness cosmopolitan foundations in the creation of the United Nations (see Archibugi), in the codification of universal human rights (see Pogge), in the furthering of international law (see Habermas), in continued calls for humanitarian assistance (see Barry), humanitarian intervention (see Kaldor), the need for democratic global governance (see Held, "Reframing"), for ecological justice (see Hayden), and in movements that call for global economic justice (see Beitz and Caney, "International Distributive Justice"). In this sense, cosmopolitanism, in its manifold manifestations, has been closely intertwined with the history of political ideas. In other words, although cosmopolitanism has enjoyed a recent resurgence due to pressing issues of globalization, its theories have always remained a meaningful source of inspiration for those who continue to believe that our "primary allegiance is to the community of human beings in the entire world."[37]

Broad themes in contemporary cosmopolitan thought

As the last section suggested, classical cosmopolitanism was largely an ethical philosophy and it only loosely connected into the realm of practical politics. For it was only after the political philosophy of Kant that a more robust transition from a moral cosmopolitan orientation to an institutional position was advanced in cosmopolitan thought.[38] This point is important to note, for most of the chapters in this Reader continue to explore and address issues at the interface between moral cosmopolitanism and its practical institutional application. In doing so, most cosmopolitans examine issues of cosmopolitan morality and its meaningful application through roughly five interrelated themes: *global justice, cultural cosmopolitanism, legal cosmopolitanism, political cosmopolitanism*, and *civic cosmopolitanism*. In this regard, like that of Kant, all cosmopolitan approaches seek to define what moral obligations we have toward fellow human beings while also attempting to establish, in various ways, what cultural, legal, political, and civic factors exist (or *should* exist) in order to foster a cosmopolitan condition. These approaches are pursued not only in response to pressing moral concerns about what justice demands globally, but also in an attempt to provide relevant responses to the various empirical conditions that threaten our shared humanity. Although these five broad themes often overlap and tackle interrelated issues, for our purposes it is useful to briefly examine them independently, and to make links with the structure of this Reader. This is done in order to understand some of the diversity involved in cosmopolitan thought and how this diversity is expressed throughout the pages of this volume.

As previously mentioned, the Reader begins with a seminal essay by Kant and with three chapters that explore his relationship with classical cosmopolitanism (see Nussbaum, "Kant and Cosmopolitanism"), with cosmopolitanism in general (see Brown, "Kant's Cosmopolitanism") and with a Kantian-inspired vision for global justice (see O'Neill). Although "Kantianism" is not a theme per se in this book, it is fair to say that all five cosmopolitan themes are influenced, directly or indirectly, by Kant's moral and political philosophy. If pressed, most scholars have traditionally placed Kant in the category of legal cosmopolitanism. This is because he was the first cosmopolitan to outline a fairly comprehensive vision of cosmopolitan law. Nevertheless, like most contemporary cosmopolitans, his interests covered the entire range of cosmopolitan thought. This is due to the fact that Kant's cosmopolitanism can be seen to incorporate aspects of cultural (see Waldron), political (see Held, "Principles"), and civil cosmopolitanism (see Habermas). Moreover, Kant wished above all else to create a universal sense of *cosmopolitan public right*, and it is for this reason that we can also understand that his cosmopolitanism acts as an important precursor for many contemporary debates about global justice (see O'Neill, Beitz, Pogge, and Caney, "International Distributive Justice").

The first and most ancient theme in cosmopolitanism relates to issues concerning *global justice*.[39] As was seen in the last section, cosmopolitan philosophers from ancient Greece through to the Enlightenment were often concerned with delineating what a condition of universal justice requires and, from this ethical position, sought to criticize what they saw as the unjust moral and political practices of their time. In this sense, as with the theories of yesteryear, we can understand that contemporary cosmopolitanism is ultimately concerned with what constitutes a condition of global justice and the exploration of what moral, political, and economic responsibilities are owed to every member of the human species. Responding to this concern for global justice can take many forms in contemporary cosmopolitan thought. Like the classical thinkers, it can still relate specifically to our ethical thinking about humanistic moral duties and what is owed to all humans globally (see O'Neill). Alternatively, it may relate to global institutional structures and to resolving questions about how justly these institutions distribute fundamental rights and duties (see Pogge). Contemporary arguments might also focus more acutely on how to develop a sense of global justice through education processes that foster sympathies for the plight of those beyond one's border (see Nussbaum, "Patriotism"). Furthermore, a concern for justice can pertain more specifically to how institutional systems at the global level should be to the mutual advantage of all human beings (see Beitz and Barry); or how these structures should in some profound sense secure universal human rights and the basic entitlements that these rights command (see Pogge). In addition, these institutional approaches to global justice can be pursued from a more Rawlsian-inspired argument in order to derive fair principles of justice at the global level (see Beitz), or more practically as a means to examine and critique unjust structures at the global level (see Caney, "International Distributive Justice"). As the chapters in this Reader will explore in greater and more exact detail, the theme of global justice involves deep questions about global cooperation (see Beitz), the appropriate principles of global cohabitation (see Held, "Principles"), and the extent to which cosmopolitan principles should guide our global social order (see Beck). Nevertheless, what is common among all cosmopolitans is a commitment to the basic ethical orientation outlined throughout this Introduction and to the principles of universal and equal individual worth beyond the traditional nation-state paradigm.

If the theme of global justice pertains to questions about what is owed to others as a matter of justice, then *cultural cosmopolitanism* can be understood as relating to how we might be able to cultivate a sense of global justice in a culturally pluralistic world. In its most basic form, cultural cosmopolitanism argues for moral duties and obligations that supersede or transgress localized obligations based solely on aspects of ethnicity, culture, and nationality. In this pursuit, cultural cosmopolitanism often has two interrelated elements. First, cultural cosmopolitans generally assert that all individuals are made up of multifarious cultural identities and influences and that human beings already identify with a multiplicity of cultural obligations (see Waldron). If multi-layered obligations are possible, and the existential worth of an individual does not have to be psychologically anchored to only one cultural identity or obligation, then it is possible that human beings, as well as various cultures, can accommodate a cosmopolitan identity beyond their immediate cultural border without also abandoning the important features of their cultural belonging. In this regard, cultural cosmopolitanism is attempting to offer a response to communitarian critiques that often restrict the scope of justice to communal borders of nationality (see Miller and a cosmopolitan response by Tan), existing state structures (see Nagel and a cosmopolitan response by Caney, "Global Distributive Justice and the State"), and culture (see Kymlicka and a cosmopolitan response by Waldron). Second, and related to the first point, cultural cosmopolitanism often relates to the search for common universal principles that encompass all human activities and cultural structures. By locating common human traits like human reason, a universal requirement for basic needs, or the capacity to be harmed, cultural cosmopolitans support unifying moral duties and rights by locating principles of the human condition that encourage our common human culture. The fostering of this ethical orientation can be through a broadened educational process (see Nussbaum, "Patriotism"), through globalization and universal perceptions of a "global risk society" (see Beck), through the slow codification of international legal norms (see Habermas), or through responsible states that self-prescribe a cosmopolitan foreign policy (see Kaldor; Hayden; Archibugi; Held, "Reframing"; Waldron; Brown, "Cosmopolitan Legal Theory"; and Caney, "Global Distributive Justice and the State"). Like the early Stoic philosophy of Seneca, cultural cosmopolitans insist that humans occupy two worlds and thus have duties and responsibilities to both; that is, to a local culture given to you by birth and to a human culture that is "truly great and truly common."

If cultural cosmopolitanism is concerned with how to foster a condition of global justice in a culturally pluralistic world, then *legal cosmopolitanism* can be understood as examining how international law should/could be constituted from, and constrained by, the moral and normative principles of global justice and from cosmopolitan principles more generally (see Brown, "Cosmopolitan Legal Theory"). There are three elements involved in this effort. First, many legally minded cosmopolitans use principles of justice in order to "evaluate certain fundamental aspects of the existing international legal order . . . [And] propose legal norms and practices which, if implemented with reasonable care, would make the system more just."[40] Second, through a critical examination of current international law and the cosmopolitan norms associated with its expansion, many legal cosmopolitans focus on how these norms can act as part of a process of constitutionalization, from which a more robust cosmopolitan legal order may evolve (see Habermas; Brown, "Cosmopolitan Legal Theory"). The third approach moves beyond a critical approach and builds upon the Kantian notion "that an additional level of law is necessary to secure human dignity and legal obligation beyond the traditional state-centric model of international law."[41] Although most legal cosmopolitans recognize that states can be meaningful institutions in the furtherance of human rights and that they can form an important part of a cosmopolitan condition (see Brown, "Cosmopolitan Legal Theory," and Caney, "Global Distributive Justice and the State"), most legal cosmopolitans reject a system of law predicated exclusively on a Westphalian state-centric model that confers overriding legal authority to state sovereignty. What is needed, many cosmopolitans argue, is the establishment of an additional level of cosmopolitan law as a supplement to international law, in order to bring states and people under the normative and legal guidance of cosmopolitan moral theory. This is because most, if not all, legal cosmopolitans argue that what is required "are more robust international legal tenets that bind states to recognizable rules of conduct and sovereign legitimacy, which if properly practiced could create a cosmopolitan legal condition."[42]

Although tightly related to the themes of its legal counterpart, *political cosmopolitanism* maintains a distinct emphasis on global governance and on reforming international political institutions in line with cosmopolitan ideals. Cosmopolitan institutions and organizations of regional and global governance are considered a necessary supplement to those of the state. Cosmopolitans offer a number of reasons for this, including the threats derived from common global risks (see Beck) or the challenges of "overlapping communities of fate" (see Held, "Reframing"). Of course, nation-states have often found it necessary to collaborate and establish international institutions in order to solve collective action problems. However, the rationale for such institutions has been grounded in "reasons of state," and thus they have been shaped through the calculus of power politics. The result has been a system of global governance that, by and large, freezes the prevailing power structures, and is ill adapted to a more complex and interconnected world. Nearly all cosmopolitans agree that existing institutions are in need of reform, yet they remain divided over how cosmopolitan institutions should be designed if they are to take seriously the principle of the equal moral worth of individuals (see Habermas, and Brown, "Cosmopolitan Legal Theory"). Held and Archibugi, for example, differ over whether the concept of sovereignty as an ordering principle needs to be modified (see Held, "Reframing") or discarded altogether (see Archibugi). There are also disagreements over the architecture of cosmopolitan institutions, with some theorists emphasizing the primacy of the legal (see Habermas; Brown, "Cosmopolitan Legal Theory"), while others argue for the centrality of politically driven change (see Hayden, for instance). Various theorists also offer unique conceptualizations of how cosmopolitan principles might apply to and improve the governance of specific issue areas, such as conflict (see Kaldor) and the environment (see Hayden). Kaldor, for instance, argues in favor of a cosmopolitan approach to humanitarian intervention, stressing the need for establishing legitimacy and the rule of law by enforcing cosmopolitan norms such as human rights rather than engaging in peacekeeping, which emphasizes the separation of belligerents rather than the protection of civilians. Similarly, Hayden argues that framing environmental issues in terms of basic rights, particularly the right to a healthy environment, as implied by the right to life, can contribute to a heightened sense of global responsibility and equity, making it easier for countries to find common ground in order to provide effective global environmental governance.

The overlaps between *civic cosmopolitanism* and its political, legal and cultural counterparts are such that at times they appear indistinguishable from each other. That said, we are able to locate one definitional nuance that delineates this theme. Whereas political cosmopolitanism is generally concerned with exploring issues involved with constructing supranational political organizations of some kind, civil cosmopolitanism places emphasis on constructing a sense of cosmopolitan citizenship. Like the Stoics, many contemporary cosmopolitans advocate a form of universal citizenship that can bind all members of humanity together. This theme can take many forms with a variety of strengths. Some cosmopolitans seek to create a metaphorical sense of cosmopolitan citizenship via the growth of a universal human culture (see Nussbaum, "Patriotism"). Other cosmopolitans pursue the protection of universal human rights within existing global and national systems as a way to confer something like the legal rights and responsibilities usually associated with the concept of citizenship (see Pogge). Similarly, many legal cosmopolitans seek to create a non-national sense of citizenship through the constitutionalization of human rights at the global level, establishing an order in which international law focuses on the rights of the individual and not on the sovereign rights of states (see Habermas). Another more political form of civil cosmopolitanism might involve granting political rights for democratic participation in processes of global governance as a form of global citizenship (see Archibugi; Held, "Reframing"). Lastly, some cosmopolitans strongly fuse political and civil themes together in order to advocate the creation of a cosmopolitan citizenship that is more analogous to those practiced within states, by advocating a robust global institutional model that resembles something similar to a world state.[43]

Nevertheless, these general characteristics of cosmopolitan thought only loosely capture some common principles associated with cosmopolitan thinking. For, like any distinct political theory, cosmopolitan thought is itself made up of various sub-fields that contain their own unique and distinct idiosyncrasies. In the broadest of terms, we have presented contemporary cosmopolitan thinking as containing the five elements listed above and we have structured this Reader largely along those lines. However, as the pages in this Reader will show, cosmopolitanism is a rich and expansive political theory that covers a broad range of moral and practical issues. Furthermore, cosmopolitanism certainly has its distracters and we have included Section VI in this Reader in order to represent various strands of critical reflection. This section covers issues of national sentiment and the limits this imposes on cosmopolitan thought (see Miller), the institutional difficulties of establishing global justice (see Nagel), internal contradictions within the philosophical language of cosmopolitanism (see Derrida), cultural identity as a limiting factor to a cosmopolitan ethos (see Kymlicka), and the institutional impossibilities of establishing cosmopolitan democracy (see Dahl). Lastly, because this Reader is unable to cover everything, it was necessary to leave out many seminal and important works that have been involved in the development of cosmopolitan thought. In order to provide some inclusion of these works, we have added a comprehensive bibliographical overview of cosmopolitan thought and its critics to the end of this Reader in the hope that this will encourage further examination.

We live in a global age, in an age of overlapping communities of fate, where the fate and fortunes of countries are increasingly entwined with one another. Cosmopolitanism does not derive from this order; it has its origins in earlier times. Yet it is of growing interest and relevance because it is a philosophy and ethical orientation that takes account of the dense enmeshment of human beings – the connections between them, the bonds that link them, the interests that divide them, and the clashes of ethical and political outlook. Cosmopolitanism is a philosophy for the age of human interconnectedness, and generates a politics for a "small world."

Notes

1 Catherine Lu, "The One and Many Faces of Cosmopolitanism," *Journal of Political Philosophy*, 8, 2 (2000): 245.
2 Thomas Pogge, see p. 114.
3 Charles Beitz, "International Liberalism and Distributive Justice: A Survey of Recent Thought," *World Politics*, 51 (1992): 287. See this volume, pp. 95–8.
4 Charles Beitz, "Cosmopolitan Liberalism and the State System," in C. Brown (ed.), *Political Reconstruction in Europe: Ethical Perspectives* (London: Routledge, 1994), p. 124.
5 Brian Barry, see p. 101.
6 David Held, see p. 295.
7 Martha Nussbaum, see p. 155.
8 Huge Harris, "The Greek Origins of the Idea of Cosmopolitanism," *The International Journal of Ethics*, 38, 1 (1927): 1–10.
9 Moses Hadas, "From Nationalism to Cosmopolitanism in the Greco-Roman World," *Journal of the History of Ideas*, 4, 1 (1943): 105–11.
10 Diogenes Laertius, *The Lives of Eminent Philosophers*, Vol. I, trans. R. Hicks (Cambridge: Loeb Classical Library, 1925), p. 65.
11 D. Dudley, *A History of Cynicism* (London, 1937), p. 34.
12 J. L. Moles, "Cynic Cosmopolitanism," in R.B. Branham and M. Goulet-Caze (eds.), *The Cynics* (Berkeley: California University Press, 1996).
13 John Sellars, "Stoic Cosmopolitanism and Zeno's Republic," *History of Political Thought*, 38, 1 (2007): 1–29.
14 Zeno of Citium, *The Fragments of Zeno and Cleanthes*, ed. Alfred Pearson (London: C. J. Clay and Co., 1891), p. 102.

15 Plutarch, "On the Fortune of Alexander," in A. Long and D. Sedley (eds.), *The Hellenistic Philosophers*, Vol. II (Cambridge: Cambridge University Press, 1987), p. 429.
16 Marcus Cicero, *De officiis*, ed. M. Griffin and E. Atkins (Cambridge: Cambridge University Press, 1991), p. 21.
17 Marcus Aurelius, *The Meditations* (New York: Hackett, 1983), Sect. 14.
18 Seneca, *De otio*, ed. A. Long and D. Sedley (Cambridge: Cambridge University Press, 1987), p. 431.
19 Ibid.
20 Marcus Cicero, *The Republic and The Laws*, ed. J. Powell and trans. N. Rudd (Oxford: Oxford University Press, 1998), 3:28.
21 Ibid.
22 Bartolome de las Casas, *A Short Account of the Destruction of the Indies*, ed. Nigel Griffin (London: Penguin Books, 1992), p. 14.
23 Lewis Hawk, *All of Mankind is One: A Study of the Disputation Between Bartolome de Las Casas and Juan Gines de Sepulveda in 1550 on the Intellectual and Religious Capacity of the American Indians* (De Kalb: Northern Illinois Press, 1974).
24 Las Casas, *A Short Account*, p. 6.
25 Francisco de Vitoria, "On Civil Power," in *Political Writings*, ed. A. Padgen and J. Lawrence (Cambridge: Cambridge University Press, 1991), p. 40.
26 Georg Cavallar, *The Rights of Strangers* (Aldershot: Ashgate Publishing, 2002), p. 94.
27 T. Schrereth, *The Cosmopolitan Ideal in Enlightenment Thought* (Indiana: Notre Dame Press, 1977).
28 John Locke, *Two Treaties of Government*, ed. M. Goldie (London: J. Dent, 1993), p. 117.
29 Thomas Paine, "Letter to Abbé Raynal," in *The Complete Writings of Thomas Paine*, ed. P. Foner (New York: The Citadel Press, 1945), p. 256.
30 Denis Diderot, "Cosmopolitain ou cosmopolite," in *Encyclopédie* (Geneva: Jean-Leonard Pellet, Imprimeur de la Republique, 1779), p. 600.
31 Karen O'Brien, *Narratives of Enlightenment: Cosmopolitan History from Voltaire to Gibbon* (Cambridge: Cambridge University Press, 2005).
32 Immanuel Kant, "Perpetual Peace," in Hans Reiss (ed.), *Kant's Political Writings* (Cambridge: Cambridge University Press, 1970), p. 107 [8:360].
33 Immanuel Kant, see p. 20: Reiss, *Kant's Political Writings*, p. 51 [8:28].
34 Immanuel Kant, *The Metaphysics of Morals*, ed. and trans. M. Gregor (Cambridge: Cambridge University Press, 1996), p. 121 [6:352].
35 Immanuel Kant, *The Critique of Pure Reason*, trans. J. Meiklejohn (New York: The Colonial Press, 1900) [3:247].
36 Kant, "Perpetual Peace," p. 108 [8:360–1].
37 Martha Nussbaum, see p. 155.
38 Daniele Archibugi, "Immanuel Kant, Cosmopolitan Law and Peace," *European Journal of International Relations*, 1, 4 (1995): 429–56.
39 Global justice is also sometimes referred to as universal justice, international justice, cosmopolitan justice, and via its distinct sub-focus on economic distributive principles: global distributive justice, global economic justice, and cosmopolitan distributive justice. However, for the most part, these signifiers are relating essentially the same general idea, that whatever cosmopolitan justice is, it is universal in its scope and application, and can reasonably include all persons globally.
40 Allen Buchanan, *Justice, Legitimacy, and Self-determination: Moral Foundations for International Law* (Oxford: Oxford University Press, 2004), p. 4.
41 Garrett Wallace Brown, "Cosmopolitan Legal Theory," see p. 254.
42 Garrett Wallace Brown, *Grounding Cosmopolitanism: From Kant to the Idea of a Cosmopolitan Constitution* (Edinburgh: Edinburgh University Press, 2009), p. 12. Cf. David Held, *Democracy and the Global Order* (Cambridge: Polity Press, 1995), ch. 10.
43 Luis Cabrera, *Political Theory of Global Justice: A Cosmopolitan Case for a World State* (New York: Routledge, 2004), and Raffaele Marchetti, *Global Democracy: For and Against: Ethical Theory, Institutional Design and Social Struggles* (Oxford: Routledge, 2008).

Part I

Kant and Contemporary Cosmopolitanism

Introduction

The philosophy of Immanuel Kant has had tremendous influence on contemporary cosmopolitanism. This is because Kant was the first philosopher to provide a thorough-going discussion of the moral dimensions of cosmopolitanism and then to apply these principles to the international concerns of his time. As Kant argues in the "Idea for a Universal History with a Cosmopolitan Purpose," "the greatest problem for the human species, the solution of which nature compels him to seek, is that of attaining a civil society which can administer justice universally." In this regard, according to Kant, "the highest task which nature has set for mankind must therefore be that of establishing a society in which freedom under external laws would be combined to the greatest possible extent . . . in other words of establishing a perfectly just civil constitution." As Kant contends, establishing this condition has become morally and politically necessary because the world is increasingly interdependent and interconnected to a point where the security and rights of one state or peoples cannot be maintained independently of others. Although Kant recognized that creating this civil order is extremely difficult in practice, he nevertheless argues that this idea remains morally and practically feasible in spite of existing hindrances. As Kant maintains, cosmopolitanism provides a moral compass towards a "matrix within which all the original capacities of the human race may be developed," and it is within his essay on universal history that Kant provides his broadest overview of why we might remain enthusiastic about the creation of an eventual cosmopolitan order.

Nevertheless, as discussed in the Editors' Introduction, Kant was not the first philosopher to discuss the idea of cosmopolitan order or to espouse tenets of moral cosmopolitanism. Furthermore, Kant was not the first philosopher to apply the use of practical moral reasoning in attempts to move cosmopolitan moral theory to institutional practice. As Martha Nussbaum's chapter on "Kant and Cosmopolitanism" highlights, we can see that Kant owes a considerable debt to the work of the Stoics, who were themselves concerned about how cosmopolitan principles could underwrite political practice. As Nussbaum argues, Kant and the Stoics give contemporary theorists a relevant and applicable paradigm for political life, which seeks to move beyond a world full of violence to one where human dignity moves front and center, toward a more mutually rewarding cosmopolitan existence.

Although Nussbaum's chapter makes useful connections between Kant and the Stoics, there are still considerable ambiguities involved with Kant's cosmopolitan theory, as well as questions with respect to its pertinence for contemporary cosmopolitan thought. For example, questions remain regarding what Kant's cosmopolitanism requires morally. In addition, how do these moral requirements translate into a demand for cosmopolitan law? Does Kant's notion of a universal history rely on an untenable and unrealistic teleology? If not, how are we to interpret Kant's strong use of natural metaphor? Furthermore, how can we extrapolate what a Kantian form of cosmopolitan justice might look like? And how applicable is this Kantian approach to contemporary debates about global cohabitation?

In many ways, the chapters by Garrett Wallace Brown and Onora O'Neill attempt to address and outline some general responses to these questions. In the chapter by Brown, background connections are made between Kant's critical philosophy and the moral foundations involved with his cosmopolitan thought. From this, the foundations for establishing a basic condition of cosmopolitan justice are outlined and connected to contemporary debates about human dignity and the moral and institutional requirements that a cosmopolitan position demands. In addition, Brown seeks to resolve the claim that this cosmopolitan vision relies on an unrealistic teleology by setting out an alternative treatment of Kant's cosmopolitan history and by suggesting that this interpretation links coherently with Kant's more defendable argument for cosmopolitan law.

Whereas Brown seeks to present a coherent picture of Kant's overall vision of cosmopolitanism, O'Neill focuses specifically on what a Kantian approach to global justice might involve and seeks to provide an argument as to why this approach has contemporary relevance. To do so, O'Neill examines, compares, and then rejects utilitarian, libertarian, and rights-based approaches to global justice. As she suggests, these theories fail to capture key elements regarding the relationships between generating moral obligations and satisfying human needs. According to O'Neill, a Kantian approach to global justice can overcome this lacuna because it provides a means to derive duties of justice while also recognizing the importance of satisfying the needs of vulnerable beings. Nevertheless, as we will see in Section II, not all cosmopolitans share O'Neill's interpretation of Kant and each theorist generates their own unique understanding of cosmopolitan global justice.

1

Idea for a Universal History with a Cosmopolitan Purpose
Immanuel Kant

Whatever conception of the freedom of the will one may form in terms of metaphysics, the will's manifestations in the world of phenomena, i.e. human actions, are determined in accordance with natural laws, as is every other natural event. History is concerned with giving an account of these phenomena, no matter how deeply concealed their causes may be, and it allows us to hope that, if it examines the free exercise of the human will *on a large scale*, it will be able to discover a regular progression among freely willed actions. In the same way, we may hope that what strikes us in the actions of individuals as confused and fortuitous may be recognised, in the history of the entire species, as a steadily advancing but slow development of man's original capacities. Thus marriages, births, and deaths do not seem to be subject to any rule by which their numbers could be calculated in advance, since the free human will has such a great influence upon them; and yet the annual statistics for them in large countries prove that they are just as subject to constant natural laws as are the changes in the weather, which in themselves are so inconsistent that their individual occurrence cannot be determined in advance, but which nevertheless do not fail as a whole to sustain the growth of plants, the flow of rivers, and other natural functions in a uniform and uninterrupted course. Individual men and even entire nations little imagine that, while they are pursuing their own ends, each in his own way and often in opposition to others, they are unwittingly guided in their advance along a course intended by nature. They are unconsciously promoting an end which, even if they knew what it was, would scarcely arouse their interest.

Since men neither pursue their aims purely by instinct, as the animals do, nor act in accordance with any integral, prearranged plan like rational cosmopolitans, it would appear that no law-governed history of mankind is possible (as it would be, for example, with bees or beavers). We can scarcely help feeling a certain distaste on observing their activities as enacted in the great world-drama, for we find that, despite the apparent wisdom of individual actions here and there, everything as a whole is made up of folly and childish vanity, and often of childish malice and destructiveness. The result is that we do not know what sort of opinion we should form of our species, which is so proud of its supposed superiority. The only way out for the philosopher, since he cannot assume that mankind follows any rational *purpose of its own* in its collective actions, is for him to attempt to discover a *purpose in nature* behind this senseless course of human events, and decide whether it is after all possible to formulate in terms of a definite plan of nature a history of creatures who act without a plan of their own. Let us now see if we can succeed in finding a guiding principle for such a history, and then leave it to nature to produce someone capable of writing it along the lines suggested. Thus nature produced a Kepler who found an unexpected means of reducing the eccentric orbits of the planets to definite laws, and a Newton who explained these laws in terms of a universal natural cause.

First proposition

All the natural capacities of a creature are destined sooner or later to be developed completely and in conformity with their end. This can be verified in all animals by external and internal or anatomical examination. An organ which is not meant for use or an arrangement which does not fulfil its purpose is a contradiction in the teleological theory of nature. For if we abandon this basic principle, we are faced not with a law-governed nature, but with an aimless, random process, and the dismal reign of chance replaces the guiding principle of reason.

Second proposition

In man (as the only rational creature on earth), *those natural capacities which are directed towards the use of his reason are such that they could be fully developed only in the species, but not in the individual.* Reason, in a creature, is a faculty which enables that creature to extend far beyond the limits of natural instinct the rules and intentions it follows in using its various powers, and the range of its projects is unbounded. But reason does not itself work instinctively, for it requires trial, practice and instruction to enable it to progress gradually from one stage of insight to the next. Accordingly, every individual man would have to live for a vast length of time if he were to learn how to make complete use of all his natural capacities; or if nature has fixed only a short term for each man's life (as is in fact the case), then it will require a long, perhaps incalculable series of generations, each passing on its enlightenment to the next, before the germs implanted by nature in our species can be developed to that degree which corresponds to nature's original intention. And the point of time at which this degree of development is reached must be the goal of man's aspirations (at least as an idea in his mind), or else his natural capacities would necessarily appear by and large to be purposeless and wasted. In the latter case, all practical principles would have to be abandoned, and nature, whose wisdom we must take as axiomatic in judging all other situations, would incur the suspicion of indulging in childish play in the case of man alone.

Third proposition

Nature has willed that man should produce entirely by his own initiative everything which goes beyond the mechanical ordering of his animal existence, and that he should not partake of any other happiness or perfection than that which he has procured for himself without instinct and by his own reason. For nature does nothing unnecessarily and is not extravagant in the means employed to reach its ends. Nature gave man reason, and freedom of will based upon reason, and this in itself was a clear indication of nature's intention as regards his endowments. For it showed that man was not meant to be guided by instinct or equipped and instructed by innate knowledge; on the contrary, he was meant to produce everything out of himself. Everything had to be entirely of his own making – the discovery of a suitable diet, of clothing, of external security and defence (for which nature gave him neither the bull's horns, the lion's claws, nor the dog's teeth, but only his hands), as well as all the pleasures that can make life agreeable, and even his insight and circumspection and the goodness of his will. Nature seems here to have taken pleasure in exercising the strictest economy and to have measured out the basic animal equipment so sparingly as to be just enough for the most pressing needs of the beginnings of existence. It seems as if nature had intended that man, once he had finally worked his way up from the uttermost barbarism to the highest degree of skill, to inner perfection in his manner of thought and thence (as far as is possible on earth) to happiness, should be able to take for himself the entire credit for doing so and have only himself to thank for it. It seems that nature has worked more with a view to man's rational *self-esteem* than to his mere well-being. For in the actual course of human affairs, a whole host of hardships awaits him. Yet nature does not seem to have been concerned with seeing that man should live agreeably, but with seeing that he should work his way onwards to make himself by his own conduct worthy of life and well-being. What remains disconcerting about all this is firstly, that the earlier generations seem to perform their laborious tasks only for the sake of the later ones, so as to prepare for them a further stage from which they can raise still higher the structure intended by nature; and secondly, that only the later generations will in fact have the good fortune to inhabit the building on which a whole series of their forefathers (admittedly, without any conscious intention) had worked without themselves being able to share in the happiness they were preparing. But no matter how puzzling this may be, it will appear as necessary as it is puzzling if we simply assume that one animal species was intended to have reason, and that, as a class of rational beings who are mortal as individuals but immortal as a species, it was still meant to develop its capacities completely.

Fourth proposition

The means which nature employs to bring about the development of innate capacities is that of antagonism within society, in so far as this antagonism becomes in the long run the cause of a law-governed social order. By antagonism, I mean in this context the *unsocial sociability* of men, that is, their tendency to come together in society, coupled, however, with a continual resistance which constantly threatens to break this society up. This propensity *is* obviously rooted in human nature. Man has an inclination to *live in society*, since he feels in this state more like a man, that is, he feels able to develop his natural capacities. But he also has a great tendency to *live as an individual*, to isolate himself, since he also encounters in himself the unsocial characteristic of wanting to direct everything in accordance with his own ideas. He therefore expects resistance all around, just as he knows of himself that he is in turn inclined to offer resistance to others. It is this very resistance which awakens all man's powers and induces him to overcome his tendency to laziness. Through the desire for honour, power or property, it drives him to seek status among his fellows, whom he cannot *bear* yet cannot *bear to leave*. Then the first true steps are taken from barbarism to culture, which in fact consists in the social worthiness of man. All man's talents are now gradually developed, his taste cultivated, and by a continued process of enlightenment, a beginning is made towards establishing a way of thinking which can with time transform the primitive natural capacity for moral discrimination into definite practical principles; and thus a *pathologically* enforced social union is transformed into a *moral* whole. Without these asocial qualities (far from admirable in themselves) which cause the resistance inevitably encountered by each individual as he furthers his self-seeking pretensions, man would live an Arcadian, pastoral existence of perfect concord, self-sufficiency and mutual love. But all human talents would remain hidden for ever in a dormant state, and men, as good-natured as the sheep they tended, would scarcely render their existence more valuable than that of their animals. The end for which they were created, their rational nature, would be an unfilled void. Nature should thus be thanked for fostering social incompatibility, enviously competitive vanity, and insatiable desires for possession or even power. Without these desires, all man's excellent natural capacities would never be roused to develop. Man wishes concord, but nature, knowing better what is good for his species, wishes discord. Man wishes to live comfortably and pleasantly, but nature intends that he should abandon idleness and inactive self-sufficiency and plunge instead into labour and hardships, so that he may by his own adroitness find means of liberating himself from them in turn. The natural impulses which make this possible, the sources of the very unsociableness and continual resistance which cause so many evils, at the same time encourage man towards new exertions of his powers and thus towards further development of his natural capacities. They would thus seem to indicate the design of a wise creator – not, as it might seem, the hand of a malicious spirit who had meddled in the creator's glorious work or spoiled it out of envy.

Fifth proposition

The greatest problem for the human species, the solution of which nature compels him to seek, is that of attaining a civil society which can administer justice universally.

The highest purpose of nature – i.e. the development of all natural capacities – can be fulfilled for mankind only in society, and nature intends that man should accomplish this, and indeed all his appointed ends, by his own efforts. This purpose can be fulfilled only in a society which has not only the greatest freedom, and therefore a continual antagonism among its members, but also the most precise specification and preservation of the limits of this freedom in order that it can co-exist with the freedom of others. The highest task which nature has set for mankind must therefore be that of establishing a society in which *freedom under external laws* would be combined to the greatest possible extent with irresistible force, in other words of establishing a perfectly *just civil constitution*. For only through the solution and fulfilment of this task can nature accomplish its other intentions with our species. Man, who is otherwise so enamoured with unrestrained freedom, is forced to enter this state of restriction by sheer necessity. And this is indeed the most stringent of all forms of necessity, for it is imposed by men upon themselves, in that their inclinations make it impossible for them to exist side by side for long in a state of wild freedom. But once enclosed within a precinct like that of civil union, the same inclinations have the most beneficial effect. In the same way, trees in a forest, by seeking to deprive each other of air and sunlight, compel each other to find these by upward growth, so that they grow beautiful and straight – whereas those which put out branches at will, in freedom and in isolation from others, grow stunted, bent and twisted. All the culture and art which adorn mankind and the finest social order man creates are fruits of his unsociability. For it is compelled by its own nature to discipline itself, and thus, by enforced art, to develop completely the germs which nature implanted.

Sixth proposition

This problem is both the most difficult and the last to be solved by the human race. The difficulty (which the very idea of this problem clearly presents) is this: if he lives among others of his own species, man is *an animal who needs a master.* For he certainly abuses his freedom in relation to others of his own kind. And even although, as a rational creature, he desires a law to impose limits on the freedom of all, he is still misled by his self-seeking animal inclinations into exempting himself from the law where he can. He thus requires a *master* to break his self-will and force him to obey a universally valid will under which everyone can be free. But where is he to find such a master? Nowhere else but in the human species. But this master will also be an animal who needs a master. Thus while man may try as he will, it is hard to see how he can obtain for public justice a supreme authority which would itself be just, whether he seeks this authority in a single person or in a group of many persons selected for this purpose. For each one of them will always misuse his freedom if he does not have anyone above him to apply force to him as the laws should require it. Yet the highest authority has to be just *in itself* and yet also a *man.* This is therefore the most difficult of all tasks, and a perfect solution is impossible. Nothing straight can be constructed from such warped wood as that which man is made of. Nature only requires of us that we should approximate to this idea.* A further reason why this task must be the last to be accomplished is that man needs for it a correct conception of the nature of a possible constitution, great experience tested in many affairs of the world, and above all else a good will prepared to accept the findings of this experience. But three factors such as these will not easily be found in conjunction, and if they are, it will happen only at a late stage and after many unsuccessful attempts.

Seventh proposition

The problem of establishing a perfect civil constitution is subordinate to the problem of a law-governed external relationship with other states, and cannot be solved unless the latter is also solved. What is the use of working for a law-governed civil constitution among individual men, i.e. of planning a *commonwealth*? The same unsociability which forced men

---

* Man's role is thus a highly artificial one. We do not know how it is with the inhabitants of other planets and with their nature, but if we ourselves execute this commission of nature well, we may surely flatter ourselves that we occupy no mean status among our neighbours in the cosmos. Perhaps their position is such that each individual can fulfil his destiny completely within his own lifetime. With us it is otherwise; only the species as a whole can hope for this.

to do so gives rise in turn to a situation whereby each commonwealth, in its external relations (i.e. as a state in relation to other states), is in a position of unrestricted freedom. Each must accordingly expect from any other precisely the same evils which formerly oppressed individual men and forced them into a law-governed civil state. Nature has thus again employed the unsociableness of men, and even of the large societies and states which human beings construct, as a means of arriving at a condition of calm and security through their inevitable *antagonism*. Wars, tense and unremitting military preparations, and the resultant distress which every state must eventually feel within itself, even in the midst of peace – these are the means by which nature drives nations to make initially imperfect attempts, but finally, after many devastations, upheavals and even complete inner exhaustion of their powers, to take the step which reason could have suggested to them even without so many sad experiences – that of abandoning a lawless state of savagery and entering a federation of peoples in which every state, even the smallest, could expect to derive its security and rights not from its own power or its own legal judgement, but solely from this great federation (*Fœdus Amphictyonum*), from a united power and the law-governed decisions of a united will. However wild and fanciful this idea may appear – and it has been ridiculed as such when put forward by the Abbé St Pierre and Rousseau (perhaps because they thought that its realisation was so imminent) – it is nonetheless the inevitable outcome of the distress in which men involve one another. For this distress must force the states to make exactly the same decision (however difficult it may be for them) as that which man was forced to make, equally unwillingly, in his savage state – the decision to renounce his brutish freedom and seek calm and security within a law-governed constitution. All wars are accordingly so many attempts (not indeed by the intention of men, but by the intention of nature) to bring about new relations between states, and, by the destruction or at least the dismemberment of old entities, to create new ones. But these new bodies, either in themselves or alongside one another, will in turn be unable to survive, and will thus necessarily undergo further revolutions of a similar sort, till finally, partly by an optimal internal arrangement of the civil constitution, and partly by common external agreement and legislation, a state of affairs is created which, like a civil commonwealth, can maintain itself *automatically*.

Whether we should firstly expect that the states, by an Epicurean concourse of efficient causes, should enter by random collisions (like those of small material particles) into all kinds of formations which are again destroyed by new collisions, until they arrive *by chance* at a formation which can survive in its existing form (a lucky accident which is hardly likely ever to occur); or whether we should assume as a second possibility that nature in this case follows a regular course in leading our species gradually upwards from the lower level of animality to the highest level of humanity through forcing man to employ an art which is nonetheless his own, and hence that nature develops man's original capacities by a perfectly regular process within this apparently disorderly arrangement; or whether we should rather accept the third possibility that nothing at all, or at least nothing rational, will anywhere emerge from all these actions and counter-actions among men as a whole, that things will remain as they have always been, and that it would thus be impossible to predict whether the discord which is so natural to our species is not preparing the way for a hell of evils to overtake us, however civilised our condition, in that nature, by barbaric devastation, might perhaps again destroy this civilised state and all the cultural progress hitherto achieved (a fate against which it would be impossible to guard under a rule of blind chance, with which the state of lawless freedom is in fact identical, unless we assume that the latter is secretly guided by the wisdom of nature) – these three possibilities boil down to the question of whether it is rational to assume that the order of nature is *purposive* in its parts but *purposeless* as a whole.

While the purposeless state of savagery did hold up the development of all the natural capacities of human beings, it nonetheless finally forced them, through the evils in which it involved them, to leave this state and enter into a civil constitution in which all their dormant capacities could be developed. The same applies to the barbarous freedom of established states. For while the full development of natural capacities is here likewise held up by the expenditure of each commonwealth's whole resources on armaments against the others, and by the depredations caused by war (but most of all by the necessity of constantly remaining in readiness for war), the resultant evils still have a beneficial effect. For they compel our species to discover a law of equilibrium to regulate the essentially healthy hostility which prevails among the states and is produced by their freedom. Men are compelled to reinforce this law by introducing a system of united power, hence a cosmopolitan system of general political security. This state of affairs is not completely free from *danger*, lest human energies should lapse into inactivity, but it is also not without a principle of *equality* governing the *actions and counter-actions* of these energies, lest they should destroy one another. When it is little beyond the half-way mark in its development, human nature has to endure the hardest of evils under the guise of outward prosperity before this final step (i.e. the union of states) is taken; and Rousseau's preference for the state of savagery does not appear so very mistaken if only we leave out of consideration this last stage which our species still has to surmount. We are *cultivated* to a high degree by art and science. We are *civilised* to the point of excess in all kinds of social courtesies and proprieties. But we are still a long way from the point where we could consider ourselves *morally* mature. For while the idea of morality is indeed present in culture, an application of this idea which only extends to the semblances of morality, as in love of honour and outward propriety, amounts merely to civilization. But as long as states apply all their resources to their vain and violent schemes of expansion, thus incessantly obstructing the slow and laborious efforts of their citizens to cultivate their minds, and even deprive them of all support in these efforts, no progress in this direction can be expected. For a long internal process of careful work on the part of each commonwealth is necessary for the education of its citizens. But all good enterprises which are not grafted on to a morally good attitude of mind are nothing but illusion and outwardly glittering misery. The human race will no doubt remain in this condition until it has worked itself out of the chaotic state of its political relations in the way I have described.

Eighth proposition

The history of the human race as a whole can be regarded as the realisation of a hidden plan of nature to bring about an internally – and for this purpose also externally – perfect political constitution as the only possible state within which all natural capacities of mankind can be developed completely. This proposition follows from the previous one. We can see that philosophy too may have its *chiliastic* expectations; but they are of such a kind that their fulfilment can be hastened, if only indirectly, by a knowledge of the idea they are based on, so that they are anything but over-fanciful. The real test is whether experience can discover anything to indicate a purposeful natural process of this kind. In my opinion, it can discover *a little*; for this cycle of events seems to take so long a time to complete, that the small part of it traversed by mankind up till now does not allow us to determine with certainty the shape of the whole cycle, and the relation of its parts to the whole. It is no easier than it is to determine, from all hitherto available astronomical observations, the path which our sun with its whole swarm of satellites is following within the vast system of the fixed stars; although from the general premise that the universe is constituted as a system and from the little which has been learnt by observation, we can conclude with sufficient certainty that a movement of this kind does exist in reality. Nevertheless, human nature is such that it cannot be indifferent even to the most remote epoch which may eventually affect our species, so long as this epoch can be expected with certainty. And in the present case, it is especially hard to be indifferent, for it appears that we might by our own rational projects accelerate the coming of this period which will be so welcome to our descendants. For this reason, even the faintest signs of its approach will be extremely important to us. The mutual relationships between states are already so sophisticated that none of them can neglect its internal culture without losing power and influence in relation to the others. Thus the purpose of nature is at least fairly well safeguarded (if not actually furthered) even by the ambitious schemes of the various states. Furthermore, civil freedom can no longer be so easily infringed without disadvantage to all trades and industries, and especially to commerce, in the event of which the state's power in its external relations will also decline. But this freedom is gradually increasing. If the citizen is deterred from seeking his personal welfare in any way he chooses which is consistent with the freedom of others, the vitality of business in general and hence also the strength of the whole are held in check. For this reason, restrictions placed upon personal activities are increasingly relaxed, and general freedom of religion is granted. And thus, although folly and caprice creep in at times, *enlightenment* gradually arises. It is a great benefit which the human race must reap even from its rulers' self-seeking schemes of expansion, if only they realise what is to their own advantage. But this enlightenment, and with it a certain sympathetic interest which the enlightened man inevitably feels for anything good which he comprehends fully, must gradually spread upwards towards the thrones and even influence their principles of government. But while, for example, the world's present rulers have no money to spare for public educational institutions or indeed for anything which concerns the world's best interests (for everything has already been calculated out in advance for the next war), they will nonetheless find that it is to their own advantage at least not to hinder their citizens' private efforts in this direction, however weak and slow they may be. But eventually, war itself gradually becomes not only a highly artificial undertaking, extremely uncertain in its outcome for both parties, but also a very dubious risk to take, since its aftermath is felt by the state in the shape of a constantly increasing national debt (a modern invention) whose repayment becomes interminable. And in addition, the effects which an upheaval in any state produces upon all the others in our continent, where all are so closely linked by trade, are so perceptible that these other states are forced by their own insecurity to offer themselves as arbiters, albeit without legal authority, so that they indirectly prepare the way for a great political body of the future, without precedent in the past. Although this political body exists for the present only in the roughest of outlines, it nonetheless seems as if a feeling is beginning to stir in all its members, each of which has an interest in maintaining the whole. And this encourages the hope that, after many revolutions, with all their transforming effects, the highest purpose of nature, a universal *cosmopolitan existence*, will at last be realised as the matrix within which all the original capacities of the human race may develop.

Ninth proposition

A philosophical attempt to work out a universal history of the world in accordance with a plan of nature aimed at a perfect civil union of mankind, must be regarded as possible and even as capable of furthering the purpose of nature itself. It is admittedly a strange and at first sight absurd proposition to write a *history* according to an idea of how world events must develop if they are to conform to certain rational ends; it would seem that only a *novel* could result from such premises. Yet if it may be assumed that nature does not work without a plan and purposeful end, even amidst the arbitrary play of human freedom, this idea might nevertheless prove useful. And although we are too short-sighted to perceive the hidden mechanism of nature's scheme, this idea may yet serve as a guide to us in representing an otherwise planless *aggregate* of human actions as conforming, at least when considered as a whole, to a *system.* For if we start out from *Greek* history as that in which all other earlier or contemporary histories are preserved or at least authenticated, if we next trace the influence of the Greeks upon the shaping and mis-shaping of the body politic of *Rome*, which engulfed the Greek state, and follow down to our own times the influence of Rome upon the *Barbarians* who in turn destroyed it, and if we finally add the political history of other peoples *episodically*, in so far as knowledge of them has gradually come down to us through these enlightened nations, we shall discover a regular process of improvement in the political constitutions of our continent (which will probably legislate eventually for all other continents). Furthermore, we must always concentrate our attention on civil constitutions, their laws, and the mutual relations among states, and notice how these factors, by virtue of the good they contained, served for a time to elevate and glorify nations (and with them the arts and sciences). Conversely, we should observe how their inherent defects led to their overthrow, but in such a way that a germ of enlightenment always survived, developing further with each revolution, and prepared the way for a subsequent higher level of improvement.

All this, I believe, should give us some guidance in explaining the thoroughly confused interplay of human affairs and in prophesying future political changes. Yet the same use has already been made of human history even when it was regarded as the disjointed product of unregulated freedom. But if we assume a plan of nature, we have grounds for greater hopes. For such a plan opens up the comforting prospect of a future in which we are shown from afar how the human race eventually works its way upward to a situation in which all the germs implanted by nature can be developed fully, and in which man's destiny can be fulfilled here on earth. Such a *justification* of nature – or rather perhaps of *providence* – is no mean motive for adopting a particular point of view in considering the world. For what is the use of lauding and holding up for contemplation the glory and wisdom of creation in the non-rational sphere of nature, if the history of mankind, the very part of this great display of supreme wisdom which contains the purpose of all the rest, is to remain a constant reproach to everything else? Such a spectacle would force us to turn away in revulsion, and, by making us despair of ever finding any completed rational aim behind it, would reduce us to hoping for it only in some other world.

It would be a misinterpretation of my intention to contend that I meant this idea of a universal history, which to some extent follows an *a priori* rule, to supersede the task of history proper, that of *empirical* composition. My idea is only a notion of what a philosophical mind, well acquainted with history, might be able to attempt from a different angle. Besides, the otherwise praiseworthy detail in which each age now composes its history must naturally cause everyone concern as to how our remote descendants will manage to cope with the burden of history which we shall bequeath to them a few centuries from now. No doubt they will value the history of the oldest times, of which the original documents would long since have vanished, only from the point of view of what interests *them*, i.e. the positive and negative achievements of nations and governments in relation to the cosmopolitan goal. We should bear this in mind, and we should likewise observe the ambitions of rulers and their servants, in order to indicate to them the only means by which they can be honourably remembered in the most distant ages. And this may provide us with another *small* motive for attempting a philosophical history of this kind.

Kant and Cosmopolitanism
Martha C. Nussbaum

> *The peoples of the earth have . . . entered in varying degrees into a universal community, and it has developed to the point where a violation of laws in one part of the world is felt everywhere. The idea of a cosmopolitan law is therefore not fantastic and overstrained; it is a necessary complement to the unwritten code of political and international law, transforming it into a universal law of humanity.*
>
> – Kant, "Toward Perpetual Peace"[1]

1

In recent years it has become fashionable for philosophers to look to the ancient Greeks for alternatives to the Enlightenment and its idea of a political life based on reason. Under the influence of Nietzsche, eminent thinkers of quite different sorts have felt dissatisfaction with a politics based on reason and principle, and have believed that in the ancient Greek *polis* we could find an alternative paradigm for our own political lives, one based less on reason and more on communal solidarity, less on principle and more on affiliation, less on optimism for progress than on a sober acknowledgment of human finitude and mortality. Thinkers in this Nietzschean tradition have differed about which Greeks they take to be the good Greeks – since usually it will be granted that reason took over and killed off the good developments at some point. For Nietzsche, famously, the bad times begin with Euripides. For Heidegger, they seem to have begun even sooner, with the death of Parmenides or Heraclitus, whichever came first. For Bernard Williams,[2] things do not get really bad until Plato, but then they get very bad quite rapidly. And for Alasdair MacIntyre,[3] it would seem that the good times persist at least through the lifetime of Aristotle and his medieval successors, and do not get really awful until Hume and Kant.

Nor do thinkers in this tradition agree precisely about what they take to be good in the Greeks and bad in their Enlightenment successors. For Nietzsche and for Bernard Williams, who is the closest of this group to Nietzsche's original idea, the good thing was to base politics on the recognition that the world is horrible and fundamentally unintelligible; the bad thing was to pretend that it has an intelligible rational structure *or* anything to make us optimistic about political progress. In a paper written after his book,[4] Williams has criticized more or less all of Western political philosophy, and in particular the philosophies of Hegel and Kant, for bringing us "good news," and has praised Sophoclean tragedy for directing us simply to contemplate "the horrors." For MacIntyre and for Heidegger – and there are certainly elements of this position in Williams also – the good thing is to suppose that in a well-ordered community we execute our tasks without reflection; the bad thing is to suppose that each political act needs, and can have, a rational justification [. . .]. All agree, at any rate, in their opposition to a hopeful, active, and reason-based politics grounded in an idea of reverence for rational humanity wherever we find it.

It is not my purpose to quarrel with these thinkers' interpretation of the Greek *polis* – though in fact I believe that they vastly underrate the importance of rational justification and rational argument to the fifth-century *polis* and fifth-century tragedy, and hence underrate the continuity between the *polis* and its philosophers.[5] I have more sympathy, in this regard, with the view of G. E. R. Lloyd, who throughout his career has perceptively stressed the difference that a rational style of political life made to the unfolding of science and philosophy in the ancient Greek world.[6] Nor is it my purpose to quarrel directly with the lessons these thinkers take from the Greeks and apply to modern political thought – although in some respects it will become clear what my attitude to those lessons is.

My purpose in this paper, instead, is to begin writing a different chapter in the history of our classical heritage, one from which I think we can derive lessons of direct political worth. For all the Nietzschean thinkers I have named, perhaps the arch-foe is Immanuel Kant. Kant, more influentially than any other Enlightenment thinker, defended a politics based upon reason rather than patriotism or group sentiment, a politics that was truly universal rather than communitarian, a politics that was active, reformist, and optimistic, rather than given to contemplating the horrors [. . .]. The struggle between Kantians and Nietzscheans is vigorous in the Germany of today, as Habermas's Kantian program for politics does battle with the legacy of Heidegger. The same struggle is joined in the Anglo-American world, as the Kantian politics of John Rawls is increasingly at odds with forms of communitarian political thought favored by Williams, MacIntyre, and others. In 1995 we had a special reason to reassess Kant's political legacy, since we celebrated the two-hundredth anniversary of the publication of "Toward Perpetual Peace," in which he mapped out an ambitious program for the containment of global aggression and the promotion of universal respect for human dignity. My aim in this paper will be to trace the debt Kant owed to ancient Stoic cosmopolitanism. It will be my contention that Kant – and, through him, Seneca, Marcus Aurelius, and above all Cicero – present us with a challenge that is at once noble and practical; that trying to meet this challenge will give us something far better to do with our time than to wait [. . .] to contemplate the horrors, many though there surely are to contemplate – that, in short, if we want to give the world a paradigm from the ancient Greco-Roman world to inform its engagement with the political life, in a time of ethnic violence, genocidal war, and widespread disregard for human dignity, it is this one that we should select.

2

Kant's "Toward Perpetual Peace" is a profound defense of cosmopolitan values. The term "cosmopolitan" occurs frequently throughout Kant's political writings, often in close proximity to classical citations and references.[7] Although his own version of cosmopolitanism grows out of a distinctive eighteenth-century tradition, both the tradi-tion itself and Kant's own approach to it are saturated with the ideas of ancient Greek and especially Roman Stoicism, where the idea of the *kosmou politês* (world citizen) received its first philosophical development.[8] Although Kant characteristically dis-cusses Stoic ideas only in a brief and general way, without precise textual detail, he seems nonetheless to have been profoundly shaped by them, or at least to have found in them a deep affinity with his own unfolding ideas about cosmopolitan humanity. Some of the Stoic influence on him derives, certainly, from his reading of modern writings on natural law that are themselves heavily indebted to Cicero and other ancient thinkers. But Kant's deep familiarity with the major Roman authors shapes his engagement with their ideas in a very close and detailed manner. We know, for example, that Cicero's *De Officiis*, a pivotal text in the moral philosophy of the period, was especially important to Kant at the time when he was writing the *Groundwork* and the later ethical/political works. Klaus Reich has shown in detail that the argument of the *Groundwork* follows Cicero closely, especially in its way of connecting the idea of a universal law of nature with the idea of respect for humanity.[9] Seneca seems to have been important throughout this period also. The influence of Marcus Aurelius appears to have been less direct, but one may still discern its presence, especially in Kant's fondness for the term "citizen of the world."[10]

The attempt proves of interest in part because of similarities it discloses; even more fascinating, however, are some profound differences of aim and philosophical sub-stance that come to light. Seeing where Kant diverges from thinkers with whom he is so solidly allied, with respect to the twin goals of containing aggression and fostering respect for humanity, assists us in no small measure in understanding his political project. I shall therefore first set out in a schematic way the general outlines of Stoic cosmopolitanism as Kant was aware of it, combining, as he does, the contributions of various thinkers, including Cicero, Seneca, and Marcus; then I shall show the extent of Kant's affinity with those ideas. Finally, I shall explore two important differences between the Kantian and the Stoic projects concerning aggression, war, and peace in the areas of *teleology* and *theory of passions*.

3

Asked where he came from, Diogenes the Cynic replied "I am a citizen of the world."[11] He meant by this, it appears, that he refused to be defined by his local origins and local group memberships, so central to the self-image of a conventional Greek male. He insisted on defining himself, primarily, in terms of more universal aspirations and concerns. It would appear that these concerns focused on the worth of reason and moral purpose in defining one's humanity. Class, rank, status, national origin and location, and even gender are treated by the Cynics as secondary and morally irrelevant attributes. The first form of moral affiliation for the citizen should be her affiliation with rational humanity; and this, above all, should define the purposes of her conduct.[12]

We know relatively little about what more the Cynics made of these ideas, although it is obvious that they had a major influence on later Greco-Roman cosmopolitan thought. The Stoics, who followed the Cynics' lead, developed the image of the *kosmo-politês* (world citizen) more fully, arguing that each of us dwells, in effect, in two com-munities: the local community of our birth and the community of human argument and aspiration. The latter is, in Seneca's words, "truly great and truly common, in which we look neither to this corner nor to that, but measure the boundaries of our nation by the sun."[13] The Stoics held that this community is the source of our most fundamental moral and social obligations. Plutarch summarizes:

> The much admired *Republic* of Zeno is aimed at this one main point, that we should not organize our daily lives around the city or the deme, divided from one another by local schemes of justice, but we should regard all human beings as our fellow demesmen and fellow citizens, and there should be one way of life and one order, just as a herd that feeds together shares a common nurturance and a common law. Zeno wrote this as a dream or image of a well-ordered and philosophical community.[14]

It is not clear whether the Greek Stoics really wished to establish a single world state. Zeno did propose an ideal city, but we know very little about its institutional structure.[15] More important by far is the Stoics' insistence on a certain way of perceiving our standing in the moral and social world. We should view ourselves as fundamentally and deeply linked to humankind as a whole, and take thought in our deliberations, both personal and political, for the good of the whole species. This idea is compatible with the maintenance of local forms of political organization, but it does direct political as well as moral thought. In the Roman world the directly political side of cosmopolitanism could come into its own in a very practical way, as Roman Stoic philosophers had a major influence on the conduct of political life. Cicero, following the Middle Stoic Panaetius, applies Stoic precepts to the conduct of affairs in the Roman Republic. Seneca was regent of the emperor under Nero; Marcus Aurelius was, of course, emperor at the height of Roman influence. Both closely connected their philosophical with their political endeavors.[16] Also during the Roman period, Stoicism provided the impetus for some republican anti-imperial movements, such as the conspiracies of Thrasea Paetus and Piso during the reign of Nero.

According to the Stoics, the basis for human community is the worth of reason in each and every human being.[17] Reason, in the Stoic view, is a portion of the divine in each of us. And each and every human being, just in virtue of being rational and moral (for Stoics, reason is above all a faculty of moral choice) has boundless worth. Male or female, slave or free, king or peasant, all are of boundless moral value, and the dignity of reason is worthy of respect wherever it is found. This reason, the Stoics held, makes us fellow citizens. Zeno, it would appear, already spoke of rational humanity as grounding a common idea of law.[18] Similarly, Cicero in the *De Officiis* (III, 27–28) holds that nature ordains that every human being should promote the good of every other human being just because he is human: "And if this is so, we are all subject to a single law of nature, and if this is so we are bound not to harm anyone."[19] Marcus develops this idea further (IV, 4): "If reason is common, so too is law; and if this is common, then we are fellow citizens. If this is so, we share in a kind of organized polity. And if that is so, the world is as it were a city state."[20]

This being so, Stoic cosmopolitans hold, we should regard our deliberations as, first and foremost, deliberations about the problems common to all human beings emerging in particular concrete situations, not problems growing out of a local or national identity that confines and limits our moral aspirations. The accident of where one is born is just that, an accident; any human being might have been born in any nation. As Marcus puts it (X, 15), "It makes no difference whether a person lives here or there, provided that, wherever he lives, he lives as a citizen of the world."[21] Recognizing this, we should not allow differences of nationality or class or ethnic membership or even gender[22] to erect barriers between us and our fellow human beings. We should recognize humanity wherever it occurs, and give its fundamental ingredients, reason and moral capacity, our first allegiance and respect.

Even in its Roman incarnations, this proposal is not, fundamentally, a proposal for a world state. The point is more radical still: that we should give our first moral allegiance to *no* mere form of government, no temporal power. We should give it, instead, to the moral community made up by the humanity of all human beings. One should always behave so as to treat with equal respect the dignity of reason and moral choice in each and every human being. And, as Marcus holds, this will generate both moral and legal obligations.

The attitude of the world citizen is held to be strategically valuable in social life. We will be better able to solve our problems if we face them in this way, as fellow human beings respecting one another. [. . .]

Furthermore, the political stance of the cosmopolitan is intrinsically valuable, for it recognizes in persons what is especially fundamental about them, most worthy of reverence and acknowledgment. This aspect may be less colorful than some of the more eye-catching morally irrelevant attributes of tradition, identity, and group membership. It is, however, the Stoics argue, both deeper and ultimately more beautiful.[23]

[. . .]

The Stoics stress that to be a world citizen one does not need to give up local identifications and affiliations, which can be a great source of richness in life. Hierocles, a Stoic of the first and second centuries AD, using an older metaphor found also in Cicero's *De Officiis,* argued that we should regard ourselves not as devoid of local affiliations but as surrounded by a series of concentric circles. The first circle is drawn around the self; the next takes in one's immediate family; then follows the extended family; then, in order, one's neighbors or local group, one's fellow city dwellers, and one's fellow countrymen. Outside all these circles is the largest one, that of humanity as a whole. Our task as citizens of the world will be to "draw the circles somehow toward the center," making all human beings more like our fellow city dwellers, and so forth.[24] In general, we should think of nobody as a stranger, as outside our sphere of concern and obligation. Cicero here borrows Terence's famous line "Homo sum: humani nihil a me alienun puto." ("I am a human being; I think nothing human alien to me.")[25] In other words, we may give what is near to us a special degree of attention and concern. But, first, we should always remember that these features of placement are incidental and that our most fundamental allegiance is to what is human. Second, we should consider that even the special measure of concern we give to our own is justified not by any intrinsic superiority in the local but by the overall requirements of humanity. To see this, consider the rearing of children. Roman Stoics tend to disagree strongly with Plato and with their Greek Stoic forebears, who seem to have followed Plato in abolishing the nuclear family. The Roman Stoics held, it seems, that we will not get good rearing of children by leaving all children equally to the care of all parents. Each parent should care intensely for his or her own children, and not try to spread parental concern all around the world. On the other hand, this should be done not from a sense that my children are really more worthwhile than other people's children, but from a sense that it makes most sense for me to do my duties where I am placed, that the human community is best arranged in this way. That, to a Stoic, is what local and national identities should be like, and that is how they can be fortified and encouraged without subverting the primary claim of humanity.

Stoic cosmopolitans are aware that politics divides people and that it encourages them to think of other groups as alien and hostile. They therefore insist strongly on a process of empathetic understanding whereby we come to respect the humanity even of our political enemies, thinking of ourselves as born to work together and inspired by a common purpose. In the words of Marcus, who develops this idea especially fully, we should "enter into the mind" of the other, as far as is possible, and interpret the other's action with understanding (VI, 53; VIII, 51; XI, 18).

A favored exercise, in this process of world thinking, is to conceive of the entire world of human beings as a single body, and its many people as so many limbs. Referring to the fact that it takes only the change of a single letter in Greek to convert the word *melos* ("limb") to *meros* ("[detached] part"), Marcus concludes (VII, 13): "If, changing the word, you call yourself merely a [detached] part rather than a limb, you do not yet love your fellow men from the heart, nor derive complete joy from doing good; you will do it merely as a duty, not as doing good to yourself." Adoption of this organic model need not entail the disregard of the separateness of persons and the importance of political liberty: Stoics were intensely concerned about both of these things, in their own way, and never conceived of the satisfactions of different persons as fusable into a single system. But it does entail that we should think at all times of the way in which our good is intertwined with that of our fellows, and indeed conceive of ourselves as having common goals and projects with our fellows.

[. . .]

The Stoics are aware that the life of the cosmopolitan, and the cosmopolitan's concern with goals of world cooperation and respect for personhood, may be difficult to sell to citizens who are hooked on local group loyalties, with their colorful slogans and the psychological security they can inspire. The life of the world citizen is, in effect, as Diogenes the Cynic said, a kind of exile[26] – from the comfort of local truths, from the warm nestling feeling of local loyalties, from the absorbing drama of pride in oneself and one's own. In the writings of Marcus especially, one sometimes feels a boundless loneliness, as if the removal of props of habit and local boundaries had left life bereft of a certain sort of warmth and security. A person who as a child loved and trusted his parents is tempted to want to reconstruct citizenship along the same lines, finding in an idealized image of a group or a nation a surrogate parent who will do his thinking for him. Cosmopolitanism, in contrast, requires a nation of adults who do not need a childlike dependence upon omnipotent parental figures.

Whatever form political institutions take, they should be structured around a mature recognition of equal personhood and humanity. Cicero, following Panaetius, took this to entail certain duties of hospitality to the foreigner and the other (*De Officiis* I, 51ff.). Marcus insisted on the duty to educate oneself about the political affairs of the world as a whole, and to engage actively in those affairs in a way that shows concern for all world citizens. All Stoics took cosmopolitanism to require certain international limitations upon the conduct of warfare – in general, the renunciation of aggression and the resort to force only in self-defense, when all discussion has proven futile (ibid., 34), and also the humane treatment of the vanquished, including, if possible, the admission of the defeated people to equal citizenship in one's own nation (ibid., 35). In general, all punishments meted out to wrongdoers, whether as individuals or collectively, must preserve respect for human dignity in them (ibid., 89). Wars motivated by group hatred and wars of extermination come in for especially harsh condemnation.

4

Kant's debt to Stoic cosmopolitanism cannot be well understood if the discussion is confined to the political sphere and the political writings. That is why, in my own characterization of Stoicism, I have started from the moral core of the Stoics' ideas about reason and personhood, rather than from a more superficial description of their institutional and practical goals. It is this deep core that Kant appropriates – the idea of a kingdom of free rational beings, equal in humanity, each of them to be treated as an end no matter where in the world he or she dwells. In Kant as in Stoicism, this idea is less a specific political proposal than a regulative ideal that should be at the heart of both moral and political reflection and that supplies constraints upon what we may politically will. It also supplies moral motives of respect and awe that provide powerful incentives to fulfill the moral law. One can easily recognize these ideas as formative in the *Groundwork*, where, as Reich has argued, Kant's way of connecting the Formula of Universal Law to the Formula of Humanity is his own nonteleological recasting of the argument of *De Officiis*, where Cicero interprets the Stoic idea of life in accordance with nature as entailing a universal respect for humanity (III, 26–27). (As Reich shows, there are so many other points of contact between the two works that it appears likely that Kant followed the lines of Cicero's argument closely.) Stoic ideas also appear formative in the Second Critique, whose famous conclusion concerning the mind's awe before the starry sky above and the moral law within closely echoes the imagery of Seneca's Letter 41, expressing awe before the divinity of reason within us. A particularly important reference to Stoic ideas of world citizenship occurs in the *Anthropology*, where Kant, apparently following Marcus or at least writing in his spirit,[27] insists that we owe it to other human beings to try to understand their ways of thinking, since only that attitude is consistent with seeing oneself as a "citizen of the world" (*Anthropologie*, 2). And one can see these core notions of humanity and world citizenship as formative in the political writings too, especially in "Toward Perpetual Peace."

As do Marcus and Cicero, Kant stresses that the community of all human beings in reason entails a common participation in law (*ius*), and, by our very rational existence, a common participation in a virtual polity, a cosmopolis that has an implicit structure of claims and obligations regardless of whether or not there is an actual political organization in place to promote and vindicate them. When Kant refers to "the idea of a cosmopolitan law" and asserts that this law is "a necessary complement to the unwritten code of political and international law" (*PP*, 108), he is following very closely the lines of analysis traced by Cicero and Marcus. So too when he insists on the organic interconnectedness of all our actions: "The peoples of the earth have thus entered in varying degrees into a universal community, and it has developed to the point where a violation of laws in *one* part of the world is felt *everywhere*." (*PP*, 107–108)

In the details of his political proposals, Kant's debt to Cicero's *De Officiis* is, as in the *Groundwork*, intimate and striking. Kant's discussion of the relationship between morality and politics in the first appendix follows closely Cicero's discussions of the relation between morality and expediency (see II, 83 and III, 16ff.). Both thinkers insist on the supreme importance of justice in the conduct of political life, giving similar reasons for their denial that morality should ever be weighed against expediency. There are close parallels between the two thinkers' discussions of the hospitality right (II, 64; cf. *PP*, 105), and between their extremely stringent accounts of proper moral conduct during wartime and especially of justice to the enemy (Cicero I, 38ff.; cf. *PP*, 96ff.). Both insist on the great importance of truthfulness and promise keeping even in war, both denounce cruelty and wars of extermination, and both insistently oppose all treacherous conduct even toward the foe. Kant is again close to the Stoic analysis when he speaks of the right of all human beings to "communal possession of the earth's surface" (106), and of the possibility of "peaceful mutual relations which may eventually be regulated by public laws, thus bringing the human race nearer and nearer to a cosmopolitan constitution" (ibid.).

Especially fascinating is the way in which Kant appropriates Cicero's ideas about the duty of the philosopher to speak freely for the public good. In an Appendix entitled "Secret Article of a Perpetual Peace" he tells the reader that the containment of aggression has one condition that governing bodies will not want to admit publicly, and therefore will not write into their public documents. The "secret article" is that governing bodies working on this issue need help from philosophers:

> Although it may seem humiliating for the legislative authority of a state, to which we must naturally attribute the highest degree of wisdom, to seek instruction from *subjects* (the philosophers) regarding the principles on which it should act in its relations with other states, it is nevertheless extremely advisable that it should do so. The state will therefore invite their help *silently*, making a secret of it. In other words, it will *allow them to speak* freely and publicly on the universal maxims of warfare and peace-making, and they will indeed do so of their own accord if no-one forbids their discussions.

There remain some important differences between the Roman Stoics and Kant. For example, the Stoics did not and could not conclude, as Kant does (*PP*, 106–107), that colonial conquest is morally unacceptable. Seneca certainly could not have uttered such sentiments had he had them, and Marcus focuses on the task of managing the existing empire as justly and wisely as he can rather than on the question whether he ought not instead to dismantle it. But we should observe that what Kant objects to in colonialism is the oppressive and brutal treatment of the inhabitants (106) more than the fact of rule itself; and, on the other hand, Marcus, in his dying words, insists, not altogether implausibly, that he has ruled his empire by persuasion and love rather than fear: ". . . neither can any wealth, however abundant, suffice for the incontinence of a tyranny, nor a bodyguard be strong enough to protect the ruler, unless he has first of all the good-will of the governed."[28] If we make allowances for the differences of station in which life located these two philosophers, we may perhaps say that they pursued the goals of cosmopolitanism in parallel ways, each executing as well as possible the task of world citizenship in the sphere of life and work to which luck and talent assigned him.

Again, both the Stoics and Kant have blind spots, and not always in the same place. Kant's cosmopolitanism allows him to fall short of the Greek and even the Roman Stoics with regard to the equal person-hood and dignity of women,[29] and the Stoics' general tendency to accept the institution of slavery, if not all the practices associated with it, is especially shocking. For both Kant and the Stoics, there is sometimes and in some ways a tendency to treat the moral imperative as displacing the political imperative, respect for dignity at times taking the place of rather than motivating changes in the external circumstances of human lives, given that for both the good will is invulnerable to disadvantages imposed by these circumstances. But one should not exaggerate the indifference of either the Stoics or Kant to political change. Both hold that we have a duty to promote the happiness of others, and both hold that this entails constructive engagement with the political life. Cicero is especially vehement on this point, and it is the example of Cicero that Kant follows most closely.

In general, we may say that Kant's conception of a world politics in which moral norms of respect for humanity work to contain aggression and to promote mutual solidarity is a close adaptation of Cicero's Stoic ideas to the practical problems of his own era.

5

But there are two deep philosophical differences between Kant and his Stoic forebears that have important implications for the argument of "Toward Perpetual Peace." These differences concern *teleology* and *the view of the passions*.

It is, of course, fundamental to Kant's moral philosophy, and a central point in his criticism of ancient Greek moral theories throughout his work, that practical reason may not rely on any metaphysical picture of the world of nature, and therefore *a fortiori* may not rely on a picture of nature as teleologically designed by a beneficent and wise deity for the sake of the overall good. It is precisely on such a picture of nature that Stoic ethics rests – although the importance of this idea to the moral arguments of the Stoic thinkers has been disputed, and although it may have different degrees of importance for different Stoic thinkers.

In Kant's political writings, however, things are more complex. The idea of Providence appears, in something like a Stoic form, but Kant is careful to qualify his allegiance to it. In "On the Common Saying, 'This May be True in Theory, but it does not Apply in Practice,' " Kant, discussing the envisaged progress in international justice as seen "from a universal, i.e. cosmopolitan point of view," makes use of a very Stoic notion of nature's providential design:

> If we now ask what means there are of maintaining and indeed accelerating this constant progress toward a better state, we soon realize that . . . [we] must look to nature alone, or rather to *providence* (since it requires the highest wisdom to fulfill this purpose), for a successful outcome which will first affect the whole and then the individual parts.

This appeal to providence returns in "Toward Perpetual Peace," with especially fascinating ambiguity, in the section entitled First Supplement: On the Guarantee of a Perpetual Peace:

> Perpetual peace is *guaranteed* by no less an authority than the great artist *Nature* herself (*natura daedala rerum*). The mechanical process of nature visibly exhibits the purposive plan of producing concord among men, even against their will and indeed by means of their very discord. This design, if we regard it as a compelling cause whose laws of operation are unknown to us, is called *fate*. But if we consider its purposive function within the world's development, whereby it appears as the underlying wisdom of a higher cause, showing the way towards the objective goal of the human race and predetermining the world's evolution, we call it *Providence*. We cannot actually observe such an agency in the artifices of nature, nor can we even *infer* its existence from them. But as with all relations between the form of things and their ultimate purposes, we can and must *supply it mentally* in order to conceive of its possibility by analogy with human artifices. . . . But in contexts

such as this, where we are concerned purely with theory and not with religion, we should also note that it is more in keeping with the limitations of human reason to speak of *nature* and not of *Providence*, for reason, in dealing with cause and effect relationships, must keep within the bounds of possible experience. *Modesty* forbids us to speak of providence as something we can recognize, for this would mean donning the wings of Icarus and presuming to approach the mystery of its inscrutable intentions.

In this complex paragraph (which is accompanied by an even more complex and very obscure footnote on the different varieties of Providence), Kant first states confidently that perpetual peace is guaranteed by nature's design; following the Stoics, he gives this design the dual names "fate" and "Providence." Already here, however, there is complexity: the Latin phrase that characterizes nature is taken from Lucretius's *De Rerum Natura*, a work much loved by Kant but one that resolutely denies that any teleological design is to be discerned in the workings of nature. Kant now goes on to make this uncertainty official, reminding his readers that we must not speak of providence with any confidence, since that would be to attempt to transcend the limits of human nature. In other words, he repudiates the Stoic approach that insists on grounding cosmopolitanism in a securely asserted teleology.

In the next paragraph, however, Kant goes straight back to the Stoic picture as if no qualification had intervened: "We may next enquire in what manner the guarantee is provided. Nature's provisional arrangement is as follows." What is especially fascinating to a classicist is that the material that ensues seems to be evidence that the strange reference to Lucretius is no accident. Kant follows closely the course of Lucretius's actual argument denying providential design in nature, but simply asserts the contradictory at every point. Lucretius says that more than half of the earth is simply uninhabitable because of climate, and that the rest is extremely inhospitable to humans on account of the presence of wild beasts. Kant asserts, without argument, that nature "has taken care that human beings are able to live in all the areas where they are settled" and has "see[n] to it that men *could* live everywhere on earth." Again, Lucretius cites war as an example of the disordered and nonprovidential nature of things; Kant immediately cites war as part of nature's providential design, in order to cause humans to scatter, inhabiting "even the most inhospitable regions." For Lucretius, legal arrangements originated because human beings, finding themselves in an intrinsically disordered universe, decided to agree to their own order; for Kant, in the next sentence, legal arrangements result from strife that is caused, in turn, by nature's providential design.

In short, I think there can be little doubt that Kant is struggling against Lucretius's anti-teleological view of nature and allying himself with Stoic providential religion. His argument gives many signs of this internal debate: for example, in a strange footnote he ponders a hypothetical objection that settlers in remote Arctic lands might someday run out of driftwood, and responds that the settlers will be able to barter for wood by using "the animal products in which the Arctic coasts are so plentiful." This is of course not an objection to teleology to be found in Lucretius; but it is just the *sort* of point Lucretius does raise, and just what we would expect an eighteenth-century Epicurean to assert. Kant, then, appears to enroll himself as an enthusiastic partisan of Stoic views, despite the modesty that his official view enjoins.

There remains, however, a large difference between Kant and the Stoics – or at least between Kant's claim about all human beings and what Stoics claim about the sage. (With respect to non-sages the Stoics' view is difficult to distinguish from Kant's.) The

Stoic sage knows with certainty the design of the universe in all its workings, and knows that it is providential. He is like Zeus in his knowledge, with the one exception that he lacks knowledge of future contingent particular events. Kant's human being, by contrast, hopes for providence, and makes up arguments about it, but thinks it inappropriate to claim actually to recognize it or to approach the mystery of its intentions – however much Kant himself appears at times to do all this. Providence is, at best, a "practical postulate," a confidently held practical hope.

How important is this hope to Kant's cosmopolitanism? This is obviously of great concern to us, since what appears attractive in Kant's version of Stoic cosmopolitanism is its attempt to preserve the moral core of the view without pinning it to a teleology that most of us can no longer believe. Here I am in agreement with Bernard Williams: if the good news that Kant's Stoicism brings us is inseparable from a view that rational purpose is inherent in the universe, we are much less likely to accept it.

The hope of Providence was clearly of importance to Kant personally, and he seems to think it important that cosmopolitans should be able to share it. That is why, in "Toward Perpetual Peace" more than elsewhere, his rhetoric is full of appeals to that hope. But I believe it is clear that the moral core of Kant's argument is altogether separable from this sort of wishful thinking – and I believe that he is correct to think that one may appropriate this moral core of Stoicism without its teleology of design. We are told that our moral acts must take their bearings from the equal worth of humanity in all persons, near or far, and that this moral stance leads politics in a cosmopolitan direction; we are told that morality should be supreme over politics, giving political thought both constraints and goals. Following Cicero, Kant focuses on that moral imperative and its basis in reverence for humanity, and adds the appeals to providence only as a kind of reassurance to the faint-hearted.

Do we need to follow Kant in alluding to providence as at least a practical postulate, a reasonable hope, if we wish either to be cosmopolitans or to persuade others that they should define themselves in accordance with cosmopolitan aims and aspirations? I believe we do not. Humanity can claim our respect just as powerfully whether we think the universe is intrinsically well ordered or whether, with Lucretius, we think that things look pretty random and unprovidential. However humanity emerged, whether by design or by chance, it is what it is and it compels respect. In a sense there is a special dignity and freedom in the choice to constitute our community as universal and moral in the face of a disorderly and unfriendly universe, for then we are not following anyone else's imperatives but our very own.

6

We now arrive at what is perhaps the central difference between Kant and the Stoics. For Kant, the search for peace requires a persistent vigilance toward human aggression, which Kant views as innate, ineliminable from human nature, and more or less brutish and ineducable. "War," he writes (*PP*, 111), "does not require any particular kind of motivation, for it seems to be ingrained in human nature." If we were looking only at a single nation, he says, we could deny that bad things result from "any inherent wickedness rooted in human nature" (120), and blame them instead on "the deficiencies of their as yet underdeveloped culture (i.e. their barbarism)." But Kant concludes that the fact that all states, however developed, behave badly in their external relations gives "irrefutable" evidence of inherent wickedness. Similarly, in "Idea for a Universal History" he says that when one contemplates human actions one sees that "everything as a whole is made up of folly and childish vanity, and often of childish malice and destructiveness" (42). Influenced, it would appear, both by Augustinian Christianity and by Romanticism's strong distinction between passion and culture, Kant appears throughout his career to conceive of the passions, including aggression, as natural, precultural, and not removable from human nature.

For the Stoics, however, none of the passions is seated in human nature. Bodily appetites do, of course, have an innate bodily basis. But the passions themselves (grief, fear, love, hatred, envy, jealousy, anger) not only require learning and belief; they are actually identified by the Stoics with a certain type of evaluative judgment – that is, with an assent to a certain sort of value-laden view of the way things are. The common characteristic of all these value-laden views is that they ascribe considerable importance, with respect to the person's own flourishing, to things and persons outside the self that the person does not control.[31] They all involve, therefore, a kind of passivity toward the world of nature, a form of life in which one puts oneself at the mercy of the world by allowing one's good to reside outside the boundaries of that which one can control. To a Stoic, such a form of life is profoundly irrational, because it is always bound to lead to instability and pain, and indeed very likely to lead, through retaliatory aggression, to the infliction of harm on others. It is always in our power to withhold assent to these ways of seeing the importance of external things, no matter how pervasive they are in our society, and to judge that one's own virtue is sufficient for one's flourishing.

It is, then, a consequence of this view that there will be no passions of anger and hatred, and no desire for retaliation, if there are no unwise attachments to external things and persons. The Stoics' diagnosis – like and the basis for Spinoza's – is that anger does not derive from any innate aggressive instinct in human nature. They see no reason to posit such an instinct, and much reason in the early behavior of children, to doubt it.[32] On the other hand, when we become attached to things outside our will – our possessions, our reputation, our honor, our bodily good looks and health – we put our dignity at the world's mercy, setting ourselves up to be slighted and damaged. To those slights and damages, anger will be the natural response – natural in the sense that a judgment that an important element of my good has been damaged or slighted is a sufficient condition for it, but not in the sense that the response itself is instinctual or (apart from the questionable value judgments) inevitable.

Nor will the Stoics accept the claim (made by Aristotelians in their philosophical culture,[33] and by many ordinary people consulting their intuitions) that anger is an essential part of public life in the sense of being a necessary motivation for valuable actions defending oneself, one's family, or one's country. They like to point out that an angry army is very likely to be an inept, aggressive army, and that actions in defense of one's own can appropriately be taken by consulting duty alone. If one acts because the action is right, not because one is oneself aggrieved, one's action will be more likely to be a balanced and measured one. The Stoics certainly do not envisage that putting an end to anger will put an end to war, for, like Kant, they conceive of some wars as appropriate responses to the aggression of others. But they do believe, as I have said, that human beings are born for mutual aid and mutual concord, and that the removal of anger will remove the vindictive and destructive elements in war and cut down greatly on the world's total of conflict.

To what extent do Stoics think that the passions – and in particular anger and hatred – can really be removed from human life? In any actual society (say, Seneca's Rome), the roots of the passions are taught so early in a child's moral education that the adult who undertakes a Stoic education will have to labor all his life against his own habits and habit-based inclinations. Seneca examines himself at the end of every day,[34] noting that he has become inappropriately angered at this or that slight to his honor – being seated too low at a dinner table and so forth. This sort of patient self-examination and self-criticism is necessary for passional enlightenment. But as it is carried on with increasing success, the personality becomes enlightened all the way down, so to speak. Reason and respect for humanity will gradually infuse the whole of Seneca's personality, shaping not only his philosophical and juridical ruminations but also his very propensities for fear, for grief, for anger and hatred. Because these passions are not a part of the soul apart from thought but rather a certain sort of (misguided) thought, they can themselves be enlightened. And therefore the Stoics hold out the hope that the society they live in, through the patient labors of individual souls, can itself become an enlightened one.

It is especially important to see how the Stoics link the goal of world citizenship to the goal of passional enlightenment. Briefly put, their recipe is that love of humanity as such should be our basic affective attitude. This will not be a passion in the technical sense in which passion is linked with upheaval and instability, but it will be a reliable motivation that will steer us in the world and give us joy. At the same time, their instructions about the proper way to view the alien, the other, or the enemy – not as objects of fear and hate, but as members of one common body with one set of purposes – provide powerful devices for the undoing of the negative attitudes that often inform situations of national or ethnic conflict. Their claim is that these attitudes are constructed by social evaluations and can be undone by the patient work of philosophy.

To enlighten the passions need not mean to remove them, although it is this goal that the Stoics actually adopt. Another sort of cognitive passion-theorist, say an Aristotelian, can hold that the passions can be enlightened in such a way that they still are on the scene in some cases but they always select appropriate objects – so that anger, for example, manifests itself only toward the appropriate targets at the appropriate time. (For the Stoics no such targets are appropriate; for Aristotle it is right to be angry about certain damages to one's body, one's loved ones, or one's country.) Such an Aristotelian view of the passions has wide currency throughout history. (It is, for example, the dominant view of emotion in the Anglo-American common-law tradition of criminal law, and is responsible for standard definitions of notions such as "reasonable provocation" and duress.) So it is important to state that we can adopt the Stoics' goal of passional enlightenment without adopting the specific content they give to that notion, which requires a radical detachment from some attachments that we might judge it reasonable to foster, even in a cosmopolitan society.

Kant cannot set such a high goal for human personal enlightenment; his related conception of social enlightenment must therefore be defined in terms of the suppression of the evil forces in human beings rather than in terms of their education. It is more than a little odd, it seems to me, that Kant, familiar as he clearly was with Stoic ideas, including ideas about the passions,[35] did not seriously consider their view as a candidate for truth in this area. This fact is all the odder given that Spinoza adopted the Stoic picture more or less unchanged and made the adoption of that picture and

its associated conception of enlightenment a linchpin of his own project of cosmopolitan reform. Rousseau, moreover, though he did not analyze the passions in detail,
seems to have been convinced of the natural goodness of humanity, and he discussed
the formation of passion against the background of that commitment.[36] It seems clear
to me that Kant could have taken over the Stoic/Spinozistic analysis of passion with
very few other changes in his overall moral and political view, and that the Stoic conception would in many ways have served his view better than the one he in fact
adopted. The pessimistic view of human evil implied by his acceptance of innate aggression is always a difficulty for him, and he must struggle against it to find a place for
his own characteristic political optimism, an optimism he clearly shares with Spinoza
and Rousseau. In "Theory and Practice," for example, he begins the section on international justice with the question "Is the human race as a whole likable, or is it an object
to be regarded with distaste?" And he shortly declares that a belief in immutable
natural evil can cause us to turn our backs on our fellow human beings, and on
ourselves:

> . . . however hard we may try to awaken feelings of love in ourselves, we cannot avoid
> hating that which is and always will be evil, especially if it involves deliberate and general
> violation of the most sacred laws of humanity. Perhaps we may not wish to harm men,
> but shall not want to have any more to do with them than we can help. (87)

Seneca's arguments against the idea of innate aggression would have provided Kant
with a strong counterweight to these pessimistic thoughts, and would have opened
up prospects of enlightenment that would give new substance to the hope for
cosmopolitanism.

Suppose, now, we substitute the Stoic view of passions for the view Kant actually
holds, and consider the prospects of human enlightenment in the perspective of that
view. How much hope does the Stoic picture give us, with respect to the containment
of anger and aggression in our own world? Not much, without some fairly radical
changes in moral education on a large scale, so that people will increasingly define
themselves in terms of their reason and character rather than in terms of honor, status,
wealth, power, and the other things that are the common occasions of slights and
damages and thus of retaliatory anger.

Furthermore, seeing the Stoic analysis of passions as based on a certain type of evaluative belief does not, as I have said, commit us to the normative Stoic view. We will
have to ask, on Kant's behalf and on our own, to exactly what extent the goal of a
complete eradication of anger is an appropriate moral goal. I myself would not have
us follow the Stoics in refusing anger at social injustice, or at damages to loved ones,
or to our own bodily integrity. I would support a more Aristotelian course. But this
qualification means that some appropriate causes of anger will still remain in human
life, and peace will still require Kant's careful institutional guarantees.

However, certain especially pernicious forms of anger and hatred can indeed be
eradicated by patient reform following Stoic conceptions. The hatred of members of
other races and religions can be effectively addressed by forms of early education that
address the cognitive roots of those passions by getting children to view these people
in the Stoic cosmopolitan way, as similarly human, as bearers of an equal moral
dignity, as members of a single body and a single set of purposes, and as no longer
impossibly alien or threatening. If one looks at the way in which racial hatred and
aggression can be and occasionally has been eradicated in a person or a community

(if, for example, one looks at successes in the rearing of nonracist children), one sees that the success, insofar as there is success, is a Stoic success, achieved through enlightenment of the images we bring to our encounters with the other, through gradual changes in *evaluation*, rather than through suppression of a brute and undiscriminating urge to harm. Consider how the equal respect for women is fostered (when it is) in an individual or a group. Once again, I believe that it is achieved in the Stoic way, well described by Musonius Rufus: it is through enlightenment of the images of rational and moral humanity that we bring to our mutual encounters, rather than through suppression of an allegedly innate and unreasoning misogyny. The powerful Stoic idea that our destructive passions are socially constructed and fostered in the images of self and other we use suggests a program of reform that, while unlikely to achieve full success, can quite realistically be expected to shape the ways our children regard one another and the ways in which marriages and partnerships of all sorts take shape. Again, where we see suspicion and hatred of the foreigner, we can always try to address it through programs of education that will make the Stoics' and Kant's idea of world citizenship real in our schools and universities, teaching young people to regard the alien, with Marcus, as one from whom they might actually learn something, and, indeed, someone who, given a change of situation, they might themselves be. We may make the same point about contempt distributed along lines of wealth and social class. Recognizing the cogency of the Stoic view of passions gives us a duty: it tells us that we have great power over racism, sexism, and other divisive passions that militate against cosmopolitan humanism, if we will only devote enough attention to the cognitive moral development of the young. [. . .] In its best form this is not in the least a totalitarian idea, but one connected with the Stoic and the Kantian ideas of a truly free person. This ideal gives us a lifetime full of work to do if only we will do it.

Moreover, where such enlightenment of divisive passions cannot be achieved in the lives of individuals, we may view it as a regulative ideal and design institutions in ways that appropriately reflect the respect for humanity involved in it. Where we cannot altogether eradicate racial hatred, we can ensure that heavy penalties for ethnic and racial hate crimes are institutionalized in our codes of criminal law – and this is now being done. Where we cannot altogether ensure that foreigners be treated with Ciceronian hospitality, we can always seek to enact constitutional protections for the alien on our soil, and for that alien's children. Where we see the rights of women, or racial or ethnic minorities, being grossly violated anywhere in the world, we can support approaches to these problems through the international human rights movement, through nongovernmental organizations of many types, and through, let us hope, our own governments, if they will show themselves capable of minimal courage. We do not need to have exaggerated optimism about the triumph of enlightenment in order to view these as goals toward which we may sensibly strive, and in order to believe that this striving may achieve many local victories.

One must acknowledge that we do not see a triumph for cosmopolitanism right now in the United States, which seems increasingly indifferent to cosmopolitan goals and increasingly given over to a style of politics that does not focus on recognizing the equal humanity of the alien and the other; which seems increasingly hostile, too, to the intellectuals whom Kant saw as crucial to the production of such an enlightenment. We may well conjecture that were either Kant or Cicero and Marcus Aurelius to look at America they would see much that would distress them: not just the dominance of anger and aggression, but also an indifference to the well-being of the whole world that would make them think of America as one of the cut-off limbs of the world body that Marcus was so fond of describing in scathing and mordant language.[37]

Nor is it only in America that cosmopolitanism seems to be in grave jeopardy. The state of things in very many parts of the world gives reason for pessimism: when, 200 years after the publication of Kant's hopeful treatise, we see so many regions falling prey to ethnic and religious and racial conflict; when we find that the very values of equality, personhood, and human rights that Kant defended, and indeed the Enlightenment itself, are derided in some quarters as mere ethnocentric vestiges of Western imperialism; when, in a general way, we see so much more hatred and aggression around us than respect and love.

And yet we may agree with Kant here as well: certain postulates of practical reason, and therefore certain hopes for at least a local and piecemeal sort of progress – even though they are not clearly supported by what we can observe – should be adopted because they appear necessary for our continued cultivation of our humanity, our constructive engagement in political life. Concerning this hope, Kant writes:

> . . . however uncertain I may be and may remain as to whether we can hope for anything better for mankind, this uncertainty cannot detract from the maxim I have adopted, or from the necessity of assuming for practical purposes that human progress is possible.
>
> This hope for better times to come, without which an earnest desire to do something useful for the common good would never have inspired the human heart, has always influenced the activities of right-thinking people.[38]

This hope is, of course, a hope in and for reason. When, as scholars, we turn to classical antiquity in order to bring its resources to our own political world, we would do better, I believe, to appropriate and follow this Stoic/Kantian tradition of cautious rational optimism than to look to ancient Athens for a paradigm of a politics that simply directs us, as Bernard Williams puts it, to contemplate the horrors. There are always too many horrors, and it is all too easy to contemplate them. But, as Kant and his Stoic mentors knew, it is also possible to stop contemplating and to act, doing something useful for the common good.

Notes

1   All citations from Kant's political writings are taken from the second enlarged edition of *Kant: Political Writings*, ed. H. Reiss (Cambridge University Press, 1991). I have, however, in some cases differed with Nisbet about the translation of some terms, and have in those cases altered the translation.
2   Bernard Williams, *Shame and Necessity* (University of California Press, 1993).
3   Alasdair MacIntyre, *After Virtue* (Notre Dame University Press, 1981); MacIntyre, *Whose Justice? Which Rationality?* (Notre Dame University Press, 1987).
4   "The Women of Trachis: Fictions, Pessimism, Ethics," in *The Greeks and Us: Essays in Honor of Arthur W. H. Adkins*, ed. R. Louden (University of Chicago Press, 1996). This paper is continuous with and further develops the picture of the development of Greek ethics presented in Williams's important book *Shame and Necessity* (University of California Press, 1993).
5   See my "Aristotle on Human Nature and the Foundations of Ethics," in *World, Mind, and Ethics: Essays on the Ethical Philosophy of Bernard Williams*, ed. J. Altham and R. Harrison (Cambridge University Press, 1995).
6   G. E. R. Lloyd, especially *Magic, Reason, and Experience* (Cambridge University Press, 1981).
7   The ancient authors referred to in the political works include Epicurus, Lucretius, Virgil, Horace, Cicero, Seneca, Marcus Aurelius, and Persius. All of these but Epicurus and Marcus are Latin authors, and Kant clearly read them in the original.

8   The term *kosmou politês* is apparently Cynic in origin: Diogenes the Cynic, asked where he came from, replied "I am a *kosmopolitês*." (Diogenes Laertius VI, 3) Marcus generally prefers not the single coined term but the phrase *politês tou kosmou*.

9   Klaus Reich, "Kant and Greek Ethics," *Mind* 48 (1939): 338–354, 446–463.

10   See the reference to Kant's *Anthropology* below.

11   Diogenes the Cynic, in Diogenes Laertius, *Lives of the Philosophers*, VI, 63. For an English version see the Loeb translation by R. D. Hicks (Harvard University Press, 1970). All translations from Greek and Latin are my own unless noted otherwise.

12   See, among other sources, Griffin, "Le movement cynique"; *The Cynics*, ed. B. Branham (University of California Press, 1996); D. R. Dudley, *A History of Cynicism* (Ares, 1980).

13   Seneca, *De Otio*, 4.1, translated as in *The Hellenistic Philosophers*, ed. A. Long and D. Sedley (Cambridge University Press, 1987), p. 431.

14   Plutarch, *On the Fortunes of Alexander*, 329A–B, my translations; see Long and Sedley, p. 429. For other relevant texts see Long and Sedley, pp. 429–437.

15   See Malcolm Schofield, *The Stoic Idea of the City* (Cambridge University Press, 1991).

16   See M. Griffin, *Seneca: A Philosopher in Politics* (Clarendon, 1976); see also her "Philosophy, Politics, and Politicians at Rome," in *Philosophia Togata*, ed. M. Griffin and J. Barnes (Clarendon, 1989). On Marcus see R. B. Rutherford, *The Meditations of Marcus Aurelius: A Study* (Clarendon, 1989).

17   I discuss these matters at greater length, with references to many texts, in chapter 9 of *The Therapy of Desire: Theory and Practice in Hellenistic Ethics* (Princeton University Press, 1994).

18   See the Plutarch passage cited above; for discussion see Schofield, *The Stoic Idea*.

19   Although Cicero in book III comes close to asserting that our obligation to humanity takes priority over all other obligations, he is far less confident in book I, and indeed makes many more concessions to local affiliation than other Stoic thinkers. On his view of our diverse obligations, see Christopher Gill, "The Four *Personae* in Cicero's *De Officiis*," *Oxford Studies in Ancient Philosophy*.

20   See also Marcus I, 14 in *The Meditations* (Hackett, 1983): he thanks his teachers for giving him a grasp of the idea of a polity "with the same laws for all, governed on the basis of equality and free speech." See also V, 16.

21   See also VI, 44: "My city and my country, as I am Antoninus, is Rome; as I am a human being, it is the world."

22   See Schofield, *The Stoic Idea*, for an excellent discussion of Stoic attitudes to sex equality. In the Stoics' ideal city, men and women would be citizens on an equal footing; even distinctions of dress would be abolished (Diogenes Laertius VII, 33).

23   See also Cicero, *De Officiis* I, 107, according to which we have two characters: one universal, arising from our rationality, and one individual, deriving from our particular talents and abilities.

24   For the Hierocles fragment, and Long and Sedley, p. 349. For Cicero's use of the circle metaphor, see *De Officiis* I, 50ff. (See the fine annotated translation *Cicero: On Duties*, ed. M. Griffin and E. Atkins (Cambridge University Press, 1991).)

25   Terence, *Heautontimoroumenos*, paraphrased in *De Officiis* (I, 30) and quoted by Kant on p. 460 of *Metaphysics of Morals* (*Kant's Ethical Writings* (Hackett, 1983), p. 125).

26   Diogenes Laertius VI, 49: "When someone spoke scornfully of his exile, he said, 'You poor man – that was how I became a philosopher.'"

27   Here is an instance in which the influence of the Stoics may have reached Kant indirectly through the mediation of natural-law writers who were ultimately much influenced by Marcus.

28   The speeches ascribed to Marcus are collected at the end of the Loeb Classical Library edition of his work (Harvard University Press, 1916).

29   On the equality of women in the Stoic ideal community, see Schofield, *The Stoic Idea*.

30   Reiss edition, p. 87.

31   See my discussion in *Therapy of Desire*.

32   This conclusion is by now widely accepted in developmental psychology and anthropology. See, for example, John Bowlby, *Attachment* (Basic Books, 1973); W. R. D. Fairbairn, *Psychological Papers* (Edinburgh, 1952); Jean Briggs, *Never in Anger* (Harvard University Press, 1980). For related primate research, see F. de Waal, *Peacemaking among Primates* (Harvard University Press, 1980), and the article on bonobo society in the March 1995 *Scientific American*.

33   See especially Seneca, *On Anger*, book I (discussed in chapter 11 of *Therapy of Desire*).

34   *On Anger* III, 36 (discussed in chapter 11 of *Therapy of Desire*).

35   See the discussion of pity in the Doctrine of Virtue of *The Metaphysics of Morals*, which alludes explicitly to the Stoic conception.

36 See especially *Emile*, book IV. On natural goodness, see Joshua Cohen, "The Natural Goodness of Humanity" (forthcoming). Rousseau's views seem close to those expressed by Seneca in book I of *On Anger*.

37 See for example VIII, 34: "If you have ever seen a dismembered hand or foot or a head cut off, lying somewhere apart from the rest of the trunk, you have an image of what a person makes of himself . . . when he . . . cuts himself off or when he does some unneighborly act. You have somehow made yourself an outcast from the unity which is according to Nature; for you came into the world as a part and now you have cut yourself off."

38 "Theory and Practice," p. 89.

Kant's Cosmopolitanism
Garrett Wallace Brown

"It makes no difference whether a person lives here or there, provided that, where he lives, he lives as a citizen of the world" – Marcus Aurelius

Introduction

In *Idea for a Universal History with a Cosmopolitan Purpose*, Immanuel Kant defines cosmopolitanism as being "the matrix within which all the original capacities of the human race may develop."[1] In the broadest sense, Kant's cosmopolitanism can be understood as being concerned with the cultivation of a global environment within which everyone can fully develop his or her human capacities. Kant expands on what establishing this matrix entails when he proclaims that, "the greatest problem for the human species, the solution of which nature compels him to seek, is that of attaining a civil society, which can administer justice universally."[2] There are two important distinctions that should immediately be made from these passages when understanding Kant's cosmopolitanism. One distinction involves understanding the components embroiled in creating a matrix of cosmopolitan law. This includes formulating what is to be meant by universal justice, a global civil society and the moral value assigned to human capacities. The other involves synthesizing these principles with Kant's assertion that nature compels us to administer justice universally and that all human beings have original capacities that nature obliges us to fully develop. In this regard, there exist two strands in Kant's cosmopolitanism. One is concerned with what some might consider a naturalistic teleology and the other is concerned with the formal principles involved in creating universal justice and cosmopolitan law. The distinctions are important, for whereas Kant's cosmopolitan theory of history sought to discover various motivations behind the formation of a cosmopolitan order, cosmopolitan law was specifically dedicated to inaugurating principles of jurisprudence necessary for a condition of universal justice to exist. Although both concepts are linked, they sustain two distinctive functions within Kant's cosmopolitanism and should not be lumped tightly together as has been traditionally done.

What the two quotes also help to highlight is that there are three interrelated elements involved in both aspects of Kant's cosmopolitanism. First, individuals represent the unit of ultimate moral concern equally and that our human capacities can only be fully developed within a condition of universal justice. Second, the attainment of universal justice requires the broader cultivation of a cosmopolitan civil society, one based solely on our humanity alone, without reference to nationality, localized political affiliation or place of birth. Third, the sole concern of cosmopolitan law is with establishing this matrix of universal justice and with formulating the necessary fundamental normative principles that underwrite a cosmopolitan constitution. It is in this sense that there is a connection between Kant and the quote used at the beginning of this chapter by Marcus Aurelius. The connection stems from a shared cosmopolitan belief that it makes no difference where a person lives, as long as that person is also understood as embedded within the larger human community. The foundations of that larger community should be based on a conception of universal justice and the establishment of a global condition where the development of everyone's capacities is to be considered as if they were equal citizens of the world.

Although many cosmopolitan scholars have invoked Kant's moral philosophy and aspects of his cosmopolitan theory as the foundational basis for their own arguments, they have often disagreed on the exact nature of Kant's cosmopolitanism. This is because there is considerable ambiguity and complication involved in the development of Kant's cosmopolitan matrix. The purpose of this chapter is to help clarify some of these ambiguities by outlining the basic elements that underwrite a Kantian form of cosmopolitanism. In doing so, this chapter will look at the ethical principles behind Kant's cosmopolitanism, the problem of Kant's cosmopolitan teleology, and develop a brief overview of Kant's more coherent principles of cosmopolitan law. [. . .] To do this, the chapter is divided into four sections. In Section I, a connection is made between Kant's critical philosophy and the moral foundations of Kant's cosmopolitan vision. The second section will then outline Kant's cosmopolitan theory of history and suggest that it is based on a problematic teleology. It is in this section that a more plausible treatment of Kant's cosmopolitan history is provided. The third section discusses the concept of cosmopolitan law and couches it in Kant's overall theory of universal justice. The aim of the fourth section is to tie the various aspects of Kant's cosmopolitanism into a single coherent narrative. [. . .]

I. Moral foundations of Kant's cosmopolitanism

The easiest way to capture the essence of Kant's moral philosophy is to state his philosophical intention. It is generally accepted that Kant's goal was to give meaning to human experience without relying on pure rationalism or empiricism. Although this is stated very broadly, it does capture Kant's basic intent, which was to provide philosophical meaning to both the realm of scientific and empirical experience, but also to metaphysical concepts such as the *idea of morality*. In opposition to David Hume's empiricism, Kant believed that the forces of nature were not to be discovered by experience alone, but also through *a priori* constructions which gave significant human meaning to these experiences. [. . .] What Kant stressed in his critical philosophy was the necessary element of independent principles of human reason, which were prior to experience and which gave order to what he called "the experience of nature." In other words, the critical philosophy of Kant was an attempt to establish a system of *a priori* principles for the purpose of understanding the external world. This understanding could only be one from the human mind, which gives meaning not only to our empirical experiences, but also provides meaningful order to the world around us.

It is in Kant's discussions of morality that his epistemological considerations transfer into political foundations. The question for Kant was how to understand the idea of morality beyond the realm of empirical experience, where the idea of morality has the ability to provide guiding principles that can be confirmed by practical reason. For Kant, the idea of morality starts with the *transcendental deduction* and the inherent assumption that individuals are free to make moral decisions. If humans are not free to determine the imperative force behind moral values, then morality no longer represents a self-imposed duty, but rather a meaningless coerced action. In order for morality to have subjective imperative, individuals must be understood as having the capacity for self-prescribed duty. The idea of morality, in order to remain internally consistent, must contain this corresponding imperative action. These moral decisions are not made in the context of determined causes alone, but find imperative weight principally through choices of our *free will*. In order to justify the idea of having a moral choice, human beings must be considered not only as phenomenal beings, but also as noumenal beings that are free. The idea of morality demands the *freedom of will* to make reasoned judgements, which in turn enable humans to make meaningful moral judgements that act in accordance with self-imposed duties. According to Kant, the capacity to self-legislate is the power to be autonomous moral agents and represents the ultimate source of human dignity. Thus, "by acting in accordance with moral principles prescribed by his own reason, man asserts his independence from the natural world and establishes what is distinctively human in his nature."[3]

Nevertheless, morality is different from other cognitive decisions because the latter command action in relation to self-imposed belief or agreed-upon social rules. Kant understands that choices as profoundly important as moral decisions must be conceived in relation to whether the moral duty can also be conceived as universally valid. It is in regard to determining what are correct rules of moral action that the idea of morality metaphysically necessitates practical synthetic *a priori* judgements of the *categorical imperative* which states, "act only according to the maxim whereby you can at the same time will that it should become a universal law."[4] It is from variations of the categorical imperative that Kant derives two important principles of cosmopolitan universality. One derivative affirms that we should "act in such a way that you treat humanity, whether in your own person or in the person of another, always at the same time as an end, and never as a means."[5] Another derivative maintains that legislative maxims are only valid if they "can at the same time have for their object themselves as universal laws of nature."[6] In other words, since everyone has the capacity to be moral lawgivers, it is therefore rational to treat all humans with respect and a sense of universal human dignity. Kant consequently defines our human capacity for freedom as an innate right when he states, "freedom (independence from being constrained by another's choice) insofar as it can coexist with the freedom of every other in accordance with a universal law, is the only original right belonging to every man by virtue of his humanity."[7] This original right translates into the maxim that individuals should thus never be used simply as means, but should be understood as having ends in themselves. We determine the validity of this maxim by understanding that we could never justify the violation of this right, for one could never rationally demand the violation of this maxim as a universal law of nature.

As Linklater has pointed out, the moral theory of Kant has two significant implications in regard to its transition to the realm of political theory. The first relates to the transcendental deduction and a moral claim that "human beings do not submit to a morality which has its source outside them."[8] The second implication relates to the categorical imperative and the principle that because individuals are moral beings, they must also have an "awareness of participating with others in a law-making community."[9] Kant himself describes this principle as a universal principle of hypothetical community when he suggests that humans should act "as if one were through his maxims always a law-making member in the universal kingdom of ends."[10] The implications derived from these principles are complex but simply summarized. Human beings should be allowed to exercise their capacity to be moral beings and that by exercising this equal capacity, we must come to understand our political and legal structures as vehicles for the development of our mutual co-legislation and external freedom.

It is therefore from a combination of the transcendental deduction and the categorical imperative that Kant formulates his *principle of universal justice* and *public right*. Kant's justice and the corresponding condition of public right are defined as "the sum of conditions under which the choice of one can be united with the choice of another in accordance with a universal law of freedom."[11] From the short discussion above, we can understand Kantian justice as an attempt to facilitate a civil condition where autonomous agents can socially coexist in accordance with universal freedom, which is for Kant the capacity of co-legislation and the voluntary subjugation to moral laws legislated by themselves. Nevertheless, there is an important distinction that should be made between the categorical imperative as used in Kantian ethics and his principle of universal justice. Whereas the first formulation of the categorical imperative describes how universal laws of morality can be determined, the principle of universal justice is concerned with what legitimate restrictions to individual freedom should exist in order to create a condition of universal public right. In this regard, justice necessitates that a legal condition of public right should exist so that "the freedom of the individual is limited in such a way as to secure the equal freedom of all."[12] The justification for this restriction of freedom is derived through the categorical imperative and a universal respect for the dignity of human beings as ends in themselves. The fact that we should see humans as moral decision makers and therefore also as having ends in themselves is derived from the transcendental deduction and the idea of morality.

The broader cosmopolitan implications of Kant's critical and moral philosophy are nicely encapsulated in the *Critique of Pure Reason*. The following quote not only represents Kant's first transition point from his critical writings to his political writings, but also provides an outline of his entire cosmopolitan project. In addition, the quote illustrates the transition of the categorical imperative into a scheme of constitutional public right. Kant's guiding principle of the categorical imperative is outlined as a shared idea of equal and universal justice when Kant suggests:

> A constitution allowing the *greatest possible human freedom in accordance with laws which ensure that the freedom of each can coexist with the freedom of all the others* (not one designed to provide the greatest possible happiness, as this will in any case follow automatically), is at all events a necessary idea which must be made the basis not only of the first outline of a political constitution but of all laws as well. It requires that we should abstract at the outset from present hindrances, which perhaps do not arise inevitably out of human nature, but are rather occasioned by neglect of genuine ideas in the process of legislation . . . Even if the latter should never come about, the idea which sets up this maxim as an archetype, in order to bring the legal constitution of mankind nearer and nearer to its

greatest possible perfection, still remains correct. For no one can or ought to decide what the highest degree may be at which mankind may have to stop progressing, and hence how wide a gap may still of necessity remain between the idea and its execution. For this will depend on freedom, which can transcend any limit we care to impose.[13]

There are five important elements that should be taken from Kant's moral theory to the realm of Kantian cosmopolitan theory. First, the source of ultimate moral concern is located within individuals as having ends in themselves and with their equal capacity to be free and autonomous law-givers within a universal *kingdom of ends*.[14] Second, the normative purpose of all civil law is to provide a constitution that can universalize a condition of equal freedom where "the freedom of each can coexist with the freedom of all the others."[15] In this sense, the concept of public right is an egalitarian principle of formal jurisprudence, since it affirms the equal restriction of everyone's external freedom in order to promote a mutually consistent level of equal freedom between individuals.[16] Third, the concept of cosmopolitan justice is universal, since it demands the universal restriction of freedom in order to maximize the equal freedom of everyone, in all places and at all times. Fourth, Kant's theory of justice is an *a priori* ideal and is meant to provide the normative grounding to which all external laws are to be legislated. Kant believes that an ideal constitution can be discovered through the use of metaphysical philosophy and should be seen as providing a moral compass toward which the establishment of universal justice is possible. In this regard, Kantian justice is also meant to provide an ideal standard from which all existing civil legislation is to be judged. Finally, despite the fact that present hindrances demonstrate a difficulty with manifesting a cosmopolitan ideal, this does not mean that it is not what mankind should strive for or that it is necessarily an impossible undertaking.

All of these principles essentially express the same conviction in Kant's thought, namely that global justice necessitates "a condition in which each individual's external freedom is restricted so as to make it consistent with the freedom of all others in the framework of a common law or system of laws."[17] For it is only within a condition of public right that humans can enjoy an environment of secured external freedom and the possibility to fully develop their moral capacities. As Kant argues, "such is the requirement of pure reason, which legislates *a priori*, regardless of all empirical ends."[18] It is from the philosophical backdrop provided in this section that a further extrapolation of a cosmopolitan framework of law will be made in Section III. However, before discussing cosmopolitan law, it is necessary to understand how Kant saw the ultimate formulation of a cosmopolitan matrix as a result of human history. It is in the next section that an outline of Kant's theory of history is provided and what implications this has for his cosmopolitanism.

II. Cosmopolitanism, globalization and Kant's problematic theory of history

The most useful way to understand Kant's cosmopolitan theory of history is by examining the teleological implications of *Idea for a Universal History with a Cosmopolitan Purpose* and *Perpetual Peace*. Critics of Kant have accused the ambitiously titled essays as proof that Kant maintained a spurious conception of human perfectibility with a correspondingly idealistic and impalpable teleology. Although critics are right to point out some inherent difficulties involved in Kant's vision of history, a different interpretation of these aspects can be provided that can salvage Kant's cosmopolitan enthusiasm without being obliged to the notion that nature mechanically compels humans toward a universal purpose. For we can interpret an alternative view of Kantian history that is more modest than Kant perhaps may have delineated. [. . .]

As was pointed out at the beginning of the chapter, Kant maintained that "the greatest problem for the human species, the solution of which nature compels him to seek, is that of attaining a civil society, which can administer justice universally."[19] Kant further grounds the development of universal justice and the corresponding condition of perpetual peace in what is often seen as a naturalistic teleology:

> Perpetual peace is *guaranteed* by no less than the great artist *Nature* herself (*natura daedala rerum*). The mechanical process of nature visibly exhibits the purposive plan of producing concord among men, even against their will and indeed by means of their very discord.[20]

This passage generates a difficult conundrum for any consistent account of Kantian cosmopolitanism. This is because the passage seems to directly contradict Kant's critical philosophy and the necessary element of independent *a priori* principles of human reason. The most problematic element within this quote is the seemingly determined and mechanical "intention of nature" and the corresponding guiding force of what Kant later describes as "providence."[21] If humans are in fact determined by a natural purpose and therefore "guaranteed" to action by the mechanical forces of providence, then this has dangerous implications for Kantian ideas of free will and moral autonomy. As Karl-Otto Apel has pointed out, if Kant's theory of history is teleological in the sense that it is determined, then it puts "nearly every presupposition of the Kantian sketch into question."[22] In relation to some implications involved in Kant's cosmopolitan vision, the problem arises that nature's *providence* not only seems to provide the motivation to adopt a cosmopolitan constitution, but also guarantees all the means for its inevitable construction.

To this end, Kant makes four teleological comments about human evolution and the way in which history can be understood as having a cosmopolitan purpose. First, Kant believes that nature has enabled humans to "live in all the areas they have settled" and has fashioned humans so that they can adapt to the most inhospitable conditions.[23] Second, Kant explains that nature has driven humans "in all directions by means of war," so that they willingly inhabit even the most inhospitable regions of the earth.[24] Third, nature has compelled all humans to develop legal relationships in order to avoid war and thus to live in communities of law. Fourth, "nature has chosen war as a means of attaining this [civil] end" and the forces of war will continue until legal relationships are broadened and a cosmopolitan matrix is ultimately procured.[25] As Kant clearly states, "the distress produced by the constant wars in which the states try to subjugate or engulf each other must finally lend them, even against their will, to enter into a cosmopolitan constitution."[26]

However, Kant claims that war is not the only mechanism that nature employs to create an inevitable "concord among men." Although Kant never used the term *globalization* specifically, he did believe that the world was becoming increasingly interconnected and that the forces of nature were organized in such a way that it would eventually produce a cosmopolitan condition. As Kant suggests, "trade between nations . . . [creates] peaceful relations with one another, and thus achieves mutual understanding, community of interests and peaceful relations, even with the most distant of their fellows."[27] However, Kant notes that the growth of commerce is also dialectical in the sense that it can have inadvertent consequences.[28] In the case of Kant's understanding of globalization, although commerce can establish communities of mutual interest, it can also "provide the occasion for troubles in one place on our globe to be felt all over it."[29] In relation to nature's use of war, Kant maintained that "the spirit of commerce sooner or later takes hold of every people, and it cannot exist side by side with war."[30] Therefore, providence employs a carrot and stick method to motivate humanity toward a cosmopolitan condition. Humans are forced to socially relate with one another through forces of global commerce and mutual interest while also being continuously threatened by the global effects and ramifications of destructive war Kant stresses the "unsocial sociability" involved in human nature and how this natural antagonism is actually the "intention of nature" when he claims that it is a "purposive plan of producing concord among men, even against their will and indeed by means of their very discord."[31]

What is often considered dubious about Kant's understanding of globalization is that he seems to argue that nature has created the dialectics involved with interconnectedness as a way to force humans to seek peace and a universal condition of justice. In this regard, "it is the unintended consequences of global interconnectedness that propel human beings toward peace, so long as they can solve the problems that this form of order poses."[32] Nonetheless, a problem ensues from the fact that Kant's globalization does not simply supply the empirical circumstances of human experience that are to inform a possible cosmopolitan solution. As we have seen, Kant's concept of globalization also appears to entail much more. For as many ascribe to Kant, global interconnectedness is not simply an empirical fact of experience, it is the "intention of nature" and compels us to resolve problems associated with globalization in order for humanity to fully develop a cosmopolitan matrix and the predetermined natural capacities of the human species.

Despite the fact that textual evidence might often support the notion that Kant is grounding his cosmopolitanism in a naturalistic teleology, there is another way to interpret Kant's intended use of historical prognosis. This is because we can interpret a Kantian vision of history that is divorced from what Karl Popper called teleological "futurism."[33] To do so, Kant's history must be understood as hermeneutic in the sense that human experiences have inadvertently brought us to where we are and that these experiences highlight the various empirical considerations from which a metaphysics of morals must take into account. In this regard, history is comprised of the empirical considerations that Kantian metaphysics must attempt to understand *as if it is possible* to derive a moral purpose behind human existence. As Apel has similarly suggested, "a morally grounded ought demands that we think hypothetically and fallibly about progress in history – that is, in terms of a possible historical process to which morally informed practice can be tied."[34] This does not mean however that the purpose of history is actually determined or guaranteed, but only that a metaphysics of morals can provide a hypothetically possible vision of historical progress from which conflicts in history might be understood as resolvable through the establishment of a cosmopolitan matrix. It is from the fact that we cannot fully understand the forces of history that we can suggest the possibility that human beings could be reflective moral participants towards this cosmopolitan ideal. Apel has understood this interpretation of Kant as a form of *reflective judgement*, where history provides practical considerations from which it is our moral concern to attempt to resolve.

Allen Wood has offered a similar interpretation of Kant's theory of history. According to Wood, "the right way to describe his [Kant's] approach is to say that he proceeds from considerations of theoretical reason, projecting the 'idea' (or *a priori* rational concept) of a purely theoretical program for making comprehensible sense of the accidental facts of human history."[35] In other words, Wood suggests that Kant's natural teleology is "heuristically motivated . . . for obtaining and systematizing theoretical knowledge about history."[36] In doing so, Kant only attempts "to make sense of human history as a process involving an unconscious and unintended teleology of nature" in order to derive possible "regulative principles of reason,"[37] and not as a means to provide predictive evidence about how "this end will actually come about."[38]

What these interpretations suggest is that a tenable conception of Kantian cosmopolitanism must reject the inherent complications involved in understanding Kant's theory of history as promoting a determined natural teleology. Whether or not Kant's theory of history was actually meant as a scheme of reflective judgement as Apel claims, or as a "perverted" form of dialectical science as charged by Popper, any practical construction of Kantian cosmopolitanism must distance itself from the possible teleological ramifications of "guaranteed" human progression. Nevertheless, as Apel has noted, adopting this interpretation of Kant's vision of history might be in contrast to what Kant may have actually believed. [. . .] However, there are two areas connected to Kant's vision of history where application of this reinterpretation could be helpful in understanding a vision of Kantian cosmopolitanism.

The first area where determined empirical considerations inform Kant's cosmopolitanism is in relation to the development of human capacities. As was suggested in the last section, human capacities relate to the transcendental deduction and to the metaphysical idea of morality. The base for Kant's discussion of moral agency stems from the empirical fact that humans generally live in moral communities and that when we speak of moral actions we usually speak in terms of people being either morally right or morally wrong. The language of morality implies freedom of will and the ability of individuals to make autonomous moral choices. This is because when someone has acted wrongly from a moral point of view the implication is that the person could have and therefore should also have acted differently. For Kant, humans have the power to be moral agents and this capacity for moral reasoning is a universal attribute of the human species.

Nevertheless, Kant also affirmed that morality is not an action of pure reason outside of social context. This is because Kant understood that human capacities can be only fully developed within a civil society and that human reason cannot mature without social interaction and instruction. In addition, the capacity for moral agency is only valid when determined in relation to social context and when it can be conceived as consistent with a possible universal natural law. Otherwise, moral actions cannot be conceived as a subjective power inherent to the human condition, but as anomalistic impulses outside of cognitive influence or beyond the spectrum of practical and social considerations. It is for this reason that Kant claims that human capabilities can only be fully developed within a social condition of civil public right and justice. For it is only within a just social arrangement that individual capacities will be held as having an end in themselves, so that "the choice of one can be united with the choice of another in accordance with a universal law of freedom."[39]

Despite the fact that humans have the capacity for moral agency, this does not mean that all humans believe in the same moral norms or that they will always act upon their own moral judgements. This is due to the empirical fact that a plurality of ethical perspectives exists in the world and that not every individual has developed the equal capacity to relate morally toward others. Consequently, it is a fact of human existence that antagonisms exist between various societies and that there are degrees to which individuals formulate moral imperatives. Antagonism in itself is not the problem, for Kant firmly believes that it is through antagonistic relationships that the exchange of ideas and the evolution of the human species is possible. Nonetheless, if this condition of natural antagonism is to be understood as having a historical purpose for humanity, it must also be thought as having a universal purpose for humanity. As Kant explains, "this purpose can be fulfilled only in a society which has not only the greatest freedom, and therefore a continual antagonism among its members, but also the most precise specification and preservation of the limits of this freedom in order that it can coexist with the freedom of others."[40] It is in this regard that the practical concern for cosmopolitanism is with creating a global environment where various individuals can mutually develop their capacities without the consequences of conflict that have been witnessed throughout history. Therefore, the cosmopolitan ideal of history is meant to illustrate that if antagonism and human agency are to be both understood as having a universal human end, we should also reflectively conclude that they must accord with universal principles of right which can guarantee the development of these purposeful ends.

This leads to the second area where determined empirical considerations inform Kant's metaphysics and the cosmopolitan prescription for a political boundary limited only by the spherical shape of the earth. The significance of the symbolism of earth's sphere is paramount to Kant's cosmopolitanism, because it provides the only natural political boundary for Kant's use of practical reason. In fact, the idea of confined global space in conjunction with a diverse global population provides for Kant's insistence that humans should enter into a cosmopolitan order. In this regard, the spherical confine of the globe provides the empirical conditions that inform his metaphysics of morals while also providing the motivation behind why we should establish cosmopolitan law. Since the world is not an infinite plane, but a sphere where individuals must necessarily occupy a finite space next to one another, reason dictates the establishment of a system of public right. As Kant proclaimed, "the peoples of the earth have thus entered in various degrees into a universal community and it has developed to the point where the violation of rights in one part of the world is felt *everywhere*."[41] However, this does not mean that humans are in fact actual members of a universal community, but that empirical conditions are such that we can metaphysically infer that humans are embroiled in something like an actual community of mutual interest. From this empirical consideration, reason dictates that we should theorize about mutual interests and universal public right from a global perspective. As Katrin Flikschuh has suggested of Kant's position, it "includes all those who because they cannot avoid occupying a place on earth, claim such a right to such a place."[42] In this regard, the bounded sphere of the earth acts as "an unavoidable constraint of nature within the limits of which finite rational beings must resolve conflicts of external freedom and justice."[43]

The elimination of Kant's naturalistic teleology does not require the rejection of his cosmopolitan enthusiasm or weaken the force of logic that underpins its relevance. This is because we can understand history as providing empirical considerations from which our normative reflection must seek to resolve. In the case of globalization and human evolution, humans have found themselves inextricably interconnected where history has proven a need to peacefully adjudicate disagreement between cohabitants of a spherically bounded world. In a fusion of empirical experience with normative principles, Kant maintains that humans cannot avoid physical contact with one another and therefore should enter into a civil order that secures mutual right and the conditions for human capabilities to develop. In this regard, Kantian cosmopolitanism is an attempt to come to terms with the plurality of various societies in some sort of minimally recognized framework of cosmopolitan law.

III. Cosmopolitan jurisprudence and the foundation for a cosmopolitan matrix

The formalization of Kant's cosmopolitan matrix rests on two related ideas of jurisprudence. The first involves Kant's concept of a universal condition of public right, or as it is referenced in the context of global relations, *cosmopolitan right*. As was mentioned before, the condition of public right is linked directly to Kant's theory of justice, namely, "the sum of the conditions under which the choice of one can be united with the choice of another in accordance with a universal law of freedom."[44] Mary Gregor defines the jurisprudence behind the concept of public right as simply "the sum of laws that need to be publicized in order to produce a rightful condition, one in which individuals, nations and states can enjoy their rights."[45] In this regard, Kant's jurisprudence is both concerned with the creation of a legal framework of mutually negative restraints on external freedom (justice), while also concerned with positive *laws of publicity* which are necessary in order to promote a condition of cosmopolitan right.[46] In the global context, cosmopolitan right refers to an equal right of all individuals to inhabit the earth, the subsequently legal condition of mutual public right and the formulation of consistent legal obligations that are based solely on our humanity alone.

The second area of Kant's jurisprudence involved in the formalization of a cosmopolitan matrix relates to cosmopolitan law and universal justice. As Kant argued, a condition of public right cannot exist unless the very idea of rightful coexistence is grounded and propagated within a greater framework of cosmopolitan law and universal public right. In this case, cosmopolitan law refers to the framework of global law that must exist in order for any mutually consistent condition of right to be possible. As Kant maintained in *Perpetual Peace*, a cosmopolitan legal condition must not only be concerned with the rightful relations between individuals within states, but also with the rightful relations that should exist between state actors and their rightful treatment of all human beings.[47] It is through this legal condition that both justice and perpetual peace should be maintained, for they are codependent and one cannot exist exclusive of the other.

In order to formalize this cosmopolitan legal condition, Kant advances a tripartite system of jurisprudence divided into *domestic law, international law* and *cosmopolitan law*. As the tripartite suggests, a judicial system of public right is to be maintained through the three corresponding forms of rights and law, which in tandem create a universal condition where "the freedom of each can coexist with the freedom of all the others."[48] However, Kant believed that the tripartite system of jurisprudence could not guarantee a condition of right when operated solely as independent cells. As Kant suggests, "the problem of establishing a perfect civil constitution is subordinate to the problem of a law governed external relationship with other states, and cannot be solved unless the latter is also solved."[49] This is because a thoroughgoing condition of public right cannot exist when certain violations of international right persistently threaten to undermine already established micro systems of domestic justice. In other words, since the world has become inextricably linked and interconnected, "if the principle of outer freedom limited by law is lacking in any one of these three possible forms of rightful condition, the framework of all the others is unavoidably undermined and must finally collapse."[50] It is from this reality of global interconnectedness that reason dictates the establishment of cosmopolitan law and a universal condition of public right.

As mentioned above, the framework of universal justice demands three corresponding forms of law and rightful condition: domestic justice and internal state law; international justice and international law; and global justice and cosmopolitan law. Within Kant's legal tripartite framework, domestic law involves the rights and duties that should exist between citizens and their governments (citizen to citizen, state to citizen). [. . .] Domestic justice is the cornerstone of Kant's overall cosmopolitan vision. This is because Kant believed that states represent the most rational form of social organization from which individual capacities could fully be allowed to develop.[51] Nonetheless, Kant also firmly believed that only a republican constitution is suitable to secure and maintain justice both internally and externally. This is because well-constituted states have the ability to function as both the providers of justice and human development, while poorly constituted states have historically been the greatest violators of public right and human dignity.

For Kant, the first principle of global justice rests on the secured justice of state law and public right. According to Kant, a well-constituted state is based on three *a priori* principles; "the freedom of every member of society as a human being; the equality of each with all the others as subject; and the independence of each member of a commonwealth as a citizen."[52] Based on this domestic foundation, international law should be primarily concerned with the rightful condition that must exist between various state actors as representative entities (state to state). As was stated before, Kant believed that domestic justice could not flourish without the state also being secured in its external relations through a legal condition of international right. In order to secure international right, Kant suggests that a federation of independent states should be established in which the members uphold the various interlocking levels of justice in order to form a unified system of universal law. These principles of right are to be cemented into universal law not by a world government, but by the willing concomitants of various communities and states that are dedicated to preserving this condition of universal public right.

However, Kant's cosmopolitanism is concerned with more than the strict prerogative of international relations. This is because Kant's political theory is preoccupied with the moral worth and rightful condition of all human beings everywhere. To this end, cosmopolitan law is ultimately concerned with establishing a universal rightful condition that should exist between all humans and all states, regardless of national origin or state citizenship (state to all humans, humans to all humans, especially non-citizens). [. . .] Kant's cosmopolitan law was primarily concerned with the hospitable treatment of everyone by everyone, whether as individuals or as political entities. By hospitality Kant means "the right of a stranger not to be treated with hostility when he arrives on someone else's territory."[53] This hospitable treatment was not merely a philanthropic principle, but "a principle having to do with rights."[54] In addition, cosmopolitan right applied to visiting foreigners and to the inhabitants of newly discovered lands. For cosmopolitan hospitality strictly forbids foreign powers from exploiting native inhabitants or from using their territory without the explicit consent of the native population.[55] As Charles Covell suggests, cosmopolitan law "was the body of public international law . . . constituting the juridical framework for the intercourse of men and states, considered in their status as bearers of the attributes of citizenship . . . that extended to embrace all mankind."[56] In this regard, "the idea of a cosmopolitan right . . . is necessary complement to the unwritten code of political and international right, transforming it into a universal right of humanity."[57]

IV. Cosmopolitan jurisprudence and the development of a Kantian cosmopolitan matrix

The first order of Kantian cosmopolitanism is to provide a legal framework that prevents any violation of public right and establishes a universal system of justice. Nevertheless, the establishment and propagation of a cosmopolitan matrix goes beyond Kant's legal foundation to include the optimistic cultivation of a broader sense of shared community, where everyone is considered as if they were mutual citizens of the world. It is in this realm that principles of cosmopolitan law and hospitality are meant to provide the grounding for a broadened sense of global community. As Kant suggests, we "stand in a community [confined by the global sphere] of possible interaction, that is, in a thoroughgoing relation of each to all others of offering to engage in commerce with any other, and each has the right to make this attempt."[58] Although current circumstances may restrict the free movement of commerce and relations, "this possible abuse cannot annul the right of citizens of the world to try to establish community with all, and to this end, to visit all regions of the earth."[59]

In this regard, cosmopolitan law goes beyond mutual security and is also meant as the legal foundation for continued interconnection and development that may eventually bring human beings closer to understanding each other as mutual citizens. However, this does not necessarily mean that they are actually citizens in the sense usually used in discussions of political obligation and national citizenship. For Kant himself defines cosmopolitan right simply as a means for a future cosmopolitan enthusiasm by suggesting that "hospitality does not extend beyond those conditions which make it possible for them to attempt to enter into relations with native inhabitants. In this way, continents distant from each other can enter into peaceful mutual relations which may eventually be regulated by public laws, thus bringing the human race nearer and nearer to a cosmopolitan constitution."[60] What this quote highlights is Kant's optimism that by creating a minimal system of cosmopolitan law which governs actions both within the *pacific federation* and externally with other communities, individuals will gradually engage with one another to the point where critical distinctions of tension disintegrate. In this sense, cosmopolitan law, and its corresponding feature of cosmopolitan right, is meant to provide the basic legal mechanism necessary for individuals to peacefully and rightfully associate, trade, communicate and exchange ideas without conflict or mistreatment. [. . .]

Furthermore, the provision of hospitality illustrates the Kantian notion for the equal freedom of individuals to be unfettered in the process of communication and political emancipation. For it is only through "the freedom to make public use of one's reason" that broader social change and global civil advancement can hope to be achieved.[61] This in turn also reflects Kant's beliefs regarding enlightenment and a possible human evolutionary progression toward a cosmopolitan condition. As Kant himself proclaims, "the public use of man's reason must always be free, and it alone can bring about enlightenment among men."[62] We can understand Kant as addressing all of humanity when he further claims that a violation of this freedom "would be a crime against human nature, whose future lies precisely in such progress."[63]

Cosmopolitan law therefore acts as the protective mechanism for the possibility of continued transnational deliberation and dialogue. As James Bohman has suggested, Kant's enlightenment and the successful propagation of a cosmopolitan sense of community requires an "unrestricted audience" from which transnational dialogue can foster.[64] It is through cosmopolitan law and its corresponding principle of a cosmopolitan right to hospitality from which various individuals can engage with one another to communicate, criticize, remonstrate, debate, evince, expostulate and to have their own conceptions measured by critical examination. Since I have argued that a coherent form of Kantian cosmopolitanism should not rely on a naturalistic teleology, a construction of Kantian cosmopolitanism must rely on mechanisms of public deliberation and reasoned dialogue as a means to further cosmopolitan enthusiasm. As Sharon Anderson-Gold has suggested, "public reason is then ultimately the basis for the development of a cosmopolitan community."[65]

Consequently, we can understand cosmopolitan law and the right to hospitality as containing two distinctive features of public right and deliberation underwriting Kant's cosmopolitan enthusiasm. The first stipulates that every human being should enjoy the right of free movement in order to associate, trade and communicate. Following from this, the second principle of public right demands that all individuals should have the freedom to reason freely with one another without dogmatic external hindrances or the fear of prosecution. Kant stresses that an ability for public reason is paramount to human advancement when he writes, "these rights of man must be held sacred . . . there are no half measures here . . . for all politics must bend the knee before right, [if] politics may hope in return to arrive, however slowly, at a stage of lasting brilliance."[66]

Nevertheless, it is difficult to understand how we should apply Kant's cosmopolitan enthusiasm in the modern context. The difficulty arises from the fact that human relationships need to reach a certain stage of maturity in order to adopt and implement cosmopolitan law. However, reaching this stage of maturity requires an already existing amount of hospitality and mutual relations from which this sense of community can flourish. Although this does not create a strict "chicken and egg" dilemma, it does call into question how we are to determine exactly where human relationships stand as far as the practical application of a Kantian system of cosmopolitan law. Some have suggested that Kant's minimal requirement for global hospitality is absolutely necessary if human beings are to engage in a continued process of mutual education toward a sense of cosmopolitan community.[67] Many contemporary scholars have suggested that cosmopolitan right is synonymous with current discussions of universal human rights and that the language of human rights has developed to a point where Kant's cosmopolitanism is conceivable.[68] Some contemporary cosmopolitans have argued that humans currently exist at a point in our development and maturity where human interdependence has made cosmopolitan law a necessarily viable alternative to the existing global order.[69] Finally, many contemporary cosmopolitans argue that the legal foundations for a cosmopolitan condition are already in some sense visible and that what is needed is a continued dedication to "cosmopolitan law enforcement"[70] and to emerging principles of "political cosmopolitanism."[71]

The practical and empirical considerations that give substance to these issues are complex and multifaceted. Nevertheless, we can say with a reasonable amount of certainty that we no longer live in a world of community isolation. Humanity has evolved, for whatever reasons, into an extremely interdependent, culturally transient and globalized environment. If this environment of global interdependence is to have a greater chance to peacefully evolve, it is important to find recognizable ethical and juridical principles that not only facilitate greater cooperation, but that also protect the valuable pluralist and autonomous concerns of various communities impacted by global cohabitation. For although we can claim that humans have reached a level of interdependence that has forced us to "relate" with one another, this very same interdependence does not necessarily mean that how we "relate" with one another could be labeled as developing a sense of shared humanity. It is in this sense that the normative principles behind Kant's cosmopolitan law are both relevant to contemporary global issues, even perhaps necessary, if we are going to tackle the problems associated with the benefits and burdens of confined global cohabitation. [. . .]

As has been discussed, Kant's cosmopolitanism is firmly grounded in his moral philosophy and the recognition of human beings as moral agents deserving of universal respect and dignity as co-legislators within a *kingdom of ends*. Therefore, individual human capacities represent the ultimate unit of moral concern equally and it is the prerogative of Kant's cosmopolitanism that these capacities should be allowed to fully develop within a condition of universal public right. It was from this moral platform that it is possible to understand Kant's cosmopolitanism as being preoccupied with providing the normative principles that are meant to ground the motivation, the formation and the maintenance of a cosmopolitan matrix. In addition, the attainment of this cosmopolitan matrix requires the cultivation of a cosmopolitan civil society; one based solely on our humanity alone, grounded in a system of cosmopolitan law. Although Kant is both ambiguous and at times inconsistent as to what forces are behind the formation of this cosmopolitan matrix, I have argued that it is still possible to maintain a defendable enthusiasm for taking Kant's cosmopolitanism seriously. It is in this vein that the subsequent chapters will provide a more detailed analysis of cosmopolitan law, the cosmopolitan federation, the place for cultural diversity within cosmopolitan law, a possible form of Kantian global distributive justice and how a connection between Kantian theory and real world application might be understood as possible.

Notes

1   Immanuel Kant. "Idea for a Universal History with a Cosmopolitan Purpose," in H. Reiss (ed), H. B. Nisbet (trans) *Kant's Political Writings* (Cambridge: Cambridge University Press, 1970), p. 51. [8:28].
2   Ibid., p. 45. [8:22].
3   Andrew Linklater, *Men and Citizens in the Theory of International Relations*. 2nd edn (Basingstoke: Macmillan, 1990), pp. 98–9.
4   Immanuel Kant, *Grounding for the Metaphysics of Morals*, J. Ellington (trans), (Cambridge: Hackett Publishing Company, 1981), pg. 30. [4:421].
5   Ibid., p. 36. [4:429].

6   Ibid., p. 42. [4:437].

7   Immanuel Kant, *The Metaphysics of Morals*, M. Gregor (ed & trans), (Cambridge: Cambridge University Press, 1996), p. 30. [6:237].

8   Linklater, p. 101.

9   Ibid., p. 102.

10 Kant, *Grounding for the Metaphysics of Morals*, p. 40. [4:434].

11 Kant, *The Metaphysics of Morals*, p. 24. [6:230].

12 Charles Covell, *Kant and the Law of Peace: A Study in the Philosophy of International Law and International Relations* (New York: Palgrave, 1998), p. 49.

13 Immanuel Kant Appendix, "Transcendental Logic II, Dialectic I, Ideas in General," in J. M. D. Meiklejohn (trans.), *The Critique of Pure Reason* (New York: The Colonial Press, 1900), [3:247].

14 The *kingdom of ends* is a metaphysical ideal of justice understood as "a systematic union of different rational beings through common laws" which is determined by "universal validity." A participant in the *kingdom of ends* is someone who "legislates in it universal laws while also being themselves subject to such laws." For these quotes see Kant, *Grounding for the Metaphysics of Morals*. pp. 39–45. [4:433–440].

15 Ibid.

16 Thomas Pogge, "Kant's Theory of Justice," *Kant-Studien*, 79 (1988).

17 Allen Rosen, Kant's *Theory of Justice* (New York: Cornell University Press, 1993), p. 9.

18 Immanuel Kant, "On the Common Saying, This May be True in Theory, But it Does not Apply in Practice," in Hans Reiss (ed), H. B. Nisbet (trans) *Kant's Political Writings* (Cambridge: Cambridge University Press, 1970), p. 73 [8:290].

19 Kant, "Idea for a Universal History with a Cosmopolitan Purpose," p. 45. [8:22].

20 Kant "Perpetual Peace: A Philosophical Sketch," in Hans Reiss (ed), H. B. Nisbet (trans), *Kant's Political Writings* (Cambridge: Cambridge University Press, 1970), p. 108. [8:360–1].

21 Ibid., [8:361–2].

22 Karl-Otto Apel, "Kant's Toward Perpetual Peace as Historical Prognosis from the Point of View of Moral Duty," in J. Bohman and M. Lutz-Bachmann, *Perpetual Peace: Essays on Kant's Cosmopolitan Ideal* (Cambridge: MIT Press, 1997), p. 81.

23 Kant, "Perpetual Peace," pp. 109–10. [8:363].

24 Ibid., p. 110.

25 Ibid., p. 111. [8:364].

26 Kant, "On the Common Saying: This May be True in Theory, But it Does not Apply in Practice," p. 90. [8:310–11].

27 Kant, "Perpetual Peace," p. 111. [8:364].

28 I use the term dialectic in the Habermasian form Namely that global interconnectedness both promotes more interconnectedness (thesis) while also creating new and unforeseen forces of opposition (antithesis) that ultimately are to be resolved through a synthesis of resolution. In Kant's case, synthesis of human history will be the result of a teleology, which culminates in a cosmopolitan condition.

29 Kant, *The Metaphysics of Morals*, p. 121. [6:353].

30 Kant, "Perpetual Peace," p. 114. [8:368].

31 Ibid., 108. [8:360–1].

32 James Bohman & Matthias Lutz-Bachmann (eds), *Perpetual Peace: Essays on Kant's Cosmopolitan Ideal* (Cambridge: MIT Press, 1997), p. 8.

33 Karl Popper, *The Poverty of Historicism* (London: Routledge, 1957).

34 Apel, p. 83.

35 Allen W. Wood, "Kant's Philosophy of History," in Pauline Kleingeld (ed), *Toward Perpetual Peace and Other Writings on Politics, Peace and History* (New Haven: Yale University Press, 2006), p. 245.

36 Ibid., p. 256.

37 Ibid., p. 254.

38 Ibid., p. 257.

39 Kant, *The Metaphysics of Morals*, pg. 24. [6:230].

40 Kant, "Idea for a Universal History with a Cosmopolitan Purpose," p. 45. [8:22].

41 Kant, "Perpetual Peace," pp. 107–8. [8:360].

42 Katrin Flikschuh, *Kant and Modern Political Philosophy* (Cambridge: Cambridge University Press, 2000), p. 179.

43   Ibid.
44   Kant, *The Metaphysics of Morals*, p. 24. [6:230].
45   Mary Gregor, "Kant's Approach to Constitutionalism," in A. Rosenbaum (ed), *Constitutionalism: The Philosophical Dimension* (New York: Greenwood Press, 1988), p. 71.
46   As Kant argues, "all maxims which require publicity if they are not to fail their purpose can be reconciled both with right and with politics." Kant, "Perpetual Peace," p. 130. [8:386].
47   Ibid., p. 126. [8:381–2].
48   Kant, *The Metaphysics of Morals*, p. 24. [6:230].
49   Kant, "An Answer to the Question 'What is Enlightenment?'," in Hans Reiss (ed.), H. B. Nisbet (trans), *Kant's Political Writings* (Cambridge: Cambridge University Press, 1970), p. 47. [8:24].
50   Kant, *The Metaphysics of Morals*, p. 89. [6:311].
51   Jeremy Waldron, "Kant's Theory of the State," in Pauline Kleingeld (ed.), *Toward Perpetual Peace and Other Writings on Politics, Peace and History* (New Haven: Yale University Press, 2006).
52   Kant, "On the Common Saying: This May be True in Theory, But it Does not Apply in Practice," pg. 74. [8:290]. Also see *The Metaphysics of Morals*, p. 91. [6:314].
53   Kant, "Perpetual Peace," p. 105. [8:357–8].
54   Kant, *The Metaphysics of Morals*, p. 121. [6:352].
55   Ibid., p. 122. [6:353].
56   Covell, p. 141.
57   Kant, "Perpetual Peace," p. 108. [8:360–1].
58   Kant, *Metaphysics of Morals*, p. 121. [6:352].
59   Ibid., [6:353].
60   Kant, "Perpetual Peace," p. 106. [8:358].
61   Kant, "An Answer to the Question 'What is Enlightenment?'," p. 55. [8:36–7].
62   Ibid.
63   Ibid., p. 57. [8:39].
64   James Bohman, "The Public Spheres of the World Citizen," in Bohman & Lutz Bachmann (eds), *Perpetual Peace: Essays on Kant's Cosmopolitan Ideal* (Cambridge: The MIT Press, 1997).
65   Sharon Anderson-Gold, *Cosmopolitanism and Human Rights* (Cardiff: University of Wales Press, 2001), p. 40.
66   Kant, "Perpetual Peace," p. 125. [8:380].
67   Martha Nussbaum, *Cultivating Humanity* (Cambridge: Harvard University Press, 1997).
68   Sharon Anderson-Gold, *Cosmopolitanism and Human Rights*, op cit.
69   David Held, "Cosmopolitanism: Globalization Tamed?," *Review of International Studies*. 29 (2003), pp. 465–80.
70   Mary Kaldor, *Global Civil Society: An Answer to War* (Cambridge: Polity Press, 2003).
71   Patrick Hayden, *Cosmopolitan Global Politics* (Burlington: Ashgate, 2005).

4

A Kantian Approach to Transnational Justice
Onora O'Neill

Justice across boundaries

The discussion of international distributive justice is both new and messy. It is new because global distribution is a fairly new possibility. It is messy because principles of distributive justice are contentious, and because it is unclear to whom arguments about international distributive justice should be addressed. Neither the agents of change nor its beneficiaries (or victims) are easily identified.

[. . .]

Today questions of global distributive justice will arise whether or not we can find the theoretical resources to handle them. Modern technical and institutional possibilities make far wider intervention not only possible but unavoidable. We can now hardly avoid asking how individuals, institutions and societies may change (exacerbate, alleviate) distant poverty and distress. Current answers range from the *laissez-faire* view that it is permissible, or even obligatory, to do nothing, to claims that global redistribution is mandatory and even that it is obligatory to use any surplus to alleviate distress wherever it may be.

These answers are not only contentious but often ill-focused. To make them more precise we would have to establish *who* is (or is not) obliged to take *which* sorts of action for *whom*. Here the messiness begins. The agents and agencies whose action and operation constitute and achieve distributions of resources are not only numerous but heterogeneous. They include not only individual actors, but also states (and their various government agencies), international organizations (e.g. the World Bank, the UN and regional organizations), and both corporations and other non-governmental organizations (NGOs), some of which are confined within national frontiers while others operate transnationally (e.g. BP and OXFAM). Even those corporations and NGOs which operate only within state frontiers often have intimate links with and a degree of dependence on others that operate transnationally, and those that operate transnationally also operate within frameworks that are defined and constituted both by state law and by international agreements. Equally, those who may be wronged by the present international economic order are scattered through many regions and jurisdictions, and have a vast array of differing forms of involvement with and dependence on the international economic order. The very transformations that have made an international economic order a reality and international distributive justice a possibility have vastly expanded the web of actions, practices and institutions that might be challenged by judgements about international distributive justice.

This suggests that any discussion of international distributive justice needs to take account of the diversity of capacities and scope for action of these various agents and agencies, and of the possibility and limits of their transformation. In practice discussions of principles of distributive justice have mainly been conducted on the basis of very incomplete views of agency. Some writers assume that the only relevant agents are individuals; others allow for the agency of states as well as individuals; most are vague about the agency or ethical responsibilities of corporations, government and international agencies and charities. While economists and development specialists are quite ready to use the vocabulary of action, obligation and responsibility when speaking of a wide variety of agencies and institutions, discussions of the ethical issues lag behind for lack of any general and convincing account of the responsibilities of collectivities. Sometimes the issue is bracketed and an abstract account of ethical requirements offered without allocating particular obligations to specified agents and agencies.

Such abstraction may be all that can readily be achieved: but it makes it hard to question or investigate the justice of present institutional structures. It fails to identify where the obligations of justice should fall, and for whom the benefits or rights that justice might achieve should be secured. If agents of change are not identified, discussions of international distributive justice will lack focus, and may proceed in terms that seem irrelevant to those whose practice is challenged. If recipients of change are not identified, the changes sought may neither find advocates nor meet the most urgent injustices. In particular, it may prove hard to connect demands for economic justice directly to claims of need and poverty.

Much modern ethical thought makes no use of the category of needs. In utilitarian thinking needs can be considered only if reflected in desires or preferences; and this is an imperfect reflection. Discussions of human rights often take no account of needs at all; and where they try to do so, strains are placed on the basic structure of rights theory, and the identification of needs is sketchy. A full account of international distributive justice would require a complete theory of human needs, which I shall not provide. This is partly a matter of prudence and ignorance, but is perhaps defensible in discussions that must take hunger and poverty seriously. It is not controversial that human beings need adequate food, shelter and clothing appropriate to their climate, clean water and sanitation, and some parental and health care. When these basic needs are not met they become ill and often die prematurely. It is controversial whether human beings need companionship, education, politics and culture, or food for the spirit – for at least some long and not evidently stunted lives have been lived without these goods. But these issues do not have to be settled for a discussion of hunger and destitution to proceed; discussion of international distributive justice can at least begin with a rudimentary account of needs.

Given the complexity and intractability of questions about agency and need, most writing on international distributive justice has understandably bracketed both topics and has concentrated on working out the implications various ethical positions would have for international distribution *if* there were agents and recipients for whom these implications were pertinent. In what follows I shall sketch and criticize a number of these positions, propose an alternative and then consider how far it can illuminate questions of agency and need. I begin with a consideration of positions that have least to say about international justice; for if these positions are convincing there will be little need to go further.

Community and cosmopolis

The deepest disagreement about international justice is between those who think that there is at least something to be said about duties beyond borders, and those who think that ethical concern cannot cross boundaries.[1] Liberal and socialist thinkers view justice as universal in scope, and *a fortiori* as having cosmopolitan implications. No doubt both liberal and socialist practice has usually subordinated these to the demands of nation and state; but this has been seen as a practical and temporary rather than a fundamental concession. However, various forms of relativism and historicism deny that the category of justice has implications or even makes sense beyond the boundaries of nation-state or communities. Burke's critique of the *Rights of Man*, and his insistence that the revolutionaries of France would have done better to appeal to the traditional rights of Frenchmen, is a classical version of this thought. Contemporary communitarian critics of "abstract" liberal justice repeat and develop many points raised by early critics of rights.[2]

One frequently made criticism of liberal, and particularly rights-based, accounts of justice is that they are too abstract.[3] However, abstraction taken strictly is neither objectionable nor avoidable. We abstract as soon as we make claims whose truth does not depend on the satisfaction or non-satisfaction of some predicate. Abstraction, in this sense, is essential to all language and reasoning; it is the basis for bringing any plurality of cases under a single principle. The critics of "abstract liberalism" themselves do not and cannot avoid abstraction. Even if we think that justice differs in Athens and in Sparta, the justice of Athens will be formulated in principles that apply to Athenians who differ in any number of ways, from which Athenian justice abstracts.

If abstraction in itself is unavoidable, critics of "abstract liberalism" probably have something else in mind. One point that many make is that abstract principles do not merely have universal scope but mandate mindlessly uniform treatment of differing cases. This would be true if abstract principles were algorithms that fully determine action; but if they are side constraints that regulate but do not wholly determine action, as most liberals hold, there is no reason why they should mandate uniform treatment of differing cases. In fact, abstract principles sometimes mandate differentiated treatment. A principle of proportioning taxation to ability to pay uses an abstract account of taxpayers and is universal in scope; but it mandates uniform treatment only when everyone has the same ability to pay. Even abstract principles that do not prescribe differentiated treatment may require differentiated applications. The actions required of those who are committed to such abstract aims as relieving poverty or combating imperialism or maximizing profit vary greatly depending on context. Universal principles can guide highly differentiated practice: applying abstract principles to varying cases needs painstaking adjudication rather than mechanical implementation.

A second and more serious objection to "abstraction" complains of ethical and political reasoning that assumes enhanced, "idealized" accounts of individual rationality and independence and of national sovereignty. This is a serious objection, but what it objects to is not strictly abstraction. Idealized reasoning does not simply *omit* predicates that are true of the objects and agents to which it is applied; it applies only to hypothetical agents who satisfy predicates that actual agents or agencies do not (fully) satisfy. Speaking strictly, idealized reasoning applies only in those ideal worlds inhabited (for example) by rational economic men with perfect information, fully transitive preferences and unlimited capacities to calculate. By contrast, merely abstract reasoning applies to agents whether or not they satisfy the predicates from which it abstracts. Since much liberal and socialist thought uses idealized models of the human agent, and of other agents such as classes and states, objections to idealized reasoning have a serious point.

Communitarians have positive as well as negative things to say about justice. Many of them contend that the categories, the sense or at least the authority of any ethical discourse is anchored within a specific community or tradition, and that attempts to apply such reasoning universally detach it from the forms of life and thought on which it depends. On this account, international justice is illusory, because it assumes that everyone shares categories and principles, whereas, as Michael Walzer put it, the largest sphere of justice is the political community. Walzer does not wholly dismiss international justice, for he allows that the admission of individual aliens to membership of the community and conflicts between states raise issues of justice. Other communitarian critics of "abstract liberalism" see the boundaries of justice as coterminous with those of community. For example, MacIntyre argues that ethical reasoning must be internal to a particular tradition, which it seeks to further, and sees an irresolvable tension between the demands of liberalism and of nationalism. Rawls, in his most nearly communitarian writing,[4] anchors his principles of justice in the outlook of citizens of a modern liberal democratic polity, and offers no reasons why others should accept them.

If communitarians are correct, international distributive justice is not an issue: compatriots have legitimate priority.[5] International distributive justice would indeed be unthinkable if the boundaries between states, and between modes of discourse and ideologies, were total and impervious. This, however, is the very respect in which the modern world is different from its predecessors. It is not a world of closed communities with mutually impenetrable ways of thought, self-sufficient economies and ideally sovereign states. What is more, communitarians acknowledge this in practice as much as anyone else. Like the rest of us they expect to interact with foreigners, and rely on practices of translation, negotiation and trade that cross boundaries. If complex, reasoned communication and association breach boundaries, why should not principles of justice do so too? Although the internationalist images of a "world community" or "global village" may be sentimental slogans, the view that boundaries of actual communities are impervious is sheer nostalgia; and often it is self-serving nostalgia. Questions of international distributive justice cannot now be ruled out of order.

Consequentialist reasoning and global distribution

Consequentialist reasoning has two great advantages and two massive defects for thinking about global distributive justice. First, the advantages. The most salient feature of the present global distribution of resources is that it produces harm. The distribution is not only uneven but leaves hundreds of millions in profound poverty and with all its associated insecurities, ill-health and powerlessness. Consequentialist thought, and specifically utilitarian thought, is geared to register harms and benefit. The second advantage is that by concentrating on results rather than on action, consequentialist reasoning can (it seems) not merely bracket but wholly avoid intractable questions about agency.

These advantages have been widely embraced, and there is plenty of consequentialist reasoning about global distribution. It ranges from the simple publicity of some charities that operate in the Third World ("Save a child's sight for £5.00") to sophisticated economic models. The more sophisticated, specifically ethical, consequentialist reasoning usually deploys a utilitarian account of value, and judges between policies and actions by reference to their probable contribution to human happiness or well-being. Right acts (whether for individuals, institutions or states) are those that maximize global expected well-being.

Consequentialist, and specifically utilitarian, reasoning about global distributive justice has been used to support a remarkable variety of incompatible courses of action. There are those who think that it requires the rich to transfer resources to the poor until further transfer would reduce aggregate well-being. Marginalist considerations suggest that any given unit of resources will be more valued by the poor than by the rich, and so that transfers would have to go a long way towards an equal distribution of resources before justice was achieved.[6] There are others, especially various neo-Malthusian writers, who use consequentialist reasoning to argue that the rich should transfer nothing to the poor: they claim that transfers of resources encourage the poor to have children they cannot support and so lead to "unsustainable" population growth and, eventually, to maximal aggregate harm.[7] There are those who think that utilitarian considerations justify selective redistribution from rich to poor: for example, they justify development aid which aims to make people self-sufficient, but not forms of food aid which merely perpetuate a "culture of dependency".[8]

The plasticity which produces these radical disagreements is the first major defect of consequentialism. Consequentialism raises hopes with the prospect of replacing conflicts by calculation, but dashes them by providing overly pliant instruments of calculation. Consequentialist principles provide an algorithm for action only when we have a method for generating all the "options" to be compared, adequate causal understanding for predicting the likely results of each "option" and an adequate theory of value (utilitarian or other) for evaluating each result with sufficient precision to enable the "options" to be ranked. This procedure can perhaps be approximately followed for limited and local problems. It is a non-starter for dealing with international justice. Here neither "problems" nor "options" for solving them can be uncontentiously listed; for most options, the results are uncertain and of disputed value. The supposedly precise recommendations which consequentialism might in principle provide elude us; in their stead we find recommendations whose spurious precision reflects contextual (perhaps ideologically contentious) views of the available "options", their likely results and the value of those results. Consequentialist reasoning about actual problems is impressionistic rather than scientific.[9]

This defect is internal to consequentialism. The second major defect is external. Consequentialism cannot capture matters that non-consequentialists think peculiar and distinctive about justice. Two aspects of this are particularly significant. First, in taking the production of benefit as the criterion for right action it permits some lives to be used and used up in order to produce benefit (happiness or well-being) in other lives. Secondly, when consequentialists use a subjective account of the good as the measure of benefit, they treat all preferences as on a par: meeting urgent needs may have to take second place to filling strong preferences. The latter is not trivial in the context of global distributive justice, because extreme deprivation can blunt rather than sharpen preferences. Even if we knew (how?) that actual preferences did not overlook urgent need, the use of some for others' benefit raises countless questions in development ethics. How far is it permissible to take what some have produced to alleviate others' poverty? Or to demand a "generation of sacrifice" (or many generations) for the benefit of future generations? Or to use non-renewable resources or to increase population if this will harm future generations? How much freedom may be traded for how much equality? The justice of proposed population, immigration, investment and resource policies is subject to endless dispute within consequentialist accounts of global justice.

Action-based reasoning: rights and obligations

If consequentialist ethical reasoning cannot avoid these problems, the most appealing alternative may be to retreat to less ambitious forms of ethical reasoning, and specifically to action-based ethical reasoning. Such reasoning looks for morally significant constraints on action (i.e. a decision procedure to establish rightness or obligatoriness) rather than for an algorithm for producing optimal results. Most contemporary action-based approaches to justice try to identify the claims of right-holders against others. Older approaches often began from an account of obligations of justice.

Beginning with rights rather than obligations has two advantages. First, it seemingly allows those who conceive of justice in terms of required action to shelve disputes about agency while they work out the requirements of justice. Secondly, the political resonance of appeals to rights can be harnessed to issues of international distributive justice. However, there are also costs to beginning with an account of rights, and it is worth seeing what these are before considering specific accounts of global distributive justice which begin with rights.

If we consider the matters of obligation and of right sufficiently abstractly, there seems to be no distinction between principles of obligation and principles of right. Whenever it is right either for some identifiable agent, A, or for unspecified parties, to have some action, x, done or omitted by B, then it is obligatory for B to do or to omit x either for A or for unspecified parties. One and the same principle defines what it is right for A (or for unspecified parties) to receive from B, and what it is obligatory (indeed, right) for B to do for A (or for unspecified parties). In many European languages the same word conveys the abstract notions of right and of obligation: "*droit*" and "*Recht*", for example, can translate either. At this level of abstraction the only difference appears to be that the vocabulary of obligation looks at ethical relationships from the perspective of agency and the vocabulary of right looks at them from the perspective of recipience. This correlativity is the most fundamental feature of action-centred ethical reasoning. Without it claims about what some are owed do not imply that action ought to be taken, and claims about what is owed by some do not imply that anyone, specified or unspecified, has been wronged if nothing is done.

At a less abstract level correlativity fails. This happens when discussion shifts from *right action* to *rights*. So long as we talk about what it is right for some agent or agency to do we need not distinguish between what is owed to specified others and what is owed indeed, but not to specified others. Once we start talking about *rights* we assume a framework in which performance of obligations can be *claimed*. The fulfilment of rights has to be allocated to specified obligation-bearers: otherwise claiming is impossible. In rights-based reasoning, rights can either be claimed of *all* obligation-bearers (here the obligation is *universal*) or can be claimed of some *specified* obligation-bearer(s) (here the obligation is *special*). Obligatory action which neither can be performed for all, nor is based on any special relationship, remains unallocated, so cannot be claimed: for it is not specified against whom any particular claim should be lodged. Reasoning which begins from rights can take no account of obligations which are neither universal nor special, where no connection is made between (universal or *specified*) bearers of obligations and holders of rights. Since the discourse of rights requires that obligations are owed to *all* others or to *specified others*, *unallocated* right action, which is owed to unspecified others, drops out of sight. It may be right to help those in need, or to treat others with courtesy – but if these traditional obligations lack counterpart rights they will not be recognized by theories that treat rights as basic. Beyond the most abstract level of action-centred reasoning, a gap opens between rights and obligations. This gap is important in many contexts, including in action-centred reasoning about human needs and international distributive justice.

The shift from discussion of right to discussion of rights adopts not merely the passive perspective of the *recipient* of others' action, but the narrower perspective of the *claimant* of others' action. Within the recipient perspective, the attitude of claimants is indeed *less* passive than other possible attitude. Claimants are not humble petitioners or loyal subjects. They do not beg boons or favours. They speak as equals who are wronged and demand others' action. The early modern innovation of the perspective of rights had both heady power and political import. It could be used by the downtrodden to reject and hector existing powers and their categories. This rhetoric was vibrant in a world of rulers and subjects, and still resonates in the later worlds of empires and colonies, of superpowers and their clients. Nevertheless, those who claim rights view themselves within an overall framework of recipience. Rights are demands on *others*. Even liberty and authority rights are rights in that they demand that *others* not interfere with or obstruct the right-holder. Rights to goods and services patently demand that *others* provide, and permit right-holders to remain entirely passive. The perspective of rights may therefore be an inappropriate one for the more powerful agents and agencies who affect international distribution. For the powerful, a focus on obligations, which make direct demands for action or restraint, may be more important.

This suggests that the rhetoric of rights is not the fundamental idiom of action-centred reasoning, but a derivative (and potentially rancorous) way of thought in which others are seen as the primary agents and right-holders as secondary agents, whose action depends on opportunities created by others. This may be the most nearly active form of ethical and political discourse for the needy and vulnerable. For the more powerful, who could end or reduce others' need, concentration on rights and recipience could mask recognition of power and its obligations, and so constrict moral vision and concern.

Part of this narrowing of vision is reflected in the disappearance of unallocated obligations within a rights framework. When obligations are unallocated it is indeed right that they should be met, but nobody can have a right – an enforceable and claimable right – to their being met. In discussion of rights it is often noted that action such as helpfulness (generosity, care, etc.) is not allocated to specified obligation-bearers, and so that there can be no rights to receive help (generous, caring, etc. treatment). *Perfect* obligations can be handled within a rights approach, but unallocated obligations cannot. These *imperfect* obligations are not owed to specified others and hence cannot be claimed; they can be thought of only as features of agents – as traits of character or virtues – and not as relating recipients to agents.

Two reactions are possible. Some writers on global issues try to restore moral standing to the social virtues by "promoting" them, and showing that they are really perfect obligations with corresponding rights, (see below). However, if the claimants of supposed "rights" to help (beneficence, care, etc.) cannot find where to lodge their claims, these are empty "manifesto" rights. For example, if a "right to food" is promulgated without any obligation to provide food for particular right-holders being allocated to specified agents and agencies, this so-called right will provide meagre pickings. This is not merely because obligation-holders may flout their obligation, but for the deeper reason that no obligation-holders have been specified. The prospects of the hungry would be transformed if specified others were obliged to provide each with adequate food; but unless obligations to feed the hungry are a matter of allocated justice rather than unallocated beneficence, a so-called "right" to food, and many other "rights" that would be important for the needy, will be only "manifesto" rights.[10]

An alternative response to shifting from the discourse of right action to that of rights is that obligations to help unspecified others may be not "promoted" to the status of perfect obligations, but rather denied. When this is done, such help will no longer be seen as obligatory, let alone as required by justice, and is likely to be viewed as optional or supererogatory, at best a virtue of individual characters and not of public institutions. This move assimilates mundane acts of kindness, generosity or helpfulness to heroic or saintly action, which indeed goes beyond all duty. The strongest and most far-reaching result of shifting discussion from matters of right to matters of rights is that there is then nothing between justice and supererogation.[11]

When taken in this way the choice of rights discourse as the idiom for ethical deliberation drives a wedge between questions of justice and matters of help and benefit. Justice is seen as a matter of assignable, hence claimable and potentially institutionalizable and enforceable rights, which only the claimant can waive. Beneficence and help are seen as unassignable, hence unclaimable, unenforceable, and *a fortiori* unwaiveable. This theoretical wedge is reflected in many contemporary institutional structures and ways of thought. Legal and economic structures are held to define the limits of justice; "voluntary" and "private" activities, including charity work and personal relationships, are seen as the domain of the virtues of beneficence and care, which afford the poor no entitlements. Others' need, even their hunger and destitution, will then be thought injustice only if we can show either that there is a universal right to be fed or that specific hungry persons have special rights to food. Contemporary economic structures, national and transnational, patently leave many either without special claims for food, or with claims only against kin and neighbours, which will probably fail whenever needs are sharpest. Yet, as we shall see, it is also uphill work to show that there is a universal right to be fed. If there are neither special nor universal rights to be fed, it may matter if ethical reasoning within a rights framework dismisses help, beneficence and care as action that we may bestow where we will, or denies that they are any sort of duty. In such accounts, need will have no independent weight; help may legitimately be confined to kin or compatriots; and virtuous action will be seen as a "private" affair. Either theories of rights must bring need under the heading of justice, by demonstrating universal rights to welfare, or they must relegate global famine and destitution to the withering inadequacy of private, optional charity.

These general features of theories of rights are significant in many contexts other than discussions of global distributive justice. More specific problems of international distributive issues stand out most clearly against the backdrop of specific accounts of rights. I shall sketch three such accounts, and comment on some of the difficulties each has in handling global distributive justice.

Libertarian justice

The most minimal accounts of human rights and the correlative obligations of justice are offered by libertarian writers, who insist that there are only negative, liberty rights. Any more extensive set of rights – for example, rights to welfare or to aid – would impose obligations that violate some obligation-bearer's supposed rights to liberty. Libertarians see taxation for others' benefit, including foreign aid from wealthier to poorer states, as unjustly taking property from those taxed. The central demand of libertarian justice, whether national or international, is: do not redistribute.

[. . .]

The insistence that redistribution by state powers or agencies is unjust determines libertarian views on aid, welfare and poverty. Libertarians hold that voluntary giving or charity are the only responses to others' needs which do not violate justice; and that even these are wrong if they foster dependence.[12] Voluntary giving, however, is entirely inadequate for dealing with massive phenomena such as global poverty.[13]

Moreover, neither, libertarians nor other liberals who pronounce themselves "agnostic about the good for man", and so reject any objective account of the good or of virtues, are well placed to say much in favour of charity. Since they deny themselves the conceptual resources which could make sense of obligations that are not the corollaries of rights, they have nothing to say about imperfect obligations, nor, therefore, about the virtues. Some may give matters a rosy gloss by suggesting that charity, since it is not a matter of obligation, is supererogatory. This is only rhetorical flourish: without an account of what makes action that goes "beyond" duty morally admirable, libertarians would be more accurate to describe charitable giving just as one possible expression of personal preference.

Despite their embargo on redistribution, libertarians could hold positions that have powerful and perhaps helpful implications for the poor of the Third World. Since they base their thought on respect for individuals and their rights, and judge any but minimal states unjust, libertarians view actual states, none of which is minimal, as exceeding their just powers. In particular, both libertarian and other liberals may hold that all interferences with individuals' movement, work and trade violate liberty. On an obvious reading this suggests that those who live in the Third World should have the right to migrate anywhere, that those who are willing to work for less have the right not to be excluded by residence and trades union restrictions and that protective trade policies violate liberties. Libertarians are known for advocating free trade, but not for advocating the dismantling of immigration laws. This may be because their stress on property rights entails an attrition of public space that eats into the freedom of movement and rights of abode of the unpropertied, even within national jurisdictions.

It is hard to see the global import of such radically cosmopolitan libertarianism. Presumably such policies would greatly weaken the position of the relatively poor within rich economies, by undercutting their bargaining power. Ostensibly "perfected" global markets might spread resources more and more evenly across the world's population: in practice it is doubtful whether a removal of restrictions on movement, abode and trade would achieve this. In an era of automated production, the poor might no longer have *anything* marketable to sell: even their labour power may lack market value. Concentrations of economic power have been able to form and survive in relatively "free" internal markets; international economic powers could presumably ride the waves of wider competition equally successfully.

Compensatory justice and world poverty

There is one other way by which even a minimal, libertarian account of rights (let alone stronger accounts) can approach international justice. This is to argue that the poor, even if they lack general rights to be helped, either by fellow-citizens or across national boundaries, sometimes have *special* rights against certain others who owe them compensation for past or present injustice.[14]

On one account these special rights are rooted in special, historical relationships. The present plight of the underdeveloped world was caused in part by past actions by the states, companies and individuals of the developed world. (No doubt it was also partly caused by more local agents and forces.) Colonialism began with invasion and massive violations of liberty. Many Third World economies were developed to the advantage of the imperial powers. Profits made in the South were "repatriated" rather than reinvested; colonial industry and trade were restricted; development in the North was partly based on exploitation of the South.

However, the actual patterns of colonial violation of economic rights are complex and obscure: in the heart of darkness nothing is definite. Many former colonies were economically backward when colonized; some colonial powers did a good deal to modernize and develop their colonies; in some cases Third World economies are *less* prosperous now than they were under colonial administrations. And it is always uncertain what the present would have been had the past not been colonial. *If* the present plight of the poor in the Third World could be traced to past colonial or imperial injustices inflicted by surviving agents or agencies, we might perhaps be able to show that some have rights to be compensated by those agents and agencies. However, the individuals whose rights were violated in the colonial past, and those who violated them, are long dead, and the relevant institutions often transformed or defunct. Since we have no adequate account of institutional agency, we cannot say where supposed obligations to compensate for past injustices are now located, nor who (if anyone) has inherited rights to be compensated. Past exploitation provides an indeterminate basis for claiming that present individuals, groups, states or regions have special rights to compensation. The bearers of special obligations to compensate have to be identifiable as those who wronged others, and rights to compensation will be no stronger than the proof of identification. If we cannot be sure how far the predicaments of the present were produced by ancient wrongs, nor which of our contemporaries have been harmed by such wrongs, nor which have benefited, nor which have special obligations to bear the costs of just compensation, rights to compensation will have few implications for action.

[. . .]

Poverty in the Third World cannot easily be remedied by compensatory justice. To claim special rights we must show a special relationship; but the causal links between specific individuals or institutions who harmed and were harmed, or who now harm others and suffer harms, are not clear enough to allocate rights of compensation; and without allocation rights are only the rhetoric of manifestos. In addition, some of the poorest peoples in the world have hardly been touched by the colonial period; hence their needs would be ignored in an account of international distributive justice that relied mainly on appeals to special rights to compensation for the injuries of colonialism.

Rights to welfare and international justice

A third, more ambitious approach to international distributive justice by way of a theory of rights argues that human beings have more than liberty rights and those special rights (such as rights to compensation) that can arise once any universal rights are acknowledged. Several theories of justice claim that there are also rights to (some level of) economic welfare, and some that there are specifically rights to whatever goods and services are required to meet basic needs. This position is sanctioned by the UN Universal Declaration of Human Rights of 1948, and widely endorsed. A position that allows for welfare rights should surely provide friendly terrain for an account of international distributive justice. Yet this is not always the case.

One well-known account of justice that includes (although it does not begin with) welfare rights is John Rawls's *A Theory of Justice*.[15] His account was proposed as a theory of justice for the basic structure of a society, conceived of as a more or less self-contained national community. He argues for two principles of justice for such societies. The first concurs with the libertarian view that all should have equal and maximal liberties; the second, the so-called difference principle, demands that inequalities be instituted only if they would be to the advantage of the representative worst-off person. Since the construction assumes the framework of the nation-state, the representative worst-off person is not thought of as one of the most disadvantaged in the world. When Rawls finally relaxes the assumption that justice is internal to states he argues only for selected principles of international justice. He repeats the thought experiment of the original position on the hypothesis that the parties are representatives of nation-states, conceived of as relatively self-sufficient entities. The principles of international justice which this is said to yield are analogues only of Rawls's *first* principle of justice: non-intervention, self-determination, *pacta sunt servanda*, principles of self-defence and of just war. There is no international analogue of the second principle of justice, hence no account of international distributive justice.

Rawls's omission here has been well discussed by Charles Beitz.[16] He points out that even assuming the self-sufficiency of states it is reasonable to think that representatives of future states, meeting behind a veil of ignorance, would choose principles of resource distribution that insure against the contingency of having only resource-poor territories. More centrally he argues that the premise that states are relatively self-sufficient is false, and hence that there are as good grounds for thinking that their representatives will agree on principles of international distributive justice as there were grounds for thinking that the parties to the original position would agree on a domestic principle for distributive justice.

The actual implications of this extension of Rawlsian thought are hard to discern. Rawls's account of justice constrains institutions: his second principle demands the evaluation and comparison of entire institutional structures. Some of the difficulties of evaluation and comparison which plague consequentialists recur here: in this context a maximin principle needs the information with which to make maximizing judgements about very complex phenomena. Since international interdependence is intricate, it is hard to know which institutional changes would *most* improve the lot of the poorest in the world.

Other accounts that go beyond a libertarian view of rights propose that we think of individuals as having rights to basic well-being, which require that their material needs be met. On such accounts – for example those of Gewirth and Shue[17] – arrangements will be unjust if they fail to meet basic needs. Without minimal standards of subsistence, agency itself fails, and so the point of liberty of action and hence even of liberty rights is gone. The point is not, of course, to neglect institutional arrangements: the basic needs of many millions could only be secured by building an appropriate economic order. The point is to find some set of arrangements that secures welfare rights.

Welfare rights, so conceived, are demands on other agents and agencies. To move from this level of abstraction towards an account of just institutions requires that the obligations that are the counterparts of these rights be identified and allocated, for a universal right without corresponding obligations is only a "manifesto right." Usually rights theorists assume that the counterparts to universal rights are universal obligations, although aspects of fulfilling and enforcing the corresponding institutional right may be allocated to specific agencies. This assumption sits well in discussions of liberty rights, where the corresponding obligations are negative. A right to liberty is not respected unless all agents and agencies refrain from violating that liberty.

Welfare rights are different. It is impossible for everyone to take on the same obligations here, for example by making the same contribution to ending poverty or hunger. A universal right to be fed or to receive basic shelter or health care is unlike a universal right not to be killed or to speak freely. It is plausible to think that rights not to be killed or to speak freely are matched by and require universal obligations not to kill or not to obstruct free speech; but a universal right to food cannot simply be matched by a universal obligation to provide an aliquot amount of food. The asymmetry of liberty and "welfare" rights, on which libertarians rest so much of their refusal to broaden their conception of justice, is I think well grounded. (This offers little comfort to libertarians if they cannot establish that liberty has priority or what maximal liberty comprises.)

The aim of welfare rights theories is to broaden their account of justice so that it includes rights to claim basic needs. The available theories do this by identifying welfare rights so abstractly that they need not fix their allocation to obligation-bearers. These theories do not determine against whom claims may be lodged. Such theories allow us to *talk* quite fluently about rights to food or to a minimal standard of life or to basic health care, but obscures the point that there is a real asymmetry between rights to such goods and services and "negative" rights not to be (for example) killed or injured or coerced.

Some advocates of welfare rights challenge the distinction between liberty and welfare rights on which these observations are based. Shue, for example, correctly points out that once we start talking about the *enforcement* of rights the distinction between liberty rights which demand only non-interference and "welfare" rights which require positive action fades. He writes: "the very most 'negative'-seeming right to liberty . . . requires positive action by society to protect it and . . . to restore it when avoidance and protection both fail."[18] However, enforcement cannot be discussed or take place until obligations are identified and allocated. It is, after all, obligations, and not rights, that will need enforcing. Arguments from the demands of enforceability cannot settle questions about what rights there can consistently be or actually are, or who holds the corresponding obligations. While it is true that the enforcement of a right not to be tortured demands positive action, just as enforcement of a right to food does, the difference between the two rights remains. Suppose we think there are both rights not to be tortured and rights to food. If, in the absence of enforcement, A tortures B, we are quite clear who has violated B's right; but if A does not provide B with food, nor even with an aliquot morsel of food, we are not sure whether A has violated B's rights. There nothing shows that it is *against A* that B's claim to food should be lodged or enforced.[19]

Universal obligations and international justice

Theories of rights come close to providing a framework for thinking about international distributive justice. What is missing from the positions just outlined is a way of combining an account of the allocation of obligations with acknowledgement of the claims of need and poverty. Libertarians allocate obligations, but overlook need; other liberals acknowledge need but fail to allocate some obligations. I shall try to meet both demands by sketching an account of obligations among finite, needy beings.

Those who make rights basic to their account of justice start with the thought that all have equal rights. An analogous approach to identifying obligations of justice would look for principles of action that can be universally adopted. As is well known, this is the basic move of the Kantian ethical enterprise.[20] Kant identifies principles of obligation as those which must be adopted if principles that cannot be universally held are rejected. Injustice on this account is a matter of adopting fundamental principles which not all can adopt. To make non-universalizable principles fundamental, to institutions or to lives, presumes status and privilege that cannot be open to all. Justice on such accounts is a matter of acting only on principles on which all *could act* (not either *would* or *should* act, as in many quasi-Kantian approaches).

A Kantian construction of principles of obligation is in one crucial way less ambitious than the constructions of human rights discussed above. Those constructions aim to determine the greatest possible liberty, or the best set of liberty and welfare rights. At some stage in these constructions an *optimum* or *maximal* arrangement must be identified. Just as the poles of a wigwam cannot stand in isolation, so these constructions of rights are all-or-nothing affairs: if one component right of "the most extensive liberty" is identified, so are all the rest; if less than the full set is established, none is established. When principles of obligations are constructed on Kantian lines they are identified *seriatim*. The construction uses a procedure for checking whether any proposed principle could be fundamental for all institutions and lives. A Kantian construction of obligations can identify *some* principles of obligation without establishing *all* of them.

Discovering which principles must be adopted if non-universalizable principles are rejected is not a matter of finding out which specific types of action ought to be done. Act descriptions which refer to particular times, places, persons or scarce resources cannot be universally satisfied, yet clearly acts, including permissible and obligatory acts, must fall under such descriptions. Superficial and detailed act descriptions need not and cannot be universalizable. We cannot all of us eat the same grain, nor share the same roof. A Kantian approach aims to identify *fundamental* principles (Kant's maxims) which may be used to govern lives and institutions. Justice on this account is a matter of not basing actions, lives or institutions on principles that cannot be universally shared; it is not a matter of uniform action.[21]

Two examples of obligations that can be identified by the Kantian method of construction are those of rejecting reliance on fundamental principles either of coercion or of deception. The background arguments here show that it is impossible for a principle of coercion to be universally shared – for those who are coerced are (at least temporarily) denied agency and so *cannot* (in principle) share their coercers' principles of action, and those who are deceived are denied knowledge of their deceiver's underlying principle (if they knew, the deception would be discredited, so ineffective) so again *cannot* share the plan to deceive. Such arguments do not show that all coercion or deception is unjust: they show only that actions, institutions and lives which make coercion or deception fundamental are unjust.

So far it may seem that a Kantian construction would identify as principles of obligation only those which correspond to the rights libertarians identify. If a construction of obligations could only proceed in this way, it could not take account of needs. However, this less ambitious approach can go beyond theories of rights in two important respects. Both follow from Kant's insistence that obligations are relevant to *finite* rational beings. (On Kant's account, idealized rational beings would in any case find principles of obligation redundant.)

Justice and the virtues

The first way in which a Kantian approach via obligations yields more than theories of rights can provide is that it can offer an account of virtue as well as of justice. It allows for the construction both of imperfect obligations, whose performance is not allocated to right-holders, and of perfect obligations, whose performance can be claimed as a right. Principles of imperfect obligation, on a Kantian account, reflect human finitude. Finite beings are inescapably needy, and their obligations cannot be based on denying this. The principles of imperfect obligation for which Kant argued are ones that must be adopted if non-universalizable principles are rejected by beings of limited capacities. Two (slightly adapted) examples are the following. First, beings who (like human beings) find that their individual abilities are not adequate to achieve their ends must (if rational) be committed to relying (to some extent) on others' help; hence, if they reject non-universalizable principles, they must be committed to a principle of offering (at least some) help to others. This commitment is a matter of rejecting principled non-beneficence rather than commitment to a determinate level of beneficence. Secondly, beings who have to develop their abilities, rather than relying on instinct or maturation, know that they will have ends that require various abilities, so will, if rational, be committed to developing some range of abilities in themselves and in others.

This construction of principles of imperfect obligation is not subjective: it does not refer to actual ends or desires. It does take the needs of finite beings into account. The line of thought can be paraphrased as follows. Rational beings whose desires, unlike those of creatures of instinct, standardly outrun both their own resources and those of their fellows will (regardless of the specific content of their desires) discover that they cannot universally act on principles of neglecting needs. They cannot rationally will that they should be part of a world in which either a principle of refusing needed help or a principle of refusing to develop abilities and resources is universally adopted. Hence their fundamental principles must include some commitment to helping others and to developing human (and other) potential. However, the non-universalizability of neglecting to help or to develop human potential does not entail that there are obligations to help all others in all their projects or to develop all possible potentials: indeed, these are impossible commitments. Nor does this account of the social virtues determine required levels of help or commitment to development. However, those who do nothing reveal that their underlying principle is to neglect both virtues. They act wrongly even if their victims cannot be identified.

In distinguishing the demands of perfect and imperfect obligations a Kantian construction respects the asymmetry of obligations to refrain and obligations to intervene. The advantage of an account of imperfect obligations is that it neither insists that what have traditionally been thought of as imperfect duties have corresponding rights nor treats them as in no way obligatory. In short, the approach leaves room, as rights-based approaches do not, for a non-trivializing account of the social and institutional virtues. Yet, unlike most contemporary accounts of the virtues, it does not rely on historicist or communitarian claims, and still allows us to talk about rights, considered as the reciprocal of perfect obligations. When it is either relevant or politic to adopt the perspective of recipience, the idiom of rights can be used to discuss and demand justice.

Justice, abilities and needs

All of this, however, does not show how an account of the claimable, perfect obligations of justice can take account of need. If perfect duties, and specifically matters of justice, are a matter of non-interference, how could meeting needs be a matter of *justice*? And if the allocation of help to those who need it is undetermined by fundamental ethical considerations, may we not allocate it capriciously among the needy? If so, what advantage does a Kantian approach offer for considering international distributive justice, where a guaranteed and reliable allocation of help and of the development of human resources is crucial? No doubt a capacity to offer a serious, non-relativist account of social and institutional virtues is an advantage, but Kantian justice still looks like an obligation-based analogue of libertarian justice.

A Kantian construction can, however, guide a non-selective approach to basic human needs within a theory of justice; and herein lies its second advantage over rights-based theories. Kant stresses repeatedly that *all* principles of obligation are principles for *finite* rational beings, and in particular that human beings are finite not only in rationality but in many other ways. In deliberating about what it takes to apply and institutional-ize fundamental principles of rejecting coercion or deception, human finitude, need and vulnerability must be taken into account.

We cannot interpret what it is to reject a principle of coercion without an account of what constitutes coercion in the human condition. It is generally agreed that physical force is coercive for human agents: when A pushes B, B's movement does not reflect B's agency, which is preempted. However, it is also generally thought that threat and duress constitute coercion, and the notion of a threat cannot be expli-cated without reference to context. What constitutes a threat depends on what powers a threatener has to harm particular victims – hence also on the reciprocal of power, i.e. on the vulnerability of those threatened. It is impossible to determine what consti-tutes a threat in abstraction from an account of the respective capacities of those who threaten and are threatened. Human finitude can take many shapes: each shape constitutes a specific configuration of need and vulnerability, which others can exploit or respect.

Here the task cannot be to judge particular cases, but only to suggest which consid-erations would be relevant in deciding how to ensure that lives and institutions eschew fundamental principles and practices of coercion and deception. Marx's slogan, "From each according to his abilities; to each according to his needs", is a suggestive way into this topic. The slogan gestures towards a vision of social relations in which antago-nisms are overcome. This victim was of the far future. For the present, Marx acknowl-edged, progress would be marked by forms of bourgeois right and law; many of his followers thought, in particular, that Marxism could bracket internationalist commit-ments and pursue socialism in one country. Socialist practice, like liberal practice, has long subordinated underlying cosmopolitan commitments to the sovereignty of nation-states. It is only in a distant future, in which states would have withered away, that justice – or rather, the full human emancipation that would succeed justice – would not be confined by state boundaries. These reminders might suggest that socialist thought has little to contribute to present issues of international justice, except perhaps by way of its influence on theories of economic development. However, Marx's slogan brings together the two issues that other theories so often sever. I shall sketch a way of reading a joint emphasis on *abilities* and *needs* into the construction of principles of justice just attempted.

Principles of obligation are relevant only for agents (perhaps some individual and others institutional). Agents must have at least some abilities or capacities for indepen-dent action: they must combine some cognitive and some executive abilities. Without these they could not act, and practical reasoning would be irrelevant for them; in short, they would not be agents. The agents and agencies who affect international distribu-tions of goods are highly diverse. However, all of them have fairly limited abilities. This is evidently true of human agents, whose abilities are reciprocal to their needs. It is also true of the many agents and agencies and even of those supposedly sovereign bodies, the nation-states. Even superpowers are limited powers; so, of course, are those new global operator's, the transnational corporations. The steps that this motley range of finite agents must take if they are to reject fundamental principles and policies of coercing or deceiving others are clearly enormously diverse. However, two aspects of their action can be clearly distinguished.

To reject principled coercion is a matter of not relying on any policy or practice of treating others in ways to which they *could not* consent. (The claim is modal; it does not invoke actual preferences.) This may seem too weak a claim: surely overriding others' actual dissent, even when they could have consented, is already coercive. However, provided action is tailored to make others' dissent *possible*, actual dissent will be registered by refusing or renegotiating others' proposals. It is action that is pushed through in the face of dissent, and makes refusal impossible, that coerces: such "offers" cannot be refused.

Relations between the powerful and the powerless are often governed by principles of coercion. This is evident in relations between developed and underdeveloped states, agencies and enterprises. Those who are weak cannot refuse or renegotiate the "offers" of the strong, unless the strong adjust these offers to the actual lack of abilities and weakness of those to whom they are made. Poor and powerless states and institutions, like poor and powerless individuals, may make dismal bargains, trading their only resources for inadequate returns, "agreeing" to damaging terms of trade and taking out loans that they cannot service. Poor states may agree to accept dirty manufacturing and to offer massive tax concessions for foreign investors. All of this reflects their vulnerability and need. Miscalculation apart, neither individuals nor institutions would accept such arrangements unless they were vulnerable.

For just transactions with vulnerable others it is not enough to meet standards that would not coerce or deceive others of equal or greater power. To act justly, the rich and powerful must adopt policies that are not based on coercing or deceiving those with whom they interact. It is not enough to observe outward forms of contract, bargain and negotiation (as libertarians might think), or to secure others from destitution (as advocates of welfare rights would insist). It is necessary to reject fundamental policies, principles or practices which deny those on the receiving end, with their specific vulnerabilities and needs, the possibility of refusing or renegotiating. Just agents and agencies allow others, including those most vulnerable to them, the space to refuse and to renegotiate offers.

A commitment not to take advantage of others' weakness is in itself frail. The strong are easily tempted – and, after all, they are not that strong; most of them live amid many competitors and stronger powers. It is hardly realistic to demand that institutions and agents, who will be squeezed by others, if they do not pursue their own advantage, not lean on the weak, unless the demand is given "teeth". Hence a genuine, action-guiding commitment to enacting principles of justice in a world of disparate agents, many of them vulnerable to others' powers, cannot be *only* a demand for justice in transactions. It must also, and crucially, be a commitment to transform the structure of institutions and the characters and powers of individual agents, i.e. the presuppositions of transactions, so as to reduce powerlessness and vulnerability.

More specifically, international markets, transactions and relations will require as much regulation as internal markets and transactions and domestic social relations, if differentials of power are not to undercut the lives and plans of the weak. This point does not impugn or challenge the presumed performance of *ideal* markets, or the *relpolitik* of *ideally* sovereign states, or the decision-making of *idealized* rational choosers. It does recognize the vast gap between the idealized agents and agencies modelled by social scientists and their actual prototypes. Without regulation, actual markets may magnify rather than minimize the implications of disparities in power and vulnerability, actual states may oppress their own and other peoples, and ruthless individuals may dominate others. Powerlessness and vulnerability are the reciprocals of others' power: a commitment to control the coercive potential of differentials of power is a commitment to reduce or restrain the capacities of the most powerful agents and to increase those of the most vulnerable. A commitment to lessen both economic and political inequality therefore follows from a serious, action-guiding commitment to justice among unequals.

Which forms of regulation would best achieve these results is a vast and selectively discussed matter. The stock antithesis between "state regulation" and "non-interference", which structures many discussions, may itself be obsolete, and there may be as much reason to look at the social and discursive practices that discipline and foster certain types of agent and institution as at the legal and administrative frameworks that constrain them. Questions of good practice may be as vital as questions of legal limits.

The present international economic order is the product of a vast and interlocking range of institutional changes and transformations. Many of the actors on this stage did not exist at the end of the Second World War. There were then no transnational corporations of the modern sort; there were few independent ex-colonies other than those whose population was of European descent. The international bodies, development agencies and NGOs that operate transnationally are new types of agencies. Some of them may have exacerbated international distributive injustice; others may have reduced it. Such a process of institution-building and transformation, including the education and transformation of human capacities, is endlessly extendable. A full commitment to international distributive justice would be a matter of seeking to transform the present institutional structure into one better able to ensure that the powers and abilities it constructs and fosters serve rather than exploit actual needs and reduce vulnerabilities.

At this point the initial question of audience can be raised again. For whom are these discussions of justice relevant? By the very arguments pursued, there is no unique locus of responsibility. But it does not follow that there are agents or agencies who have no responsibilities. The fact that nobody and no agency can do *everything* does not entail that they can do nothing. This is true not only of rich but of poor individuals, not only of governments and institutions in the North, but of those in the South; and it is true of the manifold international, multinational and transnational agencies that have proliferated in the global economy.

An account of principles of obligation among finite and mutually vulnerable beings has powerful and complex implications for issues of development and international justice. Many steps are needed for effective institutionalization of the principles defended here. The salient contrasts with other accounts of justice show some of the strengths and limitations of approaching questions of international justice by relying on a constructivist account of obligations. First some limits: the approach does not yield algorithms either for identifying principles of justice, or for their implementation. Then some strengths: the programme offers a procedure for identifying certain principles of justice, and arguments to show why their institutionalization and implementation should take account of relationships of power and vulnerability. The position shares both the libertarian recognition of the asymmetry between negative and positive principles of obligation, and the welfare rights theorists' recognition of the importance of meeting the needs whose satisfaction underpins capacities to act. It also recognizes that in many contexts there are reasons for using the vocabulary of rights, while denying that this vocabulary and the related perspective of recipience can be fundamental in an account of transnational justice among finite and needy rational beings.

Notes

1 For discussions of problems of duties that cross borders see Charles Beitz, *Political Theory and International Relations* (Princeton, Princeton University Press, 1979) and "Cosmopolitan ideals and national sentiments", *Journal of Philosophy*, 1983, pp. 591–600, Robert Goodin, "What is so special about our fellow countrymen?", *Ethics*, 1988, pp. 663–86, Stanley Hoffman, *Duties Beyond Borders On the Limits and Possibilities of Ethical International Politics* (Syracuse, Syracuse University Press, 1981), Luper-Foy (ed), *Problems of International Justice*, David Miller, "The ethical significance of nationality", *Ethics*, 1988, pp. 647–62, Onora O'Neill, *Faces of Hunger. An Essay on Poverty, Development and Justice* (London, Allen & Unwin, 1986), and "Ethical reasoning and ideological pluralism", *Ethics*, 1988; Henry Shue, "Mediating Duties", *Ethics*, 98 (1988), pp. 705–22 and Michael Walzer, *Spheres of Justice: A Defense of Pluralism and Equality* (Oxford, Martin Robertson, 1983).
2 On the communitarian critique of liberalism see Michael Sandel, *Liberalism and the Limits of Justice* (Cambridge, Cambridge University Press, 1982), Alasdair MacIntyre, *After Virtue* (London, Duckworth, 1981), "Is patriotism a virtue" and *Whose Justice? Which Rationality?* (London, Duckworth, 1988) and Walzer, *Spheres of Justice*, as well as the discussion and bibliographical essay in Jeremy Waldron, *Nonsense Upon Stilts: Bentham, Burke and Marx on the Rights of Man* (London, Methuen, 1987).
3 For fuller discussion of the contrasts between abstraction and idealization, and their relevance to international issues, see Onora O'Neill "Abstraction, idealization and ideology", in J. G. D. Evans (ed.), *Ethical Theories and Contemporary Problems* (Cambridge, Cambridge University Press, 1988) "Ethical reasoning and ideological pluralism", *Ethics*, 98 (1988), pp. 705–22 and "Gender, justice and international boundaries", *British Journal of Political Science*, 20 (1990), pp. 439–59.
4 John Rawls, "Justice as fairness; political not metaphysical", *Philosophy and Public Affairs*, 14 (1985), pp. 223–51.
5 On the question of priority for compatriots see Goodin, "What is so special about our fellow countrymen?" and Miller "The ethical significance of nationality".
6 See Peter Singer, "Famine, affluence and morality", *Philosophy and Public Affairs*, 1 (1972), pp. 229–43.
7 Garret Hardin, "Lifeboat ethics: the case against helping the poor", *Psychology Today*, 8 (1974), pp. 38–43. For further discussion of and references to neo-Malthusian writing on world hunger see O'Neill, *Faces of Hunger*, chs 2 and 4.
8 Tony Jackson with Deborah Eade, *Against the Grain* (Oxford, Oxfam, 1982).
9 O'Neill, *Faces of Hunger*, chs 4 and 5.
10 For the phrase "manifesto right" see Joel Feinberg, "The nature and value of rights", in *Rights, Justice and the Bounds of Liberty, Essays in Social Philosophy* (Princeton, Princeton University Press, 1980).
11 For discussions of philanthropy and supererogation see the papers in Ellen Frankel Paul et al. (eds), *Beneficence, Philanthropy and the Public Good* (Oxford, Blackwell, 1987), esp. Alan Gewirth, "Private philanthropy and positive rights", pp. 55–78.
12 See the papers in Paul et al. (eds), *Beneficence, Philanthropy and the Public Good*, esp. John O'Connor, "Philanthropy and selfishness", pp. 113–27.
13 Thomas Nagel, "Poverty and food: why charity is not enough", in Peter Brown and Henry Shue (eds), *Food Policy: The Responsibility of the United States in Life and Death Choices* (New York, Free Press, 1977).
14 See George Sher, "Ancient wrongs and modern rights", *Philosophy and Public Affairs*, 1981, David Lyons, "The new Indian claims and original rights to land", in Paul (ed.), *Reading Nozick* and Onora O'Neill, "Rights to Compensation", *Social Philosophy and Public Policy*, 5 (1986), pp. 72–87.
15 John Rawls, *A Theory of Justice* (Cambridge, Mass, Harvard University Press, 1970).
16 Beitz, *Political Theory and International Relations*; relevant sections are reprinted in Luper-Foy (ed), *Problems of International Justice*, pp. 27–54.
17 Alan Gewirth, "Starvation and human rights", in *Human Rights. Essays on Justification and Applications* (Chicago, University of Chicago Press, 1982); Shue, *Basic Rights*.
18 Shue, *Basic Rights*, p. 53.

19 O'Neill, *Faces of Hunger*, ch. 6, and also Shue, *Basic Rights* and "Mediating Duties", *Ethics*, 98 (1988), pp. 687–704.
20 The Kantian texts that lie behind this are mainly *Groundwork of the Metaphysic of Morals* and *The Critique of Practical Reason*; for a reading which applies them to problems of international distributive justice see O'Neill, *Faces of Hunger*, chs 7 and 8.
21 The level of description that is important – that of the Kantian maxim of action – is that of the principle which is *fundamental* to a given action. The maxim is the guiding or controlling principle of an action, the principle that makes sense of and orchestrates ancillary aspects of action. On Kant's account neither agents nor others have privileged knowledge of maxims. Although we cannot judge either others' actions or our own definitively, deliberation can identify action which would not express a non-universalizable action. Agents can strive to avoid acting on nonuniversalizable principles even if they cannot guarantee that they have succeeded. See O'Neill, *Constructions of Reason*.

Part II

Cosmopolitan Global Justice

Introduction

The preceding section examined Immanuel Kant and his call for the establishment of a cosmopolitan civil condition that would provide the necessary institutional conditions from which all individuals could secure a mutual sense of cosmopolitan public right. Underwriting this argument for a condition of universal public right was Kant's principle of justice, which stipulates that the freedom of each should be institutionally organized in such a way that it can coincide with the freedom of others under a mutual condition of universal law. In this regard, not only should a condition of justice be mutually fulfilling, but it should also be equally restrictive, so that this condition can reasonably reconcile the will of one person with the will of everyone within a universal kingdom of ends.

Although Kant provides a compelling cosmopolitan argument, he has certainly not laid the matter of cosmopolitan justice to rest. This is because there remains considerable debate regarding what rights and duties are required in order to create a mutually consistent condition of cosmopolitan global justice. For example, there are still lingering questions about when justice applies and what it demands of us morally (see Beitz and Caney). Furthermore, there are questions about why we should have moral duties to those outside of our immediate community (see Barry versus Miller); or why individuals might be entitled to certain rights of justice and welfare (see Pogge). In addition, if we do have a moral duty of global justice, then is it the same type of duty as we have to our fellow patriots, ethnic groups, religious groups, or local communities? If justice applies to basic institutional structures of social cooperation, as John Rawls suggests, then does this also apply at the global level (see Beitz)? If this is so, how can any meaningful sense of justice be maintained outside the authoritative structures of the state (see Caney, "International Distributive Justice," versus Nagel)? Do these principles of cooperative justice apply to international markets (see Beitz, Barry, and Pogge)? If so, then what distributive mechanisms must also apply? Lastly, how does a cosmopolitan moral position inform our normative thinking about justice at the global level and what difference, if any, can this moral orientation make in a world of independent states (see Caney, "Global Distributive Justice and the State")?

In attempts to provide a cosmopolitan response to these questions, this section begins with Charles Beitz and with his seminal piece on "Justice and International Relations." According to Beitz, affluent countries have an obligation to poorer people and these obligations are not limited solely to acts of humanitarian assistance, but relate more specifically to principles of global distributive justice. In order to substantiate this claim, Beitz builds upon John Rawls' *A Theory of Justice* and suggests that international economic interdependency has come to resemble something like the conditions of social cooperation that originally motivated Rawls' domestic concern for distributive justice. In this regard, according to Beitz, the current global order and its economic structure represents an institutional condition that is analogous to the conditions under which Rawls' own claims for justice apply. Although Beitz recognizes that Rawls himself has limited the boundary of justice to nation-states, Beitz suggests that this national limitation is morally inappropriate and that Rawls' two principles of justice should be applied at the global level. As Beitz argues, under Rawls' own logic, "if evidence of global economic and political interdependence shows the existence of a global scheme of social cooperation, we should not view national boundaries as having fundamental moral significance." Beitz goes on to argue that this is in fact the case and it is therefore appropriate to apply a modified version of the original position at the global level, one where appeals to nationality and citizenship would be excluded behind a global veil of ignorance.

Building upon Beitz' moral cosmopolitanism, Brian Barry suggests that cosmopolitan justice, and justice more generally, requires the satisfaction of a principle of impartiality. This form of impartial moral cosmopolitanism "shows itself to be distinctive in its denial that membership of a society is of deep moral significance when the claims that people can legitimately make on one another are addressed." This is because cosmopolitanism morally demands that "human beings are in some fundamental sense equal" and that to satisfy this moral principle would require further principles of impartial justice that "others could not reasonably reject." As Barry argues in greater detail, when these demands of justice are applied to the current global order they result in an argument for robust principles of economic distributive justice and global institutional reform. As Barry suggests, applying this model has considerable implications concerning how to organize just global institutions, since he argues that the demands of cosmopolitanism would be "best satisfied in a world in which rich people wherever they lived would be taxed for the benefit of poor people wherever they lived." For Barry this conclusion is not only what a cosmopolitan perspective demands, but also what any impartial system of justice requires.

Whereas Beitz and Barry outline a broadly positive form of cosmopolitan global justice, Thomas Pogge's chapter on "Cosmopolitanism and Sovereignty" examines the demands of global justice from a more rights-based approach that focuses on the protection of negative liberties. For Pogge, there are injustices involved within the current global order and these institutional structures systematically violate the basic human rights of others. As Pogge argues, since justice demands that we do not violate the human rights of others, it is reasonable to suggest that one's involvement with any institutional structure that systematically violated these human rights would also amount to a violation of basic negative duties of justice. The uniqueness of Pogge's argument is his insistence that human rights allow individuals to make moral claims on social institutions that greatly impact upon their lives and that these claims demand global institutional reform. Furthermore, his argument calls attention to our involvement in perpetuating unjust global structures and implicates us as the responsible agents to reform those systems. As Pogge suggests, if the global institutional order impacts negatively upon people's lives, then these people have legitimate claims for the reform of these institutional structures. If this is so, and since the current global institutional order often violates the human rights of individuals, then reform of these institutions is what justice and basic human rights require. The implications of this oblige a vertical dispersal of sovereignty so that institutional structures can better represent those who are most vulnerable (and forgotten) within the current global order.

The last chapter in this section provides a useful and precise overview of cosmopolitan distributive justice. In broadly outlining a cosmopolitan approach, Simon Caney defends the idea of cosmopolitan global justice from three of its most prominent critiques. In offering a defense, Caney examines and then responds to the nationalist claim that there are special duties to co-nationals that restrict justice to the national level, the claim that global justice grossly violates the value of state sovereignty, and the realist claim that cosmopolitanism is exceedingly idealistic in a world based on state-interest maximization. By responding to these critiques, Caney not only argues that cosmopolitan global justice is coherent and tenable in the face of these oppositions, but that it has direct political relevance to issues that plague our contemporary global order.

5

Justice and International Relations
Charles R. Beitz

Do citizens of relatively affluent countries have obligations founded on justice to share their wealth with poorer people elsewhere? Certainly they have some redistributive obligations, founded on humanitarian principles requiring those who are able to help those who, without help, would surely perish. But obligations of justice might be thought to be more demanding than this, to require greater sacrifices on the part of the relatively well-off, and perhaps sacrifices of a different kind as well. Obligations of justice, unlike those of humanitarian aid, might also require efforts at large-scale institutional reform. The rhetoric of the United Nations General Assembly's "Declaration on the Establishment of a New International Economic Order" suggests that it is this sort of obligation which requires wealthy countries to substantially increase their contributions to less developed countries and to radically restructure the world economic system. Do such obligations exist?

This question does not pose special theoretical problems for the utilitarian, for whom the distinction between obligations of humanitarian aid and obligations of social justice is a second-order distinction. Since utility-maximizing calculations need not respect national boundaries, there is a method of decision available when different kinds of obligations conflict. Contractarian political theories, on the other hand, might be expected to encounter problems in application to questions of global distributive justice. Contractarian principles usually rest on the relations in which people stand in a national community united by common acceptance of a conception of justice. It is not obvious that contractarian principles with such a justification underwrite any redistributive obligations between persons situated in different national societies.

This feature of contractarian principles has motivated several criticisms of Rawls' theory of justice.[1] These criticisms hold, roughly, that it is wrong to take the nation-state as the foundation of contractarian principles, that, instead, such principles ought to apply globally.[2] I want to pursue this theme here, in part because it raises interesting problems for Rawls' theory, but also because it illuminates several important features of the question of global justice, a question to which too little attention has been paid by political philosophers. In view of increasingly visible global distributive inequalities, famine, and environmental deterioration, it can hardly be denied that this question poses a main political challenge for the foreseeable future.

My discussion has four parts. I begin by reviewing Rawls' brief remarks on international justice, and show that these make sense only on the empirical assumption that nation-states are self-sufficient. Even if this assumption is correct, I then claim, Rawls' discussion of international justice is importantly incomplete, for it neglects certain problems about natural resources. In part three, I go on to question the empirical foundation of the self-sufficiency assumption, and sketch the consequences for Rawlsian ideal theory of abandoning the assumption. In conclusion, I explore the relation of an ideal theory of international justice to some representative problems of politics in the nonideal world.

[. . .]

I

Justice, Rawls says, is the first virtue of social institutions. Its "primary subject" is "the basic structure of society, or more exactly, the way in which the major social institutions distribute fundamental rights and duties and determine the division of advantages from social cooperation" (7). The central problem for a theory of justice is to identify principles by which the basic structure of society can be appraised.

Rawls' two principles characterize "a special case of the problem of justice." They do not characterize "the justice of the law of nations and of relations between states" (7–8) because they rest on morally significant features of an ongoing scheme of social cooperation. If national boundaries are thought to set off discrete schemes of social cooperation, as Rawls assumes (457), then the relations of persons situated in different nation-states cannot be regulated by principles of social justice. As Rawls develops the theory, it is only after principles of social justice and principles for individuals (the "natural duties") are chosen that principles for international relations are considered, and then only in the most perfunctory manner.

Rawls assumes that "the boundaries" of the cooperative schemes to which the two principles apply "are given by the notion of a self-contained national community" (457). This assumption "is not relaxed until the derivation of the principles of justice for the law of nations" (457). In other words, the assumption that national communities are self-contained is relaxed when international justice is considered. What does this mean? If the societies of the world are now to be conceived as open, fully interdependent systems, the world as a whole would fit the description of a scheme of social cooperation and the arguments for the two principles would apply, a fortiori, at the global level. The principles of justice for international politics would be the two principles for domestic society writ large, and their application would have a very radical result, given the tendency to equality of the difference principle. On the other hand, if societies are thought to be *entirely* self-contained – that is, if they are to have no relations of any kind with persons, groups, or societies beyond their borders – then why consider international justice at all? Principles of justice are supposed to regulate conduct, but if, ex hypothesi, there is no possibility of international conduct, it is difficult to see why principles of justice for the law of nations should be of any interest whatsoever. Rawls' discussion of justice among nations suggests that neither of these alternatives describes his intention in the passage quoted. Some intermediate assumption is required. Apparently, nation-states are now to be conceived as largely self-sufficient, but not entirely self-contained. Probably he imagines a world of nation-states which interact only in marginal ways; perhaps they maintain diplomatic relations, participate in a postal union, maintain limited cultural exchanges, and so on. Certainly the self-sufficiency assumption requires that societies have no significant trade or economic relations.

Why, in such a world, are principles of international justice of interest? Rawls says that the restriction to ideal theory has the consequence that each society's external behavior is controlled by its principles of justice and of individual right, which prevent unjust wars and interference with human rights abroad (379). So it cannot be the need to prohibit unjust wars that prompts his worries about the law of nations. The most plausible motivation for considering principles of justice for the law of nations is suggested by an aside regarding the difficulties of disarmament (336), in which Rawls suggests that state relations are inherently unstable despite each one's commitment to its own principles of justice. Agreement on regulative principles would then be a source of security for each state concerning each other's external behavior, and would represent the minimum conditions of peaceful coexistence.

For the purpose of justifying principles for nations, Rawls reinterprets the original position as a sort of international conference:

> One may extend the interpretation of the original position and think of the parties as representatives of different nations who must choose together the fundamental principles to adjudicate conflicting claims among states. Following out the conception of the initial situation, I assume that these representatives are deprived of various kinds of information. While they know that they represent different nations each living under the normal circumstances of human life, they know nothing about the particular circumstances of their own society. . . . Once again the contracting parties, in this case representatives of states, are allowed only enough knowledge to make a rational choice to protect their interests but not so much that the more fortunate among them can take advantage of their special situation. This original position is fair between nations; it nullifies the contingencies and biases of historical fate [378].

While he does not actually present arguments for any particular principles for nations, he claims that "there would be no surprises, since the principles chosen would, I think, be familiar ones" (378). The examples given are indeed familiar; they include principles of self-determination, nonintervention, the *pacta sunt servanda* rule, a principle of justifiable self-defense, and principles defining *jus ad bellum* and *jus in bello*.[3] These are supposed to be consequences of a basic principle of equality among nations, to which the parties in the reinterpreted original position would agree in order to protect and uphold their interests in successfully operating their respective societies and in securing compliance with the principles for individuals which protect human life (378, 115).

One objection to such reasoning might be that there is no guarantee that all of the world's states are internally just, or if they are, that they are just in the sense specified by the two principles. If some societies are unjust according to the two principles, some familiar and serious problems arise. [. . .] More generally, one might ask why a principle which defends a state's ability to pursue an immoral end is to count as a moral principle imposing a requirement of justice on other states.

Such an objection, while indicating a serious problem in the real world, would be inappropriate in this context because the law of nations, in Rawls, applies to a world of just states. Nothing in Rawls' theory specifically requires this assumption, but it seems consonant with the restriction to ideal theory and parallels the assumption of "strict compliance" which plays a role in arguments for the two principles in domestic societies. It is important to see, however, that the suggested justification of these traditional rules of international law rests on art ideal assumption not present in most discussions of this subject. It does not self-evidently follow that these rules ought to hold in the nonideal world; at a minimum, an additional condition would be required, limiting the scope of the traditional rules to cases in which their observance would promote the development of just institutions in presently unjust societies while observing the basic protections of human rights expressed by the natural duties and preserving a stable international order in which just societies can exist.

Someone might think that other principles would be acknowledged, for example, regarding population control and regulation of the environment. Or perhaps, as Barry suggests, the parties would agree to form some sort of permanent international organization with consultative, diplomatic, and even collective security functions.[4] However, there is no obvious reason why such agreements would emerge from an international original position, at least so long as the constituent societies are assumed to be largely self-sufficient. Probably the parties, if confronted with these possibilities, would reason that fundamental questions of justice are not raised by them, and such issues of policy as arise from time to time in the real world could be handled with traditional treaty mechanisms underwritten by the rule, already acknowledged, that treaties are to be observed. Other issues that are today subjects of international negotiation – those relating to international regulation of common areas such as the sea and outer space – are of a different sort. They call for a kind of regulation that requires substantive cooperation among peoples in the use of areas not presently within the boundaries of any society. A cooperative scheme must be evolved which would create new wealth to which no national society could have a legitimate claim. These issues would be excluded from consideration on the ground that the parties are assumed not to be concerned with devising such a scheme. As representatives of separate social schemes, their attention is turned inward, not outward. In coming together in an international original position, they are moved by considerations of equality between "independent peoples organized as states" (378). Their main interest is in providing conditions in which just domestic social orders might flourish.

II

Thus far, the ideal theory of international justice bears a striking resemblance to that proposed in the Definitive Articles of Kant's *Perpetual Peace*.[5] Accepting for the time being the assumption of national self-sufficiency, Rawls' choice of principles seems unexceptionable. But would this list of principles exhaust those to which the parties would agree? Probably not. At least one kind of consideration, involving natural resources, might give rise to moral conflict among states and thus be a matter of concern in the international original position. The principles given so far do not take account of these considerations.

We can appreciate the moral importance of conflicting resource claims by distinguishing two elements which contribute to the material advancement of societies. One is human cooperative activity itself, which can be thought of as the human component of material advancement. The other is what Sidgwick called "the utilities derived from any portion of the earth's surface," the natural component.[6] While the first is the subject of the domestic principles of justice, the second is morally relevant even in the absence of a functioning scheme of international social cooperation. The parties to the international original position would know that natural resources are distributed unevenly over the earth's surface. Some areas are rich in resources, and societies established in such areas can be expected to exploit their natural riches and to prosper. Other societies do not fare so well, and despite the best efforts of their members, they may attain only a meager level of well-being due to resource scarcities.

The parties would view the distribution of resources much as Rawls says the parties to the domestic original position deliberations view the distribution of natural talents. In that context, he says that natural endowments are "neither just nor unjust; nor is it unjust that men are born into society at any particular position. These are simply natural facts. What is just or unjust is the way that institutions deal with these facts" (102). [. . .] Rawls' objection is that those who are less advantaged for reasons beyond their control cannot be asked to suffer the pains of inequality when their sacrifices cannot be shown to advance their position in comparison with an initial position of equality.

Reasoning analogously, the parties to the international original position, viewing the natural distribution of resources as morally arbitrary, would think that they should be subject to redistribution under a resource redistribution principle. This view is subject to the immediate abjection that Rawls' treatment of natural talents is troublesome. It seems vulnerable in at least two ways. First, it is not clear what it means to say that the distribution of talents is "arbitrary from a moral point of view" (72). While the distribution of natural talents is arbitrary in the sense that one cannot deserve to be born with the capacity, say, to play like Rubinstein, it does not obviously follow that the possession of such a talent needs any justification. On the contrary, simply having a talent seems to furnish prima facie warrant for making use of it in ways that are, for the possessor, possible and desirable. A person need not justify his possession of talents, despite the fact that he cannot be said to deserve them, because they are already *his*; the prima facie right to use and control talents is fixed by natural fact.

The other point of vulnerability is that natural capacities are parts of the self, in the development of which a person might take a special kind of pride. A person's decision to develop one talent, not to develop another, as well as his choice as to how the talent is to be formed and the uses to which it is to be put, are likely to be important elements of his effort to shape an identity. The complex of developed talents might even be said to constitute the self; their exercise is a principal form of self-expression. Because the development of talents is so closely linked with the shaping of personal identity, it might seem that one's claim to one's talents is protected by considerations of personal liberty. To interfere with the development and use of talents is to interfere with a self. Or so, at least, it might be argued.

While I believe that Rawls' discussion of talents can be defended against objections like these, that is not my concern here, I want to argue only that objections of this sort do not apply to the parallel claim that the distribution of natural resources is similarly arbitrary. Like talents, resource endowments are arbitrary in the sense that they are not deserved. But unlike talents, resources are not naturally attached to persons, resources are found "out there," available to the first taker. Resources must be appropriated before they can be used, whereas, in the talents case, the "appropriation" is a fait accompli of nature over which persons have no direct control. Thus, while we feel that the possession of talents confers a right to control and benefit from their use, we may feel differently about resources. Appropriation may not always need a justification; if the resources taken are of limited value, or if, as Locke imagined, their appropriation leaves "enough and as good" for everyone else, justification may not present a problem. In a world of scarcity, however, the situation is different. The appropriation of valuable resources by some will leave others comparatively, and perhaps fatally, disadvantaged. Those deprived without justification of scarce resources needed to sustain and enhance their lives might well press claims to equitable shares.

Furthermore, resources do not stand in the same relation to personal identity as do talents. It would be inappropriate to take the sort of pride in the diamond deposits in one's back yard that one takes in the ability to play the *Appassionata*. This is because natural resources come into the development of personality (when they come in at all) in a more casual way than do talents. [. . .] The resources under one's feet, because they lack this natural connection with the self, seem to be more contingent than necessary elements of the development of personality. Like talents, resources are used in this process; they are worked on, shaped, and benefited from. But they are not there, as parts of the self, to begin with. They must first be appropriated, and prior to their appropriation, no one has any special natural claim on them. Considerations of personal liberty do not protect a right to appropriate and use resources in the same way as they protect the right to develop and use talents as one sees fit. There is no parallel, initial presumption against interference with the use of resources, since no one is initially placed in a naturally privileged relationship with them.

I conclude that the natural distribution of resources is a purer case of something's being "arbitrary from a moral point of view" than the distribution of talents. Not only can one not be said to deserve the resources under one's feet; the other grounds on which one might assert an initial claim to talents are absent in the case of resources, as well.

The fact that national societies are assumed to be self-sufficient does not make the distribution of natural resources any less arbitrary. Citizens of a nation which finds itself on top of a gold mine do not gain a right to the wealth that might be derived from it *simply* because their nation is self-sufficient. But someone might argue that self-sufficiency, nevertheless, removes any possible grounds on which citizens of other nations might press claims to equitable shares. A possible view is that no justification for resource appropriation is necessary in the global state of nature. If, so to speak, social cooperation is the root of all social obligations, as it is on some versions of contract theory, then the view is correct. All rights would be "special rights" applying only when certain conditions of cooperation obtain.[7]

I believe that this is wrong. It seems plausible in most discussions of distributive justice because their subject is the distribution of the benefits of social cooperation. Appropriate distributive principles compensate those who are relatively disadvantaged by the cooperative scheme for their participation in it. Where there is no social cooperation, there are no benefits of cooperation, and hence no problem of compensation for relative disadvantage. (This is why a world of self-sufficient national societies is not subject to something like a global difference principle.) But there is nothing in this reasoning to suggest that our *only* moral ties are to those with whom we share membership in a cooperative scheme. It is possible that other sorts of considerations might come into the justification of moral principles. Rawls himself recognizes this in the case of the natural duties, which are said to "apply to us without regard to our voluntary acts" (114) and, apparently, without regard to our institutional memberships.

In the case of natural resources, the parties to the international original position would know that resources are unevenly distributed with respect to population, that adequate access to resources is a prerequisite for successful operation of (domestic) cooperative schemes, and that resource supplies are scarce. They would view the natural distribution of resources as arbitrary in the sense that no one has a natural prima facie claim to the resources that happen to be under his feet. The appropriation of scarce resources by some requires a justification against the competing claims of others and the needs of future generations. Not knowing the resource endowments of their own societies, the parties would agree on a resource redistribution principle which would give each national society a fair chance to develop just political institutions and an economy capable of satisfying its members' basic needs.

There is no intuitively obvious standard of equity for such matters; perhaps the standard would be population size, or perhaps it would be more complicated, rewarding nations for their efforts in extracting resources and taking account of the differential resource needs of nations with differing economies. The underlying principle is that each person has an equal prima facie claim to a share of the total available resources, but departures from this initial standard could be justified (analogously to the operation of the difference principle) if the resulting inequalities were to the greatest benefit of those least advantaged by the inequality (cf. 151). In any event, the resource redistribution principle would function in international society as the difference principle functions in domestic society. It provides assurance to resource-poor nations that their adverse fate will not prevent them from realizing economic conditions sufficient to support just social institutions and to protect human rights guaranteed by the principles for individuals. In the absence of this assurance, these nations might resort to war as a means of securing the resources necessary to establish domestic justice, and it is not obvious that wars fought for this purpose would be unjust.

[. . .]

In failing to recognize resource problems, Rawls follows other writers who have extended the social contract idea to international relations.[8] Perhaps this is because they have attributed a greater symmetry to the domestic and international contracts than is in fact appropriate. Resource problems do not arise as distinct questions in the domestic case because their distribution and conservation are implicitly covered by the difference principle and the just savings principle. When the scope of social cooperation is coextensive with the territorial boundaries of a society, it is unnecessary to distinguish natural and social contributions to the society's level of well-being. But when justice is considered internationally, we must face the likelihood of moral claims being pressed by members of the various social schemes which are arbitrarily placed with respect to the natural distribution of resources. My suggestion of a resource redistribution principle recognizes the fundamental character of these claims viewed from the perspective of the parties' interests in securing fair conditions for the development of their respective schemes.

III

Everything that I have said so far is consistent with the assumption that nations are self-sufficient cooperative schemes. However, there are strong empirical reasons for thinking that this assumption is no longer valid. As Kant notes in the concluding pages of *The Metaphysical Elements of Justice*, international economic cooperation creates a new basis for international morality.[9]

The main features of contemporary international interdependence relevant to questions of justice are the result of the progressive removal of restrictions on international trade and investment. Capital surpluses are no longer confined to reinvestment in the societies where they are produced, but instead are reinvested wherever conditions promise the highest yield without unacceptable risks. It is well known, for example, that large American corporations have systematically transferred significant portions of their capitalization to European, Latin American, and East Asian societies where labor costs are lower, markets are better, and profits are higher. A related development is the rise of an international division of labor whereby products are manufactured in areas having cheap, unorganized labor and are marketed in more affluent areas. Because multinational businesses, rather than the producing countries themselves, play the leading role in setting prices and wages, the international division of labor results in a system of world trade in which value created in one society (usually poor) is used to benefit members of other societies (usually rich). It is also important to note that the world economy has evolved its own financial and monetary institutions that set exchange rates, regulate the money supply, influence capital flows, and enforce rules of international economic conduct.

The system of interdependence imposes burdens on poor and economically weak countries that they cannot practically avoid. Industrial economies have become reliant on raw materials that can only be obtained in sufficient quantities from developing countries. In the present structure of world prices, poor countries are often forced by adverse balances of payments to sell resources to more wealthy countries when those resources could be more efficiently used to promote development of the poor countries' domestic economies. Also, private foreign investment imposes on poor countries patterns of political and economic development that may not be optimal from the point of view of the poor countries themselves. Participation in the global economy on the only terms available involves a loss of political autonomy. Third, the global monetary system allows disturbances (e.g. price inflation) in some national economies to be exported to others that may be less able to cope with their potentially disastrous effects.

Economic interdependence, then, involves a pattern of relationships which are largely nonvoluntary from the point of view of the worse-off participants, and which produce benefits for some while imposing burdens on others. These facts, by now part of the conventional wisdom of international relations, describe a world in which national boundaries can no longer be regarded as the outer limits of social cooperation. Note that this conclusion does not require that national societies should have become entirely superfluous or that the global economy should be completely integrated. It is enough, for setting the limits of cooperative schemes, that some societies are able to increase their level of well-being via global trade and investment while others with whom they have economic relations continue to exist at low levels of development.

In view of these empirical considerations, Rawls' passing concern for the law of nations seems to miss the point of international justice altogether. In an interdependent world, confining principles of social justice to national societies has the effect of taxing poor nations so that others may benefit from living in "just" regimes. The two principles, so construed, might justify a wealthy nation's denying aid to needy peoples if the aid could be used domestically to promote a more nearly just regime. If the self-sufficiency assumption were empirically acceptable, such a result might be plausible, if controversial on other grounds.[10] But if participation in economic relations with the needy society has contributed to the wealth of the "nearly just" regime, its domestic "justice" seems to lose moral significance. In such situations, the principles of domestic "justice" will be genuine principles of justice only if they are consistent with principles of justice for the entire global scheme of social cooperation.

How should we formulate global principles? As several others have suggested, Rawls' own two principles, suitably reinterpreted, could themselves be applied globally.[11] The reasoning is as follows: if evidence of global economic and political interdependence shows the existence of a global scheme of social cooperation, we should not view national boundaries as having fundamental moral significance. Since boundaries are not coextensive with the scope of social cooperation, they do not mark the limits of social obligations. Thus, the parties to the original position cannot be assumed to know that they are members of a particular national society, choosing principles of justice primarily for that society. The veil of ignorance must extend to all matters of national citizenship. As Barry points out, a global interpretation of the original position is insensitive to the choice of principles.[12] Assuming that the arguments for the two principles are successful as set out in Rawls' book, there is no reason to think that the content of the principles would change as a result of enlarging the scope of the original position so that the principles would apply to the world as a whole.

Rawls' two principles are a special case of the "general conception" of social justice. The two principles hold when a cooperative scheme has reached a level of material well-being at which everyone's basic needs can be met. The world, conceived as a single cooperative scheme, probably has not yet reached this threshold. Assuming that this is the case, on Rawls' reasoning, we should take the general conception, which does not differentiate the basic liberties from other primary goods, as the relevant standard for assessing global economic institutions. [. . .]

The globalization of the two principles (or of the general conception, if appropriate) has the consequence that principles of justice for national societies can no longer be viewed as ultimate. The basic structure of national societies continues to be governed by the two principles (or by the general conception), but their application is derivative and hence their requirements are not absolute. A possible view is that the global principles and the principles applied to national societies are to be satisfied in lexical order. But this view has the consequence, which one might find implausible, that national policies which maximize the welfare of the least-advantaged group within the society cannot be justified if other policies would be more optimal from the point of view of the lesser advantaged elsewhere. Furthermore, no society could justify the additional costs involved in moving from the general to the special conception (for example, in reduced productivity) until every society had, at least, attained a level of well-being sufficient to sustain the general conception.

These features of the global interpretation of Rawlsian principles suggest that its implications are quite radical – considerably more so even than their application to national societies. While I am not now prepared to argue positively that the best theory of global justice consists simply of Rawls' principles interpreted globally, it seems to me that the most obvious objections to such a theory are not valid. In the remainder of this section, I consider what is perhaps the leading type of objection and suggest some difficulties in giving it theoretically compelling form.

Objections of the type I have in mind hold that considerations of social cooperation at the national level justify distributive claims capable of overriding the requirements of a global difference principle. Typically, members of a wealthy nation might claim that they deserve a larger share than that provided by a global difference principle because of their superior technology, economic organization, and efficiency.

Objections of this general sort might take several forms. First, it might be argued that even in an interdependent world, national society remains the primary locus of one's political identifications. If one is moved to contribute to aggregate social welfare at any level, this level is most likely to be the national level. Therefore, differential rates of national contribution to the global welfare ought to be rewarded proportionally. This is a plausible form of the objection; the problem is that, in this form, it may not be an objection at all. The difference principle itself recognizes the probability that differential rates of reward may be needed as incentives for contribution; it requires only that distributive inequalities which arise in such a system be to the greatest benefit of the world's least-advantaged group. To the extent that incentives of the kind demanded by this version of the objection actually do raise the economic expectations of the least advantaged without harming them in other ways, they would not be inconsistent with the difference principle.

Such objections count against a global difference principle only if they hold that a relatively wealthy nation could claim more than its share under the difference principle. That is, the objection must hold that some distributive inequalities are justified even though they are not to the greatest benefit of the world's least-advantaged group. How could such claims be justified? One justification is on grounds of personal merit, appealing to the intuition that value created by someone's unaided labor is properly his, assuming that the initial distribution was just.[13] This sort of argument yields an extreme form of the objection. It holds that a nation is entitled to its relative wealth because each of its citizens has complied with the relevant rules of justice in acquiring raw materials and transforming them into products of value. [. . .]

This interpretation of the objection is strictly analogous to the conception of distributive justice which Rawls calls the "system of natural liberty." He objects to such views that they allow people to compete for available positions on the basis of their talents, making no attempt to compensate for deprivations that some suffer due to natural chance and social contingency. These things, as I have said, are held to be morally arbitrary and hence unacceptable as standards for distribution (cf. 66–72). I shall not rehearse this argument further here. But two things should be noted. First, the argument seems even more plausible from the global point of view since the disparity of possible starting points in world society is so much greater. The balance between "arbitrary" and "personal" contributions to my present well-being seems decisively tipped toward the "arbitrary" ones by the realization that, no matter what my talents, education, life goals, etc., I would have been virtually precluded from attaining my present level of well-being if I had been born in a less developed society. Second, if Rawls' counterargument counts against natural liberty views in the domestic case, then it defeats the objection to a global difference principle as well. A nation cannot base its claim to a larger distributive share than that warranted by the difference principle on factors which are morally arbitrary.

A third, and probably the most plausible, form of this objection holds that a wealthy nation may retain more than its share under a global difference principle, provided that some compensation for the benefits of global social cooperation is paid to less fortunate nations, and that the amount retained by the producing nation is used to promote domestic justice, for example, by increasing the prospects of the nation's own least favored group. The underlying intuition is that citizens owe some sort of special obligation to the less fortunate members of their own society that is capable of over-riding their general obligation to improve the prospects of lesser advantaged groups elsewhere. This intuition is distinct from the intuition in the personal desert case, for it does not refer to any putative individual right to the value created by one's labor. Instead, we are concerned here with supposedly conflicting rights and obligations that arise from membership in overlapping schemes of social cooperation, one embedded in the other.

An argument along these lines needs an account of how obligations to the sectional association arise. One might say that the greater degree or extent of social cooperation in national societies (compared with that in international society) underwrites stronger intranational principles of justice. To see this objection in its strongest form, imagine a world of two self-sufficient and internally just societies, A and B. Assume that this world satisfies the appropriate resource redistribution principle. Imagine also that the least-advantaged representative person in society A is considerably better off than his counterpart in society B. While the members of A may owe duties of mutual aid to the members of B, it is clear that they do not have parallel duties of justice, because the two societies, being individually self-sufficient, do not share membership in a cooperative scheme. Now suppose that the walls of self-sufficiency are breached very slightly; A trades its apples for B's pears. Does this mean that the difference principle suddenly applies to the world which comprises A and B, requiring A to share all of its wealth with B, even though almost all of its wealth is attributable to economic interaction within A? It seems not; one might say that an international difference principle can only command redistribution of the benefits derived from international social cooperation or economic interaction. It cannot touch the benefits of domestic cooperation.

It may be that some such objection will turn out to produce modifications on a global difference principle. But there are reasons for doubting this. Roughly, it seems that there is a threshold of interdependence above which distributive requirements such as a global difference principle are valid, but below which significantly weaker principles hold. I cannot give a systematic account of this view here, but perhaps some intuitive considerations will demonstrate its force.

Consider another hypothetical case. Suppose that, *within* a society, there are closely-knit local regions with higher levels of internal cooperation than the level of cooperation in society as a whole. Certainly there are many such regions within a society such as the United States. The argument rehearsed above, applied to closely-knit localities within national societies, would seem to give members of the localities special claims on portions of their wealth. This seems implausible, especially since such closely-knit enclaves might well turn out to contain disproportionate numbers of the society's most advantaged classes. Why does this conclusion seem less plausible than that in the apples and pears case? It seems to me that the answer has to do with the fact that the apples and pears case looks like a case of voluntary, free-market bargaining that has only a marginal effect on the welfare of the members of each society, whereas we assume in the intranational case that there is a nonvoluntary society-wide system of economic institutions which defines starting positions and assigns economic rights and duties. It is these institutions – what Rawls calls "the basic structure" (7–11) – that stand in need of justification, because, by defining the terms of cooperation, they have such deep and pervasive effects on the welfare of people to whom they apply regardless of consent.

The apples and pears case, of course, is hardly a faithful model of the contemporary world economy. Suppose that we add to the story to make it resemble the real world more closely. As my review of the current situation (above, pp. 373–375) makes clear, we would have to add just those features of the contemporary world economy that find their domestic analogues in the basic structure to which principles of justice apply. As the web of transactions grows more complex, the resulting structure of economic and political institutions acquires great influence over the welfare of the participants, regardless of the extent to which any particular one makes use of the institutions. These features make the real world situation seem more like the case of subnational, closely-knit regions.

These considerations suggest that the amount of social and economic interaction in a cooperative scheme does not provide a straightforward index of the strength of the distributive principle appropriate to it. The existence of a powerful, nonvoluntary institutional structure, and its pervasive effects on the welfare of the cooperators, seems to provide a better indication of the strength of the appropriate distributive requirements. This sort of consideration would not necessarily support a global difference principle in the apples and pears case; but it does explain why, above a threshold measure of social cooperation, the full force of the difference principle may come into play despite regional variations in the amount of cooperation.

Proponents of this objection to a global difference principle might have one last resort. They might appeal to noneconomic features of national societies to justify the special obligations that citizens owe to the less fortunate members of their own societies. On this basis, they could claim that the difference principle applies to national societies despite regional variations in cooperation but not to international society. Probably the plausibility of this sort of argument will depend on the degree to which it psychologizes the ties that bind the members of social institutions. There are problems, however. First, it needs to be shown that psychological ties such as national loyalty are of sufficient moral importance to balance the international economic ties that underwrite a global difference principle. Second, even if this could be persuasively argued, any account of how institutional obligations arise that is sufficiently psychological to make plausible a general conflict of global and sectional loyalties will probably be too psychological to apply to the large modern state (cf. 477).

[. . .]

IV

We have now reached two main conclusions. First, assuming national self-sufficiency, Rawls' derivation of the principles of justice for the law of nations is correct but incomplete. He importantly neglects resource redistribution, a subject that would surely be on the minds of the parties to the international original position. But second, the self-sufficiency assumption, upon which Rawls' entire consideration of the law of nations rests, is not justified by the facts of contemporary international relations. The state-centered image of the world has lost its normative relevance because of the rise of global economic interdependence. Hence, principles of distributive justice must apply in the first instance to the world as a whole, then derivatively to nation-states. The appropriate global principle is probably something like Rawls' general conception of justice, perhaps modified by some provision for intranational redistribution in relatively wealthy states once a threshold level of international redistributive obligations has been met. Rawls' two principles become more relevant as global distributive inequalities are reduced and a higher average level of well-being is attained. In conclusion, I would like to consider the implications of this ideal theory for international politics and global change in the nonideal world. In what respects does this interpretation of the social contract doctrine shed light on problems of world order change?

We might begin by asking, in general, what relevance social ideals have for politics in the real world. Their most obvious function is to describe a goal toward which efforts at political change should aim. In Rawls' theory, a very important natural duty is the natural duty of justice, which "requires us to support and to comply with just institutions that exist and . . . constrains us to further just arrangements not yet established, at least if this can be done without too much cost to ourselves" (115). By supplying a description of the nature and aims of a just world order, ideal theory "provides . . . the only basis for the systematic grasp of these more pressing problems" (9). Ideal theory, then, supplies a set of criteria for the formulation and criticism of strategies of political action in the nonideal world, at least when the consequences of political action can be predicted with sufficient confidence to establish their relationship to the social ideal. [. . .]

Ideal justice, in other words, comes into nonideal politics by way of the natural duty to secure just institutions where none presently exist. The moral problem posed by distinguishing ideal from nonideal theory is that, in the nonideal world, the natural duty of justice is likely to conflict with other natural duties, while the theory provides no mechanism for resolving such conflicts. For example, it is possible that a political decision which is likely to make institutions more just is equally likely to involve violations of other natural duties, such as the duty of mutual aid or the duty not to harm the innocent. Perhaps reforming some unjust institution will require us to disappoint legitimate expectations formed under the old order. The principles of natural duty in the nonideal world are relatively unsystematic, and we have no way of knowing which should win out in case of conflict. Rawls recognizes the inevitability of irresolvable conflicts in some situations (303), but, as Feinberg has suggested, he underestimates the role that an intuitive balancing of conflicting duties must play in nonideal circumstances.[14] Rawls says that problems of political change in radically unjust situations must rely on a utilitarian calculation of costs and benefits (352–353). If this is true, then political change in conditions of great injustice marks one kind of limit of the contract doctrine, for in these cases the principles of justice collapse into utilitarianism. It seems to me, however, that this conclusion is too broad. At least in some cases of global justice, non-ideal theory, while teleological, is not utilitarian. [. . .]

The duty to secure just institutions where none exist endows certain political claims made in the nonideal world with a moral seriousness which does not derive merely from the obligations that bind people regardless of the existence of cooperative ties. When the contract doctrine is interpreted globally, the claims of the less advantaged in today's nonideal world – claims principally for food aid, development assistance, and world monetary and trade reform – rest on principles of global justice as well as on the weaker duty of mutual aid. Those who are in a position to respond to these claims, despite the absence of effective global political mechanisms, must take account of the stronger reasons provided by the principles of justice in weighing their response. Furthermore, by interpreting the principles globally, we remove a major source of

justifying reasons for not responding more fully to such claims. These reasons derive
from statist concerns, for example, a supposed right to reinvest domestic surpluses in
national societies that are already relatively favored from a global point of view. The
natural duties still require us to help members of our own society who are in need,
and a wealthy nation would be justified on this account in using some of its resources
to support domestic welfare programs. What cannot be argued is that a wealthy
nation's general right to retain its domestic product always overrides its obligation to
advance the welfare of lesser-advantaged groups elsewhere.

[. . .] The extension of economic and cultural relationships beyond national borders
has often been thought to undermine the moral legitimacy of the state; the extension
of the contract doctrine gives a systematic account of why this is so, and of its
consequences for problems of justice in the nonideal world, by emphasizing the role
of social cooperation as the foundation of just social arrangements. When, as now,
national boundaries do not set off discrete, self-sufficient societies, we may not regard
them as morally decisive features of the earth's social geography. For purposes of moral
choice, we must, instead, regard the world from the perspective of an original position
from which matters of national citizenship are excluded by an extended veil of
ignorance.

I do not believe that Rawls' failure to take account of these questions marks a pivotal
weakness of his theory; on the contrary, the theory provides a way of determining
the consequences of changing empirical circumstances (such as the assumption of
national self-sufficiency) for the concept of justice. The global interpretation is
the result of recognizing an important empirical change in the structure of world
political and social life. In this way the theory allows us to apply generalizations
derived from our considered judgments regarding familiar situations to situations
which are new and which demand that we form intelligent moral views and act on
them when action is possible and appropriate. This is no small achievement for a moral
theory. Some might think, however, that our moral intuitions are too weak or unreliable to support such an extension of the theory. I doubt that this is true; rather, it
often seems to be a convenient way to beg off from unpleasant moral requirements.
But if I am wrong about this – if we cannot expect moral theory to provide a firm guide
for action in new situations – one might wonder whether moral theory has any practical point at all.

Notes

1   John Rawls, *A Theory of Justice* (Cambridge, Mass., 1972). Page references are given parenthetically
    in the text.
2   Such criticisms have appeared in several places. For example, Brian Barry, *The Liberal Theory of
    Justice* (Oxford, 1973), pp. 128–133; Peter Danielson, "Theories, Intuitions and the Problem of
    World-Wide Distributive Justice," *Philosophy of the Social Sciences* 3 (1973), pp. 331–340; Thomas M.
    Scanlon, Jr., "Rawls' Theory of Justice," *University of Pennsylvania Law Review* 121, no. 5 (May 1973),
    pp. 1066–1067.
3   These principles form the basis of traditional international law. See the discussion, on which
    Rawls relies, in J.L. Brierly, *The Law of Nations*, 6th ed. (New York, 1963), especially chaps. 3 and 4.
4   Barry, *The Liberal Theory of Justice*, p. 132.
5   Trans. and ed. Lewis White Beck (Indianapolis, 1957), pp. 10–23.
6   Henry Sidgwick, *The Elements of Politics* (London, 1891), p. 242; quoted in S.I. Benn and R.S. Peters,
    The Principles of Political Thought (New York, 1959), p. 430. Sidgwick's entire discussion of putative
    national rights to land and resources is relevant here – see *Elements*, pp. 239–244.

7   William N. Nelson construes Rawlsian rights in this way in "Special Rights, General Rights, and Social Justice," *Philosophy & Public Affairs* 3, no. 4 (Summer 1974): 410–430.

8   Two classical examples are Pufendorf and Wolff. See Walter Schiffer, *The Legal Community of Mankind* (New York, 1954), pp. 49–79.

9   Trans. John Ladd (Indianapolis, 1965), pp. 125ff.

10 For example, on utilitarian grounds. See Peter Singer, "Famine, Affluence, and Morality," *Philosophy & Public Affairs* 1, no. 3 (Spring 1972): 229–243.

11 For example, Barry, *The Liberal Theory of Justice*, pp. 128–133; and Scanlon, "Rawls' Theory of Justice," pp. 1066–1067.

12 Barry, *The Liberal Theory of Justice*, p. 129.

13 This, roughly, is Robert Nozick's view in *Anarchy, State, and Utopia* (New York, 1974), chap. 7.

14 Joel Feinberg, "Duty and Obligation in the Nonideal World," *Journal of Philosophy* 70 (10 May 1973): 263–275.

6

International Society from a Cosmopolitan Perspective
Brian Barry

The cosmopolitan idea

Instead of offering my own definition of cosmopolitanism, I shall therefore take over the definition put forward by Charles Beitz in, *Political Restructuring in Europe*. According to Beitz, the two essential elements defining a cosmopolitan view are that it is inclusive and nonperspectival. "If local viewpoints can be said to be partial, then a cosmopolitan viewpoint is impartial."[1] What I am concerned with here is what Beitz calls "moral cosmopolitanism," of which he says that "it applies to the whole world the maxim that answers to questions about what we should do, or what institutions we should establish, should be based on an impartial consideration of the claims of each person who would be affected by our choices."[2]

Beitz distinguishes this moral cosmopolitanism from what he calls "institutional cosmopolitanism." It is important to recognize that moral cosmopolitanism leaves open the question of the ideal constitution of international society. Institutional cosmopolitanism is one answer to that question, or more precisely a family of answers. Thus, institutional cosmopolitanism "pertains to the way political institutions should be set up – to the political constitution of the world, so to speak. . . . Although the details may vary, the distinctive common feature is some ideal of world political organization in which states and state-like units have significantly diminished authority in comparison with the status quo and supranational institutions have more."[3]

As Beitz says, "there is no necessary link between moral and institutional cosmopolitanism."[4] Thus, one may be a moral cosmopolitan without believing that its precepts would best be satisfied by institutions of the kind commended by institutional cosmopolitanism. At the level of domestic politics, it is quite consistent to start from a utilitarian position and then argue for a minimum state. Similarly, there is no inconsistency in counting the interests of everyone in the world equally and concluding that those interests will tend to be best advanced by a state-centered system with only weak international authority. Whether or not this is thought to be so will depend on what one takes the main interests of human beings to be and on the way in which one thinks the world works.

Conversely, one may support the policy conclusions embodied in institutional cosmopolitanism on a basis other than that of moral cosmopolitanism. Beitz himself says that "it is hard to think of anyone who has defended institutional cosmopolitanism on other than cosmopolitan moral grounds."[5] But it is easy to see that the case for a strengthening of international authority vis-à-vis states can plausibly be derived from Hobbesian premises under contemporary conditions. Warfare between countries now has a potential for almost unlimited destruction, and only concerted action can address global problems such as ozone depletion, the "greenhouse effect," and pollution of the oceans. I believe, therefore, that universal self-interest would support a shift toward institutional cosmopolitanism, as Beitz defines it. In addition, I believe that moral cosmopolitanism leads to the endorsement of international redistribution of a kind that Hobbesian premises do not appear to underwrite. My reasons for thinking this will appear later.

[. . .] There is no automatic move from the ethical premises to any particular conclusion about the ideal world constitution. Where moral cosmopolitanism shows itself to be more distinctive is in its denial that membership of a society is of deep moral significance when the claims that people can legitimately make on one another are assessed. [. . .]

I should explain what I mean by saying that membership of a society does not have *deep* moral significance. We can in a variety of ways acquire obligations that we owe to some people and not to others. There is no reason for doubting that the members of a politically constituted society can acquire obligations to one another that they do not owe to others. What moral cosmopolitanism insists on, however, is that it should be possible to justify this special treatment on grounds that can in principle be accepted by those excluded. A standard way of doing this is, of course, to point out that those who are excluded can and do acquire special obligations to members of their own societies in exactly the same way. The point has been put well by Thomas Hill, Jr., in the following way:

> All the impartiality thesis says is that, if and when one raises questions regarding fundamental moral standards, the court of appeal that one addresses is a court in which no particular individual, group, or country has *special* standing. Before that court, declaring "I like it," "It serves *my* country," and the like, is not decisive; principles must be defensible to anyone looking at the matter apart from his or her special attachments, from a larger, human perspective.[6]

Some cosmopolitan principles

At the heart of moral cosmopolitanism is the idea that human beings are in some fundamental sense equal. All claims are to be weighed in the same balance. But how is this balancing to be carried out? An answer that naturally presents itself is that we reduce all claims to interests and then resolve conflicts of interest by saying that the outcome that most satisfies interests (the one in which the greatest sum of interest satisfaction obtains) is the best. If "interests" are given a subjective interpretation this is the utilitarian prescription. It is objectionable on two grounds. First, it is not true that all claims can be expressed in a single currency: claims are irreducibly heterogeneous in their nature. And, second, the formula is indifferent to issues of distribution. Nobody has any good reason for accepting that he or she should do very badly merely because this is the most effective means of maximizing some aggregate good, however defined.

Rather than canvassing a number of alternatives, let me simply present what seems to me the best way of giving content to the idea of impartial treatment that underlies moral cosmopolitanism. Following an idea put foxward by T. M. Scanlon, I propose that we should ask of any rule or principle whether or not it could reasonably be rejected by somebody who was motivated by "the desire to find principles which others similarly motivated could not reasonably reject."[7] We thus posit a hypothetical negotiating situation marked by equality (since everybody stands on an equal footing and is equipped with a veto to protect interests that cannot reasonably be denied) and freedom (since nobody can coerce anybody else into accepting an agreement by the exercise of superior power). Principles of justice are those principles that would emerge from a process taking this form.

We may envisage a variety of different sets of people making choices in such a hypothetical situation. By far the most effort has gone into the case in which the choice is made by people who are members of the same politically organized society. But for the present purpose I want to focus on the case in which the choice is made by all the people in the world, since it is quite possible to imagine a world in which each country is internally just but the system as a whole is extremely unjust. On the criterion of justice proposed here, this would be so if the rules governing relations between countries could reasonably be rejected by some people.

[. . .]

Following Rawls, I shall take justice to be the highest-order organizing concept within political philosophy.[8] The following are, I wish to maintain, four principles of justice. I shall say a little (but only a little) in defense of each as I go along. A point to be made about all of them together is that they meet the two objections to utilitarianism: their subject-matter is heterogeneous and they are sensitive to questions of distribution.

First principle: the presumption of equality. All inequalities of rights, opportunities, and resources have to be justifiable in ways that cannot reasonably be rejected by those who get least.

This principle does not immediately generate specific conclusions. But it is important in directing attention toward those who have the best prima facie reasons for rejecting some proposal. It emphasizes that any inequality must make sense to them. As it stands, it may appear a very weak principle, and it is undeniably lacking in content. In spite of this, what impresses me is how many relations of inequality at all levels cannot meet its demands. These relations are maintained by unequal power relationships, or (not quite the same thing) by inertia, forming part of a pattern which it would not be advantageous to anyone acting alone to disturb. Thus, those disadvantaged by an inequality may well choose to act in ways that sustain it, even though they would reject it in a hypothetical ideal-choice situation.

[. . .]

Second principle: personal responsibility and compensation. It is prima facie acceptable for people to fare differently if the difference arises from a voluntary choice on their part; conversely, victims of misfortunes that they could not have prevented have a prima facie valid claim for compensation or redress.

The first clause embodies the basic idea that human agency must be respected. It is an essential aspect of a fully human life that one's decisions should have some impact on the world, and that can happen only if what they do makes a difference to what actually happens. There is a great deal of evidence, both from surveys of opinion and from studies of freely accepted inequalities, to support the notion that the first clause would emerge from a hypothetical choice situation.

What the formulation leaves open is, of course, the conditions under which a choice counts as being voluntary. The clause about personal responsibility sets the terms of the debate, however, and, I believe, imposes definite limits on the range of reasonable disagreement."[9]

The second clause is the obverse of the first. It may be said to embody what Richard Arneson has described as "the intuition that when people's lives go badly through no fault or voluntary choice of their own, it is morally incumbent on others to offer aid to the disadvantaged so long as the cost of providing aid is not excessive."[10] I should, however, wish to approach the proviso at the end of this statement with some care. What makes the cost "excessive"? Not, I think, simply that the cost is high: if the loss is great, the cost is liable to be high, but that does not affect the force of the claim. The valid form of the proviso is, I suggest, that the obligation is weakened or in extreme cases extinguished altogether if the cost of providing the aid is greatly disproportional to the benefit gained by the recipient(s).

[. . .]

Third principle: priority of vital interests. In the absence of some compelling consideration to the contrary, the vital interests of each person should be protected in preference to the nonvital interests of anyone. Vital interests include security from physical harm, nutrition adequate for the maintenance of health, clean drinking water and sanitary arrangements, clothing and shelter appropriate to the climate, medical care, and education to a level sufficient to function effectively within one's society.

It should be observed that this principle expresses priorities not in terms of persons (as the first principle did) but in terms of types of claim. The idea underlying it is that there are certain minimum requirements of living a good life that can be acknowledged to be such by almost everyone, whatever his or her own particular conception of the good may be.[11] If the second principle is related to the idea of desert, this third principle is related to that of need. Thus, the second and third principles capture what are the commonly accepted bases for moral claims. The first principle is concerned with a third basis – the allocation of rights.

Fourth principle: mutual advantage. Whenever it would be to the prospective advantage of everyone to depart from the application of the above principles (compared with the results of applying them), it is permissible to do so. Where more than one arrangement has this property, the one to be preferred is that which maximizes the gain of those who gain least from the departure.

This principle is one of collective rationality: it endorses Pareto improvements over the baseline set by the operation of the other three principles. The second half of it provides a way of choosing between potential Pareto improvements and incorporates the idea of "the priority of the worst off." [. . .] Here the worst off are defined in relation to the baseline created by applying the other principles. Those who stand to gain least by applying the fourth one may not be those who were the worst off from the application of the other three.

Read carelessly, the fourth principle may look as if it renders the others nugatory and simply gets us back to utilitarianism. It is important to recognize that this is not so. The other three principles retain their integrity. They can be supplemented by the fourth principle but they cannot be displaced by it. For those who like the vocabulary, we may say that the first three principles jointly have lexicographic priority over the fourth. This, of course, leaves us without a formula for resolving conflicts among the first three principles, but who said that ethical problems should be easy?

Justice denied

The principles of justice I have put forward are intended to function as guides to debate: they should be capable of specifying kinds of argument that can be accepted as valid while ruling out other considerations that might be put forward. This structuring of moral discourse is what I believe principles should do. Clearly, for the full development of a theory of justice we would need to see how the principles put forward here work together to produce some conclusions about the kinds of institution they underwrite. In the space at my disposal, I have no hope of doing that. What I shall focus on, [. . .] are the largest-scale global implications, extended into the distant future.

The most striking feature of the world as it exists at present, if we line it up against the principles of justice, is the extent to which the third principle is violated. Probably half the total world population lacks the material conditions that are necessary for the satisfaction of their vital interests. [. . .] These conditions coexist – in contravention of the principle of the priority of vital interests – with over a quarter of the world's population living at material standards vastly in excess of anything required to meet their basic needs.

A second observation is that there is no tendency toward an equalization of average incomes between rich and poor countries. On the contrary, the richest countries are continuing to increase their affluence (if slowly), while many poor countries have actually become poorer in the past decade, especially as a result of debt repayments. (On balance, poor countries now make net transfers to rich ones.) Moreover, within poor countries, the burden of the "adjustment" imposed by the IMF and the World Bank falls mainly on the poor, who are hit by increased unemployment and the disappearance of basic public services.

It is, of course, conceivable that the prima facie injustice arising from the wholesale violation of the third principle is nullified by the application of one or more of the other principles. There are two candidates: the second and the fourth. Under the second, it might be argued that the plight of those whose vital interests are not being met is entirely their own fault. This is immensely implausible. Insofar as natural resources make some countries better off than others, this is clearly a matter of pure good fortune. [. . .]

The other weapon of the apologists for the justice of the status quo is the fourth principle: any attempt to improve the lot of the worst off by redistributive measures, it is sometimes claimed, would have such an inhibiting effect on the efforts of the better off that in the end everybody would be worse off than they would be under a policy of leaving the outcome to market forces. Looking at the inequalities in many poor countries and in the world as a whole, this would be hard to believe, even if indefinite increases in global production were feasible.

[. . .] We cannot know how people in the future will live or what inventions and discoveries they will make. But we know that they will need an inhabitable planet, with such amenities as an ozone layer, land that is neither desert nor eroded, relative freedom from air and water pollution, and a diversity of species. This requires that the current generation should not leave its successors with conditions that are worse in these respects, or if this is impossible that the current generation at least moves as far toward "substainability" as is feasible. What is crucial is that the capacity of the planet to regenerate depleted natural resources and render toxic wastes harmless (metals such as mercury, lead, and cadmium, and nuclear waste, for example) is strictly limited. Some people say that we need not worry about any of this because people in the future *may* come up with some "technological fix" that will solve all the problems. This, however, is scarcely consistent with taking seriously the interests of future generations, since if we acted on the optimistic assumption and it turned out to be wrong the consequences would be catastrophic.[12]

There is apparently little disagreement [. . .] that current production levels globally are unsustainable. The only question is how far they would have to be reduced to become sustainable. A widely held view is that the world left the path of sustainability in the early 1950s. To the extent that processes of production are modified to use fewer natural resources and create less pollution, we can avoid the conclusion that production levels must go back to those prevalent in the early 1950s, but they would still have to be reduced substantially. Even if sustainability entails only freezing total production, this is enough to demand a fundamental reorientation of virtually all thinking in the last fifty years (and most of that in the preceding hundred) about distributive justice. For a common theme running through the work of thinkers on both the left and the right of the political spectrum has been that production is not a zero-sum game. What unites these thinkers is the "productivist" premise that "a rising tide lifts all boats." Inequalities of income are therefore of no moment in themselves. Only simpleminded people, according to the conventional wisdom, believe that the poor are poor because the rich are rich; on the contrary, the poor are as well off as they are only because the rich are rich. Inequality increases the size of the cake, so that even those with the smallest slices get more.

If we drop the presupposition of an indefinitely expandable cake, the older idea that the poor are poor because the rich are rich comes into its own again. Let us suppose that we are at the sustainable maximum, and that it would be possible to stay at this maximum while shifting income from rich to poor. Then it does become true that anyone with a large slice of the cake is directly responsible for somebody else having a small one. Internationally it means that poor countries can expand production (within the limits of global sustainability) only if the rich countries cut back to make room.

This would be true even if sustainability demanded only that total production level out at its current volume. Now suppose (as seems to me more plausible) that long-run sustainability entails a substantial overall reduction in what is produced. Then further implications can be derived. Thus, the rationale (widely acted on in all western European countries in the past decade) for cutting high marginal rates of taxation – that the incentive effect of letting high earners keep more increases economic growth – has to go into reverse. Since, however, the evidence suggests that reducing marginal tax rates from their previous levels has had negligible effects on effort, it seems likely that post-tax earnings could be almost equalized before production fell by a substantial amount. The limits on equalization would perhaps lie rather in those imposed by the second principle, which permits the consequences of voluntary choice to be reflected in outcomes. People who are particularly keen to make more money should be able to do so by working at a job within their capabilities involving longer or less convenient hours or more unpleasant conditions than other jobs open to people with their capabilities. It should be observed, however, that the second principle does not legitimize inequalities that do not result from choice, and I believe that it would not therefore underwrite the vast majority of existing earned income inequalities. The only ones it would support would be of an essentially compensatory nature.

A parallel argument may be made about transfers from one country to another. Even if unlimited expansion of production were feasible, it would be grossly implausible to maintain that even a low level of transfer from rich to poor countries would hamper production in the rich countries so much that in the long run everyone would lose. There seems to me no real case for thinking that production in rich countries would necessarily be reduced at all by some modest level of transfer. Even if it were, poor countries would still be better off with transfers. For unless some of the increased wealth of the rich countries is deliberately channeled to poor countries, there does not appear to be any mechanism that automatically results in the increased wealth of the rich countries creating more in the poor ones. There is certainly one force moving in the other direction, which is that technological progress tends to make the rich countries less and less dependent on the raw materials (jute and sisal, for example) that are the export staples of some poor countries.

Now suppose that global production will have to be reduced if pollution and resource depletion are not to place an unfair burden on future generations. In this case, any inhibiting effect on production of the extra taxation imposed on rich countries by international redistribution becomes a positive advantage. Assuming that aggregate global output needs to come down substantially, I should be very surprised if that goal could be accomplished solely through the drag on production in the rich countries imposed by international transfers. Governments in rich countries would still have to introduce deliberate measures to curb the propensity of their economies to produce more than is compatible with long-run sustainability.

Moral cosmopolitanism and international redistribution

Moral cosmopolitanism is, in essence, an individualistic doctrine in that it focuses on how individuals fare. This does not mean that it slights the importance of families, communities, and countries. But it treats their value as derivative: they are of value to exactly the extent that they contribute to the welfare of individuals (both those within the group and those outside it, weighting their interests equally).

This moral individualism, taken together with the considerations advanced in the previous section, leads to a radical conclusion. The demands of cosmopolitanism would, I suggest, be best satisfied in a world in which rich people wherever they lived would be taxed for the benefit of poor people wherever they lived. On the revenue-raising side, the model would be that of the United States, where the federal government imposes a federal income tax, leaving the states to raise whatever taxes (including income taxes) they like. The expenditure side is rather more messy. I believe that a large proportion of the payout would have to be to individuals, either in the form of a universal unconditional basic income or an income dependent on status (youth, age, sickness and disability, unemployment). But it would clearly be advantageous for some of the resources to go to the improvement of communal facilities in areas where the most deprived people are concentrated.

[. . .] Nevertheless, it is clear that any such system would constitute a considerable derogation of state sovereignty. [. . .] It seems to me that the least one can say is that any such scheme would be unimaginable unless it had been preceded by a long period in which transfers of a systematic kind between countries had become a well-established practice. On this alternative understanding, "international redistribution" means redistribution among countries.

[. . .] Given a world that is made up of states, what is the morally permissible range of diversity among them? I shall postpone the discussion of this question of diversity until the next section. In the rest of this one, I shall leave on one side the question of the way in which the money is to be spent within countries and focus on the mechanism of transfer between countries.

We are looking for an alternative to a system in which an international authority levies taxes directly on individuals. The simplest alternative is to assess countries for contributions according to their gross national product at some standard rate (for example, one percent) provided their average income per head is above some level (roughly, that of the OECD countries). One percent is an amount that would scarcely be noticed, but it is vastly in excess of the amounts currently transferred and would make a large difference. I do not doubt that moral cosmopolitanism calls for more, but the point is that even that amount would represent a real transformation in the level of international transfers.

A scheme in which the levy is proportional to GNP, above some cutoff point of average income, is the simplest, as I have said. It would, obviously, be possible to make it more fancy by introducing an element of progressivity, so that (within the set of contributors) richer countries paid a larger amount in proportion to their GNP. There is no need to pursue such refinements here. The essential feature common to all is that each state would be assessed by some international authority according to some schedule and it would then be up to the state to determine how the money was to be raised – whether by direct or indirect taxes, for example. An example of such a system that is effective is the system prevailing within the European Union whereby constituent countries have to provide a sum each year, part of which is disbursed (as "solidarity" funds) to the poorer regions.

The case for taking something like income per head as the basis of assessment is twofold. [. . .] In terms of classical taxation theory, the criterion is "ability to pay." In terms of the principles of justice set out earlier, it is that a rich country can afford to collect the money demanded without jeopardizing the vital interests of anybody in it. [. . .] There is a second argument as well, and this is that income per head is a proxy for the use of natural resources and the degradation of the global environment. It is not, it must be admitted, precise: the United States, for example, is much more profligate in the resources it expends for a given unit of production than other countries at a roughly similar economic level. Nevertheless, there is enough of a correlation to add support to the case derived from ability to pay.

This argument, however, suggests an alternative way of raising money for an international redistributive authority: a system of user fees (as an alternative to a rationing scheme that would create windfall gains) and taxes on the infliction of global environmental damage. The object here would be twofold. In part it would be driven by considerations of equity: those who make use of inherently limited facilities should pay, and those who impose burdens on the rest of the world should compensate for the damage they cause. But it would also work to modify behavior by providing an incentive to economize on scarce resources, and to reduce pollution.

Some recently proposed ideas are a surcharge on air tickets, a charge on ocean maritime transport, a special fee for maritime dumping of waste, parking fees for geostationary satellites, charges for the use of the electromagnetic spectrum, and charges for fishing rights in certain areas. A more ambitious extension would include a "carbon tax" on emissions contributing to global warming, [. . .] Ideally, they would be gathered directly from the users or polluters. Only this would ensure that the cost entered into their calculations. It appears to me, however, that many charges would, as a practical matter, have to be levied against governments. [. . .] The result of assessing governments is that it would be possible for a country to pay its "carbon tax" by, in turn, assessing taxpayers at large rather than by imposing, say, a levy on the burning of coal and petroleum. There is, however, no way in which such slippage can be prevented. What can at least be said is that the system of fees and taxes would put some pressure on governments to reduce their liability.

It is worth noticing that this kind of indirect taxation has a different status vis-à-vis the taxation of individual incomes from a levy based on GNP per head. Both of the rationales for taxing national income would be better served by taxing individual income: ability to pay would be more sensitively captured by taxing individuals, and individual income acts as a proxy for resource use wherever the person with the income lives. The fees and taxes I have just been proposing, however, would be desirable regardless of the way in which the direct tax element might be collected. How much it could be expected to raise would depend entirely on the rates set and the scope of the tax net. Adding a "carbon tax" could make it substantial. I believe, though, that direct taxation based on "ability to pay" is inevitably going to be required. For the indirect taxes would fall on poor countries as well as rich ones. No doubt by the nature of the case rich countries will pay the bulk, but poor countries pursuing "dirty" industrialization (for example China) will also have to pay. So they should: the whole point is to attach a realistic cost to their conduct. But the scheme as a whole can be acceptable only if there is also an element of straight transfer from rich to poor countries.

It may well be said that it is slightly absurd for me to pass over the idea of [. . .] international tax-collecting [. . .] on the ground that it is politically infeasible when everything else I am advocating is politically infeasible. Let me begin a response by saying that it still makes good sense to say that one proposal is much *more* politically infeasible than another, even if both seem a long way off adoption. Turning to the question of feasibility head on, I suggest that we should divide it into two. What is commonly seen as the major problem is that of coercing recalcitrant states to play their part. I think the seriousness of this problem can be exaggerated. The European Union collects from its member states because that is the price of staying in, and there are perceived to be advantages in not being excluded. There is no suggestion that troops would be sent to storm the treasury of a nonpaying member. Similarly, the World Trade Organization has the authority to rule on violations, and has at its disposal the sanctions of expulsion or, short of that, denial of certain advantages available to adherents. Generalizing from this, the relatively wealthy countries (the only ones that concern us in this context) belong to a whole network of international agreements, and if the assessed contribution to the fund for international redistribution were the price for remaining a member in good standing, it would be worth paying.

The real problem is not so much coercing backsliders as setting up the scheme in the first place. I do not underestimate the scale of this problem, but I want to emphasize that the kind of political will required to create such a scheme will have to stem from moral motivation. Hobbesian reasoning, as I suggested at the beginning of this chapter, will go quite a way, but it will not underwrite international redistribution. Attempts are, of course, made regularly to argue that it is in the self-interest of rich countries to transfer resources to poor ones. I have the strong impression, however, that those who make such arguments are themselves led to the conclusion by cosmopolitan moral considerations. It is therefore hardly surprising that their arguments fail to convince. All I can suggest here, then, is that, unless the moral case is made, we can be sure nothing good will happen. The more the case is made, the better the chance.

The limits of diversity

I take it as axiomatic that, in comparison with many other approaches (especially those of a communitarian cast), moral cosmopolitanism tends toward an endorsement of universally applicable standards. (In this it is not, however, differentiated from the Kantian or natural law approaches, [. . .]. Indeed, they might quite perspicuously be thought of as alternative ways of working through the moral cosmopolitan project, making use of alternative mediating premises.) Although I do not have the space to argue it here, I believe that the hypothetical contractarian approach taken here will underwrite the familiar list of basic human rights.[13] Anybody whose human rights are violated – say, by being denied freedom of speech or freedom of religious worship – has a legitimate complaint, according to moral cosmopolitanism, regardless of the opinions of others in the society. Even if there is something approaching a consensus on the legitimacy of executing religious deviants, that is still a proposition that the nonbeliever in the society's orthodoxy can reasonably reject.

It follows from this that morality is socially constituted only to a limited extent. The principles of justice are valid for all societies. This is far less a straitjacket than it might appear. As I have already pointed out, the principles require interpretation, and there is a good deal of room for interpreting them differently. It should also be emphasized that there is a very wide range of possible institutional embodiments of the principles of justice. In particular, the significance of individualism in the specification of the moral cosmopolitan position should not be misunderstood. What it insists is that every institution be judged by its impact on individual human beings. It rules out appeals to the destiny of a class, race, or nation that are not reducible to claims about the rights, interests, and welfare of individuals. But it is not committed to the idea that these are best advanced in a society that imposes very weak social obligations, another sense of "individualism" that is logically quite distinct. Thus, it is quite consistent with cosmopolitan principles of justice that people may find their greatest fulfillment within a dense network of family and community obligations.

At the same time, however, a cautionary note must be sounded. Enthusiasts for "multiculturalism" have a tendency to sentimentalize traditional arrangements that are grossly oppressive and exploitative when looked at close up.[14] The ultimate test is that nobody affected could reasonably reject the arrangement: the principles of justice are advanced as guidelines to give some structure to that judgment. Unfortunately, the norms constituting extended families and wider (but still small-scale) communities all too often create inequalities (characteristically but not exclusively in relations between the sexes) that could reasonably be rejected by those whose position is the worst under them.

Moral cosmopolitanism would be satisfied if the high level of interdependence and cooperation were retained but its terms reformed so as to be acceptable to all. Where there seems to be no prospect of this happening, however, those who subscribe to the moral cosmopolitan doctrine will typically welcome a weakening of the existing social bonds, and the opening up of an "exit" option for those who wish to get out from under the oppressive set-up. From the point of view of the worst-off, this may well backfire. For the "exit" option is most attractive to those who have most to gain by leaving, and those may well be the stronger rather than the weaker members of the group. The lot of the worst-off may thus even deteriorate as the obligations of the better-off are relaxed or evaded altogether. Nevertheless, the belief that moral cosmopolitanism endorses individualism in this sense is no doubt sustained by the tendency of those who despair of reform to welcome and encourage the dissolution of traditional institutions.

A common move among the multiculturalists is to suggest that social institutions may rest on consensus, even if outsiders might consider them to be radically unjust. It is then argued that it is nobody else's business if there is general acceptance among those actually concerned. In all such cases, however, the quality of the consent given by those who do poorly must be suspect. Often, it does not exist in any form: the exploited and oppressed know perfectly well that they are being treated badly, and the consensus that is blandly asserted to obtain is actually to be found only among the more articulate and powerful members of the group. Even when acceptance is genuine, it is invalidated if the person giving it is too ill-educated or restricted in access to relevant information about alternative forms of organization to be able to make an informed judgment. We must also distinguish acceptance from resignation: if there is no realistic prospect of improvement, it is less psychically costly to put aside any thoughts of justice or injustice and concentrate on survival.

There is nothing in our hypothetical construction, however, to rule out the theoretical possibility that a social arrangement failing to satisfy the principles of justice might be freely accepted as just by all the participants. Suppose, for example, that they all subscribe to a religious system according to which different hereditary groups have higher or lower spiritual status, and that this has strongly inegalitarian implications for the distribution of rights, opportunities, and resources in this world. (The Hindu Varna system is the obvious model here.) On the basis of this, let us stipulate that they all freely accept a social system that violates the principles of justice. What follows?

What does not follow is that the set-up is just. It could still reasonably be rejected (even though it happens not to be), because anybody could reasonably reject basing an inegalitarian social system on a set of religious beliefs. For these beliefs could themselves reasonably be rejected. (It does not follow that they could not reasonably be accepted.) The case for saying that it is just has to rest, it seems to me, on the maxim *Volenti iniuria non fit*. But this maxim is rejected by all municipal legal systems: there are rights to bodily integrity and liberty that cannot validly be surrendered by the consent of the party concerned. We need not, however, draw from this the conclusion that unjust inequalities that are accepted as just by the parties should, if possible, be suppressed. Whether something is unjust is one question; what, if anything, should be done about it by outsiders is another. It can be argued that if people choose freely to live in unjust conditions of powerlessness and material degradation in furtherance of their religious beliefs, then their own view of their greater good should be respected. I have to say that I regard the whole question as purely conjectural, however, since I do not believe that the problem will ever present itself in this way. In any society that meets the information condition, I predict that there will always be found some people who reject the religious system that legitimizes unjust inequalities.

Intranational injustice and international redistribution

My primary focus [. . .] is on the distribution of income, and I want in this final section to return to it. Here, the range of legitimate variation is inherently limited, since the principles of justice bear directly on the distribution of income. The great majority of existing countries have a degree of inequality greatly in excess of that which could reasonably be justified under the principles of justice set out here. How does this affect the case for international redistribution, whether conceived as transfers from rich to poor individuals (regardless of location) or as transfers from rich to poor countries?

The answer is perhaps surprising. Take first a scheme in which an international authority collected income taxes from relatively wealthy individuals and gave money to relatively poor individuals. [. . .] The contributors to the scheme could afford to take a quite relaxed attitude to the distribution of income within recipient countries both before and after the transfers had been made. So long as governments in the recipient countries did not use their taxing powers to take away the benefits gained by the poor, it could be said that at any rate the scheme was working in that resources were being transferred from rich to poor individuals.

Now think about a scheme in which the governments of relatively rich countries transfer resources in some systematic way to the governments of relatively poor countries. Here the distribution of income within the recipient countries becomes a matter of legitimate concern. There are two reasons for this. The first is that the whole notion of the transferred resources going to the poor is now less than transparent. The only way of determining that the results of whatever the government does can be said to constitute a transfer of the money to the poor is to ask if the poor have collectively benefited to the extent of the money provided. This requires close attention to the actual distribution of income and a comparison between it and what the distribution might be hypothesized to have been in its absence.

The second point is rather more subtle. We can best approach it by observing that the individualistic scheme treats national boundaries as having no significance (for this purpose, anyway). In contrast to this, any scheme that makes countries the units of redistribution immediately throws an emphasis on the internal distribution of income. Suppose that the distribution of income in a poor country is extremely unjust (as it actually is in virtually all cases). What implications, if any, does this have for the obligations of those in rich countries to pay taxes in order to provide the resources for transfers to be made to poor countries?

[. . .] One case: that in which not only is the distribution of internally generated income unjust but also any additional income from outside would be appropriated by the ruling elite. Here there can be no morally compelling reason for making transfers. There is, instead, a case for international intervention to displace the government and, if necessary, place the country under international trusteeship until more adequate institutions can be created. This intervention will have to be military rather than taking the form of economic sanctions. For (as the examples of Haiti and Iraq illustrate) a government can ensure that the worst burden of economic sanctions falls upon the poorest, and there is no reason to suppose that a government that had already proved itself indifferent to the suffering of its poorest citizens would be motivated to reform by the prospect of their plight becoming even worse as a result of economic sanctions.

The wisdom of military intervention can be challenged, and recent United Nations efforts (in the Horn of Africa, for example) are scarcely encouraging. I cannot here enter into that argument. I assert only the principle that cosmopolitan morality cannot object to intervention under the circumstances I have outlined except on grounds of inefficacy of counterproductiveness. For whatever can be said in favor of state autonomy as a contribution to the well-being of the citizens holds only contingently. Any government which is little more than a gang of looters (as in much of sub-Saharan Africa) forfeits any respect for its independence. If it can be toppled without making things worse, that has to be a (relatively) just outcome.

Bypassing cases in which the poor gain some from international transfers but less than by the amount of the transfers, let us consider now a case in which all the benefit of the transfers goes to those who should justly receive it. It might be suggested that this still does not create an obligation to make the transfer. To put the case in its strongest form, suppose that many people in the country are failing to have their vital needs met, but that there is an economically (though not politically) feasible internal redistribution of income that would enable everybody's vital needs to be met. [. . .] It could be said then that justice begins at home: why should people elsewhere make sacrifices that would not be called for if the rich in the poor country were to behave justly?

We are here, as so often in matters of justice, confronted with the problem of the second best. If some people are not doing their bit, does that mean that others do not have to step in? If they do not, the vital needs of the poor in poor countries will continue to go unmet. If they act, vital needs will be met and the cost will be spread over hundreds of millions of people. It seems an inescapable conclusion that justice will be advanced by making the transfer. This is especially clear in the (normal) case in which even a just internal distribution would leave a need for international transfers. It would surely be unconscionable to use the lack of internal redistribution as an excuse for not acting. This is not to say that efforts should not be made to provide the government of the recipient country with strong incentives to do its bit for its poorer citizens. It would be reasonable to deny the country any development aid, for example, and this might well have some effect on the willingness of the better-off members of society to accept a measure of internal redistribution.

The obligation on rich countries to transfer resources to internally unjust poor countries might under certain conditions be challenged in another way. Imagine a country in which everyone accepts the unjust internal inequality. Can the victims of this injustice reasonably demand that their material position be improved by transfers from outside the country if they have no complaint against it themselves? This is obviously a variant of the argument from consent whose strength and scope I assessed in the previous section.

The best case would be a democracy in which a majority persistently voted for parties that did little or nothing when in government to make the distribution of income more just. The electoral success in India since independence of either the Congress Party or parties economically to its right might be advanced as a case in point, given that neither has done anything significant to tackle the maldistribution of wealth and income that the new state inherited. The argument is weak, however, even in this most favorable case. Suppose we were to accept that majority support for the status quo implied majority acceptance of the justice of status quo, a majority is far from the consensus that the argument needs. But there is no reason to make that deduction. As Gunnar Myrdal observed many years ago, India is a "soft state," marked by lack of administrative effectiveness, and in particular the cooptation of officials by the wealthy and powerful in each locality. An attitude of passive resignation on the part of the poor in the face of the failure and subversion of tax and land reform legislation is therefore scarcely to be wondered at. It cannot plausibly be deduced from passivity that they accept the moral legitimacy of the status quo.

This reply, of course, brings us back to the question of the efficacy of international transfers. If the administration of a state is so liable to derailment by powerful interests that its internal efforts at reform are hijacked, what are the prospects of external funds going to the poor rather than being misappropriated? I can only repeat in conclusion that there is no case from cosmopolitan justice for making transfers unless they do get to the people for whom they are intended. But in a second-best world, that does not provide any reason for not making transfers in the remaining cases. The outcome is more just if that is done than it would otherwise be. Needless to say, it is a question of immense practical importance how great a limitation on the scope of international redistribution this proviso imposes. But the answer to that question does not affect the validity of the idea that transfers should be made where they are called for by the principles of justice and will be efficacious in making the situation more just.

Notes

1 Charles R. Beitz, "Cosmopolitan Liberalism and the States System," in Chris Brown, ed., *Political Restructuring in Europe: Ethical Perspectives* (London: Routledge, 1994), 123–36, quotation at 124.
2 Beitz, "Cosmopolitan Liberalism," 124–25.
3 Beitz, "Cosmopolitan Liberalism," 124.
4 Beitz, "Cosmopolitan Liberalism," 125.
5 Beitz, "Cosmopolitan Liberalism," 126.
6 Thomas E. Hill, Jr., "The Importance of Autonomy," in Eva Kittay and Diane Meyers, eds., *Women and Moral Theory* (Totowa, NJ: Rowman and Allanheld, 1987), 132.
7 T. M. Scanlon, "Contractualism and Utilitarianism," in Amartya Sen and Bernard Williams, eds., *Utilitarianism and Beyond* (Cambridge: Cambridge University Press, 1982), 103–28, quotation at 116, n. 2. For an elaborated exposition of this idea, see my *Justice as Impartiality*, Vol. 2 of *A Treatise on Social Justice* (Oxford: Oxford University Press, 1995), esp. 67–72.
8 John Rawls, *A Theory of Justice* (Cambridge, MA: Harvard University Press, 1971).
9 This conclusion is arrived at in an article whose general line I endorse: Arthur Ripstein, "Equality, Luck, and Responsibility," *Philosophy & Public Affairs* 23 (1994): 3–23.
10 Richard Arneson, "Property Rights in Persons," *Social Philosophy and Policy* 9 (1992): 201–30, at 209.
11 See T. M. Scanlon, "Preference and Urgency," *Journal of Philosophy* 72 (1975): 655–69.
12 See Stein Hansen, "Entropy Implications for Global Development," Centre for the Study of Global Governance, London School of Economics, 1993.
13 For an argument to this purpose, I must refer readers to my *Justice as Impartiality*, especially ch. 4.
14 For a representative example, see Bhikhu Parekh, "The Cultural Particularity of Liberal Democracy," in David Held, ed., *Prospects for Democracy*, published as a special issue of *Political Studies* 40 (1992).

7

Cosmopolitanism and Sovereignty
Thomas Pogge

Introduction

The human future suddenly seems open. This is an inspiration; we can step back and think more freely. Instead of containment or détente, political scientists are discussing grand pictures: the end of history, or the inevitable proliferation and mutual pacifism of capitalist democracies. And politicians are speaking of a new world order. My inspiration is a little more concrete. After developing a rough, cosmopolitan specification of our task to promote moral progress, I offer an idea for gradual global institutional reform. Dispersing political authority over nested territorial units would decrease the intensity of the struggle for power and wealth within and among states, thereby reducing the incidence of war, poverty, and oppression. In such a multilayered institutional order, borders could be redrawn more easily to accord with the aspirations of peoples and communities.

Institutional cosmopolitanism based on human rights

Three elements are shared by all cosmopolitan positions. First, *individualism*: the ultimate units of concern are *human beings*, or *persons* – rather than, say, family lines, tribes ethnic, cultural, or religious communities, nations, or states. The latter may be units of concern only indirectly, in virtue of their individual members or citizens. Second, *universality*: the status of ultimate unit of concern attaches to *every* living human being *equally* (cf. n. 90) – not merely to some subset, such as men, aristocrats, Aryans, whites, or Muslims. Third, *generality*: this special status has global force. Persons are ultimate units of concern *for everyone* – not only for their compatriots, fellow religionists, or suchlike.

   Let me separate three cosmopolitan approaches by introducing two distinctions. The first is that between legal and moral cosmopolitanism. *Legal* cosmopolitanism is committed to a concrete political ideal of a global order under which all persons have equivalent legal rights and duties – are fellow citizens of a universal republic.[1] *Moral* cosmopolitanism holds that all persons stand in certain moral relations to one another: we are required to respect one another's status as ultimate units of moral concern – a requirement that imposes limits on our conduct and, in particular, on our efforts to construct institutional schemes. This view is more abstract, and in this sense weaker than, legal cosmopolitanism: it may support the latter for certain empirical circumstances, but it may, for different circumstances, support less uniform arrangements such as a system of autonomous states or even a multitude of self-contained communities. Here I present a variant of moral cosmopolitanism before examining below whether this position supports reforms that would bring our global order closer to the ideal of legal cosmopolitanism.

The central idea of moral cosmopolitanism is that every human being has a global stature as an ultimate unit of moral concern. Such moral concern can be fleshed out in countless ways. One may focus on subjective goods and ills (human happiness, desire fulfillment, preference satisfaction, or pain avoidance) or on more objective ones (such as human-need fulfillment, capabilities, opportunities, or resources). Also, one might relativize these measures, for instance by defining the key ill as *being worse off than anyone need be, as being dominated by others*, or as *falling below the mean* – which is equivalent to replacing straightforward aggregation (sum-ranking or averaging) by a maximum or egalitarian standard. In order to get to my topic quickly, I do not discuss these matters, but simply opt for a variant of moral cosmopolitanism that is formulated in terms of *human rights* with straightforward interpersonal aggregation.[2] In doing so, I capture what most other variants likewise consider essential. And my further reflections can, in any case, easily be generalized to other variants of moral cosmopolitanism.

My second distinction lies *within* the domain of the moral. It concerns the nature of the moral constraints to be imposed. An *institutional* conception postulates certain fundamental principles of social *justice*. These apply to institutional schemes and are thus second-order principles: standards for assessing the ground rules and practices that regulate human interactions. An *interactional* conception, by contrast, postulates certain fundamental principles of *ethics*. These principles, like institutional ground rules, are first-order in that they apply directly to the conduct of persons and groups.

Interactional cosmopolitanism assigns direct responsibility for the fulfillment of human rights to other individual and collective agents, whereas institutional cosmopolitanism assigns such responsibility to institutional schemes. On the latter view, the responsibility of persons is, then, indirect – a shared responsibility for the justice of any practices one helps to impose: one ought not to cooperate in the imposition of a coercive institutional order that avoidably leaves human rights unfulfilled without making reasonable efforts to protect its victims and to promote institutional reform.

Institutional and interactional conceptions are compatible and thus may be combined in a mutually complementary way.[3] Here I focus, however, on a variant of institutional cosmopolitanism while leaving open the question of its supplementation by a variant of interactional cosmopolitanism. I hope to show that making the institutional view primary leads to a more plausible and more pertinent overall morality. To do this, let me begin by exploring how the two approaches yield different understandings of human rights and their fulfillment.

On the interactional view human rights impose constraints on conduct, while on the institutional view they impose constraints, in the first instance, upon shared practices. The latter approach has two straightforward limitations. First, its applicability is contingent, in that human rights are activated only through the emergence of social institutions. Where such institutions are lacking, human rights are merely latent, incapable of being either fulfilled or unfulfilled. Thus, if we accept a purely institutional conception of human rights, then we need some additional moral conception to formulate moral constraints on conduct in a disorganized state of nature.

Second, the cosmopolitanism of the institutional approach is contingent as well, in that the *global* moral force of human rights is activated only through the emergence of a *global* institutional order, which triggers obligations to promote any feasible reforms of this order that would enhance the fulfillment of human rights. So long as there is a plurality of self-contained cultures, the responsibility for unfulfilled human rights does not extend beyond their boundaries. [. . .] It is only because all human beings are now participants in a single, global institutional order – involving such institutions as the territorial state, a system of international law and diplomacy, as well as a global economic system of property rights and markets for capital, goods, and services – that all unfulfilled human rights have come to be, at least potentially, everyone's responsibility.[4]

These two limitations do not violate generality. Each person has a duty toward *every* other not to cooperate in imposing an unjust institutional order upon her, even while this duty triggers human-rights-based obligations only to fellow participants in the same institutional scheme. This is analogous to how the duty to keep one's promises is general even while it triggers obligations only toward persons to whom one has actually made a promise.

We see here how the institutional approach makes available an appealing intermediate position between two interactional extremes: it goes beyond simple libertarianism, according to which we may ignore harms that we do not directly bring about, without falling into a utilitarianism of rights, which commands us to take account of all relevant harms whatsoever, regardless of our causal relation to them. [. . .]

Consider, for example, a human right not to be enslaved. On an interactional view, this right would constrain persons, who must not enslave one another. On an institutional view, the right would constrain legal and economic institutions: ownership rights in persons must not be recognized or enforced. This leads to an important difference regarding the moral role of those who are neither slaves nor slaveholders. On the interactional view, such third parties have no responsibility toward existing slaves, unless the human right in question involved, besides the negative duty not to enslave, also a positive duty to protect or rescue others from enslavement. Such positive duties have been notoriously controversial. On the institutional view, by contrast, those involved in upholding an institutional order that authorizes and enforces slavery – even those who own no slaves themselves – count as cooperating in the enslavement, in violation of a *negative* duty, unless they make reasonable efforts toward protecting slaves or promoting institutional reform. The institutional view thus broadens the circle of those who share responsibility for certain deprivations and abuses beyond what a simple libertarianism would justify, and it does so without having to affirm positive duties.

To be sure, promoting institutional reform is doing something (positive). But the duty requiring one to do so may nonetheless be negative for those who would otherwise, through their involvement in upholding the relevant institutional order, be harming its victims. This is analogous to how the libertarians' favorite negative duty may entail positive obligations: one must do what one has promised or contracted to do pursuant to one's negative duty not to promise/contract without performing. In both cases, the negative duty gives rise to positive obligations only through prior voluntary conduct: one's promise, or one's involvement in upholding a coercive institutional order.

The move from an interactional to an institutional approach thus blocks one way in which today's rich and mighty in the world's affluent regions like to see themselves as morally disconnected from the fate of the poor in the developing countries. It overcomes the claim that one need only refrain from violating human rights directly, that one cannot reasonably be required to become a soldier in the global struggle against human-rights violators and a comforter of their victims worldwide. This claim is not refuted but shown to be irrelevant. We are asked to be concerned about avoidably unfulfilled human rights not simply insofar as they exist at all, but only insofar as they are [produced by coercive social institutions in whose imposition we are] involved. Our negative duty not to cooperate in the imposition of unjust coercive institutions triggers obligations to protect their victims and to promote feasible reforms that would enhance their fulfillment of human rights.

One may think that a shared responsibility for the justice of any social institutions one is involved in imposing cannot plausibly extend beyond our national institutional order, in which we participate as citizens, and which we can most immediately affect. But such a limitation is untenable. The existing global institutional order is neither natural nor God-given, but shaped and upheld by the more powerful governments and by other actors they control (such as the EU, NATO, UN, WTO, OECD, World Bank, and IMF). At least the more privileged and influential citizens of the more powerful and approximately democratic countries bear then a collective responsibility for their governments' role in designing and imposing this global order and for their governments' failure to reform it toward greater human-rights fulfillment.

There are two main strategies for attempting to limit the practical importance of this shared responsibility. A more philosophical strategy seeks to show that any institutional order should be held responsible only for deprivations it *establishes*, that is, mandates or at least authorizes. A human-rights standard should then classify such an order as acceptable so long as no severe deprivations are established by it, irrespective of any severe deprivations this order merely – however predictably and however avoidably – *engenders*. And we should therefore not count against the current global order the fact that it tends to engender a high incidence of war, torture, and starvation, because nothing in the existing written or unwritten international ground rules calls for such deprivations; they actually forbid both torture and the waging of aggressive war. The prominence of these evils therefore indicates no flaw in our global order and, *a fortiori*, no violation of negative duties on our part (though we may be responsible if our own government engages in torture or an unjust war).

This position is implausible. It would be irrational to assess social institutions without regard to the effects they predictably engender – irrational, for instance, to design a penal code or a tax code without regard to the effects it will actually produce through, for example, the compliance and reward incentives it provides. Longer jail terms may lower crime rates thus reducing aggregate jail time, and lower tax rates may expand the tax base thus increasing tax revenues – or they may have the opposite effect. A legislature would not be doing its job if it made such decisions without regard to their engendered consequences. It would be similarly irresponsible to think about the design and reform of global institutions without regard to *their* engendered consequences.

It does not follow that a plausible standard for assessing social institutions must treat established and engendered consequences on a par. A human right to physical security, for instance, though it should be sensitive to the risks an institutional order may impose on (some of) its participants through the high crime rate it engenders, should certainly be *more* sensitive to the risks it produces through officially authorized or even mandated assaults. (We should not, to give a simple illustration, authorize a "reform" of police procedures that would cause an extra 90 assaults by police against suspects, even if its contribution to deterrence would also reduce by 100 the number of similarly severe assaults by criminals against citizens.) These differentiations can and should be incorporated into any plausible conception of human rights, which should avoid, then, the kind of purely recipient-oriented view of deprivations that is embodied in consequentialist and contractualist (veil-of-ignorance) theorizing. With these differentiations in place, we can count engendered deprivations (such as poverty in a market system or insecurity due to crimes) as relevant to the fulfillment of human rights without committing to a purely recipient-oriented assessment of social institutions that would assign to engendered deprivations the same weight as it assigns to equally severe established deprivations.

[. . .]

A second, more empirical strategy for attempting to limit the practical importance of our shared responsibility for global institutions seeks to downplay the extent to which our global institutional order is causally responsible for current deprivations:

> Unfulfilled human rights and their distribution have local explanations. In some countries torture is rampant, while it is virtually non-existent in others. Some regions are embroiled in frequent wars, while others are not. In some countries democratic institutions thrive, while others bring forth a succession of autocrats. And again, some poor countries have developed rapidly, while others are getting poorer year by year. Therefore our global institutional order has very little to do with the deplorable state of human-rights fulfillment on earth.[5]

This challenge appeals to true premises but draws an invalid inference. Our global institutional order can obviously not figure in the explanation of *local* variations in the underfulfillment of human rights, but only in the *macro*explanation of its *global* incidence. This parallels how Japanese culture may figure in the explanation of the Japanese suicide rate or how the laxity of US handgun legislation may figure in the explanation of the North American homicide rate, without thereby explaining particular suicides/homicides or even intercity differentials in rates. In these parallel cases the need for a macroexplanation is obvious from the fact that there are other societies whose suicide/homicide rates are significantly lower. In the case of *global* institutions, the need for a macroexplanation of the overall incidence of unfulfilled human rights is less obvious because – apart from some rather inconclusive historical comparisons – the contrast to observable alternative global institutional schemes is lacking. Still, it is highly likely that there are feasible (i.e. practicable and accessible) alternative global regimes that would tend to engender lower rates of deprivation. This is clear, for example, in regard to economic institutions, where our experience with various national and regional schemes suggests that free markets must be regulated or complemented in certain ways if extreme poverty, entailing effective exclusion from political participation as well as from educational and medical opportunities, is to be avoided. This supports a generalization to the global plane, to the conjecture that the current global economic order must figure prominently in the explanation of the fact that our world is one of vast and increasing inequalities in income and wealth, with consequent huge differentials in rates of infant mortality, life expectancy, disease, and malnutrition. Such a macroexplanation does not explain why one poor country is developing rapidly while another is not. It explains why so few are while so many are not.

Let me close the more abstract part of the discussion with a sketch of how this institutional view might understand social and economic human rights and how it might thus relate to the notion of distributive justice. A man sympathetic to the moral claims of the poor, Michael Walzer, has written: "the idea of distributive justice presupposes a bounded world, a community, within which distributions take place, a group of people committed to dividing, exchanging, and sharing, first of all among themselves."[6] This is precisely the picture of distributive justice that Robert Nozick has so vigorously attacked. To the notion of dividing he objects that "there is no *central* distribution, no person or group entitled to control all the resources, jointly deciding how they are to be doled out."[7] And as for the rest, he would allow persons to do all the exchanging and sharing they like, but would strongly reject any enforced sharing effected by some redistribution bureaucracy.

The institutional approach involves a conception of distributive justice that differs sharply from the one Walzer supports and Nozick attacks. Here the issue of distributive justice is not how to distribute a given pool of resources or how to improve upon a given distribution but, rather, how to choose or design the economic ground rules that regulate property, cooperation, and exchange and thereby condition, production and distribution. (On the particular view I defend, for example, we should aim for an economic order under which each participant would be able to meet her basic social and economic needs.) A conception of distributive justice understood in this way, as providing a standard for the moral assessment of alternative feasible schemes of economic institutions, is prior to both production and distribution occurring under such schemes and therefore involves neither the idea of an already existing pool of stuff to be doled out nor the idea of already owned resources to be *re*-distributed.

The institutional conception of distributive justice also does not presuppose the existence of a community of persons committed first of all to share with one another. Rather, it has a far more minimal rationale: we face a choice of economic ground rules that is partly open – not determined by causal necessity, nor preempted by some God-given or natural or neutral order that we must choose irrespective of its effects. This choice has a tremendous impact on human lives, an impact from which persons cannot be insulated and cannot insulate themselves. Our present global economic order produces a stable pattern of widespread malnutrition and starvation among the poor, with some 18 million persons dying each year from poverty-related causes, and there are likely to be feasible alternative regimes that would not produce similarly severe deprivations. If this is so, the victims of such avoidable deprivations are not merely poor and starving, but impoverished and starved through an institutional order coercively imposed upon them. There is an injustice in this economic order, which it would be wrong for its more affluent participants to perpetuate. And that is so quite independently of whether we and the starving are united by a communal bond or committed to sharing resources with one another – just as murdering a person is wrong irrespective of such considerations. This is what the assertion of social and economic human rights amounts to within the proposed institutional cosmopolitanism.

[. . .]

The idea of state sovereignty

Before discussing how we should think about sovereignty in the light of the proposed institutional cosmopolitanism, let me define this term, in a somewhat unusual way, as a two-place relation: A is *sovereign* over B if and only if

(1) A is a governmental body or officer ("agency"), and
(2) B are persons, and
(3) A has unsupervised[8] and irrevocable authority over B
    (a) to lay down rules constraining B's conduct, or
    (b) to judge B's compliance with rules, or
    (c) to enforce rules against B through preemption, prevention, or punishments, or
    (d) to act in B's behalf toward other agencies (ones that do or do not have authority over B) or persons (ones whom A is sovereign over, or not).

A has *absolute sovereignty* over B if and only if

(1) A is sovereign over B, and
(2) no other agency has any authority over A or over B which is not both supervised and revocable by A.

Any A having (absolute) sovereignty over some B can then be said to be an (absolute) sovereign (the one-place predicate).

Central to contemporary political thought and reality is the idea of autonomous territorial state as the preeminent mode of political organization. In the vertical dimension, sovereignty is very heavily concentrated at a single level – it is states and only states that merit separate colors on a political map of our world. For nearly every human being, and for almost every piece of territory, there is exactly one government with preeminent, authority over, and primary responsibility for, this person or territory. And each person is thought to owe primary political allegiance and loyalty to this government with preeminent authority over him or her. Such governments check and dominate the decision-making of political subunits, as well as supranational decisions which tend to be made through intergovernmental mental bargaining.

From the standpoint of a cosmopolitan morality – which centers on the fundamental needs and interests of individual human beings, and of *all* human beings – this concentration of sovereignty at one level is no longer defensible. What I am proposing instead is not the idea of a centralized world state, which is really a variant of the preeminent-state idea. Rather, the proposal is that governmental authority – or sovereignty – be widely dispersed in the vertical dimension. What we need is *both* centralization *and* decentralization – a kind of second-order decentralization away from the now dominant level of the state. Thus, persons should be citizens of, and govern themselves through, a number of political units of various sizes, without any one political unit being dominant and thus occupying the traditional role of state. And their political allegiance and loyalties should be widely dispersed over these units: neighborhood, town, county, province, state, region, and world at large. People should be politically at home in all of them, without converging upon any one of them as the lodestar of their political identity.[9]

Before defending and developing this proposal by reference to the institutional cosmopolitanism set forth above, let me address two types of objection to any vertical division of sovereignty.

Objections of type 1 dispute that sovereignty can be divided at all. The traditional form of this objection rests on the belief that a *juridical condition* (as distinct from a lawless state of nature) presupposes an absolute sovereign. This dogma of absolute sovereignty arises (e.g. in Hobbes and Kant) roughly as follows. A juridical condition, by definition, involves a recognized decision mechanism that uniquely resolves any dispute. This mechanism requires some agency because a mere written or unwritten code (constitution, holy scripture) cannot settle disputes about its own interpretation. But so long as this agency is limited or divided – whether horizontally (i.e. by territory or by governmental function) or vertically (as in my proposal) – a juridical condition has not been achieved because there is no recognized way in which conflicts over the precise location of the limit or division can be authoritatively resolved. A genuine state of peace requires then an agency of last resort – ultimate, supreme, and unconstrained. Such an agency may still be limited by codified or uncodified obligations. But these can obligate merely *in foro interno* (in conscience) because to authorize subjects, or some second agency, to determine whether the first agency is overstepping its bounds would enable conflicts about this question for which there would be no reliable legal path of authoritative resolution.

This argument, which – strictly construed – would require an absolute world sovereign, has been overtaken by the historical facts of the last 200 years or so, which show conclusively that what cannot work in theory works quite well in practice. Law-governed coexistence is possible without a supreme and unconstrained agency. There is, it is true, the possibility of *ultimate* conflicts: of disputes in regard to which even the legally correct method of resolution is contested. To see this, one need only imagine how a constitutional democracy's three branches of government might engage in an all-out power struggle, each going to the very brink of what, on its understanding, it is constitutionally authorized to do. From a theoretical point of view, this possibility shows that we are not insured against, and thus live in permanent danger of, constitutional crises. But this no longer undermines our confidence in a genuine division of powers: we have learned that such crises need not be frequent or irresolvable. From a practical point of view, we know that constitutional democracies can endure and can ensure a robust juridical condition.

This same point applies in the vertical dimension as well. Just as it is nonsense to suppose that, in a juridical condition, sovereignty *must* rest with one of the branches of government, it is similarly nonsensical to think that in a multilayered order sovereignty *must* be concentrated on one level exclusively. As the history of federalist regimes clearly shows, a vertical division of sovereignty can work quite well in practice, even while it leaves some conflicts over the constitutional allocation of powers without a reliable legal path of authoritative resolution.

Objections of type 2 oppose, more specifically, any *vertical* dispersal of sovereignty: there are certain vertically indivisible governmental functions that constitute the core of sovereignty. Any political unit exercising these core functions must be dominant – free to determine the extent to which its subunits may engage in their own local political decision-making, even while its own political process is immune to regulation and review by larger political units of which it forms a part. If there is to be any vertical distribution of sovereignty at all, it must therefore be lopsided in favor of those governments in the vertical order that have authority over the core functions. The political units coordinate to these dominant governments, and only they, deserve the title of "country" or "state" (excepting the use of this word within the US).

To be assessable, such a claim stands in need of two clarifications, which are rarely supplied. First, when one thinks about it more carefully, it turns out to be surprisingly difficult to come up with examples of indivisible governmental functions. Eminent domain, economic policy, foreign policy, judicial review; the control of natural resources, security forces, education, health care, and income support; the regulation and taxation of resource extraction and pollution, of work and consumption, can all be handled at various levels and indeed *are* so handled in existing federal regimes and confederations. So what are the governmental functions that supposedly are vertically indivisible? And, second, is their indivisibility supposed to be derived from a conceptual insight, from empirical exigencies, or from moral desiderata? And which ones?

Since I cannot here discuss all possible type 2 objections, let me concentrate on one paradigm case. Walzer claims that the authority to fix membership, to admit and exclude, is at least part of an indivisible core of sovereignty: "At some level of political organization something like the sovereign state must take shape and claim the authority to make its own admissions policy, to control and sometimes to restrain the flow of immigrants."[10] Walzer's "must" does not reflect a conceptual or empirical necessity, for in those senses the authority in question quite obviously *can* be divided – for example, by allowing political units on all levels to veto immigration. It is on moral grounds that Walzer rejects such an authority for provinces, towns, and neighborhoods: it would "create a thousand petty fortresses."[11] But if subunits are to be precluded from controlling the influx of new members, then immigration must be controlled at the state level: "Only if the state makes a selection among would-be members and guarantees the loyalty, security, and welfare of the individuals it selects, can local communities take shape as 'indifferent' associations, determined only by personal preference and market capacity."[12] The asserted connection is again a moral one. It is certainly factually possible for local communities to exist as indifferent associations even while no control is exercised over migration at all; as Walzer says, "the fortresses too could be torn down, of course."[13] Walzer's point is, then, that the insistence on openness (to avoid a thousand petty fortresses) is asking too much of neighborhoods, unless the state has control over immigration: "The distinctiveness of cultures and groups depends upon closure. . . . If this distinctiveness is a value . . . then closure must be permitted somewhere."[14]

But is the conventional model really supported by the rationale Walzer provides? To be sure, Walzer is right to claim that the value of protecting cohesive neighborhood cultures is better served by national immigration control than by no control at all. But it would be served even better if the state could admit only immigrants who are planning to move into a neighborhood that is willing to accept them. Moreover, since a neighborhood culture can be as effectively destroyed by the influx of compatriots as by that of immigrants, neighborhoods would do even better, if they had some authority to select from among prospective domestic newcomers or to limit their number. Finally, neighborhoods may often want to bring in new members from abroad – persons to whom they have special ethnic, religious, or cultural ties – and they would therefore benefit from a role in the national immigration control process that would allow them to facilitate the admission of such persons. Thus there are at least three reasons for believing that Walzer's rationale – cohesive neighborhood cultures ought to be protected without becoming petty fortresses – is actually *better* served by a division of the authority to admit and exclude than by the conventional concentration of this authority at the level of the state.

Some main reasons for a vertical dispersal of sovereignty

Having dealt with some preliminary obstacles, let me now sketch four main reasons that favor, over the status quo, a world in which sovereignty is widely distributed vertically.

Peace and security

In the existing global order, interstate rivalries are settled ultimately through military competition, including the threat and use of military force. Moreover, within their own territories, national governments are free to do virtually anything they like. Such governments therefore have very powerful incentives and very broad opportunities to develop their military might. This is bound to lead to the further proliferation of nuclear, biological, chemical, and conventional weapons of mass destruction. And in a world in which dozens of competing governments control such weapons, the outbreak of devastating wars is only a matter of time. It is unlikely that national control over weapons of mass destruction can be abolished within the existing world order – through a disarmament program that depends upon the voluntary acceptance and compliance of each and every national government, for example. The continuation of this order would thus probably lead to more and more national governments gaining the capacity to trigger a major catastrophe, and possibly to attempts by some preemptively to disarm others. Nonproliferation and gradual abolition of weapons of mass destruction presuppose a substantial centralization of authority and power at the global level – in violation of the prevalent idea of state sovereignty. Such centralization can best be accomplished in the context of a multilayered global order, that is, in the course of a process of second-order decentralization. If such global institutional reform process also reduced repression and economic injustice, its disarmament component might well win broad support from peoples and governments – provided it increases the security of all on fair terms that are effectively adjudicated and enforced. The attempt to advance disarmament in this way would in any case be far less dangerous than continuing the status quo.

Reducing oppression

In the current global order, national governments are effectively free to control "their" populations in whatever way they see fit. Many make extensive use of this freedom by torturing and murdering their domestic opponents, censoring information, suppressing and subverting democratic procedures, prohibiting emigration, and so forth. These massive violations of human rights could be reduced through a vertical dispersal of sovereignty over various layers of political units that would check and balance one another as well as publicize one another's abuses.

Global economic justice

The magnitude and extent of current economic deprivations call for reforms of the prevailing global economic order. One plausible reform would involve a global levy on the use of natural resources to support the economic development in the poorest areas. Such a levy would assure the poor of their fair share of the value of natural resources extracted and would also encourage conservation. Reforms for the sake of economic justice would again involve some centralization – though without requiring anything like a global welfare bureaucracy.

Global economic justice is an end in its own right, which requires, and therefore supports, some reallocation of political authority. But it is also quite important as a means toward the first two objectives. War and oppression result from the contest for power within and among political units, which tends to be the more intense the higher the stakes. In fights to govern states, or to expand their borders or spheres of influence, far too much is now at stake by way of control over people and resources. We can best lower the stakes by dispersing political authority among several levels *and* by institutionally securing economic justice at the global level.

This important point suggests why my first three considerations – though each supports some centralization – do not on balance support a centralized world state. While such a world state could lead to significant progress in terms of peace and economic justice, it also poses significant risks of oppression. Here the kind of multilayered order I propose has the great advantages of affording plenty of checks and balances and of assuring that, even when some political units turn tyrannical and oppressive, there will always be other, *already fully organized* political units – above, below, or on the same level – which can render aid and protection to the oppressed, publicize the abuses, and, if necessary, fight the oppressors. The prospect of such organized resistance would have a deterrent effect as governments would understand that repression is more likely to reduce than enhance their power.

There are two further important reasons against a centralized world state. Cultural and social diversity are likely to be far better protected when the interests of cultural communities at all levels are represented (externally) and supported (internally) by coordinate political units. And the order I propose could be reached *gradually* from where we are now (through what I have called second-order decentralization), while a centralized world state – involving, as it does, the annihilation of existing states – would seem reachable only through revolution or in the wake of some global catastrophe.

Ecology/democracy

Modern processes of production and consumption are liable to generate significant negative externalities that, to a large and increasing extent, transcend national borders. In a world of competing autonomous states, the internalization of such externalities is generally quite imperfect because of familiar isolation, assurance, and coordination problems. Treaties among a large number of very differently situated actors require difficult and time-consuming bargaining and negotiations, which often lead to only very slight progress, if any. And even when treaties are achieved, doubts about the full compliance of other parties tend to erode each party's own commitment to make good-faith efforts toward compliance.

One may object that this fourth reason goes beyond my institutional cosmopolitanism, because there is no recognized human right to a clean and healthy environment. Why should people not be free to live in a degraded natural environment if they so choose? In response: perhaps they should be, but for now they will not have had a choice. The degradation of our natural environment inescapably affects us all. And yet, most people are effectively excluded from any say about this issue which, in the current state-centric model, is regulated by national governments unilaterally or through intergovernmental bargaining heavily influenced by huge differentials in economic and military might.

This response suggests replacing *Ecology* with a deeper and more general fourth reason labeled *Democracy*: persons have a right to an institutional order under which those significantly and legitimately affected by a political decision have a roughly equal opportunity to influence the making of this decision – directly or through elected delegates or representatives. Such a human right to equal opportunity for political participation also supports greater local autonomy in matters of purely local concern than exists in most current states or would exist in a world state, however democratic. In fact, it supports just the kind of multilayered institutional order I have proposed.

[. . .]

Given a human right to equal opportunity for political participation so conceived, the proper vertical distribution of sovereignty is determined by considerations of three kinds. The first favor decentralization, the second centralization, while the third may correct the resulting balance in either direction.

First, decision-making should be decentralized as far as possible. This is desirable in part for minimizing the decision-making burdens upon individuals. But there are more important reasons as well. Insofar as decisions are morally closed, outsiders are more likely to lack the knowledge and sensitivities to make responsible judgments – and the only practicable and morally acceptable way of delimiting those who are capable of such judgments is by rough geographical criteria. Insofar as decisions are morally open, the goal must be to optimize persons' equal opportunity to influence the social conditions that shape their life. This opportunity should not be diluted for the sake of enhancing persons' opportunities to influence decisions of merely local significance elsewhere. Perhaps political units should be free to trade such opportunities by mutual consent for the sake of creating common decision-making mechanisms. (Here one must bear in mind that such exchanges are likely to reflect the differential bargaining power of the parties and may thus aggravate existing inequalities.) Such discretionary centralization may be rational, for example, in cases of conflict between local and global rationality (tragedy-of-the-commons cases: fishing, grazing, pollution) and also in regard to desired projects that require many contributors because they involve coordination problems or economies of scale, for example, or because they are simply too expensive (construction and maintenance of transportation and communication systems, research and technology, space programs and so forth).

Considerations of the second kind favor centralization insofar as this is necessary to avoid excluding persons from the making of decisions that significantly and legitimately affect them. The practical unavoidability of such decisions follows directly from Kant's insight that human beings cannot avoid affecting one another: through direct contact and through their impact upon the natural world in which they coexist. The relevant decisions concern two – possibly three – types of issues. First, inhabiting the same natural environment and being significantly affected by what others do to it, our human right to equal opportunity for political participation extends to regulating the use of this environment. In the present global order, most people have no political influence over how the common environment is treated, on resource extraction, for example, or pollution. Second, since the lives of human beings are very significantly shaped by prevailing social institutions – those defining property rights and markets, for instance, and those structuring child rearing and the exercise of political authority – our human right to equal opportunity for a political participation extends to the choice and design of such institutions. The existing international order engenders dangerous arms races, oppressive governments, as well as extreme poverty and inequality which greatly affect all human beings; yet most people have no political influence on the structure of these institutional rules. A right to participate in deciding issues of the third type is more controversial. There are contexts, one might say, in which we act as a species and thus should decide together how to act. Examples might be planned modifications of the human gene pool, conduct toward other biological species (extinction, genetic engineering, cruelty), treatment of the cultural heritage of humankind (ancient skeletons and artifacts, great works of art and architecture places of exceptional natural beauty), and ventures into outer space. In all these cases it would seem wrong for one person, group, or state to take irreversible steps unilaterally.

The significance of considerations of the second kind depends heavily upon empirical matters, though it does so in a rather straightforward and accessible way. These considerations in favor of centralization have clearly become much more significant over the past few centuries. This is so partly because of rising population density, but much more importantly because of heightened global interdependence. Such interdependence is to some extent due to vastly more powerful technologies, which bring it about that what a population does within its own national territory – stockpiling weapons of mass destruction, cutting down vegetation essential for the reproduction of oxygen, emitting pollutants that are destroying the ozone layer and cause global warming – now often imposes very significant harms and risks upon outsiders. These externalities bring into play the political human rights of these outsiders, thereby morally undermining the conventional insistence on an absolute right to national self-determination. [. . .] As persons become ever more heavily affected by the structure of the global economic order, they have an ever stronger moral claim to an equal opportunity for political participation in shaping this order. This claim is not fulfilled when its design is determined by free bargaining among states. For such negotiations do not satisfy the equal-opportunity principle so long as many people are excluded from effective political participation within their state, and many states are much too weak significantly to affect the outcome of such negotiations (e.g. in the context of the WTO).[15]

Taken by themselves, considerations of the first two kinds yield the result that any political decision should rest with the democratic process of a political unit that (i) is as small as possible but still (ii) includes as equals all persons significantly and legitimately affected by this decision. In the real world, these two desiderata must be balanced against each other because there cannot always be an established political unit that includes all and only those significantly affected. A matter affecting the populations of two provinces, for example, might be referred to the national parliament or be left to bargaining between the two provincial governments. The former solution serves (ii) at the expense of (i), involving many persons who are not legitimately affected. The latter solution serves (i) at the expense of (ii), giving the persons legitimately affected not an equal opportunity to influence the matter, but one that depends on the relative bargaining power of the two provincial governments.

Considerations of the first two kinds would suffice on the ideal-theory assumption that any decisions made satisfy all moral constraints with regard to both procedure (the equal-opportunity requirement) and output (human rights). But this assumption is never strictly true. And so consideration of a third kind comes into play: what would emerge as the proper vertical distribution of sovereignty from a balancing of the first two considerations alone should be modified – in either direction – if such modification significantly increases the democratic nature and reliability of the decision-making. Let me briefly outline how considerations of this third kind might make a difference.

On the one hand, one must ask whether it would be a gain for human-rights fulfill-ment on balance to transfer decision-making authority "upward" to larger units – or, perhaps more plausibly, to make the political process of smaller units subject to regula-tion and/or review by the political process of the next more inclusive one. Such author-ity would allow the larger political unit, solely on human-rights grounds, to require revisions in the structure of the political process of the subunit and/or to invalidate its political decisions, and perhaps also to enforce such revisions and invalidations. Even when such a regulation and review authority really does protect human rights, it has some costs in terms of the political human rights of the members of the subunit. But then, of course, the larger unit's regulation and review process may itself be unreliable and thus may produce unfulfilled human rights either by overturning unobjectionable structures or decisions (at even greater cost to the political human-rights of members of the subunit) or by forcing the subunit to adopt structures and decisions that directly lead to unfulfilled human rights.

On the other hand, there is also the less familiar inverse question: whether the third consideration might support a move in the direction of *decentralization*. Thus one must ask to what extent the political process of a larger unit is undemocratic or unreliable, and whether it might be a gain for human-rights fulfillment on balance to transfer decision-making authority "downward" to its subunits – or to invest the political process of such subunits with review authority. Such an authority might, for instance, allow provincial governments, solely on human-rights grounds, to block the application of national laws in their province. This authority is justified if and only if its benefits (laws that were passed in an undemocratic manner or would have led to unfulfilled human rights are not applied) outweigh its costs (unob-jectionable laws are blocked in violation of the political rights of members of the larger unit).

How such matters should be weighed is a highly complex question, which I cannot here address with any precision. Let me make two points nonetheless. First, a good deal of weight should be given to the actual views of those whose human rights are unful-filled and invoked in justification of a vertical shift in authority. If most blacks in some state of the US would rather suffer discrimination than see their state government constrained by the federal government, then the presumption against such an author-ity should be much weightier than if the opposition came only from whites. This is not to deny that victims of injustice may be brainwashed or may suffer from false con-sciousness of various sorts. But it must be shown that this is so; and thus it is harder to make the case for instituting a regulation and/or review authority when its pur-ported beneficiaries are opposed to it.

Second, commonalities of language, religion, ethnicity, or history are irrelevant. Such commonalities do not give people a claim to be part of one another's political lives, nor does the lack of such commonalities argue against restraints. Their presence or absence may still, however, have empirical significance. Thus suppose that the members of some political subunit share religious or ethnic characteristics that in the larger unit are in the minority (e.g. a Muslim province within a predominantly Hindu country). Historical experience with such cases may well suggest that a regulation and review authority by the larger unit would probably be frequently abused or that a review authority by the subunit would tend to enhance human-rights fulfillment overall. The relevance of such information brings out that the required balancing does not depend on value judgments alone. It also depends on empirically grounded expectations about how alternative arrangements would actually work in one or another concrete context.

Considerations of the third kind are also relevant to determining where decisions about the proper allocation of decision-making should be made. For example, there may be disputes between an agency of a larger political unit and an agency of one of its subunits over which of them should be in charge of some specific set of decisions. And the question is then which agency of which political unit ought to be in charge of settling such disputes. Here, again, a particular locus of decision-making must be justified by showing that it is likely to be more reliable in terms of human-rights fulfillment than its alternatives.

Nothing definite can be said about the ideal number of levels or the exact distribution of legislative, executive, and judicial functions over them. These matters might vary in space and time, depending on the prevailing empirical facts relevant to the second and third considerations (externalities, interdependence; unreliability problems) and on persons' preferences as shaped by the historical, linguistic, religious, or other cultural ties among them. Democracy may take many forms, as the human right to equal opportunity for political participation leaves room for a wide variety, hence regional diversity, of decision-making procedures – direct or representative, with or without political parties, and so on. This right does require, however, that the choice and implementation of any such procedure within a political unit be accepted by the majority of its citizens.

The shaping and reshaping of political units

One great advantage of the proposed multilayered order is that it can be reached gradually from where we are now. This requires moderate centralizing and decentralizing moves involving the strengthening of political units above and below the level of the state. In some cases, such units will have to be created, and so we need some idea about how the geographical shape of new political units is to be determined. Or, seeing that there is considerable dissatisfaction about even the geographical shape of existing political units, we should ask more: broadly: what principles ought to govern the geographical delimitation of political units on any level?

Guided again by the human right to equal opportunity for political participation, I suggest these two procedural principles as a first approximation:

1 The inhabitants of any contiguous territory may decide, through some majoritarian or supermajoritarian procedure, to join an existing political unit whose territory is

contiguous with theirs and whose population is willing – as assessed through some majoritarian or supermajoritarian procedure – to accept them as members. This liberty is subject to two conditions: the territory of the newly enlarged political unit must have a reasonable shape; and any newly contracted political unit must either remain viable in a contiguous territory of reasonable shape or be willingly incorporated, pursuant to this same liberty, into another political unit or other political units.

2 The inhabitants of any contiguous territory of reasonable shape, if sufficiently numerous, may decide, through some majoritarian or supermajoritarian procedure, to constitute a new political unit. This liberty is constrained in three ways. First, there may be subgroups whose members are free, pursuant to principle 1, to reject membership in the unit to be formed in favor of membership in another political unit. Second, there may be subgroups whose members are free, pursuant to principle 2, to reject membership in the unit to be formed in favor of forming their own political unit. And third, any newly contracted political unit must either remain viable in a contiguous territory of reasonable shape or be willingly incorporated, pursuant to the first clause of principle 1, into another political unit or other political units.

It will be said that acceptance of such principles would trigger an avalanche of applications. It is surely true that many existing groups are unhappy with their current membership status. There is a significant backlog, so to speak, that might pose a serious short-term problem. But once this backlog had been worked down, attempts at redrawing political borders would become much less frequent as most people would then be content with their political affiliations and most borders would be supported by stable majorities.

Moreover, with the advocated vertical dispersal of sovereignty, conflicts over borders would lose much of their intensity. In our world, many such conflicts are motivated by morally inappropriate considerations – especially the following two. There is competition over valuable or strategically important territories and groups because control over them importantly affects the distribution of international bargaining power (economic and military potential) for the indefinite future. And there are attempts by the more affluent (white South Africans, Slovenes, northern Italians) to separate themselves from people poorer than themselves in order to circumvent widely recognized duties of distributive justice among compatriots. Under the proposed multilayered order – in which the political authority currently exercised by national governments is both constrained and dispersed over several layers, and in which economic justice is institutionalized at the global level and thus inescapable – territorial disputes on any level would be only slightly more intense than disputes about provincial or county lines are now. It is quite possible that my two principles are not suitable for defining a right to secession in our present world of excessively sovereign states.[16] But their plausibility will increase as the proposed second-order decentralization progresses.[17]

[. . .]

The conventional alternatives to voluntaristic principles for settling the borders of political units reserve a special role either for historical states and their citizens (compatriots) or for nations and their members (fellow nationals). The former version is inherently conservative, the latter potentially revisionist (by including, e.g. the Arab, Kurdish, and Armenian nations and by excluding multinational states like the Soviet

Union or the Sudan). The two key claims of such a position are: (a) only (encompassing) groups of compatriots/fellow nationals have a right to self-government in one political unit; (b) the government of such a unit may extend its rule even to areas inhabited by unwilling subgroups of compatriots/fellow nationals, who are to have at most a right of individual emigration. Those who hold such a conventional position are liable to reject the cosmopolitan view as excessively individualist, contractualist, or voluntaristic. Examples of this sentiment are easy to find: "the more important human groupings need to be based on shared history, and on criteria of nonvoluntaristic (or at least not wholly contractarian) membership to have the value that they have."[18] Insofar as this is an empirical claim – about the preconditions of authentic solidarity and mutual trust, perhaps – I need not disagree with it. If indeed a political unit is far more valuable for its members when they share a common descent and upbringing (language, religion, history, culture), then people will recognize this fact and will themselves seek to form political units along these lines. It is quite possible that the groups seeking to change their political status under the two principles would for the most part be groups characterized by such unchosen commonalities.

But would I not allow any other group to change its political status, even if this means exchanging a more valuable for a less valuable membership? Margalit and Raz ridicule this idea through their examples of "the Tottenham Football Club supporters," "the fiction-reading public," and "the group of all the people whose surnames begin with a 'g' and end with an 'e.' "[19] Yet these cases – apart from being extremely unlikely to arise – are ruled out by the contiguity requirement, which a "voluntarist" can and, I think, should accept in light of the key function of government: to support common rules among persons who cannot avoid influencing one another through direct interaction and through their impact upon a shared environment. A more plausible example would then be that of the inhabitants of a culturally and linguistically Italian border village who prefer an *ex hypothesi* less valuable membership in France over a more valuable membership in Italy. Here I ask: do they not, France willing, have a right to err? Or should they be forced to remain, or to become, Italians against their will?

This example brings out the underlying philosophical value conflict. Institutional moral cosmopolitanism is committed to the freedom of individual persons and therefore envisions a pluralist global order. Such an institutional order is compatible with political units whose membership is homogeneous with respect to some partly unchosen features (nationality, ethnicity, native language, history, religion, etc.), and it would certainly engender such units. But it would do so only insofar as persons *choose* to share their political life with others who are like themselves in such respects. It would not entitle persons to partake in one another's political life merely because they share certain unchosen features.

One strategy for justifying the conventional alternative involves rejecting the individualist premise that only human beings are ultimate units of moral concern.[20] One could then say that, once the moral claims of states/nations are taken into account alongside those of persons, one may well find that, all things considered, justice requires institutional arrangements that are inferior, in human-rights terms, to feasible alternatives – institutional arrangements, for example, under which the interest of Italy in its border village would prevail over the villagers' interest in deciding about their own citizenship.

This justificatory strategy faces two main problems. It is unclear how states/nations can have interests or moral claims that are not reducible to interests and moral claims of their members (which can be accommodated within a conception of human rights). This idea smacks of bad metaphysics,[21] and also is dangerously subject to political and ideological manipulations, as exemplified by Charles de Gaulle, who was fond of adducing the interests of *la nation* against those of his French compatriots. Moreover, it is unclear why this idea should work here, but not in the case of other kinds of sub- and supranational political units, not in that of religious, cultural, and athletic entities. Why need we not also take into account the moral claims of Catholicism, art, or soccer?

These problems suggest the other justificatory strategy, which accepts the individualist premise but then formulates the political rights of persons with essential reference to the state/nation whose members they are. This strategy has been defended, most prominently, by Michael Walzer, albeit in a treatise that focuses on international ethics (interactions) rather than international justice (social institutions). Walzer approvingly quotes Westlake: "The duties and rights of states are nothing more than the duties and rights of the men who compose them," adding "the rights . . . [to] territorial integrity and political sovereignty . . . belong to states, but they derive ultimately from the rights of individuals, and from them they take their force. . . . States are neither organic wholes nor mystical unions."[22]

The key question is, of course, how such a derivation is supposed to work. There are two possibilities. The direct route would be to postulate either a human right to be jointly governed with one's compatriots/fellow nationals,[23] or a human right to participate in the exercise of sovereignty over one's compatriots/fellow nationals. The former of these rights is implausibly demanding upon others (the Bavarians can insist on being part of Germany, even if all the other Germans were to want nothing to do with them) and would still fail to establish claim (b), unless it were also unwaivable – a duty, really. The latter right is implausibly demanding upon those obligated to continue to abide by the common will merely because they have once, however violently, been incorporated into a state or merely because they have once shared solidarity and sacrifices.

The indirect, instrumental route would involve the empirical claim that human rights (on a noneccentric definition) are more likely to be fulfilled, or are fulfilled to a greater extent, if there is, for each person, one political unit that decisively shapes her life and is dominated by her compatriots/fellow nationals. This route remains open on my cosmopolitan conception (via the third consideration), though the relevant empirical claim would not seem to be sustainable on the historical record.

If this empirical claim indeed fails, then the institutional moral cosmopolitanism here proposed would favor a global order in which sovereignty is widely distributed vertically while the geographical shape of political units is determined, in accordance with principles 1 and 2, by the autonomous decisions of the person concerned.

Conclusion

From our angle, the world seems in good shape. We live in clean and healthy surroundings, economically and physically secure under an alliance of governments that have "won the Cold War." We have every reason to be content with the global order we have shaped. But resting content with it is doubly myopic. It ignores that we are only 15 percent of humankind: much larger numbers must live, despite hard work, on incomes with $\frac{1}{50}$ the purchasing power of ours and hence in constant confrontation with infant mortality, child labor, hunger, squalor, and disease. Fully one-third of all human beings still die from poverty-related causes. In view of such massive deprivations and unprecedented inequalities, we cannot decently avoid reflection on global institutional reform.

Resting content with the status quo also ignores the future. More and more, the transnational imposition of externalities and risks is becoming a two-way street, as no state or group of states, however rich and well armed, can effectively insulate itself from external influences – from military and terrorist attacks, illegal immigrants, epidemics and the drug trade, pollution and climate change, price fluctuations as well as scientific, technological, and cultural innovations.

Bringing these potentially highly disruptive risks and externalities under effective control requires a global institutional reform with significant reductions in national sovereignty. To be morally acceptable and politically feasible, such reform must be capable of functioning without heavy and continuing enforcement and hence must bring to poorer societies not merely a reduction in their formal sovereignty, but also economic sufficiency and democratic governance. [. . .]

Notes

1   One argument for a world state is advanced in Nielsen, "World Government, Security, and Global Justice."
2   I have in mind here a rather minimal conception of human rights, one that rules out truly severe abuses, deprivations, and inequalities while still being compatible with a wide range of political, moral, and religious cultures.
3   This is done, for example, by Rawls, who asserts both a natural duty to uphold just social institutions as well as various other natural duties that do not presuppose shared social institutions, such as duties to avoid injury and cruelty, duties to render mutual aid, and a duty to bring about just social institutions where none presently exist. See Rawls, *A Theory of Justice*, pp. 98–9 and 293–4.
4   These two limitations are compatible with the belief that we have a duty to *create* a comprehensive institutional order. Thus Kant believed that any persons and groups who cannot avoid affecting one another ought to enter into a juridical condition See *Kant's Political Writings*, pp. 73.
5   The explanatory move urged in this fictitious interjection is common among social theorists and philosophers.
6   Walzer, *Spheres of Justice*, p. 31.
7   Nozick, *Anarchy, State and Utopia*, p. 149.
8   This means that A has no supervisor with authority to give directives with regard to A's exercise of authority over B. Unsupervised authority in this sense is compatible with judicial review.
9   Many individuals might, of course, identify more with one of their citizenships than with the others. But in a multilayered order such prominent identifications would be less frequent and, most important, would not converge: Even if some residents of Glasgow would see themselves as primarily British, others would identify more with Europe, with Scotland, with Glasgow, or with humankind at large.
10 Walzer, *Spheres of Justice*, p. 39.
11 Ibid.
12 Ibid., pp. 38–9.
13 Ibid., p. 39.
14 Ibid.
15 This argument withstands the communitarian claim that we must renounce supranational democratic processes for the sake of safeguarding national self-determination. Such renunciation may indeed enhance the national autonomy of the privileged populations of the developed countries. But their gains in autonomy come at the expense of poorer populations who, despite their legal independence, have virtually no control over the most basic parameters that shape their lives.

16 *This* topic is extensively discussed by Buchanan. He takes the current states system for granted and realistically adjusts his theory of secession to it. Departing from this system, I see yet one more reason for a muitilayered global order in the fact that it would allow implementation of a morally more appealing theory of secession. A more sustained argument for the moral appeal of this theory in terms of democratic self-government is provided in Philpott, "In Defense of Self-Determination." See also Wellman, "A Defense of Secession."

17 For example, as European states continue to transfer important governmental functions to international organizations such as the EU and to subnational political units, the conflict over whether there should be one or two states in the present territory of Belgium will become ever less important – for the two cultural groups as well as for any third parties.

18 Margalit and Raz, "National Self-Determination," p. 456.

19 Margalit and Raz, "National Self-Determination," pp. 443 and 456.

20 For an example, see Barry, "Do Countries Have Moral Obligations?," pp. 27–44.

21 Rawls makes this point: "we want to account for the social values, for the intrinsic good of institutional, community, and associative activities, by a conception of justice that in its theoretical basis is individualistic. For reasons of clarity among others, we do not want to . . . suppose that society is an organic whole with a life of its own distinct from and superior to that of all its members in their relations with one another" (*A Theory of Justice*, pp. 233–4).

22 Walzer, *Just and Unjust Wars*, p. 53. See also Walzer, "The Moral Standing of States," p. 219.

23 Walzer suggests this tack: "citizens of a sovereign state have a right, insofar as they are to be ravaged and coerced at all, to suffer only at one another's hands" (*Just and Unjust Wars*, p. 86).

References

Barry, Brian, "Do Countries Have Moral Obligations?" In *The Tanner Lectures on Human Value II*, Edited by S. McMurrin (Salt Lake City: University of Utah Press, 1981).

Buchanan, Allen, *Secession*, (Boulder: Westview Press, 1991).

Kant, Immanuel, *Kant's Political Writings*, Edited by Hans Reiss (Cambridge: Cambridge University Press, 1970).

Margalit, Avishai and Raz, Joseph, "National Self-determination," *Journal of Philosophy*, Vol. 57, (1990): 439–61.

Neilsen, Kai, "World Government, Security, and Global Justice," in *Problems of International Justice*, Edited by Steve Luper-Foy (Boulder: Westview Press, 1988).

Nozick, Robert, *Anarchy, State and Utopia*, (New York: Basic Books, 1974).

Philpott, Daniel, "In Defense of Self-determination," *Ethics*, Vol. 105 (1995): 352–85.

Rawls, John, *A Theory of Justice* (Cambridge: Harvard University Press, 1971).

Walzer, Michael, "The Moral Standing of States," *Philosophy and Public Affairs*, Vol. 9 (1980): 209–29.

Walzer, Michael, *Just and Unjust Wars* (New York: Basic Books, 1983).

Walzer, Michael, *Spheres of Justice* (New York: Basic Books, 1983).

Wellman, Christopher, "A Defense of Secession and Political Self-determination," *Philosophy and Public Affairs*, Vol. 24 (1995): 142–71.

8

International Distributive Justice
Simon Caney

Political philosophers have traditionally assumed that ideals of distributive justice should operate if they operate at all within countries. On this view principles of distributive justice should be adopted at the state-level or nation-level and may require the redistribution of wealth from the wealthy within the state or nation to the less advantaged members of that society. The standard assumption thus has been that what has been called the "scope of justice" – the account specifying *from whom* and *to whom* goods should be distributed – should include other members of one's state or one's nation.[1] It should not however, include everyone. Recently, however this assumption has been vigorously challenged and a number of political philosophers have argued that there are global principles of justice. Principles of distributive justice, that is, should have a global scope.

This review article examines recent work on international distributive justice. Within the literature on global justice one can distinguish between a number of competing approaches. In this article, I shall focus on four commonly expressed approaches. In particular I shall examine the *cosmopolitan* contention that distributive principles should operate globally (first section) before then examining three responses to this position, namely the *nationalist* emphasis on special duties to fellow-nationals (second section) the *society-of-states* claim that principles of global distributive justice violate the independence of states (third section) and *realist* claims that global justice is utopian and that states should advance the national interest (fourth section).

Cosmopolitanism

[. . .] let us begin with contemporary defences of global principles of distributive justice. Recently a number of political philosophers – including Brian Barry, Charles Beitz, Thomas Pogge among others – have advocated what has come to be known as a cosmopolitan position, arguing that principles of distributive justice should be applied to the world as a whole.[2] Duties of distributive justice thus apply to all human beings. To get a full picture of the cosmopolitan perspective and the various forms it takes, it is important to bear four further points in mind.

First, it is important to distinguish between what might be termed "radical" and "mild" cosmopolitanism.[3] Radical cosmopolitanism, as I define it makes the two following claims: first there are global principles of distributive justice (tire positive claim), and, second, there are no state-wide or nation-wide principles of distributive justice (tire negative claim). Mild cosmopolitanism by contrast simply affirms the positive claim. As such it can accept the claim, denied by radical cosmopolitanism that people have special obligations of distributive justice to fellow nationals or fellow citizens. Now cosmopolitans differ in their position here. Whereas some like Charles Beitz, do affirm the radical view that "state boundaries can have derivative, but they cannot have fundamental, moral importance" (Beitz, 1988, p. 92, cf also Beitz, 1999c, p. 182), others, like Brian Barry, Martha Nussbaum and Amartya Sen do not (Barry, 1999, p. 59; Nussbaum, 1996, pp. 9 and 13; Sen, 1996, pp. 112–5).

Secondly, it is worth noting Thomas Pogge's distinction between "institutional" and "interactive" forms of cosmopolitanism. The former maintains that principles of justice concern the distribution of resources within institutions and the focus of attention is on the fairness of the institution(s). The latter, on the other hand, maintains that principles of justice concern the behaviour of individuals and one has obligations to other humans independently of whether they are members of the same institutions or not.[4] Pogge defends the institutional approach and argues that given the degree of international economic interdependence, there is a global basic structure and hence that there are global principles of distributive justice (1994a, pp. 91–7). Other cosmopolitans, however, most notably consequentialists like Peter Singer would claim that persons can have obligations to help others even if those others do not belong to the same institutions (1972, pp. 229–43).

A third feature of contemporary cosmopolitan accounts of distributive justice concerns *who* is entitled to the goods transferred. Here it is clear that most contemporary cosmopolitans affirm that duties are owed to individuals (and not states). This, for example is made clear by Beitz (1999c, pp. 152–3) and Pogge (1994b, p. 202). An alternative view has been taken by Barry who once argued that states were entitled to receive resources (1991c, pp. 203–8; 1991d, pp. 239–40). In recent publications, however, he rejects this position. And indeed given cosmopolitanism's individualist assumptions, his later position is most in keeping with cosmopolitan tenets (Barry, 1998, pp. 159–60; 1999, pp. 35–40).

Finally, it is worth drawing attention to the practical measures affirmed by contemporary cosmopolitans. These vary considerably. Some like Beitz (1999c, pp. 150–3) and David Richards (1982, pp. 287–93 (especially pp. 292–3)) have endorsed a global difference principle arguing that is, that resources should be distributed to maximize the condition of the least well-off humans. Others like Hillel Steiner have argued that everyone is entitled to an equal proportion of the Earth's resources (1994, pp. 235–6, 262–5, 270; 1999, pp. 173–7). Barry has defended four principles of global justice. These require in turn, that we affirm (i) an overridable commitment to equality, (ii) a principle compensating people for involuntary disadvantages, (iii) a commitment to protecting people's basic needs, and (iv) the claim that where these three principles are already met we may prefer that arrangement which is most mutually advantageous (Barry, 1998, pp. 147–9). Finally Pogge has defended what he terms the global resources dividend – a scheme under which persons pay a dividend when they use the Earth's natural resources (Pogge, 1994b, pp. 199–205; 1992a, pp. 96–7; 1998, pp 501–36). Space precludes a full examination of the respective merits and demerits of the various schemes proposed. What is more important is that they all have in common the conclusion that the current system is extremely unjust and that a redistribution of wealth from the affluent to the impoverished is required.

Now that we have an approximate understanding of the claims advanced by contemporary cosmopolitans we need to examine the reasoning underlying their position. Here it is instructive to consider what leading cosmopolitans – like Barry, Beitz and Pogge – claim are the central tenets of cosmopolitanism. They all argue that cosmopolitanism contains (and derives its plausibility from) the following intuitively appealing claims: (a) individuals have moral worth, (b) they have this equally, and (c) people's equal moral worth generates moral reasons that are binding on everyone.[5] Now, as they then point out, if we accept these (very plausible) ethical claims it would be mysterious to claim that the duties imposed by a theory of justice should include only fellow citizens or fellow-nationals (van den Anket, 1998, pp. 8–9). These universalist considerations imply that the scope of distributive justice should be global.

Cosmopolitans develop this point further by analysing the moral relevance of cultural identities. As Pogge, among others, points out, on all accounts of justice no reference is made to someone's ethnic identity or their status or their sex. These are all deemed to be irrelevant. But then given this, it is puzzling why these are morally irrelevant but someone's membership of a nation or state is relevant.[6] Furthermore, as Samuel Black, Charles Jones and Robert Goodin all point out, the considerations standardly adduced to defend redistribution refer to features (like the capacity for autonomy) that are possessed by humans throughout the world. Thus, if we invoke such considerations to defend redistribution they justify it to all who possess these properties whether they are fellow nationals or not.[7] In short the fundamental thesis advanced by contemporary cosmopolitans states that:

> the *principal cosmopolitan claim*: given the reasons we give to defend the distribution of resources and given our convictions about the irrelevance of people's cultural identity to their entitlements: it follows that the scope of distributive justice should be global.

To employ a Rawlsian term, the *principal cosmopolitan claim* makes a claim about peoples' "moral personality" (1999b, pp. 11, 17, 442–6). In stating that all persons (whatever their creed, culture, ethnicity or nation) should be included in the scope of justice, it affirms a universalist moral personality according to which none of these factors is ethically relevant.

This cosmopolitan claim can be found throughout recent cosmopolitan literature generally and in all of the many different arguments given in defence of the redistribution of wealth throughout the world. To see this, we need to consider some of the different cosmopolitan theories advanced, focusing on (a) contractarian, (b) rights-based, and (c) goal-based brands of cosmopolitan justice.[8]

A: The contractarian version

Beitz is famous for employing Rawls's contractarian device – the original position – and arguing that instead of asking what people in individual societies would agree to, one should hold a global original position. Although he once argued in *Political Theory and International Relations* that everyone should be included in a global original position on the grounds (i) that principles of justice should dictate the distribution of goods generated by a system of co-operation (1999c, p. 131) and (ii) that there now existed a global system of economic co-operation (1999c, pp. 144–52, 154), he has rejected this argument. In its place, Beitz argued that everyone should be included in a global hypothetical contract because the morally relevant features of humans are universal properties like their capacity for forming and revising their conception of the good and that their nationality is not morally significant (Beitz, 1983, pp. 593, 595–6). The *principal cosmopolitan claim* is also affirmed by Richards who writes that one should adopt a global original position because "one's membership in one nation as opposed to another and the natural inequality among nations may be as morally fortuitous as any other natural fact" (1982, p. 290, see also 1982, pp. 278–82, 289–93). The same point is sustained if we consider the brand of contractarian cosmopolitanism defended by Barry. Drawing on Thomas Scanlon's model of contractualism, Barry argues that just principles are principles that no person in a global hypothetical contract could reasonably reject (1998, pp. 146–7). Now, as Barry would happily agree, this device – a hypothetical contract which includes everyone – is legitimate only if we assume that everyone (independently of ethnicity and nationality) should be consulted. As Barry explicitly points out, he views his brand of contractarianism as the best way of giving content to the idea of impartial treatment that underlies moral cosmopolitanism (1998, p. 146). The *principal cosmopolitan thesis* is also present in David Held's contractarian vindication of his cosmopolitan account of distributive justice. In his important and influential *Democracy and the Global Order*, Held affirms an ideal of autonomy (1995, pp. 145–56). He argues, moreover, that we can explicate the implications of this ideal by employing a "democratic thought experiment" in which we ask what free and equal persons would agree to (1995, pp. 160–7, especially pp. 161–2). On this basis, he defends seven kinds of core right to protect and enable people to engage in autonomous action (1995, pp. 191–201, especially pp. 192–4). Held's democratic principle is however, as he makes clear predicated on a commitment to the cosmopolitan principle that *all persons* have a right to autonomy.[9] Held's contractarian argument, thus like the other contractarian arguments for global principles of distributive justice, articulates and embodies the *principal cosmopolitan thesis* defended above.

B: The rights based version

The same point can be made about the rights-based cosmopolitan theories of justice defended by Pogge, Shue, Steiner and most recently Charles Jones. Although their work differs in a number of respects, what they have in common is the belief that all humans have rights, and among these rights are rights to economic resources. Thus in his important and influential *Basic Rights*, Shue argues that if we accept civil and political rights we should also accept subsistence rights as well since the latter are essential for the former.[10] In his *Global Justice*, Jones also defends subsistence rights, arguing that they protect important human interests (Jones, 1999, Chapter 3). A rather different rights-based position is defended by Steiner who argues that everyone has a right to equal freedom and accordingly each is entitled to an equal amount of the Earth's resources (1994, pp. 235–6, 262–5, 270). Finally, Pogge has written a number of important papers which defend global economic rights. In particular he is keen to provide a defence of welfare rights such as Article 25 (1) of the Universal Declaration of Human Rights which states that everyone has the right to a standard of living adequate for the health and well-being of himself and of his family, including food, clothing, housing and medical care and necessary social services . . .[11] Now my aim here is not to evaluate these individual theories. It is to record that in each we find the principal cosmopolitan claim outlined above – namely the claim that a person's nationality or citizenship should not determine their entitlements. Both Pogge and Steiner, for instance, make explicit their commitment to the latter in their writings on distributive justice (Pogge, 1989, p. 247; Pogge, 1994b, p. 198; and Steiner, 1994, pp. 262, 265).

C: Goal-based versions

The most famous of the goal-based theories of justice is, of course, utilitarianism. So it is worth pointing out that from a utilitarian perspective, justice demands that the welfare of *all* human beings should be factored in and maximized. According to such a theory what matters is people's welfare and no reference is made to people's citizenship or nationality except insofar as these affect people's level of utility. This is clear in the work of utilitarians like Singer (1972). Underlying his moral theory is a commitment to moral equality and this requires that principles of justice incorporate everyone's utility (1979, pp. 14–23, especially p. 23) Accordingly he criticizes the idea that people should allocate aid to those who are of the same race on the grounds that race is irrelevant, adding that "[t]he same point applies to citizenship or nationhood. [I]t would be arbitrary to decide that only those fortunate enough to be citizens of our own community will share in our surplus" (1977, p. 43. See also 1979, pp. 171–2).

It is also worth recording here that non-utilitarian consequentialist cosmopolitan theories of distributive justice are also animated by the same principles. Richard Falk, for example, presents such a theory in his recent work *On Humane Governance* in which he argues that people's basic needs and fundamental interests should be met. On his account of justice, the current global system is deeply unfair for two reasons: *first*, it permits poverty, infant mortality, oppression and militarization (what Falk terms "avoidable harm") (1995, pp. 55–74) and *second*, it permits environmental degradation (what he terms "eco-imperialism") (1995, pp. 74–8). Central again to this cosmopolitan theory, therefore, is the claim that persons have needs and their citizenship or nationality is not pertinent to whether these needs should be met.

From this brief survey of contemporary brands of cosmopolitanism we can see then *both*, (1) that there is a great variety of different cosmopolitan theories of distributive justice *but* also (2) that they are united in their commitment to an account of "moral personality" according to which, people's entitlements are independent of their culture, race, and nationality. The same point would I believe be sustained if we analysed other recent defences of cosmopolitanism – like Philippe van Parijs's vindication of an unconditional basic income "for all" (van Parijs, 1995, pp. 227–8) and Onora O'Neill's distinguished contributions in her *Towards Justice and Virtue* (1996) and *Bounds of Justice* (2000). Many, however, have expressed misgivings about the cosmopolitan ideal and in the remaining sections of this review I shall examine some of these misgivings.

Nationalism

Let us start with those who emphasize the moral relevance of membership in a nation. Recent years have seen a number of important defences of a nationalist perspective, including David Miller's *On Nationality* (1995) and Yael Tamir's *Liberal Nationalism* (1993). In this section I shall examine the nationalist perspective on international distributive justice. Before we do so, however, we must address the question of how to define a nation since the cogency of the nationalist position depends on having a clear understanding of the entity in question. Miller and Tamir make it clear that nations are, for them, distinct from both states and ethnic groups.[12] What then is a nation? Miller provides the fullest characterization, defining a nation as "a community (1) constituted by shared belief and mutual commitment, (2) extended in history, (3) active in character, (4) connected to a particular territory, and (5) marked off from other communities by its distinct public culture" (1995, p. 27).[13] No reference is therefore made to either a common membership of a state or a common ethnic identity.

Having analysed the concept of a nation, we may evaluate the claims advanced by nationalists. Within contemporary nationalist political theory one can find three claims: what might be termed the "national duties" thesis, the "viability" thesis and the "allocation of duty" thesis which I examine in turn.

A: The "national duties" thesis

Many contemporary nationalists argue that cosmopolitanism is flawed because it fails to recognize the ethical ties generated by membership of a nation. More precisely, they argue that cosmopolitans overlook the following claim:

> the *national duties* thesis: individuals bear special obligations of distributive justice to other members of their nation.

This claim is strongly affirmed by both Miller and Tamir, who are keen to emphasize the local obligations one has to fellow nationals (Miller, 1995, Chapter 3, pp. 83–5, 98; Tamir, 1993, pp. 104–11). Why, however, should we accept this argument? Sometimes nationalists are content simply to argue that we should accept this claim on the grounds that it is intuitively plausible – an argument that has met with much criticism.[14]

Some, however, have proffered other considerations in support of their claim that individuals are subject to obligations of distributive justice to other members of their nation. In his contribution to an edited volume on *The Morality of Nationalism*, Jeff McMahan, for example, has defended the *national duties* thesis on the grounds: first, that individuals have special duties to others if they engage in a joint cooperative system and second that a nation is such a system (1997, p. 129). It is also interesting to note that Miller appeals on several occasions to the concept of "reciprocity" in his defence of special obligations (1995, pp. 65–7).

Some, like Barry, have criticized this argument claiming that it actually supports obligations to fellow-citizens rather than fellow-nationals (1996, p. 431). This also receives some support from Richard Dagger, who in *Civic Virtues* invokes what he terms the "argument from reciprocity" to defend special duties to fellow citizens (1997, pp. 46–60 (especially pp. 46–8, 59–60)). More radically, the central problem with this argument, however, is that it is implausible to think of nations as systems of reciprocity. Members of nations do not participate in any common enterprise. Many, for example, live overseas; others do not engage in any co-operation since they are handicapped; others live in multi-national states and engage in co-operation with people from different nations.

It is also worth recording here that even if the "national duties" thesis is vindicated, this would not contradict the cosmopolitan position. It simply challenges the negative claim affirmed by some cosmopolitans but does not challenge the positive cosmopolitan thesis that there are global principles of justice. This last point is important because it shows that the common perception of nationalism and cosmopolitanism as being straightforwardly incompatible is simplistic. Of course, even if the national duties thesis and the cosmopolitan claim that there are global principles of distributive justice are compatible, nationalists and cosmopolitans can disagree in several ways. First, they might disagree on the *content* of the cosmopolitan claim. Nationalists might tend to defend more minimal cosmopolitan principles. Second, they might disagree on the *ranking* of national duties in relation to cosmopolitan duties. The point remains, however, that cosmopolitan claims that individuals have duties to everyone are consistent with nationalist claims that they are under special duties to others of their nation.

B: The "viability" thesis

Let us turn to a second claim advanced by some nationalists who have expressed misgivings about the viability of global systems of distributive justice. Miller, for example, has argued that people must be willing to comply with a system of justice if it is to be successfully implemented. He then argues that people will adhere to such systems when that involves redistributing to fellow-nationals but they are not willing to see their money go to foreigners. Given this, cosmopolitan accounts of distributive justice should be rejected. We should therefore accept the following:

> the *viability* thesis: this states that systems of distributive justice, to be feasible, must map onto national communities and hence that global systems of distributive justice are unworkable.

Cosmopolitans can and do, however, make a number of replies to this argument. First, as Beitz (1994) and Pogge (1994a) argue, what cosmopolitans are committed to are certain moral criteria and not any specific political policies or institutional structures. Thus even if nationalists are right to argue that global institutional schemes for redistribution are simply not viable this does not undermine the moral claims affirmed by cosmopolitans. Cosmopolitans can simply reply that we should adopt whichever feasible system closest approximates their standards. Secondly, it is worth questioning the model of human motivation this argument employs. The viability argument presupposes an ahistorical and unchanging account of human nature assuming that we are necessarily only willing to make sacrifices for fellow-nationals. As Robert Goodin and others have pointed out, however, such an account is too static and neglects the fact that people's willingness to adhere to principles depends considerably on political institutions, the behaviour of others and prevalent social norms.[15] After all, in earlier periods in history the idea that people would identify with and be willing to make sacrifices for a group of 58 million would have seemed quite fantastic. It would therefore be erroneous simply to make the *a priori* assumption that the motivations people currently have are invariant. Third, and relatedly, the viability thesis relies on an impoverished moral psychology, assuming that people are motivated solely by loyalties and attachments to members of their community. It thereby underestimates people's ability to be motivated by their moral values. People might for example, seek to combat something (like apartheid or landmines or cruelty to animals or child abuse) not because they necessarily share the same identity as the oppressed (or feel themselves to be part of the same community) but because of their commitment to principles of universal rights. Given this, however, it seems reasonable to suggest, against Miller (1995, pp. 57–8), that people may be motivated by cosmopolitan distributive ideals. Consider, in this light, Falk's claim that the current world order is a form of "global apartheid" and is analogous in morally relevant ways to South African apartheid (1995, pp. 49–55). It does not seem far fetched to me to think that showing that this analogy holds may affect people's behaviour. By employing analogies like this, cosmopolitan ideals can harness already existing powerful motivations.

Finally, we should note that in his most recent work, Miller himself has propounded three principles of international distributive justice. These include a principle of human rights, a commitment to non-exploitation and a commitment to provide political communities with enough to be self-determining (2000b, pp. 174–8). It is difficult, however, to square these commitments with the viability thesis and Miller must explain why these escape his general criticism.

C: The "allocation of duty" thesis

A third thesis does not deny the cosmopolitan contention that people have entitlements as specified by a global theory of justice. But it does take exception to the claim that everyone has the same duties to ensure that people receive their just entitlements. It makes the following claim:

> the *allocation of duty* thesis: nations have special duties to ensure that their members receive their just entitlements as defined by a cosmopolitan theory of distributive justice.

Miller, for example, defends this claim in *On Nationality*. He agrees with Shue's (cosmopolitan) claim that individuals have a human right to liberty, security and subsistence but he maintains that the duty to ensure that people receive their entitlements belongs mainly to fellow-nationals (1995, pp. 74–7, cf also 1999, pp. 200–2). Again this illustrates the point that the contrast between cosmopolitanism and nationalism is more complex than is normally imagined since Miller's claim does not challenge the cosmopolitan affirmation of rights. Furthermore, the claim that not everyone has a duty to ensure that other people receive their cosmopolitan entitlements is also made by cosmopolitans like Shue – although he would not claim that nations have special duties to protect their own member's rights (Shue, 1988, pp. 687–704).

Miller's claim that the duties to ensure that people receive their just entitlements should not be borne equally by everyone is plausible. His argument for the "allocation of duty" thesis is, however, unpersuasive. He defends his claim that individuals should promote the basic rights of their fellow-nationals on the following grounds: (PI) Human beings have certain basic rights (P2) Individuals are under special obligations to their fellow-nationals. *Therefore*, (C) Individuals are under a special obligation to ensure that their fellow-nationals' basic rights are observed. Thus he writes: "*Who* has the obligation to protect these basic rights? Given what has been said so far about the role of shared identities in generating obligations, we must suppose that it falls in the first place on the national and smaller local communities to which the rights-bearer belongs" (1995, p. 75).

This argument, however, fails for two reasons. First, (P1) and (P2) do not imply (C). One can, for example, accept both premises and deny (C). Just because X has a right to alpha and I have a duty to X, does not show that I have a duty to provide X with alpha. Suppose for example, that a married man, A, has a right to a job. Now, A's spouse, we believe, has special duties to A. These two claims do not, however, imply that the central responsibility for ensuring that A's right is observed should be borne by his wife. A second problem with this argument is that it succeeds only if we also accept the "national duty" thesis's claim that individuals bear special obligations of distributive justice to co-nationals and as I have argued above, this thesis is implausible.

The society of states approach

Having examined cosmopolitan and nationalist perspectives on global justice, it is worth discussing a third recent approach to global justice. According to what I have termed the "society of states" approach, international justice requires that sovereign states respect other states' independence. Accordingly they should not seek to implement cosmopolitan ideals of distributive justice which some states would reject (Nardin, 1983). More recently similar claims have also been made by Rawls first in his Amnesty Lecture on "The Law of Peoples" (1993a, pp. 41–82) and then in his book also called *The Law of Peoples* (1999a). Although many cosmopolitan theories of justice have been influenced by Rawls, he himself rejects such an approach. He eschews defences of civil, political and economic rights that invoke the principal cosmopolitan claim (1999a, pp. 68, 81, 119–20). In their stead he presents international principles which, he argues are fair because they would be adopted by liberal and decent non-liberal societies.

Rawls's theory has four important features. First, at its heart is the concept of a "people." Rawls argues that this should not be confused with the concept of a state and he would thus resist the description of his theory as defending a society of states (1999a, pp. 17, 23–30, 35, 44–5). Two points should be made here: first, Rawls operates with a very idiosyncratic conception of "states". He defines states as necessarily being entitled to (a) pursue their national interest no matter what its impact is on non-citizens and (b) treat their own subjects as they see fit (1999a, pp. 25–7, 35). States, says Rawls, lack "moral motives" (1999a, p. 17) being concerned only with their own power and wealth (1999a, p. 28). However, neither (a) nor (b) is a defining feature of the "state" as it is ordinarily used: we can make perfect sense of liberal reasonable tolerant states. Second, his discussion of "peoples" throughout *The Law of Peoples* ascribes to them the standard features of states as normally defined. Thus peoples have (i) political institutions (1999a, p. 23), (ii) governments (1999a, pp. 3, 23–4, 26) and (iii) electoral systems and constitutions (1999a, p. 24).[16] Rawls's protestations notwithstanding then, it is fair to define his position as affirming a Society of morally respectable States.

The second essential feature of Rawls's position concerns his distinction between five types of society, namely: "liberal peoples", decent peoples, outlaw states, "societies burdened by unfavorable conditions" and "benevolent absolutisms" (1999a, p. 4). These are defined as follows: *liberal peoples* endorse the core freedoms, deem them to be of great value and distribute economic resources to their needy citizens (1999a, p. 14, see also pp. 49–51). *Decent peoples* are societies that Rawls deems to be morally acceptable societies although they are not liberal. He outlines one kind of decent people, that is, decent hierarchical peoples. These (i) adopt a non-expansionist foreign policy, and (ii) for their domestic policy recognize some basic rights, treat their subjects as members of a co-operative system, act according to an ideal of the common good and incorporate some consultation in their political processes (1999a, pp. 63–78). *Outlaw states* are those societies committed to aggression which do not abide by norms of respect (1999a, pp. 4–5). This leaves *burdened societies* (those societies that are unable to be well-ordered because they face unfavourable economic or cultural circumstances) (1999a, pp. 4–5) and *benevolent absolutisms* (1999a, p. 4).

The third important feature of Rawls's argument is his stipulation that fair principles are those that would be adopted by liberal and decent societies. Rawls defends this stipulation on the grounds that there are morally respectable forms of political society other than liberal ones and they should be tolerated. It is thus quite wrong for egalitarian liberals to argue (in the manner suggested by the thinkers analysed in the first section) that their egalitarian principles of justice should govern the global economy.

This leaves the fourth and final part of Rawls's theory, his proposed principles of international justice. Liberal and decent hierarchical societies, Rawls states, would endorse the following: (1) the freedom of peoples, (2) keeping treaties, (3) the equality of peoples, (4) non-intervention, (5) self-defence, (6) human rights, (7) principles of just warfare, and (8) a duty to assist burdened societies (1999a, p. 37). Two principles are especially important here. First, liberal and hierarchical societies are committed to human rights and these include, for Rawls, subsistence rights (1999a, p. 65; and, more generally on human rights, see pp. 78–81). Second, liberal and hierarchical societies accept an obligation to help burdened societies develop into internally just regimes. This duty of assistance, however, does not necessarily require the transfer of resources Rawls asserts three guidelines about honouring this duty. These are first, that wealth is not essential for a well-ordered society; second, that what is important is a country's political culture; and third that the rationale for any assistance is that it enables societies to operate in a "decent" fashion (1999a, pp. 106–12).

Rawls's work is suggestive and it is not possible to do justice to its claims in such a short space. In what follows I want simply to draw attention to some aspects that are open to criticism. Four areas are worthy of enquiry. One major problem concerns Rawls's justification for eschewing "liberal" ideals of distributive justice, namely his desire to avoid foisting liberal values on other societies who do not affirm these values. This commitment is what animates his theory of international justice and he explicitly rejects global norms that rely on the *principal cosmopolitan* analysed in section I (1999a, pp. 65, 81). This argument is, however, vulnerable in two ways: first, it is incomplete. Liberal and hierarchical societies can accept Rawls's eight principles only because he defines both types of society to do so. In other words, the argument is made prior to the contract.[41] Given this, before we accept the moral legitimacy of what liberal and hierarchical peoples consent to, we need to be given a reason why they both represent morally acceptable forms of society. Rawls, however, does not provide any such argument and without this we do not have any reason to accept his conclusions. Secondly, and relatedly, Rawls's contract is ad hoc. Both liberal and hierarchical societies are defined as being committed to some rights (1999a, pp. 37, 69). But Rawls gives us no reason for his inclusion of some rights or his exclusion of others. As Thomas McCarthy has pointed out, he is sometimes willing to be ethnocentric and other times he is not (1997, p. 212). Without giving a reason for his commitment to some ideals (like freedom of conscience) but not to others (like equality of opportunity) his account is criterionless and arbitrary. And his rejection of more substantive liberal cosmopolitan proposals is undermined.[17]

A second problem concerns his rejection of more expansive forms of global redistribution. Why would peoples not agree to more global redistribution? One reason is that Rawls defines peoples in such a way that they will not (1999a, pp. 29, 32, 34, 44–5). But to this we might ask, as Pogge has done, why we should assume that liberal and decent societies have no interest whatsoever in having more resources rather than less? (Pogge,

1994b, pp. 208–11). Why, in particular, would members of liberal societies want more primary goods in the domestic contract but not want more primary goods in the international contract? (Pogge, 1994b, pp. 210–11; Wenar, 2001, p. 88). Furthermore, even if one works within the motivations Rawls specifies, there are three reasons why the societies in a Rawlsian international contract would choose greater international redistribution. First, Rawls says that the parties wish to preserve their equal standing (1999a, p. 115); however as Beitz and Buchanan argue, given that genuine independence requires material wealth the parties can argue that political equality and independence require redistribution (Beitz, 2000, pp. 693–4; Buchanan, 2000, pp. 708–10, 711–15). Second, Rawls says that the parties wish to protect their self-respect (1999a, p. 114); again, however, this can justify global redistribution for, as Beitz, Buchanan and Wenar argue, international inequalities can corrode self-respect (Beitz, 2000, p. 693; Buchanan, 2000, pp. 708–9; Wenar, 2001, p. 88). Consider, finally, Rawls's account of stability. He maintains that the parties will be concerned about stability and that this will be secured only if the societies in the Society of Peoples each enjoy "success" where success includes "the decent economic wellbeing of all its people" (Rawls, 1999a, p. 45). Again, however, given this, the parties will ensure that distributive principles are in place so that no society is disaffected with the Society of Peoples because of its low (absolute or relative) standard of living. In short, then, Rawls's argument is vulnerable to an imminent critique for even operating within his parameters there are cogent (Rawlsian), arguments for embracing much more egalitarian principles of global justice than the meagre ones that he countenances.

A third vulnerable aspect of Rawls's treatment of international justice concerns his account of the nature of the duties to burdened societies. Rawls, as we have seen, thinks that wealth is not of critical importance and hence wealthy liberal and decent societies are not required to redistribute it. Rawls's analysis is, however, problematic in a number of respects. First, whilst his empirical claim about the insignificance of natural resources may be true, it is a bold and sweeping claim and we do need more empirical confirmation for his contention than he supplies. Rawls cites one book in support of his claim, namely David Landes (1998) *The Wealth and Poverty of Nations* (Rawls, 1999a, p. 117, fn 51). However, for all his emphasis on culture, even Landes explicitly disavows any "monocausal explanations" of growth, stating that "culture does not stand alone" (1998, p. 517). Second, Rawls's claim that domestic factors and not international factors are the prime cause of a society's development can be correct only if the former are unaffected by the latter. But as both Beitz and Pogge observe, a society's political structure and culture may be greatly affected by international factors (Beitz, 1999a, p. 279, more generally, pp. 279–80, 285–6; Beitz, 1999b, p. 525, more generally, pp. 524–6; and Pogge, 1994b, pp. 213–4). To argue that the political structure of a society is the prime determinant of economic growth is therefore highly questionable. Third, and relatedly, in his analysis of the factors influencing a people's standard of living, Rawls concentrates almost exclusively on domestic factors (like the culture of a country) or physical factors (like a country's natural resources). Accordingly as almost all commentators on *The Law of Peoples* observe, he fails to recognize the tremendous role played by transnational phenomena.

The deepest problem, from a cosmopolitan point of view, however, lies in Rawls's assumption that what matters is the condition of societies. He explicitly contrasts his position with the cosmopolitan tenet that political regimes have value only insofar as they serve people's interests (1999a, pp. 119–20). This commitment to the worth of societies independently of their effects on persons, however, seems mysterious and implausible. Why should we care about the condition of a society except insofar as it furthers the interests of persons?

Realism

Having analysed three strands prevalent in the contemporary literature on international distributive justice, I now want, in this penultimate section, to analyse the ethical claims advanced by a fourth approach, namely realist perspectives. As with all the other perspectives, the term "realism" is imprecise and its use contested. For the purposes of this review, I shall, however, assume that realists make the ethical claim that the state should advance its national interest and should not seek to further the standard of living of those living abroad. Defined as such, of course, it contrasts starkly with the claim that we have duties to distribute resources to the impoverished abroad. I think it is fair to say that whilst there has been a great deal of descriptive and explanatory work by realists recently there has not been as much explicitly directed towards ethical issues. There is no recent sustained defense of a realist ethical perspective in the same way that there have been sustained defences of nationalist or cosmopolitan positions. This is not to say, however, that realist value-judgements are widely rejected or dismissed. On the contrary, many are sympathetic to realist misgivings about the wisdom of seeking to further cosmopolitan principles of justice and, one can discern three distinct realist challenges to global justice within the contemporary literature.

A: Human nature

Some have misgivings about cosmopolitan ideals because they hold a pessimistic account of human nature. In a recent discussion of the rights of free movement, David Hendrickson, for example, grounds his realism on "certain psychological facts . . . of human nature" (1992, p. 215). Similarly in his work *Cosmopolis* Danilo Zolo argues against cosmopolitanism on the grounds that humans are naturally inclined to aggression and uncooperative behaviour (1997, pp. 82, 146–50, 166). They adopt, in other words, what Kenneth Waltz has termed a first-image explanation, explaining the character of international politics by reference to the nature of human beings (1959).

This kind of argument, however, fails to get to the core tenets underlying cosmopolitanism. Even if we accept their account of human nature it does not impugn the claims cosmopolitans advance about how we should behave and what criteria should be employed to judge how people behave. Their factual claims about what people *do* are quite compatible with the moral claims affirmed by cosmopolitans about what people *should do*. This is not to say that claims about human nature are irrelevant. They should be taken into account when proposing specific policies and measures. It is just that to claim that someone will not do something does not show that they have no obligation to do so.[18]

B: The international system

Other realist challenges to cosmopolitanism take a different tack and adopt what Waltz has called a third image perspective (Waltz, 1959). That is, they explain world politics in terms of the character of the international system, arguing that the system is such that states have no choice but to fend for themselves and can not seek to improve the quality of life of those outside their borders (Art and Waltz, 1983, especially pp. 6–7; Mearsheimer, 1995, especially p. 48 fn 182; Zolo, 1997, p. 69). In this way the state's pursuit of the national interest is vindicated.

This argument, however, entails its conclusion only if we assume that all the actions of states are determined by the international system and they have no capability for choice at all. Only then can we say that states have no choice but to advance the national interest. But, as Andrew Linklater points out, it is implausible to claim that states are *unable* to pursue policies other than those which advance their own ends (1998, chapter 1 (especially pp. 18–22), pp. 215–6). States are able to devote part of their GNP to overseas aid, to admit the impoverished who wish to immigrate to their country, and to co-operate with other states in cancelling third world debt. It is therefore not plausible to reject cosmopolitanism on the grounds that the international system *compels* states simply to further their national interest. Within the parameters set by the international system, states do have leeway and thus are able to further cosmopolitan ideals.

Conclusion

This brings us to the end of the review of contemporary discussions of international distributive justice.[19] I would like to conclude by emphasizing two central points and then drawing attention to future avenues for research

(1) first, we have seen that underlying all the very different cosmopolitan theories there is a common claim and justificatory move, namely the contention that persons' entitlements should not be determined by factors such as their nationality or citizenship.
(2) second, an analysis of the literature suggests that the extent to which cosmopolitanism conflicts with the other perspectives should not be exaggerated. Nationalists, for example, make claims – like the "national duties" thesis and the "allocation of duty" thesis – that are quite consistent with cosmopolitanism. In addition, acceptance of nationalist concerns about viability does not undermine cosmopolitanism. The same points can be made about the relationship between cosmopolitanism and realism. Indeed, as we have just seen, those realist critiques of humanitarian and "idealistic" foreign policy which take a consequentialist form do not dispute the cosmopolitans' fundamental moral tenets. Furthermore realist claims about human nature do not challenge cosmopolitan moral standards.

Where does this leave future research? Several options are worth pursuing. First, current discussions about international distributive justice are very abstract and there is room for more analysis of which specific practical measures should be adopted. What, for example, are the implications of principles of international justice for cancelling debt or regulating the environment or immigration policy (Bader, 1997; Black, 1991; Barry and Goodin, 1992) or humanitarian intervention? This in turn, points to a need for philosophical analyses of international distributive justice to be integrated with empirical and theoretical explanations of the nature of global politics.

Some scholars do this already (distinguished examples including Beitz, Barry, Brown and Pogge), but, in general, this is an area which could and should be developed further. To illustrate this point, consider the proposal to tax international currency markets and to spend the proceeds on alleviating poverty. The original idea was proposed by Nobel laureate James Tobin (1982, pp. 488–94) as a mechanism for stabilizing currency markets but it has subsequently been supported (by, among others, groups like War on Want (War on Want, 2001, p. 19)) as a source of raising revenue to meet basic needs. This idea has received considerable support from activists and politicians. In the light of this, it would be appropriate to have more analyses of measures like the Tobin Tax.

A second important area for research concerns the institutional implications of ideals of international distributive justice. One important contribution to this debate has been made by Sen who has persuasively argued that democratic structures prevent the occurrence of famine [. . .] (1999b, pp. 4–5, 10–11, 51–3, 147–54, 157–8, 178–88). Sen has tended to work within a system of states. Recently there have been important examinations (notably by Held (1995) and Linklater (1998)) of the question of whether states should be supplemented with, or replaced by, transnational political institutions. This work, however, has tended to focus on the (legitimate) question of whether a commitment to democracy requires cosmopolitan democratic structures rather than on the question "if one accepts principles of international distributive justice what political institutions should one accept?" There have been a number of illuminating discussions – including, for example those of Beitz (1994), Jones (1999, pp. 206–30), O'Neill (2000, pp. 139–42, 170–2, 179–85, 199–202). Pogge (1994a) and Singer (2001) – but quite what the appropriate answers are still remains very unclear. Furthermore, and relatedly, what is lacking are normative discussions of the role and legitimacy of institutions like the WTO, IMF, World Bank, UN and ILO.

Third, as was remarked at the beginning of this review, much of the debate concerning international distributive justice focuses very much on the question of whether there are global principles of distributive justice or on whether distributive justice should be implemented at the state-level. It is, however, worth exploring the applicability of principles of distributive justice to bodies such as the European Union, which fall between states and nations, on the one hand, and, the whole world, on the other. Some redistribution already takes place (via the cohesion fund) and it is appropriate to ask whether such intermediate forms of co-operation can be the subject of principles of justice.

A final area worth exploring concerns non-western ethical traditions. The approaches discussed in this review all draw almost exclusively on western thinkers, whether they are Hobbes, Thucydides, Herder, Kant or Rawls. If, however, we wish to analyse global norms and principles of distributive justice then it is of vital importance to explore traditions of thought other than those prevalent in the west.

Notes

1 For this term see C. Jones, 1999, pp. 5–7; O. O'Neill, 1994, pp. 79–84; and Welch, 1993, p. 200ff.
2 Each of these has written a great deal on cosmopolitan ideals of distributive justice. See, among other works, Barry (1998, 1999); Beitz (1999c); and Pogge (1989, part III). The discussion of cosmopolitanism below will also incorporate many of their other writings on global justice.
3 This distinction is also made by Miller, who prefers the terms "strong and weak" cosmopolitanism: Miller (1998, pp. 166–7). The two distinctions differ only in that mine distinguishes between

two types of cosmopolitan account of justice whereas Miller's is a distinction between two types of cosmopolitan account of morality in general.

4   This distinction is a feature of much of Pogge's work on global justice. See for example, Pogge (1988, pp. 227–32; 1992a, pp. 90–101; 1994a, pp. 90–8; 1995, pp. 113–19; 2000, pp. 51–69). In focusing on the basic structure as the subject of distributive justice Pogge is following Rawls (1999b, pp. 6–10).

5   See Barry (1999, section IV, especially pp. 35–6); Beitz (1979, pp. 417–20; 1983, pp. 593, 595–6; 1988, pp. 191–3; 1994, pp. 124–5); Pogge (1994a, pp. 89–90). As all these three point out, all of the diverse cosmopolitan theories of global justice share and develop this set of intuitively plausible claims.

6   See Pogge (1989, p. 247; 1994b, p. 198) and Nussbaum (1996, p. 14).

7   See Black (1991, especially pp. 355–79); C. Jones (1999, pp. 6, 8); and Goodin (1985, especially pp. 11, 154).

8   This typology adopts and modifies one made by Dworkin (1977, pp. 171–2). For good critical analyses of many of the arguments outlined below see Brown (1992, pp. 155–92); C. Jones (1999, chapters 2, 3 and 4); and O'Neill (2000, pp. 115–42).

9   See, for example, 1995, pp. 169, 186. For a fuller discussion of Held's theory see Caney (2001b).

10 For Shue's defence of the right to security and subsistence see (1996, pp. 13–34). For a discussion of the duties generated by these rights and a rebuttal of those who distinguish between positive and negative rights see (1996, pp. 35–64).

11 See, for example, "A Global Resources Dividend" which cites Article 25 of the UDHR (1998, p. 501). For Pogge's affirmation of rights see Pogge (1992a, pp. 89–101; 1994a, p. 90; 1995, pp. 103–20; 2000, pp. 45–69).

12 For the distinction between nations and states, see Miller (1995, pp. 18–9) and Tamir (1993, pp. 58–63). For the distinction between nations and ethnic groups see Miller (1995, pp. 19–21) and Tamir (1993, p. 65).

13 See more fully, Miller (1995, pp. 22–5).

14 See Miller (2000a, pp. 25–6, 39–40); For criticism see Caney (1996, pp. 125–6).

15 See Goodin (1985, p. 167). Goodin also cites Singer (1972, pp. 29–30) and Beitz (1999c, pp. 155–6) on this point.

16 For similar criticism of Rawls see Buchanan (2000, pp. 698–700).

17 I have examined Rawls's use of toleration to criticize cosmopolitanism and its flaws at much greater length elsewhere: Caney (2001c).

18 This point is made clearly by Goodin: see his (1992, pp. 248–9, 252–4).

19 It is not possible to examine, in this review article all recent works on international distributive justice. Space has precluded an analysis of Jacques Derrida's recent writings on cosmopolitanism and hospitality (Derrida, 2000, 2001). It has also precluded a discussion of recent theological discussions on global distributive justice (such as Gorringe, 1999; Northcott, 1999).

References

Art, R. and Waltz, K. (1983) "Technology Strategy, and the Uses of Force," in R. Art and K. Waltz (eds), *The Use of Force. International Politics and Foreign Policy*, 2nd ed, Lanham MD: University Press of America, pp. 1–32.

Bader, V. (1997) "Fairly Open Borders," in V. Bader (ed.), *Citizenship and Exclusion*, Basingstoke: Macmillan, pp. 28–60.

Barry, B. (1991c) "Humanity and Justice in Global Perspective," in *Liberty and Justice. Essays in Political Theory, Volume 2*, Oxford: Clarendon, pp. 182–210.

Barry, B. (1991d) "Justice as Reciprocity," in *Liberty and Justice. Essays in Political Theory, Volume 2*, Oxford: Clarendon, pp. 211–41.

Barry, B. (1996) "Nationalism versus Liberalism?" *Nation and Nationalism* 2, 430–5.

Barry, B. (1998) "International Society From a Cosmopolitan Perspective," in D. Mapel and T. Nardin (eds), *International Society Diverse Ethical Perspectives*, Princeton NJ: Princeton University Press, pp. 144–63.

Barry, B. (1999) "Statism and Nationalism: a Cosmopolitan Critique," in I. Shapiro and L. Brilmayer (eds), *Global Justice NOMOS, Volume XLI*, New York: New York University Press, pp. 12–66.

Barry, B. and Goodin, R. (eds) (1992), *Free Movement: Ethical Issues in the Transnational Migration of People and of Money*, Pennsylvania PA: Pennsylvania State University Press.

Beitz, C. (1983) "Cosmopolitan Ideals and National Sentiment," *Journal of Philosophy* 80 (10), 591–600.

Beitz, C. (1988) "Recent International Thought," *International Journal* 43, 183–204.

Beitz, C. (1994) "Cosmopolitan Liberalism and the States System," in C. Brown (ed.), *Political Restructuring in Europe. Ethical Perspectives*, London: Routledge, pp. 123–36.

Beitz, C. (1999a) "International Liberalism and Distributive Justice: a Survey of Recent Thought," *World Politics* 51 (2), 269–96.

Beitz, C. (1999b) "Social and Cosmopolitan Liberalism," *International Affairs* 75 (3), 315–29.

Beitz, C. (1999c) *Political Theory and International Relations* with a new afterword by the author, Princeton NJ: Princeton University Press.

Beitz, C. (2000) "Rawls's Law as Peoples," *Ethics* 110 (4), 669–96.

Black, S. (1991) "Individualism at an Impasse," *Canadian Journal of Philosophy* 21 (3), 347–77.

Brilmayer, L. (1994) *American Hegemony. Political Morality in a One-Superpower World*, New Haven CT: Yale University Press.

Brown, C. (1992) *International Relations Theory, New Normative Approaches*, Hemel Hempstead: Harvester Wheatsheaf.

Brown, C. (2000a) "Justice and International Order," in T. Coates (ed.) *International Justice*, Aldershot: Ashgate, pp. 27–45.

Buchanan, A. (2000) "Rawls's Law of Peoples: Rules for a Vanished Westphalian World," *Ethics*, 110 (4), 697–721.

Caney, S. (1996) "Individuals, Nations and Obligations," in S. Caney, D. George and P. Jones (eds), *National Rights International Obligations*, Oxford: Westview, pp. 119–38.

Caney, S. (2001b) "British Perspectives on Internationalism, Justice and Sovereignty: from the English School to Cosmopolitan Democracy," *The European Legacy* 6 (2), 265–75.

Caney, S. (2001c) "Survey Article: Cosmopolitanism and the Law of Peoples," *Journal of Political Philosophy*, 9.

Dagger, R. (1997) *Civic Virtues: Rights, Citizenship, and Republican Liberalism*, New York: Oxford University Press.

Derrida, J. (2000) *Of Hospitality. Anne Dufourmantelle invites Jacques Derrida to respond*, translated by R. Bowlby. Stanford CA: Stanford University Press.

Derrida, J. (2001) *On Cosmopolitanism and Forgiveness*, translated by M. Dooley and M. Hughes with a preface by S. Critchley and R. Kearney, London: Routledge.

Dworkin, R. (1977) *Taking Rights Seriously*, London: Duckworth.

Falk, R. (1995) *On Humane Governance: Toward a New Global Politics*, Cambridge: Polity Press.

Goodin, R. (1988) "What is So Special about Our Fellow Countrymen?" *Ethics*. 98 (4), 663–86.

Goodin, R. (1992) "Commentary: The Political Realism of Free Movement," in B. Barry and R. Goodin (eds), *Free Movement, Ethical issues in the Transnational Migration of People and of Money*, Pennsylvania PA: Pennsylvania State University Press, pp. 248–64.

Gorringe, I. (1999) *Fair Shares, Ethics and the Global Economy*, London: Thames and Hudson.

Held, D. (1995) *Democracy and the Global Order from the Modern State to Cosmopolitan Governance*, Cambridge: Polity Press.

Hendrickson, D. (1992) "Migration in Law and Ethics: a Realist Perspective," in B. Barry and R. Goodin (eds), *Free Movement, Ethical Issues in the Transnational Migration of People and of Money*, Pennsylvania PA: Pennsylvania State University Press, pp. 213–31.

Jones, C. (1999) *Global Justice: Defending Cosmopolitanism*, Oxford: Oxford University Press.

Landes, D. (1998) *The Wealth and Poverty of Nations. Why some are so rich and some so poor*, London: Little, Brown and Company.

Linklater, A. (1998) *The Transformation of Political Community Ethical Foundations of the Post-Westphalian Era*, Cambridge: Polity.

McCarthy, I. (1997) "On the Idea of a Reasonable Law of Peoples," in J. Bohman and M. Lutz-Bachmann (eds), *Perpetual Peace. Essays on Kant's Cosmopolitan Ideal*, Cambridge, Massachusetts MA: MIT Press, pp. 201–17.

McMahan, J. (1997) "The Limits of National Partiality," in R. McKim and J. McMahan (eds), *The Morality of Nationalism*, New York: Oxford University Press, pp. 107–38.

Mearsheimer, J. (1995) "The False Promise of International Institutions," *International Security*, 19 (3), 5–49.

Miller, D. (1995) *On Nationality*, Oxford: Clarendon Press.

Miller, D. (1998) "The Limits of Cosmopolitan Justice," in D. Mapel and T. Nardin (eds). *International Society Diverse Ethical Perspectives*, Princeton NJ: Princeton University Press, pp. 164–81.

Mitter, D. (2000a) "In Defence of Nationality," in *Citizenship and National Identity*, Cambridge: Polity, pp. 24–40.

Miller, D. (2000b) "National Self-Determination and Global Justice," in *Citizenship and National Identity*, Cambridge: Polity, pp. 161–79.

Nardin, J. (1983) *Law, Morality and the Relations of States*, Princeton NJ: Princeton University Press.

Northcott, M. (1999) *Life after Debt. Christianity and Global Justice*, London: SPCK.

Nussbaum, M. (1996) "Patriotism and Cosmopolitanism," in M. Nussbaum with Respondents edited by J. Cohen, *For Love of Country Debating the Limits of Patriotism*, Boston MA: Beacon Press, pp. 2–17.

O'Neill, O. (1996) *Towards Justice and Virtue: a Constructive Account of Practical Reasoning*, Cambridge: Cambridge University Press.

O'Neill, O. (2000) *Bounds of Justice*, Cambridge: Cambridge University Press.

Pogge, T. (1989) *Realizing Rawls*, Ithaca NY: Cornell University Press.

Pogge, T. (1992a) "An Institutional Approach to Humanitarian Intervention," *Public Affairs Quarterly*, 6 (1), 89–103.

Pogge, T. (1994a) "Cosmopolitanism and Sovereignty," in C. Brown (ed.), *Political Restructuring in Europe Ethical Perspectives*, London: Routledge, pp. 89–122.

Pogge, T. (1994b) "An Egalitarian Law of Peoples," *Philosophy and Public Affairs*, 23 (3), 195–224.

Pogge, T. (1995) "How should Human Rights be Conceived?" *Jahrbuch für Recht und Ethik*, 3, 103–20.

Pogge, T. (1998) "A Global Resources Dividend," in D. Crocker and T. Linden (eds), *Ethics of Consumption: The Good Life, Justice and Global Stewardship*, Lanham MD: Rowman and Littlefield, pp. 501–36.

Pogge, T. (2000) "The International Significance of Human Rights," *The Journal of Ethics*, 4, 45–69.

Pogge, T. (2001) "Rawls on International Justice," *The Philosophical Quarterly*, 51 (203), 246–53.

Rawls, J. (1993a) "The Law of Peoples," in S. Shute and S. Hurley (eds), *On Human Rights: The Oxford Amnesty Lectures 1993*, New York: Basic Books, pp. 41–82.

Rawls, J. (1999a) *The Law of Peoples with The Idea of Public Reason Revisited*, Cambridge MA: Harvard University Press.

Rawls, J. (1999b) *A Theory of Justice Rev* (ed) Oxford: Oxford University Press.

Richards, D. (1982) "International Distributive Justice," in J. Pennock and J. Chapman (eds), *Ethics Economics and the Law: NOMOS XXIV*, New York: New York University Press, pp. 275–99.

Sen, A. (1996) "Humanity and Citizenship," in M. Nussbaum with Respondents edited by J. Cohen. *For Love of Country Debating the Limits of Patriotism*, Boston MA: Beacon Press, pp. 111–18.

Sen, A. (1999b) *Development as Freedom*, New York: Anchor Books.

Shue, H. (1988) "Mediating Duties," *Ethics* 98 (4), 687–704.

Shue, H. (1996) *Basic Rights: Subsistence, Affluence and U. S. Foreign Policy*, 2nd ed, with a new afterword, Princeton NJ: Princeton University Press.

Singer, P. (1972) "Famine Affluence and Morality," *Philosophy and Public Affairs*, 1 (3), 229–43.

Singer, P. (1977) "Reconsidering the Famine Relief Argument," in P. Brown and H. Shue (eds), *Food Policy, the Responsibility of the United States in the Life and Death Choices*, London: Collier Macmillan, pp. 36–53.

Singer, P. (1979) *Practical Ethics*, Cambridge: Cambridge University Press.

Singer, P. (2001) "Dream of a World Where People Come before Power," *Times Higher Education Supplement*, 23 February, p. 17. This is a shortened version of Professor Singer's 2001 Amnesty Lecture.

Steiner, H. (1994) *An Essay on Rights*, Oxford: Blackwell.

Steiner, H. (1999) "Just Taxation and International Redistribution," in I. Shapiro and L. Brilmayer (eds), *Global Justice: NOMOS Volume XLI*, New York: New York University Press, pp. 171–91.

Tamir, Y. (1993) *Liberal Nationalism*, Princeton NJ: Princeton University Press.

Tobin, J. (1982) "A Proposal for International Monetary Reform," in *Essays in Economics Theory and Policy*, Cambridge MA: MIT Press, pp. 488–94.

van den Anker, C. (1998) Global Justice as Impartiality. Paper presented to the conference on "International Justice" organized by the *UK Association for Legal and Social Philosophy, 25th Anniversary* (Reading, April 2–4, 1998).

van Parijs, P. (1995) *Real Freedom for All What (if anything) Can Justify Capitalism?* Oxford: Clarendon Press.

Waltz, K. (1959) *Man, the State and War: a Theoretical Analysis*, New York: Columbia University Press.

Wenar, L. (2001) "Contractualism and Global Economic Justice," *Metaphilosophy*, 32 (1/2), 79–94.

Zolo, D. (1997) *Cosmopolis Prospects for World Government*, translated by David McKie, Cambridge: Polity.

Part III

Cosmopolitanism, Nationality, States, and Culture

Introduction

A consistent debate between cosmopolitans and non-cosmopolitans pertains to when the principles of justice apply. As was evident in the preceding section, this debate is underpinned by a disagreement about what special obligations we might have to fellow nationals, patriots, and cultural groups, and to what degree these identification relationships restrict the application of justice beyond borders. For more communitarian minded scholars, justice does not apply beyond immediate national, state, and cultural boundaries, since a condition of justice requires a fairly robust identification relationship between fellow participants (see Miller). Furthermore, for some, justice only applies to formal social and political orders that have a delineated institutional form and that it is unreasonable to suggest that the current global order resembles anything like what is found within existing national, state, and cultural structures (see Nagel, Dahl, and Kymlicka). In contrast, for those who are more cosmopolitan minded, the place of one's birth, and thus one's communal association, is morally arbitrary from the standpoint of justice and it should not delimit the basic considerations of justice toward others (see Caney, "Global Distributive Justice and the State"). In addition, as has been argued throughout Section II, many cosmopolitan scholars believe that the international environment has become increasingly interconnected to a point where circumstances have established a condition in which considerations about global justice apply (see Beitz, Barry, and Pogge).

Nevertheless, these arguments largely rest on whether or not there is enough of an identification relationship between peoples at the global level to motivate duties of global justice and whether this sense of cosmopolitan identity could/should be cultivated. In other words, the argument between cosmopolitans and anti-cosmopolitans largely involves issues of common humanity, our identification with this common humanity, and whether this cosmopolitan identity is strong enough to provide the foundations for a cosmopolitan order. It is in regards to these concerns that this section will attempt to explore and develop a cosmopolitan response. As will be seen, cosmopolitans have constructed many convincing arguments for why we should reject communitarian, nationalist, cultural, and statist claims and offer several arguments for why we should remain enthusiastic about the possibility of cultivating a future cosmopolitan identity. However, as will be evident in the critiques of cosmopolitanism involved in Section VI, this debate clearly continues to dominate the discussion and there remain forceful as well as compelling arguments on both sides of the divide.

The first chapter of this section is an influential piece by Martha Nussbaum on "Patriotism and Cosmopolitanism." This piece was particularly influential because Nussbaum's article received considerable attention from academia as well as the general public. As a result, the piece sparked an important debate between intellectuals about the values associated with patriotism and about whether this form of national identity should be necessarily opposed to a cosmopolitan ethic. As Nussbaum suggests, in making strong appeals to patriotism and national pride we often ignore issues of common humanity and global interdependency. For Nussbaum, this narrow vision of what it means to be a patriot unfortunately dominates our current educational processes (particularly in the United States) and thus limits the ability for individuals to understand that we share a world in common. In response, Nussbaum offers the groundwork for an alternative form of "cosmopolitan education" as a means to help transgress the inwardness of patriotism, toward a more global sense of cosmopolitan citizenship.

In "What is Cosmopolitan?", Jeremy Waldron examines two issues involved with what a cosmopolitan position represents. First, Waldron seeks to explore the implications of a cosmopolitan orientation as it relates to one's cultural identity. By examining some definitional elements of culture, Waldron provides an argument that suggests it is possible to be a member of one's local community while also maintaining a sense of cosmopolitan identity. In this regard, although individuals require cultural material in order to maintain meaningful lives, there is no theoretical reason to suggest that they can only derive meaningful existence from one single culture or that holding multiple identification relationships would necessarily render one's culture obsolete. Second, Waldron further seeks to explore how a relationship between cultural identity and the Kantian idea of cosmopolitan law can be mutually reinforcing. As Waldron contends, "we are always likely to find ourselves alongside others who we disagree with," and it is for this reason that justifiable legal mechanisms for cosmopolitan coexistence could be generated. Since cultures share common concerns for right and security, they also share common universal foundations for coordinating a condition of cosmopolitan law.

As mentioned previously, cosmopolitans and anti-cosmopolitans often debate the extent to which special communal and national obligations negate the prospect of cosmopolitan global justice. In particular, many anti-cosmopolitans argue not only that national identity prohibits a cosmopolitan identity from taking root, but that national obligations should also trump duties beyond borders (see Miller). These claims are not only prevalent among non-liberal thinkers, but are also often defended by liberal nationalists, who believe that a strong sense of national identity is necessary for any meaningful condition of justice to exist (see Miller, Dahl, and Kymlicka). In response to this, the chapter by Kok-Chor Tan argues that liberal nationalism is compatible with cosmopolitan justice when both are properly defined and identified. Furthermore, according to Tan, many of the extrapolated arguments associated with liberal nationalism, such as claims to national self-determination and national culture, cannot be consistently maintained within its own normative logic and therefore should not be considered as a theoretical roadblock to cosmopolitan arguments, as is often assumed.

Up until this point, the section has covered three interconnected challenges to cosmopolitanism as they relate to anti-cosmopolitan sentiments of national *patriotism*, anti-cosmopolitan sentiments of *culture* and anti-cosmopolitan sentiments of *national identity*. In the final chapter of this section, a response to statist claims against cosmopolitanism are examined and refuted by Simon Caney. As with previous anti-cosmopolitan arguments, statists argue that the state is a necessary entity involved with defining the scope of egalitarian distributive justice and that this gives it an inherent normative value that is necessarily threatened by cosmopolitanism (see Nagel). By way of a thorough examination of these anti-cosmopolitan critiques, Caney argues that these critiques remain unconvincing and that it is possible to generate a more compatible relationship that maintains the normative importance of the state while also increasing its active role in constituting a condition of cosmopolitan global justice.

9

Patriotism and Cosmopolitanism*
Martha C. Nussbaum

I

In Rabindranath Tagore's novel *The Home and the World*, the young wife Bimala, entranced by the patriotic rhetoric of her husband's friend Sandip, becomes an eager devotee of the *Swadeshi* movement, which has organized a boycott of foreign goods. The slogan of the movement is *Bande Mataram* (Hail Motherland). Bimala complains that her husband, the cosmopolitan Hindu landlord Nikhil, is cool in his devotion to the cause:

> And yet it was not that my husband refused to support *Swadeshi*, or was in any way against the Cause. Only he had not been able wholeheartedly to accept the spirit of *Bande Mataram*.
> "I am willing," he said, "to serve my country; but my worship I reserve for Right which is far greater than my country. To worship my country as a god is to bring a curse upon it."

Americans have frequently supported the principle of *Bande Mataram*, giving the fact of being American a special salience in moral and political deliberation, and pride in a specifically American identity and a specifically American citizenship a special power among the motivations to political action. I believe, as do Tagore and his character Nikhil, that this emphasis on patriotic pride is both morally dangerous and, ultimately, subversive of some of the worthy goals patriotism sets out to serve – for example, the goal of national unity in devotion to worthy moral ideals of justice and equality. These goals, I shall argue, would be better served by an ideal that is in any case more adequate to our situation in the contemporary world, namely the very old ideal of the cosmopolitan, the person whose allegiance is to the worldwide community of human beings.

My articulation of these issues is motivated, in part, by my experience working on international quality-of-life issues in an institute for development economics connected with the United Nations. It is also motivated by the renewal of appeals to the nation, and national pride, in some recent discussions of American character and American education. In a well-known op-ed piece in the *New York Times* (13 February 1994), philosopher Richard Rorty urges Americans, especially the American left, not to disdain patriotism as a value, and indeed to give central importance to "the emotion of national pride" and "a sense of shared national identity." Rorty argues that we cannot even criticize ourselves well unless we also "rejoice" in our American identity and define ourselves fundamentally in terms of that identity. Rorty seems to hold that

* The author would like us to alert you to the fact that her views on this topic have changed in significant ways. For her latest argument, please see M. Nussbaum, "Toward a Globally Sensitive Patriotism," Daedalus, vol. 137, no. 3 (2008): pp. 78–93.

the primary alternative to a politics based on patriotism and national identity is what he calls a "politics of difference," one based on internal divisions among America's ethnic, racial, religious, and other subgroups. He nowhere considers the possibility of a more international basis for political emotion and concern.

This is no isolated case. Rorty's piece responds to and defends Sheldon Hackney's recent call for a "national conversation" to discuss American identity. As a participant in its early phase, I was made vividly aware that the project, as initially conceived, proposed an inward-looking task, bounded by the borders of the nation, rather than considering ties of obligation and commitment that join America to the rest of the world. As with Rorty's piece, the primary contrast drawn in the project was between a politics based on ethnic and racial and religious difference and a politics based on a shared national identity. What we share as both rational and mutually dependent human beings was simply not on the agenda.

One might wonder, however, how far the politics of nationalism really is from the politics of difference. *The Home and the World* (better known, perhaps, in Satyajit Ray's haunting film of the same title) is a tragic story of the defeat of a reasonable and principled cosmopolitanism by the forces of nationalism and ethnocentrism. I believe that Tagore sees deeply when he observes that, at bottom, nationalism and ethnocentric particularism are not alien to one another, but akin – that to give support to nationalist sentiments subverts, ultimately, even the values that hold a nation together, because it substitutes a colorful idol for the substantive universal values of justice and right. Once someone has said, I am an Indian first, a citizen of the world second, once he or she has made that morally questionable move of self-definition by a morally irrelevant characteristic, then what, indeed, will stop that person from saying, as Tagore's characters so quickly learn to say, I am a Hindu first, and an Indian second, or I am an upper-caste landlord first, and a Hindu second? Only the cosmopolitan stance of the landlord Nikhil – so boringly flat in the eyes of his young wife Bimala and his passionate nationalist friend Sandip – has the promise of transcending these divisions, because only this stance asks us to give our first allegiance to what is morally good – and that which, being good, I can commend as such to all human beings.

Proponents of nationalism in politics and in education frequently make a weak concession to cosmopolitanism. They may argue, for example, that although nations should in general base education and political deliberation on shared national values, a commitment to basic human rights should be part of any national education system, and that this commitment will in a sense hold many nations together.[1] This seems to be a fair comment on practical reality; and the emphasis on human rights is certainly necessary for a world in which nations interact all the time on terms (let us hope) of justice and mutual respect.

But is it sufficient? As students here grow up, is it sufficient for them to learn that they are above all citizens of the United States but that they ought to respect the basic human rights of citizens of India, Bolivia, Nigeria, and Norway? Or should they – as I think – in addition to giving special attention to the history and current situation of their own nation, learn a good deal more than they frequently do about the rest of the world in which they live, about India and Bolivia and Nigeria and Norway and their histories, problems, and comparative successes? Should they learn only that citizens of India have equal basic human rights, or should they also learn about the problems of hunger and pollution in India, and the implications of these problems for the larger issues of global hunger and global ecology? Most important, should they be taught that they are, above all, citizens of the United States, or should they instead be taught that they are, above all, citizens of a world of human beings, and that, while they happen to be situated in the United States, they have to share this world with the citizens of other countries? I suggest four arguments for the second concept of education, which I call *cosmopolitan education*. But first I introduce a historical digression, which traces cosmopolitanism to its origins, and in the process recover some excellent arguments that have traditionally supported it.

II

When Diogenes the Cynic replied, "I am a citizen of the world," he meant, apparently, that he refused to be defined by his local origins and group memberships, so central to the self-image of the conventional Greek male; instead, he defined himself in terms of more universal aspirations and concerns. The Stoics, who followed his lead, further developed his image of the *kosmou politês* (world citizen) arguing that each of us dwells, in effect, in two communities – the local community of our birth, and the community of human argument and aspiration that "is truly great and truly common, in which we look neither to this corner nor to that, but measure the boundaries of our nation by the sun" (Seneca, *De Otio*). It is this community that is, fundamentally, the source of our moral obligations. With respect to the most basic moral values, such as justice, "We should regard all human beings as our fellow citizens and neighbors" (Plutarch, *On the Fortunes of Alexander*). We should regard our deliberations as, first and foremost, deliberations about human problems of people in particular concrete situations, not problems growing out of a national identity that is altogether unlike that of others. Diogenes knew that the invitation to think as a world citizen was, in a sense, an invitation to be an exile from the comfort of patriotism and its easy sentiments, to see our own ways of life from the point of view of justice and the good. The accident of where one is born is just that, an accident; any human being might have been born in any nation. Recognizing this, his Stoic successors held, we should not allow differences of nationality or class or ethnic membership or even gender to erect barriers between us and our fellow human beings. We should recognize humanity wherever it occurs, and give its fundamental ingredients, reason and moral capacity, our first allegiance and respect.

This clearly did not mean that the Stoics were proposing the abolition of local and national forms of political organization and the creation of a world state. Their point was even more radical: that we should give our first allegiance to no mere form of government, no temporal power, but to the moral community made up by the humanity of all human beings. The idea of the world citizen is in this way the ancestor and the source of Kant's idea of the "kingdom of ends," and has a similar function in inspiring and regulating moral and political conduct. One should always behave so as to treat with equal respect the dignity of reason and moral choice in every human being. [. . .]

Stoics who hold that good civic education is education for world citizenship recommend this attitude on three grounds. First, they hold that the study of humanity as it is realized in the whole world is valuable for self-knowledge: we see ourselves more clearly when we see our ways in relation to those of other reasonable people.

Second, they argue, that we will be better able to solve our problems if we face them in this way. No theme is deeper in Stoicism than the damage done by faction and local allegiances to the political life of a group. Political deliberation, they argue, is sabotaged again and again by partisan loyalties, whether to one's team at the Circus or to one's nation. Only by making our fundamental allegiance to the world community of justice and reason do we avoid these dangers.

Finally, they insist that the stance of the *kosmou politês* is intrinsically valuable, for it recognizes in people what is especially fundamental about them, most worthy of respect and acknowledgment: their aspirations to justice and goodness and their capacities for reasoning in this connection. These qualities may be less colorful than local or national traditions and identities [. . .] but they are, the Stoics argue, both lasting and deep.

The Stoics stress that to be a citizen of the world one does not need to give up local identifications, which can be a source of great richness in life. They suggest that we think of ourselves not as devoid of local affiliations, but as surrounded by a series of concentric circles. The first one encircles the self, the next takes in the immediate family, then follows the extended family, then, in order, neighbors or local groups, fellow city-dwellers, and fellow countrymen – and we can easily add to this list groupings based on ethnic, linguistic, historical, professional, gender, or sexual identities. Outside all these circles is the largest one, humanity as a whole. Our task as citizens of the world will be to "draw the circles somehow toward the center" (Stoic philosopher Hierocles, 1st–2nd CE), making all human beings more like our fellow city-dwellers, and so on. We need not give up our special affections and identifications, whether ethnic or gender-based or religious. We need not think of them as superficial, and we may think of our identity as constituted partly by them. We may and should devote special attention to them in education. But we should also work to make all human beings part of our community of dialogue and concern, base our political deliberations on that interlocking commonality, and give the circle that defines our humanity special attention and respect.

In educational terms, this means that students in the United States, for example, may continue to regard themselves as defined partly by their particular loves – their families, their religious, ethnic, or racial communities, or even their country. But they must also, and centrally, learn to recognize humanity wherever they encounter it, undeterred by traits that are strange to them, and be eager to understand humanity in all its strange guises. They must learn enough about the different to recognize common aims, aspirations, and values, and enough about these common ends to see how variously they are instantiated in the many cultures and their histories. Stoic writers insist that the vivid imagining of the different is an essential task of education, and that it requires, in turn, a mastery of many facts about the different. Marcus Aurelius gives himself the following advice, which might be called the basis for cosmopolitan education: "Accustom yourself not to be inattentive to what another person says, and as far as possible enter into that person's mind" (VI. 53). "Generally," he adds, "one must first learn many things before one can judge another's action with understanding."

A favored exercise in this process of world thinking is to conceive of the entire world of human beings as a single body, its many people as so many limbs. Referring to the fact that it takes only changing a single letter in Greek to convert the word "limb" (*melos*) into the word "part" (*meros*), Marcus says: "If, changing the word, you call yourself merely a [detached] part rather than a limb, you do not yet love your fellow men from the heart, nor derive complete joy from doing good; you will do it merely as a duty, not as doing good to yourself" (VII. 13). It is important to recall that, as emperor, he gave himself that advice in connection with daily duties that required coming to grips with the cultures of remote and, initially, strange civilizations, such as Parthia and Sarmatia.

I would like to see education adopt this cosmopolitan Stoic stance. The organic model could, of course, be abused – if, for example, it was taken to deny the fundamental importance of the separateness of people and of fundamental personal liberties. Stoics were not always sufficiently attentive to these values and to their political salience; in that sense, their thought is not always a good basis for a scheme of democratic deliberation and education. But as the image is primarily intended – as a reminder of the interdependence of all human beings and communities – it has fundamental significance. There is clearly a huge amount to be said about how such ideas might be realized in curricula at many levels. Instead of beginning that more concrete task, however, I focus on the present day and offer four arguments for making world citizenship, rather than democratic or national citizenship, the focus for civic education.

III

1. Through cosmopolitan education, we learn more about ourselves

One of the greatest barriers to rational deliberation in politics is the unexamined feeling that one's own preferences and ways are neutral and natural. An education that takes national boundaries as morally salient too often reinforces this kind of irrationality, by lending to what is an accident of history a false air of moral weight and glory. By looking at ourselves through the lens of the other, we come to see what in our practices is local and nonessential, what is more broadly or deeply shared. Our nation is appallingly ignorant of most of the rest of the world. I think this means that it is also, in many crucial ways, ignorant of itself.

To give just one example of this: If we want to understand our own history and our choices about child-rearing and the structure of the family, we are helped immeasurably by looking around the world to see in what configurations families exist, and through what strategies children are in fact being cared for. (This would include a study of the history of the family, both in our own and other traditions.) Such a study can show us, for example, that the two-parent nuclear family, in which the mother is the primary homemaker and the father the primary breadwinner, is by no means a pervasive style of child-rearing in today's world. The extended family, clusters of families, the village, women's associations – all these groups, and others, in various places in the world have major child-rearing responsibilities. Seeing this, we can begin to ask questions – for example, about how much child abuse there is in a family that involves grandparents and other relatives in child-rearing, as compared with the relatively isolated Western-style nuclear family; or about how the different structures of child care support women's work.[2] If we do not undertake this kind of educational project, we risk assuming that the options familiar to us are the only ones there are, and that they are somehow "normal" and "natural" for all humans. Much the same can be said about conceptions of gender and sexuality, about conceptions of work and its division, about schemes of property holding, or about the treatment of children and the aged.

2. We make headway solving problems that require international cooperation

The air does not obey national boundaries. This simple fact can be, for children, the beginning of the recognition that, like it or not, we live in a world in which the destinies of nations are closely intertwined with respect to basic goods and survival itself. The pollution of third-world nations that are attempting to attain our high standard of living will, in some cases, end up in our air. No matter what account of these matters we will finally adopt, any intelligent deliberation about ecology – as, also, about the food supply and population – requires global planning, global knowledge, and the recognition of a shared future.

To conduct this sort of global dialogue, we need knowledge not only of the geography and ecology of other nations – something that would already entail much revision in our curricula – but also a great deal about their people, so that in talking with them we may be capable of respecting their traditions and commitments. Cosmopolitan education would supply the background necessary for this type of deliberation.

3. We recognize moral obligations to the rest of the world that are real and that otherwise would go unrecognized

What are Americans to make of the fact that the high living standard we enjoy is one that very likely cannot be universalized, at least given the present costs of pollution controls and the present economic situation of developing nations, without ecological disaster? If we take Kantian morality at all seriously, as we should, we need to educate our children to be troubled by this fact. Otherwise we are educating a nation of moral hypocrites who talk the language of universalizability but whose universe has a self-serving, narrow scope.

This point may appear to presuppose universalism, rather than being an argument in its favor. But here one may note that the values on which Americans may most justly pride themselves are, in a deep sense, Stoic values: respect for human dignity and the opportunity for each person to pursue happiness. If we really do believe that all human beings are created equal and endowed with certain inalienable rights, we are morally required to think about what that conception requires us to do with and for the rest of the world.

Once again, that does not mean that one may not permissibly give one's own sphere a special degree of concern. Politics, like child care, will be poorly done if each thinks herself equally responsible for all, rather than giving the immediate surroundings special attention and care. To give one's own sphere special care is justifiable in universalist terms, and I think this is its most compelling justification. To take one example, we do not really think our own children are morally more important than other people's children, even though almost all of us who have children would give our own children far more love and care than we give others'. It is good for children, on the whole, that things work this way, and that is why our special care is good, rather than selfish. Education may and should reflect those special concerns – for example, in a given nation, spending more time on that nation's history and politics. But my argument does entail the idea that we should not confine our thinking to our own sphere, that in making choices in both political and economic matters we should most seriously consider the right of other human beings to life, liberty, and the pursuit of happiness, and that we should work to acquire the knowledge that will enable us to deliberate well about those rights. I believe this sort of thinking will have large-scale economic and political consequences.

4. We make a consistent and coherent argument based on distinctions
we are prepared to defend

In Richard Rorty's and Sheldon Hackney's eloquent appeals to shared values, there is something that makes me very uneasy. They seem to argue effectively when they insist on the centrality to democratic deliberation of certain values that bind all citizens together. But why should these values, which instruct us to join hands across boundaries of ethnicity, class, gender, and race, lose steam when they get to the borders of the nation? By conceding that a morally arbitrary boundary such as the boundary of the nation has a deep and formative role in our deliberations, we seem to deprive ourselves of any principled way of persuading citizens they should in fact join hands across these other barriers.

For one thing, the very same groups exist both outside and inside. Why should we think of people from China as our fellows the minute they dwell in a certain place, namely the United States, but not when they dwell in a certain other place, namely China? What is it about the national boundary that magically converts people toward whom we are both incurious and indifferent into people to whom we have duties of mutual respect? I think, in short, that we undercut the very case for multicultural respect within a nation by failing to make central to education a broader world respect. Richard Rorty's patriotism may be a way of bringing all Americans together; but patriotism is very close to jingoism, and I'm afraid I don't see in Rorty's argument any proposal for coping with this very obvious danger.

Furthermore, the defense of shared national values in both Rorty and Hackney, as I understand it, requires appealing to certain basic features of human personhood that obviously also transcend national boundaries. So if we fail to educate children to cross those boundaries in their minds and imaginations, we are tacitly giving them the message that we don't really mean what we say. We say that respect should be accorded to humanity as such, but we really mean that Americans as such are worthy of special respect. And that, I think, is a story that Americans have told for far too long.

IV

Becoming a citizen of the world is often a lonely business. It is, as Diogenes said, a kind of exile – from the comfort of local truths, from the warm, nestling feeling of patriotism, from the absorbing drama of pride in oneself and one's own. In the writings of Marcus Aurelius (as in those of his American followers Emerson and Thoreau), a reader can sometimes sense a boundless loneliness, as if the removal of the props of habit and local boundaries had left life bereft of any warmth or security. If one begins life as a child who loves and trusts his or her parents, it is tempting to want to reconstruct citizenship along the same lines, finding in an idealized image of a nation a surrogate parent who will do one's thinking for one. Cosmopolitanism offers no such refuge; it offers only reason and the love of humanity, which may seem at times less colorful than other sources of belonging.

[. . .] let me conclude with a story of cosmopolitanism that has a happy ending. It is told by Diogenes Laertius about the courtship and marriage of the Cynic cosmopolitan philosophers Crates and Hipparchia (one of the most eminent female philosophers of antiquity), in order, presumably, to show that casting off the symbols of status and nation can sometimes be a way to succeed in love. The background is that Hipparchia is from a good family, attached, as most Greek families were, to social status and pedigree. They resent the cosmopolitan philosopher Crates, with his strange ideas of world citizenship and his strange disdain for rank and boundaries.

> [Hipparchia] fell in love with Crates' arguments and his way of life and paid no attention to any of her suitors nor to wealth or high birth or good looks. Crates, though, was everything to her. Moreover, she told her parents that she would kill herself if she were not married off to him. So Crates was called on by her parents to talk their daughter out of it; he did all he could, but in the end he didn't persuade her. So he stood up and threw off his clothes in front of her and said, "Here is your bridegroom; these are his possessions; make your decision accordingly – for you cannot be my companion unless you undertake the same way of life." The girl chose him. Adopting the same clothing and style of life she went around with her husband and they copulated in public and they went off together to dinner parties. And once she went to a dinner party at the house of Lysimachus and there refuted Theodorus the Atheist, with a sophism like this: "If it wouldn't be judged wrong for Theodorus to do something, then it wouldn't be judged wrong for Hipparchia to do it either; but Theodorus does no wrong if he beats himself; so Hipparchia too does no wrong if she beats Theodorus." And when Theodorus could not reply to her argument, he ripped off her cloak. But Hipparchia was not upset or distraught as a woman would normally be. (DL 6.96–8)[3]

I am not exactly recommending Crates and Hipparchia as the marital ideal for students in my hypothetical cosmopolitan schools (or Theodorus the Atheist as their logic teacher).[4] But the story does reveal this: that the life of the cosmopolitan, who puts right before country and universal reason before the symbols of national belonging, need not be boring, flat, or lacking in love.

Notes

1 A recent example of this argument is in Amy Gutmann's "Multiculturalism and Democratic Education," presented at a conference on "Equality and Its Critics" held at Brown University in March 1994. My article originated as a comment on Gutmann's paper.
2 For some related questions about women and work, see the articles in Martha C. Nussbaum and Jonathan Glover, eds., *Women, Culture, and Development* (Oxford: Clarendon Press, 1995).
3 I am grateful to Brad Inwood for permission to use his unpublished translation of this section.
4 I exempt Hipparchia from criticism, since she was clearly trying to show him up and she did not endorse the fallacious inference seriously.

10

What is Cosmopolitan?
Jeremy Waldron

I. Introduction

[. . .]

We talk, in the first instance, of cosmopolitan attitudes and cosmopolitan lifestyles, where the adjective is supposed to indicate a way of being in the world, a way of constructing an identity for oneself that is different from, and arguably opposed to, the idea of belonging to or devotion to or immersion in a particular culture. In his *Dictionary of Political Thought*, the English conservative Roger Scruton gave the following definition of "cosmopolitanism":

> The belief in, and pursuit of, a style of life which . . . [shows] acquaintance with, and an ability to incorporate, the manners, habits, languages, and social customs of cities throughout the world. . . . In this sense, the cosmopolitan is often seen as a kind of parasite, who depends upon the quotidian lives of others to create the various local flavors and identities in which he dabbles.[1]

Personally, I feel the sting in the tail of this definition quite acutely – the cosmopolitan as *parasite* – because the charge of dabbling rootlessly in a plurality of cultures, each of which has taken generations or millennia to develop as a single living organism, seems to apply exactly to the idealized self-description I used in an article published a few years ago in *The Michigan Journal of Law Reform*, an article entitled "Minority Cultures and the Cosmopolitan Alternative."[2] There I characterized the cosmopolitan lifestyle, or rather the cosmopolitan approach to lifestyle, in terms of a person who lives in California, but came there from Oxford via Edinburgh, and came in turn to Oxford from the other side of the world, the southwestern corner of the Pacific Ocean, whither his English and Irish ancestors emigrated in the mid-nineteenth century. I spoke of someone who did not associate his identity with any secure sense of place, someone who did not take his cultural identity to be defined by any bounded subset of the cultural resources available in the world. He did not take his identity as anything definitive, as anything homogenous that might be muddied or compromised when he studied Greek, ate Chinese, wore clothes made in Korea, worshipped with the Book of Common Prayer, listened to arias by Verdi sung by a Maori diva on Japanese equipment, gave lectures in Buenos Aires, followed Israeli politics, or practised Buddhist meditation techniques. I spoke of this person as a creature of modernity, conscious, even proud, of living in a mixed-up world and having a mixed-up self. And I said that as long as a person can live like that, it is evident that people do not need what the proponents of cultural identity politics claim they do need, claim in fact that they are entitled to as a matter of right, namely, immersion in the secure framework of a single culture to which, in some deep sense, they belong.[3]

The characterization I gave in "Minority Cultures" has elicited a number of responses. I am exercised particularly by a question that Will Kymlicka posed in his recent book *Multicultural Citizenship*, when he asked in effect, "What exactly is *cosmopolitan* about this style of life that Waldron describes?" It is not, said Kymlicka, a genuine mixing of cultures; it is simply a case of someone "enjoying the opportunities provided by the diverse societal culture which characterizes the Anglophone society of the United States."[4] One of the things I want to do in this paper is answer that question. And I want also to correct what I think now is the rather unfortunate impression I gave in "Minority Cultures" that there can be nothing cosmopolitan about the life or lifestyle of someone who stays where he is, immersed in the traditions, language and practices of a particular culture.

That is one topic. I would also like to discuss the use of the term "cosmopolitan" in political philosophy and in the philosophy of law. There we find that the adjective is used in various ways, some of them differing quite significantly in their logic from the use we have just been discussing. On the one hand, there is what we might call the cosmopolitan political ideal – that is, the substantive utopian ideal of a *polis* or polity constructed on a world scale, rather than on the basis of regional, territorially limited states.

[. . .] On the other hand, the term cosmopolitan is used sometimes in legal and political philosophy not so much to pick out a particular ideal as to denote an area or department of juridical concern.

Here I have in mind the use of the term in the political writings of Immanuel Kant. Kant did not use "cosmopolitan" to designate any particular view about how the world should be organized. This is not to deny that he held such a view. [. . .] Kant thought that "the distress produced by the constant wars in which states try to subjugate or engulf each other must finally lead them, even against their will, to enter into a *cosmopolitan* constitution."[5] He was of course well aware that this view was regarded as a non-starter – "ridiculed by great statesmen, and even more by heads of state, as pedantic, childish and academic ideas"[6] – which is perhaps why he discussed it, among other places, in an essay with the laborious title, "On the Common Saying: 'This May be True in Theory, but it does not Apply in Practice.'" But apart from that substantive ideal of world government or a permanent and pacific League of Nations, Kant used the term "cosmopolitan" as a label for a topic or a department of law and legal philosophy. He used the phrase "cosmopolitan right" rather in the way we use the phrase "international law," not so much as a substantive thesis about what the law ought to be, but as a way of designating an area of human life and interaction with which law, right and justice ought to be concerned.[7] His own belief in some sort of grand federation of states is thus a thesis *in* cosmopolitan right (as his republicanism is a thesis in constitutional jurisprudence), rather than being, so to speak, the essence of the cosmopolitan.

We have to be careful here. I do not want to pretend that using a term like "cosmopolitan" as a name for a department of legal inquiry is unrelated to its use as the name of a substantive thesis. The terms we use for departments of legal study are never *entirely* neutral from a substantive point of view. [. . .] *Similarly*, I think Kant's phrase "cosmopolitan right" does not *merely* pick out a form, a topic or a level of legal analysis;

it does also connote a kind of substantive view or attitude about the basis on which he thinks we ought to proceed when we are considering law and rights at a global level. One would not talk about cosmopolitan right if one believed the peoples of the world were entitled to prey upon one another in a manner largely unregulated by law; and on the other hand, one also would not talk about cosmopolitan right if one believed that, for the sake of cultural purity or cultural integrity, the peoples of the world should have as little as possible to do with one another. Cosmopolitan right, for Kant, is the department of jurisprudence concerned with people and peoples' sharing the world with others, given the circumstance that this sharing is more or less inevitable, and likely to go drastically wrong, if not governed by juridical principles.

Thus Kant's use of "cosmopolitan" in this context is more subtle and challenging than the one that was at issue in my article on "Minority Cultures." It is challenging not least because it draws our attention to aspects of human relations, aspects of the human condition, that legal, political and constitutional theorists have to come to terms with, or ought to come to terms with, whether they like it or not, whether they are cultural cosmopolitans or not, and whether or not their political ideologies commit them to world government as an aspiration.

So there we have two topics to discuss: cosmopolitanism in culture, and the Kantian idea of cosmopolitan right. The two are connected of course. They are connected by way of our thinking about the relation between culture and *identity* – where "identity" has something to do with the way we sometimes think we are entitled to present ourselves to others, the sort of non-negotiable side of our cultural preferences. At the end of this paper, I want to draw some implications from the Kantian discussion for the politics of cultural identity. I want to suggest that cosmopolitan right, in Kant's sense, makes demands on the way we behave and comport ourselves in domestic politics. In particular, I shall argue, it calls into question the virtue of what we call "identity-politics" – which I understand as a way of presenting oneself and one's cultural preferences *non-negotiably* to others in the present circumstances of the world.

II. Cosmopolitan culture

Let us begin with the cosmopolitan in culture. In "Minority Cultures," I made the misleading suggestion that a cosmopolitan lifestyle differs necessarily in its content and format from the lifestyle of one who is immersed in the practices of a particular culture. I implied that someone immersed in the life of a particular culture swallows his culture whole, so to speak, so that his identity is as secure as the identity of the culture, uncontaminated by the intrusion of alien practices or ideas; whereas someone who lives the cosmopolitan experience wears a coat of many colors, "a bit of this and a bit of that,"[8] an identity composed of many fragments, or perhaps more accurately just many fragments of culture coexisting in the life of a single person, with the question of identity sidelined or rejected as distracting, redundant or irrelevant.

I think now that this contrast is mistaken. It is certainly wrong to imply that immersion in the particular culture of the society in which one has been brought up is incompatible with what Kant would call a cosmopolitan attitude towards sharing the world with others. It is wrong for a number of reasons.

First – and this is the truth in Kymlicka's critique of the original picture I painted – many cultures in the world have *already* something of a cosmopolitan aspect. A person who grows up in Manhattan, for example, cannot but be aware of a diversity of cultures, a diversity of human practices and experiences, indeed a diversity of languages clamoring for his attention. They are there on the streets, in Greenwich Village or on the Upper West Side. It is another matter whether we call this a single culture – "New York culture" – a culture of diversity, or whether we say (as I think) that it is just *many fragments* that happen to be available at a given place and time and that that does not amount to the existence of a *single* culture in any socially or philosophically interesting sense of "singularity." However we describe it, the fact is that someone who makes a life in this milieu is already making a life *in the world*, whether he has particular affection for one of the available cultures or not. Even if he spends his whole life in Manhattan, he is by virtue of his location necessarily open to new practices and new experiences in a cosmopolitan sort of way.

A second point follows from this, and I think it is more important.[9] Cities like New York, Paris, London and Bombay are the urban centers of world culture; they are great centers of trade, tourism and migration, where peoples and their traditions mingle and interact. They pay tribute to a central fact about human nature which the cosmopolitan, above all, ought to be in the business of emphasizing and extolling. Humans are curious and adventurous animals: they travel, they migrate, they trade, they fight, and they plunder. And they report back what they have found out about the ways in which others live (and trade and fight etc.). They bring back tales of exotic customs as well as the exotic goods they have purchased or stolen. One result of this is that custom, practice, language, and social and military organization seldom stay local. The pure culture, uncontaminated in its singularity, is for this reason an anomaly; it is an exception usually explained by historical contingency and extraordinary geographical isolation. For human cultures, it is the rule, not the exception, that ideas and ways of doing things are propagated and transmitted, noticed and adapted. No doubt – from a purist's point of view – they are violated and distorted in the process; but my point is that there is nothing normative about the purist's point of view.

Thus we should certainly expect that neighboring communities – communities within regular trading or shooting distance from one another – will have many similarities in their respective cultures. One sometimes hears it said that what is important about each culture is its *distinctiveness*, and that respecting another culture is a matter of cherishing diversity, celebrating difference, focusing attention on those aspects that clearly distinguish it from one's own. That may be a useful educational strategy in, say, elementary schools. When children in the United States have Guatemala Day at school, we do not want them all to make a special ceremony of wearing Levi jeans and drinking Coca-Cola, even if that is what Guatemalans in fact like to wear and drink. In that context, we have reason to highlight the differences between culture in Guatemala and *Norteatnericano* culture. But the general view that it is *distinctiveness* that counts may be seriously mistaken if it is intended as a description of the consciousness of those who live in the communities in question or as a prescription about what respect for another culture ought essentially to involve.

Consider the example I just mentioned, Guatemala; and compare it to a culture on the other side of the world, say, the culture of Eire (or Ireland). To the extent that a Guatemalan or an Irish person actually thinks self-consciously about her culture (a problematic notion to which I want to return in a page or two), is it the *distinctiveness* of the culture that will be important to her – that is, the respects in which her culture differs from others, as opposed to the respects in which it is similar? I doubt that we can assume this. It seems perfectly possible, for example, that an inhabitant of Guatemala would regard the teachings and sacraments of the Roman Catholic Church as among the most important aspects of her culture. If so, it may be both implicit in and essential to that thought that her Church be regarded as *catholic* with a small "c", in the sense of universal – that is, catholic in precisely the sense of being something shared by many other communities. That feature of her life – that *as a Guatemalan* she shares a faith and a church with the Irish, and also with Italians, Poles, Brazilians, Japanese Catholics and Filipinas – may be much more important to her identity than anything which (say) a Tourist Board or an elementary school teacher would use to highlight the cultural distinctiveness of Guatemala. Thus, participation in this particular culture already has a cosmopolitan dimension. The humble, local and earthy practice of worshiping God and taking the sacraments may be unintelligible except as an implicit faith in and attachment to an institution *because* it exists on a world scale and because it claims potentially to unite all mankind.

It follows, I think, that the "essence" of a culture (if indeed that idea makes sense) need not consist in its distinctiveness. One culture does not need to be clearly and importantly *different* from another, either in its appearance to an outsider or in the consciousness of its practitioners, in order to be the culture that it is. A cultural *taxonomist* may be interested in qualitative differentiation, and we as multiculturalism may want there to be lots of colorful differences in costume, language and ritual so that we can *display* our commitment to multiculturalism to even the most superficial glance. But all that may be beside the point so far as the culture itself is concerned. A culture just is what it is, and its practices and rituals are constitutive of it in virtue of their place in a shared way of life, not in virtue of their perceived peculiarity.

The point can be taken a step further. In general, we should not assume that thoughts about one's culture – whether they are thoughts about its distinctiveness or anything else – loom very large in one's own involvement in the cultural life of one's community. What one does in a community is simply speak or marry or dance or worship. One participates in a form of life. *Advertising* or *announcing* that this is what one is doing is participation in *another* form of life – a *different* form of life – a form of life only problematically related to the first. When one speaks or marries or dances or worships, one does not *say* anything about the distinctive features of, say, the Irish heritage, or the peculiarities of Guatemalan wedding festivities. One keeps faith with the mores of one's community by just following them, not by announcing self-consciously that it is the mores of one's community that one is following.

This point has a broader importance, beyond the scope of cultural participation. It calls in question some of the self-conscious posturing often associated with nationhood. In a famous essay on "Nationalism," Isaiah Berlin suggested that nationalism

> entails the notion that one of the most compelling reasons, perhaps the most compelling, for holding a particular belief, pursuing a particular policy, serving a particular end, living a particular life, is that these ends, beliefs, policies, lives are *ours*. This is tantamount to saying that these rules or doctrines or principles should be followed not because they lead to virtue or happiness or justice or liberty, or are good and right in themselves, rather they are to be followed because these values are those of *my* group – for the nationalist, of *my* nation . . . [10]

I am sure Berlin was right to see this as an aspect of explicit nationalist consciousness. (I do not think this was his own view, although discerning that is often quite difficult.) It seems to me that this self-consciousness is characteristic, too, of a great deal of modern cultural identity politics. People say: "I dress this way or I speak this language or I follow these marriage customs *because they are the ways of my people*." But if you pause and think about it, this is a very peculiar attitude to take – to insert the cultural provenance of a norm or value into what H. I. A. Hart would call its "internal aspect."[11] It seems very odd to regard the fact that something is "our" norm – that is, that this is what we Irishmen or we Maori or we Americans do – as part of the *reason*, if not the central reason, for having the norm, and for sustaining and following it. For consider: social norms and practices do not exist *in order* to make up a colorful distinctive culture for us to display and immerse ourselves in. They exist in a context of reasons and reasoning. There is always a story to be told, a story internal to the norm – part, as I said, of its internal aspect – as to why doing things this way is better or appropriate or obligatory or required. If, for example, I ask an elder of the group to which I belong why we have and follow a norm of monogamy, he may tell me a story about the need for reciprocity and equality between lovers and explain why this is difficult or impossible in polygamous relationships, or he may tell me a story about the sun and the moon and about there being only one of each. Either way, *that* is the sort of thing that counts, in the group, as a *reason* for having and following the monogamy custom. True, I may not accept the reasoning that the group associates with the norm; or I may find the sun-and-moon story bewildering or unsatisfying. But if I do, that is all there is to say about the matter: I no longer understand or respect the norm on the basis on which it claims my respect and understanding I certainly do not show any respect for it – rather I show a vain and self-preoccupied contempt for the norm itself – by gutting it of *its* reasons, and replacing them *as reasons* with my own need to keep faith with my own cultural roots. That is not the point of the monogamy requirement, and to think of it as the point, or part of the point, or even as one reason among others, may be to give a quite misleading impression of how important the norm is supposed to be in this culture and what that importance is based upon.

In other words: if there are norms and practices that constitute "our" way of life and that matter to us, then the thing to do is embrace them wholeheartedly, not in a way that leaves it open for us to comment to others in the sort of stage whisper that characterizes modern identity-politics: "I am following the practices of my community," or "What I am doing here is revisiting my roots." It is not and has not been the nature of *our* moral practices to go around saying that sort of thing about them ("I am telling my wife the truth because that is what we do around here"); and I doubt that it is the practice of very many other groups either. On the contrary, to congratulate oneself on following "the norms of my community" is already to take a point of view somewhat external to those norms, rather than to subscribe wholeheartedly to the substantive commitments that they embody.

The same point can be taken one step further. If you accept what I have said so far, then it is no longer evident that the abstract idea of moral universalism is the sort of gigantic *affront* to cultural particularity that practitioners of identity politics take it to be. Humans and human groups take their norms seriously, and to take them seriously is to think of them as embedded in a structure of reasons and reasoning. Whatever we think of them from the outside, from the inside they are not like the rules of games or the norms of fancy dress – that is, things one can cast off as soon as it seems no longer important to display oneself as a member of a particular group. They make deep claims, powerful claims about what is important and what sort of things are at stake in the areas of life that they govern. Those claims are usually held to be *true* (by those who make them), which means that they claim to offer to give a better account of what really matters than the reasoning associated with the different norms and practices of the society next door or across the sea. Now, that reasoning may bewilder and disconcert us; it is no part of my argument that it should be familiar or congenial or just like *our* reasoning over here. But it is like ours at least in this: that it represents or claims to represent some repository of human wisdom as to the best way of doing things. As such it necessarily makes its reasoning available – though, as I have said now several times, not always easily or comfortably available – to understanding and assessment on the basis of what else there is in the world in the way of human wisdom and experience on questions such as those that the norm purports to address. And *that*, I think, is what is cosmopolitan – or what has the potential to be universal and cosmopolitan – about the character of genuine as opposed to fake or patronizing participation in the life and practice of one's particular community.

III. Cosmopolitan right

The second thing I said I wanted to discuss in this paper was Immanuel Kant's use of the term "cosmopolitan right," understood in the first instance as the designation of a topic of inquiry in the philosophy of law, an area of legal concern which – as much as crime and punishment, or contract, or marriage – a decent jurisprudence ought to be in the business of saying something about.

How are we to define this topic or understand this area of concern? We may proceed by analogy with other departments of law. Criminal law responds to the potential for violence and depredation in human affairs. Its presuppositions – or, to adapt a phrase from John Rawls, the "circumstances" of criminal law[12] – are our mutual vulnerability, our limited strength of will, and the hundred and one reasons there may be for one individual to attack, or to fear attack from, another. [. . .] These are familiar explications of the point of familiar bodies of law. What are the corresponding presuppositions or circumstances of cosmopolitan right?

The starting point of Immanuel Kant's analysis of circumstances of cosmopolitan right is an entertaining mixture of the abstract, the bizarre and the almost amateurishly concrete. Nature, Kant says, has given us as a world a *sphere* to live on, not an infinite plain so that those whose actions, beliefs, customs and attitudes offend each other could disperse over the horizon beyond each others' apprehensions. We live on the surface of a sphere so that if I go far enough away from you in one direction, I will sooner or later find myself approaching you from the other direction. The world of course is very large, and different regions are separated from one another by uninhabitable stretches of desert or ocean. But even then, Kant says, "the *ship* or the *camel* (the ship of the desert) make it possible for [men] to approach their fellows over these ownerless tracts, and to utilize as a means of social intercourse that *right to the earth's surface* which the human race shares in common."[13] Indeed, and rather curiously, Kant thinks of the existence of camels, along with marine mammals and driftwood, as evidence of nature's purpose that we should spread out over the whole globe, not just the forested regions.

> [E]vidence of design in nature emerges even more clearly [i.e. even more clearly than in the case of the camel] when we realize that the shores of the Arctic Ocean are inhabited not only by fur-bearing animals, but also by seals, walruses and whales, whose

flesh provides food and whose fat provides warmth for the native inhabitants. Nature's care arouses most admiration, however, by carrying driftwood to these treeless regions, without anyone knowing exactly where it comes from. For if they did not have this material, the natives would not be able to construct either boats, or weapons, or dwellings in which to live.[14]

I do not know whether Kant took driftwood as a prototype for "the crooked timber of humanity,"[15] but at any rate the spherical shape of the earth, together with seals, camels and driftwood, are for Kant what David Hume would call the "outward circumstances" of cosmopolitan right.[16]

There are also circumstances of "natural temper,"[17] that is, circumstances relating to human motivation and attitude. Humans seem disposed to wander, travel, explore, and settle new regions. Or, if this is not an *innate* disposition, it is at the very least a disposition to respond to certain other vicissitudes of life – such as famine, climate change, overpopulation or attack by other groups – by wandering, traveling, exploring and settling. At the same time, there are familiar temptations accompanying this movement, exploration and settlement: the temptation to plunder and conquer, and exploit, enslave, or even exterminate others when one finds that the lands to which one travels are already inhabited.

And there is finally the exasperating fact of what Kant called man's "unsocial sociability,"[18] which in the present context combines man's cosmopolitan curiosity about how others live, and about practices and traditions other than his own, with an extraordinary human reluctance to take others' practices seriously, as competitors or alternatives to his own views about what he actually owes to others in the way of forbearance and respect. Kant thinks of man, even in the blood-soaked context of migration, conquest and settlement, as *sociable* in a certain (no doubt limited) willingness to restrain his own inclinations for the sake of others. Indeed, man is even potentially moral, in this sphere. But he is at the same time *un*sociable in the sense (and this is Kant's phrase) "of wanting to direct everything in accordance with his own ideas,"[19] not others' ideas, of what he owes to others in the way of forbearance and respect. It is not that his own sociability is just a cover for self-interest and that is why he is reluctant to accept others' accounts of what sociability requires. It is rather that each of us – each individual or each society – takes his own moral thinking very seriously, and finds some terrible affront, some sort of obstacle of self-righteousness, in taking seriously the different moral thinking of others, especially when it leads to different conclusions. This is the key to Kant's political philosophy of course – the famous paragraph 44 of the *Rechtslehre*[20] – but it is also, I believe, a crucial presupposition, a crucial part of the problematic, of cosmopolitan right. So, to summarize: we share the earth with those who may have ways of doing things that are different from our own, perhaps ways of doing things that we can barely understand, and who may make demands on us, for cooperation or forbearance, that are quite different from the demands with which we are prepared to comply. And we have an inclination to move across and around the surface of a bounded sphere. As a result there is no telling who in particular, or what groups, one is likely to discover as one's neighbors. There is no telling on what terms one will have to cooperate, or to what practices one will have to adapt.

As Kant himself developed it, towards the end of the *Doctrine of Right*, cosmopolitan right was understood primarily in terms of a set of constraints governing what a people was entitled to do in the course of this process as they came alongside strangers, or what they were entitled to do as strangers moved closer to them.[21] (Much of this is a vehicle for Kant's indignation at some of the bloodthirsty abuses associated with contemporary imperialism and the European colonization of Africa and America.)[22]

Each person, he said, and each group has the right to approach others with a view to engaging in commerce. Though this right is often terribly abused, still "such abuse cannot annul the right of citizens of the world to try to establish community with all [others] and, to this end, to visit all regions of the earth."[23] This is not, Kant insists, the same as a right of settlement in lands which are already inhabited; for *that* a genuine agreement is required, an agreement that does not allow one or other party unscrupulously to take advantage of the other so far as the acquisition of land is concerned.[24]

It is less clear what Kant thinks should happen once violations of this principle have become established, that is, once settlement and intermingling have taken place, and become fixed and more or less permanent, perhaps without the agreement of the original inhabitants. All he says in the *Doctrine of Right* is that the stain of injustice cannot be erased from such settlement; but that does not help us very much in figuring out what now is to be done about the resulting situation.

My hunch, however – and this is where my argument becomes constructive, not just interpretive – is that Kant held the view of commonsense here. If a new settlement – originally wrong and unlawful under principles of cosmopolitan right – becomes established over several generations, then the descendants of the original settlers are likely to have nowhere to return to. They and the descendants of those whom their ancestors invaded and expropriated now have nothing to do but come to terms with one another – as people who, whatever the history, now happen to be "unavoidably side by side" – and establish a fair basis for sharing the lands and resources that surround them. Certainly, this is what is suggested by the general tenor of Kant's observation that people and peoples move out across a surface that is not infinite. Apart from the illegitimate possibilities we have just been considering, there are a hundred and one legitimate ways in which people might find themselves living side by side with others of different cultures. In general, in a mobile, migratory world, there is no telling who we will end up living alongside of, no telling who our neighbors may turn out to be. This means that cosmopolitan right is bound to have some interesting implications for the social and political organization of particular territorial states, quite apart from the more glamorous business of international law, federations of states or cosmopolitan commonwealths.

IV. Cosmopolitan right and civic responsibility

In the last part of this paper, I shall explore some of these implications. I shall attempt to map some of what Kant said about cosmopolitan right onto other parts of his work that address more familiar topics in legal and political philosophy, namely, the basis on which we are required to live together with our fellow citizens in an ordinary middle-sized republic.

The heart of Kant's political philosophy is – as I said earlier – paragraph 44 of the *Rechtslehre*. There he maintains that, apart from positive law, the natural situation of human beings is conflict. It is not necessarily conflict for Hobbesian reasons, that is, a struggle of the self-interest or the survival interest of each against the self-interest or survival interest of all others. For Kant, the idea of conflict in the state of nature is the idea of a war raised under competing and hostile banners of justice and right. He says that people "can never be secure against acts of violence from one another, since each will have his own right to do what seems right and good to him, independently of the opinion of others."[25] Now the fact that you and I have different views about rights and justice is not a matter of concern if our interests do not converge on the same space for action, or the same objects or land or resources. But if we are, in Kant's words, "unavoidably side by side" with one another (whatever the historical reasons for our current proximity), then we have no choice but to attempt to come to terms with one another in some sort of common framework of law. Without that (I mean, without that coming to terms), no determinate principles of freedom and no relations of property are going to be possible – which means of course that there will be no shared basis, no mutually recognized basis, and thus no commonly *assured* basis, on which people around here can act and live their lives and make use of the material resources that are useful to and necessary for their subsistence.[26]

In both liberal – particularly Rawlsian – and also in recent communitarian and Walzerian political philosophy, there has been a tendency to insist that a well-ordered society should be thought of as something constructed among those who *share* certain fundamental understandings which are constitutive of justice.[27] The idea seems to be that whatever else citizens disagree about, either they share understandings that are constitutive of justice in the abstract, or they share understandings that are constitutive of what justice in various forms is for them. By contrast, the great virtue of Kant's work, it seems to me, and the reason why all this bears the sort of weight I am trying to put on it, is that he begins from *the opposite assumption*. He assumes that we are always likely to find ourselves alongside others who disagree with us about justice; and he argues that if there is to be community or a common law, a common framework for living, it has to be created in the form of positive law, constructed by good-hearted citizens out of an array of individual and cultural understandings that are initially disparate and opposed.

The need for a common body of positive law is, as I said, relative to this geographical relation of being *unavoidably side by side with others*. Cultural relativists and participants in identity politics posit – at least as an ideal – that people begin in proximity to those with whom they share a common morality: we start off in tidily homogenous communities and these are only disrupted by imperialism, attempted genocide, etc. The point of Kant's cosmopolitan right, however, is that this geographical relation – being unavoidably side by side with others – is no guarantee whatever that common moral views and shared understandings can be taken for granted, not even ideally, let alone as initially given. We cannot pick and choose the people with whom we are required to come to terms, in Kant's theory. Of those who surround us, competing for the use and control of the same action-space and the same resources, we cannot say, "We will enter into civil society with A and B, who share our understandings, but not with C because C is not a person who shares our traditions." The discipline of politics is that there is no alternative to our coming to terms with C. Humans live side by side, clustered together in circumstances where they simply *have* to deal with one another, whatever the initial disparity between their views of justice, morality and right.

All this is true of individuals holding different views. And it is true, I think, in *spades* of whole peoples – and of disparate cultures – who find themselves unavoidably side by side. If humans have fanned out over the face of the earth (as they have), then a way has to be found, when they cluster together in particular fertile or hospitable territories, to bring into relation with one another the views of each group and individual concerning justice and right with the views of all of the other groups and individuals in that locality. Or to put the matter a little more carefully, since groups may not help-fully *label* their views as "views about justice and rights": if we live alongside another group, a way has to be found to bring our views about justice and right into relation with whatever views of the *other* group – traditional, political, metaphysical, theologi-cal – serve *the function* of views of justice and right. By "serve the function of views about justice and right," I mean simply that, for practical purposes, they are (actually or potentially) at odds with, and compete with, our views about justice and right with regard to the resources and territory that we somehow need to share.

This brings me finally to the points I wanted to make about civic virtue and the poli-tics of cultural identity.

Cosmopolitan right – one's willingness to do what is required by the general prin-ciple of sharing this limited world with others – is rightly regarded by Kant as not just one ethical idea among others. However dusty and quaint it sounds, cosmopolitan right is not, he says, a mere "philanthropic principle of ethics, but a principle of right".[28] It imposes a certain juridically-based *discipline* in politics, a discipline rooted in our diver-sity, our potential disagreements, and our need nevertheless for law. Because we hold disparate views about justice and follow different traditions but still live unavoidably side by side with one another, we have to come to terms with one another. Our need to come to terms has an impact, then, on the way in which we are entitled to present ourselves as partisans of different views or participants in disparate traditions.

In Part II of this paper, I attempted to distinguish a mode of allegiance to the tradi-tions of a particular culture that was not in principle incompatible with this discipline of cosmopolitan right. If one participates straightforwardly in a way of life, without the self-consciousness that multiculturalism often involves, then paradoxically one is often *more* open to outsiders than one is if cultural participation is always presented as "revisiting my roots" or "following the traditions of my people" or "here's what's distinctive about us." If one acts directly in response responding to the reasons that internally support a given way of life, then, however peculiar one's practices, they are at least amenable to reasoned challenge or inquisitive reasoning from the outside. If someone says, "Why do you people insist on monogamy," we can give him a substan-tive answer (which is not simply "This is how we do things round here"); and in prin-ciple our answer can be brought into dialectical relation with his reasons – the outsider's reasons – for thinking that polygamy is a superior structure. On the other hand, I want to suggest that what *is* incompatible with cosmopolitan right is the presentation of one's engagement with a particular set of cultural norms and practices as though they were brute aspects of one's identity, like one's sex or one's color, and therefore non-negotiable by anyone who takes seriously and respects one's identity, one's self. This mode of engagement – cultural engagement as identity – treats the norms and prac-tices of one's community or culture as though they were costumes or attributes rather than intelligent and intelligible structures of reasoning. To repeat then: if we take a tradition or practice of our culture seriously, then we should treat it not simply as a costume for display or as an attribute of our identity, but as a standard which does some normative work in the life of one's community. Moreover, to take it seriously is to treat it as a standard with a point – a standard which does work in the society which might (in principle or at least as a matter of logical possibility) have been performed by other norms, alternative standards, and which therefore cannot be understood except in terms of its association with an array of reasons that explain why in fact it is *this* norm rather than *that* – monogamy, for example, rather than polygamy – which is the standard we happen to uphold. Only if one's *initial* allegiance to the practices of one's culture is held and presented in this sort of spirit can it be presented to others of different cultures (others who hold different norms) as a first move in the complicated business – involving bargaining, deliberation, compromise, voting, authority – of coming to terms with those who with whom we need to come to terms (rather than simply those with whom we would like to come to terms).

Thus, the discipline of cosmopolitan right in domestic politics is not that I must give up my intense and particularistic allegiances and become the sort of shallow gadfly or parasite that Roger Scruton excoriated in the definition we considered at the beginning of this paper. It is rather that I should take the norms of my culture for what they really are – not aspects of my "identity" (or my cultural vanity), but solutions or purported solutions, which have been developed in one group over time and funded deeply by the distinctive experience of the members of this group, to problems and conflicts which we may possibly find ourselves sharing with others who have developed different (and rival) approaches funded by different experiences.

That is the discipline; and it seems to me that what is cosmopolitan about it is, accordingly, much more complicated than the raffish airs of an insecure young man, thousands of miles from home, and grasping at whatever cultural straws he can reach to concoct an identity for himself. I fear that this paper has been more autobiography than moral philosophy; but one speaks of what one knows, and I hope that these remarks help to mark out some common ground between those who are engaged wholeheartedly in the life of some particular culture and those who believe – with Immanuel Kant – that it is important also simply to live *in the world* and to regard nothing human as alien.

Notes

1   Roger Scruton, *A Dictionary of Political Thought* (London: Macmillan, 1982), p. 100.
2   Jeremy Waldron, "Minority cultures and the cosmopolitan alternative," *University of Michigan Journal of Law Reform*, 25 (1992), 751–92; reprinted in *The Rights of Minority Cultures*, ed. Will Kymlicka (Oxford: Oxford University Press, 1995), pp. 93–119.
3   See, e.g., Will Kymlicka, *Liberalism, Community, and Culture* (Oxford: Clarendon Press, 1989).
4   Will Kymlicka, *Multicultural Citizenship* (Oxford: Clarendon Press, 1995), p. 85.
5   Immanuel Kant, "On the common saying: this may be true in theory, but it does not apply in practice," *Kant: Political Writings*, ed. Hans Reiss, enlarged edn. (Cambridge: Cambridge University Press, 1991), 61–92, at p. 90 (cited hereinafter as Kant, "Theory and practice"). However, no sooner did Kant announce this aspiration for world government than he backed away from it, saying apprehensively: "Or if such a state is in turn even more dangerous to freedom, for it may lead to the most fearful despotism (as has indeed occurred more than once with states which have grown too large), distress must force men to form a state which is not a cosmopolitan commonwealth under a single ruler, but a lawful federation under a commonly accepted international right" (idem).
6   Ibid., p. 92.
7   Thus the term "right" in "cosmopolitan right" is a translation of "Recht." It is not necessarily an indication that there are cosmopolitan rights, e.g., alongside civil rights, cultural rights, or socio-economic rights. Whether cosmopolitan right yields a distinctive theory of rights (whether individual rights or group rights) must be regarded as an open question (I am grateful to George Fletcher for some conversations on this point).
8   The phrase is taken from Salman Rushdie's defense of *The Satanic Verses* in a collection of his essays entitled *Imaginary Homelands: Essays and Criticism 1981–1991* (London: Granta Books, 1991), p. 394:

"Those who oppose the novel most vociferously today are of the opinion that intermingling with a different culture will inevitably weaken and ruin their own. I am of the opposite opinion."

9   Much of what follows is taken from my discussion of multiculturalism in Jeremy Waldron, "Multiculturalism and melange," *Public Education in a Multicultural Society. Policy, Theory, Critique*, ed. Robert K. Fullinwider (Cambridge: Cambridge University Press, 1996), pp. 90–118, at pp. 99–100.

10   Isaiah Berlin, *Against the Current: Essays in the History of Ideas* (Oxford: Oxford University Press, 1981), pp. 342–3.

11   See H. L. A. Hart, *The Concept of Law*, 2nd edn. (Oxford: Clarendon Press, 1994), pp. 88 ff.

12   John Rawls, *A Theory of Justice* (Oxford: Oxford University Press, 1971), pp. 126–30 (on the circumstances of justice). See also Jeremy Waldron, "The circumstances of integrity," *Legal Theory*, 3 (1997), 1–22, at pp. 2–5.

13   Immanuel Kant, "Perpetual peace: a philosophical sketch," *Kant's Political Writings*, pp. 93–130, at p. 106.

14   Ibid., p. 110.

15   Cf. Immanuel Kant, "Idea for a universal history with a cosmopolitan purpose," *Kant: Political Writings*, at p. 46: "Nothing straight can be made from such warped wood as that which man is made of." Compare the title of Isaiah Berlin, *The Crooked Timber of Humanity: Chapter in the History of Ideas* (New York: Knopf, 1990).

16   Cf. David Hume, *A Treatise of Human Nature*, ed. L. A. Selby-Bigge (Oxford: Clarendon Press, 1888), Bk III, Part II, sect ii, pp. 486 ff.

17   Idem.

18   Kant, "Idea for a universal history," p. 44.

19   Idem.

20   See Immanuel Kant, *The Metaphysics of Morals* in *Kant: Political Writings*, p. 137. See note 36 below.

21   Ibid., pp. 172–5.

22   See, e.g., ibid., p. 173.

23   Ibid., p. 172.

24   Ibid., p. 173. [A]nd even then, Kant adds, "there must be no attempt to exploit the ignorance of the natives in persuading them to give up their territories" (idem).

25   Immanuel Kant, from section 44 of the *Rechtslehre*, i.e. the first part of *The Metaphysics of Morals*, in *Kant: Political Writings*, p. 137.

26   I have developed this argument at length in Jeremy Waldron, "Kant's legal positivism," *Harvard Law Review*, 109 (1996), 1535–66.

27   See John Rawls, *Political Liberalism* (New York: Columbia University Press, 1996), p. 35; see also Michael Walzer, *Spheres of Justice* (New York: Basic Books, 1983), pp. 8–10 and 312 ff.

28   Kant, *Metaphysics of Morals*, p. 172.

11

Nationalism and Cosmopolitanism
Kok-Chor Tan

[. . .] A growing number of liberal theorists argue that implicit in liberalism is a theory of nationalism. The resurgence of nationalist movements in different parts of the world in recent years and the renewed challenges of multiculturalism and migration within liberal democracies have prompted a burgeoning interest among liberal theorists in the idea of nationalism.[1] One outcome of this confrontation with nationalism is the growing consensus among contemporary liberal theorists that liberalism and nationalism, far from being contradictory ideals as once commonly thought, are not only compatible but indeed mutually reinforcing ideals. As nationalism needs liberalism to tame it and to set moral constraints on it, so liberalism needs nationalism in order to achieve its ends. As liberal nationalists argue, it is within the context of a national culture that "the core liberal values" of individual autonomy, social justice and democracy are best realized (Kymlicka 2001a, pp. 224–9; also D. Miller 1995; Nielsen 1999; and Tamir 1992). A theory of nationalism, therefore, undergirds (even if unacknowledged) most liberal theories of justice, thus prompting Yael Tamir's observation that "most liberals are liberal nationalists" (Tamir 1992, p. 139).

What these liberal nationalists argue is that much of the liberal theorizing on justice has simply assumed the existence of a single national community *within* which liberal principles of justice are to apply (Tamir 1992, pp. 119–20; Kymlicka 1995, chap. 5; cf Rawls 1971, p. 4), and so it has become more of an open question as to whether these principles do in fact apply outside the context of the nation. The liberal ideal, that the individual is entitled to equal respect and concern, is thus exposed to be more parochial than it was once thought to be: it is meant primarily to apply to individuals qua fellow nationals, and not necessarily to *all* individuals as such.

If it is correct that implicit to liberalism is a doctrine about nationality, then my claim that liberals ought also to be cosmopolitans seems to face a problem. This is because it is often thought that nationalism and cosmopolitanism are diametrically opposed ideals. Consequently, if one is a liberal nationalist, one cannot also be a cosmopolitan liberal. So if it is true that implicit and integral to liberal political philosophy is a theory of nationalism, then the attempt to derive cosmopolitan justice from liberalism is apparently doomed to failure. With the increasing prominence and acceptance of the doctrine of liberal nationalism in the current philosophical literature, it is not surprising that there has been, lately, a noticeable skepticism or agnosticism, even among liberals, concerning the cosmopolitan aspiration to liberal justice.[2]

The cosmopolitan liberal confronted by this challenge has two possible options by way of defending cosmopolitanism. One is by denying the doctrine of liberal nationalism. That is, the incompatibility between cosmopolitanism and nationalism is accepted and the central task for cosmopolitans is, on this view, to deny the doctrine of liberal nationalism (e.g., Barry 1999; Brock 2002; Lichtenberg 1998; Moellendorf 2002, pp. 51–4). Another option open to cosmopolitans, however, does not deny liberal nationalism, but instead rejects the alleged incompatibility between cosmopolitanism and nationalism. That is, cosmopolitan liberalism is defended, on this approach, by showing how it can be reconciled with the demands of liberal nationalism. I want [. . .] to explore this second way of defending cosmopolitanism.

The conciliatory approach seems to me to be a more fruitful defense of cosmopolitan justice. First, given the growing support for liberal nationalism, a defense of cosmopolitanism that depends on the rejection of liberal nationalism risks alienating many liberals whom the cosmopolitan should want on her side. (Cosmopolitans should not want to be fending off nonliberals on one flank and liberals on another; the former is challenge enough.) Second, and more importantly, [. . .] a cosmopolitan theory that cannot accommodate certain forms of associative ties that characterize the lives of individuals, including the ties of nationality, is prima facie implausible. Such an account of cosmopolitanism would be morally rigoristic, and would be likely rejected as a *reductio ad absurdum*. The traditional view, that liberals should be cosmopolitans, gains more plausibility if it does not rule out nationalism *in toto*, particularly liberal forms of nationalism.

In what follows, I will argue that the alleged tension between cosmopolitanism and liberal nationalism is only apparent. Once the goals and content of cosmopolitan global justice, on the one hand, and the parameters of *liberal* nationalism, on the other, are properly defined and identified, the perceived conflict between liberal nationalism and cosmopolitanism disappears. After sorting out the conceptual terrain of cosmopolitan justice and liberal nationalism, I will consider some common nationalistic objections against cosmopolitan justice, and I will try to show that to the extent that these arguments do tell against cosmopolitan global justice, they cannot be *liberal* nationalist arguments.

Given that my goal is to show that cosmopolitans need not reject liberal nationalism, I shall largely grant the liberal nationalist position.[3] However, to the extent that one commonly raised objection against liberal nationalism is that it violates the universality so commonly associated with liberalism, including its acclaimed (by many liberals) commitment to global equality, my conclusion, if successful, will have the bonus of defending liberal nationalism against this common objection.

To start, I provide a brief outline of liberal nationalism, noting in particular two of its features that have been commonly thought to render it antithetical to cosmopolitanism. This will be largely a descriptive task and there is no pretense that all possible objections against the specific liberal nationalist position I shall put forward have been taken into account beyond any doubt. I intend only to present and clarify one plausible and reasonable account of liberal nationalism that also happens to pose the greatest challenge for cosmopolitan justice compared to other plausible accounts.

Liberal nationalism

Liberal nationalism is a form of nationalism in that it affirms the general nationalist thesis that all states, including liberal ones, should promote and inculcate a sense of shared nationality among their respective citizens. This sense of common belonging is thought by nationalists to be necessary for grounding a common citizenship among individuals in the modern state, a problem that is especially poignant in the context of the liberal democratic state where individuals seek diverse and sometimes incompatible ends. The nation, as understood here, is the "historic community," to adopt Walzer's phrase (1980), that underlies the state and that makes it realizable. Yet liberal nationalism is a *liberal* form of nationalism because liberal principles set constraints on the kinds of nationalist goals that may be legitimately pursued and the strategies that may be deployed to further these goals.

Liberal nationalists do not make the error commonly charged against them, namely, that they assume that states are homogeneous nation states. On the contrary, liberal nationalists recognize that states are rarely unified around a common national membership, and it is precisely this recognition of the lack of congruity between state and nation that motivates the nationalists' main thesis that states do and/or ought to take a more active role in inculcating a sense of shared nationality among its citizens.

What state-level nation-building might mean, morally speaking, for minority nationalities within the state is understood differently by different liberal nationalists. Some theorists recognize that in the case of multinational countries, the aspiration for a uniform citizenship irrespective of the diversity in nationality may be a futile one in addition to being an unjust imposition, and they recommend instead some form of differentiated citizenship along these national cultural lines. This may require granting minority nationalities certain group rights, including some form of self-government rights for minority nationalities, to offset the potential injustices of majority state nation-building (Kymlicka 2001a, chap. 5; 1995). Others are less receptive of minority rights on account of the belief that fostering a viable and cohesive nation state precludes such concessions to minorities (D. Miller 1998, p. 269). [. . .] State nation-building presents potential problems for domestic justice (the problem of minorities) and for cosmopolitan justice (the problem of nonmembers). A complete defense of liberal nationalism will, therefore, have to address both these dimensions of justice. My question concerns the latter, namely, whether liberal nationalism can be compatible with the requirements of cosmopolitan justice. Because I am focusing on state nation-building, I will take "nation" to mean the ideal of the nation state unless otherwise noted, and "nationalism" to mean specifically state-level nationalism, again unless otherwise noted.

Some liberal nationalists have tried to reconcile cosmopolitanism and liberal nationalism by defining liberal nationalism as *civic* nationalism in contrast with *ethnic* nationalism (Barry 1999, pp. 53–60). Civic nationalism is supposedly organized around political ideals rather than around a culture; it "envisages the nation as a community of equal rights-bearing citizens" united only in their common allegiance to shared political ideals and practices (Ignatieff 1993, pp. 6–7). Thus, unlike ethnic nationalism, which begins from the basic premise that "an individual's deepest attachments are inherited [through one's culture], not chosen" (1993, pp. 7–8), civic nationalism is allegedly neutral about culture, and hence is, in principle, inclusive and universalistic rather than exclusive and parochial (Barry 1999, pp. 53–5). The idea of civic nationalism is obviously tempting for liberals. After all, it is a nationalism that is based on (liberal) principles, and thereby not exclusive but inclusive of all persons willing to embrace these principles. It is a form of nationalism that is seemingly based on rationally defensible principles rather than on unchosen, narrow and seemingly exclusive factors such as ethnicity and culture.

Thus Brian Barry argues that once we limit liberal nationalism to civic nationalism, the incompatibility between liberal nationalism and cosmopolitanism largely disappears. He writes:

> There is no reason for civic nationalism to be opposed to this [global] redistribution. On the contrary, anyone who wishes to see the spread of civic nationalism must recognize that it has material preconditions. Transferring resources from rich countries to poor ones does nothing to injure civic nationalism in the rich ones (almost all of them were the same in that respect when they were half as rich) but offers at least the chance to the poor countries of creating civic nations of their own (Barry, 1999, pp. 58–60, quotation at p. 60).

In short, because the principles and ideals of civic nationalism are universal, and indeed cosmopolitan, ideals, liberal nationalism *understood as* civic nationalism is a form of nationalism that "has no principled position on boundaries" (1999, p. 56), and is hence conceptually consistent with cosmopolitanism.

But this attempt to reconcile liberal nationalism and cosmopolitanism, by distinguishing liberal nationalism from nonliberal nationalism in terms of civic versus ethnic nationalism, succeeds only by "misunderstanding" nationalism (Kymlicka 2001a, chap 12). As Will Kymlicka has argued, all forms of nationalism, liberal or nonliberal, necessarily have a cultural component that is reflected and reinforced in the public and social institutions of a nation and the shared language(s) under which these institutions operate (Kymlicka 2001a). What distinguishes liberal nationalism from nonliberal nationalism is not the issue of cultural neutrality, but the content, scope, and inclusiveness of the national *culture* that is being fostered and promoted (Kymlicka 2001a, pp. 258–61). A liberal state would promote a "thin" national culture, which Kymlicka calls a "societal culture," that is characterized by a shared language and a set of public institutions covering different areas of social life, including the law, education, and the economy, rather than a "thick" ethno-culture that is characterized by (say) shared religious beliefs, family customs, and personal lifestyles.

The civic/ethnic nationalism divide thus plays into the long-taken-for-granted myth of state ethnocultural neutrality. But once this myth is exposed as such, we see that even our paradigmatic cases of so-called ethnoculturally neutral states, like the United States, are not really neutral in this way, but have (historically and currently) taken active steps to foster and preserve their respective "societal cultures" (Kymlicka 2001a, pp. 244–5; cf. Walzer 1994). The civic/ethnic nationalism distinction, thus, not only does not help to demarcate liberal from nonliberal nationalisms, but is in fact an altogether inaccurate and misleading distinction on account of its false understanding of the nature of nationalism. To try to reconcile liberal nationalism and cosmopolitanism by defining liberal nationalism as civic nationalism too conveniently side-steps the issue by defining away the realities of nationalism.

Besides the fact that state neutrality with respect to culture is a nonstarter, many liberal nationalists have also offered positive arguments for why liberals should also be actively promoting a particular national cultural identity: why, that is, liberals must also be liberal nationalists. One main line of argument, as briefly noted above, is that it is within the context of a national culture that the core liberal values of individual autonomy and self-identity, social justice, and democracy are best realized (Kymlicka 2001a, pp. 224–9; also Gutmann 1996; Tamir 1992; D. Miller 1995; Nielsen 1999).

Simply put, membership in a national culture provides individuals with "the context of choice" within which to form, pursue and revise their conceptions of the good life (Kymlicka 1989, 1995; Tamir 1992, chap 1), as well as the basis of self-identity (Nielsen 1999, pp. 452ff). Moreover, common nationality provides the crucial bond for what David Miller has called a "community of obligation" (Miller 1995, pp. 83–4) through which separate and unrelated individuals can come to see themselves as mutually indebted and morally engaged to begin with, providing thus the requisite grounding and motivation for social justice commitments among citizens. Finally, common nationality ensures a certain degree of trust and mutual respect among fellow citizens that is necessary for a functioning deliberative democracy. Mutual respect, with its attendant ideal of reciprocity, ensures that individuals will only forward arguments that "others, as free and equal citizens might also reasonably be expected reasonably to endorse" (Rawls 1999a, p. 140); and mutual trust insures that they will abide by democratic results that are not in their favor, with the understanding that should results be in their favor next time, others would likewise concede (Kymlicka 2001a, chaps. 10 and 11; D. Miller 1995, pp. 96–8). Also, and very importantly, democratic politics is, in Kymlicka's neat phrase, "politics in the vernacular" in that "debating political issues" is best done in people's own national tongue (2001a, p. 213).

So, many liberal nationalists are nationalists with respect to culture, and hence the attempt to reconcile liberal nationalism with cosmopolitanism by rendering the concept of liberal nationalism culturally vacant is not a reconciliation strategy that they can accept.

In addition to the cultural content of nationalism, there is another feature of nationalism that is often thought to be contradictory to the cosmopolitan ideal. This has to do with the institutional implications of national self-determination. Self-determination, in its most fundamental interpretation, is a claim for a public political sphere in which a nation's cultural identity can be expressed, reflected and fostered. Such a sphere is crucial because, as Yael Tamir writes, "[i]n order to preserve their *national* identity, *individuals* must be given the opportunity to express this identity, both privately and publicly. . . . The existence of a shared public space is a necessary condition for ensuring the preservation of a nation as a vital and active community" (Tamir 1992, p. 73, italics in original). Nationality is a *publicly* shared identity characterized by a common language that must be allowed expression in a public sphere if it is to be sustained and promoted. "[A]ny language which is not a public language becomes so marginalised that it is likely to survive only amongst a small elite, or in ritualised form, not as a living and developing language underlying a flourishing culture" (Kymlicka 1995, p. 78). A "private" nationality, like a private language, would be no nationality at all.

[. . .] The crucial point here is that central to the idea of nationalism is the securing and maintaining of a relatively autonomous set of public and nationalized *institutions*, in one appropriate form of political arrangement or another, so that a given national culture may be publicly expressed and fostered.

In sum, liberal nationalism is a form of nationalism with a *cultural* content which, as with all brands of nationalism, commands the establishment of certain *nationalized institutions* for the purpose of promoting and securing a cultural identity in the name of self-determination. It is for these reasons that nationalism is often alleged to be *by definition* anti-cosmopolitan. First, the establishment and maintenance of nationalized institutions seem to go against a common understanding of cosmopolitanism as an argument for specific kinds of global and transnational institutions that would eventually supersede national institutions in significance. Second, the cultural content of nationalism seems to be incompatible with a common understanding of cosmopolitanism as a doctrine that is neutral about, and indeed suspicious of, individual attachments to particular cultures.

As is clear from the above, the "culturally based" nationalism is not endorsed by all professed liberal nationalists (e.g., it is not endorsed by those who argue for civic nationalism), and I do not pretend to have given a full defense of this view of liberal nationalism even though I have suggested its greater plausibility. But a culturally based nationalism, in addition to being the dominant account of nationalism among many important liberal nationalists writing today, is also, more to my purpose, the form of liberal nationalism that presents the greatest challenge for cosmopolitanism. (As we saw, liberal nationalists who adopt civic nationalism see no problem of consistency at all between liberal nationalism and cosmopolitanism.) By taking the culturally based liberal nationalism described above to be representative of liberal nationalism, I am therefore setting the bar higher for a successful reconciliation of liberal nationalism and cosmopolitanism, rather than begging the question in my favor. My arguments, if successful, will in any case apply a fortiori to forms of liberal nationalism that stress cultural neutrality. So, for the purpose of the present discussion, I will endorse the account of liberal nationalism that takes cultural belonging seriously, and I hope to show how this idea of nationalism can nonetheless be consistent with cosmopolitan distributive justice.

Variants of cosmopolitanism

As we have seen, cosmopolitan global justice is often thought to be inherently anti-nationalistic with respect to its views on national institutions and culture. Yet, so I shall argue, once we identify the different strands of cosmopolitanism, and disentangle them from each other, we can see that the cosmopolitan idea of distributive justice does not depend on, nor entail, either of these anti-nationalistic claims. In particular, we can sort out two different sets of cosmopolitan distinctions. On the one hand, we can distinguish between (a) cosmopolitanism as a *moral* claim as opposed to cosmopolitanism as an *institutional* claim; and, on the other, (b) cosmopolitanism as a claim about *justice* as opposed to cosmopolitanism as a claim about *culture*. While cosmopolitanism as an institutional claim and as a claim about culture is indeed at odds with the idea of nationalism, cosmopolitanism understood as a moral claim and as a claim about justice is not necessarily at odds with nationalism. The cosmopolitan idea of global justice, as we shall see, entails only these latter variants of cosmopolitanism.

Moral and institutional cosmopolitanism

It is often charged that cosmopolitanism is inherently anti-nationalistic because it calls for the creation of a world state (or some similar global institutional form) and, consequently, the cultivation of world citizenship. This is how one prominent critic of cosmopolitanism, Danielo Zolo, understands the cosmopolitan position – consequently,

Zolo goes on to reject the cosmopolitan ideal by showing that the idea of a world state is a non-starter (Zolo 1997). Nationalism, in contrast, enjoins the right to national self-determination, which may take the form of sovereign statehood or, if not feasible, other forms of autonomous political arrangements such as a multinational federalism (Tamir 1992, p. 9). In either case, national self-determination calls for the establishment and strengthening of certain major public institutions (e.g., in education, immigration/naturalization policies, official language policies, etc.) at the national level, in order to bring about (relatively) autonomous political institutions that "members might see as 'their own,'" and a public sphere in which the national culture may be expressed (Tamir 1992). Thus cosmopolitanism understood as "world statism" is obviously in some tension with nationalism. Each makes opposing institutional demands – one aiming to concentrate and locate political sovereignty in a centralized world body, the other to keep sovereignty decentralized and dispersed at the national level.

But few contemporary cosmopolitans, *pace* Zolo, actually support the idea of a world state and the subsequent outright rejection of national self-determination. Adapting Charles Beitz's terminology, I shall call the above interpretation of cosmopolitanism *institutional* cosmopolitanism, and contrast it with *moral* cosmopolitanism (Beitz 1999b, p. 287). Unlike institutional cosmopolitanism, which calls for the establishment of a world state, moral cosmopolitanism makes no necessary *institutional* demands or recommendations. Moral cosmopolitanism simply says that the individual is the ultimate unit of moral worth and concern, and that how we ought to act or what kinds of institutions we ought to establish "should be based on an impartial consideration of the claims of each person who would be affected" by our choices (Beitz 1999b). In other words, moral cosmopolitanism is not concerned *directly* with the question of how global *institutions* are to be ordered, but with the *justificatory basis* of these institutions. And nothing in this interpretation of cosmopolitanism necessitates the idea of a world state. On the contrary, a moral cosmopolitan can as well defend national self-determination if she believes that the ideal of equal and impartial concern for individuals is best realized by respecting their claims to national sovereignty. So there is no necessary conflict between moral cosmopolitanism and the idea of national self-determination.

It is plain that the cosmopolitan conception of distributive justice depends fundamentally on the cosmopolitan moral view – that individuals are the ultimate units of moral worth and are entitled to equal and impartial concern regardless of their nationality. But it is far from evident that this idea of justice must also depend on institutional cosmopolitanism (i.e., a world government). We can think of different *feasible* global institutional arrangements for redistributing wealth and resources globally without recourse to the punitive and administrative powers of a world state. Proposals like the Tobin Tax (that would tax short-term capital flows and currency speculation), or Thomas Pogge's global resource tax (that would tax countries for extracting natural resources) are global distributive schemes that are not tied to the idea of a world state (Pogge 1994).

[. . .]

Some might insist that the goals of moral cosmopolitanism are realizable only through institutional cosmopolitanism, that it is only through the institutionalizing of a world state and its accompanying idea of global citizenship can the well-being of *all* individuals be effectively accorded equal moral concern. If this is correct, the cosmopolitan vision is practically, if not conceptually, incompatible with nationalism.

But this claim would be too hastily made. As said, we can imagine certain global distributive arrangements that could realize the ends of moral cosmopolitanism without the benefit (or, more precisely, the drawbacks) of a global state. Indeed, as we can recall, many liberals have argued that certain moral cosmopolitan goals are *best* achieved in the context of the national community, rather than in the context of a global state (e.g., Kymlicka 2001a, pp. 212–16; Nielsen 1999, pp. 461ff). As Amy Gutmann points out, the aims of cosmopolitanism are better achieved through cultivating a strong sense of democratic citizenship than through a global transplanting of the nation-state system: "Democratic citizens have institutional means at their disposals that solitary individuals, or citizens of the world, do not. Some of those institutional means are international in scope, . . . but even those tend to depend on the cooperation of sovereign societies for effective action" (Gutmann 1996, p. 71). Global democracy, thus, is best achieved not through some account of democratic global citizenship, but through the strengthening of local and nationally based democratic citizenship (Thompson 1996).[4]

The claim that cosmopolitan justice has no specific institutional entailment does not contradict the general point that justice is concerned primarily with institutions. Cosmopolitan justice does not call for a world state, even though its principles are to regulate and determine the justness of institutions. It is open to the possibility that a range of institutional forms can serve the moral ideal that individuals are entitled to equal moral consideration.

[. . .] If anything, the goals of moral cosmopolitanism are furthered, rather than thwarted, by liberal nationalism.

[. . .]

Culture and justice

Another reason for the alleged incompatibility between cosmopolitan justice and nationalism is that cosmopolitanism is often thought to be primarily a doctrine about culture. Specifically, it is thought that cosmopolitanism is a thesis about the irrelevance of membership in a particular culture. On this cosmopolitan account, the truly free and autonomous individual is a free-wheeling and culturally unattached person who is able to transcend, and even renounce, her own cultural particularities, and to borrow, adapt and learn from a selection of different cultural options (e.g., Waldron 1992, p. 778). In contrast, the kind of nationalism that I am considering has a cultural content. That is, it begins from the basic idea that a given national culture is worth protecting and fostering; hence the importance of national self-determination. Whether or not cosmopolitanism about culture is defensible is a question I will leave aside. The point here is that cosmopolitanism so understood is clearly at odds with the cultural premise central to liberal nationalism.

But it is important to keep distinct "cosmopolitanism as a doctrine about culture," and "cosmopolitanism as a doctrine about justice" (Scheffler 2001, p. 111). Unlike cosmopolitanism about culture, cosmopolitanism about justice says nothing about the (ir)relevance of cultural membership. Cosmopolitanism about justice holds that the baseline distribution of material goods and resources among individuals should be decided *independently* of the national and state boundaries within which individuals happen to be. Such contingencies ought not to affect one's legitimate entitlements, and the purpose of justice, accordingly, is precisely to mitigate the biased effects of such arbitrary factors on people's life chances. Nothing, positively or negatively, is asserted here about the moral significance of cultural membership for individuals.

Cosmopolitanism about culture, on the other hand, is not directly concerned with how material goods and resources are to be distributed, but is concerned with the question as to whether cultural membership is a *relevant good* to be distributed; and, as noted above, cosmopolitans about culture want to deny that it is. But there is no necessary correlation between this view of cosmopolitanism and cosmopolitan justice. It is logically possible for one to reject the cosmopolitan doctrine about culture (i.e., maintain that cultural membership is an important individual good) and at the same time affirm the cosmopolitan idea of justice (i.e., deny that the baseline distribution of material goods should be limited by membership considerations).

The cosmopolitan conception of global distributive justice obviously affirms cosmopolitanism as a doctrine about justice. It holds that our principles of distribution ought to apply to all individuals globally, and not be restricted and shaped by national boundaries. But this idea of justice, as shown above, is independent of cosmopolitanism understood as a doctrine about culture. Cosmopolitan distributive justice, fundamentally understood, says nothing about the value or disvalue of membership in a national culture. Distributive justice is foremost concerned with how resources and wealth are to be fairly allocated, and can remain neutral about the separate issue of culture and individual freedom.

[. . .]

Let me put the different forms of cosmopolitanism discussed above more perspicuously. Moral cosmopolitanism is a claim about the moral *starting point* of cosmopolitan justice, whereas institutional cosmopolitanism is a claim about its institutional *ending point;* and cosmopolitanism as a doctrine about justice speaks to the *scope* of justice, whereas cosmopolitanism as a doctrine about culture speaks to the *content* of justice. While these different variants of cosmopolitanism are clearly interrelated, it is important not to commit the category mistake of treating them as identical and inseparable aspects of cosmopolitanism.

[. . .]

The limits of reconciliation

Thus, cosmopolitan global justice presupposes neither a world state nor the irrelevance of cultural membership. Understood precisely as *moral* cosmopolitanism, and as a claim about *justice* and not about culture, cosmopolitanism is not inherently incompatible with the basic tenets of nationalism. One can recognize the importance of membership in a national culture and the importance of national self-determining institutions, without having to reject the cosmopolitan conception of global justice.

Of course, cosmopolitan global justice does not pretend to be compatible with all forms of nationalism. Clearly, "chauvinistic nationalisms" (as labeled by some commentators), which claim that only one's own nation is worthy of self-determination and respect, violate the cosmopolitan principle that all individuals count equally. Similarly, what Margaret Canovan has called "Romantic Collectivist" forms of nationalism – that is, those that take the nation to be a moral entity in and of itself, and hence able to command individual sacrifices for the sake of some abstract national end – offend against the cosmopolitan view that the individual is the ultimate unit of moral concern, and so cannot be compatible with the cosmopolitan ideal (Canovan 1996a, pp. 6–9).

But *liberal* nationalism is essentially universalist and individualist in its scope and foundation (e.g., Kymlicka 2001a, chaps. 10 and 11; Tamir 1992, pp. 90–1). Liberal nationalists accept that the right to national self-determination is a universal right of all nations, and that the reason why national self-determination is important is not because the nation itself enjoys a certain transcendental moral worth, but because of the value of nationality for individuals. As mentioned, liberal nationalists take membership in a national culture to be an important liberal good because culture provides individuals with the context of choice within which to form, pursue, and revise their conceptions of the good. The moral worth of individuals is that which is crucial here, rather than the worth of the nation independently of what individuals value. So the liberal paradigm of liberal nationalism ensures that it stays consistent with the universalist and individualist tenets of cosmopolitanism. A truly liberal nationalism, as Kai Nielsen says, must also be a *cosmopolitan nationalism* in the sense that it has to cohere with the quintessential cosmopolitan principles of normative individualism and ethical universalism (Nielsen 1999, pp. 448–50).

But it might be pointed out here that the idea of nationalism comes packaged with certain intrinsic features that render nationalism, even in its liberal incarnation, antithetical to the demands of cosmopolitan justice. I will consider two common arguments in the contemporary discourse on global justice. I will call them (a) the argument from national self-determination and (b) the argument from national affinity. I will contend that the features of nationalism invoked in these arguments, while indeed integral to nationalism, do not contradict cosmopolitan justice if they are kept within the bounds of *liberal* nationalism.

The nationalist objections

National self-determination

The self-determination objection challenges global distributive justice on two fronts. On one front, it says that the right of self-determination implies that nations have a sovereign right over resources within their borders, and hence any "outward" redistribution of such resources to other nations is at their discretion, contra the demands of global justice (D. Miller 1995, pp. 103–8). On the other, it says that self-determination means that nations are to take full responsibility for their own economic development, but global distributive principles contradict this ideal of responsibility by compensating, through redistributive channels, poor nations for their bad domestic decisions. As David Miller writes: "To respect the self-determination of other nations also involves treating them as responsible for decisions they may make about resource use, economic growth, environmental protection, and so forth" which should give us pause when advocating a more egalitarian global redistribution of wealth and resources (Miller 1995, p. 108). [. . .]

But both fronts of this argument are ill-advanced in the context of liberal nationalism. While nonliberal nationalists could invoke the self-determination argument to oppose outward distribution of resources within their borders, liberal nationalists may *not*. One of the goals of a liberal account of nationalism is to mark permissible forms and practices of nationalism from impermissible ones. Unlike chauvinistic national-ism, which recognizes no constraints on its nation-building methods, even if this means destroying other nations in the process, liberal nationalism accepts limits on how its nationalist goals may be pursued. Liberal principles set constraints on how a nation may exercise its right to self-determination, and one such constraint is that the nation does not use more than its fair share of the world's resources when exercising this right. From the liberal egalitarian point of view, the current global distribution of wealth and resources is far from just (e.g., Beitz 1999a, part III; Pogge 1989, part III). To insist, then, that self-determination implies that (well-endowed) nations may not be compelled to redistribute their resources globally is to permit the exercise of self-determination to overstep the bounds of liberal justice itself.

In other words, the "liberal" part of the liberal nationalist equation limits the ways in which national self-determination may be expressed. More precisely, if we begin from an egalitarian conception of liberalism and want to marry that understanding of liberalism to nationalism, then the liberal nationalism we get has to be an *egalitarian* liberal nationalism. And as egalitarian liberalism begins from the basic idea that there are no principled differences between individuals on the basis of contingencies, or what Rawls has called factors that are "arbitrary from a moral point of view" (Rawls 1971, p. 15), so too must egalitarian liberal nationalism discount morally arbitrary facts about persons when it comes to determining their just global entitlements. And one arbitrary factor here would be people's national membership.

It may seem odd that liberal nationalists, if they are egalitarian liberals, must con-sider nationality a morally irrelevant factor when determining the terms of global distributive justice. What does it mean to be a nationalist in this case? But this oddity dissipates once we are clear about the circumscribed place of nationality in liberal nationalist theories. The liberal framework of liberal nationalism sets limitations on how nationality may be invoked when deliberating about justice. This claim will be illustrated and reinforced, I believe, when we confront the national partiality argu-ment below.

Concerning the other front of the self-determination argument, that national self-determination means that nations must take responsibility for their domestic policies and that global distributive justice contradicts this ideal of responsibility [. . .]. The present argument, like the earlier, relies on the thesis Thomas Pogge calls "explanatory nationalism". And, [. . .] explanatory nationalism is an objectionable thesis because it falsely attributes national performance solely to domestic decisions, without recogniz-ing that global conditions do have a crucial role in determining the state of a nation's economy (Pogge 1998, p. 497; also 1994). If the ideal of national self-determination means that nations are to take responsibility for their choices, the ideal of justice would require that the background conditions against which such choices are made be fair. As mentioned earlier, there is no inconsistency with saying that the global conditions against which nations exercise their right to self-determination be regu-lated by principles of justice and that nations are to take responsibility for their choices made within the rules of just institutions.

The aim of global justice is in part to redress, or help buffer weaker nations from, the detrimental effects of the decisions and policies of richer and more powerful nations. To say that global distributive justice would undermine self-determination (by failing to hold nations responsible for their own policies) simply overlooks this fact of the vulnerability of poor nations to the decisions of more powerful ones. As we do not say, in the domestic case, that every individual failure is due entirely to poor individual choice, likewise we cannot say that every national failure is due to a nation's failure to take full responsibility for its self-determination. To do so is to assume falsely, as liberals have warned us not to in the domestic setting, that the global background context is beyond rebuke, and that the results of decisions made within that context are thus fairly and freely made.

Thus the self-determination argument, as it applies to liberal nationalism, cannot be turned against the demands of global justice. Liberal nationalism, by definition, can support only a conception of self-determination that is situated within the bounds and understanding of liberal justice. This does not mean that no *liberal* national self-determination is ever legitimate in our vastly unequal world; but it does mean, importantly, that liberal nationalists have to be actively committed to global equality if they want to fully legitimize their exercise of self-determination. Indeed, rather than arguing against global justice, the principle of self-determination tells us that we should be concerned about bringing about a more egalitarian global structure in which the preconditions for self-determination do in fact obtain universally for all.

National affinity

The national affinity argument claims that justice depends on shared meanings and common understandings about the goods to be distributed. Yet these shared meanings and common understandings are not available outside the context of a national community (Walzer 1983; also D. Miller 1995, pp. 75, 105–6). As Walzer has famously put it, "The idea of distributive justice presupposes a bounded world within which distribution takes place" (Walzer 1983, p. 31). It is only within such a bounded world that individuals can agree on the kinds of goods that they need to share and distribute.

Although this objection need not obviously present itself as a point against reconciling cosmopolitanism and nationalism, but more obviously as a claim about the conditions of justice, it can be seen as a problem for reconciliation in the following way: if nationalists hold that national affinity is necessary for justice, then a cosmopolitan framework cannot satisfactorily accommodate nationalism without giving up on its aspiration for an idea of justice that transcends national membership. The argument, in other words, draws attention to the tension between a nation-centric idea of justice and a transnational idea of justice.

Yet it seems to me that this argument can be dismissed. Development economists have long argued that the notion of individual human capabilities, as defined by a combination of such factors as life expectancy, literacy rate, income, infant mortality rate, and so on, provides us with a common cross-societal standard against which to compare developmental levels and quality-of-life globally (e.g., Sen 1999, chap. 4; also Nussbaum 2000a, chap. 1). Such indicators are currently employed by the United Nations Human Development Program in its global quality-of-life assessment. A commitment to global egalitarianism can target these general indicators of human development without invoking any controversial presuppositions about the substantive ends and goals of human life across different societies.

There is, therefore, sufficient consensus and shared understanding for us to answer the question "equality of what?" when dealing with global inequality. It is hard to deny that there is a widespread, cross-cultural agreement that longer life span, literacy, health, real income, and so on are cherished goods, and that whatever else people need or desire in life, they need these basic goods (Nussbaum 2000a, chap. 1).

But the argument from national affinity can be read as an argument about moral motivation. So understood, it is a claim about the need for a common belonging, in particular a moral community (the "bounded world") shared by individuals, before we can reasonably (and possibly) expect their compliance with the demands of justice. As Sandel writes, a distributive principle "must presuppose some prior moral tie among those whose assets it would deploy and those whose efforts it would enlist in a common endeavor" (Sandel 1992, p. 22). But unlike nations which are "historic communities" embodying a common history, language, culture and way of life, and hence embodying a viable moral community, the global society exhibits none of these shared common ideals, and hence, unlike the nation, cannot be a moral community (Walzer 1980, 1983). Thus Sandel worries that "[p]olitical associations more expansive than nations, and with fewer cultural traditions and historical memories to draw upon, may find the task of cultivating commonality more difficult still" (Sandel 1996, p. 339).

Liberal nationalists, as we can recall, do certainly endorse the claim that national affinity provides an important precondition for social justice. But this is very different from saying that nationality is the only available basis for social justice. Rawls writes that it is "the task of the statesman to struggle against the potential lack of affinity among different peoples. . . . What encourages the statesman's work is that relations of affinity are not a fixed thing, but may continually grow stronger over time as peoples come to work together in cooperative institutions they have developed" (1999a, pp. 112–13). Rawls, it should be pointed out, recognizes this need for affinity between peoples not to ground global distributive schemes, but to ground humanitarian duties between peoples. Yet his point "that the narrow circle of mutually caring peoples in the world today may expand over time and must never be viewed as fixed" is an important one and can be adapted, I would argue, to ground more than just humanitarian duties but duties of justice as well. The issue here is whether there is sufficient affinity and sense of common moral identity among individuals to motivate compliance with global principles; and Rawls's argument shows us that it would be premature to rule out this possibility just because it is not fully realized now.

Thus, although liberal nationalists have pointed to the importance of shared nationality for the purpose of grounding social justice, it is important to note that this reflects an expansionary rather than constricting moral aspiration and project. That is, the purpose of a common nationality, in the view of liberal nationalists, is to enable citizens to transcend the local and parochial bonds and ties of family, kin, and tribe, and to extend the scope of their moral universe to also encompass strangers (who are fellow citizens). Shared nationality, therefore, motivates citizens to tend to the needs of compatriots who are otherwise strangers by making them all fellow members of a shared "imagined community" (to borrow Benedict Anderson's famous phrase). This reason for cultivating a shared nationality operates as an equally compelling reason for "cultivating humanity," to borrow Nussbaum's inspiring phrase (Nussbaum 1997).

So, understood as an expansionary moral project, there is nothing in the liberal nationalist idea of affinity to suggest that our moral world has to cease suddenly at our national borders. Indeed, as Charles Jones asks, why not capitalize on this "expansionary momentum" to expand the scope of our moral concern beyond conationals to include also foreigners (Jones 1999b, p. 160)? [. . .]

The argument from national affinity tells us that it is important that the liberal nation state cultivates some sort of shared nationality among its citizens for the purpose of promoting social justice. But this alone does not mean that considerations of social justice are important only within a national community, nor does it tell us that such considerations have no basis outside the national community. Indeed, the achievements of liberal nationalism in fostering shared sentiments and affinity could serve as the basis for extending people's commitments towards global justice (Kymlicka 2002, p. 270). The search for some form of global affinity to ground global justice may be an ongoing quest, but this is not the same as saying that such searches are in principle futile or irrelevant, as the affinity argument claims. If anything, nationalism shows us that it is possible for individuals to overcome the near and the familiar and to include strangers in our moral world as well. The trick is not to exhaust this expansionary quest at the national level, and "not to lose steam when [we] get to the borders of the nation" (Nussbaum 1996, p. 14).

Conclusion

I have tried to show that once the conceptual terrain of cosmopolitan justice and liberal nationalism is properly mapped out, the alleged contradiction between the cosmopolitan ideal and liberal nationalism disappears. I then argued that certain nationalist sentiments commonly thought to be inherently anti-cosmopolitan are not so once we situate these nationalist sentiments within the context of *liberal* nationalism. [. . .]

Notes

1   See Kymlicka and Christine Straehle (in Kymlicka 2001a, chap. 11) for a helpful survey of the relatively recent explosion of interest in nationalism in contemporary political philosophy.
2   Thus some (professed) liberal nationalists have explicitly denied the cosmopolitan idea. See D. Miller (1995, 2000) and Walzer (1983, 1995).
3   For important arguments in defense of nationalism, see Kymlicka (1995, 2001a); D. Miller (1995, 2000); and Tamir (1992).
4   Thus David Held, the well-known proponent of cosmopolitan democracy, does not advocate a democratic global state as such, but differentiated levels of global governance with different levels of democratic participation (Held 1993, 1995).

References

Barry, Brian (1999) "Statism and Nationalism: A Cosmopolitan Critique," in Shapiro and Brilmayer (ed) *Global Justice*, (New York: New York University Press).
Beitz, Charles (1999a [1979]) *Political Theory and International Relations*, 2nd Edition (Princeton: Princeton University Press).
Beitz, Charles (1999b) "International Liberalism and Distributive Justice: A Survey of Recent Thought," *World Politics*, vol. 51: 269–96.
Brook, Gillian (2002) "Liberal Nationalism Versus Cosmopolitanism: Locating the Disputes," *Public Affairs Quarterly*, vol. 16, no. 4: 307–27.
Canovan, Margaret (1996a) *Nationhood and Political Theory* (Cheltenham: Edward Elgar).
Gutmann, Amy (ed.), (1994) *Multiculturalism* (Princeton: Princeton University Press).
Gutmann, Amy (1996) "Democratic Citizenship," in J. Cohen (ed.) *For Love of Country* (Boston: Beacon Press).

Held, David (1993) "Democracy: From City-States to a Cosmopolitan Order?" in D. Held (ed.) *Prospects for Democracy* (Stanford: Stanford University Press).

Held, David (ed.), (1995) *Democracy and the Global Order: From the Modern State to Cosmopolitan Governance* (Stanford: Stanford University Press).

Ignatieff, Michael (1993) *Blood and Belonging Journeys into the New Nationalism* (Toronto: Penguin Books).

Jones, Charles (1999a) *Global Justice. A Cosmopolitan Defense* (Oxford: Oxford University Press).

Jones, Charles (1999b) "Patriotism, Morality, and Global Justice," in Shapiro and Brilmayer (eds.). *Global Justice*, (New York: New York University Press).

Kymlicka, Will (1989) *Liberalism, Community and Culture* (Oxford: Oxford University Press).

Kymlicka, Will (1995) *Multicultural Citizenship* (Oxford: Oxford University Press).

Kymlicka, Will (2001a) *Politics in the Vernacular* (Oxford: Oxford University Press).

Kymlicka, Will (2002) *Contemporary Political Philosophy*, 2nd Edition (Oxford: Oxford University Press).

Lichtenberg, Judith (1998) "How Liberal can Nationalism Be?," in Beiner (ed.) *Theorizing Nationalism* (Albany: State University of New York Press).

Miller, David (1995) *On Nationality* (Oxford: Oxford University Press).

Miller, David (1998) "The Limits of Cosmopolitan Justice," in Maple and Nardin (eds.) *International Society* (Princeton: Princeton University Press).

Miller, David (2000) *Citizenship and National Identity* (Cambridge: Polity Press).

Moellendorf, Darrel (2002) *Cosmopolitan Justice* (Boulder: Westview Press).

Nielsen, Kai (1991) "Global Justice, Capitalism and the Third World," in J. Arthur and W. Shaw (eds.) *Justice and Economic Distribution*, 2nd Edition (Englewood Cliffs: Prentice Hall): 228–41.

Nielsen, Kai (1999) "Cosmopolitan Nationalism," *Monist*, vol. 82, no 3: 446–68.

Nussbaum, Martha (1996) "Patriotism and Cosmopolitanism," in J. Cohen (ed.) *For Love of Country* (Boston: Beacon Press).

Nussbaum, Martha (1997) *Cultivating Humanity* (Cambridge: Harvard University Press).

Nussbaum, Martha (2000a) *Women and Human Development* (Cambridge: Cambridge University Press).

Pogge, Thomas (1989) *Realizing Rawls* (Ithaca: Cornell University Press).

Pogge, Thomas (1994) "An Egalitarian Law of Peoples," *Philosophy and Public Affairs*, vol. 23, no. 3: 195–224.

Pogge, Thomas (1998) "The Bounds of Nationalism," in J. Couture, K. Nielsen and M. Seymour (eds.) *Rethinking Nationalism* (Calgary: University of Calgary Press).

Rawls, John (1971) *A Theory of Justice* (Cambridge: Harvard University Press).

Rawls, John (1999a) *The Law of Peoples* (Cambridge: Harvard University Press).

Sandel, Michael (1992) "The Procedural Republic and the Unencumbered Self," in S. Avineri and A. de-Shalit (eds.) *Communitarianism and Individualism* (Oxford: Oxford University Press).

Sandel, Michael (1996) *Democracy's Discontent* (Cambridge: Harvard University Press).

Scheffler, Samuel (2001) *Boundaries and Allegiances* (Oxford: Oxford University Press).

Sen, Amartya (1999) *Development as Freedom* (New York: Knopf).

Tamir, Yael (1992) *Liberal Nationalism* (Princeton: Princeton University Press).

Thompson, Dennis (1996) "Democratic Theory and Global Society" *Journal of Political Philosophy*, vol. 7, no 2: 111–25.

Waldron, Jeremy (1992) "Minority Rights and the Cosmopolitan Alternative," *University of Michigan Journal of Law Reform*, vol. 25, no 3: 751–93.

Walzer, Michael (1980) "The Moral Standing of States," *Philosophy and Public Affairs*, vol. 9, no. 3: 209–29.

Walzer, Michael (1993) *Spheres of Justice* (New York: Basic Books).

Walzer, Michael (1994) "Comments" in A. Gutmann (ed.) *Multiculturalism* (Princeton: Princeton University Press).

Walzer, Michael (1995) "Response" in D. Miller and M. Waltzer (eds.) *Pluralism, Justice, and Equality* (Oxford: Oxford University Press).

Zolo, Danielo (1997) *Cosmopolis Prospects for World Government* (Cambridge: Polity Press).

12

Global Distributive Justice and the State
Simon Caney

It is widely assumed that the state is the main, perhaps the sole, context in which principles of distributive justice should be applied. We are familiar with citizens and political philosophers arguing about which principles of justice should apply among fellow citizens. The debates frequently focus on which distributive principle is appropriate (distribution according to need, desert, equality or as the market distributes) but the scope of justice is often taken as obvious. Principles of justice, it is assumed, apply primarily (if not exclusively) within the state. This conventional wisdom has recently been challenged by some cosmopolitan political philosophers who have argued that there should be global principles of distributive justice. Many nonetheless resist this cosmopolitan critique and hold fast to the claim that principles of justice should be applied (either wholly or primarily) within states. The state, on this view, has normative significance as a context of justice. In this article I wish to explore two arguments for this type of account of the normative significance of the state, both of which draw in different ways on John Rawls' political philosophy. Neither of these arguments, I contend, succeeds in establishing that the state has the kind of normative significance they attribute to it. The article concludes with some reflections on the relationship between ideals of justice and existing political institutions and, having criticised one account of the normative significance of the state, it proposes four alternative ways in which state membership may have moral relevance.

A theoretical framework

Prior to examining the two arguments to be scrutinised, I would like to introduce a theoretical framework for thinking about the issues at stake and to give a more general overview of how one might argue for, or against, the normative significance of the state.

First, it is important to record that the views to be considered make a distinctive claim about the normative significance of the state. They maintain that the state has normative significance, in part, because it defines the scope of some (or all) principles of distributive justice. In virtue of this let us say that those who argue in this way affirm the *Statist Scope Thesis*. Second, it is also important to note that one can distinguish between two distinct versions of the *Statist Scope Thesis* – what might be termed the *Extreme Version* and the *Moderate Version*. The Extreme Version avers that all principles of distributive justice apply only within states and that none apply at the global level (Freeman, 2007, chs 8 and 9; Nagel, 2005). This position can be contrasted with the Moderate Version of the *Statist Scope Thesis*. This contends that some principles of distributive justice apply globally but that others apply only within the confines of the state. A familiar version of this position holds that some basic rights obtain at the global level and that other distributive principles like equality apply only within the state (Blake, 2001; D. Miller, 1998, esp. p. 171; 1999a; 1999b, pp. 19–20, p. 273, fn. 32; R. Miller, 1998).[1]

With this distinction between the Extreme and Moderate Views in hand we may now examine what one would need to show to establish either view. Consider the Extreme View first. To establish that principles of justice apply only within the state and not at the global level one would have to supply an account of how the domestic realm differs from the global realm in a morally significant way. More precisely, one must show that (1) all principles of distributive justice apply only when some property (or set of properties) is present; (2) that property (or set of properties) exists at the domestic level; and finally (3) that property (or set of properties) does not exist at the global level. Only if one can perform each of these three tasks can one show that principles of distributive justice obtain at the domestic level but not at the global level. By satisfying these three conditions one is providing what might be termed a *Comprehensive Disanalogy Argument*, where a *Comprehensive Disanalogy Argument*, as I define it, shows that the global realm is disanalagous to the domestic realm in such a way that none of the principles of distributive justice that apply to the latter apply to the former (Caney, 2001, pp. 117–8; 2005a, pp. 270–1).

Consider now the more moderate view that some principles of justice apply only within the state but that some other principles apply at both the domestic and the global level. These views hold that the domestic and global realms are partially disanalogous. The two realms are sufficiently analogous (so some principles that apply in the domestic realm apply in the global realm) but they do differ in some morally relevant ways (so some principles that apply in the domestic realm do not apply in the global realm). To sustain this kind of position one needs what might be termed a *Partial Disanalogy Argument*. Stated formally, *Partial Disanalogy Arguments* hold that (1) some principles of justice apply when some property (or set of properties) P is present; (2) P is present in both the domestic and global realms; (3) some other principles of justice apply only when some property (or set of properties) Q is present; and (4) Q is present in the domestic realm but not in the global realm.

These reflections are rather abstract. We can illustrate the preceding analysis by drawing on different Disanalogy Arguments. There are a variety of different Disanalogy Arguments. We might, broadly speaking, distinguish between "social," "economic" and "political" Disanalogy Arguments. To illustrate each of these arguments I am going to focus on arguments which seek to show that some principles of distributive justice apply within the state but do not apply globally. For simplicity's sake I am going to refer to arguments which claim that "equality" is appropriate at the domestic level, but of course one might hold, say, that the difference principle or a priority principle applies domestically but not globally. In referring to "equality" I am not then assuming that it is necessarily the appropriate value that would obtain at the domestic level.

Let us now consider some different Disanalogy Arguments, starting with what I am (very loosely) terming "social" Disanalogy Arguments. Such arguments defend the application of a principle of justice to the domestic realm on the grounds that the latter exhibits some social property that is absent at the global level. Three examples would be the following:

> R1: the communitarian argument – equality applies domestically (but not globally) because equality is valuable if it produces community and equality within the state can produce a sense of community (but global equality would not produce a sense of global community);
>
> R2: the stigma argument – equality applies domestically (but not globally) because equality is needed to prevent stigma and domestic inequality produces stigma (but global inequality does not result in stigma);
>
> R3: the social unity argument – equality applies domestically (but not globally) because equality is a feasible ideal only when it is supported by a sense of social unity and this can exist within the state (but not in the global realm).

Other Disanalogy Arguments invoke what we might term political properties. Consider, for example:

> R4: the political cooperation argument – equality applies domestically (but not globally) because equality applies in a system of *political cooperation* and political cooperation exists at the domestic level (but not at the global level);
>
> R5: the coercion argument – equality applies domestically (but not globally) because equality is applicable among persons governed by a *common system of coercion* and the state is a coercive actor (but the global system is not coercive) (Blake, 2001; Nagel, 2005);
>
> R6: the domination argument – equality applies domestically (but not globally) because equality is needed to prevent some citizens from *dominating* others (but global equality is not needed to prevent some members of the world from dominating others);
>
> R7: the political participation argument – equality applies domestically (but not globally) because equality is needed to enable all citizens to engage in *political participation* and political participation is appropriate at the domestic level (but not at the global level);
>
> R8: the political legitimacy argument – equality applies domestically in liberal states (but not globally) because there is *widespread support* for it within liberal states (but there is no such widespread support for it at the global level) (Rawls, 1999b).

Consider finally an argument which appeals to what we might, crudely speaking, term an "economic" property:

> R9: the economic cooperation argument – equality applies domestically (but not globally) because equality should govern systems where people join together and engage in joint economic cooperation and this takes place among co-citizens (but not at the global order level) (Rawls, 1999a).

Having laid out this typology, three further clarificatory points are in order. First, note that the above arguments have been presented as arguments showing why one distributive principle (specifically equality) applies domestically but not globally. They are, that is, not worded as claiming that all principles of justice apply domestically but not globally. I have done this in part because I believe that the Moderate View is *prima facie* more plausible than the Extreme View. We should observe, however, that some (but not all) of the above Disanalogy Arguments could be reframed so as to defend the Extreme View. One might, for example, invoke R3 to show that no principles of justice travel, as it were, from the domestic to the global realm. The thought here would be that social unity is a prerequisite for any principles of justice (and not just egalitarian ones). In addition to this, one might conceivably recast R4 to show that no principles of justice apply at the global level because political cooperation is a prerequisite for any principles of distributive justice. Alternatively, one might revise R9 to show that no principles of distributive justice apply outside economic cooperation. All the other arguments, however, depend in some way on the particular character of equality (or some closely related principle) and so cannot easily be recast so as to support a thoroughgoing anti-cosmopolitanism.

Second, and related to this first point, we should be circumspect in drawing conclusions from successful Disanalogy Arguments. Suppose that one (or indeed several) of the arguments cited above establishes that equality should apply domestically but that it (or they) does not also establish that equality applies globally. This conclusion would *not* entail that equality does not in fact apply globally. So even if, for example, we are persuaded that equality has value where it is needed to prevent stigmatisation and even if we do not think that global inequality would issue in stigmatisation (á la R2) it does not follow that inequality at the global level is not objectionable. There might be other reasons for embracing global equality. We should, therefore, be careful not to claim too much from any individual Disanalogy Argument.

A third point: thus far we have examined Disanalogy Arguments but we should also, of course, consider what I shall term *Analogy Arguments.*[2] These argue that the domestic and global realms are sufficiently alike in morally relevant ways and hence the principles of justice that obtain in the domestic realm should also obtain in the global realm. Here it is instructive to distinguish between different kinds of analogy argument. Some, like Charles Beitz (1999a), Darrel Moellendorf (2002) and Thomas Pogge (1989; 2002), maintain, first, that principles of justice pertain to systems of economic interaction and, second, that the world economy comprises a system of economic interaction. There should then be global principles of distributive justice. This kind of approach can be contrasted with a second kind of analogy argument. For some argue that persons should be included in the scope of distributive justice in virtue of their *humanity*. They then infer from this that the scope of justice must be global.[3] For the purposes of this article I shall not arbitrate between these two kinds of cosmopolitanism. My critique of the statist approach does not require us to choose between them.

The preceding discussion has, I hope, given a picture of the variety of different arguments that might be invoked to explain why some (or all) principles of justice apply only within the state. In the next four sections I propose to focus on two arguments in particular – what I shall term the "Argument from Cooperation" (the argument described in R4 above) and the "Argument from Coercion" (the argument described in R5 above). Both seek to establish the normative importance of the state as the arena in which some (or all) principles of distributive justice apply.

The "Argument from Cooperation"

What I am terming the "Argument from Cooperation" has been developed and defended by Samuel Freeman. Freeman's argument involves a close reading of Rawls' work on justice and seeks to show that Rawls' cosmopolitan critics misunderstand the nature and plausibility of Rawls' theory of justice and his repudiation of cosmopolitanism. Freeman's argument thus involves an exegesis of Rawls' theory of justice but his aim is not purely interpretive for it is Freeman's intention to show that Rawls' theory, when correctly interpreted, provides a sound foundation for thinking that distributive justice applies only within the state. Freeman is a highly distinguished political philosopher and his recent *Justice and the Social Contract* is an important contribution to Rawlsian political philosophy. His opposition to cosmopolitan theories of justice thus requires careful attention.

Freeman proceeds thus. He starts with the assumption that:

> (1) Principles of distributive justice apply to basic institutions (Freeman. 2007, pp. 305–6).

Freeman advances this as a conceptual claim. Principles of distributive justice, by their very nature, regulate the basic institutions within which people operate and make choices. Distributive justice is, thus, defined by its *modus operandi*. As such, distributive justice must not, according to Freeman and Rawls, be confused with what Rawls terms "allocative justice", where this concerns the fair distribution of already existing wealth (Freeman, 2007, p. 305, p. 306, p. 315, p. 316, p. 318, p. 319; Rawls, 2001, pp. 50–1, pp. 170–1). Principles of distributive justice are simply those principles that govern the basic institutions that structure people's lives. But what are these basic institutions? Freeman's next step is to argue:

> (2) Basic institutions involve both (i) social and (ii) political cooperation (Freeman, 2007, p. 306).

Basic institutions are social in that they comprise legal and economic rules. They include, for example, rules governing the distribution and transfer of property, contract law, tort law and so on. Crucially, however, basic institutions are also essentially political institutions (Freeman, 2007, pp 267–8). They involve self-governing and effective political bodies. The next step in Freeman's argument is:

> (3) The state is a scheme of social and political cooperation.

It follows from (1), (2) and (3) that we should accept:

> (4) Principles of distributive justice apply to the state.

Freeman, however, goes one step further and claims that:

> (5) No global basic political institutions exist (Freeman, 2007, p 308).

Global social cooperation exists, of course, but, argues Freeman, this all emanates from the decisions of states. The state is the fundamental or basic political actor and cooperation at the global level is a "secondary" or derivative phenomenon (Freeman, 2007, p. 306, compare pp. 306–8, pp. 268–9). The primary actors are states. Therefore:

> (6) Principles of distributive justice do not apply at the global level.

Two further observations are in order. First, we should note that Freeman's argument has the right structure to undermine a cosmopolitan approach for it identifies a property – social and political cooperation – and it then contends that this marks a morally relevant difference between domestic and global realms. Second, note that the main aim of this argument is to argue that cosmopolitan thinkers like Pogge have misconstrued the nature of the "basic structure". The basic structure for Freeman can only refer to sovereign systems of political cooperation – like the state – and since there is no world state there can be no global principles of distributive justice. This emphasis on *political* cooperation is an important and striking feature of Freeman's conception for without it his case against global principles of distributive justice collapses.

Objections

Freeman's argument is vulnerable to a number of different objections. The first problem is that he fails to justify his claim that distributive justice, by its very nature, regulates the basic social and political institutions that comprise the sovereign state. Four lines of reasoning can be detected in his work.

The conceptual argument (A1)

First, as noted above, sometimes Freeman's argument just appears to be a definitional one. That is, he often simply insists that principles of distributive justice must, by definition, regulate the basic structure as he has characterised it. Distributive justice, on this view, just is concerned with regulating existing economic and legal institutions: that is what it is. It is in this vein that he maintains that cosmopolitan views confuse "allocative" and "distributive" justice. So whereas distributive justice is, for Freeman, defined with respect to the legal and economic institutions that distribute property, "allocative justice" concerns the fairness of the actual distribution of resources and opportunities (Freeman, 2007, p. 305, p 306, p. 315, p. 316, p. 318, p. 319).

Several points can be made in reply to this strategy. First, it is critically important to note that there are other conceptions of the scope of distributive justice which differ from Freeman's and he says little as to why his account is superior. Consider, for example, the following widely held view: principles of distributive justice apply to all those who belong to a common system of interaction and interdependence. Let us call this the Causal Interdependence Account. We can find this account (or close variants of it) in the work of very many political philosophers. It is affirmed by Beitz in *Political Theory and International Relations* (1999a, pp. 131–2). As Beitz puts it:

> the requirements of justice apply to institutions and practices (whether or not they are genuinely cooperative) in which social activity produces relative or absolute benefits or burdens that would not exist if the social activity did not take place (Beitz, 1999a, p. 131).

A similar conception is apparent in Pogge's work (1989, pp. 8–9, pp. 262–3, pp. 273–80; 2002, esp. pp. 170–6). Other proponents include Moellendorf (2002, pp 31–6), Onora O'Neill (1996, pp. 105–6, pp. 112–3) and Iris Marion Young (2000, pp. 222–49, p. 242, pp. 246–50).

The Causal Interdependence Account is, however, quite different to Freeman's account, for the scope of distributive justice on this model does not of necessity map on to the state. It is quite possible that the links of interdependence cross borders. Indeed, very many political philosophers (like Beitz, 1999a; Moellendorf, 2002; O'Neill, 1996; Pogge, 1989; 2002; Scanlon, 1985, p. 202; Young, 2000) have drawn on exactly this model and derived from it cosmopolitan conclusions about the scope of distributive justice.

Given then that there are alternative accounts of the scope of distributive justice which have radically different implications for the scope of distributive justice, Freeman thus owes us an explanation as to why we should accept his stipulation that the scope of justice is defined by the boundaries of the state and why we should thus repudiate the account utilised by the cosmopolitan thinkers listed above.

Freeman's conceptual points about the distinction between distributive and allocative justice are also questionable. In the first place, why should we not include allocative justice under the heading of distributive justice? It concerns the distribution of benefits and burdens and so has a good claim to be included as a matter of distributive justice. Second, even if we accept the distinction between allocative and distributive justice we need an argument for Freeman's assertion that distributive justice takes priority. Without such an argument someone can claim that there should be global principles of allocative justice. Third, to focus simply on the design of legal and economic institutions without regard to allocation is a form of fetishism. Surely what matters is the extent to which people can realise their abilities and protect and pursue their interests. In the light of this, though, it seems misguided to define distributive justice without reference to the shares that people will end up having. Freeman's account of distributive justice, however, does precisely this.

The procedural justice argument (A2)

On one occasion, Freeman shifts from his conceptual argument and suggests a second (normative) consideration in defence of his conception of the basic structure. In particular he argues that one can realise the ideal of pure procedural justice only by applying principles of distributive justice to the basic institutions that comprise the state. As Freeman puts it, "The focus on basic institutions is needed to make distribution a matter of pure procedural justice" (Freeman, 2007, p. 306, fn. 17). Freeman is here following Rawls, who argues in *Justice as Fairness: A Restatement* that there are two reasons for holding that principles of justice apply to the basic structure and the first of these holds that by applying principles of justice to the basic structure one can achieve pure procedural justice (Rawls, 2001, pp. 52–5 [esp. p. 541, pp. 170–1). One can structure the institutions in such a way that they will bring about fair outcomes. This then allows one to let people make their own choices and does not sanction "interference" with these processes.

   This argument is, however, unpersuasive. One can accept this argument's emphasis on pure procedural justice but it is not clear why pure procedural justice requires that distributive justice should conform to the boundaries of a single political unit. Suppose, for example, that principles of distributive justice apply at the global level. Suppose then that a number of influential states cooperate to design the existing international regimes, practices and organisations in such a way that they jointly further some distributive goal (like a global priority principle). Such an arrangement can be said to be realising pure procedural justice since the international regimes and rules are being structured so that the actions of those acting under these regimes and rules bring about the designated principle. A concern to realise pure procedural justice does not then require us to accept Freeman's statist conception of the basic structure.

The political role argument (A3)

We still therefore lack a reason to think that principles of distributive justice apply only within sovereign political institutions. Freeman makes at least two distinct additional suggestions. The first is what I shall term the Political Role Argument. Freeman writes:

> Rawls regards the difference principle as a political principle in the sense that it is to
> guide legislators in defining and regulating the uses of property, setting commercial

> policies, specifying schemes of taxation, specifying the terms of and regulating securities and negotiable instruments, defining conditions for copyrights, patents, royalties, and other forms of intellectual property and establishing the other indefinitely many laws and regulations that structure an economy (Freeman, 2007, p. 288).

His claim here is that the role of principles of justice is to guide legislators in their policies. Freeman infers from this that the scope of principles of distributive justice must then map on to the borders of states.

In reply: it might be true that at least one role of principles of distributive justice is to guide political actors but this does not entail that the scope of distributive justice must be coextensive with the scope of a state's borders. One might think of principles of justice as providing a guide to many political actors, an account of what they should jointly strive to achieve.

The political agency argument (A4)

Given this let us consider a different line of reasoning. In what might be termed the Political Agency Argument, Freeman says that principles of distributive justice are in need of political enforcement and therefore should map on to the borders of the state. As he writes:

> the difference principle is *a political* principle: it requires legislative judicial and executive agency and judgment for its application, interpretation, and enforcement. There is no invisible hand that gives rise to the myriad complexities of the basic institutions of property, contract law, commercial instruments, and so on. If *political* design of these and other basic economic and legal institutions is primarily what the difference principle is about . . . then there must exist political authority with legal jurisdiction, and political agents to fill these functions and positions, and to monitor and "fine tune" the system (Freeman, 2007, pp. 315–6, emphases in original).

But this too is unpersuasive. The application of principles of distributive justice does need political actors but it does not follow from this that since states are sometimes reasonably effective political actors we should then define the scope of distributive justice according to state boundaries. That surely gets the process the wrong way round. Would we not want first to determine who belongs to a scheme of distributive justice and who does not and then once having established the scope of justice examine which political actors can implement this scheme, calling for reform of these actors, or even the creation of new ones, where that is necessary. To stipulate that the effective actors must be states and that we should therefore define the scope of justice along statist lines gets matters back to front. It privileges the status quo and those advantaged by it over critical inquiry. We should, in this sense, disconnect the scope of distributive justice from the scope of state action.

None of Freeman's suggestions establishes then that principles of distributive justice must map on to sovereign self-governing political institutions and his critique of cosmopolitan ideals of distributive justice is undermined.

We can go further than this, for I believe that we have positive reason to reject Freeman's account of the scope of distributive justice. Consider two arguments. First, we should note that one of the standard rationales for attributing moral significance to the basic structure is that the latter has an enormous impact on people's lives and their ability to exercise their moral powers. The basic structure, as Rawls says, has importance because of its profound impacts on people's lives (Rawls, 1999a, p. 7; 2001, pp. 55–7). If, however, this is why the basic structure matters it is arbitrary to conceive of the basic structure simply as the legal and political system that is the state, and, moreover, distributive justice should apply not just to legal and political systems but to the transnational forces that have large effects on people's lives (Beitz, 1999a, pp. 201–2; Moellendorf, 2006, pp. 32–33, pp. 36–38). [. . .]

Second, the implausibility of Freeman's account of the subject of distributive justice is further confirmed if we consider some current environmental problems – such as ozone layer depletion or threats to biodiversity or anthropogenic global climate change. Consider, for example, global climate change. As is well known, this is caused by the emission of greenhouse gases such as carbon dioxide, methane, nitrous oxide, hydrofluorocarbons (HFCs), perfluorocarbons (PFCs) and sulfur hexafluoride (SF6). Its impacts are profound and affect people's ability to subsist, their health (and vulnerability to malaria, cholera, heat stress), their property and their ability to support themselves. Importantly in this context, climate change is a fundamentally global phenomenon. The causers are primarily industrialised countries, but now also developing countries like China, and its impacts are felt globally (but notably by the global poor). Now this is surely a paradigmatic case where principles of distributive justice apply – there is a (global) distribution of benefits and burdens. Principles are thus needed to regulate the fair distribution of these advantages and disadvantages.

Now this example supports two conclusions (a third will be introduced later). First, it establishes that principles of distributive justice are appropriate even where there is no equivalent political actor or cooperative scheme. Second, this example shows the superiority of the Causal Interdependence Account of the basic structure over Freeman's statist version. The global atmosphere represents a case where people throughout the world are causally interdependent and affect and are affected by each other. The Causal Interdependence Account can thus account for why global climate change raises issues of distributive justice.

[. . .]

Suppose, now, that we grant Freeman's assumption that justice applies only to basic social and political institutions. Freeman has not given us reason to think that there is not a global basic structure. He evinces a kind of state reductionism, according to which all interaction at the global level is entirely derivative and secondary: the only relevant actors are states. While not denying that states possess agency, Freeman's strong form of statism seems to me unwarranted. First, it entirely overlooks systemic pressures imposed by the international system (Waltz, 1959). Second, we can accept Freeman's point that international laws and conventions are the creation of states and state consent and acquiescence yet reject his conclusion that states are the only basic institutions. For Freeman overlooks the fact that once these international laws, institutions and customs are created they often have a life of their own and later governments have no power to overturn them or avoid them. So states may be the creators of the institutions but this does not entail that they can undo them. Historical precedent, inertia and convention, and more generally the phenomenon of path dependence, falsify this simplistic picture (Tan, 2006, p. 331). Third, Freeman briefly addresses the suggestion that international institutions may be basic institutions and discusses the proposal that the rules governing the control of territory constitute a basic international institution. His response, however, is implausible for he simply argues that state control over territory is not analogous to the institution of property (Freeman, 2007, pp. 307–8). This may be correct but it hardly settles the matter.

The "Argument from Coercion"

Let us turn now to a second attempted vindication of the normative significance of the state. In an important and elegantly argued article Michael Blake argues that some principles of justice apply only within the state and that others apply at the global level. Put more precisely he maintains that "relative" principles of justice, like equality, apply between members of the same state and "absolute" principles apply at the global level (Blake, 2001, p. 258). Egalitarian principles (and principles seeking to combat relative deprivation) can only have their place at the state level. Like Freeman, Blake draws on Rawls' political philosophy and he presents his views as having a Rawlsian character. Freeman's argument takes the form of an exegesis of Rawls, whereas Blake's argument is inspired by Rawls and indebted to it but does not claim to be an interpretation of what Rawls actually says. However, whereas Freeman defends the normative significance of the state by arguing that the latter is a system of political cooperation, Blake defends the normative significance of the state by arguing that it is a system of political coercion (Blake, 2001, p. 289).

Blake is not the only theorist who invokes the fact of state coercion to reject a cosmopolitan viewpoint. Thomas Nagel (2005) also advances a related claim.[4] However, whereas Nagel simply assumes that justice can only apply within the kind of coercive framework that is constituted by the modern state and gives us no argument for this assumption, Blake gives us an argument for this link between coercion and distributive justice.

Blake's argument unfolds as follows. First, he starts with the assumption that:

(1) Autonomy is valuable (Blake, 2001, pp. 266–71).

Second, Blake maintains that (1) can ground a commitment to a global sufficiency principle. If the autonomy of all is valuable then each and every person is entitled to the material resources necessary for autonomous action. We should therefore accept that:

(2) Each person is entitled to attain a decent standard of living (where this is defined in absolute terms) (p. 267, p. 271).

Blake then argues that if autonomy is valuable then political coercion can be legitimate only if a justification can be given to those subject to coercion. The key point he makes here is that:

(3) A commitment to autonomy entails that a coercive political system which restricts persons' autonomy needs to be justified to those whom it coerces (pp. 272ff).

Once we add:

(4) The state is a coercive actor (pp. 273–82).

it follows that:

(5) States have a duty to justify their policies to those whom they coerce (from (3) and (4)).

Blake further argues that:

(6) A commitment to justification entails a commitment to "relative" principles of distributive justice (pp. 282–5).

Hence it follows that:

(7) States should adopt "relative" principles of distributive justice in their domestic policy (from (5) and (6)).

Blake adds, finally, that:

(8) The global order is not coercive (p. 265, p. 280).

Hence:

(9) "Relative" principles of distributive justice do not apply at the global level (p. 258) (from (3), (6) and (8)).

Blake's argument therefore defends a moderate view. There are some global principles of distributive justice (a sufficiency principle) but relative principles of distributive justice apply only within the state and not at the global level.

Objections

Blake's argument is interesting and innovative. I believe, however, that it does not succeed. Disanalogy arguments may be flawed in two distinct ways. First, it might be the case that the domestic and global realms are not disanalogous in the way that the argument contends. Second, it might be the case that the disanalogy property does not possess the moral significance attributed to it. Blake's argument can be rejected on both grounds.

One obvious objection to Blake's argument challenges his claim that only the state is coercive and that the international system is not coercive (premise (8)). The existence of a system of state borders, critics can argue, is coercive. They forcibly restrict people from movement. Blake's proposed disanalogy property is thus misconceived: coercion exists in both the domestic and the international realms and hence, on Blake's own reasoning, relative principles apply at the global level.

This criticism has been advanced by a number of critics.[5] Blake, however, does anticipate this kind of criticism and the point about immigration (Blake, 2001, p. 280, fn. 30) and within his work we can identify three different points that he makes in reply to this line of reasoning. Let us consider each in turn. First, he replies that it is true that there is international coercion but he responds that the kind of coercion that exists at the global level is not the right kind to justify relative principles. But how is it relevantly different? Blake's answer appears to be that whereas the domestic realm directly coerces individuals the global realm does not. He writes that "the difference between domestic and international legal institutions" lies in the fact that "only the former engage in direct coercion against individuals, of the sort discussed above in connection with the criminal and civil law" (Blake, 2001, p. 280). The problem with this line of argument is that it is not clear to me why it matters if international legal institutions directly coerce individuals. Why is this a morally relevant difference? Suppose, for example, that institutions exercise coercion over entities like corporations and that, as a consequence of this, they coerce individuals and in doing so jeopardise their standard of living. In these cases A is coercing B who in turn coerces C. On Blake's account there is no need for A to justify his or her conduct to C because his or her coercion is indirect. But this is counter-intuitive: the salient point is that A has led to a disadvantage being coercively imposed on C. The first objection thus stands: Blake has not identified a morally significant difference between the domestic and global realms.

Blake sometimes makes a second different suggestion. For he writes that state coercion is different because, by contrast with international coercion, it is needed for persons to achieve autonomy. Thus he writes:

> Only the state is both coercive of individuals and required for individuals to live autonomous lives. Without some sort of state coercion, the very ability to autonomously pursue our projects and plans seems impossible; settled rules of coercive adjudication seem necessary for the settled expectations without which autonomy is denied (Blake, 2001, p. 280).

Suppose that this is true. Why does this constitute a morally relevant contrast between the domestic and global domains? That an institution is not necessary for autonomy does not entail that the benefits and burdens should not be shared using a "relative" principle. For example, a joint system in which parents take turns in taking children to school is not essential for autonomy but it does not follow that each beneficiary should not do a roughly equal share. Here surely is an institution which is not needed for autonomy and yet "relative" principles seem appropriate.

Third, and perhaps separately, Blake asserts that the justification of international coercion does not require a reference to people's relative shares. He says that international coercion is either unjustified or it is justified in terms of bringing everyone up to a sufficient standard of living. The justification of international coercion, he claims, does not require a distributive principle specifying fair shares. As Blake puts it:

> What I think is true, however, is that only the sorts of coercion practiced by the state are likely to be justified through an appeal to distributive shares. . . . Other forms of coercion in the international arena, by contrast, are generally indefensible – or, if they are defensible, do not find their justification in a consideration of their distributive consequences (Blake, 2001, p. 280).

This, however, seems implausible. Consider the World Trade Organisation (WTO). It seems perfectly natural to ask of the negotiators at Ministerial Conferences not simply whether everyone affected has a sufficient standard of living but also whether the benefits and burdens are fairly distributed. Consider for example the debates and negotiations surrounding the Doha Development Agenda. The sorts of issue being discussed included agricultural subsidies and tariffs, export subsidies and market access to developed and developing countries. WTO negotiations have also included what are termed the "Singapore" issues, so named because they first arose at the 1996 Ministerial Conference in Singapore. The Singapore issues include investment, competition policy, government procurement and trade facilitation. Now it seems entirely reasonable for the parties at the WTO to seek a fair share of the benefits arising from any such decisions, where a fair share requires more than that participating parties are above a sufficiency threshold. The WTO thus undermines Blake's position. I see no reason to say that an international trade institution is inherently unjustifiable. However, it is not enough to justify it in absolute terms – it produces a positive-sum effect and so it is fair to ask how the benefits should be distributed. Furthermore the normative debates surrounding the WTO bear this out.

[. . .]

Three challenges

The two arguments examined in this article, and more generally, each of the nine arguments outlined in the first section, seek to show that the state has a certain kind of normative significance. In particular, they seek to vindicate the claim that state borders define the scope of some (the Moderate Version) or all (the Extreme Version) principles of distributive justice.

In this penultimate section I want to draw on the preceding analysis and identify three problems inherent in any approach that claims that state borders have significance because they determine the scope of some or all principles of distributive justice. I shall then, in the final section, identify four quite separate ways in which the state may have normative significance, ways which a cosmopolitan egalitarian can accept.

Moral arbitrariness

First, the thesis that the borders of some, or all, principles of distributive justice are defined by the borders of the state needs to show why state membership is morally relevant. I argued that two prominent attempts to vindicate this view fail. We can, however, go further than this. For it is hard to see how state membership could have the type of normative significance ascribed to it by the statist views under consideration. Which state someone belongs to is, in very many cases, a matter of luck. It is a matter of fortune whether someone is born into Berkshire or Bihar and it seems highly perverse to argue that such facts should affect what people are entitled to. Why, one might ask, should being born into one state have such a tremendous impact on people's prospects in life? It is hard to see why something so arbitrary – as arbitrary as one's class origin or social status or ethnic identity – should be allowed to have such normative implications (Caney, 2005a, pp. 111ff.; Pogge, 1989, p. 247; 1994, p. 198). Consider in this light the ideal of equality of opportunity. Its aim is to ensure that people's opportunities should not be shaped by morally arbitrary factors such as one's ethnicity or regional identity. But given this, why should similarly arbitrary factors such as the country into which one is born be allowed to shape people's opportunities (Caney, 2001)?

Lest this argument is misunderstood two further points should be made. First, note that it is not sufficient to reply to this argument that some versions of the statist vision (like Blake's) ascribe *some* entitlements to persons *qua* human beings. Such a position is an improvement on the view that principles of distributive justice are *entirely* defined by people's membership of a state but we still need an argument as to why state membership should have *any* such fundamental moral importance at all. Why should membership of a state be an entitlement-generating property? Second, it is important to see that the moral arbitrariness argument, alone, does not refute the *Statist Scope Thesis*. It poses a forceful challenge to any statist view but I can see no way of showing that no argument could in principle meet this objection.[6] Any conclusive analysis must consider all the possible arguments one might give for the normative significance of state borders for the scope of distributive justice. This article has considered only two attempts to meet this challenge but, as the first section attests, there are other attempts and so the moral arbitrariness argument is not conclusive. It should therefore be seen as a powerful challenge to any would-be defence of the *Statist Scope Thesis* rather than a refutation. That said, it seems to me implausible that any argument can meet this challenge. The members of a state are, in all circumstances, highly heterogeneous in terms of their abilities, willingness to work, neediness, contribution to the social product and so on and it would be remarkable if they all (and they alone) shared some property that was entitlement generating.

Incompleteness and conservatism

A second, related, concern about the statist approach is its incompleteness and its inherent conservatism. The *Statist Scope Thesis* takes it as a given that there should be a system of states. It then argues that there are distributive principles that apply solely to those included within the state. This line of reasoning is troubling in a number of respects. First, before we accept this kind of argument we need an argument as to why there should be states in the first place. Why not, for example, have a system of multi-level governance in which power is shared between global authorities, state-level authorities and sub-state institutions (Caney, 2005a, ch 5; 2006b; Pogge, 2002, pp. 168–95)? Since such momentous normative implications (are said to) follow from state-hood it is incumbent on the proponents of the *Statist Scope Thesis* to provide a defence of the state. Without this their argument is provisional and incomplete (which is not to say that it cannot be completed). Second, and relatedly, one cannot adequately determine whether there should be states or not without also taking into account the kinds of normative implication that Blake and Freeman attribute to them. It would be inappropriate to bracket out this implication, defend the state and then claim that these implications about the scope of justice follow. It is possible that if one knew that the creation of states had this anti-egalitarian implication one would decide partly on this basis that there should not be states. Third, the statist's position is methodologically suspect for it appears to get matters back to front. It starts with the world as it is and the boundaries that exist. As such it places a great deal of normative weight on the accidents of history and military conquests. [. . .]

Three additional points are worth making. First, some who defend a statist approach contest the charge that their theory is inherently conservative. Blake, for example, argues that to accept that there should be states is not to accept the correctness of their "policies" (Blake, 2001, p. 264). One can, as he points out, criticise states for their decisions and actions. This is true but does not fully meet the concern being expressed. The whole structure of a system of states may generate or encourage injustice and a theory which starts with a commitment to a system of states lacks the conceptual resources to address this kind of problem. It cannot allow the possibility that the problem lies not with the decisions of states but with the very fact that there is a system of states and, as such, it is bunkered in its moral vision.

Second, the statist view may gain some intuitive appeal on the grounds that it is more practical than cosmopolitan egalitarianism. A defender of the statist view might say that it is a realistic doctrine, and it has more practical purchase, because it takes into account the world as it is. Blake, for example, says that one advantage of his approach is that "The division of the world into distinct political units is likely to continue for the foreseeable future, and a theory that accepts this fact can provide us with more present-day guidance than one that cannot" (Blake, 2001, p. 262; compare more generally pp. 261–4). This kind of reasoning is, however, unpersuasive and depends on an ambiguity in what it means to "accept" certain facts. We should distinguish between two different ways of accepting that the world comprises a system of states – an empirical sense and a normative sense. One might, for example, "accept" the existing system of states in a purely empirical way: one recognises as a matter of fact that there are states (as well as classes, nations, ethnic divisions and so on) and any plausible political theory must bear these in mind when proposing courses of action. Or one might "accept" the existing system of states in a normative way: one thinks that the system of states has a moral significance that should be respected. Now the obvious point to make here is that what Blake terms non-"institutional" approaches are no less practical than institutional ones for they can accept the status quo in a descriptive sense. They recognise that we are living in a world of states but it does not follow from this that we should "accept" this in a normative sense. On this view, institutions should not be taken into account in the wrong way. They should be regarded as empirical factors rather than as moral parameters. As a result, they are just as practically relevant as an institutional approach.

Third, those in favour of an "institutional" approach may reply that to dispute the legitimacy of deeply entrenched institutions and, in particular, to argue about whether there should be states is pointless. They exist and there is little that anybody can do to change that. A political theory that maintains that the existing global statist framework is unjust is irrelevant and of no use. But this challenge is mistaken for three reasons. First, it is simply mistaken to assume that the status quo is unalterable. Since the Second World War, non-sovereign bodies have evolved (like the European Union) and prior to the Treaty of Westphalia we did not see a statist order. Second, and more importantly, this argument overlooks the descriptive nature of moral language. Moral language plays at least two functions – first, to identify and defend principles to be implemented and, second, to provide an accurate description of the situation. This second role applies even when there is no chance of reforming the existing institutions. [. . .]

Theoretical inadequacy

A third problem with the *Statist Scope Thesis* is that it fails to cope with problems that are both inherently global in their nature and which also raise questions about the distribution of burdens and benefits. An important, and highly significant, case in point is global climate change. We have seen earlier that global climate change undermines both Freeman's cooperation-centred argument and Blake's coercion-centred argument. We can, however, develop this point further, for global climate change has more wide-ranging implications. Two aspects are worth stressing here. First it is a wholly global (and intergenerational) problem in that the impacts of global climate change (increased temperatures, rising sea levels, greater unpredictability, and increased rainfall in some areas and decreased rainfall in others) will be felt right across the globe, though the least advantaged will suffer disproportionately. Second, climate change inescapably raises questions of (global) distributive justice. Principles of distributive justice are needed for at least three reasons (a) They are needed to determine who is entitled to what level of protection from climate change, (b) They are also needed to determine who should bear the burden of dealing with climate change (should the duty be attributed according to an ability-to-pay criterion, or according to the principle that the polluter should pay, or some other principle?) In addition to this, (c), global principles of distributive justice are needed to determine how the right to emit carbon dioxide should be distributed among different people throughout the world. Should it be distributed according to a grandfathering rule, on an equal per capita basis, to the highest bidder in an auction or according to some other distributive principle (Caney, 2005c; 2006a)? In light of these considerations there is no escaping the fact that global climate change raises questions of distributive justice and, moreover, these are questions that arise at the global (and intergenerational) level.

This has two implications. First, it renders the Extreme View untenable, for the latter lacks the conceptual resources to recognise the existence of supra-state distributive questions. It simply fails to engage with one of the central problems of the modern world. Secondly, global climate change also undermines the Moderate View. The latter, recall, holds that some principles obtain globally – namely "absolute" ones – but that other "relative" principles do not (the terminology is Blake's [2001, p. 259]). But this seems implausible here for what we are facing is the question of how certain opportunities (the right to emit greenhouse gases) should be shared among different parties. And this strongly suggests the need for some "relative" principles. Consider absolute principles. Someone might suggest that everyone should have enough emissions to function at a certain level, but what if there is a surplus. How should this be distributed? More realistically, what if there is a deficit? What if there are not enough emission rights to meet everyone's core needs – how should that shortfall be shared among the people of the world? Relative principles inescapably surface.

It is pertinent in this context to note that many activists and philosophers explicitly adopt an egalitarian approach, arguing that the right to emit carbon dioxide should be distributed equally among all persons throughout the world (Agarwal and Narain, 1991, esp. p. 13; Athanasiou and Baer, 2002, esp. pp. 76–97). This doctrine is, moreover, the basis of the highly influential "Contraction and Convergence" approach to climate change (Meyer, 2000). Now my claim is *not* that this egalitarian principle towards emissions is in fact correct. It is, rather, that to reply "this cannot be the case because equality applies only within the state" is dogmatic and lacks any persuasive power. One might reasonably challenge the equal per capita view on the grounds that some people need more than equal emissions because they are poor and have development needs (Caney, 2005c). But note that this kind of argument does not invalidate the applicability of "egalitarian" ideals at the global level. Rather it calls for a distribution of emission rights which is sensitive to the needs of the global poor to develop. So rather than watering down the initial principle of global equality the objection expands and develops it. Clearly the question of what constitutes a fair share of global carbon emissions cannot be settled here but the point made above is simply that it is hard to see any *a priori* reason why the appropriate answer could not be egalitarian in form. The case of global climate change then represents a clear case of a pressing problem that statist conceptions of distributive justice cannot adequately address.

Two further points bear mentioning. First, note that the above argument is not an argument about institutional design. The claim is not that a system of states is ill suited to combat global climate change (though I think that this is a plausible charge). It is that one major and pressing issue cannot be adequately analysed by statist accounts of the scope of distributive justice. Second, note that I am not claiming that climate change is the only instance of the theoretical inadequacy of the *Statist Scope Thesis.* I believe that the same is, for example, true of global trade negotiations. The question of how the benefits and burdens of trade should be shared among participants raises essentially distributive questions (so the Extreme View is untenable). Furthermore a threshold view is inadequate – even if everyone were above a specified level one can still meaningfully ask whether the distribution of the remaining benefits is fair. And this takes us back from absolute principles to relative ones.

Four proposals

The three reasons adduced above indicate that both Extreme and Moderate versions of the *Statist Scope Thesis* are implausible. It is important to record, however, that to register these concerns about the prevailing *Statist Scope Thesis* is not to ignore the moral importance of political institutions, including the state. There are other ways of attributing normative significance to political institutions which are not prey to the problems of moral arbitrariness, political conservatism and theoretical inadequacy. This article concludes by outlining four different ways in which the state may have normative significance, each of which can be affirmed by egalitarian cosmopolitans.

The instrumental importance of political institutions

First, an egalitarian cosmopolitan can, and should, recognise the instrumental importance of political institutions, including the state. Those who are committed to cosmopolitan principles of justice should construct institutions, and restructure existing institutions, in order to further best those cosmopolitan principles. Furthermore, states can play an important role in this. They can do so in at least two distinct ways. First, they can pursue cosmopolitan *policies* either individually, or in cooperation with other states. They can, for example, cancel debt to heavily indebted poor countries. They can practise fair trade in their dealings with other countries and eradicate harmful tariffs and barriers to trade. In addition to this, they can incentivise democratic governance in poor countries. They can also support conflict resolution in conflict-ridden societies. In addition to this, they can mitigate their greenhouse gas emissions – passing regulations which require low greenhouse gas emissions and funding research into clean technologies – and they can combine to fund "adaptation" to climate change. Second, states can construct cosmopolitan *institutions* and reform existing international institutions in a more cosmopolitan direction. This can require reforming the WTO, International Monetary Fund (IMF) and World Bank so that they better serve global principles of justice and so that they enjoy greater legitimacy. To question the *Statist Scope Thesis* then is not to turn one's back on the instrumental normative significance of the state, or the positive role it can perform.

Political institutions and the ascription of duties to uphold the cosmopolitan entitlements of co-citizens

A second way in which political institutions, like the state, may have a normative significance can be seen if we distinguish between two different components of a theory of justice. All theories of justice make claims about persons' entitlements (what are people entitled to?) and about persons' duties (who is obligated to uphold people's entitlements?). Now if the preceding arguments are correct, it is implausible to insist that what people are entitled to should depend on which state they come from. The "arbitrariness" argument, for example, undermines the relevance of people's membership of a state to their entitlements. More precisely, they are not entitled to more than others simply because of their membership of one state rather than another. However, one can accept this and yet hold that the state has normative significance for people's duties to uphold these rights. To explain: one might adhere to cosmopolitan principles of distributive justice, including perhaps fairly egalitarian ones, but also hold that as a member of the state one is under a special duty to uphold the cosmopolitan entitlements of one's fellow citizens.[7] On this view, whether someone is Indian or Swedish should not affect how much people are entitled to but it may affect the content of their duties. One has a "special" duty to protect the (cosmopolitan) entitlements of one's fellow citizens, as well as a "general" duty to protect the cosmopolitan entitlements of everyone.

A comparison can be made here with Pogge's pioneering work on global justice (Pogge, 1989; 2002). As is well known, Pogge argues that principles of justice apply to institutions and that in virtue of membership of an "institutional scheme" (Pogge, 1989, p. 8) one has a negative duty not to participate in an unjust order. The relevant point here is that, on Pogge's view, membership of institutional schemes has relevance for people's *duties of justice*. The second point I am making about states has the same structure. As a member of a state one has a duty to fellow citizens to ensure that they receive their (cosmopolitan) entitlements. Note, also, that one might think that membership in a state can generate a special duty to uphold the cosmopolitan rights of fellow citizens and at the same time also subscribe to Pogge's argument that membership in transnational institutions similarly generates duties as well.

Political identity, patriotism, guilt and shame

Finally, it is worth noting that political institutions, including the state, may have normative significance in a third sense. In very many cases people's membership of the state affects their identity. They think of themselves as members of that state and it is an integral part of their self-understanding. In virtue of this, persons often feel sentiments like shame for the injustices committed by their state. By the same token they often take pride when their state stands up for justice and behaves nobly. Of course, sometimes citizens take pride in non-moral phenomena such as their country's sporting success, its musical heritage or its scientific record. The point remains, though, that citizens often feel strong sentiments of pride or guilt in virtue of their state's moral performance. It is, moreover, notable that these sentiments of shame and pride concern not just the state's domestic record but also the justness or otherwise of its foreign policy. Citizens may feel ashamed of their state's colonial record or their state's waging of an unjust war. They may take pride in the fact that it has stood up against an evil oppressor when no-one else did or that it led to the abolition of some evil international practice like slavery.

This phenomenon draws attention to a third way in which cosmopolitans may recognise that membership in the state has moral significance. For an egalitarian cosmopolitan approach can recognise this third kind of significance. On such an account, notions of collective pride and patriotism are sound and justified when they are grounded in their state's successful pursuit of cosmopolitan ideals. In *Professional Ethics and Civil Morals*, Émile Durkheim argues that "patriotism" and "cosmopolitanism" need not be at loggerheads (Durkheim, 1992, pp. 74–5). He suggests that we distinguish between two kinds of patriotism – one that seeks to promote the wealth and power of one's nation (it is directed outwards at others) and one that takes pride in "being the most just, the best organized and in possessing the best moral constitution" (Durkheim, 1992, p. 75) (it is directed inwards). Now Durkheim conceives this second kind of patriotism as being fundamentally about having a just domestic policy. But one could – and this is my suggestion here – conceive of it as involving pride in and commitment to one's state, in part, because of the justice of its foreign policy and the nobility (in cosmopolitan terms) of its external actions.

[. . .]

We gain a further illustration of the point being made if we reflect on the claim that states act "in the name of" their citizens. In "The Problem of Global Justice", Nagel repeatedly invokes this phrase to help ground his claim that principles of distributive justice apply only within the state (Nagel, 2005, esp. p. 128, p. 129, p. 130, p. 138, p. 140, p. 142). This article has emphatically rejected Nagel's conclusion. However, the idea that states act "in the name" of their citizens is a suggestive one and can be given, and has been given, a different interpretation to that given by Nagel. In particular, it can also be appropriated by egalitarian cosmopolitans. Consider, for example, those who protested against the war in Iraq. Many of those who marched against their governments did so under the banner "not in our name". By doing so, they provide a different interpretation of what it means for a state to act "in the name" of its citizens. On this second conception, the fact that a state acts in a person's name entails both (1) that it should act in a way that is just and honourable and also (2) that if it does not then its members may, in virtue of their political identity, feel guilt or shame. On this conception, the state should not act in such a way as to make its citizens ashamed of to feel that patriotism is inappropriate. The idea that states act in the name of their citizens and thus have duties to their citizens need not therefore lead us to a Nagelian conclusion. It also fits well (arguably better) with a cosmopolitan view, according to which states (since they act in the name of their citizens) should do so honourably and justly. And if we accept the cosmopolitan conception of political morality this means that a state acts "in our name" when it discharges its (cosmopolitan) duty well and is a fit object for our loyalty. When it does not, and it jeopardises the rights of others, then its members are entitled to regard it with shame or guilt and to deny that it acts in "their name". This coheres entirely with the way that the concept of acting in "the name" of the people is used in political practice.[8]

So here then is a third way in which one can deny the statist accounts of the scope of justice but at the same time recognise and justify the normative importance of the state.

Political identity and the ascription duties of compensation

Cases where states act unjustly in their foreign policy prompt a fourth point. As was noted above, membership in a state may entail special duties – in that case, the special duty to uphold the cosmopolitan rights of one's fellow citizens. However, one's membership in a state may also entail duties to members of other countries in cases where the latter are disadvantaged and they are disadvantaged because of the unjust foreign policy of one's state. Where one state has acted unjustly towards the members of another state (through colonialism, say, or an unjust war), one may argue that its citizens can acquire duties of compensation or reparation.

This claim has considerable intuitive appeal. Consider a case where members of one state have less than their fair share according to a principle of global justice. The question then arises as to who should provide them with the support to which they are entitled. If their disadvantage stems from the unjust actions of another state then it seems entirely appropriate to argue that, other things being equal, this support should be provided by the members of the state responsible for the injustice. Egalitarian cosmopolitans can then accept that one's membership of a state may ground special duties of compensation to some non-members (where one's state has violated their cosmopolitan rights) as well as special duties to members (to uphold their cosmopolitan rights).[9]

It is important to recognise that this does not entail that members of states with an unjust historical record are, of necessity, under more onerous obligations than members of an equally wealthy state that has not wronged others. The claim is that one's political identity can affect *to whom* one is obligated and not necessarily the total *amount* that one is obligated to do.

Conclusion

Cosmopolitan thinkers from Stoics such as Seneca, Cicero and Epictetus to contemporary cosmopolitan thinkers like Beitz and Pogge have often held that people occupy two roles. They can be citizens of a state/*polis* and citizens of the world. This article has explored the normative importance of state citizenship and found wanting the conventional interpretation of it defended by Blake and Freeman. It has found no reason to think that values like equality apply only within the state. This has a considerable ethical and practical importance given the striking inequalities that persist at the global level.

Having disputed one account of the moral importance of the state, this article has, however, suggested alternative accounts of how and why the state has normative significance. In particular it has suggested that it *may* have normative significance as an instrument of cosmopolitan justice, as a source of duties and as an object of loyalty, pride or shame.

Notes

1 As such it is compatible with what I have elsewhere termed moderate cosmopolitanism (Caney, 2005a, p. 105).
2 For excellent discussions of the morally relevant analogies between the domestic and global domains see Beitz (1999a, pp. 13–66 and esp. pp. 154–61; 1999b, pp 521–4) and Pogge (2004, esp. pp. 1744–52, 1754–9).
3 I have discussed these two types of cosmopolitanism elsewhere (Caney, 2003, pp. 295–8; 2005a. pp. 111–5; 2005b; 2007) and have argued for the importance of the humanity-centred approach (See also Buchanan 1990; 2004).
4 For criticism of Nagel's argument see Cohen and Sabel (2006) and Julius (2006). For another discussion of the coercion-based approach see Pevnick (2008).
5 See for example Arneson (2005, p. 150) and K-C Tan (2004, pp. 176–7; compare also p. 173).
6 Sophisticated statists recognise the force of this challenge. See for example, Sangiovanni and his attempt to meet the challenge of "moral arbitrariness" (Sangiovanni 2007, esp. pp. 22–9. pp. 29–34).
7 Note that my claim is about membership of the *state*. Miller has argued that membership of a *nation* generates obligations to uphold the human rights of one's fellow nationals (D. Miller 1995, pp. 75–7). I have criticised Miller's position on this elsewhere (Caney, 2005a, pp. 135–6).
8 This is not the only way of effecting a reconciliation between cosmopolitanism and patriotism. For a second, distinct way see Tan (2004, part III).
9 For a discussion of the duties that arise out of historic injustice see Caney (2006c; 2008).

References

Agarwal, A. and Narain, S. (1991) *Global Warming in an Unequal World: A Case of Environmental Colonialism.* New Delhi: Centre for Science and Environment.

Arneson, R. (2005) Do Patriotic Ties Limit Global justice Duties? *Journal of Ethics.* 9 (1–2) 127–50.

Athanasiou, T. and Baer, P. (2002) *Dead Heat: Global Justice and Global Warming.* New York: Seven Stories Press.

Beitz, C. (1999a) *Political Theory and International Relations.* Princeton NJ: Princeton University Press (with a new afterword by the author).

Beitz, C. (1999b) Social and Cosmopolitan Liberalism. *International Affairs.* 75 (3) 515–29.

Blake, M. (2001) Distributive Justice State Coercion and Autonomy. *Philosophy and Public Affairs.* 30 (3) 257–96.

Buchanan, A. (1990) Justice as Reciprocity versus Subject-Centred Justice. *Philosophy and Public Affairs.* 19 (3) 227–52.

Buchanan, A. (2004) *Justice, Legitimacy, and Self-Determination: Moral Foundations for International Law.* Oxford: Oxford University Press.

Caney, S. (2001) Cosmopolitan Justice and Equalizing Opportunities. *Metaphilosophy.* 32 (1/2) 113–34.

Caney, S. (2003) Entitlements, Obligations, and Distributive Justice: The Global Level in D. A. Bell and A. de-Shalit (eds). *Forms of Justice. Critical Perspectives on David Miller's Political Philosophy.* Lanham MD: Rowman & Littlefield. pp. 287–313.

Caney, S. (2005a) *Justice Beyond Borders: A Global Political Theory.* Oxford: Oxford University Press.

Caney, S. (2005c) Cosmopolitan Justice, Responsibility and Global Climate Change. *Leiden Journal of International Law.* 18 (4) 747–75.

Caney, S. (2006a) Global Justice Rights and Climate Change. *Canadian Journal of Law and Jurisprudence.* XIX (2) 255–78.

Caney, S. (2006b) Cosmopolitan Justice and Institutional Design: An Egalitarian Liberal Conception of Global Governance. *Social Theory and Practice.* 32 (4) 725–56.

Caney, S. (2006c) Environmental Degradation. Reparations and the Moral Significance of History. *Journal of Social Philosophy.* 73 (3) 464–82.

Caney, S. (2008) Climate Change Justice and the Duties of the Advantaged. *Critical Review of International Social and Political Philosophy* (forthcoming).

Cohen, J. and Sabel, C. (2006) Extra Rempublicam Nulla Justitia? *Philosophy and Public Affairs.* 34 (2) 147–75.

Durkheim, E. (1992) *Professional Ethics and Civic Morals.* trans. C. Brookfield with a new preface by B. S. Turner. London: Routledge.

Freeman, S. (2007) *Justice and the Social Contract. Essays on Rawlsian Political Philosophy.* New York: Oxford University Press.

Julius, A. J. (2006) Nagel's Atlas. *Philosophy and Public Affairs.* 34 (2) 176–92.

Meyer, A. (2000) *Contraction and Convergence: The Global Solution to Climate Change.* Totnes: Green Books.

Miller, D. (1995) *On Nationality.* Oxford: Clarendon Press.

Miller, D. (1998) The Limits of Cosmopolitan Justice. In D. R. Mapel and T. Nard (eds). *International Society: Diverse Ethical Perspectives.* Princeton NJ: Princeton University Press. pp. 164–81.

Miller, D. (1999a) Justice and Global Inequality. In A. Hurrell and N. Woods (eds). *Inequality, Globalization, and World Politics.* Oxford: Oxford University Press. pp. 187–210.

Miller, D. (1999b) *Principles of Social Justice.* Cambridge MA: Harvard University Press.

Miller, R. (1998) Cosmopolitan Respect and Patriotic Concern. *Philosophy and Public Affairs.* 27 (3) 202–24.

Moellendorf, D. (2002) *Cosmopolitan Justice.* Boulder CO: Westview Press.

Moellendorf, D. (2006) Equal Respect and Global Egalitarianism. *Social Theory and Practice.* 32 (4) 601–16.

Nagel, T. (2005) The Problem of Global Justice. *Philosophy and Public Affairs.* 33 (2) 113–47.

O'Neill, O. (1996) *Towards Justice and Virtue. A Constructive Account of Practical Reasoning.* Cambridge: Cambridge University Press.

Pevnick, R. (2008) "Political Coercion and the Scope of Distributive Justice. *Political Studies* 56 (2) 399–413.

Pogge, T. (1989) *Realizing Rawls.* Ithaca NY: Cornell University Press.

Pogge T. (1994) An Egalitarian Law of Peoples. *Philosophy and Public Affairs.* 23 (2) 195–224.

Pogge, T. (2002) *World Poverty and Human Rights: Cosmopolitan Responsibilities and Reforms.* Cambridge: Polity.

Pogge, T. (2004) The Incoherence between Rawls's Theories of Justice. *Fordham Law Review* XXII (5) 1739–59.

Rawls, J. (1999a) *A Theory of Justice*, revised edition. Oxford: Oxford University Press.

Rawls, J. (1999b) *The Law of Peoples with The Idea of Public Reason Revisited*. Cambridge MA: Harvard University Press.

Rawls, J. (2001) *Justice as Fairness: A Restatement*. ed. E. Kelly. Cambridge MA: Harvard University Press.

Sangiovanni, A. (2007) Global Justice, Reciprocity and the State. *Philosophy and Public Affairs* 35 (1) 3–39.

Scanlon, T. M. (1985) Rawls' Theory of Justice. In N. Daniels (ed). *Reading Rawls Critical Studies of A Theory of Justice*. Oxford: Blackwell. pp. 169–205.

Tan, K.-C. (2004) *Justice without Borders. Cosmopolitanism, Nationalism, and Patriotism*. Cambridge: Cambridge University Press.

Tan, K.-C. (2006) The Boundary of Justice and the Justice of Boundaries: Defending Global Egalitarianism. *Canadian Journal of Law and Jurisprudence*. XIX (2) 319–44.

Waltz, K. N. (1959) *Man, the State and War: A Theoretical Analysis*. New York: Columbia University Press.

Young, I. M. (2000) *Inclusion and Democracy*. Oxford: Oxford University Press.

Part IV

Cosmopolitan Politics

Introduction

As was outlined in the preceding section, critics of cosmopolitanism often suggest that a cosmopolitan preoccupation with universal morality leaves its theories without a distinct motivational component and that there is not a sufficiently strong identification relationship between so-called "world citizens" to generate the type of mutual obligations that cosmopolitanism demands (see Miller and Kymlicka). In addition, many critiques of cosmopolitanism start their criticisms with inquiries involving applied theory, by suggesting that cosmopolitanism is nothing more than a moral orientation that fails to supply a relevant political and institutional dimension (see Nagel). In particular, many critics of cosmopolitanism argue that it cannot capture the political "realities" of the international realm and that it remains under-developed in regards to practical global politics (see Dahl and Kymlicka).

In response to these concerns, this section will outline some ways that cosmopolitanism can come to ground and influence global institutional reforms. To begin this endeavor, this section starts with Ulrich Beck's "The Cosmopolitan Manifesto." In this chapter, Beck discusses the impacts of globalization on nation-states and outlines several new risks associated with the current transition to a more globalized stage of modernity (what Beck calls "second modernity"). For Beck, there are challenges that affect every society on earth (climate change, economic meltdown, etc.) and these challenges need to be responded to "simultaneously" in order for them to be effectively resolved. According to Beck, because of these new global risks, there is a growing perception that humanity as a whole is involved in something like a risk society, where a sense of these universal challenges "becomes a major force of political mobilization." A growing awareness of global risk "opens public discourse" and "unites many otherwise disparate areas of new transnational politics." However, as Beck suggests, understanding the sociological conditions of a risk society still leaves many unanswered questions about how to responsibly respond to these risks. In his attempt to answer this question, Beck explores key political elements involved with the idea of cosmopolitan politics and develops a cosmopolitan manifesto that seeks to establish a "transnational framework" in which global concerns are "properly posed, debated and resolved." As Beck contends, what is needed is the creation of an additional institutional subject at the global level, one involving "cosmopolitan parties," which can connect unheard voices into the global decision-making process.

Building upon the idea that the forces of globalization have significantly changed the way we need to conceptualize global politics, David Held develops eight universal principles that normatively underwrite the cosmopolitan political project. As Held argues, these eight principles are interconnected and can be derived directly from the cosmopolitan moral position that each person has universal equal worth. In specifying these eight foundational elements, Held seeks to map out some political permutations that result from a commitment to these principles. By doing so, Held suggests that we can derive at least three institutional features involved with political cosmopolitanism. First, the principles demand the maintenance of a "layered cosmopolitan perspective" that can accommodate pluralism while also providing the institutional conditions required for these pluralistic views to peacefully cooperate and coexist. Second, in order to create the regulative conditions for this institutional order, these eight principles will need to be adopted and codified within some form of Kantian cosmopolitan law. Third, a commitment to these principles will necessitate a form of "cosmopolitan democracy" and the creation of new political institutions that can foster civic participation and decision making at the global level.

As the conclusion in Held's chapter implies, a commitment to the principles of cosmopolitan order will also require a thoroughgoing commitment to some form of cosmopolitan law and to the cosmopolitan principles it enumerates. In this sense, there is a seemingly reinforcing relationship between the requirements of political cosmopolitanism and the commands of legal cosmopolitanism. That said, there are still many questions about what a condition of cosmopolitan law actually necessitates, how it relates to our current understanding of international law, and how it might be possible to move from cosmopolitan legal theory to legal practice. In an attempt to map out a cosmopolitan response to these questions, the chapter by Garrett Wallace Brown clarifies some historical meanings of cosmopolitan law, discusses how legal cosmopolitanism can provide a transition toward institutional cosmopolitanism and further relates how cosmopolitan law corresponds with current debates in international legal theory. Through this examination, Brown suggests that legal cosmopolitanism provides a necessary linchpin between cosmopolitan morality and its institutional practice and that the idea of cosmopolitan law can offer meaningful normative criteria for reforming international law and current institutional practice.

Continuing with a focus on legal cosmopolitanism and its relationship with political order, the last chapter in this section seeks to further advance what Jurgen Habermas calls "The Kantian Project." To do so, Habermas examines the primary foundations involved in creating a Kantian cosmopolitan legal condition in which "citizens in all parts of the world can actually enjoy formally granted liberties." From this basic conception of Kantian justice, Habermas applies this interpretation to contemporary international relations, explains why democratic states depend on its success, and examines two historical trends that progressively "work in favor of the project." Through this analysis, Habermas argues that, despite some present setbacks, there is still reason to be optimistic that the world is currently embroiled in stages of constitutionalization, in which "the individual subject . . . is gradually acquiring the status of a subject of international law and a cosmopolitan citizen." As Habermas argues, the Kantian project therefore remains "realistic" and politically relevant, which, for Habermas, can be empirically substantiated by tracing the transitional global reforms "already in progress."

13

The Cosmopolitan Manifesto
Ulrich Beck

All around the world, contemporary society is undergoing radical change that poses a challenge to Enlightenment-based modernity and opens a field where people *choose* new and unexpected forms of the social and the political. Sociological debates of the nineties have sought to grasp and conceptualize this reconfiguration. Some authors lay great stress on the openness of the human project amid new contingencies, complexities and uncertainties, whether their main operative term is "postmodernity" (Bauman, Lyotard, Harvey, Haraway), "late modernity" (Giddens), the "global age" (Albrow) or "reflexive modernization" (Beck, Giddens, Lash). Others have prioritized research into new forms of experimental identity (Melucci) and sociality (Maffesoli), the relationship between individualization and political culture (Touraine), the "post-national constellation" (Habermas) or the preconditions of "cosmopolitan democracy" (Held). Others still have contributed a wave of books on the "politics of nature" (Vandana Shiva, Gernot Böhme, Maarten Hajer, John S. Dryzek, Tim Hayward, Andrew Dobson, Barbara Adam, Robin Grove-White and Brian Wynne). All agree that in the decades ahead we will confront profound contradictions and perplexing paradoxes; and experience hope embedded in despair.

In an attempt to summarize and systematize these transformations, I have for some time been working with a distinction between first modernity and second modernity. The former term I use to describe the modernity based on nation-state societies, where social relations, networks and communities are essentially understood in a territorial sense. The collective patterns of life, progress and controllability, full employment and exploitation of nature that were typical of this first modernity have now been undermined by five interlinked processes: globalization, individualization, gender revolution, underemployment and global risks (as ecological crisis and the crash of global financial markets). The real theoretical and political challenge of the second modernity is the fact that society must respond to all these challenges *simultaneously.*

If the five processes are considered more closely, it becomes clear what they have in common: namely, they are all unforeseen consequences of the victory of the first, simple, linear, industrial modernization based on the national state (the focus of classical sociology from Durkheim, Weber and Marx to Parsons and Luhmann). This is what I mean by talking of "reflexive modernization". Radicalized modernization undermines the foundations of the first modernity and changes its frame of reference, often in a way that is neither desired nor anticipated. Or, in the terms of system theory: the unforeseen consequences of functional differentiation can no longer be controlled by further functional differentiation. In fact, the very idea of controllability, certainty or security – which is so fundamental in the first modernity – collapses. A new kind of capitalism, a new kind of economy, a new kind of global order, a new kind of society and a new kind of personal life are coming into being, all of which differ from earlier phases of social development. Thus, sociologically and politically, we need a paradigm-shift, a new frame of reference. This is not "postmodernity" but a second modernity, and the task that faces us is to reform sociology so that it can provide a new framework for the reinvention of society and politics. Research work on reflexive modernization does not deal only with the *decline* of the Western model. The key question is how that model relates to the *different modernities* in other parts of the world. Which new and unexpected forms of the social are emerging? Which new social and political forces, and which lines of conflict, are appearing on the horizon?

In world risk society, non-Western societies share with the West not only the same space and time but also – more importantly – the same basic challenges of the second modernity (in different places and with different cultural perceptions). To stress this aspect of sameness – and not otherness – is already an important step in revising the evolutionary bias that afflicts much of Western social science to this day, a bias whereby contemporary non-Western societies are relegated to the category of "traditional" or "pre-modern" and thus defined not in their own terms, but as the opposite or the absence of modernity. (Many even believe that the study of pre-modern Western societies can help us understand the characteristics of non-Western societies today!) To situate the non-Western world firmly within the ambit of a second modernity, rather than of tradition, allows a *pluralization of modernity*, for it opens up space for the conceptualization of divergent trajectories of modernities in different parts of the world. [. . .]

The increasing speed, intensity and significance of processes of transnational interdependence, and the growth in discourses of economic, cultural, political and societal "globalization", suggest not only that non-Western societies should be included in any analysis of the challenges of the second modernity, but also that the specific refractions and reflections of the global need to be examined in these different sites of the emerging global society.

Reversing Marx's judgement, we could say with Shalini Randeria that many parts of the "Third World" today show Europe the image of its own future. On the positive side, we could list such features as the development of multi-religious, multi-ethnic and multi-cultural societies, the cross-cultural models and the tolerance of cultural difference, the legal pluralism observable at a number of levels, and the multiplication of sovereignties. On the negative side, we could point to the spread of the informal sector and the flexibilization of labour, the legal deregulation of large areas of the economy and work relations, the loss of legitimacy by the state, the growth of unemployment and underemployment, the more forceful intervention by multinational corporations, and the high rates of everyday violence and crime. All these aspects, together with related questions and arguments, imply that we need a new frame of reference for the world risk society (including non-Western countries) in which we live if we are to understand the dynamics and contradictions of the second modernity (see *Korean journal of Sociology*, 1998).

As the bipolar world fades away, we are moving from a world of enemies to one of dangers and risks. But what does "risk" mean? Risk is the modern approach to foresee and control the future consequences of human action, the various unintended consequences of radicalized modernization. It is an (institutionalized) attempt, a cognitive map, to colonize the future. Every society has, of course, experienced dangers. But the risk regime is a function of a new order: it is not national, but global. It is rather intimately connected with an administrative and technical decision-making process. Risks presuppose decision. These decisions were previously undertaken with fixed norms of calculability, connecting means and ends or causes and effects. These norms are precisely what "world risk society" has rendered invalid. All of this becomes very evident with private insurance, perhaps the greatest symbol of calculation and alternative security – which does not cover nuclear disaster, nor climate change and its consequences, nor the breakdown of Asian economies, nor the low-probability high-consequences risk of various forms of future technology. In fact, most controversial technologies, like genetic engineering, are not privately insured.

What has given rise to this new prominence of risk? The concept of risk and risk society combines what once was mutually exclusive – society and nature, social sciences and material sciences, the discursive construction of risk and the materiality of threats. Margaret Thatcher, the former British Prime Minister, once said: there is no such thing as society. Most sociologists believe in what can be called a "reverse Thatcherism", namely there is *nothing but society*. This "nothing but society" sociology is blind to the ecological and technological challenges of second modernity. Risk society theory breaks with this self-sufficiency and self-centredness. It argues that there is at the same time the immateriality of mediated and contested definitions of risk *and* the materiality of risk as manufactured by experts and industries world-wide. This has many implications. For example, risk analysis needs an interdisciplinary approach. Risk science without the sociological imagination of constructed and contested risk is *blind*. Risk science that is not informed about the technologically manufactured "second nature" of threats is *naïve*. The ontology of risk as such does not grant privilege to any specific form of knowledge. It forces everyone to combine different and often divergent rationality-claims, to act and react in the face of "contradictory certainties" (Schwarz and Thompson, 1990).

In world risk society the politics and subpolitics of risk definition become extremely important. Risks have become a major force of political mobilization, often replacing references to, for example, inequalities associated with class, race and gender. This highlights the new *power game* of risk and its meta-norms: who is to define the riskiness of a product, a technology, and on what grounds in an age of manufactured uncertainties? When, in 1998, the Greens entered Gerhard Schröder's government in Germany, they began to act upon and change some of those power relations of risk definition by, for example, a strategy of pluralization of experts, calling counter-experts into governmental commissions for security who had previously been excluded; or by raising the level of acceptable insurance; or by enforcing legal norms which so far have not really been taken seriously; and so on. This, within the common framework, looks of minor, negligible importance. But this is exactly the point: in risk society seemingly unimportant areas of political intervention and action are becoming extremely important and seemingly "minor" changes do induce basic long-term transformations in the power game of risk politics.

Thus the framework of risk society again connects what have been strictly discrete areas: the question of nature, the democratization of democracy and the future role of the state. Much political debate over the last twenty years has centred on the decline in the power and legitimacy of government and the need to renew the culture of democracy. Risk society demands an opening up of the decision-making process, not only of the state but of private corporations and the sciences as well. It calls for institutional reform of those "relations of definition", the hidden power-structure of risk conflicts. [. . .]

But at the same time new prominence of risk connects, on the one hand, individual autonomy and insecurity in the labour market and in gender relations, and, on the other hand, the sweeping influence of scientific and technological change. World risk society opens public discourse and social science to the challenges of ecological crisis, which, as we now know, are global, local and personal at one and the same time. Nor is this all. In the "global age", the theme of risk unites many otherwise disparate areas of new transnational politics with the question of cosmopolitan democracy: with the new political economy of uncertainty, financial markets, transcultural conflicts over food and other products (BSE), emerging "risk communities", and, last but not least, the anarchy of international relations. Personal biographies as well as world politics are getting "risky" in the global world of manufactured uncertainties.

But the globality of risk does not, of course, mean a global equality of risk. The opposite is true: the first law of environmental risks is: *pollution follows the poor.* In the last decade poverty has intensified everywhere. The UN says more than 2,400 million people now live without sanitation, a considerable increase on a decade ago; 1,200 million have no safe drinking water; similar numbers have inadequate housing, health and education services; more than 1,500 million are now undernourished, not because there is no food, or there is too much drought, but because of the increasing marginalization and exclusion of the poor.

Not only has the gap between rich and poor grown, but more people are falling into the poverty trap. Free-market economic policies, imposed on indebted countries by the West, worsen the situation by forcing countries to develop expert industry to supply the rich, rather than to protect, educate or care for the weakest. The poorest countries now spend more servicing their debt to the richest countries than they do on health and education in their own countries.

The past decade has shown that the dogmatic free-market economics imposed throughout the 1980s – and to which every world and nation forum has since signed up – has exacerbated environmental risks and problems just as much as central planning from Moscow ever did. Indeed free-market ideology has increased the sum of human misery. On the back of crucial free-trade pacts like the WTO and NAFTA, for example, consumption is now virtually out of control in the richest countries. It has multiplied six times in less than twenty-five years, according to the UN. The richest 20 per cent of the people are consuming roughly six times more food, energy, water, transportation, oil and minerals than their parents were.

Risk and *responsibility* are intrinsically connected, as are risk and *trust,* risk and *security* (insurance and safety). To whom can responsibility (and therefore costs) be attributed? Or do we live in a context of "organized irresponsibility"? This is one of the major issues in most of the political conflicts of our time. Some believe that risk induces control, so that the greater the risk the greater the need for controllability. The concept of "world risk society", however, draws attention to the *limited* controllability of the dangers we have created for ourselves. The main question is how to take decisions under conditions of manufactured uncertainty, where not only is the knowledgebase incomplete, but more and better knowledge often means more uncertainty.

We now have to recognize and act upon the *new global market risk* which is high-lighted by the Asian crisis and which demonstrates the social and political dynamics of the *economic* world risk society. The global market (risk) is a new form of "organized irresponsibility" because it is an institutional form so impersonal as to have no respon-sibilities, even to itself. Enabled by the information revolution, the global market risk allows the near-instant flow of funds to determine who, if anyone, will prosper, and who will suffer. Like the competitive terms of economic theory, no one component is large enough to shift the overall flow; nobody controls the global market risk. The components follow their own self-interest, and the results resemble those predicted by theory. Because there is no global government, the global market risk cannot be regu-lated like national markets. Nor can any national market resist it with impunity. But at the same time the constructed fatalism is an illusion too. [. . .]

Political analysts say it is still very difficult to predict exactly how the new social and political risks will spill over in individual countries. But many now argue that the risk of backlash against the West, internal crisis or even conflict between nations has increased across the region. And what was unthinkable a year or so ago is becoming real now: the global free market is falling apart and the global free-market ideology is collapsing. All over the world, politicians, including European leaders, are taking tentative steps towards a new policy: protectionism is being reinvented; some are asking for new trans-national institutions to control global financial flow, while others plead for a transna-tional insurance system or a new politics of the existing transnational institutions and regimes. The consequence is that the era of free-market ideology is a fading memory and is being superseded by its opposite: a *politicization* of global market economy.

Today you can illustrate the constitutive components of the global market risks by the experience of the Asian crisis as you could in 1986 the basic aspects of the global technological and ecological risk society with the anthropological shock of Chernobyl. So in the global financial as well as in the global ecological risk society:

* two conflicts, two logics of distribution are interconnected: the distribution of *goods* and the distribution of *bads*;
* the foundations of "risk calculation" are undermined: damages like millions of unemployed and poor cannot, for example, be compensated financially – it makes no sense to insure oneself against a global recession;
* the "*social explosiveness*" of global financial risks is becoming real: it sets off a dynamic of cultural and political change that undermines bureaucracies, challenges the dominance of classical economics and neoliberalism and redraws the boundaries and battlefields of contemporary politics;
* the institutions of the nation-state collapse;
* risk always involves the question of responsibility, so the need for "responsible glo-balization" becomes a world-wide public and political issue;
* new options are emerging: national and regional protectionism, transnational insti-tutions and democratization.

Here is the reason why I call myself neither an optimist nor a pessimist, but a pessi-mistic optimist: the world risk society is the opposite of a "postmodern constellation"; it is a self-critical, highly political society in a new sense: the transnational dialogue of politics and democracy – perhaps even sociology – has to be reinvented.

[. . .]

*

We live in an age of risk that is global, individualistic and more moral than we suppose. The ethic of individual self-fulfilment and achievement is the most powerful current in modern Western society. Choosing, deciding, shaping individuals who aspire to be the authors of their lives, the creators of their identities, are the central characters of our time.

This "me-first" generation has been much criticized, but I believe its individualism is moral and political in a new sense. In many ways this is a more moral time than the 1950s and 1960s. Freedom's children feel more passionately and morally than people used to do about a wide range of issues – from our treatment of the environment and animals, to gender, race and human rights around the world.

It could be that this provides the basis for a new cosmopolitanism, by placing globality at the heart of political imagination, action and organization. But any attempt to create a new sense of social cohesion has to start from the recognition that individualization, diversity and scepticism are written into our culture.

Let us be clear what "individualization" means. It does *not* mean individualism. It does *not* mean individuation – how to become a unique person. It is *not* Thatcherism, not market individualism, not atomization. On the contrary, individualization is *a structural* concept, related to the welfare state; it means "*institutionalized* individualism". Most of the rights and entitlements of the welfare state, for example, are designed for individuals rather than for families. In many cases they presuppose employment. Employment in turn implies education, and both of these presuppose mobility. By all these requirements people are invited to constitute themselves as individuals: to plan, understand, design themselves as individuals and, should they fail, to blame themselves. Individualization thus implies, paradoxically, a collective lifestyle.

When this is coupled with the language of ethical globalization, I am convinced that a cosmopolitan democracy is a realistic, if utopian, project – though in an age of side-effects, we must also reflect on the dark side, on the ways it can be used politically as a front for old-style imperial adventures.

Are we a "me-first" society? One might think so from the catchphrases that dominate public debate: the dissolving of solidarity, the decline of values, the culture of narcissism, entitlement-oriented hedonism, and so on. On this view, modern society lives off moral resources it is unable to renew; the transcendental "value ecology", in which community, solidarity, justice and ultimately democracy are "rooted", is decaying; modernity is undermining its own indispensable moral prerequisites.

But this conception of modern society is false. Morality, including Christian morality, and political freedom are not mutually exclusive but mutually inclusive, even if this means that an insoluble contradiction is lodged within Christian traditions.

The question is: what is modernity? And the answer is: not only capitalism (Marx), rationalization (Weber), functional differentiation (Parsons, Luhmann), but also the dynamics of political freedom, citizenship and civil society. The point of this answer is that morality and justice are not extra-territorial variables for modern society. Quite the reverse is true. Modernity has an independent (simultaneously ancient and very modern) well-spring of meaning in its midst, which is political freedom. This spring is not exhausted by daily use – indeed, it bubbles up all the more vigorously as a result. Modernity, from this point of view, means that a world of traditional certainty is perishing and being replaced – if we are fortunate – by a legally sanctioned individualism for all.

In what we have called the first modernity, the issue of who has and who has not a right to freedom was answered through recourse to such matters as the "nature" of gender and ethnicity; contradictions between universal claims and particular realities were settled by an ontology of difference. Thus until the early 1970s, even in Western countries, women were denied civil rights such as the control of property and of their own bodies.

In the second modernity, the structure of community, group and identity loses this ontological cement. After *political* democratization (the democratic state) and *social* democratization (the welfare state) a *cultural* democratization is changing the foundations of the family, gender relations, love, sexuality and intimacy. Our words about freedom start to become deeds and to challenge the basis of everyday life, as well as of global politics. Being freedom's children, we live under conditions of radicalized democracy for which many of the concepts and formulas of the first modernity have become inadequate.

[. . .]

People are better adapted to the future than are social institutions and their representatives. The decline of values which cultural pessimists are so fond of decrying is in fact opening up the possibility of an escape from the "bigger, more, better" creed, in a period that is living beyond its means both ecologically and economically. Whereas, in the old system of values, the self always had to be subordinated to patterns of the collective, the new orientations towards the "we" are creating something like a cooperative or altruist individualism. Thinking of oneself and living for others – once considered by definition contradictory – are revealed as internally and substantively connected with each other (see Wuthnow, 1991). Living alone means living socially.

As well as ignoring these aspects of institutionalized individualism most moral preachers also fail to mention that an ever larger number of men and women are compelled to treat the future as a threat, rather than as a shelter or a promised land. All we can do here is offer a few notes about how such a *political economy* of uncertainty, the political economy of world risk society, might be developed.

First, the new power-play between territorially fixed political actors (government, parliament, unions) and non-territorial economic actors (representatives of capital, finance, trade) is the central element expressed in the political economics of uncertainty and risk. To provide a simple formula: capital is global, work is local. All around the world, at the same time, *fragile* work increases rapidly, that is, part-time, self-employed work, limited-term jobs and other forms for which we have barely found proper descriptions. If this dynamic continues, in ten to fifteen years about half the employable population of the West will work under conditions of uncertainty. What used to be the exception is becoming the rule.

Second, this leads to a well-founded impression that states no longer have any leeway except to choose between (a) social protection of the growing numbers of the poor, at the price of high unemployment (as in most European countries), and (b) acceptance of glaring poverty to achieve slightly lower unemployment (as in the United States).

Third, this is bound up with the end of the work society as more and more human beings are replaced by intelligent technologies. Rising unemployment can no longer be attributed to cyclical economic crisis, but rather to the *success* of technologically advanced capitalism. Since the early 1970s the relationship between GDP growth and employment has become tenuous in all OECD countries. Considerable increases in per capita GDP have been accompanied by little or no employment growth. The old instruments of economic policy therefore fail to achieve results, and work today is, so to speak, a daily rehearsal of redundancy.

Fourth, the political economy of uncertainty describes and analyses a *domino effect*. Things which used to supplement and reinforce one another in good times – full employment, pension savings, high tax revenue, leeway for government action – now tend *mutatis mutandis* to endanger one another. As employment grows more precarious, the bases of the welfare state decay and "normal" biographies come apart; the ever-growing pressure on welfare cannot be financed from a public purse full of holes.

Fifth, orthodox defensive strategies are therefore put under pressure. "Flexibility" is demanded everywhere – or, in other words, an "employer" should be able to fire "employees" more easily. "Flexibility" also means a redistribution of risks from state and economy to individuals. The jobs available become more and more short-term and "renewable" – which is to say, "terminable". People are just asked to smile and accept it: "Your skills and abilities are obsolete, and no one can tell you what to learn so that you will be needed in the future." Consequently, the more work relations are "deregulated" and "flexibilized", the faster work society turns into a risk society that is not open to calculation by individuals or by politics. At the same time, it becomes increasingly important to resolve the contradictions that the political economy of risk implies for economics, politics and society (Beck, 1999a). One thing is clear. Endemic uncertainty is what will mark the lifeworld and the basic existence of most people – including the apparently affluent middle classes – in the years that lie ahead. So, the expression "precarious freedoms" denotes a basic ambivalence between the cultural script of individual self-fulfilment and the new political economy of uncertainty and risk. All too swiftly, the "elective", "reflexive" or "do-it-yourself" biography can become the breakdown biography.

Let us link these points up with our previous theme. How can a secular society exposed to the rigours of a global market, based on institutionalized individualization amidst a global communications explosion, also foster a sense of belonging, trust and cohesion? It can do this only through a source which, instead of being exhausted by daily use, pours forth all the stronger – only through cultural democratization and political freedom. Yet there is a basic contradiction between political freedom and the political economy of risk and uncertainty. On the road to the uncontested rule of the political economy of risk, republican institutions and the liveliness of democratic culture are the first to go by the board. As Zygmunt Bauman (1999) has put it:

> The purpose of the republic is not an imposition of a preconceived model of the "good" life, but the enabling of its citizens to discuss freely the models of life they prefer and to practise them. . . . The decoupling of income entitlements from paid work and from the labour market may serve the republic in only one, but a crucial, way: *by taking out the awesome fly of insecurity from the ointment of freedom*. But this limitation of risks and damages is precisely the most crucial of the basic-income objectives.

When, or if, this objective is reached, men and women no longer afraid to use their freedom may find the time, will and courage to tackle the challenges of the second modernity. Let there be no misunderstanding. I am not arguing for a basic assured income to raise the poor from their poverty – that is an important issue, but one relating to a special (interest) group. My argument is, I believe, stronger: namely, that we need a basic assured income as a *sine qua non* of a political republic of individuals who will create a sense of cohesion and fellow-feeling through public conflict and commitment (see Beck, 1998a).

With political freedom placed at its centre, modernity is not an age of decline of values but an age *of* values, in which the hierarchical certainty of ontological difference is displaced by the creative uncertainty of freedom. Freedom's children are the first to live in a post-national cosmopolitan world order. But what does this mean politically? Living in an age of side-effects, we have to ask very early what are the unforeseen and unwanted consequences of the new rhetoric of "global community", "global governance" and "cosmopolitan democracy".

[. . .]

Globalization implies the weakening of state structures, of the autonomy and power of the state. This has a paradoxical result. On the one hand, it is precisely collapses of the state which have produced most of the really grave human conflicts of the 1990s, whether in Somalia, East Africa, Yugoslavia, Albania or the former Soviet Union; on the other hand, the idea of "global responsibility" implies at least the possibility of a new Western *military humanism* – to enforce human rights around the globe. Consequently, the greater the success of neoliberal politics on a global level – that is, the greater the erosion of state structures – the more likely it is that a "cosmopolitan façade" will emerge to legitimize Western military intervention. The striking feature here is that imperial power-play can coexist harmoniously with a cosmopolitan mission. For the subordination of weak states to institutions of "global governance" actually creates the space for power strategies disguised as humane intervention.

Of course, there are also double standards of morality involved here. Take the example of cosmopolitan democracy itself. What would happen if the European Union wanted to become a member of the European Union? Naturally it would have to be refused. Why? Because of its glaring lack of democracy! But it must also be asked whether EU member-states such as France, Germany, Britain or Italy can really be considered democracies, when roughly half the laws passed in their parliaments merely transplant directives issued by Brussels, the World Trade Organization, and so on.

In the age of globalization, there is no easy escape from this democratic dilemma. It cannot be solved simply by moving towards "cosmopolitan democracy". The central problem is that without a politically strong cosmopolitan consciousness, and without corresponding institutions of global civil society and public opinion, cosmopolitan democracy remains, for all the institutional fantasy, no more than a necessary utopia. The decisive question is whether and how a consciousness of cosmopolitan solidarity can develop. The *Communist Manifesto* was published a hundred and fifty years ago. Today, at the beginning of a new millennium, it is time for a Cosmopolitan Manifesto. The *Communist Manifesto* was about class conflict. The Cosmopolitan Manifesto is about transnational – national conflict and dialogue which has to be opened up and organized. What is to be the object of this global dialogue? The goals, values and structures of a cosmopolitan society. The possibility of democracy in a global age.

Who will raise this question? The "me-first" generation, freedom's children. We have been witnessing a global erosion of the authority of national states and a general loss of confidence in hierarchical institutions. But at the same time, active intervention by citizens has been growing more common and breaking the bounds of past convention – especially among younger and more educated sections of the population. The spaces in which people think and act in a morally responsible manner are becoming smaller and more likely to involve intense personal relationships. They are also, however, becoming more global and difficult to manage. Young people are moved by issues that national politics largely rules out. How can global environmental destruction be avoided? How can one live and love with the threat of AIDS? What do tolerance and social justice mean in the global age? These questions slip through the political agendas of national states. The consequence is that freedom's children practise a highly political disavowal of politics.

The key idea for a Cosmopolitan Manifesto is that there is a new dialectic of global and local questions which do not fit into national politics. These "glocal" questions, as we might call them, are already part of the political agenda – in the localities and regions, in governments and public spheres both national and international. But only in a transnational framework can they be properly posed, debated and resolved. For this there has to be a reinvention of politics, a founding and grounding of the new political subject: that is, of *cosmopolitan parties.* These represent transnational interests transnationally, but also work within the arenas of national politics. They thus become possible, both programmatically and organizationally, only as national–global movements *and* cosmopolitan parties.

The underlying basis here is an understanding that the central human worries are "world" problems, and not only because in their origins and consequences they have outgrown the national schema of politics. They are also "world" problems in their very concreteness, in their very location here and now in this town, or this political organization.

Let us take the case of all the various regulation-intensive industries that have been liberalized in recent years: telecommunications is the main example; others include energy, financial services and food. Increased competition in these areas has brought the domestic regimes that regulate them into conflict, but meanwhile the problems have become global. And this is just the start. Looming ahead are new issues – environmental and labour legislation – in which regulation is even more sensitive, even more crucial. This is the challenge of the years to come. A first wave of national deregulation enforces a second wave of transnational regulation. Without a decisive step towards cosmopolitan democratization, we are heading for a post-political technocratic world society.

The first expressions of a cosmopolitan politics are already taking shape within the framework of national states – expressions that require specific points to crystallize as political movements within and between national states. This creates the opportunities for cosmopolitan movements and parties which, even if they initially win over and mobilize only minorities for cosmopolitan interests, have the basis of their power in the act of opening out the transnational domain.

This is a difficult task. The resolution of problems in all these areas is already providing conflict enough between the US and the EU – for example, over food safety questions. Difficulties will be even greater between countries that are more divergent in their cultural assumptions, political forms and income levels. So cosmopolitan parties will have to organize global debates on these highly controversial issues, both from within and from outside individual countries. Just like corporate agrarian societies and nationally based industrial or service societies, so too world society develops its own forms of social inequality and notions of justice, its own political values and ideas, its own hysterias and dilemmas, and its own questions of organization and representation.

As I learned from Martin Albrow and his group, non-territorial communities that are organized, for example, around a transnational division of labour should be understood as "socio-scapes" (Albrow, 1996; Eade, 1997). But again the question arises: how are post-national communities possible as bases for political action and collectively binding decision-making? There are many risks in life, and only some are suitable as the basis of community. But *risk-sharing* or a *"socialization of risk"* (Elkins, 1995) can, in my view, become a powerful basis of community, one which has both territorial and non-territorial aspects. So far, risk has seemed a purely negative phenomenon, to be avoided or minimized. But it may be seen at the same time as a positive phenomenon too, when it involves the sharing of risks without borders. Post-national communities could thus be constructed and reconstructed as communities of risk. Cultural definitions of appropriate types or degrees of risk define the community, in effect, as those who share the relevant assumptions. "Risk-sharing" further involves the taking of responsibility, which again implies conventions and boundaries around a "risk community" that shares the burden. And in our high-tech world, many risk communities are potentially political communities in a new sense – because they have to live with the risks that others take. There is a basic power structure within world risk society, dividing those who produce and profit from risks and the many who are afflicted with the same risks.

This idea of non-territorial communities of shared risk cannot be developed here in all its aspects. But the key questions it poses are the following. Should risks and their attendant costs be shared among certain categories of citizens or among residents of a certain place? How can global risks ever be shared? What does it mean when the socialization of risk occurs across generations? Models of post-national risk communities may be found, for example, in regional ecological treaties (for example, among states bordering the North Sea or the Mediterranean), in transnational communities, non-governmental organizations or global movements, such as ecological or feminist networks.

These movements form a "world party" in a threefold sense. First, their values and goals have not a national but a cosmopolitan foundation: their appeal (*liberty, diversity, toleration!*) is to human values and traditions in every culture and religion; they feel an obligation towards the planet as a whole. National parties, on the other hand, appeal to national values, traditions and solidarities.

Second, they are world parties because they place globality at the heart of political imagination, action and organization. Both programmatically and institutionally, they propose a politics of concrete alternatives to the firmly established and firmly guided priorities of the national sphere. Thus, for cosmopolitan parties what is at issue is never just a certain content, but always also a new concept, new structures, new institutions of politics, which for the first time offer a platform for the negotiation and enforcement of transnational issues from below.

Third, they are world parties in the sense that they are possible only as *multinational* parties. Thus, there have to be cosmopolitan movements and parties of French, North American, Polish, German, Japanese, Chinese, South African and other provenances which, by interacting with one another in the various areas of world society, struggle to bring about cosmopolitan values, mutualities and institutions. This involves strengthening the existing independent transnational institutions against national egoisms, but above all else it involves the democratization of transnational regimes and regulators.

Which groups come into consideration as bearers of such a cosmopolitan movement to expand democracy? Where are the voters who feel they are addressed and represented by cosmopolitan parties and could be mobilized and organized by them? Where globality becomes an everyday problem or the object of cooperation – in the big cities, the transnational organizations and movements, schools and universities – the milieu and mentality of a self-conscious world citizenship take shape with a post-national understanding of politics, responsibility, the state, justice, art, science and public interchange. However, the extent to which this is already so, or likely in the future, is still open, both empirically and politically.

This expanding "world citizenship" (Kant) with national cultural hues should not be confused with the rise of a global managerial class. A distinction must be drawn between "global capitalists" and "global citizens". Yet a plural world citizenship is soaring with the wind of global capital at its back. For the bourgeois must already learn to operate in his or her own interests in a transnational framework, while the citizen must still think and act within the categories of the national state.

Nevertheless, in the milieu of transnational structures, experts and counter-experts, transnational movements and networks, we can see experimental forms of organization and the expression of a cosmopolitan common sense. It comprises a mixture of scepticism about national egoisms masquerading as universal necessities, and scepticism about the mistakes and defects of national bureaucracies. Voluntary organizations play a crucial role in building a global civil society. They help to generate the public-mindedness and civic trust to open up the national agendas for transnational, cosmopolitan concerns. And they constitute a human flourishing in their own right.

How can cosmopolitan movements become possible and powerful? In the end, this question can be answered only where people ask and listen to it – in the space of political experimentation. Citizens of the world, unite!

References

Albrow, G. (1986) *The Global Age* (Cambridge: Polity Press).

Bauman, Z. (1999) *In Search of Public Space* (Cambridge: Polity Press).

Beck, U. (1998a) "Freedom's Children", in *Democracy Without Enemies* (Cambridge: Polity Press).

Beck, U. (1998b) *Democracy Without Enemies* (Cambridge: Polity Press).

Beck, U. (1999a) *What is Globalization?* (Cambridge: Polity).

Eade, J. (ed.) (1997) *Living the Global City* (London: Routledge).

Elkins, D.T. (1995) *Beyond Sovereignty* (Toronto: University of Toronto Press).

Korean Journal of Sociology (1998) vol. 39, no. 1: Special Issue on Korea: A Risk Society.

Schwarz, M. and Thompson, M. (1990) *Divided We Stand Redefining Politics, Technology and Social Choice* (New York: Harvester Wheatsheaf).

Wuthnow, R. (1991) *Acts of Compassion* (Princeton: University of Princeton Press).

14

Principles of Cosmopolitan Order
David Held

Cosmopolitanism is concerned to disclose the ethical, cultural, and legal basis of political order in a world where political communities and states matter, but not only and exclusively. In circumstances where the trajectories of each and every country are tightly entwined, the partiality, one-sidedness and limitedness of "reasons of state" need to be recognized. While states are hugely important vehicles to aid the delivery of effective regulation, equal liberty, and social justice, they should not be thought of as ontologically privileged. They can be judged by how far they deliver these public goods and how far they fail; for the history of states is marked, of course, not just by phases of bad leadership and corruption but also by the most brutal episodes. A cosmopolitanism relevant to our global age must take this as a starting point, and build an ethically sound and politically robust conception of the proper basis of political community, and of the relations among communities.

Two accounts of cosmopolitanism bear on its contemporary meaning. The first was set out by the Stoics, who were the first to refer explicitly to themselves as cosmopolitans, seeking to replace the central role of the *polis* in ancient political thought with that of the *cosmos* in which humankind might live together in harmony (Horstmann, 1976). The Stoics developed this thought by emphasizing that we inhabit two worlds – one which is local and assigned to us by birth and another which is "truly great and truly common" (Seneca). Each person lives in a local community and in a wider community of human ideals, aspirations, and argument. The basis of the latter lies in what is fundamental to all – the equal worth of reason and humanity in every person (Nussbaum, 1997b, pp. 30, 43). Allegiance is owed, first and foremost, to the moral realm of all humanity, not to the contingent groupings of nation, ethnicity, and class. Deliberation and problem solving should focus on what is common to all persons as citizens of reason and the world; collective problems can be better dealt with if approached from this perspective, rather than from the point of view of sectional groupings. Such a position does not require that individuals give up local concerns and affiliations to family, friends, and fellow countrymen; it implies, instead, that they must acknowledge these as morally contingent and that their most important duties are to humanity as a whole and its overall developmental requirements.

The second conception of cosmopolitanism was introduced in the eighteenth century when the term *Weltbürger* (world citizen) became one of the key terms of the Enlightenment. The most important contribution to this body of thought can be found in Kant's writings (above all, 1970, pp. 41–53, 54–60 and 93–130). Kant linked the idea of cosmopolitanism to an innovative conception of "the public use of reason," and explored the ways in which this conception of reason can generate a critical vantage point from which to scrutinize civil society (see Schmidt, 1998, pp. 419–27). Building on a definition of enlightenment as the escape from dogma and unvindicated authority, Kant measured its advance in terms of the removal of constraints on "the public use of reason." As one commentator eloquently remarked, Kant grounds reason "in the reputation of principles that preclude the possibility of open-ended interaction and communication . . . The principles of reason are those that can secure the possibility of intersubjectivity" (O'Neill, 1990, p. 194). Kant conceived of participation in a cosmopolitan (*weltbürgerlich*) society as an entitlement – an entitlement to enter the world of open, uncoerced dialogue – and he adapted this idea in his formulation of what he called "cosmopolitan right" (1970, pp. 105–08). Cosmopolitan right meant the capacity to present oneself and be heard within and across political communities; it was the right to enter dialogue without artificial constraint and delimitation.

Contemporary conceptions of cosmopolitanism can be found in the work of Beitz, Pogge, and Barry, among others (see, in particular, Beitz, 1979, 1994, 1998; Pogge, 1989, 1994a, 1994b, and Barry, 1998a, 1999). In certain respects, this work seems to explicate, and offer a compelling elucidation of, the classical conception of belonging to the human community first and foremost, and the Kantian conception of subjecting all beliefs, relations, and practices to the test of whether or not they allow for uncoerced interaction and impartial reasoning. In the sections that follow, I will draw on some of this writing and use it as a basis to set out the outlines of a comprehensive account of the principles of cosmopolitanism – their nature, status, justification, and political implications. I begin by stating the principles and explain how they cluster into three types. I then go on to explore their standing and scope.

Cosmopolitan principles

Cosmopolitan values can be expressed formally in terms of a set of principles (see Held, 2002, 2004). These are principles which can be universally shared, and can form the basis for the protection and nurturing of each person's equal significance in "the moral realm of all humanity." Eight principles are paramount. They are the principles of: (1) equal worth and dignity; (2) active agency; (3) personal responsibility and accountability; (4) consent; (5) collective decision-making about public matters through voting procedures; (6) inclusiveness and subsidiarity; (7) avoidance of serious harm; and (8) sustainability. The meaning of these principles needs unpacking in order that their nature and implications can be clarified. While eight principles may seem like a daunting number, they are interrelated and together form the basis of a cosmopolitan orientation.

The first principle is that the ultimate units of moral concern are individual human beings, not states or other particular forms of human association. Humankind belongs to a single moral realm in which each person is regarded as equally worthy of respect and consideration (Beitz, 1994; Pogge, 1994a). To think of people as having equal moral value is to make a general claim about the basic units of the world comprising persons as free and equal beings (see Kuper, 2000). This notion can be referred to as the principle of individualist moral egalitarianism or, simply, egalitarian individualism. To uphold this principle is not to deny the significance of cultural diversity and difference, not at all – but it is to affirm that there are limits to the moral validity of particular communities – limits which recognize, and demand, that we must treat with equal respect the dignity of reason and moral choice in every human being (Nussbaum, 1997b, pp. 42–43). In the post-Holocaust world, these limits have been recognized in the United Nations Charter and, in the human rights regime, among many other legal instruments (see Held, 2004, part 3).

The second principle recognizes that, if principle 1 is to be universally recognized and accepted, then human agency cannot be understood as the mere expression of a given teleology, fortune, or tradition; rather, human agency must be conceived as the ability to act otherwise – the ability not just to accept but to shape human community in the context of the choices of others. Active agency connotes the capacity of human beings to reason self-consciously, to be self-reflective and to be self-determining. It bestows both opportunities and duties – opportunities to act (or not as the case may be), and duties to ensure that independent action does not curtail and infringe upon the life chances and opportunities of others (unless, of course, sanctioned by negotiation or consent: see below). Active agency is a capacity both to make and pursue claims and to have such claims made and pursued in relation to oneself. Each person has an equal interest in active agency or self-determination.

Principles 1 and 2 cannot be grasped fully unless supplemented by principle 3: the principle of personal responsibility and accountability. At its most basic, this principle can be understood to mean that it is inevitable that people will choose different cultural, social, and economic projects and that such differences need to be recognized. People develop their skills and talents differently, and enjoy different forms of ability and specialized competency. That they fare differently, and that many of these differences arise from a voluntary choice on their part, should be welcomed and accepted (see Barry, 1998a, pp. 147–49). These *pima facie* legitimate differences of choice and outcome have to be distinguished from unacceptable structures of difference which reflect conditions which prevent, or partially prevent, the pursuit by some of their vital needs. Actors have to be aware of, and accountable for, the consequences of actions, direct or indirect, intended or unintended, which may radically restrict or delimit the choices of others. Individuals have both personal responsibility-rights as well as personal responsibility-obligations.

The fourth principle, the principle of consent, recognizes that a commitment to equal worth and equal moral value, along with active agency and personal responsibility, requires a non-coercive political process in and through which people can negotiate and pursue their public interconnections, interdependencies and life chances. Interlocking lives, projects and communities require forms of public reasoning, deliberation, and decision-making which take account of each person's equal standing in such processes. The principle of consent constitutes the basis of non-coercive collective agreement and governance.

Principles 4 and 5 must be interpreted together. For principle 5 acknowledges that while a legitimate public decision is one that results from consent, this needs to be linked with voting at the decisive stage of collective decision-making and with the procedures and mechanisms of majority rule. The consent of all is too strong a requirement of collective decision-making and the basis on which minorities can block or forestall public responses to key issues (see Held, 2002, pp. 26–27). Principle 5 recognizes the importance of inclusiveness in the process of granting consent, while interpreting this to mean that an inclusive process of participation and debate can coalesce with a decision-making procedure which allows outcomes which accrue the greatest support (Dahl, 1989).[1]

The sixth principle, which I earlier referred to as the principle of inclusiveness and subsidiarity, seeks to clarify the fundamental criterion of drawing proper boundaries around units of collective decision-making, and on what grounds. At its simplest, it connotes that those significantly affected by public decisions, issues, or processes, should, *ceteris paribus*, have an equal opportunity, directly or indirectly through elected representatives, to influence and shape them. By significantly affected I mean that people are enmeshed in decisions and forces that impact on their capacity to fulfil their vital needs (see Held, 2004, ch. 6). According to principle 6, collective decision-making is best located when it is closest to and involves those whose life expectancy and life chances are determined by significant social processes and forces. On the other hand, this principle also recognizes that if the decisions at issue are translocal, transnational, or, transregional, then political associations need not only to be locally based but also to have a wider scope and framework of operation.

The seventh principle is a leading principle of social justice: the principle of the avoidance of harm and the amelioration of urgent need. This is a principle for allocating priority to the most vital cases of need and, where possible, trumping other, less urgent public priorities until such a time as all human beings, *de facto* and *de jure*, are covered by the first six principles; that is to say, until they enjoy the status of equal moral value and active agency, and have the means to participate in their respective political communities and in the overlapping communities of fate which shape their needs and welfare. A social provision which falls short of the potential for active agency can be referred to as a situation of manifest harm in that the participatory potential of individuals and groups will not have been achieved; that is to say, people would not have adequate access to effectively resourced capacities which they might make use of in their particular circumstances (Sen, 1999). But even this significant shortfall in the realization of human potential should be distinguished from situations of the most pressing levels of vulnerability, defined by the most urgent need. The harm that follows from a failure to meet such needs can be denoted as serious harm, marked as it often is by immediate, life-and-death consequences. Accordingly, if the requirements specified by the principle of avoidance of serious harm are to be met, public policy ought to be focused, in the first instance, on the prevention of such conditions; that is, on the eradication of severe harm inflicted on people "against their will" and "without their consent" (Barry, 1998a, pp. 207, 231).

The eighth and final principle is the principle of sustainability, which specifies that all economic and social development must be consistent with the stewardship of the world's core resources – by which I mean resources which are irreplaceable and non-substitutable (Goodin, 1992, pp. 62–65, 72). Such a principle discriminates against social and economic change which disrupts global ecological balances and unnecessarily damages the choices of future generations. Sustainable development is best understood as a guiding principle, as opposed to a precise formula, since we do not know, for example, how future technological innovation will impact on resource provision and utilization. Yet, without reference to such a principle, public policy would be made without taking account of the finite quality of many of the world's resources and the equally valid claims of future generations to well-being. Because the contemporary economic and military age is the first age to be able to take decisions not just for itself but for all future epochs, its choices must be particularly careful not to pre-empt the equal worth and active agency of future generations.

The eight principles can best be thought of as falling into three clusters. The first cluster (principles 1–3) sets down the fundamental organizational features of the cosmopolitan moral universe. Its crux is that each person is a subject of equal moral concern; that each person is capable of acting autonomously with respect to the range of choices before them; and that, in deciding how to act or which institutions to create, the claims of each person affected should be taken equally into account. Personal responsibility means in this context that actors and agents have to be aware of, and accountable for, the consequences of their actions, direct or indirect, intended or unintended, which may substantially restrict and delimit the opportunities of others. The second cluster (principles 4–6) forms the basis of translating individually initiated activity, or privately determined activities more broadly, into collectively agreed or collectively sanctioned frameworks of action or regulatory regimes. Public power at all levels can be conceived as legitimate to the degree to which principles 4, 5, and 6 are upheld. The final principles (7 and 8) lay down a framework for prioritizing urgent need and resource conservation. By distinguishing vital from non-vital needs, principle 7 creates an unambiguous starting point and guiding orientation for public decisions. While this "prioritizing commitment" does not, of course, create a decision procedure to resolve all clashes of priority in politics, it clearly creates a moral framework for focusing public policy on those who are most vulnerable. By contrast, principle 8 seeks to set down a prudential orientation to help ensure that public policy is consistent with global ecological balances and that it does not destroy irreplaceable and non-substitutable resources.

Thick or thin cosmopolitanism?

It could be objected at this point that, given the plurality of interpretive standpoints in the contemporary world (social, cultural, religious, and so on), it is unwise to construct a political philosophy which depends upon overarching principles. For it is doubtful, the objection could continue, that a bridge can be built between "the many particular wills" and "the general will" (see McCarthy, 1991, pp. 181–99). In a world marked by a diversity of value orientations, on what grounds, if any, can we suppose that all groups or parties could be argumentatively convinced about fundamental ethical and political principles?

It is important to stress that cosmopolitan philosophy does not deny the reality and ethical relevance of living in a world of diverse values and identities – how could it? It does not assume that unanimity is attainable on all practical–political questions. The elaboration of cosmopolitan principles is not an exercise in seeking a general and universal understanding on a wide spectrum of issues concerning the broad conditions of life or diverse ethical matters (for example, abortion, animal rights, or the role of voluntary euthanasia). This is not how a modern cosmopolitan project should be understood. Rather, at stake is a more restrictive exercise aimed at reflecting on the moral status of persons, the conditions of agency, and collective decision-making. It is important to emphasize that this exercise is constructed on the assumption that ground rules for communication, dialogue, and dispute settlement are not only desirable but essential precisely because all people are of equal moral value and their views on a wide range of moral–political questions will conflict. The principles of cosmopolitan-ism are the conditions of taking cultural diversity seriously and of building a demo-cratic culture to mediate clashes of the cultural good. They are, in short, about the conditions of just difference and democratic dialogue. The aim of modern cosmopoli-tanism is the conceptualization and generation of the necessary background condi-tions for a "common" or "basic" structure of individual action and social activity (cf. Rawls, 1985, pp. 254ff).

Contemporary cosmopolitans, it should be acknowledged, are divided about the demands that cosmopolitanism lays upon the individual and, accordingly, upon the appropriate framing of the necessary background conditions for a "common" structure of individual action and social activity. Among them there is agreement that in deciding how to act, or which rules or regulations ought to be established, the claims of each person affected should be weighed equally – "no matter where they live, which society they belong to, or how they are connected to us" (Miller, 1998, p. 165). The principle of egalitarian individualism is regarded as axiomatic. But the moral weight granted to this principle depends heavily upon the precise modes of interpretation of other principles.

Two broad positions exist in the literature. There are those for whom membership of humanity at large means that special relationships (including particular moral responsibilities) to family, kin, nation, or religious grouping can never be justified because the people involved have some intrinsic quality which suffices alone to compel special moral attention, or because they are allegedly worth more than other people, or because such affiliations provide sufficient reason for pursuing particular commit-ments or actions. This does not mean that such relationships cannot be justified – they can, but only in so far as nurturing or honoring such ties is in the cosmopolitan inter-est; that is, is the best way to achieve the good for humanity overall (Nussbaum, 1996, pp. 135–36; Barry, 1998a). As Scheffler succinctly put it, "special attention to particular people is legitimate only if it can be justified by reference to the interest of all human beings considered as equals" (1999, p. 259).

The second interpretation recognizes that while each person stands in "an ethically significant relation" to all other people, this is only one important "source of reasons and responsibilities among others" (Scheffler, 1999, p. 260). Cosmopolitan principles are, in this context, quite compatible with the recognition of different "spheres" or "layers" of moral reasoning (Walzer, 1983).

In the light of this, it is useful to draw a distinction between "strong" and "weak" cosmopolitanism, or between thick and thin cosmopolitanism as I refer to it. Miller has summarized the distinction well:

> According to the strong [thick] version . . . all moral principles must be justified by showing that they give equal weight to the claims of everyone, which means that they must either be directly universal in their scope, or if they apply only to a select group of people they must be secondary principles whose ultimate foundation is universal. The weak [thin] version, by contrast, holds only that morality is cosmopolitan in part: there are some valid principles with a more restricted scope. According to . . . [thin] cosmopoli-tanism . . . we may owe certain kinds of treatment to all other human beings regardless of any relationship in which we stand to them while there are other kinds of treatment that we owe only to those to whom we are related in certain ways, with neither sort of obligation being derivative of the other (1998, pp. 166–67).

Whether cosmopolitanism is an overriding frame of reference (trumping all other moral positions) or a distinctive subset of considerations (specifying that there are some substantive global rules, norms, and principles of justice which ought to be balanced with, and take account of, those derived from individual societies or other human groupings) is not a question which will be focused on here at length (cf. Barry, 1998a; Miller, 1998). However, some comment is in order if the rationale and standing of the eight principles are to be satisfactorily illuminated.

I take cosmopolitanism ultimately to denote the ethical and political space occupied by the eight principles. Cosmopolitanism lays down the universal or regulative principles which delimit and govern the range of diversity and difference that ought to be found in public life. It discloses the proper basis or framework for the pursuit of argument, discussion, and negotiation about particular spheres of value, spheres in which local, national, and regional affiliations will inevitably be weighed. In some respects, this is a form of thick cosmopolitanism. However, it should not be concluded from this that the meaning of the eight principles can simply be specified once and for all. For while cosmopolitanism affirms principles which are universal in their scope, it recognizes, in addition, that the precise meaning of these is always fleshed out in situated discussions; in other words, that there is an inescapable hermeneutic complexity in moral and political affairs which will affect how the eight principles are actually interpreted, and the weight granted to special ties and other practical–political issues. I call this mix of regulative principles and interpretative activity neither thick nor thin cosmopolitanism, but, rather, a "layered" cosmopolitan perspective (cf. Tully, 1995). This cosmopolitan point of view builds on principles that all could reasonably assent to, while recognizing the irreducible plurality of forms of life (Habermas, 1996). Thus, on the one hand, the position upholds certain basic egalitarian ideas – those which emphasize equal worth, equal respect, equal consideration and so on – and, on the other, it acknowledges that the elucidation of their meaning cannot be pursued independently of an ongoing dialogue in public life. Hence, there can be no adequate institutionalization of equal rights and duties without a corresponding institutionalization of national and transnational forms of public debate, democratic participation, and accountability (McCarthy, 1999). The institutionalization of regulative cosmopolitan principles requires the entrenchment of democratic public realms.

A layered cosmopolitan perspective of this kind shares a particular commitment with thin cosmopolitanism insofar as it acknowledges a plurality of value sources and a diversity of moral conceptions of the good; it recognizes, accordingly, different spheres of ethical reasoning linked to everyday attempts to resolve matters concerning modes of living and social organization (Böhme, 2001). As such, it seeks to express ethical neutrality with regard to many life questions. But ethical neutrality of this sort should not be confused with political neutrality and its core requirements (see Kuper, 2000, pp. 649f). The point has been succinctly stated by Tan: "a commitment to ethical neutrality entails a particular type of political arrangement, one which, for one, allows for the pursuit of different private conceptions of the good" (1998, p. 283, quoted in Kuper, 2000, p. 649; see Barry, 1995, p. 263). Only polities that acknowledge the equal status of all persons, that seek neutrality or impartiality with respect to personal ends, hopes, and aspirations, and that pursue the public justification of social, economic, and political arrangements can ensure a basic or common structure of political action which allows individuals to pursue their projects – both individual and collective – as free and equal agents. Such a structure is inconsistent with, and, if applied systematically, would need to filter out, those ends and goods, whether public or private, which would erode or undermine the structure itself.[2] For value pluralism and social pluralism to flourish, political associations must be structured or organized in one general way – that is, according to the constituting, legitimizing, and prioritizing principles specified above (cf. Pogge, 1994a, p. 127). Arguments can be had about the exact specification of these; that is, about how these notions are properly formulated. But the eight principles themselves constitute guiding notions or regulative ideals for a polity geared to autonomy, dialogue, and tolerance.

Cosmopolitan justifications

However, while cosmopolitanism must stand by these principles, they are not, of course, self-justifying. Or, to put the point another way, from whence come these principles? From the outset, it is important to distinguish two things too often run together: questions about the origins of principles, and questions about their validity or weight (see Weale, 1998). Both kinds of question are relevant. If the first illuminates the ethical circumstances or motivation for a preference for, or commitment to, a principle or set of principles, the second is the basis for testing their intersubjective validity. In this regard, the justificatory rationale of cosmopolitan principles is dependent on two fundamental metaprinciples or organizing notions of ethical discourse – one cultural and historical, the other philosophical. These are, respectively, the metaprinciple of autonomy and the metaprinciple of impartialist reasoning.

The metaprinciple of autonomy (henceforth, the MPA) is at the core of the democratic project. Its rationale and standing are "political not metaphysical," to borrow a phrase from Rawls (1985). A basic concept or idea is political, in this sense, if it represents an articulation of an understanding latent in public political life and, in particular, if against the background of the struggle for a democratic culture in the West and later elsewhere, it builds on the distinctive conception of the person as a citizen who is, in principle, "free and equal" in a manner "comprehensible" to everyone. In other words, the MPA can be understood as a notion embedded in the public political culture of democratic societies and emerging democracies.

The MPA is part of the "deep structure" of ideas which have shaped the constitution of modern political life. It has roots in the ancient world, although many elements of its deep structure were not part of classical thinking, marked as the latter was by a very restricted view of who could count as a citizen and by a teleological conception of nature and the cosmos. It was not until the modern world that the MPA became more firmly entrenched (Held, 1996). It became entrenched in the pursuit of citizenship, which has always been marked by "an urge," as Marshall put it, to secure "a fuller measure of autonomy" for each and every person; for autonomy is the "stuff" of which modern citizenship is made (1973, p. 84). Or, to restate the point in the language used hitherto, it has been marked by an urge to realize the core elements of an egalitarian conception of the person (with its emphasis upon people as free and equal, capable of active agency and accountable for their choices), of the democratic regulation of public life (including consent, deliberation, voting, and inclusiveness) and of the necessity to ensure that, if people's equal interest in self-determination or self-governance is to be protected, attention must be focused on those who lack the capacity to participate in, and act within, key sites of power and political institutions (that is, that there must be a measure of social protection).

Another way to put these points is to say that the MPA is the guiding political thread of modern democratic societies and that the first seven cosmopolitan principles, suitably unfolded from a commitment to self-determination and autonomy, are the basis for specifying more fully the nature and form of a liberal and democratic order.[3] In short, these cosmopolitan principles are the principles of democratic public life, but without one crucial assumption – never fully justified in any case in liberal democratic thought, classic or contemporary – that these principles can only be enacted effectively within a single, circumscribed, territorially based political community (see Held, 1995). The cosmopolitan principles do not presume, as principle 6 makes clear, that the link between self-determination, accountability, democracy, and sovereignty can be understood simply in territorial terms. Hence, it is possible to have a modern democratic rendition of the Stoic aspiration to multiple forms of affiliation – local, national, and global. The cosmopolitan principles are the core elements of democratic public life, shorn of the contingent link with the borders of nation-states. How these principles should be spliced with organizations, institutions, and borders of political communities is a separate question, to which I will return.

It could be objected that the language of autonomy and self-determination has limited cross-culture validity because of its Western origins. But a distinction must be made between those political terms and discourses which obscure or underpin particular interests and power systems and those which seek to test explicitly the generalizability of claims and interests, and to render power, whether it be political, economic or cultural, accountable. What the language of autonomy and self-determination generates and, in particular, the language of the MPA, is what might be thought of as a commitment or pre-commitment to the idea that all persons should be equally free – that is to say, that they should enjoy equal liberty to pursue their own activities without arbitrary or unwarranted interference. If this notion is shared across cultures it is not because they have acquiesced to modern Western political discourse; it is, rather, that they have come to see that there are certain languages which protect and nurture the notion of equal status and worth, and others which have sought to ignore or suppress it.

To test the generalizability of claims and interests involves "reasoning from the point of view of others" (Benhabib, 1992, pp. 9–10, 121–47). Attempts to focus on this "social point of view" find their clearest contemporary elaboration in Rawls's Original Position, Habermas's ideal speech situation and Barry's formulation of impartialist reasoning (see Rawls, 1971; Habermas, 1973, 1996; Barry, 1989, 1995). These formulations have in common a concern to conceptualize an impartial moral standpoint from which to assess particular forms of practical reasoning. This concern should not be thought of as over-demanding. As one commentator aptly put it: "all the impartiality thesis says is that, if and when one raises questions regarding fundamental moral standards, the court of appeal that one addresses is a court in which no particular individual, group, or country has *special* standing" (Hill, 1987, p. 132, quoted in Barry, 1995, pp. 226–27). Before the court, suggesting "I like it," "it suits me," "it belongs to male prerogatives," "it is in the best interest of my country," does not settle the issue at hand, for principles must be defensible from a larger, human standpoint. This social, open-ended, moral perspective is a device for focusing our thoughts and testing the inter-subjective validity of our conceptions of the good. It offers a way of exploring principles, norms, and rules that might reasonably command agreement. I refer to it as the metaprinciple of impartialist reasoning (MPIR).

The MPIR is a moral frame of reference for specifying rules and principles that can be universally shared; and, concomitantly, it rejects as unjust all those practices, rules, and institutions anchored in principles not all could adopt (O'Neill, 1991). At issue is the establishment of principles and rules that nobody, motivated to establish an unco-erced and informed agreement, could reasonably discard (see Barry, 1989; cf. Scanlon, 1998). [. . .]

The MPIR cannot produce a simple deductive proof of the ideal set of principles and conditions which can overcome the deficiencies of a political order; nor can it produce a deductive proof of the best or only moral principles that should guide institutional development. Rather, it should be thought of as a heuristic device to test candidate principles of moral worth, democracy, and justice and their forms of justification (Kelly, 1998, pp. 1–8; Barry, 1998b). These tests are concerned with a process of reason-able rejectability, which can always be pursued in a theoretical dialogue open to fresh challenge and new questions and, hence, in a hermeneutic sense, can never be com-plete (Gadamer, 1975). But to acknowledge this is not to say that theoretical conversa-tion is "toothless" either with respect to principles or the conditions of their entrenchment.

In the first instance, moral impartialism has a crucial critical and debunking role. This position is emphasized most clearly by O'Neill (1991). Impartialist reasoning, in this account, is a basis for disclosing non-generalizable principles, rules, and interests, and of showing how justice is a matter of not basing actions, lives, or institutions on principles that cannot be universally shared. The impartialist vantage point has efficacy *qua* critical stance.

[. . .]

Impartialist reasoning, thus understood, is a critical device for disclosing non-gen-eralizable principles and unjust institutions, but can it state a more positive position which lays down the underlying principles of a just cosmopolitan order? I believe something more positive can be disclosed in the pursuit of principles and rules that can be universally shared. There is only space here to sketch this thought. In this regard, it is my contention that the eight cosmopolitan principles can all meet the test of impartiality, and form moral and political elements upon which all could act. For they are at the root of the equal consideration and treatment of all human beings, irrespective of where they were born or raised. The impartialist emphasis on taking account of the position of the other, of only treating political outcomes as fair and reasonable if there are good reasons for holding that they would be equally acceptable to all parties, and of only treating the position of some socioeconomic groups as legiti-mate if they are acceptable to all people irrespective of where they come in the social hierarchy, is consistent with the eight principles and does not provide grounds on which they can be reasonably rejected. The principles of equal moral status, equal public engagement, and the public justification of collective institutional arrange-ments are robust enough not to fall foul of these considerations (see Held, 2006).

Within this theoretical framework, it can be argued that individual or collective social arrangements generating serious harm (urgent unmet need) cannot be justified by reference to a special social standing, cultural identity, ethnic background, or nationality – in fact by reference to any particular grouping – if the latter sanctions closure or exclusion in relation to the core conditions of human autonomy, develop-ment, and welfare (see Caney, 2001a). To the extent that a domain of activity operates to structure and delimit life expectancy and life-chances, deficits are disclosed in the structure of action of a political association. These deficits can, furthermore, be regarded as illegitimate to the extent to which they would be rejected under the conditions of the MPIR. If people did not know their future social location and political identity, they would not find the self-interested defense of specific exclusionary processes and mechanisms convincing. These justificatory structures cannot easily be generalized and are, thus, weak in the face of the test of impartiality. Unless exceptional arguments are available to the contrary, social mechanisms and processes generating serious harm for certain groups and categories of people fall to the requirement of impartiality (see Barry, 1995, 1998a).

Impartialist reasoning is a basis for thinking about the problems posed by asymmetries of power, unevenness of resource distribution, and stark prejudices. It provides the means for asking about the rules, laws, and policies people might think right, justified, or worthy of respect. It allows a distinction to be made between legitimacy as acquiescence to existing socioeconomic arrangements, and legitimacy as "rightness" or "correctness" – the worthiness of a political order to be recognized because it is the order people would accept as a result of impartialist reasoning. The latter can be conceived not as an optional element of a political and legal understanding, but as a requirement of any attempt to grasp the nature of the support and legitimacy enjoyed by particular social forces and relations; for without this form of reasoning, the distinction between legitimacy as "acceptance" and legitimacy as "rightness" could not be drawn.

It should be emphasized that the pursuit of impartial reasoning is a social activity – not a solitary theoretical exercise. For as Arendt has written:

> The power of judgement rests on a potential agreement with others, and the thinking process which is active in judging something is not . . . a dialogue between me and myself, but finds itself always and primarily, even if I am quite alone in making up my mind, in an anticipated communication with others with whom I know I must finally come to some agreement. . . . And this enlarged way of thinking . . . cannot function in strict isolation or solitude; it needs the presence of others "in whose place" it must think, whose perspective it must take into consideration, and without whom it never has the opportunity to operate at all (1961, pp. 220–21, as cited by Benhabib 1992, pp. 9–10).

The aim of a "theoretical conversation" about impartiality is an anticipated agreement with all those whose diverse circumstances affect the realization of people's equal interest in self-determination and autonomy. Of course, as an "anticipated agreement" it is a hypothetical ascription of an intersubjective or collective understanding. As such, the ultimate test of its validity must depend in contemporary life on the extension of the conversation to all those whom it seeks to encompass. Only under the latter circumstances can an analytically proposed interpretation become an actual understanding or agreement among others (Habermas, 1988). Critical reflection must conjoin with public debate and democratic politics.

Together the MPA and MPIR provide the grounds of cosmopolitan thought. The MPA lays down the conceptual space in which impartialist reasoning can take place. For it generates a preoccupation with each person as a subject of equal moral concern; with each person's capacity to act autonomously with respect to the range of choices before them; and with each person's equal status with respect to the basic institutions of political communities, that is, with an entitlement to claim and be claimed upon (see Rawls, 1971, pp. 544–45; Barry, 1989, p. 200). It provides motives, reasons and constraining considerations to help establish agreement on reasonable terms. The MPIR is the basis for pursuing this agreement. It is a device of argument that is designed to abstract from power relations in order to disclose the fundamental enabling conditions of active agency, rightful authority, and social justice. Of course, as a device of argument it can be resisted by those who reject the language of autonomy and self-determination; but then we must be clear that this is precisely what they are doing.

From cosmopolitan principles to cosmopolitan law

Cosmopolitan law refers to a domain of law different in kind from the law of states and the law made between one state and another for the mutual enhancement of their geopolitical interests. Kant, the leading interpreter of the idea of such a law, interpreted it as the basis for articulating the equal moral status of persons in the "universal community" (1970, p. 108). For him, cosmopolitan law is neither a fantastic nor a utopian way of conceiving law, but a "necessary complement" to the codes of national and international law, and a means to transform them into a public law of humanity (see Held, 1995, ch. 10). While Kant limited the form and scope of cosmopolitan law to the conditions of universal hospitality – the right to present oneself and be heard within and across communities – I understand it more broadly as the appropriate mode of representing the equal moral standing of all human beings, and their entitlement to equal liberty and to forms of governance founded on deliberation and consent. In other words, cosmopolitan law is the form of law which best articulates and entrenches the eight principles of cosmopolitan order. If these principles were to be systematically entrenched as the foundation of law, the conditions of the cosmopolitan regulation of public life could initially be set down.

Within the framework of cosmopolitan law, the idea of rightful authority, which has been so often connected to the state and particular geographical domains, has to be reconceived and recast. Rightful authority or sovereignty can be stripped away from the idea of fixed borders and territories and thought of as, in principle, an attribute of basic cosmopolitan democratic law which can be drawn upon and enacted in diverse realms, from local associations and cities to states and wider global networks. Cosmopolitan law demands the subordination of regional, national, and local "sovereignties" to an overarching legal framework, but within this framework associations can be self-governing at diverse levels (Held, 1995, p. 234).

In this conception, the nation-state "withers away," to borrow an old Marxist phrase. But this is not to suggest that states and national democratic polities become redundant. Rather, states would no longer be regarded as the sole centers of legitimate power within their borders, as is already the case in many places (Held, McGrew, Goldblatt and Perraton, 1999, the conclusion). States need to be articulated with, and relocated within, an overarching cosmopolitan framework. Within this framework, the laws and rules of the nation–state would become but one focus for legal development, political reflection, and mobilization. Under these conditions, people would come, in principle, to enjoy multiple citizenships – political membership, that is, in the diverse communities which significantly affect them. In a world of overlapping communities of fate, individuals would be citizens of their immediate political communities, and of the wider regional and global networks which impacted upon their lives. This overlapping cosmopolitan polity would be one that in form and substance reflected and embraced the diverse forms of power and authority that already operate within and across borders. In this sense, cosmopolitanism constitutes the political basis and political philosophy of living in a global age (see Held, 2004).

Rethinking democracy for a more global age: cosmopolitan democracy

The case for cosmopolitan democracy is the case for the creation of new political institutions which would coexist with the system of states but which would override states in clearly defined spheres of activity where those activities have demonstrable transnational and international consequences (see Held, 1995, ch. 10, for an elaboration of this argument). At issue, in addition, is not merely the formal construction of new democratic institutions, but also the construction, in principle, of broad avenues of civic participation in and deliberation over decision-making at regional and global levels. How should this conception of democracy be understood? [. . .] democracy has to become not just a national but a transnational affair if it is to be possible both within a restricted geographic territory and within the wider international community. The possibility of democracy today must, in short, be linked to an expanding framework of democratic institutions and agencies.

Two distinct requirements arise: first, that the territorial boundaries of systems of accountability be restructured so that those issues which escape the control of a nation-state – aspects of monetary management, the rules of the global trading system, environmental questions, elements of security, new forms of communication – can be brought under better democratic control; and, second, that the role and place of regional and global regulatory and functional agencies be rethought so that they may provide a more coherent and effective focal point in public affairs. The basis for meeting these requirements can be elaborated by focusing on some of the institutional components of the cosmopolitan model.

A cosmopolitan polity would need to establish an overarching network of democratic public fora, covering cities, nation-states, regions and the wider transnational order. It would need to create an effective and accountable political, administrative and regulative capacity at global and regional levels to complement those at national and local levels. This would require:

- The formation of an authoritative assembly of all states and agencies – a reformed General Assembly of the United Nations, or a complement to it. The focus of a global assembly would be the examination of those pressing problems which are at the heart of concerns about life expectancy and life chances – concerns, for instance, about health and disease, food supply and distribution, the debt burden of the developing world, global warming and the reduction of the risks of nuclear, chemical and biological warfare. Its task would be to lay down, in framework-setting law, the standards and institutions required to embed the rule of law, democratic principles, and the minimum conditions for human agency to flourish.
- The creation where feasible of regional parliaments and governance structures (for example, in Latin America and Africa) and the enhancement of the role of such bodies where they already exist (the European Union) in order that their decisions become recognized and accepted as legitimate independent sources of regional and international regulation.
- The opening up of functional international governmental organizations (such as the WTO, IMF and World Bank) to public examination and agenda setting. Not only should such bodies be transparent in their activities, but they should be open to public scrutiny (on the basis perhaps of elected supervisory bodies, or functional

deliberative fora, representative of the diverse interests in their constituencies), and accountable to regional and global assemblies.

- The establishment, where IGOs are currently weak and/or lacking in enforcement capability, of new mechanisms and organizations, e.g. in the areas of the environment and social affairs. The creation of new global governance structures with responsibility for addressing poverty, welfare and related issues is vital to offset the power and influence of market-oriented agencies such as the WTO and IMF.
- The enhancement of the transparency and accountability of the organizations of national and transnational civil society, addressing the potentially disturbing effects of those who are able to "shout the loudest" and of the lack of clarity about the terms of engagement of non-state actors with IGOs and other leading political bodies (Edwards and Zadek, 2003). Experiments are necessary to find ways of improving the internal codes of conduct and modes of operation of non-state actors, on the one hand, and of advancing their capacity to be represented in IGOs and other leading political bodies preoccupied with global policy processes, on the other. Moreover, to avoid citizens of developed countries being unfairly represented twice in global politics (once through their governments and once through their NGOs) special attention and support needs to be given to enhance the role of NGOs from developing countries.
- The use of general referenda cutting across nations and nation-states at regional or global levels in the case of contested priorities concerning the implementation of core cosmopolitan concerns. These could involve many different kinds of referenda, including of a cross-section of the public, and/or of targeted and significantly affected groups in a particular policy area, and/or of the policy-makers and legislators of national parliaments.
- The development of law enforcement and coercive capability, including peace keeping and peace-making, to help deal with serious regional and global security threats. It is necessary to meet the concern that, in the face of pressing and violent challenges to fundamental human rights and democratic priorities, "covenants, without the sword, are but words" (Hobbes).

Hand in hand with these changes, the cosmopolitan model of democracy assumes the entrenchment of a cluster of rights and obligations, including civil, political, economic and social rights and obligations, in order to provide shape and limits to democratic decision-making. This requires that they be enshrined within the constitutions of parliaments and assemblies (at the national, regional and global levels); and that the influence of international courts be extended so that groups and individuals have an effective means of suing political authorities for the enactment and enforcement of key rights, both within and beyond political associations.

If the history and practice of democracy have until now been centred on the idea of locality and place (the city-republic, the community, the nation), is it likely that in the future democracy will be centred exclusively on the international or global domain, if it is to be centred anywhere at all? To draw this conclusion is, I think, to misunderstand the nature of contemporary globalization and the argument being developed here. Globalization is, to borrow a phrase, "a dialectical process": "local transformation is as much a part of globalization as the lateral extension of social connections across time and space" (Giddens, 1990, p. 64). New demands are made for regional and local autonomy as groups find themselves buffeted by global forces and by inappropriate

In sum

Cosmopolitan Democracy

Principle(s) of justification

In a world of intensifying regional and global relations, with marked overlapping "communities of fate", the principle of autonomy requires entrenchment in regional and global networks as well as in national and local polities

Key features

Short term	*Long term*
Polity/governance	
Reform of leading UN governing institutions such as the Security Council (to give developing countries a significant voice and effective decision-making capacity)	New charter of rights and obligations locked into different domains of political, social and economic power
Creation of a UN second chamber (following an international constitutional convention)	Global parliament (with limited revenue-raising capacity) connected to regions, nations and localities
Enhanced political regionalization (EU and beyond) and the use of transnational referenda	Separation of political and economic interests, public funding of deliberative assemblies and electoral processes
Creation of a new, international Human Rights Court, compulsory jurisdiction before the International Criminal Court	Interconnected global legal system, embracing elements of criminal and civil law
Establishment of an effective, accountable, international, military force	Permanent shift of a growing proportion of a nation-state's coercive capability to regional and global institutions
Economy/civil society	
Enhancement of non-state, non-market solutions in the organization of civil society	Creation of a diversity of self-regulating associations and groups in civil society
Experimentation with different democratic organizational forms in the economy	Multi-sectoral economy and pluralization of patterns of ownership and possession
Provision of resources to those in the most vulnerable social positions to defend and articulate their interests	Public framework investment priorities set through general deliberation and government decision, but extensive-market regulation of goods and labour

---

General conditions

Continuing development of regional, international and global flows of resources and networks of interaction

Recognition by growing numbers of peoples of increasing interconnectedness of political communities in diverse domains, including the social, cultural, economic and environmental

Development of an understanding of overlapping 'collective fortunes' which require democratic deliberation – locally, nationally, regionally and globally

Enhanced entrenchment of democratic rights and obligations in the making and enforcement of national, regional and international law

Transfer of increasing proportion of a nation's military coercive capability to transnational agencies and institutions with the ultimate aim of demilitarization and the transcendence of the states' war system

Note: The institutional requirements of cosmopolitan democracy, and the complexity of the major issues of reform, are only laid out here in a rudimentary manner. For further discussion see Held (1995), Held (2004).

---

or ineffective political regimes. Although these circumstances are clearly fraught with danger, and the risk of an intensification of sectarian politics, they also portend a new possibility: the recovery of an intensive, participatory and deliberative democracy at local levels as a complement to the deliberative assemblies of the wider global order. That is, they portend a political order of democratic associations, cities and nations as well as of regions and global networks. In such an order, the principle of autonomy would be entrenched in diverse sites of power and across diverse spatial domains.

The key features of this conception of democracy are set out in the box above. The model presents a programme of possible transformations with short- and long-term political implications. It does not present an all-or-nothing choice, but rather lays down a direction of possible change with clear points of orientation.

A utopian project?

In the last hundred years political power has been reshaped and reconfigured. It has been diffused below, above and alongside the nation-state. Political power is multilevel and multilayered. Globalization has brought large swathes of the world population "closer together" in overlapping communities of fate. Life chances are affected by national, international and transnational processes. Democratic and human rights values are entrenched in important sectors of international law and new regional and global courts have been set up to examine some of the more heinous crimes humans can commit. Transnational movements, agencies and corporations have established the first stages of a global civil society. These, and related developments, create anchors for the development of cosmopolitan democracy. The latter does not have to start from scratch, but can develop from legal and institutional stepping stones laid down in the twentieth century.

There are, obviously enough, many reasons for pessimism. Globalization has not just integrated peoples and nations, but created new forms of antagonism. The globalization of communications does not just make it easier to establish mutual understanding, but often highlights what it is that people do not have in common and how and why differences matter. The dominant political game in the "transnational town" remains geopolitics. Ethnic self-centredness, religious fundamentalism, right-wing nationalism and unilateralist politics are once again on the rise, and not just in the West. Yet the circumstances and nature of politics have changed. Like national culture and traditions, cosmopolitan democracy is a cultural and political project, but with one difference: it is better adapted and suited to our regional and global age. However, the arguments in support of this have yet to be articulated in the public sphere in many parts of the world; and we fail here at our peril.

It is important to add a reflection on 9/11 and to say what it means in this context. One cannot accept the burden of putting accountability and justice right in one realm of life – physical security and political cooperation among defence establishments – without at the same time seeking to put it right elsewhere. If the political and the security, the social and the economic dimensions of accountability and justice are separated in the long term – as is the tendency in the global order today – the prospects of a peaceful and civil society will be bleak indeed. Popular support against terrorism, as well as against political violence and exclusionary politics of all kinds, depends upon convincing people that there is a legal, responsive and specific way of addressing their grievances. Without this sense of confidence in public institutions the defeat of terrorism and intolerance becomes a hugely difficult task, if it can be achieved at all.

Against the background of 9/11, the current unilateralist stance of the US and the desperate cycle of violence in the Middle East and elsewhere, the advocacy of cosmopolitan democracy may appear like an attempt to defy gravity or walk on water! And, indeed, if it was a case of having to adopt cosmopolitan principles and institutions all at once or not at all, this would be true. But it is no more the case than was the pursuit of the modern state at the time of Hobbes. Over the last several decades the growth of multilateralism and the development of international law have created cosmopolitan anchors to the world. These are the bases for the further consolidation of the hold of cosmopolitan principles and institutions. Moreover, a coalition of political groupings could emerge to push these achievements further, comprising European countries with strong commitments to the multilateral order and the human rights regime; liberal groups in the US polity which support multilateralism and the rule of law in international affairs; developing countries struggling for freer and fairer trade rules in the world economic order; non-governmental organizations from Amnesty International to Oxfam, campaigning for a more just, democratic and equitable world order; transnational social movements contesting the nature and form of contemporary globalization; and those economic forces that desire a more stable and managed global economic order (see Held and McGrew, 2002, chs 8 and 9).

Although the interests of these groupings would inevitably diverge on a wide range of issues, there is potentially an important overlapping sphere of concern among them for the strengthening of multilateralism, building new institutions for providing global public goods, regulating global markets, deepening accountability, protecting the environment and ameliorating urgently the social injustices that kill thousands of men, women and children daily. Of course, how far such forces can unite around these objectives – and can overcome fierce opposition from well-entrenched geopolitical and geoeconomic interests – remains to be seen. The stakes are high, but so too are the potential gains for human security and development if the aspirations for cosmopolitan governance can be slowly realized.

[. . .]

Notes

1   Minorities clearly need to be protected in this process. The rights and obligations entailed by principles 4 and 5 have to be compatible with the protection of each person's equal interest in principles 1, 2 and 3 – an interest which follows from each person's recognition as being of equal worth, with an equal capacity to act and to account for their actions. Majorities ought not to be able to impose themselves arbitrarily upon others. Principles 4 and 5 have to be understood against the background specified by the first three principles; the latter frame the basis of their operation.
2   As Miller aptly wrote, "an institution or practice is neutral when, as far as can reasonably be foreseen, it does not favor any particular conception of the good at the expense of others" (1989, p. 7; see pp. 72–81).
3   I say "first seven cosmopolitan principles" because the eighth, sustainability, has traditionally not been a core element of democratic thinking, although it ought to be (see Held, 2006).

References

Barry, Brian (1989) *Theories of Justice* (London: Harvester Wheatsheaf).
Barry, Brian (1995) *Justice as Impartiality* (Oxford: Clarendon Press).
Barry, Brian (1998a) "International Society from a Cosmopolitan Perspective," in D. Maple and T. Nardin (eds.) *International Society* (Princeton: Princeton University Press).
Barry, Brian (1998b) "Something in the Disputation not Unpleasant," in P. Kelly (ed.) *Impartiality, Neutrality and Justice: Re-thinking Brian Barry's Justice as Impartiality* (Edinburgh: Edinburgh University Press).
Barry, Brian (1999) "Statism and Nationalism: A Cosmopolitan Critique," in I. Shapiro and L. Brilmayer (eds.) *Global Justice* (New York: New York University Press).
Beitz, Charles (1979) *Political Theory and International Relations* (Princeton: Princeton University Press).
Beitz, Charles (1994) "Cosmopolitan Liberalism and the State System," in C. Brown (ed.) *Political Restructuring in Europe: Ethical Perspectives* (London: Routledge).
Beitz, Charles (1998) "Philosophy of International Relations," in *Routledge Encyclopaedia of Philosophy* (London: Routledge).
Benhabib, S. (1992) *Situating the Self* (Cambridge: Polity Press).
Böhme, G. (2001) *Ethics in Context* (Cambridge: Polity Press).
Caney, Simon (2001a) "Cosmopolitan Justice and Equalizing Opportunities," in T. Pogge (ed.) *Global Justice* (Oxford: Blackwell).
Dahl, Robert (1989) *Democracy and its Critics* (New Haven: Yale University Press).
Gadamer, H. (1975) *Truth and Method* (London: Sheed and Ward).
Goodin, R. (1992) *Green Political Theory* (Cambridge: Polity Press).
Habermas, Jurgen (1973) "Wahrheitstheorien" in H. Fahrenbach (ed.) *Wirchlichkeit und Reflexion* (Pfullingen: Neske).
Habermas, Jurgen (1988) *Theory and Practice* (Cambridge: Polity Press).
Habermas, Jurgen (1996) *Between Facts and Norms* (Cambridge: Polity Press).
Held, David (1995) *Democracy and the Global Order: From the Modern State to Cosmopolitan Governance* (Cambridge: Polity Press).
Held, David (1996) *Models of Democracy, 2nd Edition* (Cambridge: Polity Press).
Held, David (2002) "Law of States, Law of Peoples," *Legal Theory*, Vol. 8, no. 2: 1–44.
Held, David (2004) *Global Covenant. The Social Democratic Alternative to the Washington Consensus* (Cambridge: Polity Press).

Held, David (2006) *Cosmopolitanism: A Defense* (Cambridge: Polity Press).

Held, D., McGrew, A., Goldblatt, D., Perraton, J. (1999) *Global Transformations. Politics, Economics and Culture* (Cambridge: Polity Press).

Hill, T. (1987) "The Importance of Autonomy," in E. Kittay and D. Meyers (eds.) *Women and Moral Theory* (Towata: Rowman and Allanheld)

Horstmann, A. (1976) "Kosmopolit, Kosmopolotosmus," in *Historisches Worerbuch der Philosphie*, Band 4, (Basel: Schwabe): 1156–68.

Kant, Immanuel (1970) *Kant's Political Writings*, Edited by H. Reiss (Cambridge: Cambridge University Press).

Kelly, Paul (ed.), (1998) *Impartiality, Neutrality and Justice: Re-Reading Brian Barry's Justice as Impartiality* (Edinburgh: Edinburgh University Press).

Kuper, A. (2000) "Rawlsian Global Justice: Beyond the Law of Peoples to a Cosmopolitan Law of Persons," *Political Theory*, Vol. 28: 640–74.

Marshall, T. (1973) *Class, Citizenship and the Welfare State* (Westport: Greenwood Press).

McCarthy, T. (1991) *Ideals and Illusions* (Cambridge MA: MIT Press).

Miller, David (1989) *Market, State and Community. Theoretical Foundations of Market Socialism* (Oxford: Clarendon Press).

Miller, David (1998) "The Limits of Cosmopolitan Justice," in Maple and Nardin (eds.) *International Society* (Princeton: Princeton University Press).

Nussbaum, Martha (1996) "Patriotism and Cosmopolitanism," in J. Cohen (ed.) *For Love of Country. Debating the Limits of Patriotism* (Boston: Beacon Press).

Nussbaum, Martha (1997b) "Kant and Cosmopolitanism," in J. Bohman and M. Lutz-Bachmann (eds.) *Perpetual Peace. Essays on Kant's Cosmopolitan Ideal* (Cambridge: MIT Press).

O'Neill, Onora (1990) "Enlightenment as Autonomy: Kant's Vindication of Reason," in L. Jordanova and P. Hulme (eds.) *The Enlightenment and its Shadows* (London: Routledge).

O'Neill, Onora (1991) "Transitional Justice," in D. Held (ed.) *Political Theory Today* (Cambridge: Polity Press).

Pogge, Thomas (1989) *Realizing Rawls* (Ithaca: Cornell University Press).

Pogge, Thomas (1994a) "Cosmopolitanism and Sovereignty," in C. Blown (ed.) *Political Restructuring in Europe: Ethical Perspectives* (London: Routledge).

Pogge, Thomas (1994b) "An Egalitarian Law of Peoples," *Philosophy and Public Affairs*, Vol. 23: 195–224.

Rawls, John (1971) *A Theory of Justice* (Cambridge: Harvard University Press).

Rawls, John (1985) "Justice as Fairness: Political not Metaphysical," *Philosophy and Public Affairs*, Vol. 14, no. 3.

Scanlon, T. (1998) *What We Owe Each Other* (Cambridge: Harvard University Press).

Scheffler, Samuel (1999) "Conceptions of Cosmopolitanism," *Utilitas*, II: 255–76.

Schmidt, J. (1998) "Civility, Enlightenment and Society: Conceptual Confusions and Kantian Remedies," *American Political Science Review*, Vol. 92: 227–419.

Sen, A. (1999) *Development as Freedom* (Oxford: Oxford University Press).

Tully, James (1995) *Strange Multiplicity: Constitutionalism in an Age of Diversity* (Cambridge: Cambridge University Press).

Walzer, Michael (1983) *Spheres of Justice* (Oxford: Martin Robertson).

Weale, A. (1998) "From Contracts to Pluralism," in P. Kelly, *Impartiality, Neutrality and Justice: Re-Reading Brian Barry's Justice as Impartiality* (Edinburgh: Edinburgh University Press).

15

Moving from Cosmopolitan Legal Theory to Legal Practice: Models of Cosmopolitan Law
Garrett Wallace Brown

[. . .] there has been considerable debate about how it would be possible to move from cosmopolitan normative theory to cosmopolitan legal practice. These debates range from an uncertainty about what specific moral and normative principles should underwrite cosmopolitan law, to how those requirements for equal human worth should be institutionalised at the global level. Many legal realists remain skeptical of cosmopolitan aspirations for the creation of cosmopolitan law, arguing that its universal morality is not only impossible in a world dominated by independent sovereign states, but also that it is dangerous to national self-determination, threatening to establish "a universal state . . . attempting world conquest".[1] In addition, there remains considerable debate between cosmopolitans in regard to how to institutionalise cosmopolitan law and whether it would be best served through a world government,[2] a Kantian federation of liberal states,[3] or through some intermediate system of multidimensional democratic global governance.[4] As a recent debate between Jeremy Waldron and Seyla Benhabib on cosmopolitan legal theory highlights, there seems to be no unified move by cosmopolitans as to how a jurisprudential theory of universal human worth can be operationalised into practice.[5] Furthermore, despite the fact that all cosmopolitans ground their cosmopolitan visions on some underlying principle of cosmopolitan law, these principles are often only loosely sketched, often taken for granted as self-explanatory, or assumed to be uncontested launching points for more sophisticated global institutional designs.

The purpose of this paper is to clarify the concept of cosmopolitan law and to argue that legal cosmopolitanism provides a necessary linchpin that maintains a middle ground (and necessary transitional platform) between cosmopolitan theory and more institutional forms of cosmopolitanism. In order to define legal cosmopolitanism and why it provides the baseline position for any move to an *institutional* cosmopolitan order, this paper is divided into four sections. The first section will begin by examining the historical development of legal cosmopolitanism and how contemporary forms can be distinguished from the legal tradition of Stoicism as well as from the state-centric approach of *natural law*. From this background, the second section will outline the distinctive qualities associated with legal cosmopolitanism and how it occupies a unique position within contemporary international legal theory. In the third section, the debate about applied theory and cosmopolitan law will be explored, focusing specifically on Jeremy Waldron's "thicket" analogy, through which various approaches to move cosmopolitan legal theory to legal practice will be outlined. Finally, the paper will conclude by arguing that Kantian legal cosmopolitanism represents a coherent attempt to move from cosmopolitan theory to global institutional practice. This is due to the fact that it represents a minimal and *moderate* form of legal cosmopolitanism that accepts that any move to a cosmopolitan order would need to evolve from our current order. In this regard, legal cosmopolitanism can occupy a middle position, that not only satisfies the cosmopolitan concern for human worth, but that is also not guilty of being grossly universal beyond the minimal legal principles that make the peaceful and respectful coexistence of individuals, associations, cultures, and states, in a pluralistic global society possible.

1. A brief history of legal cosmopolitanism, cosmopolitan law and the Kantian turn towards a universal kingdom of ends

The idea of a universal human community without borders is not new. In the year 300 BC, Diogenes of Sinope first coined the phrase *kosmopolites* (universal citizen) and argued that every person was a member of a common and universal fraternity. [. . .] According to Diogenes, all persons were members of a common humanity and that this commonality should result in the treatment of everyone as if they were also equal political citizens, without appeals to particular political allegiances or places of birth. However, as far as we know, Diogenes made no direct connection between cosmopolitan morality and cosmopolitan law. His focus was more concerned with the hospitable treatment of visiting strangers than whether these duties should also be objectified into some universal law of humanity.

Despite the fact that a connection between morality and law was not directly articulated, the ancient Stoa philosophy of Diogenes and other Cynics had tremendous influence on the thinking of the first legal cosmopolitans. It is through the later work of Cicero and Marcus Aurelius that the idea of cosmopolitan jurisprudence was further extrapolated and given more elaborate legal foundations. [. . .] there are three normative principles that ground cosmopolitan thought and the advocacy for its translocation into cosmopolitan law. First, the Stoics maintained that every human being is a member of the same species and should therefore be seen as members of a unified community. Secondly, the Stoics believed that the human species was unique in that it shared a common capacity for reason, communication and reflective judgement. It is from this shared capacity to reason that the Stoics believed it was possible to derive universal principles for the equal moral respect of human beings. A third theme linking Stoic thought was a belief that human reason should be in harmony with nature and universal law. The Stoics firmly believed that the human species had a unifying purpose and that this purpose served as a universal natural law with which all human law should comply. As the logic of Aurelius expresses:

> If the intellectual capacity is common to us all, common too is reason, which makes us rational creatures. If so, that reason is common which tells us to do or not to do. If so, law is common. If so, we are citizens. If so, we are fellow members of an organized community. If so, the universe is as it were a state. And from it, this universal state, we get the intellectual, the rational, and the legal instinct.[6]

The concept of legal cosmopolitanism that is implicit in Aurelius' statement maintains the *naturalist* belief that reason, morality and law are thoroughly coextensive. Due to this belief, Aurelius argues that political organisation should reflect a universal commonality between individuals, which represents a common reason for human law, and which commands that human law should reflect a shared recognition of these normative principles as the true source of that legal order.

However, there is a complication with how the Stoics imagined the relationship between legal theory and legal practice to be organised. Stoics such as Cicero argued for the expansion of Roman-centric universal law, which was to be grounded by the normative principles outlined in his famous "ideal" Roman constitution. Under this constitution, Cicero argued that Roman law would promote the equal legal treatment of any subject within the Roman Empire, regardless of race, ethnicity and religion.[7] Cicero added that anyone who believed himself subject to this universal law could be immediately considered as a universal citizen, with equal entitlement to the ownership of private property, entitlement to the military security of Rome, and to the expectation of equal legal representation as a Roman citizen.

Nevertheless, despite the fact that Cicero wishes to broaden universal citizenship, we should remain wary about Cicero's steadfast commitment to imperialism and the implications this might have for his vision of cosmopolitan law. Our wariness should stem from the fact that Cicero seems to tie universal citizenship to the additional demand that a person was also a member of the Roman Empire. The problem is that Cicero does not talk about applying cosmopolitan law to every non-citizen, or to those who actively resisted inclusion in the Roman Empire. Although Cicero might be philosophically committed to the idea of a universal citizen, in practice, he seems to be arguing for a more positivistic and imperialistic concept of legal obligation. For Cicero, universal law requires an identification relationship as well as an enforcement mechanism, which creates an unbreakable bond between the word of law and the subject of law. In other words, Cicero's concept of universal law either required a willingness by an individual to accept Roman law as universal, and thus to agree to membership in the Roman Empire, or it required someone to be "civilized" to accept this law, through the various mechanisms of imperial power. If one was to refuse Roman expansion, as did the German "Barbarians", the Caledonians, the Catevellavni and the Persian Scythians, then Roman law did not respect them as if they were "universal citizens". Many Stoics believed that without an acceptance of universal law, it was then considered justified for these "barbarians" to be viewed as unreasonable people outside the remit and protection of Cicero's universal constitution. In this regard, although it might be fair to suggest that many Roman Stoics were legal cosmopolitans at the philosophical level, it is also sensible to suggest that they were imperial legal positivists when it came to the legal practice of cosmopolitan law. This conclusion seems justified, since the Stoic prescription for how law was to be applied under Cicero's Roman constitution contradicts the original Cynic principle that every human being is a member of a universal community, regardless of place of birth, ethnicity, religion or political affiliation.

Although the idea of applied cosmopolitan law suffered an extended period of silence after the death of Marcus Aurelius, a renewed interest in universal law developed between 1500 and 1800 AD. This renewed interest sought to make a link between universal morality and international law and was largely pursued by two distinct traditions; one embodied by the *natural law* tradition and the other by what is often referred to as *perpetual peace projects*. Whereas international legal scholars such as Hugo Grotius, Samuel Pufendorf, Emeric De Vattel and Christian Wolff personify the natural law tradition, the second tradition can be said to be represented by the normative principles associated with Abbé de Saint-Pierre, Jean-Jacques Rousseau and Immanuel Kant.

There is much that could be written about the legal theories associated with both the natural law and perpetual peace traditions and it would take volumes to compare and contrast the subtle differences that exist between them. Therefore, in order to expedite a discussion on how cosmopolitan law differentiates itself from natural law, it is prudent to focus on the area where the two approaches most diverge. The significant difference between the natural law tradition and the more cosmopolitan aspirations of Kant's perpetual peace project is the range to which universal moral commitments are to be extended at the global level. Building on the foundations laid by Thomas Hobbes, most natural law theorists promoted the contractual creation of a sovereign state as the ultimate source for ethical law and human emancipation.[8] Inherent in this type of contractarian argument is the idea that self-interested individuals contract with one another to create political institutions of mutual preservation and right. Nevertheless, like Cicero's demands for Roman citizenship, contracts between individuals immediately create boundaries between contracted citizens and other non-citizens, who are not considered to be members of the legal community. Although some natural law theorists sought limitations on state power in order to promote the natural rights of individual cooperators,[9] they nevertheless did not always argue for strong principles of universal law that created imperative moral obligations between bounded political communities, or between states and non-citizens.[10]

It was from Kant's development of cosmopolitan law that stronger commitments to cosmopolitan principles were developed away from, and as a supplement to, the natural law tradition. Unlike the natural law tradition of *jus gentium*, Kant suggested that a higher level of cosmopolitan law was necessary in order to place greater limits on the *law of nations*,[11] the Treaty of Westphalia,[12] and the injustices legitimated by claims to state sovereignty made under these legal regimes. For Kant, cosmopolitan law was meant to expand the scope of *public right* beyond a strict state-centered focus to one that encompassed all members of the earth, especially non-citizens.[13] As Charles Covell suggests, cosmopolitan law "was the body of public law . . . constituting the juridical framework for the intercourse of men and states, considered in their status as bearers of the attributes of citizenship in an ideal state that extended to embrace all mankind".[14] In this regard, Kant sought to make a dramatic move away from the natural law approach by advocating an additional level of *public right* and cosmopolitan law. This condition of public right was necessary beyond the state because the "peoples of the earth have thus entered in various degrees into a universal community and it has developed to the point where a violation of rights in *one* part of the world is felt *everywhere*".[15] Since humanity is locked into a spherically bounded relationship of codependence and cohabitation, which encompasses more than just the relationships that exist between states, reason dictates that a condition of *public right* should thus also exist at this global level. To create this new level, a condition of cosmopolitan right would require "the sum of laws that need to be publicized in order to produce [this] rightful condition, one in which individuals, nations and states can enjoy their rights".[16]

Kant argued that the grounding for cosmopolitan public right was to be applied through a tripartite system of interlocking and mutually reinforcing laws. This was to be fostered and expanded through a voluntary *pacific federation* of like-minded states and peoples who are dedicated to the establishment of a more rightful condition under cosmopolitan law. The tripartite matrix of cosmopolitan law would include domestic law (laws between citizens), international law (laws between states and political units) and the creation of cosmopolitan law (laws between states and individuals, especially non-citizens, including laws between private individuals).

Like many natural law theorists, Kant also believed that only republican states with a separation of powers and an internal condition of justice were to be considered *popular sovereigns* and therefore representative of an advanced form of communal development. However, unlike most natural law theorists, Kant was willing to take an additional step at the international level, by requiring that any cosmopolitan legal order would have to be grounded on the idea that "every civil constitution of every state shall be republican".[17] This is because Kant contends that a state could not have a rightful claim as an international sovereign if it was not a popular sovereign, since it would lack a mandate from which to be considered representative of its citizens. Kant predicates the foundation of a cosmopolitan federation on a just form of domestic law because he maintained that a democratic constitution is the only order that can secure and maintain justice both internally and externally.[18] The key to Kant's demand of domestic law as popular sovereignty is that democracies seemingly promote peace between each other and that people sharing similar conditions of popular sovereignty are more likely to agree about universal principles of justice. It is due to the fact that the internal forms of justice are familiar and complementary to the establishment of an external condition of justice, that like-minded peoples are more willing to participate in organising the legal conditions necessary to underwrite a cosmopolitan legal order.

From this concomitance to justice, Kant argued that international law should rest on the foundation of a mutually contracted federation of independent states, dedicated not only to principles of popular sovereignty, peace and mutual international right, but were further committed to the establishment and protection of universal *laws of hospitality*. The basis for this federation is not to be mistaken for a world government with coercive power, but should be seen as one based on a framework of self-regulatory international law.[19] Membership in the federation was conditioned on both an acceptance of international legal norms of right, but also conditioned on the practice and enforcement of cosmopolitan law. In many ways, Kant's pacific federation resembles the positive compliance mechanisms involved with membership in the EU. For only states which are willing to act in accordance with expressed legal requirements can be awarded the benefits of membership and seen as confederates in the promotion of these universal principles. The EU is similar to Kant's vision for self-regulation, since coercion is not guaranteed through direct policing and *hard positivism*, but through *soft-positivism*, compliance rewards, discussion, communal pressure, and through the power of federated norms to establish judgements of "legitimacy" and self-legitimisation that are based on that standard.

As alluded to above, the federation is predicated on the condition that members willingly accept to enforce cosmopolitan right. However, unlike the restrictions placed on the scope of universal law by the Roman Stoics and by many natural law theorists, the Kantian laws of hospitality are to be applied both internally within the federation and externally between federated and non-federated peoples. In this regard, Kant has moved beyond a bordered conception of legal obligation and duty, to one that reaches all members of the globe as if they were equal citizens, regardless of their immediate political affiliation. Surely, it is guaranteed that various peoples outside the federation will reject the principles of hospitality and seek to exclude themselves from compliance. Nevertheless, the federation itself remains dedicated to cosmopolitan ethical behavior with non-federated members and thus sets a standard for international legal norms and minimal justice from which a future legal relationship could be established.

Although a full discussion of Kant's cosmopolitan law cannot be fully developed here, it is useful to outline five laws of hospitality that can be derived from Kant's discussions on cosmopolitan law. These are fruitful to outline because these basic legal principles will be revisited in section four, where I will argue that cosmopolitan law represents a necessary foundation for all contemporary forms of institutional cosmopolitanism. In its basic form, the laws of hospitality concern the "right of a stranger not to be treated with hostility when he arrives on someone else's territory".[20] However, the principle of hospitality is not as introverted as it may first seem. This is because Kant subtly elaborates on what a commitment to cosmopolitan hospitality demands by alluding to additional principles of cosmopolitan hospitality that should affect all global interactions between peoples. First, all human beings have a *right to exit, enter and travel*. As Kant suggests, there is "a right of citizens of the world to try to establish community with all, and to that end, to visit all regions of the earth".[21] Secondly, all human beings should have a *freedom from hostility and from negligence* that would result in imminent harm to body or property. This is an important measure of hospitality, for it protects individuals not only from direct harm, but also stipulates that a host community cannot turn individuals away if there *is* a possibility that this action will result in death or immediate harm to person and property. Thirdly, all human beings should have the *freedom of communication* and to engage in debates of public reason. This represents the Kantian belief that it is only through dialogue, exchange and "the freedom to make public use of one's reason" that broader social change and global civil advancement can hope to be achieved over time.[22] Fourthly, all humans should have the *freedom to engage in commerce* and the use of the world in common. As Kant suggests, "[humans] stand in a community of possible interaction, that is, in a thoroughgoing relation of each to all the others of offering to engage in commerce with any other, and each has the right to make this attempt".[23] Lastly, all humans should have *freedom from false, misrepresented, extorted or fraudulent contracts*. What is interesting about Kant's final two laws are the inherent principles of fairness involved, in that they demand that all dealings with non-federated members must be negotiated in good faith and in such a way that resulting conditions are seen as mutually consistent. Although this represents a very minimal form of global justice, a strong commitment to these final normative laws could go some way to correct the inequalities involved in the global market, while also creating a greater sense of fairness, cooperation, mutual right and evenhandedness at the global level.

The idea behind a consistent commitment to these basic laws of hospitality is to create:

> those conditions which make it possible for [individuals] to attempt to enter into relations with native inhabitants. In this way, continents distant from each other can enter into peaceful mutual relations which may eventually be regulated by public laws, thus bringing the human race nearer and nearer to a cosmopolitan constitution.[24]

In other words, Kant's cosmopolitan goal is to create the foundations for an ethical order of legal norms that would, with time and commitment by like-minded members, establish the grounding for the practice of a more robust cosmopolitan legal order. A legal order that transforms these minimal laws of hospitality into a more institutionalised organisation of cosmopolitan law, so as to provide "the systematic union of different rational beings through common laws . . . in a universal kingdom of ends".[25]

[. . .]

2. Legal cosmopolitanism: contemporary approaches and distinctions

In a general sense, contemporary cosmopolitan legal theory upholds the Kantian idea that international law should be constituted from, and constrained by, moral and normative principles of universal human worth, human respect and global justice. In so arguing, legal cosmopolitans generally promote two approaches, often used in tandem, but sometimes also maintained as separate projects. The first approach is critically to assess current international law and to suggest reformulation so as to bring existing practice into line with cosmopolitan moral principles. This approach, exemplified by Allen Buchanan and Fernando Teson, highlights an objective that is to "evaluate certain fundamental aspects of the existing international legal order . . . [And to] propose legal norms and practices which, if implemented with reasonable care, would make the system more just".[26] The second approach argues that an additional level of law is necessary to secure human dignity and legal obligation beyond the traditional state-centric model of international law. This approach, which is indebted largely to the aforementioned legal theory of Kant, seeks not only to change existing law, but also to create an additional set of laws at the cosmopolitan level, which create legal obligations not only between states and non-citizens, but also between individuals themselves. Common among legal cosmopolitans, however, is a basic rejection of international law that is predicated solely on the Westphalian model and therefore one that grants absolute overriding authority to the interests of state sovereignty. As mentioned above, this rejection often translates into an argument that an additional level of law, one presiding at the global level, should supplement and enhance changes to current international law, in order to bring states and people under the normative guidance of cosmopolitan moral theory. In sum, legal cosmopolitans and most cosmopolitans in general, believe that peaceful cohabitation and justice are a question of both morality and law, and that they are thoroughly coextensive, complimentary and necessary at both the international and the global level.

However, there remain some perennial questions as to whether the idea of cosmopolitan law is a tenable idea, and if so, how the normative principles that motivate cosmopolitanism are to be established into legal practice. These debates about cosmopolitan legal theory and international legal practice have traditionally been framed as being a question of *positive law, legal realism, legal naturalism* or *liberal internationalism*. Classic legal theorists of a positivist persuasion often argue that law and morality are not connected. These legal positivists believe that our obligation to any form of international law is based solely on enforcement and convention versus being based on strong moral sentiment. Since there is no institutional mechanism to enforce international law effectively, norms are therefore entirely maintained by voluntary conventions that lack the Hobbesian "sword" from which law commands strong obligation. In a similar vein, legal realists suggest that international law is predicated on the protection of state sovereignty and that the structure of the anarchic international system rules out any robust and unified system of cosmopolitan law. Legal realists argue that international law has been created by a process of voluntary state treaties and covenants to which state self-determination, security, and a protection of sovereignty are its primary concern. Since an overarching authority does not enforce international law, the idea of universal law cannot move beyond the minimal security and economic treaties that are enlivened by the self-interest of independent sovereign states.

Conversely, legal naturalism argues that morality and law are not mutually exclusive. Legal naturalism maintains that the internal aspects that underpin legal norms, and the normative foundations from which law is often created, justify and motivate the authority of law. As members of The English School argue, legal realism fails to capture the fact that states often obligate themselves to international law, despite the fact that it might not be in their immediate self-interest and despite the fact that it might limit some absolute conception of state sovereignty. For scholars like Hedley Bull, this system of self-regulation represents something more positivistic than what legal realists proclaim, because it highlights that the moral force behind law might be more prevalent at the international level than has been assumed by Hobbesian legal positivists.[27] In a similar vein, liberal internationalists start from this position of legal naturalism, but move further, suggesting that the legal concept of sovereignty should also be understood as a conditional right. In other words, liberal internationalists not only believe that law and morality are connected, but also that the idea of sovereignty itself should be justified by various conditional moral principles of human right, accountability to international norms, and from internal mechanisms for democratic *popular sovereignty*.

Understanding where legal cosmopolitanism fits into these legal traditions is often difficult to ascertain. This is because legal cosmopolitanism incorporates and then moves beyond several of the aforementioned positions, sitting somewhere beyond liberal internationalism, while also sharing liberal principles of conditional popular sovereignty and more positivist conceptions of law. [. . .] In this regard, legal cosmopolitanism often overlaps with liberal internationalism, in that both share the belief that it is only through the democratic make-up of a popular sovereign that "the freedom of every member of society as a human being" can be secured.[28] In addition, international liberals as well as many cosmopolitans place considerable stock in Kant's *democratic peace theory*, suggesting that there is an inherent quality associated with democratic law that fosters a peaceful coexistence between democratic peoples. Furthermore, many liberal internationalists stray considerably close to cosmopolitan legalism in that many argue passionately for the universal protection of human rights and for the additional requirement that these rights act as the foundation of an international legal order.

However, despite the similarities, there are subtle differences that exist between liberal internationalism and most cosmopolitans. First, like the natural law tradition, liberal internationalists often restrict themselves to a state-centric approach, operating within the language of international relations, while remaining loyal to traditional approaches of international governance and international law. Secondly, although not true of all liberal internationalists, there is certainly a predominate assumption within classic liberal internationalism that if all states were to be democratic and economically neo-liberal, then that would be enough to end war, increase cooperative interdependence and secure universal human rights. Although cosmopolitans would agree that this would go some way to alleviate many of the world's problems, cosmopolitan-

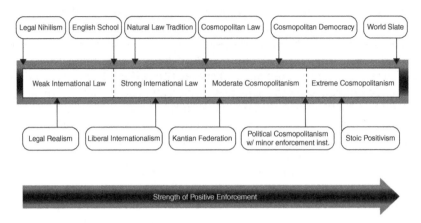

Figure 1   Distribution of global legal theory

ism demands that a more robust normative commitment to global justice also be secured. In this regard, cosmopolitan moral theory moves further than international liberalism, in that it calls for significant changes to be made to the current system of international law, economics and governance. These changes include combinations of democratic reform at the global level,[29] a solid commitment to global justice,[30] the corresponding regulation of global capitalism,[31] a more robust commitment to universal human rights,[32] institutional mechanisms to promote cross-cultural dialogue,[33] and the establishment of a global legal system that directly mirrors the cosmopolitan principles of individualism, equality and universality.[34]

Therefore, unlike liberal internationalism, cosmopolitans argue for a system of global justice that is more robust than a simple state-centric commitment to international law. As depicted in Figure 1, this system of cosmopolitan law can range from extreme forms of institutionalism to more moderate forms of cosmopolitanism that rest on a minimal conception of cosmopolitan law. However, it is important to understand that all contemporary designs for institutional cosmopolitanism are grounded on the assumption of a practiced cosmopolitan law. When surveying the literature, it becomes obvious that cosmopolitans assume and ground their more elaborate forms of institutional cosmopolitanism on some already existing level of "cosmopolitan democratic law",[35] a respect for "cosmopolitan rights", "cosmopolitan law-enforcement",[36] or a formal commitment to "political cosmopolitanism". In a move from cosmopolitan moral theory to institutional cosmopolitanism, cosmopolitans rely on a notion of cosmopolitan law and the presupposition that this law is maintained, in some thoroughgoing way, as global practice. However, what is often left ambiguous is how we can get from where we are now to where institutional and moral cosmopolitans want to be.

3. Normative roots make for healthy thickets: Waldron's thicket analogy and applied cosmopolitan legal theory

There are two analogies that capture the relationship of how cosmopolitan normative principles can come to ground, restrain and supplement the practice of international law. The first analogy, used recently by Waldron, asks us to imagine international law as a dense thicket of twisted and interlocking laws, treaties, regulations and applied norms. This thicket of "mundane" international law and norms represent, to some degree, an already functioning set of "cosmopolitan norms that structure our lives together".[37] As Waldron suggests, "if we really want to understand how the world is coming to be ordered by cosmopolitan norms, we have to look at the ordinary as well as the extraordinary, the tedious as well as the exciting, the commercial as well as the ideological".[38] For Waldron, it is through this already interlocking and growing thicket of global norms that new opportunities for the future formation of cosmopolitan law are possible. To some degree, Waldron's dense thicket resembles an English School interpretation of international law, in that there is a belief that international law is already reflective of normative principles that have some commanding force and compliance, despite the fact that there is no exclusive global authority to enforce them. In other ways, Waldron's analogy remains true to a Kantian teleology. For both Kant and Waldron seem firmly to believe that continued commerce and trade will create "peaceful relations with one another, and thus achieve mutual understanding, community of interests, even with the most distant of their fellows".[39]

In many ways this is an acceptable analogy and one that captures an important aspect of current international law. Waldron's analogy is important because it emphasises the fact that there is an already existing system of complex laws and norms that help to regulate human coexistence and which already operate without a "formal juridical apparatus". As Waldron rightly points out, it is from international commerce, global communication and the increasing interaction of peoples, that human beings have slowly, but surely, incorporated various cosmopolitan principles of cooperation, human rights, norms of hospitality and a sense of moral obligation to others. Nevertheless, scholars are right to question Waldron's analogy, suggesting that "mundane and repeated contact among different human groups is absolutely no guarantee of the spread of a cosmopolitan point of view that considers all human beings as individuals equally entitled to certain rights".[40] In addition, although Waldron is correct to suggest that some cosmopolitan norms have developed through human interaction, it is also true that the current thicket of international law fails to prevent massive inequality, injustices, war, genocide, exploitation and a sustained devaluation of human worth. In this regard, there seems to be something more Kantian missing from Waldron's analogy.

To take the analogy further, what is often missing from this thicket, are strong normative roots, which are deeply embedded in healthy cosmopolitan soil. Although Waldron is correct to suggest that the international environment has in some way embraced various cosmopolitan norms, the fact also remains that this dense thicket of international law is also weak in its universal depth and scope. This is due to the fact that the thicket has frail stalks that are often so thin, that they are frequently at breaking point, threatening to bring down huge sections of the thicket. This unhealthiness has occurred because the thicket has been allowed to grow piecemeal and in every direction, largely by the self-interest of a few gardeners who each believe in their absolute right to self-determine the final appearance of the thicket.

However, it would be disingenuous to suggest that Waldron's analogy represents complacency with an untidy and unhealthy thicket. As Waldron suggests, legal cosmopolitanism needs to focus on *both* the "ordinary as well as the extraordinary". If one were to read this generously, which I do, then it would seem that Waldron has alluded to a two-pronged approach to ground the practice of cosmopolitan law. The first prong results from the everyday practical application of existing global norms and law (established by thousands of years of interaction between peoples), and the second prong from more immediate and globally coordinated efforts which border on the extraordinary (say something like universal human rights). In this regard, the first prong suggests that the existing thicket of international law already contains some functioning cosmopolitan principles that can help form the basis for a continued cosmopolitan enthusiasm. The second prong promotes, in possible tandem with the first, the idea that this thicket could also be reinforced by nourishing its strongest normative roots and perhaps through the building of an additional canopy to help protect the more delicate parts of the thicket.

From this we can make a second analogy regarding the relationship between cosmopolitan normative principles and the idea of cosmopolitan law. Not only should the existing thicket of international law be further nourished by rich cosmopolitan soil, but an additional level of law should also be created, at the global level, which acts as an overarching canopy under which the more delicate plants in the thicket are protected. To take the analogy further, and in order to tie the analogy into contemporary debates about institutional cosmopolitanism, we should imagine that the construction of the canopy could be done in two ways.

The first option is to give authority to the most powerful gardener, in the form of a world state, to organise the resources necessary to build and protect the canopy from the various global storms that might threaten to blow it and the thicket down. As Thomas Nagel has sarcastically argued, the only way global justice can be meaningfully advanced is through a world government because justice requires "a form of organization that claims the political legitimacy and the right to impose decisions by force".[41] Nevertheless, as Kant would suggest, this option can be equally unhealthy for the thicket, since the survival of the garden would be determined solely by the whims of a single gardener, without the guarantee that the gardener would not destroy the thicket or manage it with despotic force. As Kant points out, "such a [world] state is in turn even more dangerous to freedom, for it may lead to fearful despotism".[42]

The second option is for several of the more like-minded gardeners to band together under a shared normative vision, in the form of a federation, to build the canopy and then to work together to protect that canopy from those who might seek to destroy it. Kant himself supported this option, claiming that "distrust [of a world state] must force men to form an order which is not a cosmopolitan commonwealth under a single ruler, but a lawful federation under a commonly accepted international right".[43] Kant clarifies this position further when he adds, "this federation does not aim to acquire power like that of a state, but merely to preserve and secure the freedom of each state in itself, along with that of other confederated states".[44] Therefore, unlike having only one powerful gardener, who has the ability to enforce law with impunity, the federated gardeners must use various forms of reason, communication, threats, and incentives, to try and convince non-federated gardeners to believe in the value of maintaining the canopy that protects the thicket. [. . .] Thus, although the federated thicket might not be as well kept as the world state thicket, it strikes a balance of interests and is still better than doing what is currently done, which is to let every gardener do as they wish without regard for the existence of the thicket as a whole.

Although the thicket analogy oversimplifies the complexities that are involved with the implementation of cosmopolitan law, it does render a general picture about the two primary directions from which cosmopolitan theorists have traditionally argued. However, these two directions are not always mutually exclusive of one another and many cosmopolitans combine aspects of Waldron's "mundane" bottom up approach with aspects of a top down approach, while others create a cross-pollinated hybrid representing a global variation that sits somewhere in the middle. In addition, there are several institutional formats from which cosmopolitans suggest we pursue these approaches. Most rest their institutional model somewhere between two cosmopolitan polarities along a wide distribution of legal options (see Figure 1 (above)). One model that advocates a minimal legal order of like-minded states and another model which suggests that cosmopolitan law is best enforced through something approximating a world government. It is here, between the world-state and more federated models, that a distinction between moderate and extreme forms of cosmopolitanism can be delineated. For moderate cosmopolitans believe that minimal cosmopolitan principles of law can coexist with many domestic laws of community, whereas many world state cosmopolitans argue that all legal commitments, even localised traditions, must be justified in relation to a particular cosmopolitan ideal that is centrally enforceable.

So given the plethora of cosmopolitan options, what is the best approach for applied legal cosmopolitanism and how could it be possible to establish it as cosmopolitan legal practice? First, it is prudent to postpone the world government option for some future debate. This is not to say that it is not a worthwhile theoretical exercise, but that it should be delayed simply because it is the most radical and improbable option given the current structure of international relations. Furthermore, it is logical to assume that any feasible move to a cosmopolitan condition, in whatever form that may eventually take, would necessarily have to start from current circumstances. By this I mean that any practical and meaningful world government would have to be conceived from where we stand today, which for better or for worse is a world dominated largely by nation-states. Therefore, rather than immediately negotiating the make-up of a world government from some hypothetical vacuum, it might be worthwhile to consider more moderate options with the prospect that these will ground a future legal mode of institutional practice. What seems sensible, if the transition from theory to practice is to be considered important, is to explore the necessary first step in the process of institutional cosmopolitanism.

4. Grounding cosmopolitan legal practice

It would be naive to assume that pursuing a less ambitious approach will not be mired with serious difficulties. As Benhabib has recently suggested, even a moderate move from legal theory to legal practice offers cosmopolitans with a big hurdle to jump. This is because serious questions remain about "how to create quasi-legal binding obligations through voluntary commitments . . . in the absence of an overwhelming sovereign power with the ultimate right of enforcement".[45] In this regard, Benhabib is correct to suggest that this is a crucial question facing cosmopolitanism, since any form of institutional cosmopolitanism rests on some notion of cosmopolitan legal practice. As she further argues, "the modern state system is caught between *sovereignty and hospitality*, between the prerogative to choose to be a party to cosmopolitan norms and human rights treaties, and the obligation to extend recognition of these human rights to all".[46] However, like both Waldron and Benhabib, I believe that current hindrances only represent a set of complex coordination problems, and that these difficulties do not represent a "real dilemma" for the future of cosmopolitanism on the whole. As Waldron suggests, there is already some "array of cosmopolitan norms that structure our lives together" and there is much to be enthusiastic about.[47] However, as Benhabib is also right to add, a question still remains as to how we might bolster this fledgling thicket of law so as to add additional protections on a more cosmopolitical level.

In regards to this question, I believe a key to advancing cosmopolitan legal theory to practice is to return to the Kantian model as outlined earlier. This is due to the fact that it represents a *moderate* and transitional form of legal cosmopolitanism that accepts that any move to a cosmopolitan order would need to evolve from our current order without also abandoning the cosmopolitan concern for human worth. From this baseline position, Kantian legal cosmopolitanism can occupy a middle position between a world that only reflects some cosmopolitan norms and the possible establishment of more robust cosmopolitan institutions. In order to provide some link between theory and practice the discussion below will present a brief sketch of a Kantian juridical model and how this may encourage a sustained evolution toward a condition of cosmopolitan law.

(a) Cosmopolitan law as protecting the global forum

The first order of Kantian legal cosmopolitanism is to provide a minimal legal framework that fosters a condition of public right and establishes some minimal sense of ethical obligations between peoples of the globe. Having understood the practical limitations of moving his universal moral theory to universal legal practice, Kant consciously pursued a more humble and moderate course. As Kant states, a cosmopolitan condition will be the result of international norm building and a continued enthusiasm so that these narrowest of ethical conditions will "gradually spread further and further".[48] In this regard, Kant wished to avoid making predictions as to the final institutional complexion of a cosmopolitan condition. For Kant, what is first needed, and what is critical for any advancement of institutional cosmopolitanism, are basic laws of hospitality that can help cultivate a broad sense of shared community, where everyone is considered as if they could be mutual citizens of the world.

As was outlined in the first section, Kantian legal theory begins with the idea that a federated group of like-minded democratic states obligate themselves not only to international right, but also to the furtherance and protection of cosmopolitan right. In so doing, the cosmopolitan federation would seek to embody the sum total of global public law necessary, so that "the freedom of each can coexist with the freedom of all the other".[49] In this way, the laws of hospitality would not only obligate federated states to treat all federated members with a sense of justice, but would also obligate federated states to consistently engage with all peoples of the earth in compliance with these laws. As Kant forcefully proclaimed, hospitable treatment is not merely a philanthropic principle, but a "principle having to do with right".[50] And this is, according to Kant, "a necessary complement to the unwritten code of political and international right, transforming it into a universal right of humanity".[51]

For Kant, hospitality represents those conditions which make it possible for people to enter into peaceful relations with each other so that this may eventually bring "the human race nearer and nearer to a cosmopolitan constitution".[52] As outlined earlier, implicit in Kant's laws of hospitality are five universal freedoms that are to be seen as the basic foundation for any future expansion of cosmopolitan law. These laws represent the basic legal mechanisms for humans peaceably to trade, associate, communicate, exchange ideas without mistreatment, and engage commercially with one another under a mutually consistent concept of hospitality. The idea is not immediately to create a full condition of global justice, as many contemporary cosmopolitans would wish, but a minimal condition of global law so that individuals could have the opportunity to "engage in the use of public reason" and to relate ethically toward one another to the point where critical distinctions and tensions would disintegrate over time.[53]

Kantian cosmopolitan laws of hospitality therefore act as a mechanism for the possibility for the continued deliberation and dialogue between people. It is from this baseline protection for cosmopolitan law that peoples of the earth can engage with one another, in order to exchange various *experiments in living* and for their ideas to be subject to global public reason and examination. [. . .] As Kant maintains, these exchanges must be guaranteed and fostered at the global level because it will only be through public reason and global deliberation that a future cosmopolitan condition might be obtained. [. . .] For this reason, Kant demands that "these rights must be held sacred . . . there are no half measures here . . . for all politics must bend the knee before right, [if] politics may hope to return to arrive, however slowly, at a stage of lasting brilliance".[54]

In practice, the Kantian federation needs a group of like-minded democratic states that are willing to ground these minimal laws of hospitality into their own legal codes and then to promote these laws in their dealings with all people, especially non-citizens. As Kant recommends, this should be done not only for the protection of domestic right, but also to advance these principles to all of humanity, in order to bring about a more just and cooperative cosmopolitan condition. The question then becomes why certain democratic states might be willing to obligate themselves to the laws of hospitality under a federated system and to broaden the scope of cosmopolitan right to include others.

(b) Democratic law as an intermediary between domestic and cosmopolitan justice

As was outlined in the first section, Kant predicates the foundation of a cosmopolitan federation on the *definitive article* that "the civil constitution of every state be republican". Kant grounds the expansion of cosmopolitan law on domestic democratic law because he believed that a democratic constitution is the only order that can secure and maintain justice both internally and externally. Kant believes that a domestic sense of justice between democratic peoples lends itself to viewing other democratic peoples as sharing similar values of justice and that they will seek to be more cooperative with each other. In addition, implicit in Kant's understanding of democratic law is an additional reference to democracy's intermediary quality. By intermediary, Kant suggests that democratic people not only concern themselves with the protection of domestic right, but also that they concern themselves with establishing a condition of justice with anyone who they have contact with, even non-democratic and potentially hostile peoples. This sociological element of democratic law forms the foundation for Kant's democratic peace theory, but also is held as the motivational component behind why "like-minded" democratic peoples would be more willing to create a federation that included cosmopolitan law and the laws of hospitality.

Nevertheless, Kant does not elaborate as to why democratic peoples are sociologically more accepting and thus more willing legally to protect the cosmopolitan value of those beyond their borders. In attempts to explore this prospect, Benhabib has recently suggested that democratic law creates a process of *democratic iteration* that helps to arbitrate "between universal norms and the will of democratic majorities".[55] Benhabib suggests that through a process of repeated reiteration and reconstruction, democratic law engages in progressive modification by its democratic population, resulting in what she calls "jurisgenerative politics". She argues that through continued iteration "a democratic peoples, which considers itself bound by certain guiding norms and principles, engages in iterative acts by reappropriating and reinterpreting these, thereby showing itself not only the subject but also the author of the laws".[56] Through this process of jurisgenerative politics, democratic law sequentially reflects and then expands the boundaries of ethical universalism. This occurs because the democratic concern for justice and individual autonomy are systematically incorporated into domestic positive law and that these laws in turn eventually come to guide the behaviour of that political body towards non-citizens. In order to illustrate the force behind this process, Benhabib asks us to examine the continued broadening of cosmopolitan norms between democratically liberal countries and peoples beyond their borders. Although not always representative of a progressive trajectory, liberal democracies, especially within the EU, have extended their own domestic laws to include and protect the rights of non-citizens. In addition, these same liberal democracies have sought to expand many cosmopolitan norms to the international level, as witnessed by a growing commitment to humanitarian intervention, humane migration law and to the punishment of crimes against humanity.

However, there are considerable perplexities involved with Benhabib's account of why democratic law produces progressive iterations toward a cosmopolitan ethic. Similar to Kant, Benhabib relies on the fact that cosmopolitan principles are intrinsically valid and she does not fully explain why democratic iteration would necessarily lead to universal ethical norms versus promoting nationalistic tendencies. In this regard, although democracies under the guidance of democratic law might be the most likely candidates to help advance a cosmopolitan condition under applied cosmopolitan law, it is not necessarily the case that this is inevitable.

In spite of the fact that the democratic theory of both Kant and Benhabib does not sufficiently explain why democracies necessarily promote cosmopolitanism, there is empirical justification to recommend that democratic states represent the most likely candidates for the expansion of cosmopolitan law. As the history of universal human rights law would help to illustrate, cosmopolitan principles are more likely to come from liberal democracies than from non-democratic or from more authoritarian regimes. Although theorists are not sure why democratic law can have an intermediary function between the domestic and the global, prima facie it would seem that democratic law does have an ability to move domestic concerns for justice to global laws of hospitality. Despite the fact that many cosmopolitans might view this process as insufficiently slow and without a clear linear progression, it would seem that any movement to a cosmopolitan order would have to begin with existing democratic political communities and from the enlargement of existing cosmopolitan norms. Nevertheless, this continued growth toward more applied cosmopolitan law is not guaranteed and will require prolonged deliberation and ethical acceptance through the formation of identification relationships, domestically and globally, between states and peoples, both legally and extra-legally. In addition, it will require liberal peoples consistently to apply domestic concerns for justice and the protection of human worth equally to those beyond their borders. Given the current political order, it would seem that the move to ground cosmopolitan legal theory into practice will need to come from both internal and external deliberative processes to expand domestic legal codes to include others and to then establish a condition of cosmopolitan law. Through some form of Benhabib's iterative process or Kant's intermediary system, democratic peoples will need to demand that a consistent relationship between domestic justice and global justice be maintained. Although this process as of now remains a rather intuitive speculation, it is also not totally unreasonable to suggest that there are both theoretical and empirical reasons to think this is possible, and also, as Waldron might suggest, that the world is already slowly engaged in this process.

(c) Constitutional cosmopolitanism and the codification of normative legal principles

The section above focused on the ability of democratic law to expand domestic conceptions of justice to include non-citizens and how this could in practice create a mutually consistent consanguinity between domestic justice and cosmopolitan laws of hospitality. Nevertheless, the key to this process is the establishment of robust commitments by democratic peoples and their popular sovereigns to pursue a mutually consistent condition of justice beyond their borders. This commitment must not only be held as a moral obligation, but also as a legal obligation, so as to secure cosmopolitan law as a set of legal expectations that express and facilitate the furtherance of a continued universal ethic toward others.

In many ways, Kantian cosmopolitan law seeks to provide those global norms and standards that will produce a condition of soft-positivism and compliance pull between political communities. This is because the constitution of the federation is meant to objectify the normative and juridical principles that underwrite a cosmopolitan order. It secures obligation through contractual agreement and thus commands authority through a legally binding agreement. Furthermore, the federated order establishes a condition of soft-positivism in that it generates constitutional authority to persuade compliance and obligation by setting the terms of federated membership and by setting legitimacy standards of global practice. In addition, the constitution acts as a reference point for the creation of a continued global identity and ethic, since individuals can form an identification relationship with a set of juridical standards that have positive impacts upon their lives. For Kant, a constitution refers to the totality of laws that should be publicised so as to create a rightful condition of mutual freedom between individuals, states and associations. As Kant himself proclaimed, what is ultimately needed is "a system of laws . . . for a multitude of peoples, which, because they affect one another, need a rightful condition under a will uniting them, a constitution (constitutio), so that they may enjoy what is laid down as right".[57] Although Kant did not refer specifically to a written constitutional document, he did refer to contractarian principles of self-binding obligation that were to give authority to a juridical condition of mutual public right. It is for this reason that it might be reasonable to think creatively about a Kantian based written constitution and its ability to ground self-binding commitments by political communities, individuals and states, to a cosmopolitan order.

As was stated before, in order to facilitate a continued sense of cosmopolitan community, it is necessary to create positive ethical experiences of global interaction by way of the formation of additional norms that grow through the fulfillment of existing legal and extra-legal expectations. By objectifying the minimal laws of hospitality into the written constitution of a normatively based Kantian federation, it would help to foster what Jurgen Habermas describes as a condition of *constitutional patriotism* and could help to provide a global point of reference for continued global deliberation and legal expectation.[58] This is because the continued application of juridical procedures has the ability to foster identification relationships between peoples and the normative principles that underwrite a legal constitution. Thus a sense of patriotic identification can be generated beyond local political obligations by cultivating a belief that these global legal practices have bearing and meaning on human coexistence and well-being.

Conclusion

This paper has examined the history of legal cosmopolitanism and has sought to highlight its unique position in relation to contemporary studies in international law. Through this examination, it has been argued that legal cosmopolitanism represents a middle position beyond international law, linking cosmopolitan theory to institutional cosmopolitanism. In addition, it has argued that a Kantian juridical model provides a moderate yet tenable mode for moving cosmopolitan legal theory to legal practice. In examining this model, I have sketched three factors that could give credence to a reinvigorated enthusiasm for the generation of cosmopolitan law. First, the Kantian laws of hospitality represent basic principles of applied law that are designed for the expansion of global dialogue and applied ethical norms. In this regard, they do not represent the final institutional complexion of a cosmopolitan system of justice, but act as a legal compass toward a more robust cosmopolitan condition. This not only diminishes the realist claim that cosmopolitanism aspires to utopian "world conquest," but also leaves the final conception of cosmopolitan politics open to a ongoing process of deliberative decision making. Secondly, as Kant, Benhabib and many other cosmopolitans have suggested, there is something inherent to democratic law and the democratic process that allows it to have an ability to act as an intermediary between domestic and cosmopolitan justice. Although this notion rests on a highly underdeveloped sociological pretext, there do seem to be processes involved with democratic institutions that help to facilitate a move from a condition of domestic justice to one that often includes peoples outside of its political community. Thirdly, by objectifying the minimal laws of hospitality into the constitution of a normatively based Kantian federation, it would help to foster a condition of *constitutional patriotism* and could help to provide for peaceful global deliberation, a normative point of reference and for a consistent standard of global interaction toward the establishment of a mutually secured public right. In other words, this minimal form of legal cosmopolitanism can form a linchpin between theory and practice, and can provide the minimal legal foundation necessary for more elaborate forms of institutional cosmopolitanism. Although perhaps not as robust and immediately expansive as many cosmopolitans would like, it does provide a basic matrix from which additional cosmopolitan principles can be developed and with time, be formally implemented and codified into institutional practice.

Notes

1 Martin Wright "An Anatomy of International Thought" (1987) 13 Review of International Studies 226.
2 Luis Cabrera *Political Theory and Global Justice. A Cosmopolitan Case for the World State* (New York: Routledge, 2004).
3 Garrett Wallace Brown "Kantian Cosmopolitan Law and the Idea of a Cosmopolitan Constitution" (2006) 27(3) History of Political Thought 661.
4 David Held *Democracy and the Global Order From the Modern State to Cosmopolitan Democracy* (Cambridge: Polity Press, 1995).
5 Robert Post (ed) *Another Cosmopolitanism* (Oxford: Oxford University Press, 2006).
6 Marcus Aurelius *The Meditations* (New York: Hackett, 1983) Sect. 14.
7 Clinton Walker Keyes "Original Elements in Cicero's Ideal Constitution" (1921) 42(4). The American Journal of Philology 309–323.
8 Emeric De Vattel *The Law of Nations* (Indianapolis: The Liberty Fund, 2000).
9 Christian Wolff [H. Drake (transl)] *The Laws of Nations Treated according to a Scientific Method* (Oxford: Clarendon Press, 1934).
10 Daniele Archibugi "Immanuel Kant Cosmopolitan Law and Peace" (1995) 1(4) European Journal of International Relations 429.
11 Immanuel Kant "Perpetual Peace: A Philosophical Sketch," in H. Reiss (ed) *Kant's Politics Writing* (Cambridge: Cambridge University Press, 1970).
12 Immanuel Kant "On the Common Saying: 'This May be True in Theory But it Does Not Apply in Practice' " in Reiss, ibid.
13 As outlined in Kant's *Doctrine of Right*, "right is . . . the sum of the conditions under which the choice of one can be united with the choice of another in accordance with a universal law of freedom." Immanuel Kant *The Metaphysics of Morals*, M. Gregor (ed.) (Cambridge: Cambridge University Press, 1996) p. 24.
14 Charles Covell *Kant and the Law of Peace. A Study in the Philosophy of International Law and International Relations* (New York: Palgrave, 1998) pp. 141–142.
15 Kant "Perpetual Peace," p. 107.
16 Mary Gregor, "Kant's Approach to Constitutionalism" in A. Rosenbaum (ed) *Constitutionalism: The Philosophical Dimension* (New York: Greenwood Press, 1988) p. 71.
17 Kant "Perpetual Peace," p. 107.
18 Kant *The Metaphysics of Morals*, pp. 89–95.
19 Garrett Wallace Brown "State Sovereignty Federation and Kantian Cosmopolitanism" (2005) 11 European Journal of International Relations 495.
20 Kant "Perpetual Peace," p. 106.
21 Kant *The Metaphysics of Morals*, above n 15, p. 128.
22 Kant "An Answer to the Question: 'What is Enlightenment?' ," in Reiss, above n 13, p. 55.
23 Kant *The Metaphysics of Morals*, above n 15, p. 121. Also see "Perpetual Peace," in Reiss, above n 13, p. 106.
24 Kant "Perpetual Peace," in Reiss above n 13, p. 106.
25 Immanuel Kant [J. Ellington (transl)] *Grounding for the Metaphysics of Morals* (Cambridge: Hackett Publishing Company, 1981) pp. 39–45.
26 Allen Buchanan *Justice, Legitimacy and Self-determination. Moral Foundations for International Law* (Oxford: Oxford University Press, 2004) p. 4.
27 Hedley Bull *The Anarchical Society* (London: Macmillan, 1977).
28 Kant "Theory and Practice," p. 74.
29 Daniele Archibugi and David Held *Cosmopolitan Democracy: An Agenda for a New World Order* (Cambridge: Polity Press, 1995).
30 Brian Barry "International Society From a Cosmopolitan Perspective," in D. Maple and T. Nardin (eds) *International Society* (New Jersey: Princeton University Press, 1998); Charles Beitz *Political Theory and International Relations* (New Jersey: Princeton University Press, 1999); Simon Caney *Justice Beyond Borders* (Oxford: Oxford University Press, 2005); Thomas Pogge *Global Justice* (Oxford: Blackwell, 2001).
31 Richard Falk. *On Human Governance Towards a New Global Politics* (University Park: University of Pennsylvania Press, 1995); Thomas Pogge *World Poverty and Human Rights* (Cambridge: Polity Press, 2002); Patrick Hayden *Cosmopolitan Global Politics* (Burlington: Ashgate, 2005); Caney, ibid.

32   Charles Jones. *Global Justice Defending Cosmopolitanism* (Oxford: Oxford University Press, 1999).
33   Jurgen Habermas. *The Post-National Constellation* (Cambridge: MIT Press, 2001); Jeremy Waldron "What is Cosmopolitan?" (2000) 8(2) Journal of Political Philosophy 227; Martha Nussbaum *Cultivating Humanity* (Cambridge: Cambridge University Press, 1998).
34   Fernando Teson. *A Philosophy of International Law* (Boulder: Westview, 1998).
35   David Held and Danielle Archibugi (eds.) *Cosmopolitan Democracy* (Cambridge: Polity Press, 1995).
36   Mary Kaldor *Global Civil Society An Answer to War* (Cambridge: Polity Press, 2003).
37   Jeremy Waldron "Cosmopolitan Norms," p. 83.
38   Ibid., p. 97.
39   Kant "Perpetual Peace," p. 111.
40   Seyla Benhabib "Hospitality, Sovereignty, and Democratic Iterations," p. 153.
41   Thomas Nagel "The Problem of Global Justice" (2005) 33(2) Philosophy and Public Affairs 140.
42   Kant "Theory and Practice," p. 90.
43   Ibid.
44   Kant "Perpetual Peace," p. 104.
45   Benhabib "The Philosophical Foundations of Cosmopolitan Norms," p. 23.
46   Ibid. p. 31.
47   Waldron, "Cosmopolitan Norms," p. 84.
48   Kant "Perpetual Peace," p. 104.
49   Kant *Grounding for the Metaphysics of Molls*, p. 40.
50   Kant *The Metaphysics of Morals*, p. 121.
51   Kant "Perpetual Peace," p. 108.
52   Ibid., p. 106.
53   Kant "What is Enlightenment?" p. 55.
54   Kant "Perpetual Peace," p. 125.
55   Benhabib "Democratic Iterations," p. 49.
56   Ibid.
57   Kant, *The Metaphysics of Morals*, p. 89.
58   Jurgen Habermas *Between Facts and Norms* (Cambridge: Polity Press, 1996), 499.

16

A Political Constitution for the Pluralist World Society?
Jürgen Habermas

The prospects for the success of the project of a "cosmopolitan condition" are no worse today, following the invasion of Iraq in contravention of international law, than in 1945, following the catastrophe of World War II, or in 1989–90, following the collapse of the bipolar power constellation. This does not mean that the chances are good; but we should not lose a sense of proportion either. The Kantian project only found its way onto the political agenda with the League of Nations, in other words after more than two centuries; and the idea of a cosmopolitan order only acquired an institutional embodiment with the foundation of the United Nations. The UN has gained in political significance and has evolved into an important factor in global political conflicts since the early 1990s. Even the superpower found itself compelled to engage in a confrontation with the world organization when the latter refused to succumb to pressure to provide legitimacy for a unilateral intervention. The United Nations weathered the subsequent attempt to marginalize it so well that it was able to initiate the urgently needed reform of its core organization and subsidiary agencies.

The recommendations of a reform commission appointed by the Secretary General have been on the table since December 2004. As we shall see, the proposed reforms are the product of an intelligent analysis of mistakes. This learning process is directing the political will unmistakably toward a continuation of the Kantian project. This project expresses not only the idea of an enduring state of peace. For Kant already extended the negative concept of the absence of war and violence into one of peace as an implication of legally granted freedoms. Today, the comprehensive concept of collective security also extends to the necessary resources to ensure conditions of life under which citizens in all parts of the world can actually enjoy formally granted liberties. We can still take our cue from Kant's idea of a cosmopolitan condition provided that we construe it in sufficiently abstract terms. I will first explain why I consider the Kantian alternative between a world republic and a league of nations to be incomplete (I) and how the Kantian project can be understood under contemporary conditions (II). Then I will explain why the viability of any form of democracy, including the democratic nation-state, depends on the success of this project (III) before addressing, in conclusion, two historical trends that work in favor of the project (IV and V).

I

Hobbes interpreted the relationship between law and security in functionalist terms: the state accords the citizens, as the subjects of law, the guarantee of protection in exchange for their unconditional obedience.[1] For Kant, by contrast, the pacifying function of law remains conceptually intertwined with the function of a legal condition that the citizens recognize as legitimate in promoting freedom. For the validity of law is based not only on the external threat of sanction by the state, but also on the internal reasons for the claim that it merits recognition by its addressees. Kant no longer operates with Hobbes's empiricist concept of law. However, with the idea of a transition from state-centered international law to cosmopolitan law, Kant also sets himself apart from Rousseau.

Kant breaks with the republican conception that popular sovereignty finds expression in the external sovereignty of the state – in other words, that the democratic self-determination of the people is internally linked to the collective self-assertion of a corresponding form of life, if necessary by military means. Kant recognizes that the democratic will has its roots in the ethos of a people. But that does not necessarily imply that the capacity of a democratic constitution to bind and rationalize political power must be restricted to a specific nation-state. For the universalistic thrust of the constitutional principles of a nation-state points beyond the limits of national traditions which are no doubt also reflected in the local features of a particular constitutional order.

These two operations – first, the linking of the idea of peace with a condition of legally guaranteed freedoms and, second, the separation between democratic self-determination in the domestic sphere and aggressive self-assertion toward other nations – clear the way for Kant to project the *"bürgerliche Verfassung"* (i.e. the type of constitution which had recently emerged from the American and French revolutions) from the national onto the global level. This marks the birth of the idea of a constitutionalization of international law. The extraordinary thing about this farsighted conceptual innovation was the implication that international law as a law of states would be transformed into cosmopolitan law as a law of individuals. For individuals would no longer enjoy the status of legal subjects merely as citizens of a nation-state, but also as members of a politically constituted world society.

However, Kant could construe the constitutionalization of international law exclusively as a transformation of international into intrastate relations. To the very end, he advocated the idea of a world republic, even though he proposed the "surrogate" of a league of nations [*Völkerbund*] as a first stage toward realizing such a commonwealth of nations [*Völkerstaat*]. This weak conception of a voluntary association of states that are willing to coexist peacefully while nevertheless retaining their sovereignty seemed to recommend itself as a transitional stage en route to a world republic. Many have wondered why he placed his hopes in such a conceptually flawed structure. From the vantage point of the legal and political networks of a pluralist, highly interdependent, yet functionally differentiated global society, it is easy to identify with the fortuitous hindsight of later generations the conceptual barriers that prevented Kant from overcoming this sterile alternative. Three reasons may have prevented him from conceiving the telos of the constitutionalization of international law, the "cosmopolitan condition," in sufficiently abstract terms to avoid assimilating it to the problematic model of a world republic and to prevent it from being dismissed as utopian.

The centralist French republic that served Kant as a model for a democratic constitutional state suggested that the sovereignty of the people is indivisible. In a multilevel federalist system, however, the democratic will of the people already branches out at its very source into parallel channels of legitimation through elections to local, state, or federal parliaments. The model of the United States (and the debate conducted in the "Federalist Papers") provides early testimony concerning this concept of "divided sovereignty." The image of a federalist world republic might have allayed Kant's fear that the normalizing pressure exerted by the "soulless despotism" of a global "state of nations" would rob particular nations of their cultural specificity and identity. This fear may explain his search for a "surrogate", though not yet why he felt compelled to conceptualize a cosmopolitan condition in the shape of an all-encompassing state in the first place.

The reason for this may have been another conceptual bottleneck, one which we have been able to overcome only recently as a result of the increasingly dense network of international organizations. Republicanism of the French variety explains the rationalizing effect of the subjection of political power to law in terms of a constitutive popular will that reconfigures political authority from the ground up. Rousseau's social contract implies that the state and the constitution are one because both arise *uno actu*, i.e. coevally, from the will of the people. Standing in this tradition, Kant neglected a different, competing constitutional tradition that rejects any such conceptual linkage of state and constitution. In the liberal tradition, the constitution does not have the function of constituting *authority* but only that of constraining *power*. The early modern assemblies of the estates already embodied the idea of a system of mutual checks and balances on the "ruling powers" (namely, on the aristocracy, the clergy, and the towns over against the monarch). Liberalism develops this idea further in the modern sense of the constitutional division of powers.

A political constitution primarily geared to setting limits to power founds a "rule of law" that can normatively shape existing power relations, regardless of their democratic origins, and direct the exercise of political power into legal channels. By rejecting the identity of the rulers with the ruled, a constitution of this type ensures the conceptual independence of three elements, namely, the constitution, the powers of the state, and citizenship.[2] Thus, here there is no fundamental conceptual obstacle to separating the elements that are so tightly intermeshed in the democratic state. In fact, the cooperation between different nations in multilateral networks or in transnational negotiation systems has in many cases produced the legal forms of a constitution of international organizations without state characteristics which dispense with the familiar forms of legitimation through the will of an organized citizenry. Such constitutions regulate the functional interplay among nation-states; even comprehensive global policy networks lack the "meta-competence" characteristic of states, namely, the power to define and extend their own competences.

Thus the liberal type of constitution that limits the power of the state without constituting it also provides a conceptual model for a constitutionalization of international law in the form of a politically constituted world society without a world government. With the transition from state-centered international law to a cosmopolitan legal order, nation-states will be restricted in their scope of action without being robbed of their status as subjects of a global legal order by the individual world citizens, who now acquire the additional status of subjects of cosmopolitan law. Rather, republican states can remain subjects of a world constitution without a world government alongside individual world citizens. That said, the fusion of the types of constitution that have hitherto emerged from competing legal traditions gives rise to the problem of how political decision-making above the national level can be fed back into national channels of legitimation.[3]

[. . .]

With an eye to the present-day structures, we can outline a conceptual alternative to the cosmopolitan republic (and its contemporary variants) on this basis.[4] This calls for three further adjustments within the conceptual apparatus of political theory: (a) the concept of national sovereignty must be adapted to the new forms of governance beyond the nation-state; (b) we must revise the conceptual linkage between the state's monopoly on force and compulsory law in favor of the idea that supranational law is backed up by the sanctioning powers that remain the preserve of nation-states; and (c) we must identify the mechanism that explains how nations can change their self-understanding.

(a) According to the tradition of liberal nationalism, the core norms of international law, i.e. the principle of state sovereignty and the prohibition on intervention in domestic affairs, follow from the principle of popular sovereignty. The competence of the state to assert itself toward the outside is the reflection of the democratic self-determination of the citizens within the state.[5] The state must have the right and the ability to uphold the identity and the form of life supported by the democratic community and to protect itself against other nations, if necessary with military force. Internal self-determination requires protection against the threat of foreign domination. However, this conception encounters difficulties in a highly interdependent global society. If even a superpower can no longer guarantee the security and welfare of its own population without the help of other states, then "sovereignty" is losing its classical meaning.[6]

Whereas internal state sovereignty is no longer restricted to simply maintaining law and order but also includes the effective protection of the civil rights of citizens, "external sovereignty" today calls for the ability to cooperate with partners as much as the capacity to defend oneself against external enemies. Fulfilling the social contract also presupposes that the sovereign state is willing and able to participate equally in collective efforts to address problems that arise at the global and regional levels and can only be solved within the framework of international or supranational organizations.[7] This presupposes both the renunciation of the right to go to war and the recognition of the duty of the international community to protect the population of a criminal or failing state against its own government or what is left of it.

(b) Interestingly enough, the international community can transfer this right to impose sanctions and to intervene to a world organization without at the same time equipping the latter with a global monopoly on force. Contrary to the conventional understanding of compulsory state law, a gap is opening up between supranational legislative authority and national agencies that can draw on legitimate means of force to implement that law. The individual states retain their monopoly on force, although as members of the United Nations they formally cede the right to decide on when military force should be used to the Security Council (except in the case of justified self-defense). In line with the pattern of behavior that has evolved within collective security systems, the effectiveness of a Security Council resolution to intervene in the affairs of a nation-state is ensured by a sufficient number of powerful members making their forces available for executing consensually agreed-upon missions. The European Union is a convincing example of how higher-order legal norms can have binding force, even though they are only backed in this circular way by formally subordinate member states. The means of force available to impose the sanctions called for by laws decided in Brussels and Luxembourg remain in the hands of the individual states, which then "implement" this law without resistance.

(c) This example also illustrates the hypothesis concerning the empirical effectiveness of norms without which it would be difficult to render the Kantian project of promoting a cosmopolitan condition empirically plausible. The constitutional norms and legal constructs introduced by political elites in supranational arenas exercise anticipatory effects in the sense of a *self-fulfilling prophecy*. This kind of lawmaking anticipates the change in consciousness that it provokes among the addressees only in the course of its gradual implementation. The accompanying political discourses provide the medium in which the spirit of legal regulations, whose letter is initially recognized only in a declamatory manner, can be gradually internalized. This holds for the states and their citizens alike. How national contracting parties understand their role can shift in the course of such a constructive, self-referential, and circular learning process. As collective actors used to making autonomous decisions become accustomed to forms of cooperation that are initially agreed upon in a sovereign manner, their self-understanding is transformed into the consciousness of members of international organizations with rights and duties. In this way, even sovereign states can learn to subordinate national interests to the obligations they have assumed as members of the international community or as players in trans-national networks.

II

In the light of these preliminary clarifications, I would now like to flesh out the idea of a cosmopolitan condition in a form that remains in touch with existing realities while at the same time pointing beyond them. On my understanding, the constitution-alized world society, which I have outlined elsewhere,[8] is a multilevel system that can make possible a global domestic politics that has hitherto been lacking, especially in the fields of global economic and environmental policies, even without a world government. Whereas the state-centered system of international law recognized only one type of player – the nation-states – and two playing fields – domestic and foreign policy or internal affairs and international relations – the new structure of a constituted cosmopolitan society is characterized by *three arenas* and *three kinds of collective actors*.

The *supranational arena* is dominated by a single actor. The international community assumes institutional form in a *world organization* that has the ability to act in carefully circumscribed policy fields without itself taking on the character of a state. The United Nations lacks the authority to define or expand its own powers at will. Its authority extends to the effective, and above all non-selective, fulfillment of two functions, namely, securing peace and human rights on a global scale, and is restricted to these two fundamental, but clearly circumscribed, functions. Hence, the pending reform of the United Nations must focus not only on strengthening core institutions but also on detaching them from the extensive web of special UN organizations, in particular those networked with independent international organizations.[9]

Of course, opinion- and will-formation within the world organization should be connected back to the circuits of communication within national parliaments and should be subject to more effective monitoring by NGOs and other representatives of a mobilized world public. Yet even an appropriately reformed world organization would remain composed of nation-states in the first instance and not of world citizens. In this respect, it resembles more a league of nations [*Völkerbund*] than Kant's idea of a universal state of nations [*Völkerstaat*]. For there cannot be a world parliament, however modest, without a world republic. The collective actors would not disappear *without a trace* into the new order, which they must first establish with the only instrument available to them, namely, a treaty under international law. The world organization must be permanently buttressed by power centers organized at the state level if it is to constitute the main pillar of a legal pacifism backed up by power. Alongside individuals, states remain subjects of an international law transformed into a cosmopolitan human rights regime that is capable of protecting individual citizens, if necessary even against their own governments.

As members of the international community, nation-states must retain a privileged status also with a view to the far-reaching agenda that the United Nations has recently announced under the imposing title "Millennium Development Goals." The legal guarantees spelled out in the UN's human rights compacts are no longer limited to basic liberal and political rights but include the "empowering" material conditions that would first enable the world's most vulnerable populations to make use of the rights accorded there *in abstracto*.[10] The worldwide political efforts demanded by such an agenda overtax the capacities and political will of the international community. At present we can observe this in the arena of increasingly numerous and interconnected *transnational* networks and organizations designed to cope with the growing demand for coordination of a world society that is becoming more complex.[11] However, regulation in the form of the "coordination" of governmental and nongovernmental actors is only sufficient to address a particular category of cross-border problems.

The largely institutionalized procedures of information exchange, consultation, control, and agreement are sufficient for handling "technical" issues in a broader sense (such as the standardization of measures, the regulation of telecommunications, disaster prevention, containing epidemics, or combating organized crime). Since the devil is always in the details, these problems also call for a balancing of conflicting interests. However, they differ from genuinely "political" issues that impinge on entrenched interests which are deeply rooted in the structures of national societies, such as, for example, questions of global energy and of environmental, financial, and economic policy, all of which involve issues of equitable distribution. These problems of a future world domestic policy call for regulation and positive integration, for which at present both the institutional framework and actors are lacking. The existing political networks are functionally differentiated, multilateral, and at times even inclusive international organizations in which government representatives generally bear the responsibility and have the final word, irrespective of who else is granted admission. At any rate, they do not provide a forum for legislative competences and corresponding processes of political will-formation. Even if such a framework were to be established, collective actors capable of implementing such decisions would still be lacking. What I have in mind are *regional or continental regimes* equipped with a sufficiently representative mandate to negotiate for whole continents and to wield the necessary powers of implementation for large territories.

Politics cannot intentionally meet the spontaneous need for regulation of a systemically integrated, quasi-natural global economy and society until such time as the intermediate arena is populated by a manageable number of global players. The latter must be strong enough to form shifting coalitions, to produce a flexible system of checks and balances, and to negotiate and implement binding compromises – above all on issues concerning the structure and boundary conditions of the global ecological and economic systems. In this way, international relations as we know them would continue to exist in the transnational arena in a modified form – modified for the simple reason that under an effective UN security regime even the most powerful global players would be denied recourse to war as a legitimate means of resolving conflicts. The problem that, with the exception of the United States, there are at present no viable actors at the intermediate or transnational level directs our attention to the *third level*, namely, the lower level of the nation-states.

This level began to emerge on a global scale only during the process of decolonization. An inclusive international community of nation-states arose only in the latter half of the twentieth century, during which time the number of UN member states increased from fifty-one to 192. Thus these nation-states are a comparatively recent political formation. Although, as the "original" actors, they remain the most powerful actors with the greatest scope for action, the nation-states are now coming under pressure. The growing interdependencies of the global economy and the cross-border risks of a world society are overtaxing their territorial range of operation and their chains of legitimation. Globalized networks in all dimensions have long since made nonsense of the normative assumption in democratic theory of a congruence between those responsible for political decision-making and those affected by political decisions.[12]

Thus on all continents individual nation-states find themselves compelled to establish regional alliances, or at any rate closer forms of cooperation (APEC, ASEAN, NAFTA, AU, ECOWAS, OAS, etc.). However, these regional alliances represent weak beginnings. The nation-states need to enter into closer alliances than forms of intergovernmental cooperation if they are to assume the role of collective pillars of a global domestic politics at the transnational level. Only in this way can they acquire the scope for action of global players and confer the necessary democratic legitimacy on the outcomes of transnational political accords.

[. . .]

Thus far I have not mentioned the cultural pluralism that could pose problems for a constitutionalized world society at all three levels. The current worldwide political instrumentalization of the major religions also increases tensions at the international level. Within a cosmopolitan order, this perceived clash of civilizations would above all impede the transnational negotiation systems. However, the fact that the nation-states would have to learn to change both their behavior and their self-image within the multilevel system outlined would make it easier to cope with such conflicts.

One of the required learning processes involves internalizing the norms of the world organization and acquiring the ability to pursue one's own interests by prudently merging into transnational networks. Even without formally relinquishing their monopoly on force, the sovereign states must come to see themselves in a constitutionalized world society as peaceful members of the international community and at the same time as capable players in international organizations. The other learning process relates to overcoming a stubborn mindset that is historically closely interconnected with the formation of the nation-state. Nationalism provided the basis for what is by any standards a highly abstract form of civic solidarity. This national consciousness must now be raised to an even higher level of abstraction in the process of integrating nation-states into continental regimes. A mobilization of the masses through religious, ethnic, or nationalist agitation will gradually become less likely the more the expectations of tolerance inherent in a liberal civic ethos permeate political culture also at the national level.

[. . .] Before I discuss two historical trends that may work in favor of the revised Kantian project, I would like to draw attention to the possible benefits and risks of the success or failure of this project. The issue is whether we must finally bid farewell to the very idea of constitutional democracy or whether the normative core of the vanishing world of democratic nation-states can be recovered within the postnational constellation.

III

Modern conceptions of the constitution refer explicitly to the relationship between citizens and the state. But in addition they also implicitly prefigure a comprehensive legal order encompassing the state and civil society (in the Hegelian and Marxist senses)[13] – in other words, the totality comprised of administrative state, capitalist economy, and civil society. The economy comes into play for the simple reason that the modern, tax-based state depends on market transactions regulated by civil law. In social contract theories, civil society is thematized as the network of relations among the citizens – whether, following the liberal tradition, as the relations between private utility maximizers or, following the republican tradition, as relations of solidarity between citizens.

To be sure, the legal construction of a community of free and equal citizens is the focus of any constitution. The topics of "security", "law," and "freedom" place the emphasis on the self-assertion of the political community toward the outside world, on the one hand, and on the rights that free and equal persons accord each other as members of a voluntary and self-administering association, on the other. The constitution lays down how organized force within the state is transformed into legitimate power. However, this problem of "law and freedom" cannot be solved without implicitly defining the roles that the economy, as the basic functional system, and civil society, as the arena in which public opinion and political will are formed, are supposed to play in relation to the administrative power of the state.

With the expansion of the catalogue of tasks to be performed by the state beyond the classical functions of maintaining law and order, this implicit, comprehensive character of the constitutional order becomes especially apparent. Social injustice must be overcome in a capitalist society, collective dangers must be averted in a risk society, and the equal rights of members of different religions, cultures, and ethnicities must be guaranteed in a pluralist society. In the class differences produced by capitalism, in the risks produced by science and technology, and in the tensions intrinsic to cultural pluralism, the state encounters problems that do not immediately respond to the instruments of politics and law, i.e. the means of coercion available to the state. But the state cannot simply shirk its general political responsibility either, because it depends on the systemic integration promoted by private functional systems – in the first instance, on the economy – and on the social integration fostered by civil society. The state, in its role as provider of welfare, must cope with the internal logic of functional systems and the cultural dynamics of civil society. The corporatist mode of negotiation is an indicator of this new style of state as a moderator which nevertheless continues to take its orientation from the constitution or from an interpretation of the constitution suitably adapted to the times.

The triple reference of the constitution to the state, the economy, and civil society can be explained in sociological terms by the fact that all modern societies are integrated through exactly three media, "power," "money," and "communication" (or "mutual understanding"). In functionally differentiated societies, social relations come about either through "organization," the "market," or consensus-formation (i.e. communicative actions, values, and norms). Corresponding types of social interaction assume concrete form in the bureaucratic state, the capitalist economy, and civil society (as a separate sphere differentiated from both). The political constitution is geared to shaping each of these systems by means of the medium of law and to harmonizing them so that they can fulfill their functions as measured by a presumed "common good." The constitutional design is supposed to prevent system-specific pathologies in virtue of the structuring effects of the legal system as a whole, thereby contributing to maximizing the common good.

In this way, the state is supposed to employ political power to implement law and guarantee freedom without resorting to repressive, patronizing, or normalizing force. The economy is supposed to promote productivity and affluence without violating the standards of distributive justice (by ensuring that as many people as possible are better off and nobody suffers disadvantage); and civil society is supposed to foster solidarity among independent citizens without resorting to collectivist integration or fragmentation or provoking ideological polarization. The postulated "commonweal" is jeopardized not only by "failures of the state" (legal uncertainty and repression) but likewise by "failures of the market" and by a lack of solidarity and mutual recognition among citizens. The indeterminate character of the essentially contested common good[14] results especially from the difficulty in striking a balance between these interdependent variables.

Even if the state discharges its proper tasks of maintaining security and freedom, it cannot preserve the necessary level of legitimacy in the long run unless a functioning economy fulfills the preconditions for an acceptable pattern of distribution of social rewards and unless an active civil society fosters a sufficient orientation to the common good among citizens. The converse also holds. For this reason, the constitution burdens the democratic state with the paradoxical responsibility of satisfying the economic and cultural preconditions for maintaining the society as a whole. Although the state can try to meet these demanding requirements and bring them under political control with the instruments at its disposal, such as legal regulations and political pressures, it cannot provide legal guarantees of success. Unemployment and social segmentation cannot be eliminated by prohibitions or administrative decrees any more than can a deterioration in social solidarity.

This asymmetry between the image of society inscribed in the constitution and the limited scope of the political tools available to the state was not harmful as long as the economy coincided with the nation-state and civic solidarity among a comparatively homogeneous population was sustained by a corresponding national consciousness. As long as the system of free trade with fixed exchange rates established with the 1945 Bretton Woods agreements existed, the opening of national borders to free trade did not deny nation-states a certain degree of control over economies that remained embedded in their territories. Under such conditions, governments retained a considerable scope for political regulation and intervention, one which moreover was perceived as sufficient. They could in any case be relied upon to master publicly relevant social processes by political means.

This presupposition that problems are "politically manageable" is the key to the constitutional construction of a society that has the ability to exert a formative influence upon itself through state agencies in accordance with the will of its citizens. Indeed, the democratic substance of a constitution that makes the citizens the authors of the laws to which they are at the same time subject as addressees stands or falls with this presupposition. The political autonomy of citizens acquires concrete content only to the extent that a society is capable of influencing itself by political means. This is the crucial point for the present discussion. However, the expansion of the domains of political responsibility and the new forms of corporatism have placed the channels of legitimation of the nation-state under intolerable strain.[15] And with the switch-over to a neoliberal economic regime these channels have definitively reached breaking point.

We are currently witnessing an ever more extensive privatization of public services that were hitherto provided by the nation-state for good reasons. The connection of these services to the dictates of the constitution is being loosened by their transfer to private firms. This becomes all the more risky the further privatization advances into the core areas of sovereignty, such as public security, the military, the penal system, or the energy supply. Since the globalization of the economy has developed a dynamic of its own, however, ever more processes that are vital for maintaining the rule of law, freedom, distributive justice, and equal rights are escaping political supervision and control. At any rate, the asymmetry between the responsibilities accorded the democratic state and its actual scope of action is becoming increasingly pronounced.[16]

With the deregulation of markets and the globalization of flows of traffic and information in many further dimensions, a need for regulation arises that is being absorbed and processed by transnational networks and organizations. Their decisions, even when national officials collaborate in making them, make deep inroads into the public life of nation-states without being connected with processes of legitimation at the national level. Michael Zurn has described the impact of this development as follows:

> The democratic decision-making processes within nation-states are thus losing their anchorage. They are superseded by organizations and actors who indeed are mostly accountable to their national governments one way or another, but at the same time are quite remote and inaccessible for the nationally enclosed addressees of the regulations in question. Given the extent of the intrusion of these new international institutions into the affairs of national societies, the notion of "delegated, and therefore controlled authority" in the principal and agent sense no longer holds.

If this description is accurate, then the postnational constellation confronts us with an uncomfortable alternative: either we must abandon the demanding idea of the constitution as a self-administering association of free and equal citizens and resign ourselves to a sociologically disillusioned interpretation of constitutional democracies that have been reduced to empty facades; or we must detach the fading idea of a democratic constitution from its roots in the nation-state and revive it in the postnational guise of a constitutionalized world society. Needless to say, a philosophical thought experiment describing how the normative substance of the idea can be *conceptually* preserved in a cosmopolitan society without a world government does not go far enough. The idea must also find *empirical* support in the real world.

The nation-states have long since become entangled in the interdependencies of a complex world society. The latter's subsystems effortlessly permeate national borders – with accelerated information and communication flows, worldwide movements of capital, networks of trade and production, technology transfers, mass tourism, labor migration, scientific communication, etc. This global society is also integrated through the same media of power, money, and consensus as the nation-states. Why should a constitution, which successfully drew upon these sources of integration at the national level by shaping them through politics and law, be doomed to failure at the supranational and transnational levels? There are no necessary socio-ontological reasons why solidarity between citizens and the regulatory capacity of the constitution should stop at national borders. As mentioned, however, it is not enough to show through a philosophical thought experiment how the normative content of the idea of the constitution of a nation-state can be *conceptually* translated into that of the cosmopolitan order of a constitutionalized world society.

In a multilevel global system, the classical function of the state as the guarantor of security, law, and freedom would be transferred to a *supranational* world organization specialized in securing peace and implementing human rights worldwide. However, it would not shoulder the immense burden of a global domestic policy designed to overcome the extreme disparities in wealth within the stratified world society, reverse ecological imbalances, and avert collective threats, on the one hand, while endeavoring to promote an intercultural discourse on, and recognition of, the equal rights of the major world civilizations, on the other. These problems differ in kind from violations of international peace and human rights. They call for a different kind of treatment within the context of *transnational* negotiation systems. They cannot be solved directly by bringing power and law to bear against unwilling or incapable nation-states. They impinge upon the intrinsic logic of functional systems that extend across national borders and the intrinsic meaning of cultures and world religions. Politics must engage with these issues in a spirit of hermeneutic open-mindedness through the prudent balancing of interests and intelligent regulation.

In searching for actual trends that meet the idea of a cosmopolitan constitution halfway, the distinction between the supranational and the transnational levels points, on the one hand, to the pending reform of the United Nations (IV) and, on the other, to the dynamics triggered by an ever clearer awareness of the lack of legitimacy of current forms of global governance (V).

IV

In his reflections on the gap between the is and the ought, John Rawls distinguished between "ideal" and "real" theory. This methodological distinction did not go far enough in detranscendentalizing the Kantian distinction between the world of noumena and the world of phenomena. Ideas find their way into social reality through the unavoidable *idealizing presuppositions of everyday practices* and in this way inconspicuously acquire the status of stubborn social facts. For example, citizens participate in elections because they assume from their perspective as participants that their vote counts, irrespective of what political scientists report from an observer perspective concerning the effects of electoral geography and voting procedures. Likewise, litigants do not stop going to court with the expectation that the judge will treat their case impartially and reach the correct decision, irrespective of what law professors or judges have to say about the indeterminate character of law. However, ideas produce effects only through the idealizing presuppositions of established or institutionalized practices. Only when the practices have acquired a foothold in legal institutions, for example, must the fictions or presuppositions on which participants operate be taken seriously as facts.

The United Nations is such an institution. Over the decades, normatively loaded practices and procedures have emerged within the framework of this institution of international law. I would like to examine how realistic the Kantian project is by tracing a reform of this world organization already in progress. With this we leave the terrain of a theory constructed primarily with normative arguments and shift to the constructive interpretation of a domain of enacted law [positiven Rechts] undergoing rapid development. The validity of international law has in the meantime become assimilated to the mode of validity of national law, in the process shedding its status as *soft law*. At the transnational level, "we are dealing with a novel combination of national and supranational law, of private contracts and public law"; at the supranational level "we are in addition witnessing the emergence of a global constitutional law."[18] The controversy between the dualistic conception of the relation between national and international law, on the one hand, and the monistic doctrine of the fusion of national and international law in the global legal system, on the other, has thereby been rendered moot.[19]

At any rate, many experts construe the accelerated development of international law as a process of "constitutionalization" promoted by the international community with the goal of strengthening the legal position of the individual legal subject, who is gradually acquiring the status of a subject of international law and a cosmopolitan citizen.[20] The High-Level Panel put in place by Kofi Annan[21] also starts quite naturally from the premise that the overdue reform of the world organization must pursue the line already laid down by the UN Charter with four far-reaching innovations:

(a) (in common with Kant) the Charter explicitly links the objective of securing international peace to the global implementation of human rights;
(b) the Charter backs up the prohibition on violence with the threat of sanctions, including interventions to enforce peace (and hence creates the prospect of a penalization of war as a mechanism for solving interstate conflicts);
(c) the Charter relativizes the sovereignty of the individual member states to the goal of international peace and collective security; and
(d) by admitting all nations into an inclusive world organization, the Charter creates a key condition for the precedence and universal validity of international and UN law.

(a) In contrast to the League of Nations, the UN Charter links the objective of world peace (in Article 1.1 and Article 2.4) with the "respect for human rights and for fundamental freedoms for all without distinction as to race, sex, language, or religion" (Article 1.3). This obligation to promote the worldwide validity of constitutional principles hitherto guaranteed only within nation-states has increasingly shaped the agenda of the Security Council and has led in recent decades to a progressively broader interpretation of what constitutes a breach of peace, an act of aggression, and a threat to international security. The High-Level Panel infers from this development that it is necessary to extend the "new security consensus" to include the indivisible triad of protection against basic dangers, promotion of individual liberties and rights of participation, and emancipation from unworthy and undignified living conditions. It extends the sources of danger beyond classical interstate conflicts to include not only civil war and internal conflicts, international terrorism, the possession of weapons of mass destruction, and transnational organized crime; with an eye to the developing countries, it expands this catalogue of sources of danger to cover the mass deprivation of the population through poverty and disease, social marginalization, and environmental degradation.

[. . .]

(b) The core of the UN Charter comprises the general prohibition on the use of force in connection with the authorization of the Security Council to impose the appropriate sanctions in the case of violations. With the exception of coercive measures imposed by the UN itself, the general prohibition on the use of force is only qualified by a narrowly defined right of self-defense in the case of a clearly identifiable and immediate threat of attack. The High-Level Panel reaffirms the Security Council's prerogative to object to unilateral actions of major powers that arrogate a right of preventive first strikes. At the same time, it insists on the Security Council's right to intervene militarily: "Collectively authorized use of force may not be the rule today, but it is no longer an exception" (TCC, p. 32). It emphasizes this also with regard to the now established practice of intervention in domestic conflicts: "We endorse the emerging norm that there is a collective international responsibility to protect, exercisable by the Security Council authorizing military intervention as a last resort, in the event of genocide and other large-scale killing, ethnic cleansing or serious violations of international humanitarian law which sovereign Governments have proved powerless or unwilling to prevent" (TCC, p. 66).

Based on a thorough analysis of past errors and shortcomings, the Panel proceeds to criticize the implausible selectivity of perception and the shamefully unequal treatment of relevantly similar cases (TCC, pp. 34, 65–6).[22] The report makes proposals

- for a more exact specification of possible sanctions and their monitoring;
- for a more appropriate differentiation between peacekeeping and peace-enforcing missions;
- for the correct weighting of the constructive tasks of post-conflict peace-building, which the UN must not shirk from taking on following a military intervention; and, most importantly,
- for strict conditions governing the legitimate use of force (seriousness of threat, proper purpose, last resort, proportional means, balance of consequences).

However, the High-Level Panel does not address the pressing question concerning what consequences follow for humanitarian international law from the transformation of military force into a global police force. When armed forces carry out a mission authorized by the Security Council, the focus is no longer on limiting military violence and the so-called collateral damage of warfare within civilized bounds. Once war has been overcome, the key issue becomes that of obligating a global *police force* to act on behalf of the basic rights of cosmopolitan citizens who need protection against their own criminal governments or other violent gangs operating within states.

(c) If we read the UN Charter literally, then there is a contradiction between Article 2.7, which appears to affirm the classical prohibition on intervention in the internal affairs of any sovereign state, and Chapter VII, which accords the Security Council the right of intervention. In practice, this inconsistency has often paralyzed the work of the Security Council, especially in cases of humanitarian disasters that have unfolded behind the shield of the sovereignty of a criminal or complicit regime.[23] However, the international community violates its legal obligation to protect human rights world-wide if it simply sits back and watches mass murders and mass rapes, ethnic cleansing and expulsions, or a policy of deliberately exposing people to starvation and disease, without intervening (TCC, pp. 65–6). The High-Level Panel recalls that the United Nations was not intended to be a utopian project. Rather, the establishment of the Security Council was intended to equip the principles with adequate political power and to subordinate international relations to compulsory legal regulations (TCC, p. 13).

Given the fact that the monopoly on the means of legitimate violence continues to be dispersed among so many states, this can only work if the Security Council acquires enough authority to borrow the relevant means of sanction required to enforce higher-level UN law from cooperating members in *all* cases. The proposals on reforming the Security Council as regards its composition, its voting procedures, and the provision of resources thus serve to strengthen the willingness of powerful members to cooperate and to engage a superpower that understandably has the greatest difficulty in changing its self-image from that of an autonomous player to that of one player among others.

If necessary, UN law must be implemented against opposed or ineffectual states by means of the combined capacities of the other member states, each of which still retains its monopoly on force. This is not an altogether unrealistic premise, as the example of the European Union shows; but it is certainly not yet satisfied at the supra-national level of the world organization. In this context, the High-Level Panel recommends that the Security Council should cooperate more closely with regional alliances. For neighboring armed forces bear a special responsibility when it comes to carrying out UN missions in their regions.

Assuming that member states provide the UN with the means it requires to implement higher-level law, an elegant solution to the dogmatic question of how we should understand the "sovereign equality" of states suggests itself: "In signing the Charter of the United Nations, States not only benefit from the privileges of sovereignty but also accept its responsibilities. Whatever perceptions may have prevailed when the Westphalian system first gave rise to the notion of State sovereignty, today it clearly carries with it the obligation of a State to protect the welfare of its own peoples and meet its obligations to the wider international community" (TCC, p. 17). The nation-state continues to be equipped with strong competences, but it now operates as the fallible agent of the international community. The sovereign state remains responsible for guaranteeing the human rights enshrined in constitutional basic principles within national borders; the constitutional state fulfills this function on behalf of its demo-cratically united citizenry. However, in their role as subjects of international law – as cosmopolitan citizens – these citizens have also issued the world organization a kind of indemnity that authorizes the Security Council to act on their behalf as a stand-in in cases of emergency when the primary agent, their own government, is no longer able or willing to protect their rights.

(d) Whereas the League of Nations was supposed to consist of an avant-garde of liberal nations, the United Nations, which now comprises 192 members, was designed from the outset to include all the world's nations. Alongside nations with liberal constitutions, it also includes various authoritarian, sometimes despotic or even criminal regimes, whose practices fly in the face of the wording of the UN Charter that they formally recognize and UN resolutions that they nominally support. Full inclusion thereby meets a necessary condition for the universal validity of cosmopolitan law while at the same time undermining its binding character. This consciously accepted tension between facts and norms becomes most drastic in the case of human rights violations by the major powers that enjoy veto rights and can block any Security Council resolutions directed against them. For similar reasons, the credibility of other institutions and procedures has been damaged by the use of double standards. This applies in particular to the practice of the Commission on Human Rights, which the High-Level Panel suggests should be reformed from the ground up: "Standard-setting to reinforce human rights cannot be performed by States that lack a demonstrated commitment to their promotion and protection" (TCC, p. 89).

The gap between norm and reality also works the other way round and exerts pressure to conform on authoritarian member states. The changed international perception and public stigmatization of states that violate the established standards on security and human rights have led to a materialization of the rules governing the international recognition of states. The principle of effectivity, according to which a state is recognized as sovereign if it maintains law and order within its own borders, has been largely superseded by the principle of legitimacy. The regular reports submitted by global monitoring agencies such as Human Rights Watch or Amnesty International have played a major part in stripping such "outlaw states" (John Rawls) of their legitimacy.

The desired recognition of the International Criminal Court is especially important in this context. The practice of a court that specifies what constitute violations of international law and would in future monitor the relevant Security Council resolutions would not only strengthen the binding character of supranational law vis-à-vis the sovereign claims of nations of dubious repute and in general foster the autonomy of UN institutions vis-à-vis the nation-states' monopoly over the means of legitimate violence. Such a court would also lend an authoritative voice to a diffuse global public sphere that is stirred by mass political crimes and unjust regimes.

V

This brings us to the question of the need and capacity for legitimation of political decisions in international organizations. Such organizations are founded on multilateral treaties between sovereign states. If such organizations are burdened with the tasks of "governance beyond the nation-state," the growing need for legitimacy soon outstrips the type and scope of legitimacy that international treaties can ideally enjoy in virtue of the democratic character of the signatory states. Such a discrepancy seems to exist even in the case of the world organization, which is expected to monitor international security and worldwide compliance with human rights standards.

The High-Level Panel recommends including NGOs in the consultation process for the General Assembly (TCC, p. 109), which would at least enhance the visibility of the UN and its decisions in the global public arena. Direct connections to the national parliaments in the member states might also be helpful in this regard.[24] The convention that stipulates that "foreign affairs" are the privileged domain of the executive branch becomes obsolete in any case as state sovereignty shifts from unilateral policy-making to institutionalized multilateralism. Let us not fool ourselves, however; these reforms, desirable though they may be, are not extensive enough to establish a connection between the supranational and the national levels in such a way that an uninterrupted chain of legitimation would run from the nation-states to the world organization. A gap remains.

On the other hand, we must ask whether the need for legitimacy that would arise from the future interaction of a reformed Security Council with a universally recognized ICC would require this gap to be bridged in the first place. On closer inspection, it transpires that what legitimacy requires is different at the supranational and the transnational levels. Insofar as the development of international law follows the intrinsic logic of an explication and extension of human rights and international politics increasingly conforms to this trend, the issues that the world organization faces tend to be more of a legal than a political kind. This would be even more emphatically true in a perfectly constitutionalized world society. Two reasons suggest that embedding a reformed world organization in a (for the present still under-institutionalized) global public sphere would be sufficient to confer the requisite legitimacy on decisions taken by its two central, but nonmajoritarian institutions.

Let us assume for the sake of argument that the Security Council were to deal with litigable issues of securing peace and protecting human rights in accordance with fair procedures, hence in an impartial and nonselective manner. And let us assume further that the ICC had dogmatically analyzed and defined the major crimes within its jurisdiction (presently characterized as threats to international security, acts of aggression, breaches of the peace, and crimes against humanity). Thus reformed, the world organization could count on a worldwide background consensus in a threefold sense. The agreement would be geared, first, to the political goal of a substantively expanded conception of security, second, to the legal basis of the human rights pacts and conventions of international law passed by the General Assembly and already ratified by many states (i.e. the core domain of *jus cogens*), and, third, to the procedural principles in terms of which a reformed world organization would tackle its problems. This practice can expect to gain due recognition if, as we assume, it abides by just those principles and procedures that reflect the result of long-term democratic learning processes. Confidence in the normative force of existing judicial procedures can tap into the reserve of legitimacy made available by the exemplary histories of proven democracies for the collective memory of mankind, as it were.

Of course, these assumed agreements within the background global public sphere do not yet explain why we may accord the latter a critical function. [. . .] Decisions taken at the supranational level concerning war and peace and justice and injustice do indeed attract the attention and critical responses of a global public – just think of the interventions in Vietnam, Kosovo, and Iraq, and the cases of Pinochet, Milošević, and Saddam. The dispersed society of world citizens becomes mobilized on an *ad hoc* basis through spontaneous responses to events and decisions of such import. Shared moral indignation extends across the gulfs separating different cultures, forms of life, and religions as a response to egregious human rights violations and manifest acts of aggression. Such shared reactions, including those spawned by sympathy for the victims of humanitarian and natural disasters, gradually produce traces of cosmopolitan solidarity.

The negative duties of a universalistic morality of justice – the duty not to commit crimes against humanity or to launch wars of aggression – have roots in all cultures and luckily correspond to the yardsticks used by the institutions of the world organization to justify their decisions. This is too narrow a basis, however, for regulations negotiated at the transnational level that go beyond the classical tasks of promoting security, law, and freedom. Such regulations impinge upon issues of redistribution familiar from the national arena where the corresponding policies call for the kind of legitimation that can only be provided, albeit poorly, through proper democratic channels. But once we bid farewell to the dream of a world republic, this channel is blocked at the transnational level. Thus a deficit in legitimation arises that is increasingly recognized as a problem.[25]

In conclusion, I would like to mention three responses to the legitimation problem produced by the more interesting among the new forms of governance beyond the nation-state. Over and above offering a correct description of the problem, the United Nations does not do much more than issue helpless appeals (a). For neoliberal and legal pluralist apologists of the status quo, the whole problem dwindles in importance because legal pluralism and the conception of a world society under private law deflate the supposedly misleading claims for legitimation. But the appeal to the legitimizing force of nonmajoritarian institutions does not go far enough (b). Even if we assume that the economic theory underlying the neoliberal neutralization of the problem of legitimacy is correct, the policy switch from political regulation to economic self-regulation poses a disturbing question: Can we take responsibility for promoting the worldwide political self-limitation of the leeway for possible political interventions? (c)

(a) The expansion of the concept of international security makes it unthinkable for the United Nations to restrict itself to the central tasks of peacekeeping and human rights policy. The Economic and Social Council (ESC) was originally intended to ensure the linkage between these policies and the onerous tasks of global development. But the UN quickly ran up against its limits in these areas. An international economic regime was established under the hegemony of the United States outside of the UN framework. This experience is reflected in the following sober statement: "decision-making on international economic matters, particularly in the areas of finance and trade, has long left the United Nations and no amount of institutional reform will bring it back" (TCC, p. 86). The institutional design of the United Nations offers a simple explanation for this. Assuming the sovereign equality of all members, the UN is geared more to normatively regulated consensus-formation than to political struggles over conflicts of interests, and hence it is not suited to the constructive tasks of a global domestic politics.

On the other hand, the Global Economic Multilaterals (GEMs) – first and foremost, the World Trade Organization (WTO), the World Bank (WB), and the International Monetary Fund (IMF) – are nowhere near tackling the collection of tasks emerging for the first time under the banner of the "new security consensus." This is the context of the High-Level Panel's observation concerning the "sectoral fragmentation" in the way international organizations function and cooperate. The self-referentially closed circuit of communication between ministries of finance and international monetary institutions, between ministries for international development and international development programs, and between ministries of the environment and international environmental agencies hinders even an appropriate perception of the problems:

> International institutions and States have not organized themselves to address the problems of development in a coherent, integrated way, and instead continue to treat poverty, infectious disease and environmental degradation as stand-alone threats . . . To tackle the problems of sustainable development, countries must negotiate across different sectors and issues, including foreign aid, technology, trade, financial stability and development policy. Such packages are difficult to negotiate and require high-level attention and leadership from those countries that have the largest economic impacts (TCC, p. 26).

The call for an institution in which not only technocrats and ministerial delegates with specialized expert knowledge but also responsible representatives of governments with global authority or councils of ministers meet to address the problems in context-sensitive ways, and resolve them within a broader perspective, can be understood as an implicit answer to the legal pluralist defense of a "disaggregated world order." However, the informal meetings of heads of state in the style of the G-8, or the formation of *ad hoc* coalitions such as the G-20 and G-77, can hardly be regarded as convincing starting points for constructing an enduring global domestic politics. With the exception of the United States and China (and perhaps also of Russia), today's nation-states are ill-suited for the role of global players. They would have to achieve the aggregate scale of continental or subcontinental regimes, without thereby incurring substantial democratic deficits.

(b) The counterproposal to this vision of a global domestic politics has the advantage of reinforcing the existing structure of global policy networks. From the viewpoint of legal pluralism, the functional requirements of a differentiated world society are giving rise to transnational networks that intensify communication between the expanding functional systems that were hitherto national in scope. The networked flows of information foster the spontaneous production of legal norms and promote coordination and benchmarking, the stimulation and regulation of competition, and the balancing and mutual prompting of learning processes. Beyond the nation-state, vertical, power-based dependencies are receding behind horizontal interactions and functional interconnections. Anne-Marie Slaughter links this analysis with the thesis of the disaggregation of state sovereignty.[26]

From this perspective, the functionally specified exchange relations acquire structural precedence over territorially bound power relations to the extent that the transnational networks achieve a certain degree of independence, and thus act back upon the national governments from which they originated. The centrifugal forces of transnational networks drain the sovereignty from the member states and disaggregate their centralized hierarchies. State sovereignty disintegrates into the sum of the various functionally autonomous subsidiary authorities. The state loses the competence to define its own competencies and to operate on the domestic and international stages as an actor with a single voice. This image of the disaggregation of state sovereignty also illuminates the increasing uncoupling of regulatory decisions that intervene in nation-states from above or outside from popular sovereignty as organized within the nation-state. Although the competences and decisions transferred to the GEMs remain formally within the responsibility of the governments concerned, the agreements reached in those remote organizations are *de facto* no longer exposed to public criticism, deliberation, and political reaction by affected citizens in their respective national arenas.[27] On the other hand, no substitute for this growing deficit of legitimacy at the national level is emerging beyond the nation-state either.[28]

Anne-Marie Slaughter responds to the issue of the legitimation deficit at the transnational level with a proposal that exposes and illuminates the problem without solving it: "The members of government networks [must] . . . first . . . be accountable to their domestic constituents for their transgovernmental activities to the same extent that they are accountable for their domestic activities. Second, as participants in structures of global governance, they must have a basic operating code that takes account of the rights and interests of all peoples."[29] But to whom are the delegates of the executive branch accountable when they negotiate binding multilateral regulations that their domestic electorate would not accept? And who decides what is in the interest of all of the peoples affected as long as negotiating power in transnational settings is as unequal as the military power and economic weight of the participating countries in the real world?

Another line of defense is more promising, namely, the neoliberal strategy of playing down supposedly *excessive* demands for legitimacy. The legitimizing power of democratically elected governments who send their officials as delegates to international organizations is held to be quite sufficient for international agreements, even if there is no public discussion of the relevant issue in the countries in question. On this reading, the unequal distribution of voting power and influence within the GEMs is not a serious problem, because democratic representation is simply the wrong model. What is lacking in terms of accountability can be offset (over and above increased transparency of negotiations, better information for those affected, and if necessary the involvement of NGOs) especially by the self-legitimizing force of the rationality of experts. Here the professionalism of nonmajoritarian institutions serves as a model: "Contemporary democracies have assigned a large and growing role to nonmajoritarian institutions, such as the judiciary . . . and central banks . . . The accountability of international institutions, particularly global ones, may compare favorably to these domestic analogues."[30]

However, these supposedly extenuating analogies are in fact misleading. The independence of central banks is explained by the (as it happens, controversial) assumption that the stabilization of a currency calls for complex arguments and decisions that should be left to experts. The decisions taken by the GEMs, by contrast, are politically controversial because they have major impacts on the interests of national societies and on occasion even on the structure of entire national economies. For this reason, the WTO now features a Dispute Settlement Body and an Appellate Body designed to ensure that the interests of third parties also receive due consideration. For example, they adjudicate conflicts between economic interests, on the one side, and standards for health or environmental protection and the protection of consumer or employee rights, on the other. However, this nonmajoritarian institution in the shape of an arbitrating body, whose "reports" have the function of binding "judgments," throws the lack of accountability of the WTO into sharp relief.

Within the framework of the constitutional state, the legitimacy of judicial decisions relies essentially on the fact that courts apply the law laid down by a democratic legislature and that court decisions can be corrected via the political process. In the WTO there is no legislative authority that could lay down or *amend* norms in the domain of international business law. Because cumbersome multilateral negotiations cannot serve as a substitute for such an authority, the autonomous arbitration body develops new law with its detailed reports, and thereby also implicitly performs legislative functions. Devoid of any discernible legitimation, such informal regulations could impact on national legal systems and (as in the famous dispute between the United States and the EU over artificial hormones) impose painful adjustments.

(c) The argument that governmental policy networks should be relieved of exaggerated demands for legitimation would work only on the assumption that the GEMs function as integral parts of a liberal global economic regime order that *is assumed to be legitimate* to implement the worldwide deregulation of markets against government interventions. There is an elective affinity between the neoliberal program of creating a global "civil law society"[31] and the organizational structure of the existing GEMs composed of managers and controlled by governments. The envisaged division of labor between the integration of the world society through liberalized markets, on one side, and the shifting of the costs of any remaining social and ecological obligations to the nation-states, on the other, would render any form of global governance superfluous. From this perspective, the vision of a global domestic policy is a dangerous pipedream.

But what is the real danger? The worldwide export of the project of a neoliberal world order that President Bush again impressively expounded in November 2003 on the occasion of the twentieth anniversary of the foundation of the National Endowment for Democracy[32] does not enjoy worldwide democratic support. The so-called Washington consensus rests rather on a fallible and highly controversial theory, in particular, a combination of the economic dogmas of the Chicago School and a liberal version of modernization theory. The problem is not that these theories could turn out to be wrong like any other. Far more disquieting is an implication of a long-term neoliberal restructuring of the global economy. The political goal of switching from political forms of regulation to market mechanisms tends to perpetuate such a politics, since a change in policy becomes more difficult to the extent that the scope for political intervention is curtailed. The deliberate political self-limitation of the room for political maneuver in favor of systemic self-regulation would rob future generations of the very means they would require for a future course correction. Even if every nation "consciously and democratically decides to be more of a 'competition state' than a 'welfare state,'" such a democratic decision would inevitably destroy its own foundations if it led to a form of social organization that made it impossible to overturn that very decision by democratic means.

This assessment of the consequences recommends itself not just in the foreseeable event of the failure of neoliberal forecasts. Even if the theoretical assumptions should prove to be accurate *grosso modo*, the old slogan concerning the "cultural contradictions of capitalism" could take on new meaning.[33] Competing social models of capitalism coexist even within the domain of Western culture, which is the cradle of capitalist modernization and remains the source of its dynamism. Not all Western nations are prepared to accept the social and cultural costs at home and abroad of the unrectified global disparities in wealth that the neoliberals would foist upon them for the sake of a more rapid increase in affluence for the time being.[34] The interest in maintaining a certain political scope for action is all the greater in *other* cultures which are willing to adjust and transform their own ways of life with access to the global market and acceptance of the dynamics of social modernization, but are not prepared to *abandon* these ways of life and allow them to be replaced by imported patterns. The many cultural faces of the pluralist global society, or *multiple modernities*,[35] do not fit well with a completely deregulated and politically neutralized world market society. For this would rob the non-Western cultures that are shaped by other world religions of their freedom to assimilate the achievements of modernity with their own resources.

Notes

1 In the following I draw on my essay "Does the Constitutionalization of International Law Still Have a Chance?" in Jürgen Habermas, *The Divided West*, ed and trans Ciaran Cronin (Cambridge: Polity, 2006), pp. 115–93.

2 See Gunter Frankenberg, "Die Rückkehr des Vertrages: Uberlegungen zur Verfassung der Europäischen Union," in Lutz Wingert and Klaus Günther (eds), *Die Öffentlichkeit der Vernunft und die Vernunft der Öffentlichkeit* (Frankfurt am Main: Suhrkamp, 2001), pp. 507–38.

3 Christoph Möllers analyzes this link using the European Union as an example in his introductory chapter on constitution and constitutionalization in Armin von Bogdandy (ed), *Europäisches Verfassungsrecht* (Heidelberg: Springer, 2003), pp. 1–56.

4 On "cosmopolitan democracy," see Daniele Archibugi and David Held (eds), *Cosmopolitan Democracy* (Cambridge: Polity, 1995); David Held, *Democracy and the Global Order* (Cambridge: Polity, 1995); on a federal world republic, see Otfried Höffe, *Demokiatie im Zeitalter der Globalisierung* (Munich: Beck, 1999).

5 Michael Walzer still defends this view in *Just and Unjust Wars* (New York: Basic Books, 1977) and *Arguing about War* (New Haven, Conn.: Yale University Press, 2005). See also the essays on "Twenty Years of Michael Walzer's *Just and Unjust Wars*," *Ethics and International Affairs* 11 (1997): 3–104.

6 Erhard Denninger advocates rejecting the concept of sovereignty altogether; see "Vom Ende der nationalstaatlichen Souveränität in Europa," in Denninger, *Recht in globaler Unordnung* (Berlin: Berlin Wissenschafts-Verlag, 2005), pp. 379–94.

7 See the corresponding definition of "new sovereignty" in Abram Chayes and Antonia Handler Chayes, *The New Sovereignty Compliance with International Regulatory Agreements* (Cambridge, Mass.: Harvard University Press, 1995).

8 See Habermas, *The Divided West*, pp. 115ff. and 176ff.

9 For an overview of the UN family, see David Held, *Global Covenant* (Cambridge: Polity, 2004), pp. 82f.

10 On "material equality of rights" [*Rechtsinhaltsgleichheit*], see Habermas, *Between Facts and Norms*, trans William Rehg (Cambridge: Polity, 1998), pp. 484ff.

11 Anne-Marie Slaughter offers an impressive list of the international organizations in *A New World Order* (Princeton, N J., and Oxford: Princeton University Press, 2004), pp. xv–xviii.

12 David Held and Anthony McGrew (eds), *The Global Transformations Reader* (Cambridge: Polity, 2003).

13 These two elements were not initially differentiated from each other in the classical concept of civil or bourgeois society [*bürgerliche Gesellschaft*]; see Habermas, "Further Reflections on the Public Sphere," in Craig Calhoun (ed), *Habermas and the Public Sphere* (Cambridge, Mass.: MIT Press, 1992), pp. 421–61.

14 Claus Offe, "Wessen Wohl ist das Gemeinwohl?" in Wingert and Günther (eds), *Die Öffentlichkeit der Vernunft*, pp. 459–88.

15 Dieter Grimm, *Die Zukunft der Velfassung* (Frankfurt am Main: Suhrkamp, 1991), pp. 372–96; Grimm, "Bedingungen demokratischer Rechtsetzung," in Wingert and Gunther (eds), *Die Öffentlichkeit der Vernunft*, pp. 489–506, here pp. 500ff.

16 David Held, Andrew McGrew, David Goldblatt, and Jonathan Perraton, *Global Transformations* (Cambridge: Polity, 1999).

17 Michael Zürn, "Global Governance and Legitimacy Problems, Government and Opposition," *International Journal of Comparative Politics* 39 (2004): 260–87, here 273f.

18 Anne Peters, "Wie funktioniert das Völkerrecht?" *Basler Juristische Mitteilungen* (February, 2004]: 24.

19 Hans Kelsen, "Sovereignty," in Stanley Paulson and Bonnie Litschewski Paulson (eds), *Normativity and Norms* (Oxford: Clarendon Press, 1998), pp. 525–36.

20 Christian Tomuschat, "International Law: Ensuring the Survival of Mankind on the Eve of a New Century: General Course on Public International Law," *Recueil des cours* 281 (1999), (The Hague, 2001): 163f.: "Today, the international legal order cannot be understood any more as being based exclusively on State sovereignty . . . Protection is afforded by the international community to certain basic values even without or against the will of individual States. All of these values are derived from the notion that States are no more than instruments whose inherent function is to serve the interests of their citizens as legally expressed in human rights. . . . Over the last decades, a crawling process has taken place through which human rights have steadily increased their weight, gaining momentum in comparison with State sovereignty as a somewhat formal

principle." On this, see also Armin von Bogdandy, "Constitutionalism in International Law: Comment on a Proposal from Germany," *Harvard International Law Journal* 47 (2006): 223–42.

21   On December 1, 2004, the High-Level Panel on Threats, Challenges and Change presented its report, *A More Secure World: Our Shared Responsibility* (New York: United Nations Department of Public Information, 2004; hereinafter "TCC") Kofi Annan incorporated its substance into his report to the General Assembly on the reform of the UN on March 21, 2005: "In Larger Freedom: Toward Development, Security and Freedom for All."

22   TCC, p. 19: "Too often, the United Nations and its Member States have discriminated in responding to threats to international security. Contrast the swiftness with which the United Nations responded to the attacks on 11 September 2001 with its actions when confronted with a far more deadly event: from April to mid-July 1994, Rwanda experienced the equivalent of three 11 September attacks every day for 100 days, all in a country whose population was one thirty-sixth of that of the United States."

23   TCC, p. 65: "The Charter of the United Nations is not as clear as it could be when it comes to saving lives within countries in situations of mass atrocity. It 'reaffirms faith in fundamental human rights' but does not do much to protect them, and Article 2.7 prohibits intervention 'in matters which are essentially within the jurisdiction of any State.' There has been, as a result, a longstanding argument in the international community between those who insist on a 'right to intervene' in man-made catastrophes and those who argue that the Security Council . . . is prohibited from authorizing any coercive action against sovereign States for whatever happens within their borders."

24   Andreas Brummel, *Internationale Demokratie entwickeln* (Stuttgart: Horizonte, 2005).

25   Mattias Kumm, "The Legitimacy of International Law: A Constitutionalist Framework of Analysis," *European Journal of International Law* 15 (2004): 907–31. However, this proposal focuses exclusively on legitimizing legal principles and neglects the institutional level.

26   Slaughter, *A New World Order*, pp. 12ff.

27   Michael Zürn, "Global Governance and Legitimacy Problems," pp. 273f.

28   Patrizia Nanz and Jens Steffek, "Global Governance, Participation and the Public Sphere," *Government and Opposition* 39 (2004): 314–35.

29   Anna-Marie Slaughter, "Disaggregated Sovereignty: Toward the Public Accountability of Global Government Networks," *Government and Opposition* 39 (2004): 163.

30   Miles Kahler, "Defining Accountability Up: The Global Economic Multilaterals," *Government and Opposition* 39 (2004): 133.

31   Ernst-Joachim Mestmäker, "Der Kampf ums Recht in der offenen Gesellschaft," *Rechtstheorie* 20 (1989) 273–88.

32   "President Bush Discusses Freedom in Iraq and Middle East" (www.whitehouse.gov/news/releases/2003/11/print/20031106-2.html).

33   Daniel Bell, *The Cultural Contradictions of Capitalism* (New York: Basic Books, 1976).

34   David Held, *Global Covenant. The Social Democratic Alternative to the Washington Consensus* (Cambridge: Polity, 2004), develops a social democratic alternative to the prevailing Washington Consensus.

35   Charles Taylor, "Two Theories of Modernity," *Public Culture* 11 (1999): 153–74.

Part V

Cosmopolitanism, Global Issues, and Governance

Introduction

The preceding section furnished some key foundational principles that generally underwrite discussions about political, legal, and institutional cosmopolitanism. As we saw, in defining the general characteristics of political and legal cosmopolitanism, the scholars concerned also felt it necessary to explore some essential background conditions needed before any meaningful expression of cosmopolitanism can take root. In examining these conditions, these cosmopolitans reevaluated the socializing effects of global risk, asked how we might resolve global collective action problems, explored what normative and institutional principles should underpin these responses, and investigated what political and legal elements currently exist to support these cosmopolitan reforms. Furthermore, all four chapters ended with a similar normative appeal: namely, that there are fundamental changes occurring at the global level which require a more unified political approach, and that cosmopolitanism, as a global political theory, could provide useful responses for how to alter existing practices toward a more cosmopolitical order.

Whereas the preceding section dealt specifically with outlining some general foundational elements involved with establishing a cosmopolitan political condition, the chapters in this section focus more specifically on extrapolating various cosmopolitan institutional designs and on the application of these designs to contemporary global challenges. In particular, the chapters in this section focus their attention on examining a cosmopolitan approach to global governance (see Held), cosmopolitan democracy (see Archibugi), humanitarian intervention (see Kaldor), and ecological justice (see Hayden). In other words, the chapters in this section attempt to provide a more institutionally minded examination of issues involved with cosmopolitan global governance and of how a cosmopolitan approach can be applied to some predominating concerns debated within International Relations.

To begin, the section starts with a chapter on "Reframing Global Governance" by David Held. As Held suggests, there is a paradox of our time: namely, that "the collective issues we must grapple with are growing extensively and intensely and, yet, the means for addressing these are weak and incomplete." For Held, there are three core sets of problems that humanity will have to grapple with. These problems pertain to how to ecologically share the planet, how to sustain our human needs, and how to create a general "rulebook" for global cooperation and cohabitation. As Held argues, current forms of multilateral global governance have failed to secure an effective response to these concerns, and it is for this reason that renewed thinking about cosmopolitan global governance is politically relevant as well as necessary for human survival. In order to reform these shortcomings, Held argues for the strengthening of global governance regimes in line with cosmopolitan principles. For Held, this requires a reformation toward a fully integrated system of global governance, which not only incorporates familiar global interests, such as states, but also can include voices and concerns that are currently left marginalized at the periphery. To do so, Held suggests a form of multilayered cosmopolitan social democracy as an institutional alternative to "The Washington Consensus" model. As Held argues, it is only by reframing current global governance along these cosmopolitan lines that the governance processes "can meet the tests of solidarity, justice, democracy and effectiveness."

Picking up where Held ends, the chapter by Daniele Archibugi seeks to outline a more specific constitutional structure for cosmopolitan democracy. As Archibugi acknowledges, cosmopolitan democracy represents only one form of possible global governance and not all cosmopolitan democrats will share a similar institutional architecture (for example, see the different approach by Held above). However, according to Archibugi, the democratic principles that underwrite cosmopolitan democracy have both moral and empirical justification that renders it a viable alternative to the current international system. In outlining the constitutional architecture of cosmopolitan democracy, Archibugi locates key areas of democratic intervention, the necessary levels of democratic interconnection (local, state, interstate, regional, and global), the form of constitutionalism required to integrate these levels, and what legal and political union could most appropriately capture the demands of cosmopolitan democracy. Through this discussion Archibugi argues that cosmopolitan democracy still remains an unprecedented experiment that waits to happen, but also, more importantly, that it is a political experiment whose time has come.

Unlike the grand cosmopolitan architectures provided by Held and Archibugi, the chapter by Mary Kaldor seeks to examine the particular issue of humanitarian intervention and how it might be understood from a cosmopolitan perspective. In her chapter, Kaldor argues that, although current global policy concerning humanitarian intervention has often had good intentions, this policy has nevertheless failed to capture the changing nature of "new wars" and has also failed to secure lasting and meaningful peace and security. As a response to these failures, Kaldor proposes what she labels as a cosmopolitan approach to humanitarian intervention. This is an approach that focuses on "cosmopolitan political mobilization, which embraces both the so-called international community and local populations, and which is capable of countering the submission to various types of particularism." As Kaldor argues, the cosmopolitan concerns for legitimacy, the rule of law, political inclusion, political mobilization, and civic activism must override considerations of geo-politics and short-term gains. To do this, Kaldor outlines an approach that refocuses efforts toward creating grass-roots civil movements that can enhance the legitimacy of political participation, that can shift from peacekeeping to cosmopolitan law-enforcement, and to an approach that focuses less on "assistance" and more on "reconstruction." As Kaldor argues, it is only by moving toward this cosmopolitan approach that the calamity of increased bloodshed can be appropriately mediated.

As with the specific focus on humanitarian intervention provided by Kaldor, the final chapter by Patrick Hayden concentrates its attention on issues relating to contemporary global environmental concerns and explores a cosmopolitan approach to environmental politics and ecological justice. In doing so, Hayden begins his chapter with a critique of current global policies as they relate to environmental and developmental sustainability, arguing that these approaches fail to satisfy the concerns of social justice. As an alternative, Hayden argues for cosmopolitan principles of environmental justice and the promotion of environmental citizenship, which can provide a "bridge" between environmental degradation and the political mechanisms necessary to protect our common wellbeing. From this discussion, Hayden argues that any appropriate form of cosmopolitan politics will necessarily have to include a strong environmental component, especially if we are to secure the "substantive and procedural environmental rights of all persons everywhere."

17

Reframing Global Governance: Apocalypse Soon or Reform!
David Held

The paradox of our times

The paradox of our times can be stated simply: the collective issues we must grapple with are of growing extensiveness and intensity and yet the means for addressing these are weak and incomplete. Three pressing global issues highlight the urgency of finding a way forward.

First, little, if any, progress has been made in creating a sustainable framework for the management of global warming. The concentration of carbon dioxide in the global atmosphere is now almost 35 per cent higher than in pre-industrial times (Byers, 2005). The British government chief scientist, Sir David King, has recently warned that "climate change is the most serious problem we are facing today, more serious than the threat of terrorism" (King, 2004, p. 177). Irrespective of whether one agrees with this statement, global warming has the capacity to wreak havoc on the world's diverse species, biosystems and socio-economic fabric. Violent storms will become more frequent, water access will be a battleground, rising sea levels will displace millions, the mass movement of desperate people will become more common, and deaths from serious diseases in the world's poorest countries will rise rapidly (largely because bacteria will spread more quickly, causing greater contamination of food and water). The overwhelming body of scientific opinion now maintains that global warming constitutes a serious threat not in the long term, but in the here and now. The failure of the international community to generate a sound framework for managing global warming is one of the most serious indications of the problems facing the multilateral order.

Second, little progress has been made towards achieving the millennium goals – the agreed human development targets of the international community, or, one could say, its moral consciousness. The millennium goals set down minimum standards to be achieved in relation to poverty reduction, health, educational provision, the combating of HIV/AIDS, malaria and other diseases, environmental sustainability and so on. Progress towards these targets has been lamentably slow, and there is evidence that they will be missed by a very wide margin. In fact, there is evidence that there may have been no point in setting these targets at all, so far are we from attaining them in many parts of the world. Underlying this human crisis is, of course, the material vulnerability of half of the world's population: 45 per cent of humankind live below the World Bank's $2/day poverty line; 18 per cent (or some 1,089 million people) live below the $1/day poverty line. As Thomas Pogge has appropriately put it, "people so incredibly poor are extremely vulnerable to even minor shifts in natural and social conditions. . . . Each year, some 18 million of them die prematurely from poverty-related causes. This is one third of all human deaths – 50,000 every day including 29,000 children under age five" (Pogge, 2006; cf. UNDP, 2005). And yet, the gap between rich and poor countries continues to rise, and there is evidence that the bottom 10 per cent of the world's population has become even poorer since the beginning of the 1990s (Milanovic, 2002).

Third, the threat of nuclear catastrophe may seem to have diminished but it is only in abeyance, as Martin Rees has recently argued (Rees, 2003, pp. 8, 27, 32–3, 43–4). Huge nuclear stockpiles remain nuclear proliferation among states is continuing (for example, in India, Pakistan and perhaps Iran) nuclear weapons and materials due to poor accounting records may have been purloined (after the demise of the Soviet Union) new generations of tactical nuclear weapons are being built, and dirty bomb technology (the coating of plutonium on the surface of a conventional bomb) makes nuclear terrorism a serious threat. Other dangers exist including terrorist attacks on nuclear power stations, many of which may be in countries with little protective capacity. Adding to these considerations, the disquieting risks stemming from microbiology and genetics (engineered viruses), Rees concludes that "the odds are no better than fifty-fifty that our present civilisation on Earth will survive to the end of the present century without a serious setback" (2003, p. 8). Certainly, huge questions are raised about accountability, regulation and enforcement.

These global challenges are indicative of three core sets of problems we face – those concerned with sharing our planet (global warming, biodiversity and ecosystem losses, water deficits), sustaining our humanity (poverty, conflict prevention, global infectious diseases) and our rulebook (nuclear proliferation, toxic waste disposal, intellectual property rights, genetic research rules, and trade, finance and tax rules) (Rischard, 2002, p. 66). In our increasingly interconnected world, these global problems cannot be solved by any one nation-state acting alone. They call for collective and collaborative action – something that the nations of the world have not been good at, and which they need to be better at if these pressing issues are to be adequately tackled. Yet the evidence is wanting that we are getting better at building appropriate governance capacity.

Why be concerned with global challenges?

Why do these global issues matter? The answer to this may seem intuitively obvious, but four separate reasons are worth stressing: solidarity, social justice, democracy and policy effectiveness. It is important to clarify each of these because they provide a map of the dimensions we need to keep in mind for thinking about the nature and adequacy of governance at the global level. By solidarity I mean not just empathetic recognition of another's plight, but the willingness to stand side-by-side with others in the creation of solutions to pressing collective problems. Without solidarity between rich and poor, developed and developing countries the Millennium Development Goals will not be met[1] and, as Kofi Annan simply put it, "millions of people will die, prematurely and unnecessarily" (Annan, 2005: 139). These deaths are all the more poignant because solutions are within our grasp. Insofar as challenges like global warming and nuclear proliferation are concerned we need to add to the definition of solidarity a focus on our own sustainability, never mind that of citizens of the future. Contemporary global challenges require recognition of, and active participation in, the forces that shape our overlapping communities of fate.

A second reason to focus on global challenges is social justice. Standards of social justice are, of course, controversial. To make my argument as accessible as possible, I will, following Pogge, take social justice to mean the fulfilment of human rights in an institutional order to the extent that it is reasonably possible (Pogge, 2007). Of course, most argue that social justice requires more, and so it can be claimed with some confidence that an institutional order that fails to meet these standards cannot be just. Accordingly, it can be reasoned that insofar as our existing socio-economic arrangements fail to meet the Millennium Goals, and the broader challenges of global warming and the risks of nuclear proliferation, they are unjust, or, simply, beyond justice.

The third reason is democracy. Democracy presupposes a noncoercive political process in and through which people can pursue and negotiate the terms of their interconnectedness, interdependence and difference. In democratic thinking, "consent" constitutes the basis of collective agreement and governance; for people to be free and equal there must be mechanisms in place through which consent can be registered in the determination of the government of public life (Held, 2006). Yet, when millions die unnecessarily, and billions are threatened unnecessarily, it can clearly be held that serious harm can be inflicted on people without their consent and against their will (Barry, 1998). The recognition of this reveals fundamental deficits in our governance arrangements which go to the heart of both justice and democracy.

Finally, the failure to act sooner rather than later on pressing global issues generally escalates the costs of dealing with them. In fact, the costs of inaction are high and often vastly higher than the costs of action. For instance, it has been estimated that the costs of inaction in dealing with communicable diseases in Africa are about one hundred times greater than the costs of corrective action (Conceição, 2003). Similar calculations have also been undertaken in areas of international financial stability, the multilateral trade regime, and peace and security, all of which show that the costs of deficient global public goods provision are extremely large and outweigh by significant margins the costs of corrective policies (Kaul et al., 2003). And yet, we too often stand paralysed in the face of urgent collective challenges, or actively engage in the reproduction of political and social arrangements that fail to meet the minimum standards that solidarity, justice and democracy require.

Deep drivers and governance challenges

The post-war multilateral order is threatened by the intersection and combination of humanitarian, economic and environmental crises. There are, moreover, forces pushing them from bad to worse; I call these the emergent system of structural global vulnerability, the Washington policy packages and the constellation of contemporary geopolitics. The first factor – structural global vulnerability – is a feature of our contemporary global age, and in all likelihood is here to stay. The other two factors are the outcome of clear political choices, and they can be modified. Their force is willed, even though it often presents itself in the form of inevitability. Or to put the point another way, the current form of globalization is open to transformation, even if the Doomsday clock (the logo on the Bulletin of Atomic Scientists) is rather too close to midnight.

The world we are in is highly interconnected. The interconnectedness of countries – or the process of "globalization" as it is often called – can readily be measured by mapping the ways in which trade, finance, communication, pollutants, violence, among many other factors, flow across borders and lock the well-being of countries into common patterns (Held et al., 1999). The deep drivers of this process will be operative for the foreseeable future, irrespective of the exact political form globalization takes. Among these drivers are:

- the changing infrastructure of global communications linked to the IT revolution;
- the development of global markets in goods and services, connected to the new worldwide distribution of information;
- the pressure of migration and the movement of peoples, linked to shifts in patterns of economic demand, in demography and in environmental degradation;
- the end of the Cold War and the diffusion of democratic and consumer values across many of the world's regions, alongside some marked reactions to this;
- the emergence of a new type and form of global civil society, with the crystallization of elements of a global public opinion.

Despite the fractures and conflicts of our age, societies are becoming more interconnected and interdependent. As a result, developments at the local level – whether economic, political or social – can acquire almost instantaneous global consequences and vice versa (Held, 2004, pp. 73–116; Giddens, 1990, pp. 55–78). Link to this the advances in science across many fields, often now instantly diffused through global communication networks, and the global arena becomes both an extraordinary potential space for human development as well as for disruption and destruction by individuals, groups or states (all of whom can, in principle, learn the lessons of nuclear energy, genetics, bacteriology and computer networking) (Rees, 2003, pp. 62, 65).

The second set of driving forces can be summed up in two phases: the Washington economic consensus and the Washington security agenda. I take a detailed look at these in *Global Covenant* (Held, 2004), and *Debating Globalization* (Barnett et al., 2005). Any assessment of them must be grounded on the issues each seeks to address. But they are now also connected drivers of the specific form globalization takes. Together, they promulgate the view that a positive role for government is to be fundamentally distrusted in core areas of socio-economic life – from market regulation to disaster planning – and that the sustained application of internationally adjudicated policy and regulation threatens freedom, limits growth, impedes development and restrains the good. Of course, neither exhaustively explains the current structures of globalization, but they form a core part of its political circumstances.

The thrust of the Washington Consensus is to enhance economic liberalization and to adapt the public domain – local, national and global – to market leading institutions and processes. It thus bears a heavy burden of responsibility for the common political resistance of unwillingness to address significant areas of market failure, including:

- the problem of externalities, for example, the environmental degradation exacerbated by current forms of economic growth;
- the inadequate development of *non*-market social factors, which alone can provide an effective balance between "competition" and "cooperation", and thus ensure an adequate supply of essential "public goods" such as education, effective transportation and sound health; and
- the underemployment or unemployment of productive resources in the context of the demonstrable existence of urgent and unmet need.

[. . .]

The Washington Consensus has, in sum, weakened the ability to govern – locally, nationally and globally – and it has eroded the capacity to provide urgent public goods. Economic freedom is championed at the expense of social justice and environmental sustainability, with long-term damage to both. And it has confused economic freedom and economic effectiveness. Moreover, the systematic political weaknesses of the Washington Consensus have been compounded by the new Washington security doctrines.

The rush to war against Iraq in 2003 gave priority to a narrow security agenda which is at the heart of the new American security doctrine of unilateral and pre-emptive war. This agenda contradicts most of the core tenets of international politics and international agreements since 1945 (Ikenberry, 2002). It throws aside respect for open political negotiations among states, as it does the core doctrine of deterrence and stable relations among major powers (the balance of power). We have to come to terms not only with the reality that a single country enjoys military supremacy to an unprecedented extent in world history, but also with the fact that it can use that supremacy to respond unilaterally to perceived threats (which may be neither actual nor imminent), and that it will brook no rival.

[. . .]

It would be wrong to link current threats to the multilateral order just to these policy packages, and specifically to policy shifts introduced by the Bush administrations. First, elements of the Washington Consensus clearly pre-date Bush. Second, the end of the Cold War and the huge geopolitical shifts that have come in its wake may also form a key geopolitical factor. John Ikenberry has formulated the argument thus: the rise of America's unipolar power position during the 1990s has complicated the old post-war logic of cooperation among allied democratic states. America's power advantages make it easier for it to say no to other countries or to go it alone (Ikenberry, 2005). Connected to the decline in incentives for the United States to multilateral cooperation are the divisions within Europe which make it less effective in promulgating an alternative model of global governance. The current state of the leading organizations and institutions of the multilateral order needs unfolding.

Global governance: contemporary surface trends

In a survey of the current state of key global and regional governance arrangements – the UN, EU and NATO prominent among them – Ikenberry has suggested that they have all weakened. To quote him again: "today the machinery of the post-war era is in disrepair. No leader, international body or group of states speaks with authority or vision on global challenges" (2005, p. 30). This is my judgement as well. The value of the UN system has been called into question, the legitimacy of the Security Council has been challenged as have the working practices of many multilateral bodies. While the UN still plays a vital and effective role in peacekeeping, natural disaster mitigation, protecting refugees, among other tasks, the war in Iraq dramatized the weakness of the UN system as a vehicle for global security cooperation and collective decision-making on the use of force. The management of the UN system is also under suspicion, with the oil-for-food programme in Iraq becoming a scandal and UN-helmeted troops in Africa being implicated in sexual violence and the abuse of children. In September 2005 the UN members came together to try to establish new rules and institute bold reforms. But member states were unable to agree on a new grand vision and the summit failed in many key respects (I return to these issues later). As a result, the deeply embedded difficulties of the UN system remain unresolved – the marginalization or susceptibility of the UN to the agendas of the most powerful states, the weaknesses of many of its enforcement operations (or lack of them altogether), the underfunding of its organization, the inadequacies of the policing of many environmental regimes (regional and global) and so on.

The future direction of the EU is also highly uncertain. There is a deep sense of unease in Brussels about what the next few years will bring. Anxious about the increasing success of low-cost economies, notably China, India and Brazil, and about whether the European social model can survive in its current form, voters are increasingly expressing scepticism about both European integration and expansion. The French "no" to the proposed European constitution partly reflects this, as does the Dutch "no" – although the latter was also fuelled by a perception that the Dutch "host culture" was under threat from historical waves of immigration. The capacity of Europe to project its "soft power" alternative to US "hard power" looks frail, as does its capacity to play a more active global leadership role. In the absence of the negative unity provided by the Cold War, old foreign policy rivalries and differences among the big states are reasserting themselves (Ikenberry, 2005, p. 30), and the existing generation of leaders appears as much part of the growing impasse as its solution. [. . .]

While the economic multilaterals are still functioning (although the WTO faces a critical test over whether the Doha round can be brought to a successful conclusion), many of the multilaterals that coordinate the activities of the United States, EU and other leading states all look weaker now: NATO, the G8, treaty-based arms control, among others. Since 9/11 the future of NATO has become clouded. The global redeployment of US forces: and divisions in Europe about the conditions for the use of NATO troops, have rendered the role of NATO increasingly unclear. The G8 has always been more of a "talking shop" than a vehicle for collective action, but today its meetings appear to have minimal, if any, lasting impact. [. . .]

The post-war multilateral order is in trouble. With the resurgence of nationalism and unilateralism in US foreign policy, EU disarray and the growing confidence of China, India and Brazil in world economic fora, the political teutonic plates appear to be shifting. Clear, effective and accountable global decision-making is needed across a range of global challenges; and, yet, the collective capacity for addressing these matters is in serious doubt.

Problems and dilemmas of global problem-solving

The field of contemporary geopolitics is merely the chaff, significant though it is. Prior to it, beneath it, underlying it, restricting it are the limits of the post-war settlement itself and of the institutional nexus of the multilateral order. Four deep-rooted problems need highlighting.

In the first instance there is no clear division of labour among the myriad of international governmental agencies; functions often overlap, mandates frequently conflict and aims and objectives too often get blurred. There are a number of competing and overlapping organizations and institutions all of which have some stake in shaping different sectors of global public policy. This is true, for example, in the area of health and social policy where the World Bank, the IMF and the WHO often have different or competing priorities (Deacon et al., 2003, pp. 11–35); or, more specifically, in the area of AIDS/HIV treatment, where the WHO, Global Fund, UNAIDS, the G1 (i.e. the United States) and many other interests vie to shape reproductive healthcare and sexual practices.

Reflecting on the difficulties of interagency cooperation during his time as head of the WTO, Mike Moore wrote that "greater coherence amongst the numerous agencies that receive billions of taxpayers' dollars would be a good start . . . this lack of coherence damages their collective credibility, frustrates their donors and owners and gives rise to public cynicism . . . the array of institutions is bewildering . . . our interdependent world has yet to find the mechanism to integrate its common needs" (Moore, 2003, pp. 220–3).

A second set of difficulties relates to the inertia found in the system of international agencies, or the inability of these agencies to mount collective problem-solving solutions faced with disagreement over means, objectives, costs and so on. This often leads to the situation where, as mentioned previously, the cost of inaction is greater than the cost of taking action. Bill Gates, Chairman of Microsoft, recently referred to the developed world's efforts in tackling malaria as "a disgrace"; malaria causes an estimated 500 million bouts of illness a year, kills an African child every 30 seconds, and costs an estimated \$12 billion a year in lost income, yet investment in insecticide-treated bed nets and other forms of protective treatment would be a fraction of this (Meikle, 2005). The failure to act decisively in the face of urgent global problems not only compounds the costs of dealing with these problems in the long run, but it can also reinforce a widespread perception that these agencies are not just ineffective but unaccountable and unjust.

A third set of problems emerges as a result of issues which span the distinction between the domestic and the foreign. A growing number of issues can be characterized as intermestic – that is, issues which cross the *inter*national and do*mestic* (Rosenau, 2002). These are often insufficiently understood, comprehended or acted upon. For there is a fundamental lack of ownership of global problems at the global level. It is far from clear which global public issues – such as global warming or the loss of biodiversity – are the responsibility of which international agencies, and which issues ought to be addressed by which particular agencies. The institutional fragmentation and competition leads not just to the problem of overlapping jurisdictions among agencies, but also to the problem of issues falling between agencies. This latter problem is also manifest between the global level and national governments.

The fourth set of difficulties relates to an accountability deficit, itself linked to two interrelated problems: the power imbalances among states as well as those between state and non-state actors in the shaping and making of global public policy. Multilateral bodies need to be fully representative of the states involved in them, and they are rarely so. In addition, there must be arrangements in place to engage in dialogue and consultation between state and non-state actors, and these conditions are only partially met in multilateral decision-making bodies. Investigating this problem, Inge Kaul and her associates at the UNDP have made the telling point that "the imbalances among states as well as those between state and non-state actors are not always easy to detect, because in many cases the problem is not merely a quantitative issue – whether all parties have a seat at the negotiating table." The main problem is often qualitative, "how well various stakeholders are represented" (Kaul et al., 2003, p. 30). Having a seat at the negotiating table in a major intergovernmental organization (IGO) or at a major conference does not ensure effective representation. For even if there is parity of formal representation, it is often the case that developed countries have large delegations equipped with extensive negotiating and technical expertise, while poorer developing countries often depend on one-person delegations, or have even to rely on the sharing of a delegate. The difficulties that occur range from the significant under-representation of developing countries in agencies such as the IMF – where 24 industrial countries hold 10–11 seats on the executive board while 42 African countries hold only 2 – to problems that result from an inability to develop substantial enough negotiating and technical expertise even with one person/one country decision-making procedures (Buira, 2003; Chasek and Rajamani, 2003; Mendoza, 2003). Accordingly, many people are stakeholders in global political problems that affect them, but remain excluded from the political institutions and strategies needed to address these problems.

Underlying these institutional difficulties is the breakdown of symmetry and congruence between decision-makers and decision-takers (Held, 1995, pp. 141–218). The point has been well articulated recently by Kaul and her associates in their work on global public goods. They speak about the forgotten *equivalence* principle (Kaul et al., 2003, pp. 27–8). This principle suggests that the span of a good's benefits and costs should be matched with the span of the jurisdiction in which decisions are taken about that good. At its simplest, the principle suggests that those who are significantly affected by a global good or bad should have a say in its provision or regulation. Yet, all too often, there is a breakdown of "equivalence" between decision-makers and decision-takers, between decision-makers and stakeholders, and between the inputs and outputs of the decision-making process. [. . .]

As a result, we face the challenge of:

- *Matching circles of stakeholders and decision-makers*: to create opportunities for all to have a say about global public goods that affect their lives.
- *Systematizing the financing of global public goods*: to get incentives right and to secure adequate private and public resources for these goods.
- *Spanning borders, sectors, and groups of actors*: to foster institutional interaction and create space for policy entrepreneurship and strategic issue management (Kaul et al., 2003, pp. 5–6).

Failures or inadequacies in global political processes often result from the mismatch between the decision-making circles created in international arenas, and the range of spillovers associated with specific public goods or public bads. The challenge is to align the circles of those to be consulted (or to take part in the decision making) with the spillover range of the good under negotiation (2003, p. 28).

Strengthening global governance

To restore symmetry and congruence between decision-makers and decision-takers and to entrench the principle of equivalence, requires a strengthening of global governance and a resolve to address those institutional challenges just discussed, and those underlying fault lines running through global governance provision. [. . .] In the first instance, this agenda can be thought of as comprising three interrelated dimensions: promoting coordinated state action to tackle common problems, reinforcing those international institutions that can function effectively, and developing multilateral rules and procedures that lock in all powers, small and major into a multilateral framework (Hirst and Thompson, 2002, pp. 252–3). But to do what exactly? It cannot be to pursue more of what we have had: the misleading and damaging policy packages of the Washington Consensus and the Washington security doctrines. Indeed, both need to be replaced by a policy framework that:

- encourages and sustains the enormous enhancement of productivity and wealth that the global market and contemporary technology make possible;
- addresses the extremes of poverty and ensures that the benefits are fairly shared;
- creates avenues of "voice", deliberation and democratic decision-making in regional and global public domains;
- puts environmental sustainability at the centre of global governance;
- provides international security which engages with the causes as well as the crimes of terrorism, war and failed states.

I call the approach that sets itself this task social democratic globalization and a human security agenda.

The Washington Consensus needs to be replaced by a wider vision of institutions and policy approaches. Liberal market philosophy offers too narrow a view, and clues to an alternative vision can be found in an old rival – social democracy (Ruggie, 2003; Held, 2004). Traditionally, social democrats have sought to deploy the democratic institutions of individual countries on behalf of a particular project; they have accepted that markets are central to generating economic well-being, but recognized that in the absence of appropriate regulation they suffer serious flaws – especially the generation of unwanted risks for their citizens, and an unequal distribution of those risks.

Social democracy at the level of the nation-state means supporting free markets while insisting on a framework of shared values and common institutional practices. At the global level it means pursuing an economic agenda which calibrates the freeing of markets with poverty reduction programmes and the protection of the vulnerable. Moreover, this agenda must be pursued while ensuring, on the one hand that different countries have the freedom they need to experiment with their own investment strategies and resources and on the other, that domestic policy choices uphold basic universal standards (including human rights and environmental protection). The question is: how can self-determination, markets and core universal standards coexist?

To begin with, bridges have to be built between international economic law and human rights law, between commercial law and environmental law, and between state sovereignty and transnational law (Chinkin, 1998). What is required is not only the firm enactment of existing human rights and environmental agreements and the clear articulation of these with the ethical codes of particular industries (where they exist or can be developed), but also the introduction of new terms of reference into the ground rules or basic laws of the free market and trading system. Precedents exist, for instance, in the Social Chapter of the Maastricht Agreement or in the attempt to attach labour and environmental conditions to the North American Free Trade Agreement (NAFTA) regime, for the pursuit of this objective.

At stake, ultimately, are three interrelated transformations. The first would involve engaging companies in the promotion of core UN universal principles (as the UN's Global Compact does at present). To the extent that this led to the entrenchment of human rights and environmental standards in corporate practices, that would be a significant step forward. But if this is to be something other than a voluntary initiative, vulnerable to being sidestepped or ignored, then it needs to be elaborated in due course into a set of codified and mandatory rules. The second set of transformations would, thus, involve the entrenchment of revised codes, rules and procedures – on health, child labour; trade union activity, environmental protection, stakeholder consultation and corporate governance – in the articles of association and terms of reference of economic organizations and trading agencies. The key groups and associations of the economic domain would have to adopt, within their very *modus operandi*, a structure of rules, procedures and practices compatible with universal social requirements, if the latter are to prevail. This would require a new international treaty, laying down elements of universal jurisdiction and clear avenues of enforcement. (Of course, poorly designed regulatory structures can harm employment levels, but countries with strong social democratic traditions, above all the Scandinavian, show that it is possible to be both business-friendly and welfare-orientated).

There are many possible objections to such a scheme. However, most of these are misplaced (Held, 2002a, pp. 72ff.). The framework of human rights and environmental values is sound, preoccupied as it is with the equal liberty and development possibilities of all human beings. But it cannot be implemented without a third set of transformations, focused on the most pressing cases of economic suffering and harm. Without this commitment, the advocacy of such standards can descend into *high-mindedness*, which fails to pursue the socio-economic changes that are a necessary part of such a commitment.

At a minimum, this means that development policies must be directed to promote the "development space" necessary for national trade and industrial incentives (including infant industry protection), to build robust public sectors nurturing political and legal reform, to develop transparent, accountable political institutions, to ensure long-term investment in healthcare, human capital and physical infrastructure, to challenge the asymmetries of access to the global market, and to ensure the sequencing of global market integration into a framework of fair global rules for trade and finance. Moreover, it means eliminating unsustainable debt, seeking ways to reverse the outflow of net capital assets from the South to the North, and creating new finance facilities for development purposes. In addition, if such measures were combined with a (Tobin) tax on the turnover of financial markets, and/or a consumption tax on fossil fuels and/ or a shift of priorities from military expenditure (now running at $900 billion per annum globally) to the alleviation of severe need (direct aid amounts only to some $50 billion per annum globally), then the developmental context of Western and Northern nation-states could begin to be accommodated to those nations struggling for survival and minimum welfare.

The shift in the agenda of globalization I am arguing for – in short, a move from liberal to social democratic globalization – would have pay-offs for today's most pressing security concerns. At the centre of this argument is the need to connect the security and human rights agendas and to bring them into a coherent international framework. This is the second aspect of global policy: replacing the Washington security doctrines. If developed countries want swift movement in the establishment of global legal codes that will enhance security and ensure action against the threats of terrorism, then they need to be part of a wider process of reform that addresses the insecurity of life experienced in developing societies. Across the developing or majority world, issues of justice with respect to government and terrorism, are not regarded as a priority on their own, and are unlikely to be perceived as legitimate concerns unless they are connected with fundamental humanitarian issues rooted in social and economic well-being, such as basic education, clean water and public hygiene. At issue is what I call a new "global covenant" or, as the High Level Panel on UN reform recently put it, a new "grand bargain" (Held, 2004; UN, 2004.)

Specifically, what is needed is to link the security and human rights agenda in international law; reform the United Nations Security Council to improve the legitimacy of armed intervention, with credible threshold tests; amend the now outmoded 1945 geopolitical settlement as the basis of decision-making in the Security Council and extend representation to all regions on a fair and equal footing; expand the remit of the Security Council or create a parallel Social and Economic Security Council to examine and, when necessary, intervene in the full gamut of human crises – physical, social, biological, environmental – that can threaten human agency; and found a World Environmental Organization to promote the implementation of existing environmental agreements and treaties, and whose main mission would be to insure that the world trading and financial systems are compatible with the sustainable use of the world's resources. This would be a grand bargain indeed! (See the box at the end of the chapter for a summary of the policy shifts I am arguing for to replace the Washington Consensus and the Washington security doctrines.)

[. . .] The Washington Consensus and Washington security doctrines are failing – market fundamentalism and unilateralism have dug their own graves (Held, 2004; Barnett et al., 2005). The most successful countries in the world (China, India, Vietnam, Uganda, among them) are successful because they have not followed the Washington Consensus agenda (Rodrick, 2005), and the conflicts that have most successfully been diffused (the Balkans, Sierra Leone, Liberia, Sri Lanka; among others) are ones that have benefited from concentrated multilateral support and a human security agenda (Human Security Centre, 2005). Here are clear clues as to how to proceed, and to build alternatives to both the Washington Consensus and the Washington Security Doctrines.

Global governance and the democratic question

The reflections developed so far are about taking steps toward solidarity, democracy, justice and policy effectiveness after the failures of current policy have come home to roost. Yet the problems of global governance today require a much longer time horizon as well. The problems of democracy and justice will only be institutionally secured if we grasp the structural limits of the present global political arrangements, limits which can be summed up as "realism is dead" or, to put it more moderately, *raison d'état* must know its place.

Traditionally, the tension between the sphere of decision-makers and the sphere of decision-takers has been resolved by the idea of political community – the bounded, territorially delimited community in which decision-makers and decision-takers create processes and institutions to resolve the problem of accountability. During the period in which nation-states were being forged, the idea of a close mesh between geography, political power and democracy could be assumed. It seemed compelling that political power- sovereignty, democracy and citizenship were simply and appropriately bounded by a delimited territorial space (Held, 1995). But this is no longer the case. Globalization, global governance and global challenges raise issues concerning the proper scope of democracy, and of a democracy's jurisdiction, given that the relation between decision-makers and decision-takers is not necessarily symmetrical or congruent with respect to territory.

The principle of all-inclusiveness is often regarded in democratic theory as the conceptual means to help clarify the fundamental criterion for drawing proper boundaries around those who should be involved in particular decision-making domains, those who should be accountable to a particular group of people, and why. At its simplest, it states that those significantly affected by public decisions, issues, or processes should have an equal opportunity, directly or indirectly through elected delegates or representatives, to influence and shape them. Those affected by public decisions ought to have a say in their making. But the question today is: how is the notion of "significantly affected" to be understood when the relation between decision-makers and decision-takers is more spatially complex – when, that is, decisions affect people outside a circumscribed democratic entity, as is the case, for example, with agricultural subsidies, the rules governing stem cell research, and carbon omissions? In an age of global interconnectedness, who should key decision-makers be accountable to? The set of people they affect? The answer is not so straightforward. As Robert Keohane has noted, "being affected cannot be sufficient to create a valid claim. If it were, virtually nothing could ever be done, since there would be so many requirements for consultation and even veto points" (Keohane, 2003, p. 141). This is a hard issue to think through. The matter becomes a little easier to address if the all-affected principle is connected directly to the idea of impact on people's needs or interests.

If we think of the impact of powerful forces on people's lives, then impact can be divided into three categories: strong, moderate and weak. By strong I mean that vital needs or interests are affected (from health to housing) with fundamental consequences for people's life expectancy. By moderate I mean that needs are affected in such a way that people's ability to participate in their community (in economic, cultural and political activities) is in question. At stake here is the quality of life chances. By weak I mean an effect which impacts upon particular lifestyles or the range of available consumption choices (from clothes to music). These categories are not watertight but they provide some useful guidance:

- If people's urgent needs are unmet their lives will be in danger. In this context, people are at risk of serious harm.

- If people's secondary needs are unmet they will not be able to participate fully in their communities and their potential for involvement in public and private life will remain unfulfilled. Their choices will be restricted or depleted. In this context, people are at risk of harm to their life opportunities.
- If people's lifestyle needs are unmet their ability to develop their lives and express themselves through diverse media will be thwarted. In this context, unmet need can lead to anxiety and frustration.

In the light of these considerations, the principle of all-inclusiveness needs restating. I take it to mean that those whose life expectancy and life chances are significantly affected by social forces and processes ought to have a stake in the determination of the conditions and regulation of these, either directly or indirectly through political representatives. Democracy is best located when it is closest to and involves those whose life expectancy and life chances are determined by powerful entities, bringing the circles of stakeholders and decision-makers closer together. The argument for extending this consideration to decisions and processes which affect lifestyle needs is less compelling, since these are fundamentally questions of value and identity for communities to resolve for themselves. For example, whether McDonald's should be allowed access across China, or US media products given free range in Canada, are questions largely for those countries to resolve, although clearly serious cross-border issues concerning, for example, the clash of values and consumption choices can develop, posing questions about regional or global trade rules and regulations.

The principle of all-inclusiveness points to the necessity of both the decentralization *and* centralization of political power. If decision-making is decentralized as much as possible, it maximizes the opportunity of each person to influence the social conditions that shape his or her life. But if the decisions at issue are translocal, transnational, or transregional, then political institutions need not only be locally based but also to have a wider scope and framework of operation. In this context, the creation of diverse sites and levels of democratic fora may be unavoidable. It may be unavoidable, paradoxically, for the very same reasons as decentralization is desirable: it creates the possibility of including people who are significantly affected by a political issue in the public (in this case, transcommunity public) sphere.

To restore symmetry and congruence between decision-makers and decision-takers, and to entrench the principle of all-inclusiveness, requires a redevelopment of global governance and a resolve to address those challenges generated by cross-border processes and forces. This project must take as its starting point, in other words, a world of overlapping communities of fate. Recognizing the complex processes of an interconnected world, it ought to view certain issues – such as industrial and commercial strategy, housing and education – as appropriate for spatially delimited political spheres (the city, region or state), while seeing others – such as the environment, pandemics and global financial regulation – as requiring new, more extensive institutions to address them. Deliberative and decision-making centres beyond national territories are appropriately situated when the principle of all-inclusiveness can only be properly upheld in a transnational context; when those whose life expectancy and life chances are significantly affected by a public matter constitute a transnational grouping; and when "lower" levels of decision-making cannot manage satisfactorily transnational or global policy questions. Of course, the boundaries demarcating different levels of governance will always be contested, as they are, for instance, in many local, subnational regional and national polities. Disputes about the appropriate jurisdiction for handling particular public issues will be complex and intensive; but better complex and intensive in a clear public framework than left simply to powerful geo-political interests (dominant states) of market-based organizations to resolve them alone. In short, the possibility of a long-term institutional reform must be linked to an expanding framework of states and agencies bound by the rule of law, democratic principles and human rights. How should this be understood from an institutional point of view?

Multilevel citizenship, multilayered democracy

In the long term, the realignment of global governance with solidarity, democracy and social justice must involve the development of both independent political authority and administrative capacity at regional and global levels. It does not call for the diminution *per se* of state power and capacity across the globe. Rather, it seeks to entrench and develop political institutions at regional and global levels as a necessary supplement to those at the level of the state. This conception of politics is based on the recognition of the continuing significance of nation-states, while arguing for layers of governance to address broader and more global questions. The aim is to forge an accountable and responsive politics at local and national levels alongside the establishment of representative and deliberative assemblies in the wider global order; that is, a political order of transparent and democratic cities and nations as well as of regions and global networks within an overarching framework of social justice.

The long-term institutional requirements include:

- multilayered governance and diffused authority;
- a network of democratic fora from the local to the global;
- strengthening the Human Rights Conventions and creating regional and global Human Rights courts;
- enhancing the transparency, accountability and effectiveness of leading functional IGQs; and building new bodies of this type where there is demonstrable need for greater public coordination and administrative capacity;
- improving the transparency accountability and voice of non-state actors;
- use of diverse forms of mechanisms to access public preferences, test their coherence and inform public will formation;
- establishment of an effective, accountable, regional and global police/military force for the last-resort use of coercive power in defence of international humanitarian or cosmopolitan law.

I call this agenda, and the institutions to which it gives rise, cosmopolitan democracy (Held, 1995, 2004, 2006; Archibugi and Held, 1995). Since I have elaborated it elsewhere, I will restrict myself here to the change it entails in the meaning of citizenship.

At the heart of a cosmopolitan conception of citizenship is the idea that citizenship can be based not on exclusive membership of a territorial community, but on general rules and principles which can be entrenched and drawn upon in diverse settings.

This conception relies on the availability and clarity of the principles of democracy and human rights. These principles create a framework for all persons to enjoy, in principle, equal moral status, equal freedom and equal participative opportunities. The meaning of citizenship shifts from membership in a community which bestows, for those who qualify, particular rights and duties to an alternative principle of world order in which all persons have equivalent rights and duties in the cross-cutting spheres of decision-making which affect their vital needs and interests. It posits the idea of a global political order in which people can enjoy an equality of status with respect to the fundamental processes and institutions which govern their life expectancy and life chances.

Within this context, the puzzling meaning of a cosmopolitan or global citizenship becomes a little clearer. Built on the fundamental rights and duties of all human beings, cosmopolitan citizenship underwrites the autonomy of each and every human being, and recognizes their capacity for self-governance at all levels of human affairs. Although this notion needs further clarification and unpacking, its leading features are within our grasp. Today, if people are to be free and equal in the determination of the conditions which shape their lives, there must be an array of fora, from the city to global associations, in which they can hold decision-makers to account. If many contemporary forms of power are to become accountable and if many of the complex issues that affect us all – locally, nationally, regionally and globally – are to be democratically regulated, people will have to have access to, and membership in, diverse political communities. As Jürgen Habermas has written, "only a democratic citizenship that does not close itself off in a particularistic fashion can pave the way for a *world citizenship* ... State citizenship and world citizenship form a continuum whose contours, at least, are already becoming visible" (Habermas, 1996, pp. 514–15). There is only a historically contingent connection between the principles underpinning citizenship and the national community; as this connection weakens in a world of overlapping communities of fate, the principles of citizenship must be rearticulated and re-entrenched. Moreover, in the light of this development, the connection between patriotism and nationalism becomes easier to call into question, and a case built to bind patriotism to the defence of core civic and political principles – not to the nation or country for their own sake (Heater, 2002). Only national identities open to diverse solidarities, and shaped by respect for general rules and principles, can accommodate themselves successfully to the challenges of a global age. Ultimately diversity and difference can flourish only in a "global legal community" (Brunkhorst, 2005; Held, 2002b).

There was once a time when the idea that the old states of Europe might share a set of economic, monetary and political institutions seemed improbable, to say the least. It also appeared improbable that the Cold War would be brought to an end by a peaceful revolution. The notion that Nelson Mandela would be released from jail alive, and that apartheid would be undone without substantial violence, was not anticipated by many. That China and India would be among the fastest-growing economies in the world once seemed unlikely. Let us hope that the task of reframing global governance is similarly possible, even though now it seems remote! Let us hope as well that this task is pursued with an increasing sense of urgency. For many, it is already "apocalypse now"; for the rest of us it may well be "apocalypse soon" unless our governance arrangements can meet the tests of solidarity, justice, democracy and effectiveness.

Policy shifts to replace the Washington Consensus and security doctrines

The Original Washington Consensus	Washington Consensus (augmented) The original list plus:
• Fiscal discipline • Reorientation of public expenditures • Tax reform • Financial liberalization • Unified and competitive exchange rates • Trade liberalization • Openness to foreign direct investment (FDI) • Privatization • Deregulation • Secure property rights	• Legal/political reform • Regulatory institutions • Anti-corruption • Labour market flexibility • WTO agreements • Financial codes and standards • "Prudent" capital-account opening • Non-intermediate exchange rate regimes • Social safety-nets • Poverty reduction
The Social Democratic Agenda Local • Sound macroeconomic policy • Nurturing of political/legal reform • Creation of robust public sector • State-led economic and investment strategy, enjoying sufficient development space to experiment with different policies • Sequencing of global market integration • Priority investment in human and social capital • Public capital expenditure on infrastructure • Poverty reduction and social safety-nets • Strengthening civil society	**The Social Democratic Agenda Global** • Salvaging Doha • Cancellation of unsustainable debt • Reform of trade-related intellectual property rights (Trips) • Creation of fair regime for transnational migration • Expand negotiating capacity of developing countries at international finance institutions (IFIs) • Increase developing country participation in the running of IFIs • Establish new financial flows and facilities for investment in human capital and internal country integration • Reform of UN system to enhance accountability and effectiveness of poverty reduction, welfare and environmental programmes

The Washington Security Doctrine	The Human Security Doctrine
1 Hegemonic	1 Multilateralism and common rules
2 Order through dominance	2 Order through law and social justice
3 'Flexible multilateralism' or unilateralism where necessary	3 Enhance multilateral collective security
4 Pre-emptive and preventive use of force	4 Last-resort use of internationally sanctioned force to uphold international humanitarian law
5 Security focus: geopolitical and, secondarily geoeconomic	5 Security focus: relinking security and human rights agendas: protecting all those facing threats to life whether political social, economic or environmental
6 Collective organization where pragmatic (UN, NATO), otherwise reliance on US military and political power	6 Strengthen global governance: reform UN Security Council; create Economic and Social Security Council: democratize UN
7 Leadership: United States and its allies	7 Leadership: develop a worldwide dialogue to define new global covenant
8 Aims: making world safe for freedom and democracy: globalizing American rules and justice	8 Aims: making world safe for humanity: global justice and impartial rules

Note

1   The eight Millennium Development Goals, established by the UN and agreed upon by the UN General Assembly in September 2000, are to: eradicate extreme poverty and hunger; achieve universal primary education; promote gender equality and empower women; reduce child mortality; improve health; combat HIV/AIDS, malaria and other diseases; ensure environmental sustainability; and develop a global partnership for development – all by the target date of 2015. See UN, 2000.

References

Annan, K. (2005) "Three Crises and the Need for American Leadership", in A. Barnett, D. Held and C. Henderson, eds, *Debating Globalization* Cambridge: Polity, pp. 134–40.

Archibugi, D. and D. Held, eds. (1995) *Cosmopolitan Democracy. An Agenda for a New World Order* Cambridge: Polity.

Barnett, A., D. Held and C. Henderson, eds. (2005) *Debating Globalization*, Cambridge: Polity.

Barry, B. (1998) "International Society from a Cosmopolitan Perspective", in D. Mapel and T. Nardin, eds, *International Society Diverse Ethical Perspectives* Princeton: Princeton University Press, pp. 144–63.

Brunkhorst, H. (2005) *Solidarity From Civic Friendship to Global Legal Community* Cambridge, Mass.: MIT Press.

Buira, A. (2003) "The Governance of the International Monetary Fund", in I. Kaul et al., *Providing Global Public Goods*, pp. 225–44.

Chasek, P. and I. Rajamani (2003) "Steps towards Enhanced Parity: Negotiating Capacity and Strategies of Developing Countries", in I. Kaul et al., *Providing Global Public Goods*, pp. 245–62.

Chinkin, C. (1998) "International Law and Human Rights", in T. Evans, ed., *Human Rights Fifty Years On. A Reappraisal* Manchester: Manchester University Press, pp. 105–28.

Conceição, P. (2003) "Assessing the Provision Status of Global Public Goods", in I. Kaul et al., *Providing Global Public Goods*, pp. 152–84.

Deacon, B. et al. (2003) "Global Social Governance Reform: From Institutions and Policies to Networks, Projects and Partnerships", in B. Deacon, E. Ollida, M. Koivusalo and P. Stubbs, eds. *Global Social Governance* Helsinki: Hakapaino Oy.

Giddens, A. (1990) *The Consequences of Modernity* Cambridge: Polity.

Habermas, J. (1996) *Between Facts and Norms Contribution to a Discourse Theory of Law and Democracy* trans. W. Rehg. Cambridge: Polity.

Heater, D. (2002) *World Citizenship* London: Continuum.

Held, D. (1995) *Democracy and the Global Order. From the Modern State to Cosmopolitan Governance* Cambridge: Polity.

Held, D. (2002a) "Globalization, Corporate Practice and Cosmopolitan Social Standards" *Contemporary Political Theory* 1(1): pp. 59–78.

Held, D. (2002b) "Law of States Law of Peoples: Three Models of Sovereignty" *Legal Theory* 8(1): pp. 1–44.

Held, D. (2004) *Global Covenant* Cambridge: Polity.

Held, D. (2006) *Models of Democracy* 3rd edn. Cambridge: Polity.

Held, D., A. G. McGrew, D. Goldblatt, D. J. Perraton (1999) *Global Transformations Politics Economics and Culture*, Cambridge: Polity.

Hirst, P. and G. Thompson (2002) "The Future of Globalization" *Cooperation and Conflict* 37(3): pp. 252–3.

Human Security Centre (2005) *Human Seem Report 2005 War and Peace in the 21st Century*, http://www.humansecurityreport info (accessed II February 2006).

Ikenberry, J. (2002) "America's Imperial Ambition". *Foreign Affairs*. 81(5): pp. 44–60.

Ikenberry, J. (2005) "A Weaker World". *Prospect* 116 (October): p. 32.

Kaul, I., P. Conceição, K. Le Goulven and R. V. Mendoza eds. (2003a) *Providing Global Public Goods* Oxford: Oxford University Press.

Kaul, I., P. Conceição, K. Le Goulven and R. V. Mendoza (2003b) "Why Do Global Public Goods Matter Today", in I. Kaul et al. *Providing Global Public Goods*. pp. 1–58.

Keohane, R. O. (2003) "Global Governance and Democratic Accountability", in D. Held and M. Koenig-Archibugi, eds. *Taming Globalization* Cambridge: Polity. pp. 130–59.

King, Sir David, A. (2004) "Climate Change Science: Adapt, Mitigate or ignore?" *Science*, 303 (January): pp. 176–7.

Meikle, J. (2005) "Bill Gates Gives $258m to World Battle against Malaria", *The Guardian* 31 October pp. 22.

Mendoza, R. V. (2003) "The Multilateral Trade Regime", in I. Kaul et al. *Providing Global Public Goods*, pp. 455–83.

Milanović, B. (2002) "True World Income Distribution. 1988 and 1993: First Calculation Based on Household Surveys Alone". *Economic Journal*, 112 (January): pp. 51–92.

Milanović, B. (2005) *Worlds Apart Measuring International and Global Inequality* Princeton: Princeton University Press.

Moore, M. (2003) *A World of without Walls* Cambridge: Cambridge University Press.

Pogge, T. (2007) "Reframing Economic Security and Justice", in D. Held and A. G. McGrew, eds. *Globalization Theory* Cambridge: Polity.

Rees, M. (2003) *Our Final Century* London: Arrow Books.

Rischard, J. F. (2002) *High Noon Twenty Global Problems, Twenty Years to Solve Them* New York: Basic Books.

Rodrick, D. (2005) "Making Globalization Work for Development". Ralph Miliband Public Lecture, London School of Economics. 18 November.

Rosenau, J. N. (2002) "Governance in a New Global Order", in D. Held and A. G. McGrew, eds. *Governing Globalization* Cambridge: Polity. pp. 70–86.

Ruggie, J. (2003) "Taking Embedded Liberalism Global: The Corporate Connection", in D. Held and M. Koenig-Archibugi, eds. *Taming Globalization* Cambridge: Polity. pp. 93–129.

UN (2000) "Millennium Development Goals", available at: www.unorg/millenniumgoals/ (accessed 14 February 2006).

UN (2004). "A More Secure World: Our Shared Responsibility", Report of the High-Level Panel on Threats. Challenges and Change, available at: www.unorg/secureworld/ (accessed 11 February, 2006).

UNDP (2005) *Human Development Report 2005*, Oxford/New York: Oxford University Press. Also available at: http://hdrundporg/reports/global/2005/.

18

The Architecture of Cosmopolitan Democracy
Daniele Archibugi

The global laboratory

[. . .]

This chapter sets out an ambitious project: it outlines the possible constitutional structure of a cosmopolitan democracy. A cosmopolitan democracy is but one of the possible forms of global governance, but it is one that tilts heavily toward a democratic management of the global commons. Choosing cosmopolitan democracy is based on two considerations. The first consists of asserting a conviction: democracy is better able to satisfy the demands of the world's population than any other form of governance. We cannot expect all to share this claim. The normative theory, especially when operating outside the boundaries of what has already passed the test of history, cannot provide evidence in support. Never before has the world had so many inhabitants; never before have there been such significant interconnections among the various parts. And never before has a cosmopolitan democracy been tried out. As is often the case in politics, doctrine is overwhelmed by individual interests and choices. To opt for a democratic management of global problems is a partisan choice. I make this choice, but not only as an act of faith. Just as democracy has bestowed more advantages than disadvantages on individual nations, I deem that democracy can bring long-term benefits to all the inhabitants of the Earth.

The second consideration pertains instead to the democratic goal. Looking back over the long and successful journey of democracy, we observe that it remains incomplete until such time as the problem of inclusion is solved.[1] Not only, but in the absence of any extension of the global sphere, the democratic breakthroughs achieved in individual countries are in jeopardy today. The democracy achieved inside a growing number of individual countries is liable to be sapped by globalization and will be reduced to a mere formality unless it succeeds in linking up also with the higher echelons of actual power management.[2]

Such a context sheds new light on the self-governance experiments carried out in the course of nearly three thousand years. Those experiments may actually be viewed as a laboratory in which a yet-to-be-attained goal is pursued. This is not the first time that, in order to survive, democracy has had to change its skin. When the first American settlers devised a system of participation based on the universal suffrage of all free adult men, and on a much larger scale than that of the ancient Greek cities or the Italian renaissance republics, the settlers did not even use the old word *democracy*, as this would have suggested "direct" democracy, something infeasible in their situation. Tom Paine defined direct democracy as "simple," and the authors of the *Federalist* preferred to use the term *republic*, explicitly asserting that "in a democracy the people meet and exercise the government in person; in a republic, they assemble and administer it by the representatives and agents."[3]

Yet the two systems, although different, share common values linking old democracy to the modern form: the legal equality of the citizens, the majority principle, the fact that, once established, the government must govern in the interest of all, the requirement that majorities should be transitory and not permanent, the idea that decisions must be taken after a public comparison of the various positions. These principles, which underscore the material advantages bestowed by democracy, may also be transferred with the necessary changes to the global sphere.

Areas of intervention

So what is the significance of reinventing democracy in order to enable it to govern the contemporary world? It is a matter of sharing a minimal list of substantial objectives, the responsibility for which is to be entrusted, although not necessarily in an exclusive fashion, to the global institutions. Without sharing certain minimal substantial objectives, a cosmopolitan democracy would boil down to mere procedure. These objectives must for the time being be minimalist: whatever form of transnational democracy is adopted, it is highly unlikely that it will possess the necessary resources and competencies to deal with street lighting or the ban on smoking; most competencies would therefore remain within the purview of the present-day power structures. Five areas of priority action may be listed.

(1) *Control over the use of force.* Try to keep political violence to a minimum both within and outside nation-states, until force is used solely as a last resort and regulated by previously established rules and procedures. This implies an extension of the principle of nonviolence.

(2) *Acceptance of cultural diversity.* Global system architecture must allow existing differences to be preserved and promoted. The successful attainment of a convergence of governance methods and even lifestyles must not be imposed by one party on the others, but achieved endogenously by free choice.

(3) *Strengthening of the self-determination of peoples.* It is necessary to ensure that every people is actually in a position to govern itself. This self-governance involves both the internal dimension, namely, the citizens' effective participation in the choices affecting their own political community, and the external dimension, namely, the absence of domination.

(4) *Monitoring internal affairs.* Self-determination also must be subjected to constraints in order to avoid individual political communities being governed in an authoritarian manner to the detriment of their subjects or those communities imposing their own dominion over subcommunities. It therefore becomes necessary to open up a channel of intervention in internal affairs that, although not appearing as an imposition by one party on the others, is concerned with the protection of human rights and has a place in the existing self-governance modes expressed in the

various political communities. This entails collective action being placed if necessary under the political control of external agents.

(5) *Participatory management of global problems.* Unlike other forms of global governance, cosmopolitan democracy gives prominence also to the management modes. By embracing the democratic cause, cosmopolitan governance therefore sets out to strengthen the dimension of political equality in global matters. In other words, it aims to extend the principle of political equality as far as the management of the global commons is concerned.

However minimalist, this list might conceivably be viewed as a mere pipe dream, with little relevance to the ruthless practice of world politics.[4] The daily press is full of reports on how these aims are ignored and trampled upon, and realist critics ridicule the underlying aspirations. Nevertheless, political theory has the task of setting objectives and endeavoring to identify the instruments to achieve them, if for no other reason than to identify adverse projects. Cosmopolitan democracy may best be conceived of as involving different levels of governance. These levels are bound not necessarily by hierarchical ties but rather by a set of functional relations. Five paradigmatic dimensions may be taken into consideration: local, state, interstate, regional, and global. These levels correspond to what Michael Mann termed "socio-spatial networks of social interaction."[5] It is a matter of verifying the extent to which the rules of democracy can be applied to each of these dimensions and their respective interactions. At the end of this exercise, the similarities and differences between existing state representative democracy and a possible global democracy will emerge.

The local dimension

Today it is hard to imagine a state democracy without a local network of democratic institutions, associations, and movements. This dimension is generally considered part of the normal meaning of state democracy and does not need any exhaustive treatment here. But today not even the local dimension is independent of the external dimension. There is a growing number of organizations – both governmental and not – linking together communities and local governments that do not belong to the same state.[6] In some cases, geographic proximity encourages the birth of these organizations, which are often limited by well-defined functions. However, in other cases, these organizations pursue goals that overstep the functions assigned to them as subunits of a territorial state. Nation-states rarely decide to devolve their competencies on specific issues to interlocal institutions, even when the interlocal institutions are able to involve all the stakeholders. Let us take the case of the Danube, a river that flows through at least ten countries but involves each of those countries in different ways. The relevant policies are coordinated by an IGO, the International Commission for the Protection of the Danube River, which, although involving the various port authorities and members of civil society, is the result of a convention underwritten by thirteen states. In spite of this, it is no easy matter for the commission to hammer out common policies and ensure those policies are implemented. Cosmopolitan democracy would suggest boosting the local government structure and, wherever necessary, setting up an ad hoc local government to solve problems involving separate parts of different territorial states. This approach would lend greater bargaining weight to the direct stakeholders and therefore make it easier to identify the policies most beneficial to the common good.

The state dimension

Although the democratic ideal has won converts among yesterday's adversaries, it is far from being established all over the world. The new democracies are in constant peril and are forced daily to overcome obstacles threatening their regime. Not even the more advanced democratic systems actually fully satisfy their own citizens' demands. Here the problem is not the expansion of state democracy, on which an abundant literature is available,[7] but rather the extension of democracy to the transnational sphere. I view the state as both a laboratory and an agent of cosmopolitan democracy. It is a laboratory in the sense that nowadays one of the problems on the nation-states' agenda is to acknowledge the rights of individuals who are not normally considered citizens – for instance, refugees and immigrants. A great deal still remains to be done to ensure that these individuals have the same rights that native-born citizens have. Democratic practice has to come to terms with the problem of who its citizens actually are. Are its citizens those who are born in a given community? Those living and paying taxes in the country? Those who would simply like to live there?

Even inside a given community, distinctions are beginning to be made among the rights of the various citizens and groups. One of the most significant developments in the modern theory of citizenship is the acknowledgment of the rights of communities that uphold different religious, cultural, and ethnic values. A democratic state is based not only on equality but also on the acceptance and indeed on the appreciation of these differences. The principle of political equality is gradually beginning to be interpreted flexibly and creatively. However, acknowledging the differences among members of the same political community makes its limits much harder to determine. Indeed, one sometimes wonders about the logic behind the current dividing lines that sometimes group together individuals with few or no cultural, ethnic, and religious affinities into the same state while on other occasions separate individuals with strong affinities across different states. The need for a cosmopolitan approach based on the principle of inclusion no longer arises only at the frontier but also in the schools and neighborhoods that already accommodate the whole wide range of ethnic groups.

In addition to having an internal dimension, a state is characterized by being a member of the international community. What distinguishes a good member from a bad one? John Rawls pondered what the foreign policy of a liberal state should be and noted several precepts that should unilaterally be followed by such a state.[8] We shall take his prescriptions as suggestions for guidelines for a democratic foreign policy. Rawls nevertheless left *agreements* between states in a residual role; this would allow the states – as in the pre-United Nations conception of international law – to autonomously determine their own external behavior. In the cosmopolitan democracy project, a liberal state must distinguish itself not only for the substance of its foreign policy but also because it follows a shared procedure. A nation-state wanting to be considered a worthy citizen of the international community should not only pursue a virtuous foreign policy (as suggested by Rawls) but also have the will to participate in the life of international institutions, to accept their procedures, and to respect their rules.[9]

The interstate dimension

The very existence of IGOs is an indication not only of the need to extend to interstate level at least some of the principles of democracy (formal equality among members, publicity of proceedings, rule of law) but also of the difficulties involved. It is not necessary to be an advocate of democracy and even less of cosmopolitan democracy to support the work of the IGOs: they have the aim of facilitating the functioning of states – both democratic and autocratic – as much as to restrict their sovereignty. Realists, idealists, functionalists, and federalists are all equally in favor of IGOs, even though each of these schools of thought envisages a different future for them. Are IGOs democratic institutions? If not, can they become so? The concept of democratic deficit is applied increasingly not only to the EU but also to other organizations, starting with the UN.[10] IGO members consist simply of governments accepted into the IGOs without having to pass any test of democratic legitimacy. Decisions affecting a number of countries may be taken by bodies of which both democratic and autocratic governments are members. A democratic state may have well-grounded reasons for being reluctant to accept the majority principle, for example, if many of the representatives of intergovernmental bodies have not been democratically elected, and all the more so if the competencies are extended to include matters of internal relevance.

But even if IGO composition were limited to democratic countries alone, as happens in the EU, there is no guarantee that the decision-making process will respect the will of the majority of stakeholders. IGOs are based on the formal equality of the member states, and this means that the voting rights of each country are independent of its population and of its political or military power and degree of involvement in the decisions taken. Can a decision taken by the UN General Assembly by a majority vote be considered democratic when the vote of Malta is equal to that of India and that of Grenada to the United States? In theory, nation-states accounting for only 5 percent of the world population have a majority in the GA. Would a decision approved by only six states (China, India, the United States, Indonesia, Brazil, and Russia) be more democratic even if those six states account for more than half the world's population? What majority principle would lead to a greater degree of democracy?[11]

In the Security Council, the five-country right to veto is a breach of all conventional democratic principles; in the IMF and the World Bank, decision-making power is based on wealth. At G7 or G8 summits, although these organizations are not formally IGOs owing to the absence of a statute, a small number of governments make decisions on matters regarding the entire planet. The main contemporary military alliance, NATO, although today made up entirely of democratic countries, has on several occasions intervened in the internal affairs of individual member states in order to prevent allegedly pro-Soviet parties from gaining access to government through free elections. Much remains to be done in order to ensure the IOs accept the principles of democracy.[12] The participation of individuals in IGO decisions is nonexistent or has only a decorative function. With the exception of the EU, which has an elected parliament, no other IGO sees the need to involve the people in discussing existing options. Only a small number of countries with more advanced political systems and generally of a small size allow their citizens to discuss the stance adopted by their own governments by the IGOs. In recent years, nongovernmental organizations have been consulted more often by the IGOs, albeit only in an advisory role. We are still far from having achieved anything resembling a global legislative assembly.

Dahl is certainly right when he claims that it is not easy to come up with procedures that satisfy the requirements of democracy in the IGOs, although this should be used as an incentive to ensure the problem of their democratization is placed on the agenda. There are numerous projects and campaigns aimed at the reform and democratization of both the UN and the other IGOs.[13] Let us examine choices that are political even more than theoretical. When it is a matter of demanding the abolition of the power of veto in the Security Council, of giving countries with a low quota in the IMF greater voting clout, of increasing the transparency of the World Trade Organization, where do the champions of democracy stand?

Regional dimension

Problems that do not fit into the nation-state dimension may be addressed at the regional level. In many cases the level of regional governance is more appropriate and effective for public policies. The most significant historical example of this is the EU, where the first six member states slowly but constantly developed a political system able both to strengthen itself and to strengthen its members' internal democracy. The capacity to associate first six, and then twenty-seven, and in the future an even larger number of countries, along with a parliament elected by universal franchise distinguishes Europe from all the other regional organizations. The EU is without doubt the most sophisticated but not the only case of regional organization. The past decade has witnessed an increase in the number of regional organizations and a strengthening of their functions in all quarters, above all for commercial reasons. Not surprisingly many of those regional organizations look at the EU as a model to emulate.[14]

The regional dimension can be an important factor of stability in areas where the individual components are substantially less familiar with the procedures of democracy, where state political unity has often proved unable to retain the exclusive use of force within the state and to maintain peaceful relations without it. Let us take the case of the Great Lakes region in Central Africa: the formation of nation-states has been superimposed on older communities such as the village, the ethnic group, and race. Many of the conflicts in that area, such as the endemic conflicts between rival ethnic groups, could be addressed more effectively through a regional organization that, as well as including representatives of the states, would also incorporate some representatives from the various local communities. Others have suggested using the cosmopolitan democracy model to set up regional trade zones like Mercado Común del Sur.[15]

One interesting case is that of the East African Community, which has endeavored to repeat some of the features typical of the EU even though the EAC's members have much weaker institutions and in some cases are on the brink of becoming "failed states." Already today the EAC issues passports, thus bypassing one of the monocratic powers claimed by the state, namely, to authorize its own citizens to go abroad and to decide who has the right to enter the state. There are plans to issue a common currency in 2009. It is hard to predict how far this process will go, and in all likelihood the elites will feel its influence more strongly than the masses: in Africa if you have a passport and currency you are already part of the elite. This could be a form of cosmopolitanism that is not necessarily open to the demos. This regional integration would still involve the transfer of competencies that had previously been the exclusive prerogative of the state to different institutions lacking powers of coercion. Unlike the EU, where consolidated nation-states gradually transferred competencies to the union, what is happening in East Africa shows that the process of integration can also take place between still-unconsolidated states. Such an integration can even be used as a policy to prevent the collapse of state institutions or to develop for the first time competencies hitherto not pertaining to the states.

The global dimension

It is certainly hard to imagine how global decisions can be taken on the basis of democratic procedures. But let us begin by assuming that global governance actually exists and that international society is no longer, if it ever was, entirely anarchic.[16] Existing governance is highly imperfect, as it does not always succeed in achieving the set objectives and because in many cases it eludes all control. In the case of arms, financial flows, even of trade, the regulation planned by the various international regimes often fails to keep the various economic agents under control. And, more importantly, the existing controls are often not accountable. Is it possible to constrain global governance within democratic procedures? In a global dimension, citizens should have a voice and a political franchise in parallel to and independently of those they have inside the state. This proposal is perhaps less bold than it appears. For at least a decade the opinions of subjects not having any decision-making power have been aired at the various UN summits. On the other hand, a broader-based level of governance of the range of action of states, both individually and collectively, is gradually emerging. The UN itself and its specialized agencies, although retaining their essentially intergovernmental nature, have largely transcended these barriers.

The claim to a democratization of global governance has been advanced in numerous sectors: financial movements, migratory flows, environmental issues, defense of fundamental human rights, development aid.[17] This list could be continued at length. It is therefore not surprising that, in each of these regimes, there are initiatives and campaigns aimed at enhancing representativeness, transparency, and public assessment.[18] The various initiatives proceed independently, although each initiative is pushing in the direction of a greater democratization. However, it is equally important to indicate the direction in which these individual actions are nudging the international system. In this sense, cosmopolitan democracy merely sets out to offer a framework linking what the citizens and global movements are laboriously trying to achieve in so many different areas.

The relations between levels of governance

From sovereignty to constitutionalism

The aims of cosmopolitan democracy thus take the form of the pursuit of democracy at different levels of governance that are mutually autonomous but complementary. At a time of increasing levels of governance and of the relative institutions, a question comes spontaneously to mind: how to distribute the competencies among the various bodies? Is there not a danger of creating fresh divisions among the bodies, in which each institution claims to be sovereign although none actually is? Could the existence of institutions with overlapping competencies, where each institution claims its own sovereignty, actually lead to new conflicts? Sovereignty is obviously the key concept on which the international legal system has been based since the Restoration. It is sovereignty that has defined the competencies of nation-states and established that the limits of each one should coincide, at least formally, with its own borders. To abandon the universe of sovereign states would perhaps amount to a return to the so-called neo-medievalism that Bull has already warned us of, where the loyalty of the individuals and of the institutions would again have to be split between an emperor and a pope, between local and global powers. Today this would mean that political agents would be under the authority of local authorities, national governments, IGOs, and nongovernmental associations and that any action would be subordinated to a variety of approvals. The fear is that all decision-making powers would be blocked, as decision-making capacity would no longer be linked to a legitimacy ensured by an effective power residing in sovereign states.

Cosmopolitan democracy is ideally part of that school of thought that, from Kelsen on, has considered sovereignty a dogma that must be superseded.[19] This idea is based on the assumption that it is incompatible with democracy to allow any political or institutional player to be not accountable. Whether a despot or a "sovereign" people, each political subject should be requested to come to terms with the other political subjects in the case of overlapping spheres of power. Historically, sovereignty has largely been an artificial creation, an "organized hypocrisy," that in only a small number of cases succeeded in limiting the extraterritorial interests of nation-states.[20] However, the problem arises of deciding what to replace sovereignty with, as even today the formal claim of sovereignty serves the purpose of curbing the domination of the weaker by the more powerful.

The tension between the concept of sovereignty and that of democracy demands that sovereignty be replaced, both within and between states, by constitutionalism, thereby subjecting every institution to rules, checks, and balances. The idea behind this proposal closely resembles that of the vertical dispersion of sovereignty suggested by Pogge and of the cosmopolitan model of sovereignty proposed by Held.[21] Nevertheless, the very term *sovereignty*, at least from the normative point of view, seems incompatible both with the idea of democracy and with a level of legitimacy higher than that of the individual nation-state. This draws attention to the need to redirect the conflicts of competence among the various levels of governance toward a global constitutionalism and to bring conflicts before jurisdictional bodies, as recommended by Kelsen, which would act in accordance with an explicit constitutional mandate.[22] The idea that global conflicts can be resolved by means of constitutional and legal procedures rather than by force is based on the conviction that rules may be enforced even in the absence of an ultimate power of coercion.[23] The cosmopolitan democracy project is thus seen to be much more ambitious – to transform international politics from a domain of antagonism to one of agonism. In democratic states this process has gradually become established, and it is accepted as normal practice that the various institutions experience conflicts of competence.

Redefinition of political community constituencies

We have claimed that political communities of the disjunctive type based on dividing lines between the included and the excluded are not a suitable model of the democratic management of the *res publica* in the age of globalization. But while it is easy to find evidence of numerous repeated democratic deficits, it is much more difficult to identify what the ideal political community should be like. Who must decide what? How many and which political communities must each individual belong to? We have stated several general principles that should inform democratic attitudes such as, for example, the inclination to participate of all persons involved in a decision-making process. But each person is involved to a different extent and with a different intensity. The broader the participation of stakeholders, the more important it is for each stakeholder's relative decision-making clout.

[. . .]

How can the ideal political community thus be delimited? On certain global issues, such as those related to the environment, safeguarding human rights, or future generations, there is no reason to depart from the "one person, one vote" principle. Even if each person is involved to a different extent, democratic theory assumes that individuals act as representatives of the political community. Even centenarians vote on environmental issues, the repercussions of which will be felt decades later. In a democratic political community, it is assumed that the judgment of individuals can contribute to the best decision for society regardless of whether the individuals are directly involved. However, the same principle does not hold for purely local issues, and so only the inhabitants of a given city are eligible to elect the mayor. When transplanting democratic principles at the global level, it is necessary to decide who is to wield the decision-making power. It is easy to find a Solomonic agreement based on the idea that everyone involved must be consulted, but in the end who actually decides? What is the composition of the specific decision-making bodies?

Let us return to the case of the Danube. How must the relative electoral weighting be decided in a reformed International Commission for the Protection of the Danube River? Under the existing system, Germany and Hungary have the same clout. In a reformed system, it is conceivable that an inhabitant of a city through which the river flows, such as Vienna, Budapest, or Belgrade, should have greater decision-making power than someone who lives in Berlin, Prague, or Sofia. As a first approximation, it is preferable for local matters to be self-regulated, because it is always better for the parties involved to be able to come up with institutional forms that can ensure that everyone is represented. This would entail an institutive process in which the various stakeholders decide on how decision making is to be regulated. Yet not always do the parties involved reach agreement. In the case of the Mururoa atomic experiments in 1996, the French state and the Pacific communities reached no agreement. In cases such as that, the parties should make recourse to other powers that are able to establish the relative weight of the various actors in decision making and to assign competencies. In democratic systems, this is the task assigned to the legislative assemblies and the constitutional courts. At the global level, similar institutions should also have the task of deciding on the decision-making clout of the stakeholders and of assigning competencies.[24]

What type of union of states?

The cosmopolitan project may be envisaged within the framework of the theory of unions of states. The theory of the unions of states takes in institutional relations and interactions among the various components. To accept the idea that the international system can converge on union means adopting a clear stance in favor of a specific form of global governance based on the legal coding of the interactions. Let us take the two principal models of existing state systems, confederation and federation, as our points of reference.[25] Confederation and federation will be described here as ideal models, not necessarily related to specific historical experiences. Later, I will show how the cosmopolitan democracy model differs substantially from confederation and federation and how cosmopolitan democracy proposes a kind of meta-union among states. The salient features of the three models are summed up in table 1. The question is now to see to what extent the confederal and federal models satisfy the definitions of democracy in the following dimensions: (a) within states, (b) among states, and (c) global (for the sake of simplicity, the local and regional dimensions will not be addressed although they are nevertheless easy to infer).

Table 1 Three Models of Union of States: Confederation, Federation, Cosmopolitan Democracy			
Distinctive Features	**Confederal Model**	**Federalist Model**	**Cosmopolitan Democracy Model**
Components	The members of a confederation are governments and not individuals.	The citizens are members of the federation and participate in the appointment of the federal government.	Both individuals and governments have their own representatives in the global sphere.
Citizenship	Individuals have neither rights nor duties vis-à-vis the confederation, except those envisaged by their own state.	Although the citizens are members of both individual states and of the federation, their duties vis-à-vis the former are secondary to those vis-à-vis the latter. The federation guarantees that the citizens' constitutional rights are respected in the individual states.	Together with their citizenship of the state, individuals also acquire a cosmopolitan citizenship. This envisages a minimal list of rights and duties vis-à-vis constituting cosmopolitan institutions.
Membership criteria	Merits of the candidates' political constitution are not analyzed. Accepted members are governments that have effective control of the territory whose membership is deemed advantageous to the other members.	A federation is a union of states with politically homogeneous constitutions. The member states are called upon to respect the constitutional rules governing the federation.	Admission to intergovernmental organizations is regulated by the principle of effective control over a given territory, excluding only governments that violate fundamental human rights (for instance, genocide and apartheid). Cosmopolitan institutions accept only delegates deemed to be legitimate representatives of their respective peoples.
Decision-making criterion	There is formal equality among states, embodied in the principle of "one state, one vote."	Even though the formal equality between states is maintained, the principal electoral criterion of the federation is "one citizen, one vote."	1. Intergovernmental institutions are based on equality among the states, as guaranteed by the principle of "one state, one vote". 2. Cosmopolitan institutions are based on equality among citizens, as guaranteed by the principle "one individual, one vote."
Internal sovereignty	Internal sovereignty is held by the member states.	The member states devolve their internal sovereignty to the federation, which is competent in constitutional and fiscal matters.	The internal sovereignty of the states is limited by global constitutional rules and is aimed at ensuring effective self-determination.
External sovereignty	External sovereignty is partially relinquished even though foreign and defense policy is the exclusive prerogative of state governments.	External sovereignty is firmly in the hands of the federal government, which control both foreign policy and the armed forces.	The external sovereignty of the states is replaced by a global constitutionalism. The union has the task of solving conflicts by negotiation.

Table 1 *(Continued)*			
Distinctive Features	**Confederal Model**	**Federalist Model**	**Cosmopolitan Democracy Model**
Powers of coercion	The confederation has no powers of coercion of its own. Its military actions rely on the armies of the member states.	The individual states can rely on autonomous police forces but have no armed forces, which are under the exclusive control of the federation.	The states retain their own armed forces. Humanitarian interventions to prevent acts of genocide are managed by cosmopolitan institutions.
Jurisdiction of states	No compulsory jurisdiction is envisaged. Any legal power that exists is more arbitrational than jurisdictional.	The federation's constitution provides for a compulsory jurisdiction regarding disputes between states and between a state and federation. The executive power of the federation enforces decision execution.	The member states accept the compulsory jurisdiction of the international courts. Although the union has no means of coercion to enforce the decisions, it can use sanctions.
Criminal jurisdiction	Absent. Only the national courts have jurisdiction in individual crimes.	Individual states have their own autonomous criminal jurisdictions. In the case in which the constitutional rules have been breached, the federation can intervene and call criminal jurisdiction to itself.	A criminal court is envisaged which has compulsory jurisdiction and can intervene in the case of crimes not punished or pursued by national legislations.
Participation	The participation of member states is voluntary and revocable.	Secession from the federation is possible only in accordance with precise constitutional rules, and the decision of last resort is often in the hands of federal courts and legislative assemblies.	Participation is voluntary and revocable. It nevertheless requires consulting the citizens in addition to their governments. In cosmopolitan institutions, the union can resolve to accept citizens also representing states that do not intend to participate.
Territorial delimitation	The borders delimiting each state are accepted by all members and may be modified only on a consensual basis.	In disputes among states or within the state, the federation is competent to determine the territorial limits of individual states.	In the case of disputes among states or within the state, the territorial modifications are indicated by the union with a view to enforcing individual rights and self-government.

The confederal model

A confederation is an association of sovereign states that have underwritten a treaty to agree on given questions. Some confederations have come into being as coalitions to oppose rival states or unions of states and thus have an essentially military function. NATO is a case in point. Other confederations, such as Zollverein, the European Common Market, and the North Atlantic Free Trade Agreement were set up for commercial reasons. Some confederations, including several of the oldest, such as the Universal Postal Union and the International Telegraph Union, are virtually open to every state in the world, although they have only a limited scope. However, the confederations of interest here are those with universal validity and whose main objective is to prevent war and guarantee peace, such as the League of Nations and the United Nations.

a. *Democracy within states.* The confederal model may indirectly facilitate internal democratization, as it can lead to the removal of several of the obstacles placed in the way of internal political participation by a conflictual international system. However, the confederal model makes no provision for a channel of direct intervention to promote the democracy of states. The principle of noninterference prohibits the intervention of both the confederation and its individual member states in the internal affairs of another member. Not even in the most sensational cases of fundamental human rights breaches, such as genocide, does the confederation have the right to intervene in the internal affairs of a state. The only protection afforded to individuals in a confederation is that of their own governments. Even though the confederal model envisages a partial renunciation of external sovereignty, it does not entail any renunciation of internal sovereignty. Indeed, the very existence of a mutual institutional recognition among states may increase the stability of ruling governments even when these governments are not legitimated by any democratic mandate. Actually, the confederation makes external intervention on humanitarian grounds more difficult. Like individuals also the ethnic minorities of a state who seek their own self-determination, both internal and external, have access solely to the institutions of their own state and not to those of the confederation. The problem of internal democracy thus remains wholly removed from the international system.

b. Democracy among states. In the confederal model, nondomination is guaranteed by respect for the sovereignty and autonomy of the states. Nevertheless, a genuine interstate democracy is limited by the fact that both democratic and autocratic governments enjoy the same rights. It is actually possible to envisage a world order in which decisions are made quite democratically by the several governments even when all the governments are autocratic. [. . .]

c. Global democracy. As the confederal model makes no provision for any form of participation by individuals in international politics, the making of global choices is delegated to the relations among states, which are represented by their respective governments. The citizens have no direct say in global matters except through their own governments. Global democracy thus proves impossible. Even if all the members were democratic governments, the governments of the nation-states would not necessarily represent global interests, as they are called upon to represent the specific interests of their own constituency rather than the common interest. An example of this is the EU: the Council of Ministers on which the representatives of the individual governments sit is much more reluctant to support European solutions than a body elected by universal suffrage such as the European Parliament. The reason why the confederal model fails to satisfy the criteria for global democracy is that it is based on and reinforces intergovernmental oligarchism. This model provides no opportunity for constructing cross-links between civil societies in the individual states; the individual states have no institutional channels through which to communicate with each other and have the limitation of being represented by state political forces in matters that transcend state borders.

The federalist model

The federalist model has a much more rigid constitutional structure than the confederal model. The federalist model aims at implementing principles and rules that are valid for all the members of the federation. The federalist model, which has its noblest theoretical foundations in the writings of Hamilton, Madison, and Jay, has been applied in numerous contemporary states, including the United States, Switzerland, and

Germany. These three nations grew up as confederations and gradually centralized their powers until they became constitutionally based federal states. Other earlier confederations such as the United Provinces of the Netherlands developed into a unitary state. In the important intellectual and political tradition that arose out of federalism, it is claimed that the problem of peace and democracy in the world can be resolved only by imposing strong limitations on the sovereignty of states and by giving rise to a process of centralization of power that leads to a world federal state.[26] In this tradition, it is considered that the subdivision of the world into nation-states is a transcendable historical legacy. Federalist thinking stresses the existence of human rights having universal values that may be safeguarded solely by setting up a corresponding political institution. Let us now examine whether this model of political organization satisfies the three criteria for democracy outlined above.

a. *Democracy within states.* When the federation is founded on the principles of democracy, democracy is necessarily extended to the individual members. In the case of conflict, the federal government has the authority and the necessary means of coercion to impose the respect of democratic principles on the individual nation-states. Conflicts among the various organs of a federation have been known to end in civil war. The most famous instance is the American Civil War, which led to the reinstatement of the union and the enforcement in all the states of a constitutional norm imposed by the federal government, namely, the abolition of slavery. The concept of democracy as an endogenous conquest gives rise to doubts as to whether a single model may be applied to all regions in the world. A prerequisite for the federal system is a unified system of rules among the various parties, which is unlikely to be compatible with existing cultural and anthropological differences in the world.

b. *Democracy among states.* In the narrow sense, democracy among states can no longer exist in a federation, as the sovereign states themselves have been abolished. Relations between the central authorities and the local authorities are instead regulated as conflicts of competence, as we learn from the history of existing federal states. The process of centralization giving rise to federal states has shown that the existence of external threats was what enabled different communities to accept a single sovereignty. The centralization of power that occurred in the Swiss Confederation, in the Dutch Provinces, and in the United States arose out of the need for defense against attack by other states. The question is whether the same experiment is possible at the worldwide level in which there are no external dangers. It seems that, in the absence of any threat to survival, the desire to preserve local identity outweighs the desire to give rise to a centralized power. There is always the likelihood that one party will take control over the others using coercive means, creating a sort of federal empire. However, if a means such as war is used to set up such a model, there is no reason to believe that the institution's subsequent functioning would be based on the rules of democracy.

c. *Global democracy.* A centralized federal power would have the authority and the competence to address global problems on the basis of democratic principles. It is nevertheless likely that a number of problems would be addressed at the expense of individual communities. A government for the whole world, however democratic, would be the expression of a heterogeneous majority, while the minorities that were not part of the government would be even more heterogeneous. A government of this kind would therefore constantly be tempted to find technocratic solutions to problems. In a word, this kind of government would resemble Plato's government of guardians more than an authentically democratic government.

Model of cosmopolitan democracy

Let us now examine the possibility of planning a union of states that is intermediate between the confederal model and the federalist one, that is, more centralized than the confederal model but less centralized than the federalist model. Unlike in the case of the first two models, no historically significant experiences of cosmopolitan democracy exist.

The model that comes closest to cosmopolitan democracy is the result of transient experiences: confederations that took on the essential characteristics of cosmopolitan democracy in the move toward federal arrangements. However, the requirements of democratic management were much easier to satisfy in the past than in the present. In the contemporary world, the EU is passing through this intermediate stage: it is something more than a simple confederation but not yet a federal system. It is not known whether the EU will take the typical form of a federation or whether it will retain its distinctive features. The UN already has some features that make it more sophisticated than a typical confederation.

Underlying the cosmopolitan model is the idea that it is preferable not to proceed beyond a certain degree of centralization of power, and in particular, of means of coercion, on such a large scale as that of the entire planet. When applied to the whole world, the cosmopolitan democracy model is not intended to be a temporary step toward a federal system but a permanent form of organization. Cosmopolitan democracy is therefore a project that aims to develop democracy at different levels of governance on the assumption that, although independent of each other, these levels may be pursued simultaneously. This model also shows that each level demands different procedures.

The cosmopolitan model sets out on the one hand to integrate and on the other to limit the functions of existing states by means of new institutions founded on the citizens of the world. These institutions would be competent to manage issues of global significance, such as the capability of interfering inside other states in cases of violation of human rights. The cosmopolitan system presupposes not only the existence of universal human rights protected by the states but also the formation of a hard core of rights that individuals can demand from global institutions. These rights are relevant, in the first instance, to the sphere of survival and to issues extending beyond state borders. Vis-à-vis these rights, the citizens of the world have certain obligations that should allow them, through global institutions, to perform a function of subsidiarity or of replacement with regard to the state institutions.

a. Democracy within states. Unlike the case of the federalist model, the cosmopolitan democracy model can accommodate states with different political constitutions. This does not mean, however, blind acceptance of the principle of noninterference, as applies in the confederal model. Indeed, the cosmopolitan model has the declared aim of transmitting to and disseminating among the various political communities methods and tools of government and therefore of introducing and gradually developing democracy in all the members of the international community. However, the conception of democracy on which the cosmopolitan model is based seems to indicate that, in one form or another, differences in the political systems will continue to exist, which means that an IO must accommodate different systems. The idea of including states with autocratic regimes is grounded on two assumptions: on the one hand, there is nothing like the existence of common institutions to facilitate the development of democracy from within; on the other, the elimination or reduction of the threat of war deprives autocratic governments of one of their principal arguments for imposing their own internal dominion, that is, external threat.

Since intervention by one state in the internal affairs of another can be instrumental, the cosmopolitan model entrusts to the citizens, rather than to the national governments, the task of "interfering" in the internal affairs of each state. The aim of this interference is to increase political participation inside each state and to enforce recognized human rights. It arises out of the conception of democracy as outlined above that every nation in the world, although they are at very different stages of the democratic process, has something to gain from a critical analysis of its own political system performed in the light of existing experiences in other countries.

b. *Democracy among states.* Interstate relations are regulated by IGOs. Multilateralism is the instrument used to guarantee noninterference and to prevent individual states from performing hostile acts against other members of the international community. Should the arbitration performed by the intergovernmental institutions fail to achieve the desired result, disputes among states are sent before international judicial institutions, the mandatory jurisdiction of which is accepted by the states. Should a member state refuse to obey the decision of the judicial authority, the international community can take various kinds of coercive measures, including economic, political, and cultural sanctions. Military force is used solely as a last resort when all the other political and diplomatic measures have failed. It is placed under the direct control of the union's governing bodies and must be approved in advance by the institutions of world citizens. It behooves the states participating in an armed conflict to keep war victims on both sides to a minimum. One instrument used by the international community is to appeal to the citizens of the state having violated international law to overthrow its own government and replace it with a government that complies with international legality.

c. *Global democracy.* Issues deemed to be essentially global, such as environmental matters and those regarding humankind's survival, including the rights of future generations, are referred to transnational and not only to intergovernmental institutions. Global civil society is able to access political decisions on these matters through new permanent institutions. These institutions may be endowed with specific competencies (such as the environment, demographic issues, development, and disarmament) or with broader political mandates (such as the safeguarding of fundamental human rights and the safeguarding of future generations). Some of these topics may be addressed at the local or regional level by setting up ad hoc organizations. Other topics are entrusted to true global institutions. The global institutions are intended to supplement, not to replace, existing IGOs.

[. . .]

World citizenship

A project as ambitious as that of cosmopolitan democracy also requires the availability of an innovative legal apparatus. Here we focus on two crucial aspects: citizenship and, in the next section, the global legal system.

The desire for a citizenship accommodating all human beings, such as to allow them to travel to, visit, and live in any corner of the earth, is an old and never satisfied one.

In recent times, this desire has taken on much more concrete features for increasingly large groups of individuals. Managers, rock stars, and football idols have become the symbols of a nonterritorial citizenship, but less privileged groups of individuals, whether they are immigrants, refugees, or tourists, also discover they are living in a metanational space. In the abundant recent literature on the subject, cosmopolitan citizenship is often interpreted more in a sociological than legal sense.[27] Cosmopolitan democracy is therefore aimed at representing the condition of the inhabitants of the Earth in the present era, marked by problems and interactions that transcend one's own local community. One characteristic of this sociological dimension is the extent to which it varies among different groups of persons: each individual makes use of and consumes global space in a different way. Significant studies have focused specifically on particular groups that, because of their own personal and collective history, have an identity and membership status that coincide only partly or not at all with a specific territorial state. Ethnic minorities, refugees, and immigrants are but several examples of this. In these cases, the specific social condition has drawn attention to the need for institutional instruments other than those made available by the more conventional forms of citizenship.

However, when speaking of citizenship it is useful to separate the sociological problem from the legal one, the analysis of the ongoing processes from the type of regulatory and institutional response required. This distinction, which would facilitate all studies on citizenship – even those addressing a single country – becomes essential when dealing with the transnational sphere. From the sociological point of view, we are all more or less, directly or indirectly, willy nilly, citizens of the world. [. . .] However, this social feeling in no way shows that the rights and duties of world citizenship already exist.

The distinction between the sociological and the legal dimension could not actually be more clear-cut: while individual participation in global processes increases, legal rules still link rights and duties to the territorial states. These are not abstract problems: public administrations have to cope daily with controversial issues. Let us take, for example, e-business, which accounts for a significant and increasing proportion of business transactions. There is no longer a clear link between the place in which the service is performed and the place in which taxes are levied on the service (where paying taxes is considered one of the citizens' duties). Similar problems arise in the case of different rights of citizenship: a growing number of persons, for instance, are entitled to or are denied health care in countries other than their own. In fields such as these, there is ample scope for IGOs actions directed toward harmonization.

Can the existing gap between social and legal conditions be bridged? What are the conditions to generating a global commonwealth in which citizens would have explicit rights and duties? Cosmopolitan citizenship is appealed to as an instrument of participation in and of safeguarding human rights. By virtue of the Universal Declaration of Human Rights and the subsequent pacts, individuals have been endowed with positive rights that they can claim from their own states. In addition, the states have accepted to be mutually accountable for these rights. However, despite the complexity of the international regulations governing human rights, in which governments, IGOs, and NGOs are involved, the effectiveness of those regulations has so far been very modest. Ever since its inception, the UN and the other IOs have failed both to safeguard individuals and to mete out effective sanctions against states that violate human rights despite the frequency and extreme intensity of the abuses committed. This failure has opened up a chasm between recognized rights and enforcement. This situation is closely linked to the very nature of the current regime of human rights, which is only partially able to offset the principle of noninterference and the dogma of sovereignty. One reason why the regime of human rights is so weak is linked to the fact that this regime has been managed mainly within the framework of intergovernmental relations. Condemnation and acquittal have thus often become negotiating tools in the diplomatic contest, while the most effective sanctions are still found to be those applied through denunciation to public opinion. Individuals find themselves in a hybrid situation: they possess certain rights but have no direct extrastate access channels through which to exercise those rights. The projection of individuals into a global sphere has taken place without any adjustment being made to their legal status.

The concept of world citizenship may hopefully help to close the existing gap by obliging states to observe transparency and accountability in their actions vis-à-vis nonstate institutions. Cosmopolitan democracy is not intended to replace national citizenship with world citizenship. Such a replacement would lead back to the federalist option. World citizenship should not take on all the values of nation-state citizenship but rather be restricted to several fundamental rights. This would further mean that it is necessary to identify the areas in which individuals must have certain rights and duties insofar as those individuals are world citizens in addition to their rights and duties as citizens of secular states. In some cases the areas of competence may overlap and in others those areas may be complementary. The EU has shown that it is possible to accompany the citizenship existing inside the states with some form of transnational citizenship, and this experience is becoming an example for several other regional organizations.

What spheres should world citizenship be invoked for? Let us take as our point of reference the Universal Declaration of Human Rights and the associated pacts. However sacred the principles enshrined in them are, they are so wide-ranging that it is impossible to imagine that the global institutions now being set up can manage to enforce them. Since they are not binding for anyone, the Universal Declaration has indicated such a vast array of principles that it may be considered a "book of dreams." It will be helpful to establish priorities on which world citizens hammer out an agreement to ensure that some core rights are enforced. The first priority involves the sphere of survival. The second regards the respect of fundamental human rights and the possibility of each political community to govern itself and to share in the management of global problems.

Institutions and resources are required in order to achieve these goals. As far as institutions are concerned, these tasks should be entrusted to bodies that represent a direct expression of the citizens, regardless of and parallel to the institutions of their respective states. It is possible to envisage a world parliament expressing a secretariat that is called upon to act directly in cases of glaring need. These cases would consist of natural disasters, famine, and any of the areas touching on survival. These institutions should be backed up by autonomous, albeit limited, resources that are not dependent on the member states. These resources could be funded by a small tax levy, for which numerous technical devices have been suggested, for instance, international taxes such as a surcharge on air tickets and financial transactions.[28] Only when survival is at risk because of conflicts would these institutions be entitled to request the intervention of the states, as the states have a much more powerful secular arm. However, in addition to direct intervention, world citizenship should imply a political role of intervention in global affairs backed up by a mandate adequately covering the whole range of the Universal Declaration. A world parliament would have the authority to perform these tasks. Although lacking any concrete means for carrying out direct intervention, a world parliament would still be performing a politically burdensome role, particularly for the more democratic states. These interventions would actually no longer be bound by the principle of noninterference, as they would not now be promoted by a state but by a body representing world citizens.

A contract of citizenship characterized by basic rights and minimum duties opens up the way to a global commonwealth of citizens, which could take thicker forms for certain groups of persons in conditions of extreme need. Groups of persons deprived of their national citizenship rights could find protection in a more comprehensive world citizenship in which the institutions in charge perform several administrative functions such as the issue of passports, hitherto the exclusive competence of the states.[29] Refugees often live in conditions of extreme poverty and are certainly not members of any elite. Today they number about twenty million, often living in make-shift camps, who have to fight to survive. If these persons were provided with the status of world citizenship, they could become the first group to benefit from the "right to have rights" ensured by cosmopolitan institutions and denied them by their states of origin. If refugees were granted certain rights associated with world citizenship, such as a guaranteed income and a chance to stay in a free port while awaiting repatriation, a significant discrepancy would arise between the social group to which the rights were granted and the social group having the duties. If the contributions needed to fund world citizenship were to come, as some have suggested, from taxes levied on air travel or financial transfers, it would be the elites who bore the brunt, while the beneficiaries of the rights would be groups, such as refugees, in conditions of extreme hardship.

Another significant case is that of immigrants, although this case leads to the opposite prescription. Immigrants have to live and work in countries different from their original one; they pay taxes but have fewer rights than members of the state in which they now live (for example, immigrants do not have the right to vote). If it is considered that the vast majority of immigrants gravitate toward the richer and more developed countries, it would be counterproductive to safeguard immigrants by means of a world citizenship, the legal and political strength of which would inevitably be weaker than that of the nation-state. It would seem in this case that the idea of world citizenship is more useful if used to request that the host states incorporate into their own system the extension to aliens of rights hitherto reserved to natives of these countries. In this sense, world citizenship would become an instrument for exerting pressure on the states to convince them to become champions of cosmopolitanism in their own territorial area by granting rights and duties to those who de facto participate in the life of their community.

Toward cosmopolitan law

The idea of cosmopolitan law – introduced by Kant in his well-known essay *Perpetual Peace* – has been brought back into fashion in an attempt to seek a legal framework for the demand for a generalized enforcement of human rights.[30] From the standpoint of legal construction, possibly Kant's greatest contribution is related to the subdivision of public law into three branches: public, interstate, and cosmopolitan. These branches correspond to the three organization levels that the philosopher himself had referred to in the three definitive articles of his hypothetical peace treaty. The first article was dedicated to internal constitutional law and acknowledged the republican constitution as a device that favored peace. The second article was dedicated to interstate law, inviting nation-states to form a free federation. The third article was dedicated to cosmopolitan law, observing that "the peoples of the earth have thus entered in varying degrees into a universal community, and it has developed to the point where a violation of rights in one part of the world is felt everywhere."[31]

Unfortunately the Kantian season in legal doctrine was short-lived. First the Napoleonic wars and then the Restoration were destined to support a rigid dichotomy between internal public law and interstate law. This is clearly expressed in Hegel's philosophy, to the extent that in his *Philosophy of Law* the very term *international* was replaced by the concept of external state law.[32] After the Napoleonic frenzy, during which making and unmaking states had become a party game between one battle and the next, Hegel expressed the need to bolster internal sovereignty, the negation of which had been the cause of so much bloodshed for nearly twenty years. Sovereignty was gradually reinforced in European law during the nineteenth century, becoming the legal doctrine inherited by the twentieth century. However, ever since the foundation of the UN, states are increasingly obliged to account for their actions to other states, to IOs, and even to the world public opinion. The result has been a surprising expansion of the range of action of international law: today international law includes fields that actually lie outside the purview of relations among states. Environmental law, humanitarian law, the rights of future generations, and even the right to democracy are constrained within too narrow a framework in the field of interstate relations and would deserve a different position.

What is the most appropriate response that legal doctrine can give? Is it preferable to push back the frontiers of international law to incorporate these new developments or rather to found a new branch of law? In accordance with the levels of governance outlined above, the cosmopolitan project aims to reinvigorate the three-way division of law suggested by Kant. This means making a distinction between the rules governing relations among states and the rules directly involving citizens of the world. The subdivision of competences is no easy matter. But if truly cosmopolitan institutions were to be set up, the current legal framework would be reductive. Indeed, international law would frame regulations and organizations even when the substance of the matter no longer involved the states exclusively. This leads to the need to distinguish regulations that govern interstate relations and that have their place in international law and regulations that refer to individuals and global problems and that should be included, as Kant had already suggested, in cosmopolitan law.

This reappraisal of competencies raises an important objection and a corollary. In the first instance there is indeed a danger that commitments undertaken on global issues that today are inappropriately but sometimes effectively addressed by international law will vanish and be taken over by cosmopolitan law. One example is the Kyoto Protocol on climate change: states have entered into undertakings with other states, which can enforce the agreements through a battery of instruments that would not be available to newborn cosmopolitan institutions. Should the states be accountable for their actions in environmental or human rights matters to institutions representing the citizens of the world, the states would have a counterpart that was formally endowed with greater legitimacy but that lacked the clout to drive home its point. This objection may be countered in various ways. First, it is likely that the denunciation of rights violations would be more effective if it did not come from other governments but from institutions acting in the interest of all citizens, as these institutions are perceived as objective and therefore more authoritative. This type of effect is certainly greater in countries with a vibrant public opinion. We would expect democratic governments to become more reluctant to violate given rules if this were dictated by cosmopolitan law rather than by international law, and that the opposite would be true for autocratic governments. Second, the existence of cosmopolitan law in no way means that the states should disregard these problems. Indeed, we should hope that the democratic states will be willing to act as the "secular arm" of cosmopolitan law and institutions. Third, we should hope that direct instruments of pressure, such as sanctions applied directly by the citizens (economic boycotting, investment strikes, tourism strikes, and so on), take on a more significant role as a result of the granting of cosmopolitan citizenship that also imposes obligations vis-à-vis individuals.

The implementation of the legal project originally called for by Kant does not imply that cosmopolitan law should ultimately absorb international law.[33] Should international law evolve and become cosmopolitan law, the legal corpus for interstate relations would diminish. This result will introduce a new internal/cosmopolitan dichotomy in law that would lead toward a federal system rather than toward a cosmopolitan democracy because the lack of a body of law regulating interstate relations would imply the dissolution of individual states into a world state. Conversely, adding cosmopolitan law to the already existing bodies of public law and international law will lead to an overall cosmopolitan legal system subdivided into three branches. As outlined above, conflicts of competence are likely to occur among the three levels of law, although these conflicts can be addressed with the instruments proper to law.

Notes

1 Jürgen Habermas, *The Inclusion of the Other: Studies in Political Theory* (Cambridge, MA: MIT Press, 1998); Iris M. Young, *Inclusion and Democracy* (Oxford: Oxford University Press, 2000); Raffaele Marchetti, "Global Governance or World Federalism? A Cosmopolitan Dispute on Institutional Models," *Global Society* vol. 20, no. 3 (2006): 287–305.

2 Held, *Democracy and the Global Order*.

3 Thomas Paine, *Rights of Man* (Secaucus, NJ: Citadel Press, 1794), p. 173; Alexander Hamilton, James Madison, and John Jay, *The Federalist* (Chicago: Encyclop<ae>dia Britannica, [1788] 1955), no. 14.

4 Chris Brown, *Sovereignty, Rights and Justice* (Cambridge: Polity Press, 2002), p. 226.

5 Michael Mann, "Has Globalization Ended the Rise of the Nation-State?" *Review of International Political Economy* vol. 4, no. 3 (1997): 472–96, on p. 475.

6 For a review, see Chadwick F. Alger, "Searching for Democratic Potential in Emerging Global Governance," pp. 87–105 in *Transnational Democracy: A Critical Consideration of Sites and Sources*, ed. Bruce Morrison (Aldershot: Ashgate, 2003).

7 See, for instance, Shapiro and Hacker-Cordón, *Democracy's Edges*; April Carter and Geoffrey Stokes, eds., *Democratic Theory Today* (Cambridge: Polity Press, 2002); David Beetham, Sarah Bracking, Iain Kearton, Nalini Vittal, and Stuart Weir, eds., *The State of Democracy: Democracy Assessments in Eight Nations Around the World* (Dordrecht: Kluwer, 2002).

8 Rawls, *Law of Peoples*, pp. 10 and 83.

9   See the pioneering attempt by Andrew Linklater, "What Is a Good International Citizen?" pp. 21–43 in *Ethics and Foreign Policy*, ed. Paul Keal (Sydney: Allen & Unwin Keal, 1992).

10 See, for example, Andrew Moravcsik, "Is There a 'Democratic Deficit' in World Politics? A Framework for Analysis," *Government and Opposition* vol. 39, no. 2 (2004): 336–63.

11 The issue is discussed in Derk Bienen, Volker Rittberger, and Wolfgang Wagner, "Democracy in the United Nations System: Cosmopolitan and Communitarian Principles," pp. 287–308 in *Re-imagining Political Community*, ed. Archibugi et al.; Richard Falk, *Law in an Emerging Global Village: A Post-Westphalian Perspective* (Ardsley: Transnational Publishers, 1998).

12 For an innovating attempt to define, quantify, and measure the level of democracy of several IGOs, see Thomas D. Zweifel, *International Organization and Democracy: Accountability, Politics, and Power* (Boulder, CO: Lynne Rienner Publishers, 2005). The ongoing Global Institutional Design project led by David Held, Mathias Koenig-Archibugi, Tony McGrew, and Paola Robotti at the London School of Economics is investigating similar themes, but it also takes into account private and public-private governance initiatives and explores the effectiveness of international policies.

13 For a review see Heikki Patomaki and Teivo Teivainen, *A Possible World: Democratic Transformation of Global Institutions* (London: Zed Books, 2004).

14 Mario Telò, ed., *European Union and New Regionalism* (London: Ashgate, 2001).

15 Heikki Patomaki and Teivo Teivainen, "Critical Responses to Neoliberal Globalization in the Mercosur Region: Roads towards Cosmopolitan Democracy?" *Review of International Political Economy* vol. 9, no. 1 (2002): 37–71.

16 My understanding of global governance draws, among others, on Rosenau, *Along the Domestic-Foreign Frontier*; Robert O. Keohane, "Governance in a Partially Globalized World," *American Political Science Review* vol. 95, no. 1 (2001): 1–13; Held and McGrew, *Governing Globalization*; and Koenig-Archibugi, "Mapping Global Governance."

17 For a wide range of case studies, see Held and McGrew, *Governing Globalization*; Aksu and Camilleri, *Democratizing Global Governance*; David Held and Mathias Koenig-Archibugi, eds., *Global Governance and Public Accountability* (Oxford: Blackwell, 2005); and Koenig-Archibugi and Zürn, *New Modes of Governance*.

18 Michael Edwards and John Gaventa, eds., *Global Citizen Action* (London: Earthscan, 2001); Glasius, Kaldor, and Anheier, *Global Civil Society*; David Held, *Global Covenant*.

19 Hans Kelsen, *Das Problem der Souveränität und die Theorie des Völkerrechtes. Beitrag zu einer rerren. Rechtslehre* (Tübingen: J. C. B. Mohr, 1920).

20 Stephen Krasner, *Sovereignty: Organised Hypocrisy* (Princeton: Princeton University Press, 1999).

21 Thomas Pogge, "Cosmopolitanism and Sovereignty," *Ethics* vol. 103, no. 1 (1992): 48–75, on p. 62; and David Held, "Law of States, Law of Peoples: Three Models of Sovereignty," *Legal Theory* vol. 8, no. 2 (2002): 1–44, on p. 23.

22 Hans Kelsen, *Peace through Law* (Chapel Hill: University of North Carolina Press, 1944).

23 This line of research has been investigated by Friedrich V. Kratochwil, *Rules, Norms, and Decisions: On the Conditions of Practical and Legal Reasoning in International Relations and in Domestic Affairs* (Cambridge: Cambridge University Press, 1989); Ian Hurd, "Legitimacy and Authority in International Politics," *International Organization* vol. 3, no. 2. (1999): 379–408; William Scheuerman, "Cosmopolitan Democracy and the Rule of Law," *Ratio Juris* vol. 15, no. 4 (2002): 439–57.

24 Cf. Marchetti, "Global Governance or World Federalism?"

25 A classical definition of the juridical differences between a confederation of states and a federal state is given in Hans Kelsen, *General Theory of Law and State* (Cambridge, MA: Harvard University Press, 1945), section V.D. For a theoretical and historical review of unions of states, cf. Murray Forsyth, *Unions of States: The Theory and Practice of Confederation* (Leicester: Leicester University Press, 1981). See also the stimulating essays by Martin Wight, *Systems of States* (Leicester: Leicester University Press, 1977).

26 A classical defense of federalism as a partial union among states was made by William H. Riker, *Federalism: Origin, Operation, Significance* (Boston, MA: Little, 1964). For an overview, see Lucio Levi, *Federalist Thinking* (Lanham, MD: University Press of America, 2008). A modern restatement of world federalism is provided by Myron J. Frankman, *World Democratic Federalism: Peace and Justice Indivisible* (Houndmills: Macmillan, 2004).

27 See, for example, Kimberly Hutchings and Roland Danmeuther, eds., *Cosmopolitan Citizenship* (Houndmills: Macmillan, 1999) and Nigel Dower and John Williams, eds., *Global Citizenship: A Critical Reader* (Edinburgh: Edinburgh University Press, 2002).

28 See Inge Kaul and Pedro Conceiçao, eds., *The New Public Finance: Responding to Global Challenges* (Oxford: Oxford University Press, 2006).

29 As is the case, de facto, for refugees, cf. Pierre Hassner, "Refugees: a Special Case for Cosmopolitan Citizenship?" pp. 273–86 in *Re-Imagining Political Community*, ed. Archibugi et al.

30 Daniele Archibugi, "Immanuel Kant, Peace, and Cosmopolitan Law," *European Journal of International Relations* vol. 1, no. 4 (1995): 429–56; Pavlos Eleftheriadis, "Cosmopolitan Law," *European Law Journal* vol. 9, no. 2 (2003): 241–63; Jürgen Habermas, *The Divided West* (Cambridge: Polity Press, 2006), pp. 80–81; Seyla Benhabib, *Another Cosmopolitanism* (Oxford: Oxford University Press, 2006).

31 Kant, "Towards Perpetual Peace," pp. 107–8.

32 Hegel, *Philosophy of Law*, § 330, p. 262.

33 This hypothesis is hinted at in a recent essay by Habermas, *Divided West*, p. 149, which I otherwise share.

19
Humanitarian Intervention: Towards a Cosmopolitan Approach
Mary Kaldor

At the beginning of the 1990s, there was a lot of optimism about the possibilities for solving global problems, particularly wars. In the *Agenda for Peace*, the UN Secretary-General Boutros Boutros-Ghali talked about the "second chance" for the UN now its activities were no longer blocked by the Cold War. The term "international community", implying a cohesive group of governments acting through international organizations, entered into everyday usage. Conflicts in a number of countries seemed close to resolution – Cambodia, Namibia, Angola, South Africa, Nicaragua, Afghanistan. And in those conflicts which were not resolved, the idea, enunciated by the French minister and former director of Médecins Sans Frontières Bernard Kouchner, of a right/duty to intervene for humanitarian purposes seemed to be gaining widespread acceptance.

The number of UN peacekeeping operations increased dramatically in the 1990s, as did the range of tasks they were asked to perform, including the delivery of humanitarian aid, the protection of people in safe havens, disarmament and demobilization, creating a secure environment for elections and reporting violations of international humanitarian law, in addition to the traditional tasks of monitoring and maintaining ceasefires. Mandates were also strengthened; in both Somalia and Bosnia, peacekeeping troops were authorized to act under Chapter VII of the UN Charter, which allows the use of force. Moreover, the UN was not the only umbrella for multilateral peacekeeping operations; regional organizations such as NATO, the EU, the CIS, the AU or the Economic Community of West African States (ECOWAS) were also responsible for organizing peacekeeping missions.

Yet despite the hopes and good intentions, the experience so far of what has come to be known as humanitarian intervention has been frustrating, to say the least. At best, people have been fed and fragile ceasefires have been agreed, although it is not clear whether this can be attributed to the presence of peacekeeping troops. At worst, the UN has been shamed and humiliated, as, for example, when it failed to prevent genocide in Rwanda, when the so-called safe haven of Srebrenica was overrun by Bosnian Serbs, or when the hunt for the Somali warlord Aideed ended in a mixture of farce and tragedy. Moreover, the term humanitarian intervention has been used to justify wars, as in Kosovo, and now Iraq and Afghanistan, giving rise to scepticism about the whole concept; hence the phrase "military humanism" coined by Noam Chomsky.[1]

There have been many explanations for the failures – the short-termism of politicians, the role of the media, which raises public consciousness at particular times and particular places, the lack of coordination of governments and international agencies, inadequate resources – and all of these have some merit. But the most important explanation is misperception, the persistence of inherited ways of thinking about organized violence, the inability to understand the character and logic of the new warfare. One response to the new wars has been to treat them as Clausewitzean wars in which the warring parties are states or, if not states, groups with a claim to statehood. Many of the terms used, such as "intervention", "peacekeeping", "peace-enforcement", "sovereignty", "civil war", are drawn from conceptions of the nation-state and of modern war that are not only difficult to apply in the current context, but may actually pose an obstacle to appropriate action. The other response is fatalistic. Because the wars cannot be understood in traditional terms, they are thought to represent a reversion to primitivism or anarchy, and the most that can be done, therefore, is to ameliorate the symptoms. In other words, wars are treated as natural disasters; hence the use of terms such as "complex emergencies", which are emptied of political meaning. Indeed the very term "humanitarian" acquired a non-political meaning in the 1990s. It came to be associated with the provision of humanitarian relief assistance in wars, or help to noncombatants or the wounded, rather than with respect for human rights which was implied in the classic usage of the term "humanitarian intervention."[2]

[. . .] What is needed is a much more political response to the new wars. A strategy of capturing "hearts and minds" needs to be counterposed to the strategy of sowing "fear and hate". A politics of inclusion needs to be counterposed against the politics of exclusion; respect for international principles and legal norms needs to be counterposed against the criminality of the warlords. In short, what is needed is a new form of cosmopolitan political mobilization, which embraces both the so-called international community and local populations, and which is capable of countering the submission to various types of particularism. A sceptic might argue that a form of cosmopolitan politics is already on the international agenda; certainly, respect for human rights, abhorrence of genocide and ethnic cleansing are increasingly part of the accepted rhetoric of political leaders. But political mobilization involves more than this; it has to override other considerations – geo-politics or short-term domestic concerns; it has to constitute the primary guide to policy and action which has not been the case up to now.

The reconstruction of legitimacy

The key to the control of violence is the reconstruction of legitimacy. I agree with Hannah Arendt when she says that power rests on legitimacy and not on violence. By legitimacy, I mean both consent and even support for political institutions, as well as the notion that these institutions acquire their authority on the basis of operating within an agreed set of rules – the rule of law.

[. . .]

The same point is made by Giddens. The internal pacification of modern states was achieved not by violence, but by the extension of the rule of law and, concomitantly, the administrative reach of the state, including the extension of surveillance. The monopoly of legitimate organized violence implied the control of violence and much less reliance on the use of physical coercion, except, of course, in the international arena. Pre-modern states were much more violent in domestic affairs than the modern state, but also much less powerful. In so far as external violence contributed to internal pacification, it was an indirect contribution, arising from the increased legitimacy of the state associated with the defence of territory from external enemies and the augmentation of administrative capacities.

In the new wars, the monopoly of legitimate violence has broken down. And what is crucial is not the privatization of violence, as such, but the breakdown of legitimacy. [. . .] The strategy is political control on the basis of exclusion – in particular, population displacement – and the tactics for achieving this goal are terror and destabilization. For this reason, it is virtually impossible for any of the warring parties to re-establish legitimacy. Violence may be controlled sporadically through uneasy truces and ceasefires, but in situations in which the moral, administrative and practical constraints against private violence have broken down, they rarely last long. At the same time, however, isolated citizens' groups or political parties which try to re-establish legitimacy on the basis of inclusive politics are relatively powerless in conditions of continuing violence.

"Cosmopolitanism", used in a Kantian sense, implies the existence of a human community with certain shared rights and obligations. In "Perpetual Peace" Kant envisaged a world federation of democratic states in which cosmopolitan right is confined to the right of "hospitality" – strangers and foreigners should be welcomed and treated with respect.[3] I use the term more extensively to refer both to a positive political vision, embracing tolerance, multiculturalism, civility and democracy, and to a more legalistic respect for certain overriding universal principles which should guide political communities at various levels, including the global level.

These principles are already contained in various treaties and conventions that comprise the body of international law [. . .]. Laws and customs of war which date back to early modern times were codified in the nineteenth and twentieth centuries; particularly important were the Geneva Conventions sponsored by the ICRC and the Hague Conferences of 1899 and 1907. The Nuremberg trials after World War II marked the first enforcement of "war crimes" or, even more significantly, "crimes against humanity." To what was known as international humanitarian law, human rights norms were added in the post-war period. The difference between humanitarian and human rights law has to do largely with whether violation of the law takes place in war or peacetime. The former is confined to abuses of power in wartime situations. The assumption tends to be that war is usually modern inter-state war and that such abuses are inflicted by a foreign power – in other words, aggression. The latter is equally concerned with abuses of power in peacetime, in particular those inflicted by a government against its citizens – in other words, repression.

The violations of international norms with which both bodies of law are concerned are, in fact, those which form the core of the new mode of warfare [. . .] classic distinctions between internal and external, war and peace, aggression and repression are breaking down. A war crime is at one and the same time a massive violation of human rights. A number of writers have suggested that humanitarian law should be combined with human rights law to form "humane" or "cosmopolitan" law.[4] Elements of a cosmopolitan regime do already exist. NGOs and the media draw attention to violations of human rights or to war crimes, and to some extent governments and international institutions respond through methods ranging from persuasion and pressure to, as yet tentative, enforcement. Particularly important in the latter respect has been the establishment of international tribunals with respect to violations of international humanitarian law for Rwanda and former Yugoslavia, and the creation of an International Criminal Court (ICC) to deal with "core crimes" – war crimes, crimes against humanity and genocide. War crimes tribunals were established in 1993 and 1994, and the ICC in 1998.

These tentative steps towards a cosmopolitan regime, however, conflict with many of the more traditional geopolitical approaches adopted by the so-called international community which continue to emphasize the importance of state sovereignty as the basis of international relations. This is especially true since 9/11 and the promulgation of the "War on Terror". The prevalence of geo-politics is reflected in the terminology used to describe the response of the international community to post-Cold War conflicts. The literature is replete with discussions about intervention and non-intervention.[5] Intervention is taken to mean an infringement of sovereignty and, in its strong version, a military infringement. The prohibitions against intervention, expressed in particular in Article 2(1) of the UN Charter, which refers to the "principle of sovereign equality", is considered important as a way of restricting the use of force, respecting pluralism and acting "as a brake on the crusading, territorial and imperial ambitions of states."[6]

But what does intervention and non-intervention mean nowadays? The new types of war are both global and local. There is already extensive international involvement, both private through diaspora connections, NGOs, etc, and public through patron states or international agencies providing aid or loans or other kinds of assistance. Indeed, [. . .] the various parties to the conflict are totally dependent on outside support. Likewise, these are wars usually characterized by the erosion or disintegration of state power. In such a situation, what does it mean to talk about infringements of sovereignty?

An illustration of the artificiality of these terms was the debate about whether the war in Bosnia was an international or a civil war. Those who argued that this was an international war favoured intervention to support the Bosnian state. They argued that the Bosnian state had been internationally recognized and that the war was the result of an act of aggression by Serbia. Hence, intervention was justified under Chapter VII of the UN Charter, since Serbian aggression was a "threat to international peace and security". Those who argued that this was a civil war were against intervention. They claimed that this was a nationalist war between Serbs, Croats and Bosnians to control the remnants of the Yugoslav state – intervention would have been a violation of sovereignty. Both positions missed the point. This was a war of ethnic cleansing and genocide. What did it matter whether the crime was committed by Serbs from Belgrade or by Serbs from Bosnia? [. . .] In effect, the debate about whether the conflict was an international or a civil war treated it as an old war between the fighting sides, in which violence against civilians is merely a side-effect of the war.

Moreover, because outside involvement in various forms is already so extensive in this type of conflict, there is no such thing as non-intervention. The failure to protect the victims is a kind of tacit intervention on the side of those who are inflicting humanitarian or human rights abuses.

[. . .]

An alternative cosmopolitan approach starts from the assumption that no solution is workable based on the political goals of the warring parties and that legitimacy can only be restored on the basis of an alternative politics which operates within cosmopolitan principles. Once the values of inclusion, tolerance and mutual respect are established, the territorial solutions will easily follow. [. . .]

From top-down diplomacy to cosmopolitan politics

In recent wars, the dominant approach of the international community has been to attempt a negotiated solution between the warring parties. This approach has several drawbacks.

First, the talks raise the profile of the warring parties and confer a sort of public legitimacy on individuals who may be criminals. Many people remarked on the paradox that international negotiators were seen on television shaking hands with Karadžic and Mladić, both of whom had earlier been named by the International Tribunal and by leading Western politicians as war criminals. [. . .]

Second, because of the particularistic nature of the political goals of the warring parties, it is extremely difficult to find a workable solution. One option is territorial partition – a kind of identity-based apartheid. The other option is power-sharing on the basis of identity. The record of such agreements is dismal. Partitions do not provide a basis for stability; refugees, displaced persons or newly created minorities constitute a long-term source of tension, as the history of partitions in Cyprus, India and Pakistan, Ireland or Palestine testifies. Nor do power-sharing agreements fare any better. [. . .] Today, the Washington Agreement between Croats and Muslims, the Dayton Agreement, the Oslo Agreement between Israel and the Palestinians, or the Paris Agreements on Cambodia are all displaying the strains of trying to combine incompatible forms of exclusivism.

A third drawback is that such agreements tend to be based on exaggerated assumptions about the power of the warring parties to implement agreements. Since the power of the warring parties depends largely on fear and/or self-interest and not on consent, they need an insecure environment to sustain themselves both politically and economically. Politically, identity is based on fear and hatred of the other; economically, revenues depend on outside assistance for the war effort and on various forms of asset transfer based on loot and extortion or on price distortions resulting from restrictions on freedom of movement. In peacetime, these sources of sustenance are eroded.

It is often argued that, despite these drawbacks, there is no alternative. These are the only people who can end the violence. It is true that those responsible for the violence have to end it, but it does not follow that these are the people who can make peace. Negotiations with warlords may sometimes be necessary, but they need to take place in a context where alternative non-exclusive political constituencies can be fostered. The aim is to establish conditions for an alternative political mobilization. This means that the mediators have to be very clear about international principles and standards and refuse compromises that violate those principles, otherwise the credibility of the institutions will suffer and any kind of implementation could be very difficult. The point of the talks is to control violence so that space can be created for the emergence or re-emergence of civil society. The more "normal" the situation, the greater the possibilities for developing political alternatives. There is, as it were, another potential source of power that has to be represented at the talks, involved or consulted in any compromise and, generally, made more visible. Precisely because these are not total wars, participation is low, loyalties change, sources of revenue dry up; it is always possible to identify local advocates of cosmopolitanism, people and places that refuse to accept the politics of war – islands of civility.

The example of Northwest Somaliland represents an example where local elders have succeeded in establishing relative peace through a process of negotiation. In Armenia and Azerbaijan, the local branches of the Helsinki Citizens' Assembly have succeeded in negotiating with local authorities on each side of the border, Kazakh and Echevan, and establishing a peace corridor; the corridor provides a place where hostages and prisoners of war can be released and where dialogue between women's groups, young people and even security forces can be organized. In Sierra Leone, the women's movement played a critical role in pressing for democracy and paving the way for peace.[7]

[. . .] In the Philippines, a peace zones strategy was adopted after a town in the north, Hungduan, convinced guerrillas to withdraw from the town and then acted to prevent the military from moving in; the peace zones strategy is said to have been an important factor in ending the war.

Many other examples from Northern Ireland, Central America, Vojvodina or West Africa can be enumerated. In nearly all these cases, women's groups play an important role. They are rarely reported because they are not news. They may involve local negotiations and conflict resolution between local factions or pressure on the warring parties to keep out of the area. They are often difficult to sustain because of the pressures of the war economy – influxes of refugees seeking safety, unemployment, and propaganda, especially television, radio and video cassettes controlled by the warring parties. But they need to be taken seriously and given credibility by outside support.

These groups represent a potential solution. To the extent that they are capable of mobilizing support, they weaken the power of the warring parties. To the extent that the areas they control can be extended, so the zones of war are diminished. They also represent a repository of knowledge and information about the local situation; they can advise and guide a cosmopolitan strategy.

In many places, there is a growing emphasis by governments and international organizations on the role of local NGOs and grass-roots initiatives, and they provide funding and other forms of support. In some cases, support for NGOs is seen as a substitute for action. They are supposed to undertake the tasks that the international community is unable to fulfil. But what is not understood is that, in a context of war, the survival of such groups is always precarious. Civil society needs a state. If the local state does not provide the conditions in which alternative politics can develop, there has to be support from international organizations. However courageous those engaged in NGOs, they cannot operate without law and order. The peace movement in Bosnia-Herzegovina was destroyed when the Serbs began to shoot demonstrators. What happened in Rwanda is a classic illustration of what happens to local advocates of cosmopolitanism without outside support.

Just as the warring factions depend on outside support, so there needs to be a conscious strategy of building on local cosmopolitan initiatives. What form support takes, whether or not it involves sending troops, depends on each situation and what the local groups consider necessary. But there is still a reluctance to engage in a serious dialogue on a par with the dialogue with the warring parties, to see these groups as partners in a shared cosmopolitan project and to work out jointly a mutual strategy

for developing a peace constituency. There is a tendency on the part of Western political leaders to dismiss such initiatives as worthy but insignificant; "citizens can't make
peace", said David Owen when negotiator in the former Yugoslavia. This attitude can
perhaps be explained by the horizontal character of top-level communication, the fact
that leaders generally talk only to leaders. It also has to do with the colonial mentality
that seems to grip representatives of international institutions when on missions in
faraway countries – there are widespread complaints, whether in Somalia, Bosnia or
the Transcaucasus, about the seemingly systematic failure to consult local experts or
NGOs.

[. . .]

The failure to take seriously alternative sources of power displays a myopia about
the character of power and the relationship between power and violence. An effective
response to the new wars has to be based on an alliance between international organizations and local advocates of cosmopolitanism in order to reconstruct legitimacy.
A strategy of winning "hearts and minds" needs to identify with individuals and groups
respected for their integrity. They have to be supported, and their advice, proposals
and recommendations need to be taken seriously. There is no standard formula for a
cosmopolitan response; the point is rather that, in each local situation, there has to
be a process involving these individuals and groups through which a strategy is developed. The various components of international involvement – the use of troops, the
role of negotiation, funds for reconstruction – need to be worked out jointly.

It is often argued that it is difficult to identify local cosmopolitans. Are they just
marginal groups of intellectuals? Are there moderate religious and nationalist groups
who count as cosmopolitan? There has to be, of course, widespread consultation. But
through such a consultation it is possible to situate those who are concerned about
the future of the whole society and not just sectarian interest. Women's groups usually
play a key role in a more inclusive approach. Even if the cosmopolitans are a small
minority, they are often the best source of ideas and proposals.

This argument also has implications for the way in which political pressure from
the international community is exerted on political and military leaders to reach agreement or to consent to peacekeeping forces. Typical methods include the threat of air
strikes or economic sanctions, which have the consequence of identifying the leaders
with the population instead of isolating them, treating them as representative of
"sides", as legitimate leaders of states or proto-states. Such methods can easily be counterproductive, alienating the local population and narrowing the possibilities of pressure below. There may be circumstances in which these methods are an appropriate
strategy and others where more targeted approaches may be more effective – arraign-
ing the leaders as war criminals so that they cannot travel, exempting cultural communication so as to support civil society, for example. The point is that local
cosmopolitans can provide the best advice on what is the best approach; they need to
be consulted and treated as partners.

From peacekeeping and/or peace-enforcement to cosmopolitan law-enforcement

In the literature about peacekeeping, a rigid division tends to be drawn between peacekeeping and peace-enforcement.[8] Both terms are based on traditional assumptions

about the character of war. Peacekeeping is based on the assumption that an agreement has been reached between the two sides in a war; the task of the peacekeeper is to supervise and monitor implementation of the agreement. The principles of peacekeeping as developed in the post-war period are consent, impartiality and the non-use of force. Peace-enforcement, on the other hand, which is authorized under Chapter VII of the UN Charter; is basically war-fighting; it means intervening in a war on one side. The distinction is considered important because war-fighting is assumed to involve the use of maximum force, since Clausewitzean wars tend to extremes. General Rose's preoccupation with "crossing the Mogadishu line" is about maintaining this distinction and not sliding from peacekeeping to peace-enforcement.

The analysis of new wars suggests that what is needed is not peacekeeping but enforcement of cosmopolitan norms, i.e. enforcement of international humanitarian and human rights law. Precisely because these wars are directed mainly against civilians, they do not have the same extremist logic as modern wars. Therefore, it ought to be possible to devise strategies for the protection of civilians and the capture of war criminals. The political aim is to provide secure areas in which alternative forms of inclusive politics can emerge. Many of the tactics that have been developed in recent wars are relevant – for example, the use of safety zones, humanitarian corridors, or no-fly zones – but their implementation up to now has been hampered by inflexible mandates and/or rigid adherence to what are viewed as the principles of peacekeeping. [. . .]

Cosmopolitan law-enforcement is somewhere between soldiering and policing. Some of the tasks that international troops may be asked to perform fall within traditional ambits, for example, separating belligerents and maintaining ceasefires, controlling airspace. Others are essentially new tasks, e.g. the protection of safety zones or relief corridors. And yet others are close to traditional policing tasks – ensuring freedom of movement, guaranteeing the safety of individuals, especially returned refugees or displaced persons, and the capture of war criminals. Policing has been the great lacuna of peacekeeping. Back in the 1960s, when peacekeeping forces were sent to Cyprus, they were unable to prevent communal conflict because policing was not part of their mandate. Military forces have been notoriously unwilling to undertake police tasks, but, at the same time, it has proved difficult to recruit policemen because they are needed in their own societies. However one judges their record, the British forces in Northern Ireland did undertake policing tasks. Given the unlikelihood of another old war, military forces will eventually have to be reoriented to combine military and policing tasks.

Such tasks require enforcement and therefore necessarily involve the use of force, but in terms of the principles governing their application, the tasks of cosmopolitan law-enforcement are closer to peacekeeping. It is worth spelling out those principles and showing how they would need to be reformulated.

Consent

In the scenarios that were developed when preparing the official British peacekeeping manual, it was concluded that "forcible pacification" is impracticable:

> Without the broader co-operation and consent of the majority of the local population and the leadership of the principal ruling authorities, be they parties to the dispute or government agencies, success is simply not a reasonable or realistic expectation. The risks

entailed and force levels required of an approach that dispensed with a broad consensual framework is simply not a reasonable or realistic expectation. Put simply, consent (in its broadest form) is necessary for any prospect of success.[9]

According to this argument, consent is required at both the operational and the tactical level. At an operational level, consent is required before the mission is established. At a tactical level, commanders need to negotiate local consent.

The argument that "forcible pacification" is impossible is clearly correct. [. . .] International military forces have to be seen to be legitimate – that is to say, they have to operate on the basis of some sort of consent and even support, and to be acting within an agreed set of rules. Otherwise, there is a risk that they will become just another party to the conflict, as seems to have happened to some extent to the ECOMOG peacekeeping force in Liberia, where lack of pay, equipment and training meant that soldiers became engaged in the black market and/or theft from humanitarian supplies, and where the troops veered from neutrality to support for particular factions.

However, unqualified consent is impossible; otherwise there would be no need for peacekeeping forces. If, for example, protection of humanitarian convoys is based on consent, then this can be negotiated as easily and perhaps more effectively by unarmed UN agencies or NGOs. The need for troops is based on the fact that not everyone consents and that those who prevent the convoys may have to be dealt with forcefully. For similar reasons, it may be impossible to obtain consent from *both* the local population and the warring parties. If an agreement has to be negotiated with a war criminal, then the credibility of the operation in the eyes of the local population may be damaged.

In general, international troops can expect considerable initial goodwill. In former Yugoslavia, the standing of the UN was very high; many local people had served in UN contingents. But the failure to react forcefully against those who interrupted aid convoys, to protect effectively safe havens, to capture war criminals or even to maintain the No Fly Zone greatly undermined the legitimacy of the entire organization. The same was true in Somalia, where many local people hoped that the American troops who arrived in large numbers would disarm the warring parties. There was great disappointment when the Americans announced they would not disarm the factions and opened negotiations with the warlords.

[. . .]

What *is* important is widespread consent from the victims, the local population, whether or not formal consent has been obtained from the parties at an operational level. If consent at the operational level can be obtained, without sacrificing the goals of the mission, it is clearly an advantage. Retaining and building on the consent of the local population at a tactical level may well mean acting without the consent of one or other of the parties.

Impartiality

Impartiality tends to be interpreted as not taking sides. The ICRC makes a useful distinction between impartiality and neutrality. The principle of impartiality, it stated, means that, it "makes no discrimination as to nationality, race, religious beliefs, class, or political opinions. It endeavours to relieve the suffering of individuals, being guided solely by their needs, and to give priority to the most urgent cases of distress." The principle of neutrality means that, in "order to continue to enjoy the confidence of all, the Red Cross may not take sides in hostilities or engage at any time in controversies of a political, racial, religious or ideological character".[10]

In practice, impartiality and neutrality have been confused. The distinction is important for cosmopolitan law-enforcement. The law has to be enforced impartially, that is to say, without any discrimination on the basis of race, religion, etc. Since it is almost inevitable that one side violates the law more frequently than another, it is impossible to act according to both impartiality and neutrality. Neutrality may be important for an organization such as the Red Cross which depends on consent for its activities, although the insistence on neutrality has frequently raised questions, particularly during World War II. It could also be important for the traditional concept of peace-keeping or for a purely humanitarian conception of the role of peacekeepers, i.e. the delivery of food. But if the task of the troops is to protect people and to stop violations of human rights, then insistence on neutrality is, at best, confusing and, at worst, undermines legitimacy.

In the aftermath of the bombing of the United Nations headquarters in Iraq in the summer of 2003, many NGOs and humanitarian agencies have been calling for a return to the Red Cross principles and a renewed separation of the military and those who undertake humanitarian tasks so as to preserve humanitarian space. The problem is that, in the new wars, humanitarian space has been squeezed. It is no longer possible to separate military and humanitarian activities. Rather, the military have to operate differently so as to protect humanitarian space. In Iraq, US forces were war-fighting forces and the international agencies were identified with the United States. There was no force capable of or responsible for cosmopolitan law-enforcement.

According to Mackinlay: "A UN soldier has the same approach as a policeman enforcing the law. He will uphold it regardless of which party is challenging him. But legitimacy must be intact at all levels." However, Mackinlay seems to think that, if the UN soldier enforces the rules impartially, it is possible to retain the respect of both sides.[11] The same point is made by Dobbie, one of the authors of the British peacekeeping manual, when he compares the role of the peacekeeper to the role of the referee at a football match. But these wars are not football matches; the various parties do not accept the rules. On the contrary, the nature of these wars is rule-breaking. The point is rather to persuade ordinary people of the advantages of rules so as to isolate and marginalize those who break them.

Use of force

Traditional peacekeeping insisted on the non-use of force. The new British peacekeeping manual uses the term "minimum necessary force", defined in the manual as "the measured application of violence or coercion, sufficient only to achieve a specific end, demonstrably reasonable, proportionate and appropriate; and confined in effect to the specific and legitimate target intended."[12]

The British contrast this position with what is known as the Weinberger–Powell doctrine of overwhelming force. The UN intervention in Somalia is often cited as an example of the perils of using force. It was largely an American intervention authorized under Chapter VII of the UN Charter. After an attack by his forces on Pakistani peacekeepers, the Americans began a manhunt for Mohammed Aideed. Bombardments in Southern Mogadishu resulted in many deaths and the manhunt for Aideed failed. (Owing to the refusal of the Americans to share intelligence information with the UN, a careful raid on what was supposed to be Aideed's hideout failed because it turned out to be a UN office.) The nadir for the Americans was reached when Aideed succeeded in shooting down two US helicopters, killing eighteen soldiers, whose mutilated bodies were publicly paraded in front of television cameras, and wounding seventy-five others.

The problem, as various commentators have pointed out, was not the use of force as such, but the assumption of overwhelming force and the failure to take into account the local political situation and the need to act in such a way as to lend support to legitimacy and credibility.

[. . .]

Much the same dilemma is faced by American forces in Iraq and Afghanistan.

Modern armies are uneasy about using minimum force because they are organized along Clausewitzean lines and have been trained to confront other similarly organized armies. As was shown in the case of Somalia, when confronted with the challenge of new wars, they find it extremely difficult to identify a middle way between the application of massive firepower and doing nothing. Unlike war-fighting, in which the aim is to minimize casualties on your own side whatever the cost in casualties on the other side, and peacekeeping, which does not use force, cosmopolitan law-enforcement has to minimize casualties on all sides. The significance of Nuremberg was that individuals and not collectivities were held responsible for war crimes. It is the arrest of individuals who may have committed war crimes or violations of human rights that is required for cosmopolitan law-enforcement, not the defeat of sides.

Cosmopolitan law-enforcement may mean risking the lives of peacekeepers in order to save the lives of victims. This is perhaps the most difficult presupposition to change. International personnel are always a privileged class in the new wars. The lives of UN or national personnel are valued over the lives of local people, despite the UN claim to be founded on the principles of humanity. The argument about humanitarian intervention revolves around whether it is acceptable to sacrifice national lives for the sake of people far away. The preference of Western powers, especially the United States, for air strikes, despite the physical and psychological damage caused even with highly accurate munitions, arises from this privileging of nationals or Westerners. This type of national or statist thinking has not yet come to terms with the concept of a common human community.

In effect, the proposal for cosmopolitan law-enforcement is an ambitious proposal to create a new kind of soldier-cum-policeman which will require considerable rethinking about tactics, equipment and, above all, command and training. The kind of equipment required is generally cheaper than that which national armed forces order for imagined Clausewitzean wars in the future. [. . .]

More importantly, the new cosmopolitan troops will have to be professionalized. Since they are likely to comprise multilateral forces, integrated command systems, joint exercises and standard rates of pay and conditions would need to be introduced. The new cosmopolitan troops have to become the legitimate bearers of arms. They have to know and respect the laws of war and follow a strict code of conduct. Reports of corruption or violations of human rights have to be properly investigated. Above all, the motivations of these new forces have to be incorporated into a wider concept of cosmopolitan right. Whereas the soldier, as the legitimate bearer of arms, had to be prepared to die for his or her country, the international soldier/police officer risks his or her life for humanity.

The example of Kosovo

The war over Kosovo illustrates the problem of using war-fighting techniques for humanitarian ends. The intervention was hailed as the first war for human rights. The British prime minister, Tony Blair, used the occasion of NATO's fiftieth anniversary, which took place during the air strikes, to enunciate a new "Doctrine of International Community." "We are all internationalists now whether we like it or not", he told an audience in Chicago. "We cannot refuse to participate in global markets if we want to prosper. We cannot ignore new political ideas in other countries if we want to innovate. We cannot turn our backs on conflicts and the violation of human rights in other countries if we still want to be secure."[13]

But the actual record of the war is much more ambiguous. The proclaimed goal did represent an innovation and an important precedent in international behaviour; it is to be hoped that, after Kosovo, it will be much more difficult for the international community to stand aside when tragedies such as the genocide in Rwanda take place. However, the methods were much more in keeping with a traditional conception of war and had little connection with the proclaimed goal. Because of the concern about casualties, the tactic chosen to achieve this goal was air strikes over Yugoslavia.

In practice, however, the utility of the air strikes was highly questionable. Altogether, some 36,000 sorties were flown, of which 12,000 were strike sorties. Some 20,000 "smart" bombs and 5000 conventional bombs were dropped. But it appears that not much damage was done to the Yugoslav military machine. For fifty years, the Yugoslav army had been trained to withstand a superior enemy. A vast underground network had been built, including stores, airports and barracks. Tactics had been developed which involved constructing decoys, hiding tanks and artillery, conserving air defences and avoiding troop concentrations. NATO did not succeed, in the initial stages, in knocking out the Yugoslav air-defence system: this is why NATO aircraft continued to fly at 15,000 feet. Nor did they succeed in doing much damage to Serb forces on the ground. NATO claims that the air strikes did constrain Serb forces and prevented them from bringing equipment into the open, but, nevertheless, the air strikes evidently did not prevent operations against Kosovar Albanian civilians. [. . .]

There was more success in hitting civilian targets – roads, bridges, power stations, oil depots and factories. Because of the insistence that aircraft fly above 15,000 feet, pilots could not see what was happening on the ground and were dependent on intelligence from numerous, often badly coordinated, sources. Consequently, repeated mistakes were made, as became embarrassingly clear for the duration of the air strikes. Low points included the bombing of the Chinese Embassy and of refugees inside Kosovo. Some 1400 people were killed in so-called collateral damage. Environmentalists are only now assessing the consequences of damage to industrial facilities. Historic sites were destroyed, in Novi Sad for example. A TV transmitter was blown up, killing journalists inside. And targets were hit in Montenegro, whose government had refused to participate in the war in Kosovo.

A cosmopolitan approach to the Kosovo crisis would have been aimed directly at protecting people. There should have been a humanitarian intervention on the ground designed to minimize all casualties, even if this meant risking the lives of international troops. Humanitarian intervention is different from air strikes and different from classic "old war" ground operations; the goal is the prevention of gross violations of human rights, not the defeat of an enemy. Humanitarian intervention is defensive and non-escalatory by definition. Its focus is the individual human being and not another state. Humanitarian intervention also has to involve respect for the rule of law and support for democracy. Effectively, it constitutes cosmopolitan law-enforcement and is thus more like policing than war-fighting.

If possible such an intervention should be based on consent. But instead of high-level negotiations aimed at finding a political compromise between irreconcilable parties, as happened in the period prior to the intervention, negotiations should have focused on the position on the ground. The goal was to establish an international presence in Kosovo, not to resolve the issue of status. Instead of using the threat of air strikes to strengthen the hands of the negotiators, the NATO position on the ground in neighbouring Macedonia should have been strengthened; the position of the OSCE monitors in Kosovo should also have been expanded (these were withdrawn when the bombing began; the local staff who stayed were killed).

Humanitarian intervention, by protecting people and enforcing law, can create the conditions for a cosmopolitan political response. The aim is to establish a secure environment where people can act freely without fear and where inclusive forms of politics can be nurtured. Ways have to be found to sideline those responsible for ethnic cleansing, not to elevate them through negotiations. The indictment of Milošević and some of his co-conspirators the week before the bombing ended was a constructive step in this direction. Targeted sanctions such as the denial of visas or the freezing of bank accounts could also be applied. An intervention of this kind would have made it more difficult for Milošević to justify his behaviour within Yugoslavia and it would have generated much more international support.

From humanitarian assistance to reconstruction

Mark Duffield writes about a two-tier system of economic assistance in the 1990s. On the one hand, official assistance is predicated on structural adjustment programmes or transition strategies which contribute to the decline of the formal economy. On the other hand, a safety net to cope with the consequences has been developed, largely based on contracting out the provision of assistance to NGOs.[14] A similar point is made by Alvaro de Soto and Graciana del Castillo in their discussion of the lack of coordination between the IMF and the World Bank, on the one hand, and the UN, on the other. The consequences and the cost in political and humanitarian terms of the policies of the former agencies are simply not taken into account. They describe the problems of implementing a peace programme in El Salvador against the backdrop of an IMF stabilization programme. In order to keep within the IMF spending limits, El Salvador was unable to afford to build a national civil police force and to embark on an arms-for-land programme to reintegrate guerrillas as required by the peace agreement: "The adjustment program and the stabilization plan, on the one hand, and the peace process, on the other, were born and reared as if they were children of different families. They lived under different roofs. They had little in common other than belonging roughly to the same generation."[15]

During the 1990s, there was a big increase in humanitarian assistance; in 2000 it amounted to over 10 per cent of official development assistance, and it has continued to rise. The establishment of the UN Department of Humanitarian Affairs in 1991 and of the European Community Humanitarian Office (ECHO) in 1992 reflects the growing importance of humanitarian assistance. [. . .]

Humanitarian assistance is essential; otherwise, people would starve. But it needs to be much more carefully targeted, taking the advice of local experts who really know the local situation. And it needs to be accompanied by assistance for reconstruction. By reconstruction, I mean the rebuilding of a formal political economy, based on accepted rules, and the reversal of the negative social and economic relationships. The word "reconstruction" has other connotations drawn from earlier wars. It is usually assumed to be a programme of economic assistance, on the 1947 Marshall Plan model, that is put into effect once an overall political settlement has been reached. Aid agencies often insist that no reconstruction assistance can be provided before a political settlement is reached and, indeed, that the lure of reconstruction assistance represents an incentive to reach a political settlement. But I have argued that a lasting settlement can only be reached in a situation based on alternative politics, the politics of civility – which is very difficult so long as these negative social and economic relations persist. Instead, reconstruction should be viewed as a strategy to achieve peace rather than a strategy to be implemented after peace has been established.

The situation in what might be called near war economies is not so very different from situations of war. Whether we are referring to places where ceasefires have recently been agreed to or to "bad neighbourhoods" where the negative relationships of war have spread, the symptoms are much the same – unemployment, breakdown of basic infrastructure, pervasive criminality – and these are the symptoms that contribute to the outbreak or renewal of war. In other words, reconstruction is both a pre-war and a post-war strategy, aimed at prevention and at cure.

Reconstruction has to mean, first and foremost, the rebuilding of political authorities, even if only at the local level, and the reconstruction of civil society in the sense both of law and order and of providing the conditions in which alternative political groupings can mobilize. It does not mean reconstruction of what went before. Necessarily, it must entail the restructuring of political and economic arrangements so as not to repeat the conditions that gave rise to war. The adaptation of appropriate forms of governance and the introduction of regulated market relationships take time, and have to be part of a long-term process through which different groups in society can participate.

It is often argued that reconstruction has to encompass transition, in the sense that there is clearly a need to reform the institutions that preceded the war. Unfortunately, the term transition has come to be associated with a standard formula for democratization and transition to the market, which includes the formal aspects of democracy, for example elections, as well as economic liberalization and privatization. In the absence of meaningful political institutions through which genuine debate and participation can take place, and in situations where the rule of law is weak and where trust and confidence is lacking, this standard formula can exacerbate the underlying problems, providing incentives for exclusivist politics or for criminalization of formerly state-owned enterprises. Reconstruction has to involve reform, but not necessarily along the lines of the standard transition formula.

Reconstruction should be focused on zones of civility so that they can act as models encouraging similar initiatives in other places. Where legitimate local authorities do not exist, local trusteeships or protectorates could be proposed. The experience of the EU administration in Mostar has led to scepticism about the idea of local trusteeships.

The problem there, however, was that the administration did not have adequate policing capacities and had to share power with the nationalist parties which controlled
the police forces and included notorious criminals. The rhetoric of self-help is used as
an argument against trusteeships or protectorates, but it is very difficult for people to
help themselves when they are at the mercy of gangsters.

The primary requisite is the restoration of law and order in order to create a situation in which normal life can resume and refugees and displaced persons can be repatriated. This task includes disarmament, demobilization, protection of the area, capture
of war criminals, policing and/or establishing and training local police forces, and the
restoration of the judiciary.

Despite greatly increased efforts at achieving disarmament and demobilization, the
record is mixed. It is very difficult for UN forces to achieve more than partial disarmament, and techniques such as weapons "buy-back" programmes have tended to result
in the handing back of sub-standard weapons, while the high-quality weapons remain
hidden. Moreover, there are now so many sources for acquisition, at least of small arms,
because of both the high number of producers and the availability of surplus weapons,
that the task is never-ending. Creating a secure environment may well turn out to be
more important than disarmament. Effective policing and the capture of war criminals
are essential conditions for security, whether they are undertaken by international
forces, together with civilian affairs officers, or by local police forces under international supervision, or whether local authorities can take responsibility, perhaps with
some outside support, as is the case in better-established zones of civility.

As well as disarmament and policing, law and order needs an independent and
trustworthy judiciary and an active civil society, i.e. the creation of a relatively free
public space. For this reason, investment in education and a free media are essential
to stop the relentless particularistic propaganda and to end not just physical intimidation but also psychological intimidation. These conditions are much more important
than the formal procedures of democracy. Outsiders often insist on elections as a way
of providing a timetable and terminal point for their involvement. But without the
preconditions of security, public space, reconciliation and open dialogue, elections
may end up legitimizing the warring parties, as was the case, for example, in Bosnia
after Dayton.

To create a self-sustaining zone of civility, so that law and order, education and
media can be paid for, soldiers find jobs and education, and taxes are paid, the local
economy has to be restored. As well as disarmament, demobilization is also difficult,
and not only because of the insecure environment. Indeed, the biggest weakness of
DDR (disarmament, demobilization and reintegration) programmes has been reintegration. Many soldiers would like to give up banditry and find settled jobs or, in the
case of children and young people, an education. But reintegration programmes have
not been very successful because of unemployment and labour shortages and inadequate educational facilities.

The priorities are basic services and local production. Infrastructure – water, power,
transport, post and telecommunications – needs to be restored at both local and
regional levels. As well as being necessary on grounds of need, infrastructure is vital
for the restoration of normal trade links and can be a subject of negotiation even when
there is no agreement in other areas. Even at the height of wars, it is sometimes possible to reach agreement on these kinds of concrete issue, especially where there is a
mutual interest. Gas supplies to Sarajevo were maintained more or less throughout

the war, for example. The other area is support for local production of basic necessities so as to reduce the need for humanitarian assistance, especially food, clothing, building materials, and so on. Along with public services, this is a good way to generate local employment.

In so far as reconstruction is a strategy for peace, it has to provide economic security and hope for the future so as to remove the atmosphere of fear in which people live, and to offer, to young people especially, an alternative livelihood to the army or the mafia. What needs to be done is specific in every situation, but certain principles can be specified.

First, all assistance projects should be based on the principles of openness and integration. It is all too easy, in the interests of restoring services, to accept divisions and partitions established through war and, thereby, legitimize the status quo instead of helping to change it. [. . .]

Second, assistance needs to be decentralized and to encourage local initiatives. By spreading recipients, more people are involved in the programme, there are greater possibilities to experiment and there is less risk of aid being creamed off or being distorted by political compromises. Where demobilization has taken place, it has been local community-based programmes, often organized by the veterans themselves, that seem to have been the most successful – for example, the Uganda Veterans' Board or the National Demobilization Commission in Somaliland, which developed a programme of demobilization and reintegration together with the veterans' organization SOYAAL.

[. . .]

Third, it is very important to make use of local specialists and to encourage a wide-ranging local debate about how aid should be provided. This is important in order to increase efficiency by using people who have knowledge and experience of the area, to increase transparency, to reduce corruption and to build up civic engagement. One of the worst consequences of international assistance has been the displacement of skilled people as a result of foreign contracts and a distorted pay scale. Highly skilled doctors, engineers, teachers or lawyers often take jobs as drivers and interpreters because the salaries are so much higher. Bosnia, Kosovo and Afghanistan all provide examples of this pattern of skill displacement.

Even in areas that seem the most intractable there are some possibilities for funding assistance based on these principles. The strategy of expanding zones of civility to offset the spread of "bad neighbourhoods" needs to be able to extend itself directly into the bad neighbourhoods. Poor, uncivil areas become caught in a vicious circle in which assistance is refused because of the behaviour of the local "authorities"; unemployment and criminality flourish, thereby helping to sustain the position of the particularist warlords. It is all the more important to identify ways to support certain bottom-up projects that cross war divides in order to begin to open up spaces in these areas.

Reconstruction can be thought of as a new approach to development, an alternative to both structural adjustment/transition and humanitarianism. As is the case of cosmopolitan law-enforcement, it is bound to be costly in the short term, to require greater resources than rich countries have so far been willing to commit to peacekeeping and overseas assistance. It would mean abandoning some of the neo-liberal assumptions about levels of public expenditure that have dominated international economic orthodoxy in recent years. Reconstruction means that politics, economics and security issues have to be integrated into a new type of humanistic global policy which should be capable of enhancing the legitimacy of international institutions and mobilizing popular support.

Notes

1 Noam Chomsky, *The New Military Humanism Lessons from Kosovo*, London: Pluto, 1999.
2 See Michael Walzer, *Just and Unjust Wars. A Moral Argument with Historical Illustrations*, Harmondsworth: Penguin, 1980.
3 "Perpetual Peace" (1795), in *Kant's Political Writings*, ed. Hans Reiss, Cambridge: Cambridge University Press, 1992.
4 On the references to humane or cosmopolitan law, see J. Pictet, "International humanitarian law: a definition", in UNESCO, *International Dimensions of Humanitarian Law*, Dordrecht: Martinus Nijhoff, 1988.
5 For good introductions to the literature, see Oliver Ramsbotham and Tom Woodhouse, *Humanitarian Intervention in Contemporary Conflict: A Reconceptualization*, Cambridge: Polity, 1996.
6 Adam Roberts, *Humanitarian Action in War*, Adelphi Paper 305, Oxford: Oxford University Press for the International Institute for Strategic Studies, 1996.
7 Mary Kaldor, "A decade of humanitarian intervention: the role of global civil society", in Helmut Anheier, Marlies Glasius, and Mary Kaldor (eds), *Global Civil Society 2001*, Oxford: Oxford University Press, 2001.
8 See, for example, William J. Durch (ed.), *The Evolution of UN Peacekeeping. Case Studies and Comparative Analysis*, New York: St Martin's Press, 1993.
9 Charles Dobbie, "A concept for post-Cold War peace-keeping", *Survival* (Autumn 1994).
10 Roberts, "Humanitarian action", p. 51.
11 John Mackinlay, "Improving multifunctional forces", *Survival* (Autumn 1994).
12 Quoted in Dobbie, "A concept", p. 137.
13 *Doctrine of the International Community*, speech by Tony Blair at the Economic Club, Chicago, 24 April 1999, http://www.pm.gov.uk/output/Page1297.asp.
14 Mark Duffield, "Relief in war zones: towards an analysis of the new aid paradigm", *Third World Quarterly* (1997).
15 Alvaro de Soto and Graciana del Castillo, "Obstacles to peace-building", *Foreign Policy*, 94 (Spring 1994).

20

The Environment, Global Justice and World Environmental Citizenship
Patrick Hayden

As a result of a number of global environmental threats becoming increasingly evident over the past three decades, a transnational environmental movement involving a wide range of actors united by a shared ethic of preserving the environment has emerged. During this same period management of the global environment has arisen as a major concern in world politics and environmental matters have assumed a growing importance for international relations scholars and practitioners (Vogler and Imber 1996). An indication of the significance now attached to environmental issues can be gathered from UN Secretary General Kofi Annan's recent Millennium Report to the UN General Assembly in which he describes the new global agenda as aiming to secure "freedom from want, freedom from fear, and the freedom of future generations to sustain their lives on this planet".[1] The manifestation of environmental globalization can be regarded as a consequence of the "thickening" of environmentally-centred linkages between state and nonstate actors around the world, which has occurred largely as a result of mounting concerns about the very possibility of sustaining human life in the face of severe threats to the planet's environment (Held et al. 1999; Clark 2000).

   [. . .]

   For too long many have assumed that human rights and environmentalism are contradictory concerns. However it is clear that human rights claims are predicated on the continued existence and functioning of life-sustaining ecosystems and resources that are now under severe threats and pressures. Furthermore global environmental degradation poses one of the most significant ecological security risks humanity faces and forces us to consider the complex ways in which environmental problems intersect with humanitarian problems such as conflict over land and scarce resources, forced displacement and refugees, the destruction of indigenous cultures through environmental exploitation, the spread of diseases such as HIV/AIDS in less developed and marginalised countries, and so forth. Moreover the possibility of a cosmopolitan world community only takes shape assuming the presence of a safe and healthy environment. The well-being of all human beings depends crucially on how we organize our societies in respect of the planetary environment within which our lives are sustained. For all these reasons a focus on cosmopolitanism cannot mean turning our backs on the environment.

   This essay considers the issue of environmental degradation from a cosmopolitan perspective. The first section examines the emergence of the idea of sustainable development, advancing a critique of this idea in so far as it has been interpreted and implemented in such a way as to neutralise the progressive aspects of its content with regard to fundamental issues of social justice. The second section then connects this critique to a more suitable normative and analytical framework, that of environmental justice. The concept of environmental justice creates a bridge between environmental degradation and the social and political contexts that not only give rise to such degradation but also manifest its effects on human well-being, particularly for the world's poor and marginalised. This section is followed by a survey of global environmental governance and the transnational environmental movement, and concludes with a discussion of the concept of world environmental citizenship as a vital component of contemporary cosmopolitan global politics.

Sustainable development and the turn towards global justice

Since the UN Conference on the Human Environment (UNCHE) in June of 1972, the notion of sustainable development has become central to the elaboration and understanding of contemporary international environmental law and policy. As the twenty-six principles embodied in the Stockholm Declaration adopted at the UNCHE make clear, the numerous ecological crises threatening the planet demand that questions of economic development are integrated with issues concerning protection of the environment. Principle 4, for instance, states: "Man has a special responsibility to safeguard and wisely manage the heritage of wildlife and its habitat which are now gravely imperiled by a combination of adverse factors. Nature conservation including wildlife must therefore receive importance in planning for economic development."[2]

Despite such recognition however, the Stockholm Declaration did not offer a formal definition of what is now referred to by the phrase "sustainable development". The subsequent adoption by the UN General Assembly of the World Charter for Nature in 1982 provided further support for the general principles and attitudes of environmental conservation expressed in the Stockholm Declaration.[3] Yet it was not until the publication of the Brundtland Report in 1987, entitled *Our Common Future*, that sustainable development received its first clear articulation and gained increasingly widespread attention. As drawn up by the members of the World Commission on Environment and Development (WCED), the Brundtland Report defines environmentally sustainable economic development as that which can "ensure that it meets the needs of the present without compromising the ability of future generations to meet their own needs". Moreover, "sustainable development requires meeting the needs of all and extending to all the opportunity to fulfill their aspirations for a better life" (WCED 1987: 8).

Soon after the Brundtland Report appeared the WCED established the Experts Group on Environmental Law. The purpose of this group was to formulate a substantive account of the notion of sustainable development, paying particular attention to the identification of deficiencies and the articulation of proposals with respect to international law, and economic and social policy. The Experts Group was especially concerned with clarifying complex issues concerning the legal rights and responsibilities of development as necessitated by an awareness of the limits of the earth's natural resources. The group's final report elaborated a host of carefully constructed legal principles intended to assist the effective transformation of "all

States individually and collectively" towards the goal of sustainable development and environmental protection.[4]

Little was done to implement the legal principles suggested by the Experts Group however, until the 1992 UN Conference on Environment and Development (UNCED) or "Earth Summit" held in Rio de Janeiro. Indeed as the title of the conference suggests this gathering was seen as the most significant attempt yet to address the linkage of the environment and economic development. More specifically one of the primary concerns of the Earth Summit was to evaluate problems raised by the dual need to protect the environment and enable developing nations to strengthen their economies and improve their standards of living. This was not an easy task however, given the considerable differences expressed by the conference's participants. While many of the industrialised nations argued for more stringent environmental protection along with continued economic growth, the majority of developing nations insisted that their precarious economic development – and thus the exploitation of their natural resources – could not be imperilled by an undue emphasis on environmental protection.

Despite these differences a consensus was achieved which enabled the participants to adopt three non-legally binding instruments: (1) the Rio Declaration on Environment and Development; (2) Agenda 21 (which lays out prescriptions for sustainable development in the twenty-first century); and (3) the Authoritative Statement of Principles for a Global Consensus on the Management, Conservation and Sustainable Development of All Types of Forest (or the Forest Principles). The conference also resulted in the signing of two global treaties – the United Nations Framework Convention on Climate Change and the Convention on Biological Diversity – as well as the establishment of the UN Commission on Sustainable Development (CSD), a body intended to assess and monitor progress in the implementation of Agenda 21 and to promote dialogue and build partnerships for sustainable development with relevant governmental and non-governmental actors (Birnie and Boyle 1995: 658–65).

It is widely accepted that sustainable development has attained the status of the common, regulative idea intended to guide present and future environmental law and policy at the national and international level. The centrality of sustainable development is reflected in the fact that the ten-year follow up conference to the Earth Summit held in Johannesburg, South Africa in August and September 2002, had the title "World Summit on Sustainable Development". I would suggest that despite the key status attained by the idea of sustainable development there are good reasons to adopt a critical stance towards the concept of sustainable economic development, particularly when it comes to considering its implications for the demands of global justice which emphasize the good of humanity over the narrow interests of states and multinational corporations. By examining some of the core themes of sustainable development it should become clear that the concept gives insufficient weight to matters of social injustice, economic exploitation, and the link between ecologically unsound practices and poverty.

Principle 1 of the Rio Declaration proclaims: "Human beings are at the center of concerns for sustainable development. They are entitled to a healthy and productive life in harmony with nature" (Birnie and Boyle 1995: 10). Despite the central role assumed by the idea of sustainable development in recent years it is not yet clear from our discussion what the term entails. The Brundtland Report defines sustainability as follows:

> In essence, sustainable development is a process of change in which the exploitation of resources, the direction of investments, the orientation of technological development, and institutional change are all in harmony and enhance both current and future potential to meet human needs and aspirations (WCED 1987: 46).

A review of the major agreements and statements produced in support of sustainable development enables us to identify (illustratively rather than exhaustively) the following four central elements that are thought to be entailed by the concept of sustainable development, but which are generally in tension with one another and perhaps even internally contradictory.

First, any conclusions concerning the idea of sustainable development remain subordinate to a framework which favours state and commercial interests. Consider Principles 2 and 3 of the Rio Declaration:

> Principle 2: "States have . . . the sovereign right to exploit their own resources pursuant to their own environmental and developmental policies" as long as this exploitation does not "cause damage to the environment of other States or other areas beyond the limits of national jurisdiction".

> Principle 3: "The right to development must be fulfilled so as to meet equitably developmental and environmental needs of present and future generations" (Birnie and Boyle 1995: 10–11).

These principles express two apparent rights: (1) that of state-based exploitation, in so far as the natural environment is regarded as little more than an economic resource to be utilized as any sovereign state sees fit; (2) that of development, in so far as this is assumed to be industrial and economic growth using neoliberal economic policy paradigms. The idea of the right to development began to emerge in the early 1970s when less developed or "Third World" countries sought to negotiate reforms of the world political economy around issues of trade, finance, aid and investment for the purpose of effecting an international redistribution of resources. By the mid-1980s however, arguments in support of reform of the international economic system began to be overshadowed by the structural adjustment approach favoured by the more powerful Western states (Rosas 1995: 247–56). Structural adjustment programmes were introduced as conditions on loans by the International Monetary Fund (IMF) that required developing countries to modify their economic policies in order to cut public spending, place limitations on wages, increase incentives for exports and devalue currency (UNRISD 1994: 2–3). Nevertheless in 1986 the United Nations General Assembly adopted the Declaration on the Right to Development, Article 1.1 of which states that "the right to development is an inalienable human right by virtue of which every human person and peoples are entitled to participate in, contribute to, and enjoy economic, social, cultural and political development, in which all human rights and fundamental freedoms can be fully realized".[5] [. . .]

While the Declaration on the Right to Development [. . .] suggests the need for substantive reform of the world economic system inclusive of resource transfer obligations between rich and poor countries, and emphasizes the centrality of *human* development to the right to development, these innovative features have been either diluted or explicitly rejected in subsequent years as the economic growth model of development has remained dominant (Shue 1995). The notion of human development was introduced into international debates by the United Nations *Human Development Report 1990*, as an alternative to the narrower conventional concept of development as simple economic growth. As defined in the *Human Development Report 2003*:

> Human development is about people, about expanding their choices to live full, creative lives with freedom and dignity. Economic growth, increased trade and investment, technological advance – all are very important. But they are means, not ends. Fundamental to expanding human choices is building human capabilities: the range of things that people can be. The most basic capabilities for human development are living a long and healthy life, being educated, having a decent standard of living and enjoying political and civil freedoms to participate in the life of one's community (UNDP 2003: 28).

[. . .] In contrast to the notion of human development the economic growth model conceives and measures development in terms of increases in gross national product (GNP) per capita as compared between the GNPs of different countries. If the GNP of a country increases then it is considered to be "developing" relative to industrialized countries with the highest GNPs. This approach is problematic in at least two significant ways. First, increases in aggregate GNP per capita tell us little about how wealth is being distributed and put to use within a country, and thus whether this increase is accompanied by enlarged disparities of wealth internally which may result in lower standards of living for the majority of the population (Little 2003; Sen 1999). Second, development predicated on economic growth fuelled by industrialization renders imperative the exploitation and consumption of renewable and nonrenewable natural resources, and leads to increased pollution of water, air and land, consequences which harm rather than assist human development.

A second core element of the concept of sustainable development is that the current framework within which international instruments concerning sustainable development are advanced places heavy emphasis on state sovereignty over natural resources. This is in agreement with customary principles and practices of public international law. As with Principle 2 of the Rio Declaration, international environmental instruments incorporating the idea of sustainable development explicitly affirm state sovereignty. For instance, Principle 1 (a) of the Forest Principles announces that "States have the sovereign and inalienable right to utilize, manage and develop their forests in accordance with their development needs and level of socioeconomic development".[6] While sovereignty over resources is granted the status of an inherent or "inalienable" right, state sovereignty in this respect is supposedly subject to the obligations incurred under international law although the extent of those obligations may be taken to be quite minimal. An effect of this statist orientation towards natural resources is to reinforce the misguided idea that each state not only has control over its own resources but is also solely responsible for its own development.

As a third element, Principle 3 of the Rio Declaration also points to two other important aspects of the concept of sustainable development, namely, equity and intergenerational responsibility. These two aspects are emphasized as well in Principles 5 and 8 of the Rio Declaration. Principle 5 declares: "All States and all people shall cooperate in the essential task of eradicating poverty as an indispensable requirement for sustainable development, in order to decrease the disparities in standards of living and better meet the needs of the majority of the people of the world." Principle 8 calls for the eventual elimination of unsustainable patterns of production, consumption and population growth in order to achieve "a higher quality of life for all people" (Birnie and Boyle 1995: 11). Sustainable development, it is argued, can only be achieved if each generation bears responsibility for the continued protection and functioning of ecosystems for future generations, and if worldwide poverty and other social disparities are eradicated. The proposal that issues of equity and environmental integrity must be intrinsically linked is the most progressive aspect of sustainable development theory and corresponds with several of the recommendations of the WCED. [. . .]

In view of the issues raised above, the fourth and final core element is that sustainable development is regarded as including the notion of "common but differentiated responsibilities". As expressed in Principles 6, 7, 8 and 9 of the Rio Declaration, both developed and developing nations share the responsibility to protect, conserve and restore the environment, but this responsibility weighs differently according to whether states are more developed or less developed. This differentiation of responsibilities has two facets: First, it is recognized that more developed or, industrialised nations contribute most greatly to environmental degradation and possess the economic and technological means to begin to actively redress this degradation. The United States for instance, is the world's biggest greenhouse polluter, responsible for 25 per cent of global greenhouse gas emissions despite having only 4 per cent of the world's population, while also having the world's largest economy in terms of GDP.[7] Despite this fact the George W. Bush administration withdrew the United States from the Kyoto Protocol, an international treaty drafted in 1997 according to which industrialized nations agreed to reduce substantially their emissions of greenhouse gases. Second, less developed nations are also acknowledged as contributing in their own ways to environmental degradation but are held to have less financial and technological capability of responding to such problems. Consequently the achievement of a global and equitable version of sustainable development requires a greater transfer of resources from developed to developing nations in order to, so to speak, "level the playing field".

Aspects of the first, third and fourth core elements entailed by the concept of sustainable development seem to challenge the traditional limitations placed around matters of justice in international relations. In particular they bring to our attention that programmes intended to protect the environment often disregard the differential benefits and burdens that arise between societies and generations. Consequently doing justice with regard to the aims of such programmes would require a fair distribution of these benefits and burdens. It would be unjust, for example, to continue to maintain burdens disproportionately greater for poor peoples than for rich ones, and benefits disproportionately greater for the already advantaged than for the disadvantaged.

It would appear then that the idea of sustainable development is one that is explicitly intended to further the goal of greater justice across the planet. Yet it is also an idea constrained by internal tensions or limitations that arise from the fact that it remains firmly entrenched in the terrain of state interests and the economics of consumerism. These tensions at the heart of the concept of sustainable development weaken the perception that the natural environment ought to be protected, thereby leaving the potentially progressive elements of sustainable development largely, squandered. For the most part this is a consequence of the primacy assumed by economic development in the phrase "sustainable development". Although the idea of sustainable development is promoted as the preferred paradigm for environmental action within the context of the international system, it is absurd to ignore the fact that in the absence of global regulation international capitalism is inherently unsustainable. Economic development, no matter how closely it is wrapped in "green" language, is by definition under global capitalism predicated on the expansion of commodity production and thus the continued intense consumption and exploitation of the earth's resources.

Our natural environment is considered by the crude growth and consumption paradigm of economic development to be little more than a standing reserve whose only purpose is to provide resources for human exploitation. A conceptual framework and economic system which strictly divides humanity from nature and posits nature as an object merely for human use is most likely unable to support the kinds of changes in value and belief that are needed to address effectively the extent of global environmental degradation and thus extend the scope of justice across the entire planet. If the interdependencies of human and nonhuman life are to be genuinely recognized, future environmental institutions and treaties must resist the temptation to extract human concerns from their broader natural mooring and elevate them to a separate and inherently superior status, such as with a right to economic development that would trump all environmental concerns properly situated with regard to human well-being. As I discuss in the following section, recent attempts at articulating principles that integrate human and environmental rights seem to be a positive effort in this direction.

The narrow cost-benefit approach that lies behind uncontrolled economic exploitation of the environment also poses problems for the laudable goals of intergenerational responsibility and equity included in the idea of sustainable development. While the emphasis on intergenerational issues is intended to temper the kind of short-term thinking characteristic of our conventional practices of uncontrolled exploitation of the environment, exploitation nevertheless retains a prominent place within sustainable development. It is no accident that Principle 4 of the Rio Declaration states that environmental protection constitutes only a "part" of the development process. On the one hand, it must be asked whether the sense of justice conveyed by the inclusion of intergenerational concerns can be adequately served by the belief that more economic growth is the answer to the world's environmental problems. On the other hand, the question arises as to how justice can be served if developing nations are unable to obtain a standard of living suitable to a healthy and secure life, that is, if the current social and economic inequities between North and South remain firmly entrenched.

[. . .]

Given the massive inequalities in the present global distribution of resources recourse must be made to some redistributive claims as required by the duties of justice. One such claim can be made in light of John Rawls's principle of fair equality of opportunity. In his well-known theory of justice as fairness Rawls proceeds on the belief that justice is the primary and indispensable virtue against which the laws and institutions of society must be assessed (Rawls 1999a: 3). Given the indispensable status of social justice, a society's laws and institutions must be reformed or abolished if they are unjust even though they may be good or proper according to some other criteria. The same may be said of the world community, particularly given the systematic interconnectedness and interdependency of the globalized political system and the extensive global impact of environmental destruction and pollution. The most fundamental principles of justice are designed to regulate the distribution of fundamental rights and duties, advantages and burdens, assigned to individuals by the rules of society. Clearly both individual societies and the global society have patterns of inequality that persist over time and systematic ways of allocating people to positions within their hierarchies of power, status and money. Because of these structural allocations of advantages and disadvantages, without the application of adequate principles of justice many aspects of the basic structure responsible for arbitrary inequalities would remain unaffected. A fundamental aim of justice as fairness is to ensure the existence of a just system of institutions.

One argument that highlights the importance of these structural inequalities concerns what Rawls calls "fait equality of opportunity" which he distinguishes from "formal" equality of opportunity (Rawls 1999a: 73–8). Formal equality exists when no laws unequally restrict the opportunities of anyone to acquire such social goods as wealth, income or powers of office. However, formal equality of opportunity does not concern itself with inequalities of life prospects that stem from unequal starting places in society. Thus under a scheme of formal equality of opportunity if two equally motivated and equally talented individuals start from unequal social positions it is likely that they will achieve unequal levels of wealth, income or powers of office. Consequently persons with equal talents and motivations will not have equal life prospects or expectations.

In contrast, fair equality of opportunity exists when persons with equal talents, abilities and motivations have the same or similar life prospects of expectations of attaining positions involving certain levels of income, wealth and powers of office, regardless of the social position each is born into. This requires certain institutions designed to mitigate the influence of social position on individual attainment and thus to equalize life prospects regarding the attainment of income, wealth, or the powers of office for individuals with similar abilities and motivation. For example if two similarly talented and motivated individuals happened to be born into radically different circumstances such that one of them had access to adequate educational facilities and housing as well as clean water, air and food while the other did not, the resulting disparity in life prospects could be lessened by the equal provision of basic education, housing, and a clean and safe environment. What this means is that the basic structure of society generates, in conjunction with natural and social contingencies, conditions which can be the source of significant injustices. Consequently the basic structures of domestic and global society must be regulated to eliminate as much as possible such injustices.

While the interrelationships between globalization and social justice are complex, it is nonetheless possible to recognize that there exists interdependent economic (as well as political, social and cultural) activity that produces substantial aggregate benefits, and a pattern in which international and transnational institutions (multinational corporations, international and transnational trade and investment, property rights over national territories and their resources) distribute those benefits as well as burdens. Yet global interdependence as it has functioned in the market framework preoccupied with economic growth has coincided with ever widening gaps between rich and poor countries, political inequality and inequality of opportunities among the members of different countries and, domestically, gaps between upper and lower income classes (Eichengreen 1999). Thus, while the process of globalization carries with it significant interdependencies including a reduction of barriers to the flow of goods, services, finance, people and communications, it also entails increasing gaps in economic, social, political and environmental standards within and between states which must be addressed by the world community.

Given the interdependencies of peoples throughout the world generated by globalization, it has become imperative that principles of social justice are applied globally. The shared fates and interests of persons extend beyond political boundaries as economic, environmental, social, cultural and political life becomes increasingly global. These considerations lead to the conclusion that in a world where state boundaries do not constitute the limits of social goods and bads, the confinement of principles of social justice – such as fair equality of opportunity – to the domestic sphere has the effect of unfairly burdening poor countries and poor classes therein, thereby contributing to avoidable suffering.

In characterizing sustainable development as a way of balancing ecosystem protection with the familiar rules of the global economic system we sacrifice strong consideration of the global aspect of social justice to the notion of simple conformity with the status quo of international political economy. Doing so leaves in place the basic global structures that operate to reproduce existing patterns of power, wealth, privilege and inequality. Calling for deep structural reforms in line with egalitarian distributive principles is certainly more complex than an insistence on straightforward economic development and is sure to be an unfavourable position among the affluent. Yet the principle of intergenerational equity and responsibility is one which calls for a strong sense of fairness when considering how the requirements of justice are to be balanced within and between generations. It is perhaps also the only way to ensure that both environmental and economic preservation can be fulfilled. Consequently I suggest that the discourse of sustainable *development* should give way to a discourse of sustainable or environmental *justice*.

[. . .]

From sustainable development to environmental justice

Environmental justice begins from the recognition that marginalisation of the environment and marginalisation of poor communities, most often those of ethnic or racial minorities, are strongly linked together and stem from common attitudes and practices dismissive of basic principles of justice. Environmental injustice issues therefore connect problems of racial and ethnic discrimination with those of socioeconomic inequality, which are intersecting problems affecting a vast percentage of the world's population. According to the 2002 and 2003 editions of the *Human Development Report*:

- Incomes are distributed more unequally across the world's people than in the most unequal countries.
- The richest 5 per cent of the world's people receive 114 times the income of the poorest 5 per cent.
- The richest 1 per cent receive as much as the poorest 57 per cent.
- Global inequality increased between 1987 and 1998.
- On a per capita basis the Gross Domestic Product of the world's least developed countries declined by more than 10 per cent during the 1990s.
- Per capita incomes fell in 54 countries during the 1990s, with most of these countries in sub-Saharan Africa.
- In the early 1990s children under five were 19 times more likely to die in sub-Saharan Africa than in rich countries – and today, 26 times more likely.
- Poor women and girls are hurt disproportionately by environmental degradation, often because they are responsible for collecting fuel, fodder and water.
- About 1.7 billion people, a third of the developing world's population, live in countries facing water stress (defined as countries that consume more than 20 per cent of their renewable water supply each year).

In short, these and other statistics reveal that "many environmental problems stem from poverty – often contributing to a downward spiral in which poverty exacerbates environmental degradation and environmental degradation exacerbates poverty" (UNDP 2002: 123).

Environmental justice refers to this connection between environmental concerns and social justice. The concept of environmental justice emerged initially from the work of scholars and activists in the United States which documented the dispropor-tionate economic burdens and health risks found in poor communities and especially communities of colour, associated with the siting of rubbish, landfill, hazardous and toxic waste facilities and polluting industries, and the unequal distribution of environmental benefits, resulting in a lack of access to clean land, water and air (Bryant 1995; Hofrichter 1993). Environmental justice has expanded upon this initial focus in two key ways: First, it has moved "beyond racism to include others (regardless of race and ethnicity) who are deprived of their environmental rights" and therefore are most vulnerable to the impact of environmental problems, "such as women, children and the poor" (Cutter 1995: 113). Second, it has moved beyond the context of local communities within a single state to recognition that environmen-tal injustice associated with those in lower socioeconomic groups is a feature of the global context of the international system.[8] The result has been a shift in or addition to the discourse of environmentalism, which is no longer merely an issue of resource conservation and wildlife preservation but also a social and political matter of global, justice, equity and rights with regard to all persons everywhere and their quality of life.

While it is not the purpose of this essay to rehearse arguments for and against anthropocentrism and biocentrism (or ecocentrism) within the context of environmen-tal ethics since these have been comprehensively conducted elsewhere,[9] the environ-mental justice argument is admittedly anthropocentric in so far as it focuses on human beings as the proper subjects of justice and on their claims to rights and fairness within systems of political morality. Nevertheless, environmental justice need only be consid-ered as adopting a "weak" version of anthropocentrism for two reasons. First, admit-ting human beings as the proper subjects of justice does not mean that nonhumans cannot also be a locus of moral concern. Second, its concern with human health and well-being is grounded in the recognition that the quality of human life is insepa-rable from the quality of the supporting ecosystems upon which human life depends; there is no need to presume a strict ontological distinction between human beings and the environment in which they live. It is quite possible, then, to defend pragmatically the aims of environmental justice while holding stronger biocentric beliefs. In com-parison economic rationality not only regards nonhuman nature solely in instrumen-tal terms, as resources to be exploited in the service of economic ends, but also human beings in general, as instruments to be utilized in the service of those same ends. Within the market paradigm of economic rationality human needs, health and well-being are insufficient grounds for legitimating basic human rights claims vis-à-vis the environment.

On the one hand, then, a narrow conception of environmentalism that focuses solely on the protection of the nonhuman natural environment leads to an extreme biocen-trism which fails to account for the interests of humans in general and the rights of individuals in particular. On the other hand, an equally narrow focus on the merely instrumental value of the environment for human use leads to an extreme anthropocentrism which fails to take into account potentially noninstrumental dimensions of ecosystems (such as the aesthetic, religious/spiritual, cultural and psychological) and the extent to which human life is dependent upon the environment in ways which transcend its mere exploitation as an economic resource. The environmental justice approach charts a balanced path between these extremes, accepting that the environment is not completely reducible to an economic instrumentality but that it is also fundamentally inseparable from human existence and interests. As Kristin Shrader-Frechette notes: "What affects the welfare of the planet affects us all" (Shrader-Frechette 2002: 6). For this reason environmental conditions and sociopolitical conditions reflect an interpenetration which renders it imperative to challenge practices that degrade these conditions, and the burdens of economic development must not be "shifted to the poor and the powerless" such as indigenous peoples and citizens of developing nations (Shrader-Frechette 2002: 6).

[. . .]

Environmental justice therefore focuses attention on the inequities – whether distributive or procedural and disproportionate burdens borne by poor communities and countries that arise from the inclusion of what arguably are morally irrelevant features such as race, ethnicity, economic status and political power, in environmental decision making (Bullard 2001: 8). Distributively, conventional practices have led to situations in which those who most benefit from the exploitation of natural resources and advantageous siting of harmful facilities and by-products such as toxic waste have not sustained burdens commensurate to those benefits. The unequal distribution of the burdens and benefits associated with environmental siting policies and practices can undermine fair equality of opportunity, as discussed in the previous section. Procedurally, those who traditionally have least benefited from conventional environmental practices have also been burdened incommensurately by disparities in the formulation, adoption and implementation of policies and strategies intended to improve the environmental conditions in which they must live, thereby limiting their access to and capacity for participating in environmental and economic decision-making. As Cole and Foster note an important aspect of environmental justice "is the element of democratic decision-making", and current "processes have not been effective in providing meaningful participation opportunities for those most burdened by environmental decisions" (Cole and Foster 2001: 16). All of this amounts to a violation of the condition of fairness underlying deliberations regarding principles of justice according to which basic fairness demands that the interests of all persons as human beings be given equal consideration in various decision-making processes that may have a significant affect on those interests (Hunold and Young 1998).

[. . .]

While the exact content of what environmental justice entails is open to plural interpretations it has often been framed in terms of basic rights, in particular the right to a healthy environment implied by the right to life. Environmental rights should be understood to encompass both substantive and procedural rights. Substantive environmental rights include the right to clean air and water, the right to be protected from environmental harm, and the right to natural resources used and managed according to environmentally sound practices. Procedural environmental rights which enhance and protect our ability to claim substantive rights include the right to be fully informed about the potential affects of environmental hazards, the right to participate in democratic procedures for policy-making and decision-making concerning such hazards, the right to consent to policies and decisions reached, and the right to complain about existing conditions, standards and policies.[10]

Environmental human rights contribute substantive moral and political entitlements to the doctrine of sustainable development, and the coupling of sustainable development with environmental justice leads to a more adequate perspective which might be referred to as *sustainable justice*. Sustainable justice reframes the discourse of sustainable development around notions of justice, rights and equity. Without the inclusion of principles of environmental justice into the discourse and practice of sustainable development, narrowly instrumental conceptions of economic development may end up overriding the requirements of justice and fair social practice. These *prima facie* obligations of the requirements of sustainable justice consist minimally of the equitable distribution of environmental benefits (goods) and burdens (bads) and equal environmental human rights irrespective of morally irrelevant features such as race, ethnicity and economic status. A sustainable justice approach thus advocates a more comprehensive understanding of the need to transform the social contexts that underlie and produce environmental injustice, and a long-term consideration of the ways that the capacity to pursue politically, economically and ecologically sound policies can be enhanced through local-global linkages. In this way it can contribute to a heightened sense of global responsibility and equity such as in the case of the notion of world environmental citizenship discussed in the following section.

Furthermore the discourse of environmental rights adds depth to the notion of a basic right to life intrinsic to human development, in so far as it emphasises the importance of quality of life above and beyond bodily survival (Hamm 2001). It suggests that human beings are not only entitled to live in conditions free from unreasonably adverse forms of environmental degradation, but that we have responsibilities both to protect others from such degradation and to utilize, manage and transform the earth only in ways that do not create unacceptable (and disproportionate) risks to the well-being of others. Being attentive to these environmental dimensions of human development helps to ensure that all persons have a fair share of safe and sustainable resources and are not disproportionately disadvantaged by the effects of environmental policies, thereby respecting the principle of fair equality of opportunity. Because the planetary environment is our means of survival, fair equality of opportunity within the framework of global sustainable justice must encompass concern for disparities in the basic structure of society which negatively impact human health and well-being, and thereby create unjust inequalities in life chances. The effects that human actions have on the environment have a necessary connection to concomitant effects on humans individually and collectively, now and into the future.

[. . .]

Global environmental governance and world environmental citizenship

As mentioned in the introduction, the transnational environmental movement and the importance attached to global environmental problems have occurred mainly as a result of the recent emergence of a number of well-publicized global environmental threats. Environmental organizations in both developed and less developed countries have increased the profile of these threats and have helped to move them onto political agendas by putting pressure on influential actors and institutions. For this reason, and in light of the types of concerns focused on by environmental justice discourse, global environmental change is best understood as a social rather than physical phenomenon. This is because what has occurred is not simply dramatic change in the natural environment but more significantly the growth of an environmental consciousness, which realizes the limits of human exploitation (of both the earth and other human beings) and seeks to preserve the environment as the support system necessary for human existence (Lipschutz and Meyer 1996: 20). The emergence of environmental consciousness is, then, very much the result of the "rediscovery" of human dependence on our natural surroundings, which has been masked by the modern scientific and technological illusion that nature can be mastered in a process of unlimited human expansion (Falk 1995: 252). Therefore, although the transnational environmental movement is due in large part to a number of world ecological threats becoming increasingly evident, the development of a shared global ethic seeking to limit human exploitation of the earth and the human costs of such exploitation is an important indicator of a transformative cosmopolitan politics.

Largely as a result of the emergence of the transnational environmental movement and its shared global ethic, environmental globalization is rapidly occurring. David Held defines globalization as the "stretching and deepening of social relations and institutions across time and space", a result of which is that local activities increasingly are influenced by events across the globe, while practices of local groups can have global influence (Held 1995: 20). As William C. Clark argues, if environmental globalism consists of "the existence of a rich network of environmentally mediated linkages among actors at multicontinental distance", then it is unequivocally a feature of global society. He suggests as well that if, using Held's definition, environmental globalization is the "thickening" of the linkages of environmental globalism then this process is well under way (Clark 2000: 101–2). Clark outlines three groups of environmental linkages that have noticeably increased in the past few decades, focused on what he calls the "environmental stuff" dimension of globalism, namely, the flows of materials (such as hazardous materials, toxic wastes and "greenhouse" gases) and biota around the globe, environmental ideas, and environmental governance. He cites increases in the variety, strength and density of long distance relationships among actors, the number of actors involved in those relationships, and the velocity of change in society that these relationships help to induce as persuasive proof of environmental globalization.

Clark uses the phrase "globalization of stuff" to denote the way in which flows of energy, materials and organisms throughout the natural and human environments link the actions of people in one place with people at a distance. Clark and others contend that it is necessary to understand the earth as a system that involves a vast number of complex interactions and linkages which are irreducible to a linear cause and effect conception of actions in the environment (Clark 2000: 57; Blackmore and Smyth 2002: 204). The flows of energy around the earth mean that disturbances to the planet's energy at one place can augment and create a large-scale impact in a number of other places. In addition flows of materials, which include those relocated by intercontinental transport as well as gases and particles that flow through the atmosphere, link together people in different places. Finally, biotic linkages such as the movement of pests or diseases can have significant and devastating effects on human populations and their supporting ecosystems. Because the earth's environment functions as a complex system there has always been a degree of globalism in the ways in which relationships between humans are mediated by environmental linkages. However as a result of the increase in the world's population, consumption of resources and greater economic interdependence, these linkages have thickened considerably (Clark 2000: 87–94).

[. . .]

The significant component of environmental globalization is the thickening of linkages between actors as a result of the emergence of a complex system of global governance aimed at addressing global environmental problems. Global governance refers to "collective actions to establish international institutions and norms to cope with the causes and consequences of adverse supranational, transnational, or national problems" (Värynen 1999: 25). Global governance involves both governmental institutions and nongovernmental organizations in the collective making of rules and exercising of power at the global level but unlike the formal system of government, global governance is not necessarily backed by police powers (Rosenau 1992: 4). Ernst-Otto Czempiel's description of governance as the "capacity to get things done without the legal competence to command that they be done" emphasizes the lack of coercive power inherent in the definition of governance as distinct from government (Czempiel 1992: 249). Young further defines global governance as the management of complex interdependencies among an extensive network of actors who are engaged in interactive decision-making and take actions that affect each others' welfare (Young 1996: 2). The system of global environmental governance thus includes both formal treaties and the institutions created to implement them, as well as less formal norms and rules that both constrain and enable actors' behaviour without necessarily being backed by strong coercive powers (Lipschutz and Meyer 1996: 249).

The transnational environmental movement is characterized not only by the search for collective and cooperative solutions to global environmental problems, but also by the diversity of actors involved. Although some have argued that as a result of the emergence of international regimes the state would have less power, the state remains highly influential in the governance of the environment. States alone have formal coercive power over their citizens, they negotiate the international legal instruments which form the basis of global environmental governance, and they adopt international trade and financial policies which affect the environment both directly and indirectly (Porter and Brown 1996: 2). Intergovernmental organizations such as the United Nations Environment Programme play a significant role in environmental governance as they perform a wide variety of functions and have influence on states and other governmental organizations. Private actors have also become involved in the transnational environmental movement, with a number of domestic and multinational corporations adopting environmental considerations into their operations, and through the formation of international umbrella organizations such as the World Business Council for Sustainable Development. The sector that has undergone the most significant transformation, however, is that of public nongovernmental actors. Especially since their extensive and high-profile involvement at the Rio Conference on Environment and Development in 1992, NGOs have grown rapidly in number and exert increasing influence on global environmental politics (Clark 2000: 100). Therefore although the state still plays a central role in global governance of the environment, other actors have also taken on substantial roles in world environmental politics.

Out of this general background of global environmental governance another notable feature that has evolved is the emergence of networks which involve large numbers of diverse actors united by their interest in a specific issue or project. These vast networks constitute what is now referred to as "global civil society" and engage like-minded actors from different levels and sectors of society from the local to the global. As Mary Kaldor notes, "global civil society is in the process of helping to constitute and being constituted by a global system of rules, underpinned by overlapping intergovernmental, governmental and global authorities" (Kaldor 2003: 2). These civil society networks are defined as global because the actors, in addition to being from numerous different countries, are involved in international forums, conferences and debates, and are globally linked through networks, communications and a shared ethic aimed at preserving the environment and rectifying social harms connected with environmental problems. Global civil society is fundamental in dealing with global environmental problems, as it involves local practices which are linked globally and which therefore make shared global practices plausible (Lipschutz and Meyer 1996: 49–60). These types of networks have developed in other fields of governance such as human rights and they are especially crucial in the environmental field, as without both global and local action taking place the transnational environmental movement would be rendered ineffective.

However in order to answer more fully the question of whether the transnational environmental movement provides a good example of global governance it first must be asked how to measure effective governance. Oran R. Young outlines several different dimensions of effectiveness of global governance. The most important measure is whether the problems that motivated the creations of the system of governance are being addressed adequately and whether progress is being made in their solution. Linked to this measure but not always identical to it is the extent to which the goals of a regime are attained over time. In addition both "behavioural effectiveness" which Young defines as the extent to which a regime causes its members to alter their behaviour and comply with the requirements, and "process effectiveness" which is the extent to which the provisions are implemented within the relevant political units are important. Finally, "evaluative effectiveness" denotes the extent to which a regime operates in an efficient and equitable manner (Young 1996: 8–14). Each of these facets of effectiveness can be used to analyze the efficacy of the transnational environmental movement as a system of global governance.

The traditional method of dealing with global environmental problems has been the creation of regimes which establish a system of rules, standards and procedures for each area of concern. These regimes are based on multilateral agreements out of which institutions designed to implement the negotiated provisions are formed (Porter and Brown 1996: 16). Different environmental regimes have proved to be widely divergent in terms of solving the environmental issue they were intended to address. An example of a regime which has been widely cited as bringing about measurable improvement is the ozone regime. This regime is based on the 1985 Framework Convention for the Protection of the Ozone Layer that defined the means by which actors would cooperate in reducing emissions, which was followed up in 1987 by the Montreal Protocol that outlined concrete reduction targets. These targets have been largely complied with, and between 1987 and 1996 there was an 85 per cent reduction in the worldwide consumption of chlorofluorocarbons (CFCs) (Simonis and Bruhl 2002: 108–9). The ozone and other environmental regimes generally are effective governance mechanisms in that the problems they aim to solve are diverse in character and require specialized institutional responses. However a common criticism is that there is a lack of coordination between the various regimes and thus the overall governance of environmental issues becomes too fragmented and responsibilities are spread too widely (Juma 2002: 44). Consequently although some regimes have been successful in reducing the pressure placed by humans on the environment, environmental degradation continues at a rapid pace and the system of global governance as a whole cannot yet be regarded as entirely effective in solving the problems it was designed to address.

In an effort to counteract the fragmentary nature of separate environmental regimes the United Nations Environment Programme (UNEP) was established after the UN Conference on the Human Environment (UNCHE) in 1972 to coordinate existing efforts in protecting the environment (Simonis and Bruhl 2002: 105). Although it plays a significant role in directing the attention of states to environmental problems and suggesting solutions, UNEP has been criticised as inadequate because it has limited resources, no executive authority or coercive power, and relies completely on the actions of states to implement its directions (Juma 2002: 44). Despite its shortcomings, which are due primarily to structural deficiencies of the inter-state system, UNEP has filled a highly visible role in seeking to catalyse changes in human perceptions about the environment, ensure widespread legitimacy of global environmental governance, and build consensus between industrialised and developing countries in devising cooperative norms and policies.

The extent to which the goals of a regime are fulfilled can be distinguished from the effectiveness of that regime in solving problems. There is often a substantial difference between the degree of regulation that needs to be enforced in order to halt environmental degradation and the actual provisions of a regime which are negotiated by various actors. For example although the Intergovernmental Panel on Climate Change noted that the world's greenhouse gas emissions must be reduced to 60 per cent of the 1990 levels if the earth's climate system is to be stabilised, the agreed target of reduction of emissions of greenhouse gases for the years 2008–12 outlined in the Kyoto Protocol is an average of only 5.2 per cent (Simonis and Bruhl 2002: 110). The goals set by a regime are often limited by state actors adhering to a narrow conception of national interests who are thus unwilling to make necessary changes to their own policies and practices. While the goal of the UN Conference on the Environment and Development in 1992 was to take a long-term global approach to sustainable development, the negotiating stances of the participating countries were largely determined by their short-term economic and political interests (Simonis and Bruhl 2002: 104). Although there are real differences that need to be addressed, especially between the North and the South, actors also need to be willing to revise their conception of the interests at stake in order to ensure that regime goals adequately address environmental problems.

In order for environmental regimes to operate most effectively states must comply with the measures agreed upon and there must be compliance mechanisms to enforce against those who do not comply. Only a few regimes have specific enforcement mechanisms and those which do exist are largely cooperative in nature, where signatories are bound to support a noncomplying state so that it can meet its obligations. Under the Montreal Protocol for instance, countries are questioned on the reasons for their noncompliance and a joint effort is made to identify ways to ensure future compliance, which might include measures such as sanctions, cancellation of benefits and formal admonitions, or more supportive measures such as financial and technology transfers (Simonis and Bruhl 2002: 120–21). The lack of strong enforcement mechanisms included in international regimes has been the subject of much criticism, as not all states comply with the established rules and noncompliance does not always lead to corrective action being taken. Therefore although there has been a reasonably high rate of compliance with regimes, stronger enforcement mechanisms need to be built into regimes so that they can operate more effectively.

Clearly there has been a significant amount of coordinated action based on the diffusion of environmental ideas and a shared ethic of sustainability and environmental justice, and as a result the transnational environmental movement has contributed to the creation of global civil society. While there have been some positive steps taken to make certain that global policies are adopted at local levels, ongoing efforts still are needed to ensure that citizens around the world are informed and motivated to protect the environment and thereby contribute to human development. As part of this process it is extremely important that in light of the insights offered by environmental justice, governance of the environment is regarded as equitable by all parties involved. Because many global environmental problems can be traced to the industrialized countries of the North, it is only fair that they assume a greater burden in helping to rectify these problems consistent with the global principle of fair equality of opportunity and the global nature of environmental threats.[11] The Brundtland Report makes clear that the world's political communities are bound by common interests in regard to the environment and are in need of reaching common solutions:

> National boundaries have become so porous that traditional distinctions between local, national, and international issues have become blurred. Policies formerly considered to be exclusively matters of "national concern" now have an impact on the ecological bases of other nations' development and survival. Conversely, the growing reach of some nations' policies – economic, trade, monetary, and most sectoral policies – into the "sovereign" territory of other nations limits the affected nations' options in devising national solutions to their "own" problems (WCED 1987: 312).

By linking human-centred development with environmental protection and incorporating sufficient incentives to make participation by developing countries achievable and attractive, it may be possible for the countries of the North and South to find even more common ground. The principle of common but differentiated responsibility anchored in many multilateral environmental agreements should also be given greater support in local, national and international environmental policies. Other means of making global environmental governance more equitable include debt cancellation and financial and technology transfers which enable developing countries to comply with regulations. While differing needs and capacities must be kept in mind, the transnational environmental movement has sought to make regulations equitable and therefore meaningful for both developed and developing countries.

Although systems of global environmental governance have not yet made major progress in solving environmental problems, important building blocks have been put in place in the organization of the transnational environmental movement. The most encouraging aspect of this movement is its contributing role in the emergence of global civil society in which networks of actors spanning different levels and different sectors of society are linked by their shared concern for the environment and human development, which results in local groups taking action based on globally embedded ideas. For this reason it is possible to speak of a consolidation of cosmopolitan and environmental values and ideals into a new conception of "world environmental citizenship" as a dynamic moral-political dimension of global civil society.

World environmental citizenship can be viewed as a component of the more general cosmopolitan conception of world citizenship. The idea of world citizenship refers to the individual as a member of the wider community of all humanity complementary to whatever other political communities, such as the state, of which he or she is a member. Membership in the community of humanity implies some form of identity with and commitment to the other members of that community, and to the well-being of that community as a whole. World environmental citizenship arises from an ethical concern for the social, political and economic problems associated with the environment and humanity's dependence upon it, and from a recognition of our global responsibilities for the human condition in light of humanity's interconnectedness with the environment. Thus the world environmental citizen is concerned about the common good of the human community and places particular emphasis on the fact that we are all citizens belonging to both local environments and a single global environment. One of the first attempts to define environmental citizenship was offered by Environment Canada, the department within the Government of Canada that manages environmental affairs:

> Environmental citizenship is a personal commitment to learning more about the environment and to taking responsible environmental action. Environmental citizenship encourages individuals, communities and organizations to think about the environmental rights and responsibilities we all have as residents of planet Earth (Environment Canada 1993: 1).

More recently the United Nations Environment Programme launched a new Global Environmental Citizenship Programme. According to UNEP the aim of the Global Environmental Citizenship Programme is to "assert the differentiated rights and responsibilities of various sectors of society and promote informed actions to protect life on Earth".[12] More specifically the Programme functions to broaden its constituencies beyond state governments both by facilitating the participation of major environmental groups and NGOs such as Greenpeace, Earth Action and Friends of the Earth in global environmental governance; and by strengthening links between UNEP, governments and global civil society.

The universalist values and aspirations contained in the conception of world environmental citizenship may have found its fullest expression yet in the Earth Charter, which was officially launched at the Peace Palace in The Hague on 29 June 2000. The Earth Charter is the culmination of a decade-long consultative process that involved prominent political figures, individual experts, national committees, intergovernmental organizations, and domestic and international NGOs. It is therefore the result of global civil society as a constructive partner in global governance. The impetus for the Earth Charter came from the 1987 United Nations World Commission on Environment and Development report *Our Common Future* which called for the creation of a new global charter that would set forth the fundamental principles of sustainable development. Following the 1992 Earth Summit in Rio calls for the drafting of a new charter increased, and in 1997 an Earth Charter Commission was formed with an Earth Charter Secretariat established at the Earth Council in Costa Rica. Ultimately the mission of the Earth Charter initiative transcended earlier conceptions of sustainable development and led to the adoption of a platform of global environmental justice in order to "establish a sound ethical foundation for the emerging global society and to help build a sustainable world based on respect for nature, universal human rights, economic justice, and a culture of peace".[13] A number of the Earth Charter's principles give clear expression to the idea of world environmental citizenship:

- 2 (a): Accept that with the right to own, manage, and use natural resources comes the duty to prevent environmental harm and to protect the rights of people.
- 3 (a): Ensure that communities at all levels guarantee human rights and fundamental freedoms and provide everyone an opportunity to realize his or her full potential.
- 3 (b): Promote social and economic justice, enabling all to achieve a secure and meaningful livelihood that is ecologically responsible.
- 4 (a): Recognize that the freedom of action of each generation is qualified by the needs of future generations.
- 6 (c): Ensure that decision making addresses the cumulative, long-term, indirect, long distance, and global consequences of human activities.
- 9 (a): Guarantee the right to potable water, clean air, food security, uncontaminated soil, shelter, and safe sanitation, allocating the national and international resources required.
- 9 (c): Recognize the ignored, protect the vulnerable, serve those who suffer, and enable them to develop their capacities and to pursue their aspirations.
- 10 (a): Promote the equitable distribution of wealth within nations and among nations.
- 10 (b): Enhance the intellectual, financial, technical, and social resources of developing nations, and relieve them of onerous international debt.
- 13 (a): Uphold the right of everyone to receive clear and timely information on environmental matters and all development plans and activities which are likely to affect them or in which they have an interest.
- 13 (b): Support local, regional and global civil society, and promote the meaningful participation of all interested individuals and organizations in decision making.

Finally, the Preamble to Earth Charter concludes by declaring:

> To realize these aspirations, we must decide to live with a sense of universal responsibility, identifying ourselves with the whole Earth community as well as our local communities. We are at once citizens of different nations and of one world in which the local and global are linked. Everyone shares responsibility for the present and future well-being of the human family and the larger living world.

Conclusion

These examples demonstrate that the idea of world environmental citizenship already has been exercised as an emerging identity within global civil society and that the state is no longer the only important actor in global affairs. World environmental citizens – as individuals and members of voluntary associations and networks of organizations – conceive of themselves as active and responsible members of planet Earth, participate in public decision-making regarding environmental policy, and promote values and ways of life conducive to the health and well-being of their fellow citizens of overlapping local and global environments. The responsibilities attached to world environmental citizenship derive from a commitment to sustaining the environment in light of the fact that the quality of the global ecosystem translates directly into the quality of human life, and from an understanding that without a healthy, sustainable environment it will become increasingly difficult to provide for the basic needs and human development of future generations. The activities of world environmental citizens also help to contribute to enlarging debates about humanity's proper place in the environment; to making more informed choices, policies and laws that affect the environment; and to subjecting to scrutiny the behaviour of states, international organizations and transnational corporations. All of these activities further advance the aims of environmental justice as an integral component of global governance, most importantly by improving the effectiveness of global environmental governance and securing the substantive and procedural environmental rights of all persons everywhere. Consequently the idea of world environmental citizenship urgently reminds us that we must promote the rights and responsibilities consistent with an environmentally just social and political order at the local, national and regional levels if we are to build an effective, truly global cosmopolitan politics.

Notes

1   Kofi Annan, secretary general of the United Nations, statement to the General Assembly on presentation of his Millennium Report, We the Peoples: The Role of the United Nations in the 21st Century, 3 April, 2000, UN Doc. SG/SM/7343, GA/9705; cited in Clark (2000: 101).
2   "Declaration of the UN Conference on the Human Environment, Stockholm, 5–16 June 1972," in Birnie and Boyle (1995: 1–8).
3   "World Charter for Nature, 28 October 1982," in Birnie and Boyle (1995: 15–20).
4   Experts Group on Environmental Law of the World Commission on Environment and Development (1987: 7).
5   UNGA Resolution 41/128, annex, 41 UN GAOR Supp. (No. 5.3) at 186, UN Doc. A/41/53 (1986).
6   See UN Doc. A/CONF. 151/PC/WG 1/L. 18/Rev, 1 Decision 2/13 (1992).
7   See the Intergovernmental Panel on Climate Change, Climate Change 2001 Synthesis Report (Cambridge and New York: Cambridge University Press, 2001).
8   For a helpful analysis of the relationship between domestic and international levels of environmental justice, see Anand (2004), esp. pp. 9–19.
9   See Attfield (1999: 27). Attfield defines anthropocentrism as "the traditional view that only human beings and their values and interests matter", biocentrism as the position that "recognises the moral standing of all living creatures", and ecocentrism as the view that "regards ecosystems and the biosphere as having moral significance independent of that of their members".
10 For more detailed discussions of environmental rights, see Dommen (1998), Hancock (2003), and Shelton (1991). See as well the "Draft Declaration of Principles on Human Rights and the Environment" in Hayden (2001: 669–74).
11 See the discussion of global warming in Moellendorf (2002: 97–100).
12 UNEPNews (April 1999), online at http://www.rolac.unep.mx/cionica/ing/pn0499i.htm.
13 "Mission of the Earth Charter Initiative", The Earth Charter Initiative (2002), online at http://www.earthcharter.org.

References

Anand, R. (2004) International Environmental Justice. A North–South Dimension (Aldershot: Ashgate Publishing).
Attfield, R. (1999) The Ethics of the Global Environment (Edinburgh: Edinburgh University Press).
Birnie, P. and Boyle, A (eds.) (1995) Basic Documents on International Law and the Environment (Oxford: Oxford University Press).
Blackmore, C. and Smyth, J. (2002) "Living with the Big Picture: A Systems Approach to Citizenship of a Complex Planet," in N. Dower and J. Williams (eds) Global Citizenship. A Critical Introduction (New York: Routledge).

Bryant, B. (ed.) (1995) *Environmental Justice Issues, Policies, and Solutions* (Washington: Island Press).

Bullard, R. (2001) "Decision Making," in L. Westra and B. Lawson (eds.) *Faces of Environmental Racism. Confronting Issues of Global Justice*, 2nd Edition, (Lanham: Rowman & Littlefield).

Clark, W. (2000) "Environmental Globalization," in J. Nye and J. Donahue (eds.) *Governance in a Globalizing World* (Washington: Brookings Institution Press).

Cole, L. and Foster, S. (2001) *From the Ground Up. Environmental Racism and the Rise of the Environmental Justice Movement* (New York: New York University Press).

Cutter, S. (1995) "Race, Class and Environmental Justice," *Progress in Geography*, Vol. 19, no. 1: 111–22.

Czempiel, E. (1992) "Governance and Democratization," in J. Rosenau and E. Czempiel (eds.) *Governance without Government Order and Change in World Politics* (Cambridge: Cambridge University Press).

Dommen, C. (1998) "Claiming Environmental Rights: Some Possibilities Offered by the United Nations' Human Rights Mechanisms," *Georgetown International Environmental Law Review*, Vol. 11: 1–48.

Eichengreen, B. (1999) "The Global Gamble on Financial Liberalization: Reflections on Capital Mobility National Autonomy, and Social Justice," *Ethics and International Affairs*, Vol. 13: 205–26.

Falk, R. (1995) *On Human Governance Toward a New Global Politics* (Cambridge: Polity Press).

Hamm, B. (2001) "A Human Rights Approach to Development," *Human Rights Quarterly*, Vol. 23, no. 4: 1005–31.

Hancock, J. (2003) *Environmental Human Rights Power, Ethics and Law* (Aldershot: Ashgate).

Hayden, P. (ed.) (2001) *The Philosophy of Human Rights Readings in Context* (St. Paul: Paragon House).

Held, D. (1995) *Democracy and the Global Order From the Modern State to Cosmopolitan Governance* (Cambridge: Polity Press).

Held, D., McGrew, A., Goldblatt, D., and Pertaton, J. (1999) *Global Transformations: Politics, Economic, Culture* (Cambridge: Polity Press).

Hofrichter, R. (ed.) (1993) *Toxic Struggles. The Theory and Practice of Environmental Justice* (Philadelphia: New Society Publishers).

Hunold, C. and Young, I. (1998) "Justice, Democracy, and Hazardous Siting," *Political Studies*, Vol. 46, no. 1: 82–95.

Intergovernmental Panel on Climate Change (2001), *Climate Change 2001 Synthesis Report* (Cambridge: Cambridge University Press).

Juma, C. (2002) "The Perils of Centralizing Global Environmental Governance," *Environment*, Vol. 42, no. 9: 44–5.

Kaldor, M. (2003) *Global Civil Society: An Answer to War* (Cambridge: Polity Press).

Lipschutz, R. and Meyer, J. (1996) *Global Civil Society and Global Environmental Governance* (New York: State University of New York Press).

Little, D. (2003) *The Paradox of Wealth and Poverty Mapping the Ethical Dilemmas of Global Development* (Boulder: Westview Press).

Moellendorf, D. (2002) *Cosmopolitan Justice* (Boulder: Westview Press).

Porter, G. and Brown, J. (1996) *Global Environmental Politics*, 2nd Edition (Boulder: Westview Press).

Rawls, J. (1999a) *A Theory of Justice*, Revised Edition (Cambridge: Harvard University Press).

Rosas, A. (1995) "The Right to Development," in A. Eide, C. Krause, and A. Rosas (eds.) *Economic, Social and Cultural Rights. A Textbook* (Dordrecht: Martinus Nijhoff).

Rosenau, J. (1992) "Governance, Order, and Change in World Politics," in J. Rosenau and E. Czempiel (eds.) *Governance Without Government Order and Change in World Politics* (Cambridge: Cambridge University Press).

Sen, A. (1999a) *Commodities and Capabilities* (New Delhi: Oxford University Press).

Sen, A. (1999b) *Development as Freedom* (New York: Anchor Books).

Shelton, D. (1991) "Ethics, the Environment and the Right to Environment," *Stanford Journal of International Law*, Vol. 28, no. 1: 103–38.

Shue, H. (1996) *Basic Rights, Subsistence, Affluence, and US Foreign Policy*, 2nd Edition (Princeton: Princeton University Press).

Shrader-Frechette, K. (2002) *Environmental Justice Creating Equity; Reclaiming Democracy* (Oxford: Oxford University Press).

Simonis, U. and Bruhl, T. (2002) "World Ecology: Structures and Trends," in P. Kennedy, D. Messner, and F. Nuscheler (eds.) *Global Trends and Global Governance* (London: Pluto Press).

United Nations Development Programme (2002) *Human Development Report 2002* (Oxford: Oxford University Press).

United Nations Development Programme (2003) *Human Development Report 2003* (Oxford: Oxford University Press).

United Nations Research Institute for Social Development (1994) *Structural Adjustment in a Changing World*, UNRISD Briefing Paper Series 4, (Geneva: UNRISD).

Vayrynen, R. (1999) "Norms, Compliance, and Enforcement in Global Governance," in R. Vayrynen (ed.) *Globalization and Global Governance* (Lanham: Rowman & Littlefield).

Vogler, J. and Imber, M. (eds.) (1996) *The Environment and International Relations* (London: Routledge).

World Commission on Environment and Development (1987) *Our Common Future* (Oxford: Oxford University Press).

Young, O. (1996) "Introduction: The Effectiveness of International Governance Systems," in O. Young, G. Demko and K. Ramakrishna (eds.) *Global Environmental Change and International Governance* (Hanover: University Press of New England).

Part VI

Cosmopolitan Examinations and Critiques

Introduction

Cosmopolitanism has had many detractors and it has historically received staunch criticism from scholars, politicians, and laymen alike. These criticisms of cosmopolitanism usually focus on perceived problems with its moral universalism (see Miller and Derrida), its lack of institutional feasibility (see Nagel), its lack of political capability (see Dahl) and the impossibility of establishing a common motivation and cosmopolitan identity within a pluralistic and often incommensurable world (see Miller and Kymlicka). Many of these criticisms of cosmopolitanism have already been examined, summarized, and touched upon throughout the pages of this Reader. In addition, many of the cosmopolitan arguments in this Reader have directly engaged with, referenced, and responded to the critiques and authors presented in this final section. However, in order to provide some balance of argument, we have dedicated the last section of this Reader solely to letting these anti-cosmopolitan arguments speak for themselves. This is because we realize that the art of argument does not always fairly represent the views of its opponents and that, if cosmopolitanism is to be taken seriously, then it must confront its most profound critics head-on and then prove them wrong.

It is with this in mind that this section begins with one of the most outspoken critics of cosmopolitanism, David Miller. As Miller's examination of cosmopolitanism will highlight, he is not convinced by strong versions of moral cosmopolitanism that demand egalitarian global justice at the expense of losing special obligations between co-nationals. This is because, according to Miller, national and communal sentiments are important and necessary conditions in establishing the motivations for, and the reciprocal conditions of, social justice. In addition, as Miller explains, special obligations to co-nationals can have meaningful impact upon our lives and to ignore these benefits because they are assumed to be "arbitrary" by the cosmopolitan, negates an important aspect of our human condition. As Miller emphasizes, by being indifferent to these communal forms of justice, cosmopolitanism, as a moral theory, dismantles key elements of communal belonging and pursues this theory against the intrinsic value involved in existing special duties. As an alternative, Miller briefly outlines a "split-level" approach, where special duties to co-nationals generally take precedence over international obligations, but where some "weak cosmopolitan" responsibilities to others can also exist.

The critique of cosmopolitanism by Thomas Nagel takes a different approach and begins by arguing that justice requires "a form of organization that claims the political legitimacy and right to impose decisions by force." Since this authoritative condition is missing at the global level, the idea of establishing a condition of global justice remains an unintelligible "chimera." This is because egalitarian justice requires the "internal political, economic, and social structure of nation-states and cannot be extrapolated to different contexts, which require different standards." What is a more appropriate discussion, according to Nagel, is to focus upon the fact that the nation-state, when properly constituted, is the "primary locus of political legitimacy and the pursuit of justice." This does not mean that we do not have duties to others beyond borders, but it does mean, due to our current global structure, that these are not duties of justice.

Whereas Miller and Nagel focus on a critique of cosmopolitan global justice, the chapter by Jacques Derrida offers a critical examination of the idea of cosmopolitan law and of Kant's conceptualization of a corresponding cosmopolitan right to hospitality. According to Derrida, there is a seeming contradiction in Kant's cosmopolitan law because the legal "conditions" he initiates within the laws of hospitality ultimately undermine the universality also suggested within Kant's cosmopolitan vision. As Derrida highlights, this contradiction is due to the fact that Kantian cosmopolitanism requires an unconditional hospitality on one hand (a right to travel the world and engage in public reason), while simultaneously imposing a limitation on any right to residence on the other (settlement only by agreed contract with local inhabitants). For Derrida, this built-in conditionality within cosmopolitan law creates an internal tension, one in which cosmopolitanism becomes dependent on a legal apparatus, which, for Derrida, has been abused and "perverted" by the law and the enforcers of that law, the "state police." For Derrida, this "perversion" is particularly evident in cases concerning the protection of asylum seekers, since "there is still a considerable gap separating the great and generous principles of the right to asylum inherited from the Enlightenment thinkers . . . and the historical reality or the effective implementation of these principles." As a result, for Derrida, we must reexamine and question the internal salience of cosmopolitan law and seek a different cosmopolitanism that offers "a more just response" than that found in its existing formulations.

In the chapter by Robert Dahl, the question of whether international institutions can be democratic is addressed and ultimately rejected. According to Dahl, it is already "notoriously difficult for citizens to exercise effective control over many key decisions," and he believes that there are significant reasons to expect that these difficulties will also persist, if not increase, at the international level. Furthermore, by attempting to insert democratic decision making into global institutional processes, Dahl believes that we run the risk of passing decision-making power to what are effectively elite-run or non-democratic structures. It is because of this threat that the demands of democratic accountability and legitimacy require scholars to remain skeptical of the proposed reforms advocated by cosmopolitan democrats such as David Held and Daniele Archibugi.

Lastly, the final chapter of this section offers a critique of cosmopolitan citizenship. In this chapter, Will Kymlicka investigates the relationship between globalization and the cosmopolitan claim that it creates a need for an expanded form of citizenship at the global level. Specifically, Kymlicka examines the cosmopolitan argument that globalization has eroded the structure of domestic democratic citizenship and explores whether this necessitates a strong reconsideration for redrawing the principles of democratic citizenship to include governance at the transnational level. In responding to these cosmopolitan claims, Kymlicka argues that cosmopolitans have over-hyped the effects of globalization and that domestic democratic citizenship has not eroded to the point where it is fundamentally obsolete. In this regard, Kymlicka argues that there is still "considerable scope for national policy making" and that we should not so easily abdicate the democratic worth of states and national citizenship. In addition, Kymlicka, like Dahl, is "skeptical about the idea that transnational institutions and organizations can themselves be made democratic in any meaningful sense." This is because, according to Kymlicka, there is simply not the same level of interconnection between peoples at the global level as there is between national citizens, and the obstacles involved in creating an equivalent sense of cosmopolitan citizenship are considerable. In particular, Kymlicka suggests that the democratic conditions necessary for deliberation and the formulation of the common good are stymied by transnational barriers of language, cultural difference, pluralistic conceptions of the good, as well as problems of institutional feasibility. Because of these challenges, Kymlicka concludes by suggesting that the idea of cosmopolitan democratic citizenship is institutionally unlikely as well as improbable sociologically.

Throughout this Reader, cosmopolitans have responded to, and attempted to move beyond, the logic embedded within these critiques. As we have seen, in many cases, although these critiques offer considerable food for thought, they also often remain wanting. In this regard, cosmopolitanism, as a political theory, has been able to highlight the existing shortcomings found within these traditional arguments while also providing positive alternative answers. Although cosmopolitanism is still developing and further work needs to be done to fully convince its critics, it nevertheless comes from a strong philosophical legacy and its arguments have been increasingly applied, thought about, and made relevant to present debates. Therefore, cosmopolitanism and its various approaches continue to evolve and to shape our thinking about human cohabitation on an increasingly "small world."

21

Cosmopolitanism
David Miller

I

"Cosmopolitan" is probably now the preferred self-description of most political philosophers who write about global justice. It is not hard to see the attraction of such a label. In popular speech, to be cosmopolitan is to be open-minded, sophisticated, forward-looking, etc.; conversely, the antonyms of "cosmopolitan" would include "insular", "parochial", "narrow-minded", "hidebound", and so forth. The editors of the popular fashion magazine *Cosmopolitan* knew what they were doing when they chose that title. However cosmopolitanism as a perspective on global justice must refer to something more specific than this. But what exactly? Our first task must be to try to pin down the meaning or meanings of "cosmopolitanism" more precisely, before going on to evaluate it.[1]

The term derives originally from the Greek *kosmopolites*, a citizen of the world, and it was popularized by the Stoic philosophers of antiquity. Their claim was that human beings everywhere formed a single community, governed by a law that was discovered through the use of reason – though in some versions of Stoicism cosmopolitan citizenship was reserved for the wise and the good. In what sense was this community political? The Stoics did not imagine that the *kosmopolis* either did or should have human rulers, although some envisaged it as being under divine kingship. So we should not interpret Stoic cosmopolitanism as involving a demand for world government in the conventional sense. Nonetheless, Stoic philosophy played an influential part in the ideology of the Roman Empire, and it is easy to see why: if what really matters is one's membership in the cosmic city and not the territorially bounded human city, then imperial conquest – at least by the wise and the good – does no wrong, and may do some good. Does cosmopolitanism, then, have implications for worldly politics, and might it be said always to lend support to (benign) forms of imperialism?

Before we leap to any such conclusion, we need to draw a distinction between moral and political versions of cosmopolitanism. Moral cosmopolitanism, in its most general formulation, says simply that human beings are all subject to the same set of moral laws: we must treat others in accordance with those laws no matter where in the universe they live; they likewise must treat us in the same way. Political cosmopolitanism says that this can be achieved only if everyone is ultimately subject to the same authority with the power to enforce those laws. The first of these positions does not entail the second, and indeed many would deny that moral cosmopolitanism has any specific political implications. Charles Beitz, for example, writes:

> Cosmopolitanism need not make any assumptions at all about the best political structure for international affairs; whether there should be an overarching, global political organization, and if so, how authority should be divided between the global organization and its subordinate political elements, is properly understood as a problem for normative political science rather than for political philosophy itself. Indeed, cosmopolitanism is consistent with a conception of the world in which states constitute the principal forms of human social and political organization. . . .[2]

Political cosmopolitanism is less popular today than moral cosmopolitanism, and I shall discuss it only briefly, but before doing that I want to draw attention to the way in which the ambiguity inherent in the term may be helpful to the moral version. Cosmopolitanism invites us to see ourselves as citizens of the world. But if we are not to take that in a political sense – we do not aspire to a share in political authority at global level – what does it mean? The idea of citizenship gets its moral force from the experience of people living together in cities, people who identify with one another, face common enemies, and so forth. The cosmopolitan version takes that idea and stretches it so as to embrace the whole of humanity, regardless of what relationships, if any, may exist between people across the globe. It assumes that the moral force of citizenship can survive such stretching. But this, to say the least, is something that needs to be argued for.

   [. . .]

Most advocates of political cosmopolitanism do not in fact advocate world government in its most literal sense – a government at global level enjoying the powers to make and enforce law and policy that national governments typically have today – but something far more modest, for instance a system of international law backed up by coercive sanctions, or, a world federation in which powers are divided in such a way that the centre only enjoys limited authority. It is not hard to see why world government proper appeals only to those with a strongly technocratic cast of mind.[3] It seems to run contrary to the sheer diversity of human cultures, and to the wish of people everywhere to belong to communities that are able to determine their own future paths. For liberals, the greatest appeal of world government has lain in the promise of an end to armed conflict, but even Kant ended his essay on perpetual peace by describing world government as "a universal despotism which saps all man's energies and ends in the graveyard of freedom", a view echoed more recently by Isaiah Berlin for whom a cosmopolitan world "would lead to a tremendous desiccation of everything that is human".[4]

The objections to world government, then, are twofold. If we assume that the cultural differences between societies that we find in today's world are not only well-entrenched, but are positively valuable as providing the settings within which different forms of human excellence can evolve, then the idea that a single authority should legislate for all societies despite these differences must seem far-fetched. It has proved difficult enough to create multinational states in which all the constituent communities feel equally at home, and equally represented in the public sphere, and even the European Union, sometimes held up as the forerunner of a world state to come, has achieved such legitimacy as it presently enjoys by drawing upon the common political heritage of a group of liberal states. Furthermore, it is hard to see how a world state could be subject to effective democratic control. Current nation-states are only able to practise democracy in an attenuated form – periodic elections and some government responsiveness to public opinion – and achieving even this level of democracy requires a democratic public who speak the same language (or at a minimum, participate in official bilingualism) are exposed to the same mass media, form parties and other political associations, and so forth. Again, it is the comparative absence of such a democratic public at European level that makes it difficult to speak of the European Union as itself democratic, as opposed to being a federation or confederation whose component parts are democracies. These problems would be many times worse if we try to envisage a form of government that is both genuinely global and genuinely democratic.

II

There is much more that could be said about political cosmopolitanism, but my main interest [. . .] is in moral cosmopolitanism and its implications for global justice. So what does cosmopolitanism mean as an ethical doctrine with no direct institutional implications? Here we must tread very carefully, because it is easy to slip unnoticed between weaker and stronger versions of moral cosmopolitanism, and in doing so to derive ethical principles that are quite controversial from a premise that is almost platitudinous. This weak cosmopolitan premise can be formulated in a number of slightly different ways: one formulation states that every human being has equal moral worth; another that every human being is equally an object of moral concern; yet another that we owe every human being impartial consideration of their claims upon us.[5] What these formulations have in common is the idea that we owe all human beings moral consideration of some kind – their claims must count with us when we decide how to act or what institutions to establish – and also that *in some sense* that consideration must involve treating their claims equally. [. . .] But we can perhaps get a better sense of what the premise means by seeing what kinds of behaviour it rules out. Suppose my government decides to dispose of its nuclear waste by dumping it in some foreign land, and when it is pointed out that this may prove hazardous to the people who live there, simply declares that that is of no concern to us. This amounts to failing to give any consideration at all to the needs, interests, or other claims of the people involved, which would be a clear violation of the cosmopolitan premise. Another way of violating the premise would be to treat different groups of people in different ways without giving any grounds for the unequal treatment – adopting, say, a policy whereby light-skinned people get better access to medical care than dark-skinned people, without trying to justify this in any way at all, or in any way that might conceivably serve as a relevant moral ground (just repeating "because they are light-skinned" does not qualify).

An equal consideration principle that would rule out the kinds of behaviour described in the last paragraph would be accepted by almost everyone (with the exception perhaps of a few extreme racists), so if that were all moral cosmopolitanism meant, we could safely say that we are all cosmopolitans now. But those who self-consciously describe themselves as cosmopolitans want to get something stronger out of this premise, a requirement of equal treatment that goes beyond saying that all human beings must be considered in some way when we are deciding how to act. For example, they may want to argue that our institutions and practices must be based on the principle of giving equal weight to the interests of all those affected by them. Or they may claim that we are bound to apply one or other strong, substantive principle of equality at global level, for example a principle of equal access to resources or a principle of equal opportunity. Whether such principles can be defended in their own terms, it is important to see that they cannot be derived from the weak cosmopolitan premise.

The gulf that divides weak from strong cosmopolitanism can perhaps best be explained in the following way. Weak cosmopolitanism is in the first place a claim about moral value. It says that the various good and bad things that can happen to people should be valued in the same way no matter who those people are and where in the world they live. A world in which there is a starving peasant in Ethiopia is to that extent as bad as a world in which there is a starving peasant in Poland, all else being equal. The fate of both these people makes a claim on us. But this does not by itself settle whether, as moral agents, we have an equal responsibility to respond to both claims. The fact that both cases of starvation are equally bad does not tell me whether I have more reason or less to go to the aid of the Ethiopian than to go to the aid of the Pole. On the contrary, as an agent I may well have an obligation grounded in moral reasons to act to help one of these people before the other – to take a straight-forward case, I may have entered an undertaking to support food aid to Ethiopia. This obligation cannot be defeated merely by pointing out that the condition of both people is equally a matter of moral concern.

A simple example may help to bring out this gap between our moral assessments of states of affairs, and the reasons we have for acting in relation to those states of affairs. Suppose a child goes missing and there are fears for her safety. This is equally bad no matter whose child it is, and there are some agents, for instance the police, who should devote equal resources to finding the child in all cases. But there are other agents whose reasons for action will depend on their relationship to the child. If the child is mine, then I have a strong reason, indeed an overwhelming reason, to devote all my time and energy to finding her – a *moral* reason, to be clear, not merely a strong desire, by virtue of our special relationship. If the child comes from my village, then I have a stronger reason to contribute to the search than I would have in the case of a child from another community. Of course if I have information that might help find that distant child, then I should give it to the police at once. It is not that I lack any responsibilities to the distant child. But nearly everyone thinks that I have a much greater responsibility to my own child, or to one I am connected to in some other way. The important point is that this is perfectly consistent with the view that it is equally bad, equally a matter of moral concern, when any child goes missing.

It might be said in reply here that if claims about the equal value of human beings have no implications for how we should act, they become redundant. All moral claims must in some way or other guide our behaviour. But this is acknowledged in the example just given. The value of the distant child is registered in my obligation to supply relevant information to the police. In a similar way, the cosmopolitan premise means that we cannot be wholly indifferent to the fate of human beings with whom we have no special relationship of any kind. There is something that we owe them – but weak cosmopolitanism by itself does not tell us what that something is, and certainly does not tell us that we owe them equal treatment in a substantive sense. So cosmopolitans who go on to argue that their cosmopolitan convictions are best expressed through practical doctrines such as the doctrine of human rights, or global equality of opportunity, need to add a further premise about what we owe to other human beings as such – a premise that, to repeat, is not contained in the idea of cosmopolitanism as such. Some independent reason has to be given why cosmopolitan concern should be expressed by implementing the particular conception of global justice favoured by any individual author.

When presented with examples such as that of the missing child, many cosmopolitans will concede that the weak form of egalitarianism contained in the cosmopolitan premise does not exclude special responsibilities and special obligations such as those that obtain between parents and their children. They do not object to the idea of special duties as such, but they are critical of the idea that *nations*, in particular, can serve as the source of such duties. Their cosmopolitanism, in other words, is developed in opposition to a form of nationalism that holds that we owe more to our fellow-nationals than we owe to human beings in general merely by virtue of the fact that we share with them the various cultural and other features that make up a national identity. So is it possible to move from the weak cosmopolitan premise to a stronger form of cosmopolitanism that excludes special obligations to compatriots, except in cases where it can be shown that recognizing and acting upon such obligations actually helps to serve cosmopolitan aims?[6]

III

One popular way of making such a move proceeds as follows. We start with the premise that principles of justice are principles of equal treatment – they are principles that require us not to discriminate on morally irrelevant grounds such as (in most instances) a person's race or sex. What equal treatment means more concretely does not matter here – there are different "currencies of justice" that might be used – but for the sake of concrete illustration let me assume that the relevant principle is equality of opportunity, a principle of justice that is widely recognized within nation-states as an aim that governments ought to pursue. The cosmopolitan move then involves arguing that a person's nationality is an irrelevant feature when we are considering what opportunities they should have, so the principle should be given a global application. As the argument is often put, nationality is a "morally arbitrary" feature of persons in the same way as their hair colour or the social class of their parents. So they are owed equal treatment as a matter of justice no matter which society they belong to.

If, however, we look carefully at the way this argument moves from premise to conclusion, we find that it relies on a crucial equivocation about what it means for some feature of a person to be morally arbitrary. In one sense, a person's nationality might be described as morally arbitrary because in the great majority for cases the person in question will not be morally responsible for her national membership – people are simply born into a nation and acquire the advantages and disadvantages of membership as they grow up regardless of their choice. In this spirit, Simon Caney writes that "people should not be penalized because of the vagaries of happenstance, and their fortunes should not be set by factors like nationality and citizenship".[7] Here "nationality and citizenship" are assimilated to other features for which people cannot be held morally responsible – Caney mentions "class or social status or ethnicity" – and the implicit assumption is that if someone is not morally responsible for possessing a certain feature, then unequal treatment on the basis of that feature cannot be justified.

But "morally arbitrary" may also be used to signal the conclusion of the argument as opposed to its premise. Here a morally arbitrary feature of persons is a feature that should not be allowed to affect the way they are treated – it is a morally irrelevant characteristic, something we are bound to ignore when deciding how to act towards them. Obviously, if nationality is a morally arbitrary feature in this second sense, then inequalities of treatment based on national belonging are unjustified; this follows by definition. What needs to be shown is why we should regard nationality as morally arbitrary in this second sense.

In order to link the two senses of moral arbitrariness – the argument's premise and its conclusion – we need a substantive principle. Here is a likely candidate: if two people are differentiated only by features for which they are not morally responsible (arbitrariness in sense 1), then it is wrong that they should be treated differently (arbitrariness in sense 2). This principle would certainly do the job, but unfortunately it is quite implausible. We can see this by thinking about people who have different *needs*, where these needs are not the results of actions for which their bearers are morally responsible (think for instance of people who have been handicapped from birth). Need differences are morally arbitrary in sense 1, but they are not morally arbitrary in sense 2. Virtually everyone thinks that people with greater needs should be given additional resources, whatever precise characterization of the moral duty involved they prefer to give.

So we have yet to be given a reason why it is wrong if people are better or worse off on account of their national membership. Why regard nationality as a morally irrelevant characteristic like hair colour rather than a morally relevant characteristic like differential need? The fact that in some sense it is "happenstance" that I belong to this nation rather to any other does not settle the question, for the reason just given. It is equally "happenstance" that somebody should be born with a physical handicap. There has to be a *substantive* argument for the irrelevance of nationality, not merely a formal argument that trades on the ambiguity of "arbitrariness".

An argument of the right kind would be one that showed that nationality is not the kind of human relationship that can support special obligations among members. The assumption here is that it is indeed morally permissible to recognize special obligations to members of certain groups – the family being the most obvious example – but this does not extend to just any group of which someone might happen to be a member. Indeed, it may seem obvious that there are groups that cannot possibly support such obligations – racist groups, for instance, whose existence is premised on a belief in the superiority of the favoured race. So the cosmopolitan critic of national duties can deploy a pincer strategy, arguing on the one hand that nations are not, in relevant respects, similar to groups such as the family within which almost everyone would allow special duties to obtain,[8] while on the other hand arguing that the reasons offered to support duties to compatriots would also apply to racists or to members of criminal conspiracies, who could justifiably claim that they owed special duties to other members of their race or gang. To escape this critique, we need to show what differentiates nations and other groups that can legitimately support special duties from these other attachments which have no such ethical significance.

What follows, therefore, is an attempt to defeat strong versions of cosmopolitanism by showing that nations are indeed communities of the kind that can support special obligations. It does not address those who think that there can be no local duties, duties not owed to humanity at large, not even within family groups. As I have indicated, most cosmopolitans are willing to accept such duties when presented with cases such as the missing child, but many are convinced that national obligations cannot be defended in the same way. This task having been achieved, I will conclude by asking what weak cosmopolitanism *does* imply with respect to principles of global justice.

IV

The question we must ask, then, is when do attachments legitimately ground special duties of the kind that nationhood is thought to impose? To get this question into proper focus, we need to begin by distinguishing between relationships that are merely instrumentally valuable and those that are also intrinsically valuable. Both types of relationship can support special duties, but there is a difference in the *kind* of special duties supported that can best be brought out through an example. Compare a group of friends with a group of people who associate for a specific purpose, say a group of work colleagues who decide to form a syndicate to own a racehorse. In the case of the friends, although there are certainly instrumental benefits to friendship – friends can call on each other, for help when they get into difficulties, for example – there is also the intrinsic value of the friendship itself. People's lives go better just by virtue of being involved in this kind of relationship; when friendships dissolve for one reason or another, this is a loss. The syndicate, by contrast, only exists because the members need to join to bear the cost of owning a horse. If any of them could do it single-handed, that would be better still for the lucky ones, and it does not matter if the syndicate collapses and a new consortium is formed. So the only duties that arise in the case of the syndicate are those inherent in the cooperative practice itself. These might be contractual – each member might have agreed to pay so much per month for the stabling costs of the horse when he joined – or they might be duties of fairness – each might take it in turns to drive the horse to race meetings even if there was no antecedent agreement to do this. But there is no duty to keep the syndicate in existence, and no duties to the other members over and above those that their particular relationship entails. Friendship on the other hand creates open-ended duties to support and help one's friends, to keep the relationship alive by staying in touch, and so forth, and the grounds for these are that a valuable form of relationship would be lost if these duties were not acknowledged and acted upon.

Ground-level special duties, therefore, arise only from relationships that are intrinsically valuable. Furthermore the duties in question must be integral to the relationship in the sense that the relationship could not exist in the form that it does unless the duties were generally acknowledged. In other words, the duties are not merely an ethical superstructure erected on top of an attachment whose real basis is something else – emotion, say, or self-interest – but they are central to the way that the relationship is understood by the participants. You cannot be somebody's friend unless you understand that this entails giving them certain kinds of priority in your life – being ready to drop what you are doing and go to them when they need you. [. . .] The point is that we cannot treat friendship just as an emotional attachment – say as a relationship entered into simply because of the fun we get out of being with our friends – without changing its essential character, and losing part of what gives it value.

A final condition for the existence of ground-level special duties is that the attachments that ground them should not inherently involve injustice; they should not be relationships whose very existence is premised on the unjust treatment of others. The injustice that undercuts the value of relationships can be of different kinds: it might involve the exploitative treatment of outsiders, or the unjust exclusion of would-be members. So, for example, a gang of boys, part of whose *raison d'être* is the bullying of weaker classmates, is not the kind of group to which one can have special duties; nor is the Mafia; nor is a racist group that excludes members of the disfavoured races. Once again, it is possible for attachments like these to give rise to duties of certain kinds: there can be honour among thieves, and I suppose one has some moral and not merely prudential reason to keep one's agreements with fellow mafiosi and so forth. But one does not have special duties to the members of these groupings as such. The pervasive injustice that they generate deprives them of such intrinsic value as they might otherwise have had, so they are not the kind of attachments that can legitimately support ground-level special duties.

The last condition may be difficult to apply because any group has the potential to act in unjust ways, and so it may be hard to decide whether the injustice is inherent in the group or incidental to it. Every gang is liable to humiliate those who do not belong; even groups of friends can act unfairly towards people who would like to join the circle but are not permitted to. Families may create social injustice by virtue of the undeserved advantages that they give to their offspring. This issue becomes critical when we come to the case of nations, because critics are inclined to see nations as exclusive clubs whose very existence is premised on the exclusion of outsiders both from membership and from the resources that the nation controls. I shall return to this shortly. What needs stressing at this point is the distinction between groups founded on injustice, so to speak, and groups that contingently may act in unjust ways, but without the injustice becoming an essential part of the group's distinctive character. Only groups of the first kind lack the value that can ground special duties.

So now let us ask whether nations can meet the three conditions I have identified. First, are the relationships that exist among compatriots intrinsically valuable?[9] It is sometimes argued that, in so far as national identity and national solidarity have any value at all, it is purely instrumental – it makes it possible for states with a national basis to achieve certain political goals, such as stable democracy. It is certainly true that such instrumental values feature more prominently in ethical defences of nationality than they do, for instance, in accounts of the family: we think it cheapens the value of family life when the family is characterized merely as an effective tool for socializing children, or a form of mutual insurance against hardship for the members, even though it does undoubtedly serve these ends. However the point to make about the instrumental value of nationality is that it is parasitic on its intrinsic value in the following sense: compatriots must first believe that their association is valuable for its own sake, and be committed to preserving it over time, in order to be able to reap the other benefits that national solidarity brings with it. Whatever value we as outsiders may attach to other people's sense of national belonging, a political association that was entered into and supported purely for instrumental reasons could not work in the way that a national community does. And in fact the way that most people think about their nationality reveals that its value for them is indeed intrinsic. They would, for instance, profoundly regret the loss of their distinct national identity, even if they were guaranteed the other goods that nationality makes possible, stable democracy, social justice, and so forth.

There is of course a logical gap between nationality being intrinsically *valued* and its being intrinsically *valuable*, but, echoing John Stuart Mill's famous remark that "the sole evidence it is possible to produce that anything is desirable, is that people do actually desire it",[10] the onus surely falls on those who want to deny the value of national attachments to show why people's actual valuations are misguided. One reason that is sometimes given is that whereas family or friendship relationships, say, are "real" – the bonds that link me to friends and relations are based on direct knowledge and interaction – in the case of nations the bonds are "artificial" or "imaginary", since I can have no direct experience of 99.9 per cent of my compatriots. But this critique would apply to many other attachments besides national ones, for instance to churches, or professional associations, or football supporters' clubs. In all these cases what links the members is a set of shared understandings about what it is that they are members of, and what distinguishes them from outsiders, and this is a strong enough link to create a relationship that can have genuine value.

[. . .] Cosmopolitans who deny the intrinsic value of nationality may be motivated by the worry that if they recognize special duties to compatriots, these will obliterate duties to humanity at large. If so, their worries are groundless: the question at this point is not what weight we should attach to national duties, but whether national membership has intrinsic value of the kind that can justify special duties in the first place, independently of the question whether these duties can override cosmopolitan, or for that matter familial, etc., duties. Is the cosmopolitan self really one that is indifferent to national membership, or simply one that recognizes competing attachments of many other different kinds?

The next question is whether special duties to compatriots are integral to the idea of nationhood. The counterclaim is that it is possible to value national identity in the sense of taking pleasure in the various cultural features and cultural activities that one shares with one's fellow countrymen, while thinking that this has no ethical significance and that one's moral duties are all global in scope. Now it is certainly possible to envisage cultural attachments that take this form – people might have a collective identity somewhat like the identity of a group of music fans for whom going along to concerts of blues music, say, is an important part of their lives, who enjoy mingling with other fans, and so forth, but would not say they had any special responsibilities either towards the other participants or to keep their particular brand of music alive. But such an identity would be very different from national identities as we currently experience them, and it could not function in the way that national identity now does: it could not underpin political values like social justice or deliberative democracy. [. . .] These functions presuppose that nations are ethical communities whose members have special responsibilities both to support one another and to preserve their community. Belonging to them constitutes a good that is different in kind from the good that the music fans enjoy.

Those who favour a purely cultural understanding of nationhood might reply that even if something is lost when compatriots cease to recognize special duties to one another, this is more than compensated for by the potential gain in justice overall. So this brings us to the question whether injustice is integral to national attachments in the way that it is, for instance, to membership in a racist group. Why might we think that national attachments, in their present form, are inherently unjust? In recognizing such attachments, we draw a distinction between insiders and outsiders, and regard ourselves as having more extensive and weightier obligations to our compatriots. But it may appear that this inevitably works to the disadvantage of all those who are left outside the circle, whose claims on us are now reduced. By granting ethical weight to national attachments, we unavoidably help to perpetrate global injustice.

Samuel Scheffler has called this "the distributive objection" to special responsibilities.[11] The objection holds that such responsibilities can be justified only when they are consistent with general responsibilities that show an equal regard for all human beings. To illustrate the point, he asks us to imagine three persons Alice, Beth, and Carla who initially have equal responsibilities to each other. Alice and Beth, however, join an In Group while Carla does not, and as a result acquire special responsibilities to one another that exclude Carla. This disadvantages Carla in so far as Alice and Beth, by virtue of their special relationship, can now legitimately give priority to each other's demands and needs, which means that Carla has a lesser claim on their resources. Alice and Beth have become better off than Carla by virtue of joining the In Group; but, the distributive objection concludes, this just shows that In Groups (such as nations) that entail special responsibilities are inconsistent with recognizing the equal moral claims of all persons.

Scheffler considers a number of responses to this objection; in particular he points out that the objection might be circumvented if we bring into the picture a fourth person, Denise, and consider how the creation of the Alice–Beth In Group changes her responsibilities to Carla. He suggests that because Alice and Beth are now looking out for each other, Carla and Denise can legitimately give one another greater priority even without forming a group of their own, and this restores Carla's position. The distributive objection derives its main force, Scheffler suggests, from cases where the In Group are also a privileged group in relation to the outsiders: if Americans are allowed to give special weight to the interests of their compatriots at the expense of the Third World, it will not be much comfort to the inhabitants of Chad or Bangladesh to be told that "they may rely all the more heavily on one another or . . . they may pursue their own projects unburdened by excessive concern for the welfare of affluent Westerners".[12]

Although Scheffler's diagnosis here is carefully executed, I think that his initial formulation of the problem is ambiguous in one crucial respect. When introducing the distinction between general and special responsibilities, he does not say whether such responsibilities are to be understood as requiring some form of *equal* treatment, or whether as requiring, for instance, the provision of a certain fixed level of resources. On the latter view, one might think of the general responsibilities of human beings to one another in terms of a set of human rights that must be fulfilled and protected for people everywhere. This would not be inconsistent with a special responsibility to provide a higher level of resources to some human beings but not others. How would this play out in the Alice–Beth–Carla case? Each has a responsibility to secure the human rights of the others, and this responsibility does not alter when the In Group is formed; Alice and Beth simply have to do things for each other over and above this minimum. It may be true, as Scheffler points out, that because of these extra commitments, they are less inclined to do supererogatory things for Carla. But why would this amount to any kind of injustice to her? More seriously, what if Alice cannot protect the rights of both Beth and Carla – she hasn't enough resources to secure the subsistence rights of both? With the formation of the In Group, she will acquire a special responsibility to help Beth, but again can Carla complain of injustice if the choice is simply between Alice helping Beth and Alice helping Carla? So long as the general responsibilities of Alice and Beth to Carla continue to take priority over their special responsibilities to each other, it does not seem that Carla's position is worsened in a relevant way when the In Group is formed, even under circumstances of inequality.

The force of the distributive objection to special responsibilities among compatriots therefore depends entirely on how we specify the general responsibilities that obtain beforehand. If we say that we have an obligation to treat people everywhere equally in some strong and substantive sense – provide them with equal opportunities or equal levels of welfare, for instance – then it immediately follows that by recognizing local duties we will almost certainly be causing injustice to the Carlas of the world. But this of course means that the distributive objection cannot be used to *ground* this view of global responsibilities. If our global responsibilities are to be understood in some other, non-comparative, way – for instance, as I suggested above, as an obligation to ensure that people everywhere have access to a minimum set of resources – then there is no inherent injustice involved in recognizing greater responsibilities to compatriots. Both sets of responsibilities can in principle be discharged at once. Recall that I am not here attempting to reply to those who, following the lead of William Godwin, believe that special responsibilities are never justified – that we must always decide how to act after giving equal weight to the interests of everyone who might be affected by our actions[13] – but to those who believe that such responsibilities can be justified within relationships of certain kinds – families, especially – but not within nations. What I have sought to show here is that there is no good reason to exclude nations as a source of special duties. They can meet the conditions specified earlier, namely that the relationships in question should be intrinsically valuable, the duties in question should be integral to those relationships, and maintaining the relationships does not intrinsically involve injustice to outsiders.

V

Let me take stock of where we have got to in our discussion of (moral) cosmopolitanism. The key distinction has been between weak and strong versions of cosmopolitanism, where weak cosmopolitanism requires us to show equal *moral concern* for human beings everywhere, while strong cosmopolitanism goes beyond this to demand that we should afford them equal *treatment*, in a substantive sense. I have tried to expose the flaws in various arguments that attempt to link these two positions in such a way that strong cosmopolitanism follows directly from weak cosmopolitanism. And I have tried to show that weak cosmopolitanism is consistent with the recognition that we have special responsibilities to compatriots in addition to the general responsibilities that we have to humanity at large.

But I have not yet tried to specify what such a split-level ethical position might look like, beyond pointing out that there is no inherent contradiction in recognizing both special and general duties – a contradiction arises only if we say that the general duties are duties of equal treatment, which in this context is a question-begging move. But what if, in practice, we have to choose between fulfilling the two types of responsibilities, say because there are not sufficient resources to meet both? What if our duty to promote social justice at home collides with our duty to promote global justice abroad? How should we resolve this kind of practical dilemma without abandoning weak cosmopolitanism?

We might propose giving one set of duties strict priority over the other. So, for instance, whenever local and global duties conflict, local duties should be discharged first, and then, depending on what resources are available, our global duties next. But this proposal, though logically coherent, is very implausible. It would mean, for instance, that there was no limit to the harm that we should be willing to inflict on outsiders if this proved to be necessary in the course of carrying out our local duties, say duties to provide fellow-nationals with a certain level of security. But most of us would recoil from this position. Although we may acknowledge a duty to provide our compatriots with adequate health care, for instance, this would not extend to killing foreigners in order to secure a supply of kidneys or other body parts for transplanting. In this case, our global duty to respect human rights takes precedence over an obligation of distributive justice that we owe to our compatriots. Within each category there are duties of different weight, and it is simply implausible to think that *any* duty owed to a fellow-national must be given priority over *any* duty that is global in scope.

Nor, on the other hand, does it seem plausible to give strict priority to global duties, particularly if we assume that these duties include a requirement that human beings everywhere should receive equal treatment – treatment, that is, that varies only according to personal characteristics like special need and never according to their nationality.[14] Suppose that a flu pandemic breaks out and the government only has sufficient vaccine to inoculate a limited number of vulnerable people against the disease. It does not seem wrong in this case to give priority to treating compatriots, that is to supply the vaccine to all those fellow-citizens identified by age or other relevant criteria as belonging to the vulnerable group, before sending any surplus abroad, even though it is reasonable to assume that some foreigners will be *more* vulnerable to the flu than some compatriots selected for vaccination. And this remains true even if we know that those more vulnerable foreigners will not receive the vaccine from their own health services.

If neither of these strict priority proposals is acceptable, we might next consider *weighting* duties according to whether they are local or global in scope, with local duties being given a greater weight. Under this proposal, then, the final weight of a duty would be the product of two factors – the seriousness of the duty as determined by its content, and the closeness of our attachment to the people to whom the duty is owed. But this proposal, although it might succeed in modelling our considered ethical judgements in some cases, does not seem appropriate in all of them. For instance, if we consider the duty to give aid in cases where people need our help but are not in desperate, life-threatening circumstances, something like the weighting model might apply. We owe a stronger duty to those we are attached to in some way, but if we have to choose between helping a few associates and a very much larger number of strangers, then we may think that we should help the strangers – the weight of numbers tipping the scales against the weight of association. But in other cases the weighting model looks wrong. If we return to the case of killing a stranger in order to obtain body parts, it does not seem that this can be defended by ratcheting up the closeness of our association with those who will be saved in this way. We do not think it is more justified to kill a stranger to obtain body parts for family members than it is to kill a stranger to obtain body parts for compatriots. In both cases we recognize an absolute prohibition on killing someone for this reason, and the weighting model does not allow for unconditional duties of this kind.

So a plausible split-level ethics that makes room both for global responsibilities and for special responsibilities to compatriots and others is going to have a more complex structure than either the strict priority proposal or the weighting proposal. I shall not put forward an alternative proposal in any detail here, but by way of illustration consider the responsibility to protect human rights, which I suggested above might be central to the ethics of weak cosmopolitanism. What is involved in the protection of human rights? [. . .] On the one hand, we have a duty not to assault or injure others, not to restrict their freedom of movement or expression without good cause, not to abuse them in ways that destroy their self-respect, and so forth. These are duties to *refrain* from acting in harmful ways. On the other hand, we have duties to ensure that people everywhere have access to resources such as food, drinkable water, medical aid, and so forth. These are duties to *act* in beneficial ways when it is necessary to do so – to provide the food or the medical aid in cases where people currently lack them.

The point of drawing this distinction is not to suggest that from the recipients' point of view duties of the first kind are more important than duties of the second; in general there is no reason to think that. The distinction becomes important, however, when we take up the perspective of the agent whose duty is to protect rights, for here it seems that (other things being equal) there is a more stringent duty to refrain from violating rights by causing harm than to fulfil rights positively by acting beneficially, corresponding to the familiar (though much debated) distinction in moral philosophy between acts and omissions. Furthermore, whereas negative duties clearly fall on all agents, whether individual or collective, in the case of positive duties there is a substantive question about *whose* responsibility it is to provide the resources needed to secure basic rights, whenever there are many agents each of whom could potentially discharge the duty in question. In international contexts, it may be clear enough that action is urgently needed to protect the rights of a vulnerable group of people, but much less clear which of many possible nations is the one on whom the responsibility falls.

Indeed when we think about the protection of basic rights in a world in which there are many agents whose activities may impinge upon such rights, the picture becomes more complex still. The duty to respect basic rights fragments into at least the following four sub-duties:

1. The negative duty to refrain from infringing basic rights by our own actions – for example killing or injuring innocent people.
2. The positive duty to secure the basic rights of the people we are responsible for protecting – for example supplying food to people who cannot provide it for themselves, where we have been identified as the responsible agent.
3. The positive duty to prevent rights violations by other parties – for example intervening to prevent a genocide or some lesser abuse of human rights.
4. The positive duty to secure the basic rights of people when others have failed in their responsibility – for example supplying food to people who are themselves responsible for their own hunger, or towards whom third parties have failed in their duty of aid.

These duties are not equally stringent. Their relative stringency depends on two factors: whether the duty is negative or positive in character, that is whether failing to comply with it involves an active violation of rights or merely a failure to fulfil them, and whether the agent in question is the *primary* bearer of the duty, in either case. I assume, as before, that negative duties weigh more heavily than positive ones, other things being equal, and also that it is more urgent not to violate duties oneself than to prevent others from violating theirs. On these assumptions, duty 1 is clearly considerably more stringent than duty 4, with duties 2 and 3 falling somewhere in between, though their relative weight is difficult to determine – is it more urgent to supply food aid in a famine, or to prevent someone else's genocide, if the number of victims would be the same in both cases? This variability of strength is important when we turn to consider how these duties might relate to the local duties we have to compatriots, duties either to protect *their* human rights, or duties of justice more generally. We begin to see why neither a simple priority rule nor a system of weights that makes local duties count for more gives the right answer in all cases. It will depend which of the sub-duties is at issue.

If, for instance, we take the first sub-duty, the duty to refrain from infringing basic rights, then I think that this excludes giving any greater weight to the claims of compatriots. I have already suggested that one could not justify infringing the basic rights of outsiders even where this was necessary to provide the resources to protect the basic rights of compatriots: to vary the example, the government of a nation whose members are starving would not be justified in seizing resources from another nation if this meant that some of *that* nation's members would fall below the threshold for adequate nutrition. I am also doubtful that one would be justified in infringing a stranger's rights in order to avoid infringing a compatriot's. If we think about cases modelled on the trolley problem made famous by Judith Thomson,[15] I do not think it would be justifiable to switch the trolley from a track on which it was hurtling towards a compatriot on to a track on which it would hurtle towards a foreigner. Nor do I think, if one takes the view that when the difference between the numbers on the two tracks becomes large enough, one ought to switch the trolley, that there should be any additional weighting in favour of compatriots. If one should switch the trolley to kill one in order to save ten, then the identity of the ten and the one is irrelevant. At this level, morality appears to me to require strict equality of treatment at least as far as nationality is concerned.

Turning to the second sub-duty, however – the duty to provide resources of various kinds – the picture changes quite radically. Considering first cases in which the claims we are responding to are qualitatively similar, a strong form of priority for compatriots seems to apply: if because of material shortages we have to choose between securing the subsistence rights of compatriots and the equivalent rights of others, we should favour our compatriots. But priority in this strict form does not extend to all positive duties in category 2. Even basic rights can be more or less urgent, and once it is established that we have a particular responsibility to starving people in a foreign country, this duty may take precedence over our duty to supply elementary education, say, to fellow-nationals (that governments do not act on this principle may be explained by the fact that we currently lack adequate mechanisms for assigning positive duties, so no country believes it has a special responsibility to render aid in such a case). So here perhaps we should apply a weighting model, and think of partiality towards compatriots as a matter of giving their rights-claims greater (though not absolute) weight when deciding how to use scarce resources.

If we consider cases in which our duties to foreigners take the form of sub-duties 3 and 4, then these are likely to be trumped by duties to compatriots of types 1 and 2.

In particular, where the sub-duty is of type 4, a reasonable view would be that all obligations of social justice towards fellow-nationals should take precedence over international obligations that arise from failures of responsibility by third parties – this despite the fact that the *condition* we are responding to may be much worse in the case of outsiders. How can this view be defended? It relies on the idea that the strength of a duty depends not only on the urgency of the demand it responds to but also on the role played by the agent in question in bringing that situation about: I have a much greater responsibility to rescue a child I have carelessly pushed into the river, than to rescue a child somebody else has pushed in, particularly if that somebody else could now perform the rescue with relative ease. We need of course to show that similar considerations about agency and responsibility apply to collectives, especially to nations, as they do to individuals. [. . .] I hope I have said enough to indicate how weak cosmopolitanism may be compatible with a split-level view of agents' responsibilities. No human being's claims are ever discounted entirely, but the strength of the duties they impose on us, as particular agents standing in relationships to other agents, is quite variable, and the resulting picture of global ethics is a complex one. [. . .]

Notes

1   I shall not try to examine all of the different senses of cosmopolitanism. In particular, I shall have nothing to say here about *cultural* cosmopolitanism. For discussions that range more widely, see S. Scheffler, "Conceptions of Cosmopolitanism", in S. Scheffler, *Boundaries and Allegiances: Problems of Justice and Responsibility in Liberal Thought* (Oxford: Oxford University Press, 2001); K. C. Tan, *Justice without Borders: Cosmopolitanism, Nationalism and Patriotism* (Cambridge: Cambridge University Press, 2004), ch. 1; K. A. Appiah, *Cosmopolitanism: Ethics in a World of Strangers* (London: Allen Lane, 2006).
2   C. Beitz, "International Relations, Philosophy of", in E. Craig (ed.), *Routledge Encyclopaedia of Philosophy* (London: Routledge, 1998), IV, 831.
3   And also perhaps to those with a deep fear of war between states. It appears that the high point of enthusiasm for world government occurred in the years immediately after 1945. See L. Cabrera, *Political Theory of Global Justice: A Cosmopolitan Case for the World State* (London: Routledge, 2004), ch. 5.
4   I. Kant, "Perpetual Peace: A Philosophical Sketch", in H. Reiss (ed.), *Kant's Political Writings* (Cambridge: Cambridge University Press, 1971), 114; N. Gardels, "Two Concepts of Nationalism: An Interview with Isaiah Berlin", *New York Review of Books*, 21 November 1991, 22.
5   Versions of this cosmopolitan premise can be found *inter alia* in Beitz, "International Relations, Philosophy of", 830–1; C. Beitz, "Cosmopolitanism and Global Justice", in G. Brock and D. Moellendorf (eds), *Current Debates in Global Justice* (Dordrecht: Springer, 2005), 17; B. Barry, "Statism and Nationalism: A Cosmopolitan Critique", in I. Shapiro and L. Brilmayer (eds), *Nomos 49: Global Justice* (New York: New York University Press, 1999), 35–6; T. Pogge, "Cosmopolitanism and Sovereignty", in T. Pogge (ed.), *World Poverty and Human Rights* (Cambridge: Polity Press, 2002), 169–70; Tan, *Justice without Borders*, 1 and 94.
6   I add this rider because strong cosmopolitans can of course recognize and endorse special obligations to compatriots where it can be shown that acting on these is the most effective means of bringing about global justice. For arguments of this kind, see, for instance, R. E. Goodin, "What Is So Special about Our Fellow Countrymen?", *Ethics*, 98 (1987–8), 663–86.
7   S. Caney, "Cosmopolitan Justice and Equalizing Opportunities", in T. Pogge (ed.), *Global Justice* (Oxford: Blackwell, 2001), 125.
8   These critics include H. Brighouse, "Against Nationalism", in J. Couture, K. Nielsen and M. Seymour (eds), *Rethinking Nationalism* (Calgary, Canada: University of Calgary Press, 1998) and C. Wellman, "Friends, Compatriots, and Special Political Obligations", *Political Theory*, 29 (2001), 217–36.
9   The question whether nations are intrinsically valuable communities is discussed at greater length in M. Moore, *The Ethics of Nationalism* (Oxford: Oxford University Press, 2001), ch. 2.
10 J. S. Mill, *Utilitarianism* in H. B. Acton (ed.), *Utilitarianism; On Liberty, Considerations on Representative Government* (London: Dent, 1972), 32.

11 See S. Scheffler, "Families, Nations and Strangers" and "The Conflict between Justice and Responsibility", in Scheffler, *Boundaries and Allegiances*.

12 Scheffler, "The Conflict between Justice and Responsibility", in Scheffler, *Boundaries and Allegiances*, 89.

13 The original source is W. Godwin, *Enquiry Concerning Political Justice*, I. Kramnick (ed.) (Harmondsworth, UK: Penguin, 1976), Book II, ch. 2.

14 A strict priority proposal of this kind is defended in Tan, *Justice without Borders*, ch. 7.

15 J. J. Thomson, "The Trolley Problem", in J. J. Thomson, *Rights, Restitution and Risk Essays in Moral Theory* (Cambridge, MA: Harvard University Press, 1986).

22

The Problem of Global Justice
Thomas Nagel

I

We do not live in a just world. This may be the least controversial claim one could make in political theory. But it is much less clear what, if anything, justice on a world scale might mean, of what the hope for justice should lead us to want in the domain of international or global institutions, and in the policies of states that are in a position to affect the world order.

By comparison with the perplexing and undeveloped state of this subject, domestic political theory is very well understood, with multiple highly developed theories offering alternative solutions to well-defined problems. By contrast, concepts and theories of global justice are in the early stages of formation, and it is not clear what the main questions are, let alone the main possible answers. I believe that the need for workable ideas about the global or international case presents political theory with its most important current task, and even perhaps with the opportunity to make a practical contribution in the long run, though perhaps only the very long run.

The theoretical and normative questions I want to discuss are closely related to pressing practical questions that we now face about the legitimate path forward in the governance of the world. These are, inevitably, questions about institutions, many of which do not yet exist. However imperfectly, the nation-state is the primary locus of political legitimacy and the pursuit of justice, and it is one of the advantages of domestic political theory that nation-states actually exist. But when we are presented with the need for collective action on a global scale, it is very unclear what, if anything, could play a comparable role.

[. . .]

I will approach the question by focusing on the application to the world as a whole of two central issues of traditional political theory: the relation between justice and sovereignty, and the scope and limits of equality as a demand of justice. The two issues are related, and both are of crucial importance in determining whether we can even form an intelligible ideal of global justice.

The issue of justice and sovereignty was memorably formulated by Hobbes. He argued that although we can discover true principles of justice by moral reasoning alone, actual justice cannot be achieved except within a sovereign state. Justice as a property of the relations among human beings (and also injustice, for the most part) requires government as an enabling condition. Hobbes drew the obvious consequence for the international arena, where he saw separate sovereigns inevitably facing each other in a state of war, from which both justice and injustice are absent.

The issue of justice and equality is posed with particular clarity by one of the controversies between Rawls and his critics. Rawls argued that the liberal requirements of justice include a strong component of equality among citizens, but that this is a specifically political demand, which applies to the basic structure of a unified nation-state. It does not apply to the personal (nonpolitical) choices of individuals living in such a society, nor does it apply to the relations between one society and another, or between the members of different societies. Egalitarian justice is a requirement on the internal political, economic, and social structure of nation-states and cannot be extrapolated to different contexts, which require different standards. This issue is independent of the specific standards of egalitarian justice found in Rawls's theory. Whatever standards of equal rights or equal opportunity apply domestically, the question is whether consistency requires that they also apply globally.

If Hobbes is right, the idea of global justice without a world government is a chimera. If Rawls is right, perhaps there can be something that might be called justice or injustice in the relations between states, but it bears only a distant relation to the evaluation of societies themselves as just or unjust: for the most part, the ideal of a just world for Rawls would have to be the ideal of a world of internally just states.

II

It seems to me very difficult to resist Hobbes's claim about the relation between justice and sovereignty. [. . .]

What creates the link between justice and sovereignty is something common to a wide range of conceptions of justice: they all depend on the coordinated conduct of large numbers of people, which cannot be achieved without law backed up by a monopoly of force. Hobbes construed the principles of justice, and more broadly the moral law, as a set of rules and practices that would serve everyone's interest if everyone conformed to them. This collective self-interest cannot be realized by the independent motivation of self-interested individuals unless each of them has the assurance that others will conform if he does. That assurance requires the external incentive provided by the sovereign, who sees to it that individual and collective self-interest coincide. At least among sizable populations, it cannot be provided by voluntary conventions supported solely by the mutual recognition of a common interest.

But the same need for assurance is present if one construes the principles of justice differently, and attributes to individuals a non-self-interested motive that leads them to want to live on fair terms of some kind with other people. Even if justice is taken to include not only collective self-interest but also the elimination of morally arbitrary inequalities, of the protection of rights to liberty, the existence of a just order still depends on consistent patterns of conduct and persisting institutions that have a pervasive effect on the shape of people's lives. Separate individuals, however attached to such an ideal, have no motive, or even opportunity, to conform to such patterns or institutions on their own, without the assurance that their conduct will in fact be part of a reliable and effective system.

The only way to provide that assurance is through some form of law, with centralized authority to determine the rules and a centralized monopoly of the power of enforcement. This is needed even in a community most of whose members are attached to a common ideal of justice, both in order to provide terms of coordination and because it doesn't take many defectors to make such a system unravel the kind of all-encompassing collective practice or institution that is capable of being just in the primary sense can exist only under sovereign government. It is only the operation of such a system that one can judge to be just or unjust.

According to Hobbes, in the absence of the enabling condition of sovereign power, individuals are famously thrown back on their own resources and led by the legitimate motive of self-preservation to a defensive, distrustful posture of war. They hope for the conditions of peace and justice and support their creation whenever it seems safe to do so, but they cannot pursue justice by themselves.

I believe that the situation is structurally not very different for conceptions of justice that are based on much more other-regarding motives. Without the enabling condition of sovereignty to confer stability on just institutions, individuals however morally motivated can only fall back on a pure aspiration for justice that has no practical expression, apart from the willingness to support just institutions should they become possible.

The other-regarding motives that support adherence to just institutions when they exist do not provide clear guidance where the enabling conditions for such institutions do not exist, as seems to be true for the world as a whole. Those motives, even if they make us dissatisfied with our relations to other human beings, are baffled and left without an avenue of expression, except for the expression of moral frustration.

III

Hobbes himself was not disturbed by the appearance of this problem in the international case, since he believed that the essential aim of justice, collective security and self-interest, could be effectively provided for individuals through the sovereignty of separate states.

[. . .]

The absence of sovereignty over the globe, in other words, is not a serious obstacle to justice in the relations among the citizens of each sovereign state, and that is what matters.

This position is more problematic for those who do not share Hobbes's belief that the foundation of justice is collective self-interest and that the attachment of any individual to just institutions is based solely on his own good. If Hobbes were right, a person's interest in justice would be served provided he himself lived in a stable society governed in accordance with the rules of peace, security, and economic order. But for most of us, the ideal of justice stems from moral motives that cannot be entirely reduced to self-interest.

It includes much more than a condition of legally enforced peace and security among interacting individuals, together with stable property rights and the reliability of contracts. Most modern conceptions of justice impose some limits on the powers of sovereignty – in the name of non-Hobbesian individual rights to liberty – and some condition of fairness or equality in the way the institutions of a just society treat its citizens, not only politically but economically and socially. It is this last element that creates unease over the complete absence of any comparable standards of fairness or equality of opportunity from the practices that govern our relations with individuals in other societies.

The gruesome facts of inequality in the world economy are familiar. Roughly 20 percent of the world's population live on less than a dollar a day, and more than 45 percent live on less than two dollars a day, whereas the 15 percent who live in the high-income economies have an average per capita income of seventy-five dollars a day.[1] How are we to respond to such facts?

There is a peculiar problem here for our discussion: The facts are so grim that justice may be a side issue. Whatever view one takes of the applicability or inapplicability of standards of justice to such a situation, it is clearly a disaster from a more broadly humanitarian point of view. I assume there is some minimal concern we owe to fellow human beings threatened with starvation or severe malnutrition and early death from easily preventable diseases, as all these people in dire poverty are. Although there is plenty of room for disagreement about the most effective methods, some form of humane assistance from the well-off to those in extremis is clearly called for quite apart from any demand of justice, if we are not simply ethical egoists. The urgent current issue is what can be done in the world economy to reduce extreme global poverty.

These more basic duties of humanity also present serious problems of what we should do individually and collectively to fulfill them in the absence of global sovereignty, and in spite of the obstacles often presented by malfunctioning state sovereignty. But now I am posing a different question, one that is morally less urgent but philosophically harder. Justice as ordinarily understood requires more than mere humanitarian assistance to those in desperate need, and injustice can exist without anyone being on the verge of starvation.

Humanitarian duties hold in virtue of the absolute rather than the relative level of need of the people we are in a position to help. Justice, by contrast, is concerned with the relations between the conditions of different classes of people, and the causes of inequality between them. My question is about how to respond to world inequality in general from the point of view of justice and injustice rather than humanity alone. The answer to that question will depend crucially on one's moral conception of the relation between the value of justice and the existence of the institutions that sovereign authority makes possible. There are two principal conceptions that I want to consider.

According to the first conception, which is usually called *cosmopolitanism*, the demands of justice derive from an equal concern or a duty of fairness that we owe in principle to all our fellow human beings, and the institutions to which standards of justice can be applied are instruments for the fulfillment of that duty. Such instruments are in fact only selectively available: We may be able to live on just terms only with those others who are fellow members of sufficiently robust and well-ordered sovereign states. But the moral basis for the requirements of justice that should govern those states is universal in scope: it is a concern for the fairness of the terms on which we share the world with anyone.[2]

If one takes the cosmopolitan view, the existence of separate sovereign states is an unfortunate obstacle, though perhaps for the foreseeable future an insurmountable one, to the establishment or even the pursuit of global justice. But it would be morally inconsistent not to wish, for the world as a whole, a common system of institutions that could attempt to realize the same standards of fairness or equal opportunity that one wants for one's own society. The accident of being born in a poor rather than a rich country is as arbitrary a determinant of one's fate as the accident of being born into a poor rather than a rich family in the same country. In the absence of global sovereignty we may not be able to describe the world order as *unjust*, but the absence of justice is a defect all the same.

Cosmopolitan justice could be realized in a federal system, in which the members of individual nation-states had special responsibilities toward one another that they did not have for everyone in the world. But that would be legitimate only against the background of a global system that prevented such special responsibilities from generating injustice on a larger scale. This would be analogous to the requirement that within a state, the institutions of private property, which allow people to pursue their private ends without constantly taking into account the aims of justice, should nevertheless be arranged so that societal injustice is not their indirect consequence.

Unlike cosmopolitanism, the second conception of justice does not have a standard name, but let me call it the *political* conception, since it is exemplified by Rawls's view that justice should be understood as a specifically political value, rather than being derived from a comprehensive moral system, so that it is essentially a virtue – the first virtue – of social institutions.

On the political conception, sovereign states are not merely instruments for realizing the preinstitutional value of justice among human beings. Instead, their existence is precisely what gives the value of justice its application, by putting the fellow citizens of a sovereign state into a relation that they do not have with the rest of humanity, an institutional relation which must then be evaluated by the special standards of fairness and equality that fill out the content of justice.

[. . .]

Every state has the boundaries and population it has for all sorts of accidental and historical reasons; but given that it exercises sovereign power over its citizens and in their name, those citizens have a duty of justice toward one another through the legal, social, and economic institutions that sovereign power makes possible. This duty is *sui generis*, and is not owed to everyone in the world, nor is it an indirect consequence of any other duty that may be owed to everyone in the world, such as a duty of humanity. Justice is something we owe through our shared institutions only to those with whom we stand in a strong political relation. It is, in the standard terminology, an *associative* obligation.

Furthermore, though the obligations of justice arise as a result of a special relation, there is no obligation to enter into that relation with those to whom we do not yet have it, thereby acquiring those obligations toward them. If we find ourselves in such a relation, then we must accept the obligations, but we do not have to seek them out, and may even try to avoid incurring them, as with other contingent obligations of a more personal kind: one does not have to marry and have children, for example.

If one takes this political view, one will not find the absence of global justice a cause for distress. There is a lot else to be distressed about: world misery, for example, and also the egregious internal injustice of so many of the world's sovereign states. Someone who accepts the political conception of justice may even hold that there is a secondary duty to promote just institutions for societies that do not have them. But the requirements of justice themselves do not, on this view, apply to the world as a whole, unless and until, as a result of historical developments not required by justice, the world comes to be governed by a unified sovereign power.

The political conception of justice therefore arrives, by a different route, at the same conclusion as Hobbes: The full standards of justice, though they can be known by moral reasoning, apply only within the boundaries of a sovereign state, however arbitrary those boundaries may be. Internationally, there may well be standards, but they do not merit the full name of justice.

IV

On either the cosmopolitan or the political view, global justice would require global sovereignty. But there is still a huge difference between the two views in the attitude they take toward this conclusion. On the political view, the absence of global justice need not be a matter of regret; on the cosmopolitan view, it is, and the obstacles to global sovereignty pose a serious moral problem. Let me consider the issue of principle between the two conceptions. While we should keep in mind that different views about the content of justice can be combined with either of these two conceptions of its scope, I will continue to use Rawls to exemplify the political view. But most of what I will say is independent of the main disagreements over the content of domestic justice – political, economic, or social.

[. . .]

Rawls is famous for insisting that different principles apply to different types of entities: that "the correct regulative principle for a thing depends on the nature of that thing."[3] The most noted instance of this is his argument against utilitarianism, which he criticizes for applying to a society of individuals the principles of aggregating and maximizing net benefits minus costs that are appropriate within the life of a single individual, but inappropriate for groups of individuals. "Utilitarianism," he says, "does not take seriously the distinction between persons."[4]

But the point applies more widely. Rawls's anti-monism is essential to understanding both his domestic theory of a just society and his view of the relation between domestic and international principles, as expressed in *The Law of Peoples*. His two principles of justice are designed to regulate neither the personal conduct of individuals living in a just society, nor the governance of private associations, nor the international relations of societies to one another, but only the basic structure of separate nation-states. It is the nature of sovereign states, he believes, and in particular their comprehensive control over the framework of their citizens' lives, that creates the special demands for justification and the special constraints on ends and means that constitute the requirements of justice.

[. . .]

Internationally, Rawls finds the main expression of moral constraints not in a relation among individuals but in a limited requirement of mutual respect and equality of status among peoples. This is more constraining than the traditional Hobbesian privileges of sovereignty on the world stage; it is a substantial moral order, far from the state of nature. But the moral units of the order are peoples, not individuals, and the values have to do with the relations among these collective units rather than the relations of individuals across the world.

Just as, within a state, what we owe one another as fellow citizens through our common institutions is very different from what we owe one another as private individuals, so internationally, what we owe to other inhabitants of the globe through our society's respect for the societies of which they are citizens is different both from what we owe to our fellow citizens and from what we as individuals owe to all our fellow human beings. The duties governing the relations among peoples include, according to Rawls, not only nonaggression and fidelity to treaties, but also some developmental assistance to "peoples living under unfavorable conditions that prevent their having a just or decent political and social regime."[5] But they do not include any analogue of liberal socioeconomic justice.

This limitation is rejected by cosmopolitan critics of Rawls. The issue is the choice of moral units. The monist idea is that the basic constituency for all morality must be individuals, not societies or peoples, and that whatever moral requirements apply either to social institutions or to international relations must ultimately be justified by their effects on individuals – and by a morality that governs the treatment of all individuals by all other individuals.

From this point of view it seems natural to conclude that any such morality must count all individual lives as equally valuable or important, and that in particular it must not allow international boundaries to count at the most basic level in determining how one individual should take into consideration the interests of another. The consequence seems to be that if one wants to avoid moral inconsistency, and is sympathetic to Rawls's theory of justice, one should favor a global difference principle, perhaps backed up by a global original position in which all individuals are represented behind the veil of ignorance.

But whatever we think about the original position, Rawls must resist the charge that moral consistency requires him to take individuals as the moral units in a conception of global justice. To do so would make a huge difference, for it would mean that applying the principles of justice within the bounds of the nation-state was at best a practical stop-gap.

Rawls's anti-monism is in essence a theoretical rejection of such standards for moral consistency. Just as there is no inconsistency in governing interpersonal relations by principles very different from those that govern legal institutions, so there need be no inconsistency in governing the world differently from its political subdivisions. But if what we are looking for is moral, and not just logical, consistency, the differences between the cases must in some way explain why different principles are appropriate.

The way to resist cosmopolitanism fundamentally would be to deny that there is a universal pressure toward equal concern, equal status, and equal opportunity. One could admit a universal humanitarian requirement of minimal concern (which, even in the world as it is, would not be terribly onerous, provided all the prosperous countries did their share). But the defense of the political conception of justice would have to hold that beyond the basic humanitarian duties, further requirements of equal treatment depend on a strong condition of associative responsibility, that such responsibility is created by specific and contingent relations such as fellow citizenship, and that there is no general moral requirement to take responsibility for others by getting into those sorts of relations with as many of them as possible.

This would still count as a universal principle, but it would imply a strongly differentiated system of moral obligations. If the conditions of even the poorest societies should come to meet a livable minimum, the political conception might not even see a general humanitarian claim for redistribution. This makes it a very convenient view for those living in rich societies to hold. But that alone doesn't make it false.

V

I find the choice between these two incompatible moral conceptions difficult. The cosmopolitan conception has considerable moral appeal, because it seems highly arbitrary that the average individual born into a poor society should have radically lower life prospects than the average individual born into a rich one, just as arbitrary as the corresponding difference between rich and poor in a rich but unjust society. The cosmopolitan conception points us toward the utopian goal of trying to extend legitimate democratic governance to ever-larger domains in pursuit of more global justice.

But I will not explore that possibility further. Without trying to refute cosmopolitanism, I will instead pursue a fuller account of the grounds and content of the political conception. I am going to follow this fork in the path partly because I believe the political conception is accepted by most people in the privileged nations of the world, so that, true or false, it will have a significant role in determining what happens. I also think it is probably correct.

Let me try to spell out the kind of political conception that seems to me plausible. Even though I am skeptical about grounding it in a hypothetical contract of the type Rawls proposes, its debt to the social contract tradition will be obvious.[6]

We can begin by noting that even on the political conception, some conditions of justice do not depend on associative obligations. The protection, under sovereign power, of negative rights like bodily inviolability, freedom of expression, and freedom of religion is morally unmysterious. Those rights, if they exist, set universal and prepolitical limits to the legitimate use of power, independent of special forms of association. It is wrong for any individual or group to deny such rights to any other individual or group, and we do not give them up as a condition of membership in a political society, even though their precise boundaries and methods of protection through law will have to be determined politically in light of each society's particular circumstances.

Socioeconomic justice is different. On the political conception it is fully associative. It depends on positive rights that we do not have against all other persons or groups, rights that arise only because we are joined together with certain others in a political society under strong centralized control. It is only from such a system, and from our fellow members through its institutions, that we can claim a right to democracy, equal citizenship, nondiscrimination, equality of opportunity, and the amelioration through public policy of unfairness in the distribution of social and economic goods.

In presenting the intuitive moral case for the particular principles of justice he favors as the embodiment of these ideals, Rawls appeals repeatedly to the importance of eliminating or reducing morally arbitrary sources of inequality in people's life prospects. He means inequalities flowing from characteristics of people that they have done nothing to deserve, like their race, their sex, the wealth or poverty of their parents, and their inborn natural endowments. To the extent that such factors, through the operation of a particular social system, generate differences in people's expectations, at birth, of better or worse lives, they present a problem for the justification of that system. In some respects these arbitrary sources of inequality can be eliminated, but Rawls holds that where they remain, some other justification needs to be found for permitting them.

The important point for our purposes is that Rawls believes that this moral presumption against arbitrary inequalities is not a principle of universal application. It might have considerable appeal if recast as a universal principle, to the effect that there is something prima facie objectionable to anyone's having lower life prospects at birth than anyone else just because of a difference between the two of them, such as the wealth of their parents or their nationality, over which neither of them had any control. But this is not the principle Rawls is appealing to. Rather, in his theory the objection to arbitrary inequalities gets a foothold only because of the societal context. What is objectionable is that we should be fellow participants in a collective enterprise of coercively imposed legal and political institutions that generates such arbitrary inequalities.

[. . .]

Since there are equally arbitrary extrasocietal distinctions that do not carry the same moral weight, the ground for the presumption cannot be merely that these intrasocietal inequalities have a profound effect on people's lives. The fact that they shape people's life prospects from birth is necessary but not sufficient to explain the presumption against them. So what is the additional necessary condition?

I believe it comes from a special involvement of agency or the will that is inseparable from membership in a political society. Not the will to become or remain a member, for most people have no choice in that regard, but the engagement of the will that is essential to life inside a society, in the dual role each member plays both as one of the society's subjects and as one of those in whose name its authority is exercised. One might even say that we are all participants in the general will.

A sovereign state is not just a cooperative enterprise for mutual advantage. The societal rules determining its basic structure are coercively imposed: it is not a voluntary association. I submit that it is this complex fact – that we are both putative joint authors of the coercively imposed system, and subject to its norms, i.e., expected to accept their authority even when the collective decision diverges from our personal preferences – that creates the special presumption against arbitrary inequalities in our treatment by the system.

Without being given a choice, we are assigned a role in the collective life of a particular society. The society makes us responsible for its acts, which are taken in our name and on which, in a democracy, we may even have some influence; and it holds us responsible for obeying its laws and conforming to its norms, thereby supporting the institutions through which advantages and disadvantages are created and distributed. Insofar as those institutions admit arbitrary inequalities, we are, even though the responsibility has been simply handed to us, responsible for them, and we therefore have standing to ask why we should accept them. This request for justification has moral weight even if we have in practice no choice but to live under the existing regime. The reason is that its requirements claim our active cooperation, and this cannot be legitimately done without justification – otherwise it is pure coercion.

The required active engagement of the will of each member of the society in its operation is crucial. It is not enough to appeal to the large material effects that the system imposes on its members. The immigration policies of one country may impose large effects on the lives of those living in other countries, but under the political conception that by itself does not imply that such policies should be determined in a way that gives the interests and opportunities of those others equal consideration. Immigration policies are simply enforced against the nationals of other states; the laws are not imposed in their name, nor are they asked to accept and uphold those laws. Since no acceptance is demanded of them, no justification is required that explains why they should accept such discriminatory policies, or why their interests have been given equal consideration. It is sufficient justification to claim that the policies do not violate their prepolitical human rights.

That does not mean that on the political conception one state may do anything whatever to the citizens of another. States are entitled to be left to their own devices, but only on the condition that they not harm others. Even a nation's immunity from the need to justify to outsiders the limits on access to its territory is not absolute. In extreme circumstances, denial of the right of immigration may constitute a failure to respect human rights or the universal duty of rescue. This is recognized in special provisions for political asylum, for example. The most basic rights and duties are universal, and not contingent on specific institutional relations between people. Only the heightened requirements of equal treatment embodied in principles of justice, including political equality, equality of opportunity, and distributive justice, are contingent in this way.

[. . .]

In short, the state makes unique demands on the will of its members – or the members make unique demands on one another through the institutions of the state – and those exceptional demands bring with them exceptional obligations, the positive obligations of justice. Those obligations reach no farther than the demands do and that explains the special character of the political conception.

VI

What is the overall moral outlook that best fits the political conception of justice? Although it is based on a rejection of monism and does not derive its content from a universal moral relation in which we stand to all persons, the political conception does not deny that there is such a relation. Political institutions create contingent, selective moral relations, but there are also noncontingent, universal relations in which we stand to everyone, and political justice is surrounded by this larger moral context.

The normative force of the most basic human rights against violence, enslavement, and coercion, and of the most basic humanitarian duties of rescue from immediate danger, depends only on our capacity to put ourselves in other people's shoes. The interests protected by such moral requirements are so fundamental, and the burdens they impose, considered statistically, so much slighter, that a criterion of universalizability of the Kantian type clearly supports them. I say "statistically" because the restrictions implied by individual rights can in particular cases be very demanding: you may not kill an innocent person to save your life, for example. But the importance to all of us of blanket immunity from such violation dominates the slight danger that we will be called on to lose our lives rather than violate the constraint. This is based not on a utilitarian calculation but on the great importance to each person of the kind of inviolability conferred by rights. Rights are a guarantee to each of us of a certain protected status, rather than a net benefit to the aggregate.

[. . .]

This moral minimum does not depend on the existence of any institutional connection between ourselves and other persons: It governs our relations with everyone in the world. However, it may be impossible to fulfill even our minimal moral duties to others without the help of institutions of some kind short of sovereignty. We do not need institutions to enable us to refrain from violating other people's rights, but institutions are indispensable to enable us to fulfill the duty of rescue toward people in dire straits all over the world. Further, it seems clear that human rights generate a secondary obligation to do something, if we can, to protect people outside of our society against their most egregious violation, and this is practically impossible, on a world scale, without some institutionalized methods of verification and enforcement.

The first of these roles, that of rescue, can be filled to some extent by NGOs that operate internationally but privately, providing individuals with the opportunity to contribute to relief of famine and disease. Even the second role, protection of rights, has its private institutional actors in the form of organizations like Amnesty international and Human Rights Watch. But successful action on a much larger scale would be possible through international institutions supported by governments, both with funds and with enforcement. The World Bank is in some respects such an institution, and the International Criminal Court aspires to be. The question is whether international developments will countenance the bending of national sovereignty needed to extend the authority of such institutions, both to command funds and to curb domestic rights violations with force, if necessary.

But even if this is the direction of global governance for the future, there remains a clear line, according to the political conception of justice, between the call for such institutions and a call for the institution of global socioeconomic justice. Everyone may have the right to live in a just society, but we do not have an obligation to live in a just society with everyone. The right to justice is the right that the society one lives in be justly governed. Any claims this creates against other societies and their members are distinctly secondary to those it creates against one's fellow citizens.

Is this stark division of levels of responsibility morally acceptable, or is it too radical an exclusion of humanity at large from full moral concern? The answer from the point of view of the political conception must be that there is no single level of full moral concern, because morality is essentially multilayered.

Even within the framework of a just society special obligations arise from contingent personal relations and voluntary associations or undertakings by individuals. The whole point of the political conception is that social justice itself is a rise in exclusive obligation, but with a broader associative range and from a lower moral baseline than the personal obligations. And it depends on the contingency of involuntary rather than voluntary association.

Perhaps this move to a new moral level can be best understood as a consequence of the more basic obligation, emphasized by both Hobbes and Kant, that all humans have to create and support a state of some kind – to leave and stay out of the state of nature. It is not an obligation to all other persons, in fact it has no clear boundaries; it is merely an obligation to create the conditions of peace and a legal order, with whatever community offers itself.

This requirement is based not on a comprehensive value of equality, but on the imperative of securing basic rights, which can be done more or less locally. But once the state exists, we are in a new moral situation, where the value of equality has purchase. The difference between the political and the cosmopolitan conceptions is that the latter sees the formation of the state as answering also a universal demand for equality, even if as a practical matter it can be realized only locally. On the political conception, by contrast, the only universal requirement of equality is conditional in form: We are required to accord equal status to anyone with whom we are joined in a strong and coercively imposed political community.

Some standard of universalizability underlies even this conditional requirement. It is part of a multilayered conception of morality, shaped by the Kantian ideal of a kingdom of ends whose members do not share a common set of ends. The heightened obligations that arise from contingent particular associations do not subtract from a prior condition of universal concern, but rather move our moral relations selectively to a new level, at which more ends and responsibilities are shared. The universality of this morality consists in its applying to anyone who happens to be or to become a member of our society: no one is excluded in advance, and in that sense all persons are regarded as morally equal.

Such a morality also leaves space for voluntary combinations in the pursuit of common ends, which are not in general governed by standards of equality. But political institutions are different, because adherence to them is not voluntary: Emigration aside, one is not permitted to declare oneself not a member of one's society and hence not subject to its rules, and other members may coerce one's compliance if one tries to refuse. An institution that one has no choice about joining must offer terms of membership that meet a higher standard.

[. . .]

VII

The implications of the political conception for world politics tend to be conservative, but that is not the end of the story; the conservatism comes under pressure from powerful forces in the other direction. The source of that pressure lies both in existing global or international institutions and in the increasingly felt need to strengthen such institutions and to create new ones, for three types of purpose: the protection of human rights; the provision of humanitarian aid; and the provision of global public goods that benefit everyone, such as free trade, collective security, and environmental protection. Institutions that serve these purposes are not designed to extend democratic legitimacy and socioeconomic justice, but they naturally give rise to claims for both, in respect to their design and functioning. And they put pressure on national sovereignty by their need for power to be effective. They thus present a clearly perceived threat to the limits on claims of justice imposed by the political conception.

This poses a familiar dilemma: Prosperous nations have reasons to want more governance on a world scale, but they do not want the increased obligations and demands for legitimacy that may follow in its wake. They do not want to increase the range of those to whom they are obliged as they are toward their own citizens; and this reflects the convictions of their citizens, not just of their governments.

Resistance to the erosion of sovereignty has resulted in the U.S. refusal to join the Kyoto Treaty on atmospheric emissions and the International Criminal Court, decisions that have been widely criticized. Similar questions arise over who is to determine the policies of the International Monetary Fund and the World Bank, and over the authority of the United Nations in matters of international peace and security. But by far the most important institutions from this point of view are those of the international economy itself.

The global economy, within which the familiar inequalities are now generated, requires a stable international system of property rights and contractual obligations that provide the conditions for international commerce. These include: the rights of sovereign states to sell or confer legal title to the exploitation of their natural resources internationally; their right to borrow internationally and to create obligations of repayment on successor governments; the rights of commercial enterprises in one country to establish or acquire subsidiaries in other countries, and to profit from such investments; international extensions of antitrust law; regulation of financial markets to permit the orderly international flow of capital; the laws of patent and copyright; the rules of international trade, including penalties for violations of agreed restrictions on protective tariffs, dumping, preferential subsidies, and so forth. Many of the goods that contemporary persons consume, or their components, are produced in other countries. We are clearly in some kind of institutional relation – legal and economic – with people the world over.

This brings us to an issue that is internal to the political conception, rather than being about the choice between the political and the cosmopolitan conceptions. Some would argue that the present level of world economic interdependence already brings into force a version of the political conception of justice, so that Rawls's principles, or some alternative principles of distributive justice, are applicable over the domain covered by the existing cooperative institutions.[7] This would be a very strong result, but I believe that it is not the case, precisely because such institutions do not rise to the level of statehood.

The absence of sovereign authority over participant states and their members not only makes it practically infeasible for such institutions to pursue justice but also makes them, under the political conception, an inappropriate site for claims of justice. For such claims to become applicable it is not enough that a number of individuals or groups be engaged in a collective activity that serves their mutual advantage. Mere economic interaction does not trigger the heightened standards of socioeconomic justice.

Current international rules and institutions may be the thin end of a wedge that will eventually expand to seriously dislodge the dominant sovereignty of separate nation-states, both morally and politically, but for the moment they lack something that according to the political conception is crucial for the application and implementation of standards of justice: They are not collectively enacted and coercively imposed in the name of all the individuals whose lives they affect; and they do not ask for the kind of authorization by individuals that carries with it a responsibility to treat all those individuals in some sense equally. Instead, they are set up by bargaining among mutually self-interested sovereign parties. International institutions act not in the name of individuals, but in the name of the states or state instruments and agencies that have created them. Hence the responsibility of those institutions toward individuals is filtered through the states that represent and bear primary responsibility for those individuals.

But while international governance falls far short of global sovereignty, and is ultimately dependent on the sovereignty of separate states, international institutions are not all alike. Some involve delegation of authority, by states, to a supranational institution, generally by treaty, where this amounts to a partial limitation of sovereignty. Under NAFTA, for example, the domestic courts of the United States, Canada, and Mexico are expected to enforce the judgments of its tribunals. And judgments of the European Court of justice are enforced by the national courts of member states of the European Union.

Then there are the traditional international organizations, such as the UN, the WHO, the IMF, and the World Bank, which are controlled and financed by their member states and are empowered to act in various ways to pursue agreed-upon goals, but are not, with the exception of the Security Council, empowered to exercise coercive enforcement against states or individuals. Even the coercive authority of the Security Council is primarily a form of collective self-defense exercised by traditional sovereign powers, although there is some erosion of sovereignty in the move toward intervention to prevent domestic genocide.

Finally, there are a number of less formal structures that are responsible for a great deal of international governance–structures that have been enlighteningly described by Anne-Marie Slaughter in her recent book on government networks.[8] Such networks typically bring together officials of different countries with a common area of expertise and responsibility, who meet or communicate regularly, harmonize their practices and policies, and operate by consensus, without having been granted decision-making authority by any treaty. Examples are networks of environmental regulators, antitrust regulators, central bankers, finance ministers, securities commissioners, insurance supervisors, or police officials. The Basel Committee on Banking Supervision, for example, "is now composed of the representatives of thirteen central banks that regulate the world's largest banking markets."[9] It has developed standards for the division of tasks between home-country and host-country regulators, and has set uniform capital adequacy standards. Agreements are reached by consensus and implemented by the central banks themselves, acting under the sovereign authority of their several states. Slaughter argues that networks of this kind, which link the disaggregated subparts of sovereign states sharing common competences and responsibilities rather than the (notionally) unitary states themselves, will become increasingly important in global governance, and should be recognized as the wave of the future.

It is a convincing case. It is important to recognize that the traditional model of international organizations based on treaties between sovereign states has been transcended. Nevertheless, I believe that the newer forms of international governance share with the old a markedly indirect relation to individual citizens and that this is morally significant. All these networks bring together representatives not of individuals, but of state functions and institutions. Those institutions are responsible to their own citizens and may have a significant role to play in the support of social justice for those citizens. But a global or regional network does not have a similar responsibility of social justice for the combined citizenry of all the states involved, a responsibility that if it existed would have to be exercised collectively by the representatives of the member states. Rather, the aim of such institutions is to find ways in which the member states, or state-parts, can cooperate to better advance their separate aims, which will presumably include the pursuit of domestic social justice in some form. Very importantly, they rely for enforcement on the power of the separate sovereign states, not of a supranational force responsible to all.

Individuals are not the constituents of such institutions. Even if the more powerful states are motivated to some extent by humanitarian concerns to shape the rules in consideration of the weakest and poorest members of the international community, that does not change the situation fundamentally. Justice is not merely the pursuit of common aims by unequal parties whose self-interest is softened by charity. Justice, on the political conception, requires a collectively imposed social framework, enacted in the name of all those governed by it, and aspiring to command their acceptance of its authority even when they disagree with the substance of its decisions.

Justice applies, in other words, only to a form of organization that claims political legitimacy and the right to impose decisions by force, and not to a voluntary association or contract among independent parties concerned to advance their common interests. I believe this holds even if the natural incentives to join such an association, and the costs of exit, are substantial, as is true of some international organizations and agreements. There is a difference between voluntary association, however strongly motivated, and coercively imposed collective authority.

VIII

A second, somewhat different objection to this limitation of justice to the nation-state is that it assumes an unrealistically sharp dichotomy between sovereign states and existing global institutions with respect to agency, authorization, and authority. So even if economic globalization does not trigger the full standards of social justice, it entails them in a modified form.

In fact, according to this objection, there is a sliding scale of degrees of co-membership in a nested or sometimes overlapping set of governing institutions, of which the state is only the most salient. If we accept the moral framework of the political conception, we should conclude that there is a corresponding spectrum of degrees of egalitarian justice that we owe to our fellow participants in these collective structures in proportion to our degrees of joint responsibility for and subjection to their authority. My relation of co-membership in the system of international trade with the Brazilian who grows my coffee or the Philippine worker who assembles my computer is weaker than my relation of co-membership in U.S. society with the Californian who picks my lettuce or the New Yorker who irons my shirts. But doesn't the first pair of relations as well as the second justify concern about the moral arbitrariness of the inequalities that arise through our joint participation in this system? [. . .]

Perhaps such a theory of justice as a "continuous" function of degrees of collective responsibility could be worked out. It is in fact a natural suggestion, in light of the general theory that morality is multilayered. But I doubt that the rules of international trade rise to the level of collective action needed to trigger demands for justice, even in diluted form. The relation remains essentially one of bargaining, until a leap has been made to the creation of collectively authorized sovereign authority.

On the "discontinuous" political conception I am defending, international treaties or conventions, such as those that set up the rules of trade, have a quite different moral character from contracts between self-interested parties within a sovereign state. The latter may be part of a just socioeconomic system because of the background of collectively imposed property and tax law in which they are embedded. But contracts between sovereign states have no such background: They are "pure" contracts, and nothing guarantees the justice of their results. They are like the contracts favored by libertarians, but unless one accepts the libertarian conception of legitimacy, the obligations they create are not and need not be underwritten by any kind of socioeconomic justice. They are more primitive than that.

On the political conception, the same is true of the economic relation in which I stand to Brazilian or Philippine workers. Within our respective societies the contracts and laws on which this relation depends are subject to standards of social justice. Insofar as they transcend societal boundaries, however, the requirements of background justice are filtered out and commercial relations become instead something much thinner: instruments for the common pursuit of self-interest. The representatives of distinct societies that establish the framework within which such transactions can be undertaken will be guided by the interests of their own members, including their interest in domestic social justice. But a more comprehensive criterion of global socioeconomic justice is not part of the picture.

By contrast a "continuous" or sliding scale of requirements of justice would have to depend on a scale of degrees of collective engagement. I am related to the person who assembled my computer in the Philippines through the combination of U.S. and Philippine property, commercial and labor law, the international currency markets, the international application of patent law, and the agreements on trade overseen by the World Trade Organization. The claim would have to be that since we are both participating members of this network of institutions, this puts us in the same boat for purposes of raising issues of justice, but somehow a different and perhaps leakier boat than that created by a common nation-state.

Leaving aside the practical problems of implementing even a weaker standard of economic justice through such institutions, does the idea make moral sense? Is there a plausible position covering this case that is intermediate between the political and the cosmopolitan conceptions? (The cosmopolitan conception would say that ideally, the full standards of justice should apply, but that practically, they cannot be implemented given the limited power of international institutions.) Although it is far from clear what the answer is, it seems to me that such a sliding standard of obligation is considerably less plausible than either the cosmopolitan (one-place) or political (two-place) standard. It is supposed to be a variation on the political conception, according to which one can be moved above the default position defined by human rights and collective self-interest through participation in the institutional structures that make complex economic interaction possible. But if those institutions do not act in the name of all the individuals concerned, and are sustained by those individuals only through the agency of their respective governments or branches of those governments, what is the characteristic in virtue of which they create obligations of justice and presumptions in favor of equal consideration for all those individuals? If the default really is a basic humanitarianism, permitting voluntary interaction for the pursuit of common interests, then something more is needed to move us up toward the higher standard of equal consideration. It will not emerge merely from cooperation and the conventions that make cooperation possible.

I would add two qualifications to this rather uncompromising claim. First, there are good reasons, not deriving from global socioeconomic justice, to be concerned about the consequences of economic relations with states that are *internally* egregiously unjust. Even if internal justice is the primary responsibility of each state, the complicity of other states in the active support or perpetuation of an unjust regime is a secondary offense against justice.

Secondly, even self-interested bargaining between states should be tempered by considerations of humanity, and the best way of doing this in the present world is to allow poor societies to benefit from their comparative advantage in labor costs to become competitors in world markets. WTO negotiations have finally begun to show some sense that it is indecent, for example, when subsidies by wealthy nations to their own farmers cripple the market for agricultural products from developing countries, both for export and domestically.

IX

That is more or less where we are now. But I said there was a dilemma, stemming from the need for more effective global institutions to deal with our collective problems, from global warming to free trade. It is not only the fear of tyranny but also the resistance to expanded democracy, expanded demands for legitimacy, and expanded scope for the claims of justice that inhibits the development of powerful supranational institutions. Fortunate nations, at any rate, fear such developments. They therefore face the problem of how to create a global order that will have its own legitimacy, but not the kind of legitimacy that undermines the strict limits on their responsibilities.

The resistance to expanded democracy is sometimes explained on the ground that the right kind of *demos* does not exist internationally to permit democratic government beyond the nation-state. Even in the subglobal and much less unequal space of Europe this is a serious problem, which has given rise to significant debate. If there is not now a European civil society; is there nevertheless the hope of one? Is the possibility compatible with the linguistic diversity of Europe? Could it perhaps be brought into existence as the *result* of democratic European political institutions, rather than serving as a precondition of their creation?

But this, I believe, is not the main issue. Multilingual and multinational states have their problems, and they may have functioned most successfully before the era of democracy. But if there came into being a genuine European federation with some form of democratically elected representative government, politics would eventually develop on a European scale to compete for control of this centralized power. The real problem is that any such government would be subject to claims of legitimacy and justice that are more than the several European populations are willing to submit themselves to. That reflects in part a conviction that they are not morally obliged to expand their moral vulnerabilities in this way. (The recent expansion of the European Union, by increasing its economic inequality, will almost certainly inhibit the growth of its federal power for just this reason.)

Globally there are a number of ways in which greater international authority would be desirable. Resources for development aid and emergency relief could be more effectively obtained by a systematic assessment or tax than by the present system of voluntary contributions. Global public goods like atmospheric protection and free trade could obviously benefit from increased international authority. Both the protection of human rights and the provision of basic humanitarian aid would be easier if regimes found to be responsible for the oppression or destitution of their own subjects in these respects were regarded as having forfeited their sovereign rights against outside interference. Not only the prevention of genocide but the relief of famine may sometimes require a change of government, and the intervention of collective outside forces and agencies. This would mean establishing a link between internal and external legitimacy, as a qualification of the general right of noninterference.

But all these types of increased international authority would bring with them increased responsibilities. An authority capable of carrying out these functions and imposing its decisions would naturally be subject to claims of legitimacy, pressures toward democracy, and pressures to apply standards of justice in the distribution of burdens and benefits through its policies. There is a big difference between agreements or consensus among separate states committed to the advancement of their own interests and a binding procedure, based on some kind of collective authority, charged with securing the common good. The potential costs are much more serious than the risks that led to the U.S. refusal to join the International Criminal Court.

This leaves us with the question whether some form of legitimacy is possible for the global or international case that does not depend on supranational sovereignty or democracy – let alone distributive justice – and yet can be embodied in institutions that are less cumbersome and feeble than those that depend for their creation and functioning on unanimous voluntary acceptance by sovereign states. For the moment, I do not see such a possibility, though perhaps it can be invented. The alternative to global sovereignty may not be global anarchy, but a clear and limited form of such governance remains elusive.

X

Yet in thinking about the future, we should keep in mind that political power is rarely created as a result of demands for legitimacy, and that there is little reason to think that things will be different in this case.

If we look at the historical development of conceptions of justice and legitimacy for the nation-state, it appears that sovereignty usually precedes legitimacy. First there is the concentration of power; then, gradually, there grows a demand for consideration of the interests of the governed, and for giving them a greater voice in the exercise of power. The demand may be reformist, or it may be revolutionary, or it may be a demand for reform made credible by the threat of revolution, but it is the existence of concentrated sovereign power that prompts the demand, and makes legitimacy an issue. War may result in the destruction of a sovereign power, leading to reconfigurations of sovereignty in response to claims of legitimacy; but even in that case the conquerors who exercise power become the targets of those claims.

Even in the most famous case of the creation of a democratic federation, illegitimacy preceded legitimacy. The foundation of the United States depended on the protection of slavery, without which unanimity among the thirteen ex-colonies could not have been achieved. In fighting the civil war to preserve the Union, Lincoln knew that the preservation of sovereign power over the entire territory was the essential condition for progress in the pursuit of democratic legitimacy and justice. The battle for more political and social equality has continued ever since, but it has been possible only because centralized power was kept in existence, so that people could contest the legitimacy of the way it was being used.

So I close with a speculation. While it is conceivable in theory that political authority should be created in response to an antecedent demand for legitimacy, I believe this is unlikely to happen in practice. What is more likely is the increase and deployment of power in the interests of those who hold it, followed by a gradual growth of pressure to make its exercise more just, and to free its organization from the historical legacy of the balance of forces that went into its creation. Unjust and illegitimate regimes are the necessary precursors of the progress toward legitimacy and democracy, because they create the centralized power that can then be contested, and perhaps turned in other directions without being destroyed. For this reason, I believe the most likely path toward some version of global justice is through the creation of patently unjust and illegitimate global structures of power that are tolerable to the interests of the most powerful current nation-states. Only in that way will institutions come into being that are worth taking over in the service of more democratic purposes, and only in that way will there be something concrete for the demand for legitimacy to go to work on.

This point is independent of the dispute between the political and cosmopolitan conceptions. We are unlikely to see the spread of global justice in the long run unless we first create strong supranational institutions that do not aim at justice but that pursue common interests and reflect the inequalities of bargaining power among existing states. The question is whether these conditions can be realized by units established through voluntary agreement rather than by involuntary imposition. The path of conquest, responsible for so much of the scope of sovereign authority in the past, is no longer an option on a large scale. Other historical developments would have to create the illegitimate concentrations of power that can nurture demands for legitimacy, and provide them with something that is both worth taking over and not too easy to break up.

My conclusion, though it presupposes a conception of justice that Hobbes did not accept, is Hobbesian in spirit: the path from anarchy to justice must go through injustice. It is often unclear whether, for a given problem, international anarchy is preferable to international injustice. But if we accept the political conception, the global scope of justice will expand only through developments that first increase the injustice of the world by introducing effective but illegitimate institutions to which the standards of justice apply, standards by which we may hope they will eventually be transformed. An example, perhaps, of the cunning of history.

Notes

1   These figures, from a few years ago, come from Thomas Pogge, *World Poverty and Human Rights* (Cambridge: Polity Press, 2002) pp. 97–99.
2   See Peter Singer, *One World* (New Haven, Conn: Yale University Press, 2002); Thomas Pogge, *Realizing Rawls* (Ithaca N.Y.: Cornell University Press, 1989), pp. 240–80; Pogge, *World Poverty and Human Rights*; Charles Beitz, *Political Theory and International Relations* (Princeton, N.J.: Princeton University Press, 1979). I am leaving aside here the very important differences over what the universal foundation of cosmopolitan justice is. Cosmopolitans can be utilitarians, or liberal egalitarians, or even libertarian defenders of laissez faire, provided they think these moral standards of equal treatment apply in principle to our relations to all other persons, not just to our fellow citizens.
3   John Rawls, *A Theory of Justice*, rev ed (Cambridge Mass: Harvard University Press, 1999), p. 25.

4   Ibid., p. 24.

5   John Rawls, *The Law of Peoples* (Cambridge, Mass: Harvard University Press, 1999), p. 37.

6   In "Distributive Justice, State Coercion, and Autonomy," *Philosophy & Public Affairs* 30 (2001): 257–96, Michael Blake defends very similar moral conclusions – specifically that although absolute deprivation is an international concern, relative deprivation is not. But he bases his argument on the rather different ground of autonomy and what is needed to justify coercion.

7   See Brian Barry, *The Liberal Theory of Justice* (Oxford: Oxford University Press, 1973), pp. 128–33; Beitz, *Political Theory and International Relations*, pp. 150–53.

8   Anne-Marie Slaughter, *A New World Order* (Princeton, N.J.: Princeton University Press, 2004).

9   Ibid., p. 43.

23

On Cosmopolitanism
Jacques Derrida

Where have we received the image of cosmopolitanism from? *And what is happening* to it? As for this citizen of the world, we do not know what the future holds in store for it. One must ask today whether we can still make a legitimate distinction between the two forms of the metropolis – the City and the State. Moreover, one is seeking to inquire if an International Parliament of Writers can still, as its name seems to suggest, find inspiration in what has been called, for more than twenty centuries now, cosmopolitanism: For is it not the case that cosmopolitanism has something to do either with all the cities or with all the states of the world? At a time when the "end of the city" resonates as though it were a verdict, at a time when this diagnosis or prognosis is held by many, how can we still dream of a novel status for the city, and thus for the "cities of refuge", through a *renewal* of international law? Let us not anticipate a simple response to such a question. It will be necessary therefore to proceed otherwise, particularly if one is tempted to think, as I do, that "The Charter for the Cities of Refuge" and "The International Agency for Cities of Refuge" which appear on our programme must open themselves up to something more and other than merely banal articles in the literature on international law. They must, if they are to succeed in so doing, make an audacious call for a genuine innovation in the history of the right to asylum or the duty to hospitality.

The name "cities of refuge" appears to be inscribed in gold letters at the very heart of the constitution of the International Parliament of Writers. Ever since our first meeting, we have been calling for the opening of such refuge cities across the world. That, in effect, very much resembles a new cosmo*politics*. We have undertaken to bring about the proclamation and institution of numerous and, above all, autonomous "cities of refuge", each as independent from the other and from the state as possible, but, nevertheless, allied to each other according to forms of solidarity yet to be invented. This invention is our task; the theoretical or critical reflection it involves is indissociable from the practical initiatives we have already, out of a sense of urgency, initiated and implemented. Whether it be the foreigner in general, the immigrant, the exiled, the deported, the stateless or the displaced person (the task being as much to distinguish prudently between these categories as is possible), we would ask these new cities of refuge to reorient the politics of the state. We would ask them to transform and reform the modalities of membership by which the city (*cité*) belongs to the state, as in a developing Europe or in international juridical structures still dominated by the inviolable rule of state sovereignty – an intangible rule, or one at least supposed such, which is becoming increasingly precarious and problematic nonetheless. This should no longer be the ultimate horizon for cities of refuge. Is this possible?

In committing ourselves thus, in asking that metropolises and modest cities commit themselves in this way, in choosing for them the name of "cities of refuge", we have doubtless meant more than one thing, as was the case for the name "parliament". In reviving the traditional meaning of an expression and in restoring a memorable heritage to its former dignity, we have been eager to propose simultaneously, beyond the old word, an original concept of hospitality, of the duty (*devoir*) of hospitality, and of the right (*droit*) to hospitality. What then would such a concept be? How might it be adapted to the pressing urgencies which summon and overwhelm us? How might it respond to unprecedented tragedies and injunctions which serve to constrain and hinder it?

I regret not having been present at the inauguration of this solemn meeting, but permit me, by way of saluting those here present, to evoke at least a vague outline of this new charter of hospitality and to sketch, albeit in an overly schematic way, its principal features. What in effect is the context in which we have proposed this new ethic or this new cosmo*politics* of the cities of refuge? Is it necessary to call to mind the violence which rages on a worldwide scale? Is it still necessary to highlight the fact that such crimes sometimes bear the signature of state organisations or of non-state organisations? Is it possible to enumerate the multiplicity of menaces, of acts of censorship (*censure*) or of terrorism, of persecutions and of enslavements in all their forms? The victims of these are innumerable and nearly always anonymous, but increasingly they are what one refers to as intellectuals, scholars, journalists, and writers – men and women capable of speaking out (*porter une parole*) – in a public domain that the new powers of telecommunication render increasingly formidable – to the police forces of all countries, to the religious, political, economic, and social forces of censorship and repression, whether they be state-sponsored or not. Let us not proffer an example, for there are too many; and to cite the best known would risk sending the anonymous others back into the darkness (*mal*) from which they find it hard to escape, a darkness which is truly the worst and the condition of all others. If we look to the city, rather than to the state, it is because we have given up hope that the state might create a new image for the city. This should be elaborated and inscribed in our Statutes one day. Whenever the State is neither the foremost author of, nor the foremost guarantor against the violence which forces refugees or exiles to flee, it is often powerless to ensure the protection and the liberty of its own citizens before a terrorist menace, whether or not it has a religious or nationalist alibi. This is a phenomenon with a long historical sequence, one which Hannah Arendt has called, in a text which we should closely scrutinise, "The Decline of the Nation-State and the End of the Rights of Man".[1] Arendt proposes here, in particular, an analysis of the modern history of minorities, of those "without a State", the *Heimatlosen*, of the stateless and homeless, and of deported and "displaced persons". She identifies *two great upheavals*, most notably between the two wars:

1 First, the progressive abolition, upon the arrival of hundreds of thousands of stateless people (*les apatrides*), of a right to asylum which was "the only right that had ever figured as a symbol of Human Rights in the domain of international relations". Arendt recalls that this right has a "sacred history", and that it remains "the only modern vestige of the medieval principle of *quid est in territorio est de territorio*" (p. 280) "But",

continues Arendt, "although the right to asylum had continued to exist in a world organised into nation states, and though it had even, in some individual cases, survived two world wars, it is still felt to be an anachronism and a principle incompatible with the international laws of the State". At the time when Arendt was writing this, *circa* 1950, she identified the absence in international charters of the right to asylum (for example in the Charter of the League of Nations). Things have doubtless evolved a little since then, as we shall see in a moment, but further transformations are still necessary.

2 The second upheaval (*choc*) in Europe was to follow a massive influx (*arrivée*) of refugees, which necessitated abandoning the classic recourse to repatriation or naturalisation. Indeed, we have still to create a satisfactory substitute for it. In describing at length the effects of these traumas, Arendt has perhaps identified one of our tasks and, at the very least, the background to our Charter and of our Statutes (*Statuts*). She does not speak of the city, but in the shadow of the two upheavals (*l'onde du double choc*) she describes and which she situates between the two wars, we must today pose new questions concerning the destiny of cities and the role which they might play in these unprecedented circumstances. How can the right to asylum be redefined and developed without repatriation and without naturalisation? Could the City, equipped with new rights and greater sovereignty, open up new horizons of possibility previously undreamt of by international state law? For let us not hesitate to declare our ultimate ambition, what gives meaning to our project: our plea is for what we have decided to call the "city of refuge". This is not to suggest that we ought to restore an essentially classical concept of the city by giving it new attributes and powers; neither would it be simply a matter of endowing the old subject we call "the city" with new predicates. No, we are dreaming of another concept, of another set of rights for the city, of another politics of the city. I am aware that this might appear utopian for a thousand reasons, but at the same time, as modest as it is, what we have already begun to do proves that something of this sort can, from now on, function – and this disjointed process cannot be dissociated from the turbulence which affects, over the lengthy duration of a process, the axioms of international law.

Is there thus any hope for cities exercising hospitality if we recognise with Arendt, as I feel we must, that nowadays international law is limited by treaties between sovereign states, and that not even a "government of the world" would be capable of sorting things out? Arendt was writing of something the veracity of which still holds today:

> contrary to the best-intentioned humanitarian attempts to obtain new declarations of human rights from international organisations, it should be understood that this idea transcends the *present sphere of international law which still operates in terms of reciprocal agreements and treaties between sovereign states*; and, for the time being, a sphere that is above the nations does not exist. Furthermore, this dilemma would by no means be eliminated by the establishment of a world government.[2]

It would be necessary to expand upon and refine what she says of groups and individuals who, between the two wars, lost *all status* – not only their citizenship but even the title of "stateless people". We would also have to re-evaluate, in this regard, in Europe and elsewhere, the respective roles of States, Unions, Federations or State Confederations on the one hand, and of cities on the other. If the name and the identity of something like the city still has a meaning, could it, when dealing with the related questions of hospitality and refuge, elevate itself above nation-states or at least free itself from them (s'affranchir), in order to become, to coin a phrase in a new and novel way, a *free city* (*une ville hanche*) ? Under the exemption itself *(en général)* , the statutes of immunity or exemption occasionally had attached to them, as in the case of the right to asylum, certain places (diplomatic or religious) to which one could retreat in order to escape from the threat of injustice.

Such might be the magnitude of our task, a theoretical task indissociable from its political implementation (*mise en oeuvre*) – a task which is all the more imperative given that the situation is becoming ever more bleak with each passing day. As the figures show, the right to political asylum is less and less respected both in France and in Europe. Lately, there has been talk of a "dark year for asylum seekers in France".[3] Because of such understandable despondency, the number of applications for political asylum has been regularly diminishing. In fact, OFPRA (The French Office for the Protection of Refugees and the Stateless) toughened its criteria and spectacularly reduced the number of refugees afforded asylum status. The number of those whose application for asylum has, I might add, continued to rise throughout the 1980s and since the beginning of the 1990s.

Since the Revolution, France has had a certain tendency to portray itself as being more open to political refugees in contradistinction to other European countries, but the motives behind such a policy of opening up to the foreigner have, however, never been "ethical" *stricto sensu* – in the sense of the moral law or the law of the land (*séjour*) – (*ethos*), or, indeed, the law of hospitality. The comparative drop in the birth rate in France since the middle of the eighteenth century has generally permitted her to be more liberal in matters of immigration for obvious economic reasons: when the economy is doing well, and workers are needed, one tends not to be overly particular when trying to sort out political and economic motivations. This was especially true in the 1960s, when an economic boom resulted in a greater need for immigrant workers. It is also worth noting that the right to asylum has only recently become a specifically juridical concept (*définitionelle*) and a positive juridical concept, despite the fact that its spirit was already present in the French Constitution. The Constitution of 1946 granted the right to asylum only to those characterised as persons persecuted because of their "action in the name of liberty". Even though it subscribed to the Geneva Convention in 1951, it is only in 1954 that France was forced to broaden its definition of a political refugee to encompass all persons forced into exile because "their lives or their liberties are found to be under threat by reason of their race, religion, or political opinions". Considerably broadened, it is true, but very recent nevertheless. Even the Geneva Convention was itself very limited in the manner in which it could be applied, and even at that we are still a long way from the idea of cosmopolitanism as defined in Kant's famous text on the right to (*droit de*) universal hospitality, the limits and restrictions of which I shall recall in just a moment. [. . .]

There is still a considerable gap separating the great and generous principles of the right to asylum inherited from the Enlightenment thinkers and from the French Revolution and, on the other hand, the historical reality or the effective implementation (*mise en œuvre*) of these principles. It is controlled, curbed, and monitored by implacable juridical restrictions; it is overseen by what the preface of a book on *The Crisis of the Right to Asylum in France* refers to as a "mean-minded" juridical tradition. In truth, if the juridical tradition remains "mean-minded" and restrictive, it is because it is under the control of the demographico-economic interest – that is, the interest of the nation-state that regulates asylum. Refugee status ought not to be conflated with the status of an immigrant, not even of a political immigrant. It has happened that a recognition of refugee status, be it political or economic, has only come into effect long after entry into France. We shall have to maintain a close eye on these sometimes subtle distinctions between types of status, especially since the difference between the economic and the political now appears more problematic than ever.

Both to the right and to the left, French politicians speak of "the control of immigration". This forms part of the compulsory rhetoric of electoral programmes. Now, as Luc Legoux notes, the expression "immigration control" means that asylum will be granted only to those who cannot expect the slightest economic benefit upon immigration. The absurdity of this condition is manifestly apparent: how can a purely political refugee claim to have been truly welcomed into a new settlement without that entailing some form of economic gain? He will of course have to work, for each individual seeking refuge cannot simply be placed in the care of the host country. This gives rise to an important consideration which our conventions will have to address: how can the hosts (*hôtes*) and guests of cities of refuge be helped to recreate, through work and creative activity, a living and durable network in new places and occasionally in a new language? This distinction between the economic and the political is not, therefore, merely abstract or gratuitous: it is truly hypocritical and perverse; it makes it virtually impossible ever to grant political asylum and even, in a sense, to apply the law, for in its implementation it would depend entirely on opportunistic considerations, occasionally electoral and political, which, in the last analysis, become a matter for the police, of real or imaginary security issues, of demography, and of the market. The discourse on the refugee, asylum or hospitality, thus risks becoming nothing but pure rhetorical alibis. As Legoux notes, "what tends to render the asylum laws in France ineffectual for the people of poor countries is the result of a particular conception of asylum, one with a long and complex history, and one which is becoming ever more stringent".[4]

This tendency to obstruct is extremely common, not to Europe in general (supposing that one had ever been able to speak of "Europe" in general), but to the countries of the European Union; it is a price that is oftentimes paid as a consequence of the Schengen Agreement – the accords of which, Jacques Chirac declared, have not been, up to now at least, implemented in full by France. At a time when we claim to be lifting internal borders, we proceed to bolt the external borders of the European Union tightly. Asylum-seekers knock successively on each of the doors of the European Union states and end up being repelled at each one of them. Under the pretext of combating economic immigrants purporting to be exiles from political persecution, the states reject applications for the right to asylum more often than ever. Even when they do not do so in the form of an explicit and reasoned (*motivée*) juridical response, they often leave it to their police to enforce the law; one could cite the case of a Kurd to whom a French tribunal had officially granted the right to asylum, but who was nevertheless deported to Turkey by the police without a single protest. As in the case of many other examples, notably those to do with "violations of hospitality", whereby those who had allegedly harboured political suspects were increasingly charged or indicted, one has to be mindful of the profound problem of the role and status of the police, of, in the first instance, border police, but also of a police without borders, without determinable limit, who from then on become all-pervasive and elusive, as Benjamin noted in *Critique of Violence* just after the First World War.

The police become omnipresent and spectral in the so-called civilised states once they undertake to *make the law*, instead of simply contenting themselves with applying it and seeing that it is observed. [. . .]

With respect to new police powers (national or international), one is touching here on one of the most serious questions of law that a future elaboration of our charter for the cities of refuge would have to develop and inscribe throughout the course of an interminable struggle: it will be necessary to restrict the legal powers and scope of the police by giving them a purely administrative role under the strict control and regulation of certain political authorities, who will see to it that human rights and a more broadly defined right to asylum are respected.

Hannah Arendt, in the spirit of Benjamin, had already highlighted the new and increased powers afforded to the modern police to handle refugees. She did so after making a remark about anonymity and fame which we should, particularly in an International Parliament of Writers, take seriously:

> Only fame will eventually answer the repeated complaint of refugees of all social strata that nobody here knows who I am; and it is true that the chances of the famous refugee are improved just as a dog with a name has a better chance to survive than a stray dog who is just a dog in general.
>
> The nation-state, incapable of providing a law for those who had lost the protection of a national government, transferred the whole matter to the police. This was the first time the police in Western Europe had received authority to act on its own, to rule directly over people; in one sphere of public life it was no longer an instrument to carry out and enforce the law, but had become a ruling authority independent of government and ministries.
>
> [p. 287]

We know only too well that today this problem is more serious than ever, and we could provide much evidence to this effect. A movement protesting against the charge of what has been called for some time now "violations of hospitality" has been growing in France; certain organisations have taken control of it, and, more widely, the press has become its mouthpiece. A proposal of "Toubon-law", in the spirit and beyond of the laws known as "Pasqua", has now come on to the agenda. Under examination in the parliamentary assemblies, in the National Assembly and in the Senate, is a proposal to treat as acts of terrorism, or as "participation in a criminal conspiracy", all hospitality accorded to "foreigners" whose "papers are not in order", or those simply "without papers". This project, in effect, makes even more draconian article 21 of the famous edict of 2 November 1945, which had already cited as a "criminal act" all help given to foreigners whose papers were not in order. Hence, what was a criminal act is now in danger of becoming an "act of terrorism". Moreover, it appears that this plan is in direct contravention of the Schengen accords (ratified by France) – which permit a conviction of someone for giving help to a foreigner "without papers" only if it can be proved that this person derived financial profit from such assistance.

We have doubtless chosen the term "city of refuge" because, for quite specific historical reasons, it commands our respect, and also out of respect for those who cultivate an "ethic of hospitality". "To cultivate an ethic of hospitality" – is such an expression not tautologous? Despite all the tensions or contradictions which distinguish it, and despite all the perversions that can befall it, one cannot speak of cultivating an ethic of hospitality. Hospitality is culture itself and not simply one ethic amongst others. Insofar as it has to do with the *ethos*, that is, the residence, one's home, the familiar place of dwelling, inasmuch as it is a manner of being there, the manner in which we relate to ourselves and to others, to others as our own or as foreigners, *ethics is hospitality*; ethics is so thoroughly coextensive with the experience of hospitality. But for this very reason, and because being at home with oneself (*l'être-soi chez soi – l'ipséité même –* the other within oneself) supposes a reception or inclusion of the other which one seeks to appropriate, control, and master according to different modalities of violence, there is a history of hospitality, an always possible perversion of the law of hospitality (which can appear unconditional), and of the laws which come to limit and condition it in its inscription as a law. It is from within this history that I would like to select, in a very tentative and preliminary way, some reference points which are of great significance to us here.

First, what we have been calling the city of refuge, it seems to me, bridges several traditions or several moments in Western, European, or para-European traditions. We shall recognise in the Hebraic tradition, on the one hand, those cities which would welcome and protect those innocents who sought refuge from what the texts of that time call "bloody vengeance". This urban right to immunity and to hospitality was rigorously and juridically developed and the text in which it first emerged was, without doubt, the Book of Numbers:[5] God ordered Moses to institute cities which would be, according to the very letter of the Bible itself, "cities of refuge" or "asylum", and to begin with there would be "six cities of refuge", in particular for the "resident alien, or temporary settler". Two beautiful texts in French have been devoted to this Hebraic tradition of the city of refuge, and I would like to recall here that, from one generation to the other, both authors of these essays are philosophers associated with Strasbourg, with this generous border city, this eminently European city, the capital city of Europe, and the first of our refuge cities. I am speaking here of the meditations by Emmanuel Levinas in "The Cities of Refuge" ["Les Villesrefuges", in *L'Au-delà du verset* (Minuit, 1982), p. 51], and by Daniel Payot in *Refuge Cities* [*Des villes-refuges, Témoignage et espacement* (Ed. de l'Aube, 1992), especially pp. 65ff.].

In the medieval tradition, on the other hand, one can identify a certain sovereignty of the city: the city itself could determine the laws of hospitality, the articles of predetermined law, both plural and restrictive, with which they meant to condition the Great Law of Hospitality – an unconditional Law, both singular and universal, which ordered that the borders be open to each and every one, to every other, to all who might come, without question or without their even having to identify who they are or whence they came. [. . .]

Finally, at this juncture, we could identify the cosmopolitan (*cosmopolitique*) tradition common to a certain Greek Stoicism and a Pauline Christianity, of which the inheritors were the figures of the Enlightenment, and to which Kant will doubtlessly have given the most rigorous philosophical formulation in his famous *Definitive Article in View of Perpetual Peace*: "The law of cosmopolitanism must be restricted to the conditions of universal hospitality." This is not the place to analyse this remarkable Article, or its immense historical context, which has been excised from this text without trace. It was Cicero who was to bequeath a certain Stoic cosmopolitanism. Pauline Christianity revived, radicalised and literally "politicised" the primary injunctions of all the Abrahamic religions, since, for example, the "Opening of the Gates of Israel" – which had, however, specified the restrictive conditions of hospitality so as to ensure the "safety" or "security" of the "strong city" (26, 2). Saint Paul gives to these appeals or to these dictats their modern names. These are also theologico-political names, since they explicitly designate citizenship or world co-citizenship: "no longer foreigners nor metic in a foreign land, but fellow-citizens with God's people, members of God's household" (Ephesians II, 19–20). In this sentence, "foreigners" (*xenoi*) is also translated by guests (*hospices*); and "metic" – but see also "immigrants", for "*paroikoi*" – designates as much the neighbour, from a point of view which is important to us here, as the foreigner without political rights in another city or country. I am modifying and mixing several translations, including that of Chouraqui, but it will be necessary to analyse closely the political stakes and the theological implications of these questions of semantics; Grosjean-Leturmy's translation, in the Pléiade Library, for example, could literally announce the space of what we are interpreting as the "city of refuge". But that is precisely what I would like to begin putting into question here – i.e., the secularised version of such Pauline cosmopolitanism: "And so therefore, you are no longer foreigners abroad (*xenoi, hospites*), you are fellow-citizens of the Saints, you belong to the House of God" (*sympolitai tōn hagiōn kai oikeioi tou theou; cives sanctorum, et domestics Dei*).

When, in the spirit of the Enlightenment thinkers from whom we are drawing inspiration, Kant was formulating the law of cosmopolitanism, he does not restrict it "to the conditions of universal hospitality" only. He places on it two limits which doubtless situate a place of reflection and perhaps of transformation or of progress. What are these two limits?

Kant seems at first to extend the cosmopolitan law to encompass universal hospitality without limit. Such is the condition of perpetual peace between all men. He expressly determines it as *a natural law (droit)*. Being of natural or original derivation, this law would be, therefore, both imprescriptible and inalienable. In the case of natural law, one can recognise within it features of a secularised theological heritage. All human creatures, all finite beings endowed with reason, have received, in equal proportion, "common possession of the surface of the earth". No one can in principle, therefore, legitimately appropriate for himself the aforementioned surface (as such, as a surface-area) and withhold access to another man. If Kant takes great care to specify that this good or common place covers "the surface of the earth", it is doubtless so as not to exclude any point of the world or of a spherical and finite globe (globalisation), from which an infinite dispersion remains impossible; but it is above all to expel from it what is erected, constructed, or what sets itself up above the soil: habitat, culture, institution, State, etc. All this, even the soil upon which it lies, is no longer soil pure and simple, and, even if founded on the earth, must not be unconditionally accessible to all comers. Thanks to this strictly delimited condition (which is nothing other than the institution of limit as a border, nation, State, public or political space), Kant can deduce two consequences and inscribe two other paradigms upon which it would be in our interest to reflect.

1 First of all he excluded hospitality as a *right of residence (Gastrecht)*; he limits it to the *right of visitation (Besuchsrecht)*. The right of residence must be made the object of a particular treaty between states. Kant defines thus the conditions that we would have to interpret carefully in order to know how we should proceed:

> We are speaking here, as in the previous articles, not of philanthropy, but of right; and in this sphere hospitality signifies the claim of a stranger entering foreign territory to be

treated by its owner without hostility. The latter may send him away again, if this can be done without causing his death; but, so long as he conducts himself peaceably, he must not be treated as an enemy. It is not a right to be treated as a guest to which the stranger can lay claim – a special friendly compact on his behalf would be required to make him for a given time an actual inmate – but he has a right of visitation. This right to present themselves to society belongs to all mankind in virtue of our common right of possession on the surface of the earth on which, as it is a globe, we cannot be infinitely scattered, and must in the end reconcile ourselves to existence side by side: at the same time, originally no one individual had more right than another to live in any one particular spot.[6]

It is this limitation on the right of residence, as that which is to be made dependent on treaties between states, that perhaps, amongst other things, is what remains for us debatable.

2 By the same token, in defining hospitality in all its rigour as a law (which counts in this respect as progress), Kant assigns to it conditions which make it dependent on state sovereignty, especially when it is a question of the *right of residence*. Hospitality signifies here the *public nature (publicité)* of public space, as is always the case for the juridical in the Kantian sense; hospitality, whether public or private, is dependent on and controlled by the law and the state police. This is of great consequence, particularly for the "violations of hospitality" about which we have spoken considerably, but just as much for the sovereignty of cities on which we have been reflecting, whose concept is at least as problematic today as in the time of Kant.

All these questions remain obscure and difficult and we must neither conceal them from ourselves nor, for a moment, imagine ourselves to have mastered them. It is a question of knowing how to transform and improve the law, and of knowing if this improvement is possible within an historical space which takes place *between* the Law of an unconditional hospitality, offered *a priori* to every other, to all newcomers, *whoever they may be,* and the conditional laws of a right to hospitality, without which the unconditional Law of hospitality would be in danger of remaining a pious and irresponsible desire, without form and without potency, and of even being perverted at any moment.

Experience and experimentation thus. Our experience of cities of refuge then will not only be that which cannot wait, but something which calls for an urgent response, a just response, more just in any case than the existing law. An immediate response to crime, to violence, and to persecution. I also imagine the experience of cities of refuge as giving rise to a place (*lieu*) for reflection – for reflection on the questions of asylum and hospitality – and for a new order of law and a democracy to come to be put to the test (*expérimentation*). Being on the threshold of these cities, of these new cities that would be something other than "*new* cities", a certain idea of cosmopolitanism, *an other,* has not yet arrived, *perhaps.*

   – If it has (*indeed*) arrived.
   – . . . then, one has perhaps not yet recognised it.

Notes

1 Hannah Arendt, *The Origins of Totalitarianism* (London: George Allen and Unwin Ltd, 1967), pp. 267–302.
2 Ibid., p. 285 J. D.'s italics.

3   See *Le Monde*, 27 February 1996. See also Luc Legoux, *La Crise d'asile politique en France* (Centre français sur la population et le développement (CEPED)).

4   Ibid, p. xviii.

5   Numbers XXXV 9–32 Cf 1 Chronicles 6. 42, 52, where the expression "Cities of refuge" reappears, and also Joshua 20. 1–9: "if they admit him into the city, they will grant him a place where he may live as one of themselves", *Revised English Bible with Apocrypha* (Oxford and Cambridge, 1989), p. 199.

6   In Immanuel Kant, *Perpetual Peace: A Philosophical Essay*, trans. M. Campbell Smith (New York & London, Garland Publishing, Inc., 1972), pp. 137–138.

24

Can International Organizations be Democratic?
A Skeptic's View
Robert A. Dahl

Can international organizations, institutions, or processes be democratic? I argue that they cannot be. Any argument along these lines raises the question, "What is democracy?" or, better, "What do I mean by democracy?" If I can say what democracy is, presumably I can also say what democracy is not, or to put it another way, what is not a democracy. In brief: an international organization is not and probably cannot be a democracy.[1]

Democracy

Yet to say what democracy is and is not is far more difficult than we would like. This is so for many reasons, of which I will offer three.

First, as we all know, the term democracy has been and continues to be used indiscriminately. Although the word may be applied most frequently to a form of government, it is not restricted to forms of government. What is more, government itself is a protean term. Not only do states have governments; so also do economic enterprises, trade unions, universities, churches, voluntary associations, and other human organizations of infinite variety, from families and tribes to international organizations, economic, military, legal, criminal, and the rest. Even when the word democracy is applied to governments, and further restricted to the government of a state, the concept unfolds into several complex dimensions.[2] In usage, then, the meaning of the term is virtually unbounded – indeed so unrestricted that it has even been used to signify dictatorship.[3]

To explain why international institutions and processes will be non-democratic, I intend to consider just two of the innumerable aspects of democracy. These are democracy as a system of popular control over governmental policies and decisions, and democracy as a system of fundamental rights.

When we consider democracy from the first and probably the most familiar point of view, we interpret it as consisting of rule by the people, or rather the demos, with a government of the state that is responsive and accountable to the demos, a sovereign authority that decides important political matters either directly in popular assemblies or indirectly through its representatives, chosen by lot or, in modern democracies, by means of elections. Viewing democracy from the second point of view, we interpret it as providing an extensive body of rights. These are of at least two kind. One consists of rights, freedoms, and opportunities that are essential to popular control and the functioning of the democratic institutions themselves, such as freedom of speech and assembly. The other consists of a broad array of rights, freedoms, and opportunities that, though arguably not strictly essential to the functioning of democratic institutions, tend to develop among a people who govern themselves democratically, such as rights to privacy, property, a minimum wage, non-discrimination in employment, and the like.

One may value democracy from either point of view, or, more likely, from both, and of course for other reasons as well. However that may be, I am going to focus mainly on the first perspective, democracy as a system of popular control over governmental policies and decisions, and I will offer several reasons for believing that whatever kind of government may prevail in international organizations it will not be recognizably democratic in that sense. The famous democratic deficit that has been so much discussed with respect to the European Union is not likely to be greatly reduced in the EU; elsewhere the deficit is likely to be far greater.

The second problem in saying what democracy is and is not is to determine how and where to locate the threshold or cut-off. It is not very useful to treat democracy as if we could specify a sharp, clear line between democracy and non-democracy. Imagine that we had two scales for democracy rather like scales for measuring temperatures. One would run from a theoretical system that is perfectly or ideally democratic to a theoretical system that is completely non-democratic; the other would run from actual or real-world systems that sufficiently meet ideal democratic criteria to be called democracies to the most extreme non-democratic systems that we actually observe in human experience. An analogy might be a thermometer used for weather and one going from absolute zero to the boiling point of water. If we were to place the two democracy scales alongside one another, systems at the top of the scale for measuring actual democracy would surely fall considerably short of the top of the scale on which we would locate an ideal democracy – and so too, no doubt, at the bottom. At what point on the scale of actual political systems are we justified in designating a political system as democratic or non-democratic? Unfortunately the transition from democracy to non-democracy is not like the freezing point of water. None the less, even if the threshold is pretty hazy, I want to argue that international systems will lie below any reasonable threshold of democracy.

A third difficulty in defining democracy arises because, in practice, all democratic systems, with the exception perhaps of a few tiny committees, allow for, indeed depend on, delegation of power and authority; the citizen body delegates some decisions to others. Size and complexity make delegation essential. Despite all their concern for maintaining the authority of the assembly, even Athenians could not avoid delegation. In modern representative democracies, or what I sometimes call polyarchies, the extent of delegation is enormous, in theory running from the demos to its elected representatives to higher executives to top administrators and on down the lengthy bureaucratic hierarchy. To what extent the demos effectively controls important final decisions has been, of course, a much disputed empirical question, not to say a crucial ideological issue. But we would agree, I think, that, in practice, delegation might be so extensive as to move a political system beyond the democratic threshold.

I believe this is very likely to be true with international organizations and institutions, including the European Union (hereafter, the EU).

The problem

If that judgment were shown to be justified, a democrat might say, we cannot in good conscience support such delegation of power and authority by democratic countries to international organizations and institutions. Yet this answer will not do. In both democratic theory and practice a fundamental dilemma lurks half hidden, ordinarily just out of view. Other things being more or less equal, a smaller democratic unit provides an ordinary citizen with greater opportunities to participate in governing than a larger unit. But the smaller the unit the more likely that some matters of importance to the citizen are beyond the capacity of the government to deal with effectively. To handle these broader matters, the democratic unit might be enlarged; but in doing so the capacity of the citizen to participate effectively in governing would be diminished. To put it loosely, one might say that although your government gains more control over the problem, your capacity to influence that government is diminished.

At the extreme limit, a democratic unit of, say, twenty people, could provide every member with unlimited opportunities to participate in its decisions and little or no delegation would be necessary. Yet the government would have no capacity to deal effectively with most matters that were important to the members. At the other extreme, a world government might be created in order to deal with problems of universal scope, such as poverty, hunger, health, education, and the environment. But the opportunities available to the ordinary citizen to participate effectively in the decisions of a world government would diminish to the vanishing point. To speak in this case of "delegating authority" would simply be a misleading fiction useful only to the rulers.[4]

Optimists and skeptics

In the latter half of the twentieth century this dilemma has reappeared because of the increasing use of international organizations, institutions, and processes to deal with matters that are beyond the effective capacities of the government of a single country. So the question arises: to what extent can the ideas and practices of democratic government be applied to international organizations, institutions, and processes? Those who believe that democracy can be extended to the international realm offer an optimistic answer. International institutions not only should be democratized but actually can be (Archibugi and Held 1995; Held 1995). An opposing view is offered by skeptics such as Philippe Schmitter (1996), who argues that even within "the emerging Europolity" (which is surely the most promising international site for democratization) a recognizably democratic political system is unlikely to develop. For reasons I am going to present here, I share Schmitter's skepticism, although I take a somewhat different path to reach a similar conclusion.

My skepticism applies not just to the European Union but even more to international organizations in general. I do not mean to say that we should reject the benefits of international organizations and institutions. The benefits may sometimes even include assistance in fostering democratization in non-democratic countries. But I believe we should openly recognize that international decision-making will not be democratic. Whether the costs as measured in democratic values are outweighed by gains as measured in other values, and perhaps even by gains in the democratization of non-democratic countries, obviously depends, among other things, on how much one values democracy. Overarching judgments are likely to be either vacuous or highly controversial. The only point I wish to press here, however, is that international policy decisions will not ordinarily be made democratically.

My argument is simple and straightforward. In democratic countries where democratic institutions and practices have been long and well established and where, as best we can tell, a fairly strong democratic political culture exists, it is notoriously difficult for citizens to exercise effective control over many key decisions on foreign affairs. What grounds have we for thinking, then, that citizens in different countries engaged in international systems can ever attain the degree of influence and control over decisions that they now exercise within their own countries?

Foreign affairs and popular control: the standard version

Scholars and other commentators have observed for many years that exercising popular control over foreign policy decisions is a formidable problem. Consider the United States. In the standard version[5] foreign affairs are remote from the lives, experiences, and familiar knowledge of ordinary citizens. Although a small "attentive public" may exist "before whom elite discussion and controversy takes place" (Almond 1950: 139), a great many citizens lack knowledge of foreign affairs, certainly in depth.[6] Concrete experience, personal familiarity, social and professional ties, knowledge of relevant histories, data, and trends are weak or entirely lacking and are replaced, if at all, by flickering images drawn from radio, television, or newspaper accounts. In addition, the sheer complexity of many international matters often puts them beyond the immediate capacities of many, probably most, citizens to appraise. The upshot is that crucial foreign policy decisions are generally made by policy elites without much input from or accountability to the majority of citizens.

The US decision in late 1993 to adopt NAFTA closely fits the pattern. A week before the vote on NAFTA in the House of Representatives, 79 percent of those surveyed in a CBS/*New York Times* poll were unsure or did not know whether their Congressional representative favored or opposed NAFTA. "Some Americans felt strongly about NAFTA. But the vast majority neither understood it nor cared enough about it to become well informed. As a result, public opinion was effectively neutralized on the issue and had little effect on the final outcome" (Newhouse and Mathews 1994: 31–2; see also Molyneux 1994: 28–30).

Americans are not unique. Is it realistic, for example, to expect citizens in European countries to develop informed judgments about European Monetary Union and its desirability? The editors of *The Economist* recently observed that "public debate on the subject has been dismally poor right across Europe. . . . Far from engaging in argument, the pro and anti tribes ignore each other resolutely" (*The Economist* 1996: 17).

One response to the standard account might be: So what? If the average citizen is uninterested in foreign affairs and not fully competent to make informed judgments, is it not better to leave the matter to the political leaders and activists?

We can take it as axiomatic that virtually all decisions by any government, including a democratic government, are disadvantageous to some people. If they produce gains, they also result in costs. If the trade-offs in advantages and disadvantages were identical for everyone, judgments involved in making collective decisions would be roughly equivalent to those involved in making individual decisions; but the trade-offs are not the same for everyone. Typically costs and benefits are distributed unevenly among those subject to a decision. So the perennial questions arise: What is the best decision? Who can best decide? How?

A part of the perennial answer is that the proper criterion for government decisions is the public good, the general interest, the collective good, and other similar, though perhaps not strictly equivalent, formulations. But as we all know, how to define the public good and how to achieve it are formidable problems.

Proposed solutions to the problem of the public good seem to fall into two rough categories: substantive and procedural. Substantive solutions offer a criterion, such as happiness, welfare, well-being, utility, or whatever; a metric or measure that can be summed or aggregated over the persons concerned; and a distributive principle for determining what constitutes a just or justifiable allocation of the good among persons. Procedural solutions offer a process for determining and validating decisions, such as majority rule, or a full-blown democratic process, or guardianship, or judicial determination, and so on. On closer examination, however, neither substantive nor procedural solutions are sufficient; each requires the other. Because substantive solutions are not self-enacting, they require procedures for determining the substantively best outcomes; and because procedures, including democratic procedures, are means to ends, not ends in themselves, their justification depends on more than purely procedural values.

In practice all substantive solutions are contested, indeed highly contested; none commands general acceptability, except perhaps in a purely formulaic way, such as Pareto optimality or the greatest good of the greatest number. In the absence of full agreement on substantive criteria, many people in democratic countries tend to accept procedural solutions as sufficient, at least most of the time. When we disagree, they might say, then let the majority decide, if not directly then through our representatives; though to be acceptable, the majority decision must not only follow proper procedures but must also lie within some generally agreed on boundaries as to rights, liberties, minimal standards of justice, and so on.[7]

As a practical matter, the problem of determining the general good would be easier to solve in a political unit containing a highly homogeneous population. At the limit of complete homogeneity, differences in the impact of collective decisions would vanish, but of course that limit is rarely if ever reached, even in a unit as small as a family. In any case, an increase in the size of a political unit is usually accompanied by an increase in the diversity of interests, goals, and values among the people in the unit. Thus when a democratic unit is enlarged to include new territory and people, the demos is likely to become more heterogeneous. Diversity in turn tends to increase the number of possible political interests and cleavages based on differences in economic position, language, religion, region, ethnic or racial identity, culture, national affiliation, historical memories, organizational attachments, and others.

As the number of persons and the diversity of interests increase, the idea of a common good or general interest becomes ever more problematic. Earlier I mentioned some of the cognitive and emotional obstacles to popular control over foreign policy decisions. These make it harder for citizens to perceive and understand the situations, conditions, needs, wants, aims, and ends of other citizens who are distant and different from themselves in crucial respects. Even if they acquire some grasp on these matters, their incentives to act for the benefit of the distant others when it may be to their own cost or disadvantage are weak or non-existent. Beyond the boundaries of one's own intimate attachments, altruism is uncommon, and as a steady state among many people it is too feeble to be counted on. In sum, among a large group of persons with varied and conflicting ends, goals, interests, and purposes, unanimity is unattainable, disagreement on the best policy is to be expected, and civic virtue is too weak a force to override individual and group interests.[8]

If the public good on foreign affairs were rationally demonstrable, if in fine Platonic fashion the elites possessed the necessary rationality and sufficient virtue to act on their knowledge of the public good, and if ordinary citizens had no opinions or held views that demonstrably contradicted their own best interests, then a defensible argument might be made that the political leaders and activists should be entrusted with decisions on foreign affairs. But on international issues the public good is as rationally contestable as it is on domestic questions and we have no reason to believe that the views of elites are in some demonstrable sense objectively correct. Yet the weight of elite consensus and the weakness of other citizens' views means that the interests and perspectives of some, possibly a majority, are inadequately represented in decisions. Views that might be strengthened among ordinary citizens if these views were more effectively brought to their attention in political discussion and debate remain dormant. The alternatives are poorly explored among ordinary citizens, if not among the policy elites. Yet if citizens had gained a better understanding of their interests and if their views had then been more fully developed, expressed, and mobilized, the decisions might have gone another way.

These conditions probably exist more often on foreign affairs than on domestic issues. Sometimes elites predominantly favor one of the major alternatives; many citizens are confused, hold weak opinions, or have no opinions at all; and those who do have opinions may favor an alternative that the political leaders and activists oppose. So public debate is one-sided and incomplete, and in the end the views and interests of the political leaders and activists prevail.

To provide a satisfactory account of the empirical evidence bearing on this conjecture would be a large undertaking, all the more so if one attempted to compare the experiences of several democratic countries. The best I can offer are several scattered pieces of evidence:

- As I have already indicated, the US decision about NAFTA appears to fit the pattern pretty well.
- Support for European unification was markedly higher among "opinion leaders" than among non-leaders in twelve European countries from 1973–91 (Wessels 1995: 143–4, tables 7.2 and 7.3). From evidence for changes in support over time, one author concludes that:

> a system of internationalized governance such as the EC could not expect support if there were no political leaders and activists, political parties, and attentive publics who care about it. That does not turn the European integration process into a process independent of mass opinion. Quite the contrary: because support and legitimacy are necessary, élites and political actors have to work to secure them. (Wessels 1995: 162)

The revised standard version: occasional activation

In the standard version, the views of elites tend to prevail, particularly when they pretty much agree. But suppose that the policy on which they agree is seen to cause or threatens to cause great harm to the interests, goals, and well-being of a large number of citizens. We need only recall the Vietnam War, in which US policy was initially made almost exclusively by "the best and the brightest," the elite of the elites, until the human waste and futility of the war became so evident as to create intense public opposition *and* a broadening split among the political leaders and activists. On such occasions, political leaders and activists are sharply divided, ordinary citizens are activated, mass publics develop strong views about foreign affairs, and public opinion becomes highly influential in key foreign policy decisions (Aldrich, Sullivan, and Bordiga 1989).

It is misleading to say, for example, that Americans never become involved in foreign affairs. Answering the standard Gallup question, "What do you think is the most important problem facing this country today?" in about one-third of the 150 surveys from 1935 to 1985 Americans ranked foreign affairs highest. At least once in each of eighteen years during that fifty-year interval Americans put foreign affairs highest. Not surprisingly, the importance of foreign affairs soared during wars: World War II, Korea, Vietnam. In short, their responses were appropriate to the circumstances.[9] While support for the war effort during World War II was widespread among elites and the general public, during the wars in Korea and Vietnam elite opinion, at least in some highly influential quarters, lagged behind general public opinion.

In Europe, questions about a country's relations with the EU and its predecessor, the European Community, have led to the political activation of a large part of the electorate,[10] aroused intense passions, and produced sharp divisions within the general population, sometimes in opposition to the predominant views of the political leaders and activists. Political activation and sharp divisions were particularly visible in the referendum in Norway in 1972 on membership in the EC, in France in 1992 on ratifying the Maastricht Treaty, and in Norway and Sweden in 1994 on membership in the EU. In all four referenda, citizens disagreed as sharply in their views of what would be best for themselves and their country as they would on divisive domestic issues. Voters in the French referendum on Maastricht split almost evenly (51 per cent yes to 49 percent no) along class and occupational lines.[11] By small majorities Norwegians rejected membership in the EC in a referendum in 1972 and again in the EU in 1994. In public argument, advocates of the economic, security, and cultural advantages of the EU were in conflict with opponents who tended to stress such values as democracy, absence of red-tape Brussels bureaucracy, environmental protection, welfare state values and policies, counter-culture as well as gender equality. Analysis of the vote reveals significant differences among Norwegians. "No" votes were concentrated more heavily in the northern and western periphery; in fishing and farming communities; among church members, women, and those working in primary industries or in the public sector, particularly in social and public health services. "Yes" votes were concentrated more in urbanized areas, particularly in the area around Oslo, and among voters with university education or higher incomes. Voters who identified themselves as supporters of the Christian, Agrarian, or Left Socialist parties preponderantly opposed EU membership, while both Labor and

Conservative voters strongly supported it.[12] The referendum in Sweden appears to have divided voters in a somewhat similar fashion. It is worth noting, by the way, that Swedish surveys revealed that within a year the majority in favor had declined to a minority, though by then the die was cast.

The revised standard version of the influence of public opinion on foreign policy, then, would read something like this: although citizens in democratic countries are usually less interested in foreign affairs than in domestic issues, in some circumstances they can become activated and play an influential or even decisive role in key foreign policy decisions. A policy is likely to activate citizens if it causes or threatens to cause such severe harm to the interests, goals, and well-being of a large minority, or even a majority, of citizens that they become aroused in opposition, political activists arise to champion their cause, and political leaders are themselves split. The question then begins to look very much like a hard-fought domestic issue. If the threatened costs of the policy are fairly obvious, concrete, and immediate, while the promised gains are abstract, theoretical, and distant, leaders in favor of the policy may ultimately lose.

Yet even in the revised standard version, such issues are rare: in Vietnam, casualties brought the costs home while the promised gains, like preventing the dominoes of South and Southeast Asia from falling, were to most Americans remote, uncertain, and highly theoretical. So, too, joining the EU pits assurances of long-run and somewhat abstract gains for some Europeans against more specific and understandable losses perceived by others.

But foreign policy decisions like these are uncommon. Even NAFTA did not activate many voters, despite the efforts of its opponents to generate fears of its consequences. As a result, most Americans gave it scant attention. In effect, the decision was made by political leaders and activists without much influence by ordinary citizens.

International organizations and processes

If popular control is formidably difficult within democratic countries, surely the problem will be even harder to solve in international institutions. If Norway had joined the EU, would its citizens be able to exercise anything like the degree of influence and control over the decisions in Brussels and Strasbourg that they have over the decisions of their own parliament and cabinet? Swedish citizens may now have more influence on the policy decisions of the EU than Norwegians, but would anyone contend that they exercise as much influence in the European Parliament as they do in their own? Or Danes? That these are small and relatively homogeneous countries only reinforces the point. Scale and heterogeneity matter. But the same question might be asked about a larger country such as Britain.

To achieve a level of popular control that is anywhere near the level already existing within democratic countries, international organizations would have to solve several problems about as well as they are now dealt with in democratic countries. Political leaders would have to create political institutions that would provide citizens with opportunities for political participation, influence, and control roughly equivalent in effectiveness to those already existing in democratic countries. To take advantage of these opportunities, citizens would need to be about as concerned and informed about the policy decisions of international organizations as they now are about government decisions in their own countries. In order for citizens to be informed, political and communication elites would need to engage in public debate and discussion of the alternatives in ways that would engage the attention and emotions of the public. To insure public debate, it would be necessary to create an international equivalent to national political competition by parties and individuals seeking office.[13] Elected representatives, or functional equivalents to them (whatever they might be), would need to exercise control over important international bureaucracies about as well as legislatures and executives now do in democratic countries.

How the representatives of a hypothetical international demos would be distributed among the people of different countries poses an additional problem. Given huge differences in the magnitude of the populations of different countries, no system of representation could give equal weight to the vote of each citizen and yet prevent small countries from being steadily outvoted by large countries; thus all solutions acceptable to the smaller democracies will deny political equality among the members of the larger demos. As with the United States and other federal systems, acceptable solutions may be cobbled together as one has been for the EU. But whatever compromise is reached, it could easily be a source of internal strain, particularly in the absence of a strong common identity.

Strain is all the more likely because, as I have already said, just as in national democracies most decisions are bound to be seen as harming the interests of some people, so too in international organizations. The heaviest burden of some decisions might be borne by particular groups, regions, or countries. To survive these strains, a political culture supportive of the specific institutions would help – might indeed be necessary. But developing a political culture takes time, perhaps many generations. In addition, if policy decisions are to be widely acceptable and enforceable among the losers, then it is probable that some common identity, equivalent to that in existing democratic countries, would have to develop. On present evidence, even Europeans do not now possess a common identity.[14] How then can we reasonably expect one to grow elsewhere?

In sum: if it is difficult enough for ordinary citizens to exercise much influence over decisions about foreign affairs in their own countries, should we not conclude that the obstacles will be far greater in international organizations? Just as many important policy decisions in democratic countries are in effect delegated by citizens to the political elites, will not the citizens of countries engaged in an international association delegate effective control to the international policy elites? And will not the extent of delegation in international organizations go well beyond any acceptable threshold of democracy?

Conclusions

To say that international organizations are not and are not likely to be democratic is not to say that they are undesirable. It seems evident that they are necessary to many of the same human needs and goals that advocates of democracy contend are best served by democratic governments, and, as I said at the beginning, they can sometimes assist a non-democratic country to make the difficult transition from a highly undemocratic to a more democratic government. In addition, international organizations can help to expand human rights and the rule of law, the other important aspect of democracy that I emphasized earlier. Even measured against some loss in democratic control, these are important potential gains.

Despite these possible advantages I see no reason to clothe international organizations in the mantle of democracy simply in order to provide them with greater legitimacy.

[. . .]

Notes

1   I am indebted to Martin Gilens for polling data on American opinion and to Bernt Hagtvet and Rune Premfors for providing me with articles, published and unpublished, on the referenda on membership in the European Union in the Nordic countries and Austria.

2   In my own work, for example, a minimally coherent and adequate assessment seems to me to require descriptions of ideal criteria, their moral justifications, different forms of actual political institutions that we call democratic (which is to say, more or less democratic by ideal standards), chiefly democratic polyarchy, and some conditions favorable or unfavorable for the emergence and stability of actual democratic political systems.

3   "The most explicit occurrence," according to Christophersen, "is Babeuf's statement that the terms 'democracy' and 'Robespierrism' were identical, and the latter term signified a revolutionary dictatorship, or a strict and merciless emergency rule, which was to crush anything that barred the victory of revolution" (Christophersen 1966: 304). Lenin and his followers also equated dictatorship of the proletariat with democracy, or proletarian democracy.

4   For my earlier explorations of this dilemma, see Dahl 1967: 953–70, 1989: 317ff and 1994, and Dahl and Tufte 1973: 13ff.

5   The classic and still highly relevant study is Almond 1950.

6   In surveys in the US from the 1930s to 1994, 553 questions concerned foreign affairs. Of these, "14 percent were answered correctly by at least three-quarters of survey respondents. . . . An additional 28 percent of the items were correctly answered by between half and three-quarters of those asked. . . . [M]ore than half could be answered by less than half the general public. 36 percent of the questions were known by only one-quarter to one-half of those asked. In the 1940s, this included knowledge about the forms of government of Sweden and Yugoslavia . . . and that the United States was sending military aid to Greece. Finally, nearly a quarter of the items could be answered by fewer than one-fourth of those asked. These little known facts included knowing that the United States was sharing information about the atomic bomb with England and Canada in the 1940s . . . knowing about how many soldiers had been killed in Vietnam in the 1960s, knowing how much of the federal budget goes to defense or foreign aid in the 1970s . . . " (Delli Carpini and Keeter 1996: 82–6).

7   The process of deliberation in democratic decision-making, to which democratic theorists have been giving increased attention, can be seen as a crucial procedural stage necessary if democratic decisions are to be substantively justifiable. See Guttman and Thompson 1996 and Fishkin 1991.

8   I have elaborated on this question in Dahl 1987 and 1995.

9   Thus, in 1939, the public concerns of Americans began to shift from domestic to foreign affairs, moved to first place after Hitler invaded Poland, were replaced at the end of World War II by domestic matters, which in turn were replaced by Cold War worries in the late 1940s. "From that point until the early 1960s, foreign affairs dominated public concern, ranking first in 48 of 56 surveys and often commanding over 50 percent of the public. In 1963 the hegemony of foreign affairs was interrupted by the emergence of the civil rights movement . . . until foreign affairs, boosted by the Vietnam War, regained the top position in 1965. From 1960 to 1970 Vietnam and other international issues dominated public concern. The only exception occurred in August 1967, when race riots pushed social control to the forefront . . . With minor exceptions, economics has completely dominated public concerns for the last 10 years [1974–84], often capturing 60 percent of the public" (Smith 1985).

10 The turnout on the EU referendum in Austria was 82 per cent, which exceeded the general election of 1994; in Finland, 74 percent, about the same as in the election of 1991; in Sweden, 83.3

11   percent, about 3.5 percent lower than in the immediately preceding general election; in Norway 89 percent, which exceeded turnout in all previous elections (Jahn and Storsved 1995).

11   The "no" vote was 70 percent among farm laborers, 62 percent among farmers, and 60 percent among urban manual workers. Lower white collar workers and persons in crafts and small business split almost evenly. People in big business, management, professions, academics, scientists, teachers, and health and social workers voted in favor by substantial majorities (Brulé 1992).

12   Cf. Pettersen, Jenssen, and Listhaug 1996; Hansen 1996; Bjorklund (n. d.). Although the various factors tend to overlap, multiple regression analysis indicates that those listed had significant independent effects.

13   Although his conclusions are somewhat more hopeful than mine, Ramón Vargas-Machuca (1994) addresses some of the problems.

14   "As an economic, political, and administrative construction, Europe evidently elicits evaluative attitudes, but not a real community of belonging of the kind experienced in nation states. If the European Union is able, in the future, to generate a new system of belonging, it is difficult to imagine, from what we know, what it will be like . . . For the present, a European identity is a vanguard phenomenon" (Duchesne and Frognier 1995:223).

References

Aldrich, John H., Sullivan, John L. and Bordiga, Eugene (1989) Foreign affairs and issue voting: do presidential candidates "waltz before a blind audience"? *American Political Science Review* 83(1): 124–41.

Almond, Gabriel (1950) *The American People and Foreign Policy*, New York: Harcourt Brace.

Archibugi, Daniele and Held, David (eds) (1995) *Cosmopolitan Democracy, An Agenda for a New World Order*, Cambridge: Polity Press.

Bjorklund, Tor (n.d.) Change and continuity: the "no" majority in the 1972 and 1994 referendum concerning Norwegian membership in the EU (MS).

Brulé, Michel (1992) France after Maastricht. *The Public Perspective* 4(1): 28–30.

Christophersen, Jens A. (1966) *The Meaning of Democracy*, Oslo: Universitetsvorlaget.

Dahl, Robert A. (1967) The city in the future of democracy, *American Political Science Review* 61: 953–70.

Dahl, Robert A. (1987) Dilemmas of pluralist democracy: the public good of which public? In Peter Koslowski (ed.), *Individual Liberty and Democratic Decision-Making*, Tübingen: J. C. B. Mohr, pp. 201–14.

Dahl, Robert A. (1989) *Democracy and its Critics*. New Haven: Yale University Press.

Dahl, Robert A. (1994) Democratic dilemma: system effectiveness versus citizen participation, *Political Science Quarterly* 109: 23–34.

Dahl, Robert A. (1995) Is civic virtue a relevant ideal in a pluralist democracy? In Susan Dunn and Gary Jacobsohn (eds), *Diversity and Citizenship*, Lanham, MD: Rowman and Littlefield, pp. 1–16.

Dahl, Robert A. and Tufte, Edward R. (1973) *Size and Democracy*, Stanford: Stanford University Press.

Delli Carpini, Michael X. and Keeter, Scott (1996) *What Americans Know About Politics and Why It Matters*, New Haven: Yale University Press.

Duchesne, Sophie and Frognier, André-Paul (1995) Is there a European identity? In Oskar Niedermayer and Richard Sinnott (eds), *Public Opinion and International Governance*, New York: Oxford University Press, pp. 192–226.

The Economist (1996) The wrong design. 14 December, p. 17.

Fishkin, James (1991) *Democracy and Deliberation*, New Haven: Yale University Press.

Guttman, Amy and Thompson, Dennis (1996) *Democracy and Disagreement*, Cambridge, MA: Harvard University Press.

Hansen, Tore (1996) The regional basis of Norwegian EU-resistance (MS)

Held, David (1995) *Democracy and the Global Order, From the Modern State to Cosmopolitan Governance*. Stanford: Stanford University Press.

Jahn, Deflef and Storsved, Ann-Sofie (1995) Legitimacy through referendum? The nearly successful domino-strategy of the EU referendums in Austria, Finland, Sweden and Norway. *West European Politics* 18: 18–37.

Molyneux, Guy (1994) NAFTA revisited: unified "opinion leaders" best a reluctant public. *The Public Perspective, A Roper Center Review of Public Opinion and Polling* (January/February): 28–30.

Newhouse, Neil S. and Mathews, Christine L. (1994) NAFTA revisiter: most Americans just weren't deeply engaged. *The Public Perspective, A Roper Center Review of Public Opinion and Polling* (January/February): 31–2.

Pettersen, Per Arnt, Jenssen, Anders Todal, and Listhaug, Ola (1996) The 1994 EU referendum in Norway: continuity and change. *Scandinavian Political Studies* 19(3): 257–81.

Schmitter, Philippe C. (1996) Is it really possible to democratize the Euro-policy? Unpublished.

Smith, Tom W. (1985) The Polls: America's most important problems, Part I: National and international, *Public Opinion Quarterly* 49: 264–74.

Vargas-Machuca, Ramón (1994) How to be larger and more accountable: the paradoxical challenge of European political parties. Paper presented at the Center for Advanced Study in the Social Sciences of the Juan March Institute, Madrid, 15–17 December.

Wessels, Bernhard (1995) Support for integration: elite or mass driven? In Oskar Niedermayer and Richard Sinnott (eds), *Public Opinion and International Governance*, Oxford: Oxford University Press, pp. 137–62.

25

Citizenship in an Era of Globalization
Will Kymlicka

The literature is replete with discussions of the impact of globalization on us as workers, consumers, investors, or as members of cultural communities. Less attention has been paid to its impact on us as citizens – as participants in the process of democratic self-government. This is a vitally important issue, for if people become dissatisfied with their role as citizens, the legitimacy and stability of democratic political systems may erode.

This question in fact arises at two levels – domestically, and transnationally or globally. David Held provides a clear and balanced assessment of the possible consequences of globalization for citizenship at both levels. In effect, Held argues that globalization is eroding the capacity for meaningful democratic citizenship at the domestic level, as nation states lose some of their historic sovereignty and become "decision-takers" as much as "decision-makers". If meaningful citizenship is to exist in an era of globalization, therefore, it will require democratizing those transnational institutions which are increasingly responsible for important economic, environmental, and security decisions.

[. . .] I would like to pursue a couple of Held's points in more depth. While I do not disagree with any of his substantive claims, I would like to suggest that there is more room for optimism regarding the prospects for domestic citizenship than he suggests, but perhaps less ground for optimism about global citizenship.

Domestic citizenship

First, then, let me consider the impact of globalization on citizenship at the domestic level. Like many commentators, Held argues that globalization is reducing the historic sovereignty of nation states, and so undermining the meaningfulness of participation in domestic politics. There is obviously some truth in this, but how extensive is the problem? Held gives a nuanced account of this process of globalization, and explicitly distances himself from the more exaggerated claims about the "obsolescence" of the nation state which are made by the "hyper-globalizers" [. . .]. Yet I think that Held too, in his own way, may overstate the situation.

It is certainly true that industrialized nation states have less elbow-room regarding macroeconomic policy today than they did before. (It is doubtful whether Third World states ever had much elbow-room in this area.) This became painfully clear to Canadians when a left-wing government was elected in Canada's largest province (Ontario), and announced a policy of reflationary public spending to reduce unemployment. The response from international financial markets (and bond-rating services) was rapid and severe, and the government quickly dropped the proposal. This made all Canadians aware of how truly dependent we had become on the "men in red suspenders," as our finance minister called Wall Street brokers.

But there are two possible explanations for this phenomenon. Some people see the loss of control by nation states over macroeconomic policy as an inherent and permanent feature of the new world order, which we simply have to learn to live with. This, implicitly at least, is Held's view. But other people argue that the dependence on international financial markets is not an inherent feature of globalization, but rather a contingent result of international indebtedness. On this view, states which run up large foreign debts lose control over their macro-economic policy. We are now so accustomed to governments running up billions of dollars in deficits every year that we take it as normal, even inevitable, that governments owe hundreds of billions of dollars in debt to people outside the country. But it is insane to think that a country can run up such debts for twenty years, and not have it affect their fiscal autonomy. If you put yourself in massive debt to other people, you lose some control over your life.

[. . .]

I think that Held also exaggerates the issue of capital mobility – i.e., the fear that companies will move their operations to whatever country offers the lowest taxes or wages. This is supposed to put dramatic limits on the extent to which countries can adopt more generous unemployment insurance programs, health and safety legislation, parental leave, or minimum wages. Here again, there is obviously some truth to this concern, but we need to keep it in perspective. A reporter in a large US city recently selected at random a number of companies in the Yellow Pages and asked each of them whether they had thought about relocating to another country. The number who said "yes" was negligible. The option of moving overseas is irrelevant for large sectors of the economy – health care, education and training, construction, most retail, most services, agriculture, and so on. The issue of capital mobility is most relevant for mid-to-large manufacturing companies employing low-skilled workers. This is not an insignificant portion of the economy, but it has been a declining percentage for a long time, and it is difficult to see how Third World countries can ever develop except by competing in this sector. The loss of some of these low-skilled manufacturing jobs is inevitable, and perhaps even desirable from the point of view of international justice so long as there are fair transition programs for those people thrown out of work; but there is no reason to think that large numbers of companies in other sectors will pack up and move if the government tells them to provide better parental leave to their workers.

So there remains considerable scope for national policy-making. Moreover, and equally importantly, countries continue to exercise their autonomy in very different ways, reflecting their different political cultures. Even if globalization puts similar pressures on all countries, they need not – and do not – respond in the same way. In his survey of social policy in OECD countries, Keith Banting notes that globalization puts great pressure on nation states both to respond to the social stresses created by economic restructuring and to the demands of international competitiveness. None the less, despite fears of a race to the bottom or an inexorable harmonization of social programs, the share of national resources devoted to social spending continues to inch upwards in OECD nations. While all welfare states are under pressure, "the global economy does not dictate the ways in which governments respond, and different nations are responding in distinctive ways that reflect their domestic politics and cultures" (Banting 1997).

I believe that citizens often care deeply about maintaining these national differences in social policy, and they provide considerable motivation for political participation in domestic politics. For example, the differences between Canadian and American approaches to social policy are increasing, not decreasing, and for Canadian citizens, these differences are worth keeping, and fighting for.

This points to another overstatement in Held's analysis. He argues that globalization is undermining the sense that each nation state forms "a political community of fate" [. . .]. I think he is vastly overstating the situation here. It is certainly true that "some of the most fundamental forces and processes which determine the nature of life chances" cut across national boundaries [. . .], but what determines the boundaries of a "community of fate" is not the forces people are subjected to, but rather how they respond to those forces, and, in particular, what sorts of collectivities they identify with when responding to those forces. People belong to the same community of fate if they *care* about each other's fate, and want to *share* each other's fate – that is, want to meet certain challenges together, so as to share each other's blessings and burdens. Put another way, people belong to the same community of fate if they feel some sense of responsibility for one another's fate, and so want to deliberate together about how to respond collectively to the challenges facing the community. So far as I can tell, globalization has not eroded the sense that nation states form separate communities of fate in this sense.

For example, as a result of NAFTA, North Americans are increasingly subjected to similar economic "forces and processes." But there is no evidence that they feel themselves part of a single "community of fate" whose members care about and wish to share each other's fate. There is no evidence that Canadians now feel any strong sense of responsibility for the well-being of Americans or Mexicans (or vice versa). Nor is there any evidence that Canadians feel any moral obligation to respond to these challenges in the same way as do Americans or Mexicans (or vice versa). On the contrary, Canadians want to respond to these forces *as Canadians* – that is, Canadians debate amongst themselves how to respond to globalization, and they do so by asking what sort of society Canadians wish to live in, and what sorts of obligations Canadians have to each other. Americans ask the same questions amongst themselves, as do the Mexicans.

The economic forces acting on the three countries may be similar, but the sense of communal identity and solidarity remains profoundly different, as have the actual policy responses to these forces. Despite being subject to similar forces, citizens of Western democracies are able to respond to these forces in their own distinctive ways, reflective of their "domestic politics and cultures," and most citizens continue to cherish this ability to deliberate and act as a national collectivity, on the basis of their own national solidarities and priorities.

So I do not accept the view that globalization has deprived domestic politics of its meaningfulness. Nation states still possess considerable autonomy; their citizens still exercise this autonomy in distinctive ways, reflective of their national political cultures; and citizens still want to confront the challenges of globalization as national collectivities, reflective of their historic solidarities, and desire to share each other's fate. These facts all provide meaning and significance to domestic political participation.

I would not deny that many citizens in Western democracies feel dissatisfied with their political participation, but I would argue that the main sources of dissatisfaction with citizenship in Western democracies have little to do with globalization, and in fact long predate the current wave of globalization.[1] In Canada, for example, we have an electoral system which systematically deprives smaller regions of effective political representation in Canadian political life. We have also been unable to regulate campaign financing, with the result that the political process is increasingly seen as heavily skewed towards wealthy individuals and pressure groups. Nor have we changed party nomination procedures to reduce the systematic under-representation of women, Aboriginals, visible minorities, or the working class.

Moreover, Canada has a ridiculously centralized legislative process, in which the real power rests in the hands of a few people in the inner cabinet. We have no meaningful separation between the executive and legislative functions of government, and we have rigid party discipline. As a result, individual members of parliament, whether they are in the governing party or the opposition, have no real input into legislation – at least, much less influence than their counterparts in the American Congress Parliamentary committees are supposed to provide a forum for input into the legislative process, but they are widely seen as a joke. For most Canadians, therefore, their elected MP is important only for constituency service, not as a conduit to the legislative process. What is the point in making one's views known to one's MP, when individual MPs seem to have no role in the legislative process?

These are the real problems with the political process in Canada – these are at the root of people's increasing sense that they have no real voice in political life. So far as I can tell, they have little to do with globalization. Globalization is not the cause of these problems, nor is there anything in globalization which prevents us from dealing with them.

[. . .]

Indeed, far from depriving domestic citizenship of its meaningfulness, globalization may actually be helping to renew it in important respects. For example, globalization is opening up the political process to new groups. Existing legislative and regulatory processes have been captured by entrenched interest groups for a long time now, but their traditional power bases are being eroded by globalization, and previously excluded groups are jumping in to fill the void (Simeon 1997: 307).

Also, globalization, far from encouraging political apathy, is itself one of the things which seems to mobilize otherwise apathetic people. Consider the vigorous debate over free trade in Canada, or the debate in Denmark over the Maastricht Treaty. This should not be surprising, since decisions about how to relate to other countries are themselves an important exercise of national sovereignty.

This is perhaps clearer in the European context than in North America. It is quite clear, for example, that the desire of Spain or Greece to join the EU was not simply a matter of economic gain. It was also seen as a way of confirming their status as open, modern, democratic, and pluralistic states, after many years of being closed and authoritarian societies. Similarly, the decision about whether to admit new countries from Eastern Europe to the EU will be decided not just on the basis of economic gain, but also on the basis of moral obligations to assist newly democratizing countries, and on the basis of aspirations to create a Europe free of old divisions and hatreds.

In other words, decisions by national collectivities to integrate into transnational institutions are, in part, decisions about what kind of societies people want to live in.

Being open to the world is, for many people, an important part of their self-conception as members of modern pluralistic societies, and they autonomously decide to pursue that self-conception through various international agreements and in situations. Such decisions are not a denial of people's national identity or sovereignty, but precisely an affirmation of their national identity, and a highly valued exercise of their national sovereignty.

The best example of this, perhaps, is the desire of former communist countries to join European organizations. It would be a profound misunderstanding to say that the decision by Baltic states to join the Council of Europe is an abridgment of their sovereignty. On the contrary, it is surely one of the most important symbolic affirmations of their new-found sovereignty. One of the most hated things about communism was that it prevented Baltic nations from entering into such international alliances, and acting upon their self-conception as a "European" country. Latvia's decision to join the Council of Europe was a way of declaring: "now we are a sovereign people, able to act on our own wishes. No longer can anyone tell us who we can and cannot associate with." Sovereignty is valued because it allows nations to act on their interests and identities, and the freedom to enter European organizations is an enormously important example of this sovereignty for Baltic nations.

These examples show, I think, that globalization often provides options which nations value, and decisions about whether and how to exercise these options have become lively topics for national debate. Globalization does constrain national legislatures, although the extent of this is often exaggerated. But globalization also enriches national political life, and provides new and valued options by which nations can collectively promote their interests and identities.

Cosmopolitan citizenship

So globalization need not undermine the scope for meaningful democratic citizenship at the national level. By contrast, I am rather more skeptical about the likelihood that we can produce any meaningful form of transnational citizenship. I think we should be quite modest in our expectations about transnational citizenship, at least for the foreseeable future.

I heartily agree with many aspects of Held's conception of "cosmopolitan democracy." In particular, I endorse efforts to strengthen the international enforcement of human rights, and I accept Held's idea that the rules for according international recognition to states should include some reference to democratic legitimation. Principles of democracy and human rights should indeed be seen as "cosmopolitan" in this sense – i.e., each state should be encouraged to respect these principles.

But I am more skeptical about the idea that transnational institutions and organizations can themselves be made democratic in any meaningful sense. Can we even make sense of the idea of "democratizing" such institutions? When thinking about this question, it is important to remember that democracy is not just a formula for aggregating votes, but is also a system of collective deliberation and legitimation. The actual moment of voting (in elections, or within legislatures) is just one component in a larger process of democratic self-government. This process begins with public deliberation about the issues which need to be addressed and the options for resolving them. The decisions which result from this deliberation are then legitimated on the grounds that they reflect the considered will and common good of the people as a whole, not just the self-interest or arbitrary whims of the majority.

Arguably, these forms of deliberation and legitimation require some degree of commonality amongst citizens. Collective political deliberation is only feasible if participants understand and trust one another, and there is good reason to think that such mutual understanding and trust require some underlying commonalities. Some sense of commonality or shared identity may be required to sustain a deliberative and participatory democracy.

But what sort of shared identity? If we examine existing democracies to see what sorts of commonalities have proven necessary, I think we would find that deliberative democracy does *not* require a common religion (or common lifestyles more generally); a common political ideology (e.g., right versus left); or a common racial or ethnic descent. We can find genuinely participatory democratic fora and procedures which cut across these religious/ideological/racial cleavages.

When we turn to language, however, things become more complicated. There are of course several multilingual democracies – e.g., Belgium, Spain, Switzerland, Canada. But if we look at how democratic debates operate within these countries, we find that language is increasingly important in defining the boundaries of political communities, and the identities of political actors.

There is a similar dynamic taking place in all of these countries, by which: (a) the separate language groups are becoming more territorialized – that is, each language has become ever-more dominant within a particular region, while gradually dying out outside that region (this phenomenon – known as the "territorial imperative" – is very widespread); and (b) these territorialized language groups are demanding increased political recognition and self-government powers through federalization of the political system. (These processes of territorialization and federalization are of course closely linked – the latter is both the cause and the effect of the former.) Political boundaries have been drawn, and political powers redistributed, so that territorialized language groups are able to exercise greater self-government within the larger federal system.

Held argues that globalization is undermining the territorial basis of politics, and that territory is playing a less important role in the determination of political identity [. . .]. I think this is simply untrue, at least in the context of multilingual states. On the contrary, language has become an increasingly important determinant of the boundaries of political community within each of these multilingual countries, and territory has become an increasingly important determinant of the boundaries of these language groups. These countries are becoming, in effect, federations of territorially concentrated, self-governing language groups. These self-governing language groups often describe themselves as "nations," and mobilize along nationalist lines, and so we can call these countries "multination states."

There are good reasons to think that these "national" linguistic/territorial political communities – whether they are unilingual nation states or linguistically distinct subunits within multination states – are the primary forum for democratic participation in the modern world. They are primary in two distinct senses. First, democracy within national/linguistic units is more genuinely participatory than at higher levels which cut across language lines. Political debates at the federal level in multination states, for example, or at the level of the EU, are almost invariably elite-dominated.

Why? Put simply, democratic politics is politics in the vernacular. The average citizen only feels comfortable debating political issues in their own tongue. As a general rule, it is only elites who have fluency with more than one language, and who have the continual opportunity to maintain and develop these language skills, and who feel comfortable debating political issues in another tongue within multilingual settings. Moreover, political communication has a large ritualistic component, and these ritualized forms of communication are typically language-specific. Even if one understands a foreign language in the technical sense, without knowledge of these ritualistic elements one may be unable to understand political debates. For these and other reasons, we can expect – as a general rule – that the more political debate is conducted in the vernacular, the more participatory it will be.

[. . .]

There is a second sense in which these "national" units are primary – namely, they are the most important forum for assessing the legitimacy of other levels of government. Members of these national units may wish to devolve power upwards – to the federal level in multination states, or to the European Union – just as they may wish to devolve power downwards to local or municipal governments. As I noted earlier, such upward (or downward) devolutions of power are to be expected, since they will often be in the national interest of these collectivities. But the legitimacy of these devolutions of power is generally seen as dependent on the (ongoing) consent of the national unit (and this consent will only be given if these devolutions of power do not undermine the ability of the national unit to maintain itself as a viable, self-governing society). Decisions made by larger units – whether they are federal policies in multination states, or EU policies – are seen as legitimate only if they are made under rules and procedures which were consented to by the national unit, and similarly changes to the rules are only legitimate if they are debated and approved by the national unit. Members of these national collectivities debate amongst themselves, in the vernacular, how much power they wish to devolve upwards or downwards, and periodically reassess, at the national level, whether they wish to reclaim some of these powers. The legitimate authority of higher-level political bodies depends on this ongoing process of debate and consent at the national level. These decisions are made on the basis of what serves the national interest (and not on the basis of what serves the interests of, say, Europe as a whole).

[. . .]

This is not to deny the obvious fact that we need international political institutions which transcend linguistic/national boundaries. We need such institutions to deal not only with economic globalization, but also with common environmental problems and issues of international security. At present, these organizations exhibit a major "democratic deficit." They are basically organized through intergovernmental relations, with little, if any, direct input from individual citizens. Held suggests that this is a serious problem, which can only be resolved by promoting new forms of "cosmopolitan citizenship" which enable individuals and non-government groups to participate directly in transnational organizations [. . .].

I am not so sure that there is a serious problem here, or that Held's suggestion is realistic. It seems to me that there is no necessary reason why international institutions should be directly accountable to (or accessible to) individual citizens. To be sure, if international institutions are increasingly powerful, they must be held accountable. But why can we not hold them accountable *indirectly*, by debating at the national level how we want our national governments to act in intergovernmental contexts?

It seems clear that this is the way most Europeans themselves wish to reconcile democracy with the growth of the EU. There is very little demand for a strengthened EU Parliament. On the contrary, most people, in virtually all European states, show little interest in the affairs of the European Parliament, and little enthusiasm for increasing its powers.

What they want, instead, is to strengthen the accountability of their *national* governments for how these governments act at the intergovernmental Council of Ministers. That is, citizens in each country want to debate amongst themselves, in their vernacular, what the position of their government should be on EU issues. Danes wish to debate, in Danish, what the Danish position should be *vis-à-vis* Europe. They show little interest in starting a European-wide debate (in what language?) about what the EU should do. They are keenly interested in having a democratic debate about the EU, but the debate they wish to engage in is not a debate with other Europeans about "what should we Europeans do?" Rather, they wish to debate with each other, in Danish, about what we Danes should do. To put it another way, they want Denmark to be part of Europe, but they show little interest in becoming citizens of a European demos.

This is not to say that increasing the direct accountability and accessibility of transnational institutions is a bad thing. On the contrary, I support many of Held's suggestions in this regard. I agree that NGOs should have an increased role at the UN and other international bodies [. . .], and I support the idea of a global civil society, in which people seek to mobilize the citizens of other countries to protest violations of human rights or environmental degradation in their own country. But it is misleading, I think, to describe this as the "democratization" of transnational institutions, or as the creation of democratic citizenship on the transnational level. After all, these proposals would not create any form of collective deliberation and decision-making that connects and binds individuals across national boundaries.

[. . .]

Transnational activism by individuals or NGOs is not the same as democratic citizenship. Moreover, attempts to create a genuinely democratic form of transnational citizenship could have negative consequences for democratic citizenship at the domestic level. For example, I am not convinced that it would be a good thing to strengthen the (directly elected) EU Parliament at the expense of the (intergovernmental) EU Council. The result of "democratizing" the EU would be to take away the veto power which national governments now have over most EU decisions. Decisions made by the EU Parliament, unlike those made by the Council, are not subject to the national veto. This means that the EU would cease to be accountable to citizens through their national legislatures. At the moment, if a Danish citizen dislikes an EU decision, she can try to mobilize other Danes to change their government's position on the issue. But once the EU is "democratized" – i.e., once the Parliament replaces the Council as the major decision-making body – a Danish citizen would have to try to change the opinions of the citizens of every other European country (none of which speak her language). For obvious and understandable reasons, few Europeans seek this sort of "democratization." For Danish citizens to engage in a debate with other Danes, in Danish, about the Danish position *vis-à-vis* the EU is a familiar and manageable task, but for Danish citizens to engage in a debate with Italians to try to develop a common European position is a daunting prospect. In what language would such a debate occur, and in what fora? Not only do they not speak the same language, or share the same territory, they also do not read the same newspapers, or watch the same television shows, or belong to the same political parties. So what would be the forum for such a trans-European debate?

Given these obstacles to a trans-European public debate, it is not surprising that neither the Danes not the Italians have shown any enthusiasm for "democratizing" the EU. They prefer exercising democratic accountability through their national legislatures. Paradoxically, then, the net result of increasing direct democratic accountability of the EU through the elected Parliament would in fact be to undermine democratic citizenship. It would shift power away from the national level, where mass participation and vigorous democratic debate is possible, towards the transnational level, where democratic participation and deliberation is very difficult. As Grimm argues, given that there is no common European mass media at the moment, and given that the prospects for creating such a Europeanized media in the foreseeable future "are absolutely non-existent," dramatically shifting power from the Council to the Parliament would "aggravate rather than solve the problem" of the democratic deficit (Grimm 1995: 296).

In short, globalization is undoubtedly producing a new civil society, but it has not yet produced anything we can recognize as transnational democratic citizenship. Nor is it clear to me that we should aspire to such a new form of citizenship. Many of our most important moral principles should be cosmopolitan in scope – e.g., principles of human rights, democracy, and environmental protection – and we should seek to promote these ideals internationally. But our democratic citizenship is, and will remain for the foreseeable future, national in scope.

Note

1   The following discussion draws in part on Kymlicka 1997.

References

Banting, Keith. 1997. "The internationalization of the social contract." In Thomas Courchene (ed), *The Nation State in a Global/Information Era*, pp. 255–86. Kingston, Canada: John Deutsch Institute for Policy Studies, Queen's University.

Grimm, Dieter. 1995. "Does Europe need a constitution?" *European Law Journal* 1(3): 282–302.

Kymlicka, Will. 1997. "The prospects for citizenship: reply to Simeon." In Thomas Courchene (ed), *The Nation State in a Global/Information Era*, pp. 315–25. Kingston, Canada: John Deutsch Institute for Policy Studies, Queen's University.

Simeon, Richard. 1997. "Citizens and democracy in the emerging global order." In Thomas Courchene (ed), *The Nation State in a Global/Information Era*, pp. 299–314. Kingston, Canada: John Deutsch Institute for Policy Studies, Queen's University.

26

A Comprehensive Overview of Cosmopolitan Literature
Garrett Wallace Brown and Megan Kime

Cosmopolitanism

The following provide general introductions to the ideal of cosmopolitanism, and to its various applications in moral, social, and political philosophy.

Archibugi, Daniele, ed. *Debating Cosmopolitics*. London: Verso, 2003.

Beitz, Charles R. "Cosmopolitanism and Global Justice." *Journal of Ethics* 9, nos. 1–2 (2005).

Benhabib, Seyla. *Another Cosmopolitanism*, ed. Robert Post. Oxford: Oxford University Press, 2006.

Brighouse, Harry, and Gillian Brock, eds. *The Political Philosophy of Cosmopolitanism*. Cambridge: Cambridge University Press, 2005.

Brown, Garrett Wallace, and David Held, eds. *The Cosmopolitanism Reader*. Cambridge: Polity Press, 2010.

Cheah, P., and B. Robbins, eds. *Cosmopolitics: Thinking and Feeling Beyond the Nation*. Minneapolis: University of Minnesota Press, 1998.

Cohen, R., and S. Vertovic, eds. *Conceiving Cosmopolitanism: Theory, Context, and Practice*. Oxford: Oxford University Press, 2002.

Cohen, R., and Robert Fine. "Four Cosmopolitan Moments." In *Conceiving Cosmopolitanism: Theory, Context, and Practice*, ed. R. Cohen and S. Vertovic. Oxford: Oxford University Press, 2002.

Featherstone, M. "Cosmopolis: An Introduction." *Theory, Culture, and Society* 19, nos. 1–2 (2002): 1–16.

Fine, Robert. *Cosmopolitanism*. New York: Routledge, 2007.

Lu, Catherine. "The One and Many Faces of Cosmopolitanism." *Journal of Political Philosophy* 8, no. 2 (2000): 244–67.

Pollock, S., H. K. Bhabha, C. A. Breckenridge, and D. Chakrabarty. "Cosmopolitanisms." *Public Culture* 12, no. 3 (2000): 577–89.

Scheffler, Samuel. "Conceptions of Cosmopolitanism." *Utilitas* 11 (1999): 227–43.

Van Hooft, Stan. *Cosmopolitanism*. Stocksfield: Acumen, 2009.

Waldron, Jeremy. "What is Cosmopolitan?" *Journal of Political Philosophy* 8, no. 2 (2000): 227–43.

Historical cosmopolitanism

Cosmopolitanism has roots in ancient Greek and Roman philosophy, as well as in early-modern western political thought. The following is a selection of the main primary and secondary literature on the classical development of cosmopolitan thought.

Aurelius, Marcus. *The Meditations*. New York: Hackett, 1983.

Baldry, H. C. *The Unity of Mankind in Greek Thought*. Cambridge: Cambridge University Press, 1965.

Bentham, Jeremy. "Principles of International Law." In *The Works of Jeremy Bentham*, ed. John Bowring. New York: Russell & Russell, 1962.

Brown, Eric. "Hellenistic Cosmopolitanism." In *A Companion to Ancient Philosophy*, ed. Mary Louise Gill and Pierre Pellegrin. Oxford: Blackwell, 2006.

—— "Socrates the Cosmopolitan." *Stanford Agora: An Online Journal of Legal Perspectives*, 2000.

—— *Stoic Cosmopolitanism*. Cambridge: Cambridge University Press, 2008.

Cavallar, Georg. *The Rights of Strangers*. Aldershot: Ashgate Publishing, 2002.

Cicero, Marcus. *De officiis*, ed. M. T. Griffin and E. M. Atkins. Cambridge: Cambridge University Press, 1991.

Covell, Charles. *The Law of Nations in Political Thought: A Critical Survey from Vitoria to Hegel*. Basingstoke: Palgrave, 2009.

Diogenes, Laertius. *The Lives of Eminent Philosophers*, trans. R. Hicks. Vol. II. Cambridge, MA: Loeb Classical Library, 1925.

Dudley, Donald. *A History of Cynicism: From Diogenes to the 6th century AD*. London: Ares Publishing, 1937.

Erasmus, Desiderius. "A Complaint of Peace Spurned and Rejected by the Whole World." In *Desiderius Erasmus, Works*, 289–322. Toronto: University of Toronto Press, 1986.

Fichte, Johann Gottlieb. *Foundations of Natural Right*, trans. Michael Baur, ed. Frederick Neuhouser. Cambridge: Cambridge University Press, 2000.

Fougeret de Montbron. *Le cosmopolite ou le citoyen du monde*. Woodbridge: Research Publications, 1970 [1750].

Grotius, Hugo. *The Law of War and Peace. De iure belli ac paci libri tres*, trans. Francis W. Kelsey. New York: Bobbs-Merrill, 1925 [1625].

Haddas, Moses. "From Nationalism to Cosmopolitanism in the Greco-Roman World." *Journal of the History of Ideas* 4, no. 1 (1943): 105–11.

Harris, H. "The Greek Origins of the Idea of Cosmopolitanism." *International Journal of Ethics* 381 (1927): 1–10.

Hawk, Lewis. *All Mankind is One: A Study of the Disputation between Bartolomé de Las Casas and Juan Gines de Sepulveda in 1,550 on the Intellectual and Religious Capacity of the American Indians*. De Kalb: Northern Illinois Press, 1974.

Heater, Derek. *World Citizenship and Government: Cosmopolitan Ideas in the History of Western Political Thought*. New York: St Martin's, 1996.

Jacob, Margaret C. *Strangers Nowhere in the World: The Rise of Cosmopolitanism in Early Modern Europe*. Philadelphia: University of Pennsylvania Press, 2006.

Kant, Immanuel. *Kant's Political Writings*, ed. Hans Reiss. Cambridge: Cambridge University Press, 1991.

Kleingeld, P. "Six Varieties of Cosmopolitanism in Late Eighteenth-Century Germany." *Journal of the History of Ideas* 60, no. 3 (1999): 505–24.

Las Casas, Bartolomé de. *A Short Account of the Destruction of the Indies*, trans. Nigel Griffin. London: Penguin Books, 1992.

Lu, Catherine. "The One and Many Faces of Cosmopolitanism." *Journal of Political Philosophy* 8, no. 2 (2000): 244–67.

Moles, J. L. "Cynic Cosmopolitanism." In *The Cynics: The Cynic Movement in Antiquity and its Legacy*, ed. R. Bracht Branham and Marie-Odile Goulet-Caze, 105–20. Berkeley and Los Angeles: University of California Press, 1996.

—— "The Cynics." In *The Cambridge History of Greek and Roman Political Thought*, ed. Christopher Rowe and Malcolm Schofield, 415–34. Cambridge: Cambridge University Press, 2000.

—— "The Cynics and Politics." In *Justice and Generosity: Studies in Hellenistic Social and Political Philosophy*, ed. Andre Laks and Malcolm Schofield, 129–58. Cambridge: Cambridge University Press, 1995.

Nussbaum, Martha C. "Duties of Justice, Duties of Material Aid: Cicero's Problematic Legacy." *Journal of Political Philosophy* 8, no. 2 (2000): 176–206.

—— "Kant and Stoic Cosmopolitanism." *Journal of Political Philosophy* 5, no. 1 (1997): 1–25.

O'Brien, Karen. *Narratives of Enlightenment: Cosmopolitan History from Voltaire to Gibbon*. Cambridge: Cambridge University Press, 2005.

O'Malley, Joseph, and Richard A. Davis, eds. *Marx: Early Political Writings*. Cambridge: Cambridge University Press, 1994.

Pagden, A. "Stoicism, Cosmopolitanism, and the Legacy of European Imperialism." *Constellations* 7, no. 1 (2000): 3–22.

Pufendorf, Samuel. *De iure naturae et gentium libri octo*, ed. Walter Simons. Buffalo: Hein, 1995.

Rousseau, Jean-Jacques. *The Social Contract and Other Later Political Writings* trans. and ed. Victor Gourevitch. Cambridge: Cambridge University Press, 1997.

Schlegel, Friedrich. "Essay on the Concept of Republicanism Occasioned by the Kantian Tract 'Perpetual Peace.'" In *The Early Political Writings of the German Romantics*, ed. Frederick C. Beiser, 95–113. Cambridge: Cambridge University Press, 1996.

Schlereth, Thomas J. *The Cosmopolitan Ideal in Enlightenment Thought: Its Form and Function in the Ideas of Franklin, Hume, and Voltaire, 1694–1790*. Notre Dame: University of Notre Dame Press, 1977.

Schofield, Malcolm. *The Stoic Idea of the City*. Cambridge: Cambridge University Press, 1991.

Scott, James. *The Spanish Origin of International Law: Francisco de Vitoria and his Law of Nations*. Oxford: Clarendon Press, 1934.

Sellers, John. "Stoic Cosmopolitanism and Zeno's Republic." *History of Political Thought* 28, no. 1 (2007): 1–29.

Seneca. *De Otio*, ed. A. Long and D. Sedley. Cambridge: Cambridge University Press, 1987.

Smith, Adam. *An Inquiry into the Nature and Causes of the Wealth of Nations*. Ed. R. H. Campbell and A. S. Skinner. Indianapolis: Liberty Classics, 1976.

Tarn, W. *Hellenistic Civilization*. London: Plume, 1930.

Toulmin, S. *Cosmopolis: The Hidden Agenda of Modernity*. New York: Free Press, 1990.

Tuan, Yi-fu. *Cosmos and Hearth: A Cosmopolite's Viewpoint*. Minneapolis: University of Minnesota Press, 1996.

Varouxakis, G. "'Patriotism', 'Cosmopolitanism' and 'Humanity' in Victorian Thought." *European Journal of Political Theory* 5, no. 1 (2006): 100–18.

Vattel, Emeric de. *The Laws of Nations*. Indianapolis: The Liberty Fund, 2000.

Vitoria, Francisco de. "On the American Indians." In *Political Writings*, ed. A. Padgen and J. Lawrence. Cambridge: Cambridge University Press, 1991.

—— "On Civil Power." In *Political Writings*, ed. A. Padgen and J. Lawrence. Cambridge: Cambridge University Press, 1991.

—— "On Laws." In *Political Writings*, ed. A. Padgen and J. Lawrence. Cambridge: Cambridge University Press, 1991.

—— "On the Laws of War." In *Political Writings*, ed. A. Padgen and J. Lawrence. Cambridge: Cambridge University Press, 1991.

Kant and Kantian cosmopolitanism

Immanuel Kant's development of cosmopolitanism has been especially influential in both moral philosophy and international relations theory.

Archibugi, D. "Immanuel Kant, Cosmopolitan Law, and Peace." *European Journal of International Relations* 1, no. 4 (1995): 429–56.

—— "Models of International Organization in Perpetual Peace Projects." *Review of International Studies* 18 (1992): 295–317.

Axinn, Sidney. "Kant on World Government." In *Proceedings of the Sixth Kantian Congress*, ed. G. Funke and T. Seebohm. Washington: University Press of America, 1989.

Bohman, James, and Matthias Lutz-Bachmann, eds. *Perpetual Peace: Essays on Kant's Cosmopolitan Ideal*. Cambridge, MA: MIT Press, 1997.

Brown, Garrett Wallace. *Grounding Cosmopolitanism: From Kant to the Idea of a Cosmopolitan Constitution*. Edinburgh: University of Edinburgh Press, 2009.

—— "Kantian Cosmopolitan Law and the Idea of a Cosmopolitan Constitution." *History of Political Thought* 27, no. 3 (2006).

—— "State Sovereignty, Federation and Kantian Cosmopolitanism." *European Journal of International Relations* 11, (2005).

Cavallar, G. *Kant and the Theory and Practice of International Right*. Cardiff: University of Wales Press, 1999.

Covell, C. *Kant and the Law of Peace: A Study in the Philosophy of International Law and International Relations*. Cambridge, MA: MIT Press, 1998.

Donaldson, Thomas. "Kant's Global Rationalism." In *Traditions of International Ethics*, ed. T. Nardin and D. Mapel. Cambridge: Cambridge University Press, 1992.

Doyle, Michael. "Kant and Liberal Internationalism." In *Toward Perpetual Peace and Other Writings on Politics, Peace and History*, ed. Pauline Kleingeld. New Haven: Yale University Press, 2006.

—— "Kant's Liberal Legacies and Foreign Affairs." *Philosophy and Public Affairs* 12, nos. 3 & 4 (1983): 204–35, 323–53.

Fine, Robert. "Kant's Theory of Cosmopolitanism and Hegel's Critique." *Philosophy and Social Criticism* 296 (2003): 609–30.

Flikschuh, Katrin. *Kant and Modern Political Philosophy*. Cambridge: Cambridge University Press, 2000.

Franceschet, Antonio. *Kant and Liberal Internationalism: Sovereignty, Justice and Global Reform*. New York: Palgrave, 2002.

—— "Popular Sovereignty or Cosmopolitan Democracy?: Kant, Liberalism and International Reform" *European Journal of International Relations*, 6, no. 2 (2000): 209–28.

—— "Sovereignty and Freedom: Immanuel Kant's Liberal Internationalist 'Legacy.' " *Review of International Studies*, 27, no. 2 (2001): 277–302.

Gregor, Mary. "Kant's Approach to Constitutionalism." In *Constitutionalism: The Philosophical Dimension*, ed. A. Rosenbaum. New York: Greenwood Press, 1988.

—— *The Laws of Freedom: A Study of Applying the Categorical Imperative in the Metaphysics of Morals*. New York: Barnes and Noble, 1963.

Guyer, Paul. *Kant on Freedom, Law and Happiness*. Cambridge: Cambridge University Press, 2000.

Habermas, Jurgen. *The Divided West*. Part IV. Cambridge: Polity Press, 2006.

—— "Kant's Idea of Perpetual Peace, with the Benefit of Two Hundred Years' Hindsight." In *Perpetual Peace: Essays on Kant's Cosmopolitan Ideal*, ed. James Bohman and Matthias Lutz-Bachmann. Cambridge, MA: MIT Press, 1997.

Hoffe, Otfried. *Kant's Cosmopolitan Theory of Law and Peace*. Cambridge: Cambridge University Press, 2006.

Hurrell, Andrew. "Kant and the Kantian Paradigm in International Relations." *Review of International Studies* 16, no. 3 (1990): 183–205.

Kant, Immanuel. "Ideal for a Universal History with a Cosmopolitan Purpose." In *Kant's Political Writings*, ed. H. Reiss. Cambridge: Cambridge University Press, 1970.

—— *Perpetual Peace*. Indianapolis: Hackett, 1994.

—— *Perpetual Peace*, trans. Lewis White Beck. New York: Liberal Arts Press, 1957.

—— *Kant's Political Writings*, ed. Hans Reiss. Cambridge: Cambridge University Press, 1991.

Kaufman, Alexander. *Welfare in the Kantian State*. Oxford: Clarendon Press, 1999.

Kleingeld, Pauline. "Approaching Perpetual Peace: Kant's Defence of a League of States and his Ideal of a World Federation." *European Journal of Philosophy* 12 (2004): 304–25.

—— "Kantian Patriotism." *Philosophy and Public Affairs* 29 (2000): 313–41.

—— "Kant's Cosmopolitan Law: World Citizenship for a Global Order." *Kantian Review* 2 (1998): 72–90.

Laberge, Pierre. "Kant on Justice and the Law of Nations." In *International Society: Diverse Ethical Perspectives*, ed. D. Maple and T. Nardin. Princeton, NJ: Princeton University Press, 1998.

Mertens, T. "Cosmopolitanism and Citizenship: Kant against Habermas." *European Journal of Philosophy* 4 (1996): 328–47.

Mulholland, Leslie. *Kant's System of Rights*. New York: Columbia University Press, 1990.

Nussbaum, Martha C. "Kant and Stoic Cosmopolitanism." *Journal of Political Philosophy* 5, no. 1 (1997): 1–25.

O'Neill, Onora. *Constructions of Reason: Exploration of Kant's Practical Philosophy*. New York: St. Martin's Press, 1989.

—— "Transnational Justice." In *Political Theory Today*, ed. D. Held. Cambridge: Polity Press, 1995.

Orend, Brian. *War and International Justice: A Kantian Perspective*. Waterloo: Wilfred Laurier University Press, 2001.

Pogge, Thomas W. "Kant's Theory of Justice." *Kant-Studien* 79 (1988): 407–33.

Pojman, Louis P. "Kant's Perpetual Peace and Cosmopolitanism." *Journal of Social Philosophy* 36, no. 1 (2005): 62–71.

Smith, William, and Robert Fine. "Kantian Cosmopolitanism Today: John Rawls and Jürgen Habermas on Immanuel Kant's *Foedus Pacificum*." *King's College Law Journal* 15, no. 1 (2004): 5–22.

Teson, Fernando. "Kantian International Liberalism." In *International Society: Diverse Ethical Perspectives*, ed. D. Mapel and T. Nardin. Princeton, NJ: Princeton University Press, 1998.

Tully, James. "The Kantian Idea of Europe: Critical and Cosmopolitan Perspectives." In *The Idea of Europe*, ed. A. Pagden. Cambridge: Cambridge University Press, 2002.

Waldron, Jeremy. "Kant's Legal Positivism." *Harvard Law Review* 109 (1996).

—— "Kant's Theory of the State." In *Toward Perpetual Peace and Other Writings on Politics, Peace and History*, ed. Pauline Kleingeld. New Haven: Yale University Press, 2006.

—— "What is Cosmopolitan?" *Journal of Political Philosophy* 8, no. 2, (1999): 227–43.

Williams, Howard. *Kant's Political Philosophy*. New York: St. Martin's Press, 1983.

Moral Cosmopolitanism

In modern moral philosophy the normative ideal of cosmopolitanism is often expressed as a commitment to the equal moral worth of all individuals.

Appiah, Kwame Anthony. *Cosmopolitanism: Ethics in a World of Strangers.* New York: W. W. Norton, 2006.
Beitz, Charles R. "Cosmopolitan Ideals and National Sentiment." *Journal of Philosophy* 80 (1983): 591–600.
Benhabib, Seyla. "The Philosophical Foundations of Cosmopolitan Norms." In *Another Cosmopolitanism*, ed. Robert Post. Oxford: Oxford University Press, 2006.
Canto-Sperber, Monique. "The Normative Foundations of Cosmopolitanism." *Proceedings of the Aristotelian Society* 106, no. 2 (2006): 265–81.
Gewirth, Alan. "Ethical Universalism and Particularism." *Journal of Philosophy* 85 (1988): 283–302.
Nussbaum, Martha C. "Patriotism and Cosmopolitanism." In *For Love of Country: Debating the Limits of Patriotism*, ed. Joshua Cohen. Boston: Beacon Press, 1996.
Scheffler, Samuel. *Boundaries and Allegiances.* Oxford: Oxford University Press, 2001.
Singer, Peter. "Famine, Affluence, and Morality." *Philosophy and Public Affairs* 1, no. 3 (1972): 229–43.
—— *One World.* New Haven: Yale University Press, 2002.
Unger, Peter. *Living High and Letting Die: Our Illusion of Innocence.* Oxford: Oxford University Press, 1996.

Human rights

Moral cosmopolitans usually endorse universal human rights such as those enshrined in the Universal Declaration for Human Rights. Human rights are also used as critical tools in international politics and law.

Anderson-Gold, S. *Cosmopolitanism and Human Rights.* Cardiff: University of Wales Press, 2001.
Bauer, J., and Daniel Bell. *The East Asian Challenge for Human Rights.* Cambridge: Cambridge University Press, 1999.
Beitz, Charles R. *The Idea of Human Rights.* Oxford: Oxford University Press, 2009.
Beitz, Charles R., and Robert Goodin (eds.) *Global Basic Rights.* Oxford: Oxford University Press, 2009.
Charvet, John. "The Possibility of a Cosmopolitan Order Based on the Idea of Universal Human Rights." *Millennium: Journal of International Relations*, 27, no. 3 (1998).
Donnelly, Jack. *International Human Rights.* Boulder: University of Colorado Press, 1998.
—— *Universal Human Rights in Theory and Practice.* Ithaca: Cornell University Press, 1998.
Douzinas, Costas. *Human Rights and Empire: The Political Philosophy of Cosmopolitanism.* Abingdon: Routledge, 2007.
Dunne, Timothy, and Nicholas J. Wheeler, eds. *Human Rights in Global Politics.* Cambridge: Cambridge University Press, 1999.
Falk, R. *Human Rights Horizons: The Pursuit of Justice in a Globalizing World.* London: Routledge, 2000.
Fine, Robert. "Cosmopolitanism and Human Rights: Radicalism in a Global Age." *Metaphilosophy* 40, no. 1 (2009): 8–23.
Follesdal, Andreas. "Universal Human Rights: Is a Shared Political Identity Impossible? Necessary? Sufficient?" *Metaphilosophy* 40, no. 1 (2009): 77–91.
Kelly, Erin. "Human Rights as Foreign Policy Objectives." In *The Ethics of Assistance*, ed. Dean K. Chatterjee. Cambridge: Cambridge University Press, 2004.
Kuper, Andrew, ed. *Global Responsibilities: Who Must Deliver on Human Rights?* New York: Routledge, 2005.
McGrew, Anthony. "Human Rights in a Global Age: Coming to Terms with Globalization." In *Human Rights Fifty Years On: A Reappraisal*, ed. T. Evens, 188–210. Manchester: Manchester University Press, 1998.
Pogge, Thomas W., ed. *Freedom from Poverty as a Human Right: Who Owes What to the Very Poor?* New York: Oxford University Press, 2007.
Shue, Henry. *Basic Rights: Subsistence, Affluence, and U.S. Foreign Policy.* 2nd edn. Princeton, NJ: Princeton University Press, 1996.
Sumner, L. *The Moral Foundations of Rights.* Princeton, NJ: Princeton University Press, 1987.

Humanitarian intervention

One implication of universal human rights is the question of when we should intervene in order to protect them. Recent instances of so-called "humanitarian interventions" (for example in Kosovo, Afghanistan, and Iraq) have led to a surge in literature on the topic.

Archibugi, Daniele. "Cosmopolitan Guidelines for Humanitarian Intervention." *Alternatives* 29, no. 1 (2004): 1–22.

Chandler, David. *From Kosovo to Kabul: Human Rights and International Intervention.* London: Pluto Press, 2002.

—— "The Road to Military Humanitarianism: How the Human Rights NGOs Shaped a New Humanitarian Agenda." *Human Rights Quarterly* 23, no. 3 (2001): 678–700.

Chatterjee, Dean K., ed. *The Ethics of Assistance: Morality and the Distant Needy.* Cambridge: Cambridge University Press, 2004.

Chatterjee, Dean K., and Don E. Scheid. *Ethics and Foreign Intervention.* Cambridge: Cambridge University Press, 2003.

Hayden, Patrick. "Security Beyond the State: Cosmopolitanism, Peace and the Role of Just War Theory." In *Just War Theory: A Reappraisal*, ed. M. Evans. Edinburgh: Edinburgh University Press, 2005.

Kaldor, Mary. *Global Civil Society: An Answer to War.* Cambridge: Polity Press, 2003.

Pattison, James. "Humanitarian Intervention and a Cosmopolitan UN Force." *Journal of International Political Theory* 4, no. 1 (2008): 126–45.

—— *Humanitarian Intervention and the Responsibility to Protect: Who Should Intervene?* Oxford: Oxford University Press, 2010.

Pogge, Thomas W. "An Institutional Approach to Humanitarian Intervention." *Public Affairs Quarterly* 6, no. 1 (1992): 89–103.

—— "Preempting Humanitarian Interventions." In *Freedom, Power and Political Morality*, ed. I. Carter and M. Riccardi. London: Palgrave, 2001.

Smith, William, and Robert Fine. "Anticipating a Cosmopolitan Future: The Case of Humanitarian Military Intervention." *International Politics* 44, no. 1 (2007): 72–89.

—— "Cosmopolitanism and Military Intervention." In *The Globalization of Political Violence: Globalization's Shadow*, ed. C. Hughes and R. Devetak, 46–68. London: Routledge, 2008.

Wheeler, Nicholas J. *Saving Strangers: Humanitarian Intervention in International Society.* Oxford: Oxford University Press, 2000.

Cosmopolitan Justice

One of the key tenets of cosmopolitan thought in political theory is the demand for cosmopolitan justice – often understood as global egalitarianism. Most arguments for cosmopolitan justice rely on some form of the claim that a commitment to a liberal theory of justice should lead one to the conclusion that principles of justice have global scope.

Abizadeh, Arash, and Paolo Gilabert. "Cooperation, Pervasive Impact, and Coercion: On the Scope (Not Site) of Distributive Justice." *Philosophy and Public Affairs* 35, no. 4 (2007): 318–58.

—— "Is There a Genuine Tension between Cosmopolitan Egalitarianism and Special Responsibilities?" *Philosophical Studies* 138, no. 3 (2008): 349–65.

Anderson-Gold, S. *Cosmopolitanism and Human Rights.* Cardiff: University of Wales Press, 2001.

Armstrong, Chris. "Global Egalitarianism." *Philosophy Compass* 4, no. 1 (2009): 155–71.

Arneson, Richard. "Do Patriotic Ties Limit Global Justice Duties?" *Journal of Ethics* 9, nos. 1–2 (2005): 127–50.

Barry, Brian. "Humanity and Justice in Global Perspective." In *Ethics, Economics and the Law*, ed. J. Pennock and J. Chapman. New York: Harvester Wheatsheaf, 1982.

—— "International Society from a Cosmopolitan Perspective." In *International Society: Diverse Ethical Perspectives*, ed. D. Mapel and Terry Nardin. Princeton, NJ: Princeton University Press, 1998.

—— "Spherical Justice and Global Injustice." In *Pluralism, Justice, and Equality*, ed. David Miller and Michael Walzer. Oxford: Oxford University Press, 1995.

—— "Statism and Nationalism: A Cosmopolitan Critique." In *Global Justice*, ed. Ian Shapiro and Lea Brilmayer. New York: New York University Press, 1999.

Beitz, Charles R. "Bounded Morality: Justice and the State in World Politics." *International Organisation* 33, no. 3 (1979): 405–24.

—— "Does Global Inequality Matter?" *Metaphilosophy* 32, nos. 1/2 (2001): 95–112.

—— *Political Theory and International Relations*. Princeton, NJ: Princeton University Press, 1979.

—— "Rawls's Law of Peoples." *Ethics* 110, no. 4 (2000): 669–96.

—— "Social and Cosmopolitan Liberalism." *International Affairs* 75, no. 3 (1999): 515–29.

Brock, Gillian. *Global Justice: A Cosmopolitan Account*. Oxford: Oxford University Press, 2009.

Brown, Chris. "Justice and International Order." In *International Justice*, ed. Tony Coates, 27–45. Aldershot: Ashgate, 2000.

Caney, Simon. "Cosmopolitan Justice, Responsibility and Global Climate Change." *Leiden Journal of International Law* 18, no. 4 (2005): 747–75.

—— "Cosmopolitan Justice and Equalizing Opportunities." *Metaphilosophy* 32, nos. 1/2 (2001): 113–34.

—— "Cosmopolitanism and the Law of Peoples." *Journal of Political Philosophy* 10, no. 1 (2002): 95–123.

—— "Global Distributive Justice and the State." *Political Studies* 56, no. 3 (2008).

—— "Global Justice, Rights and Climate Change." *Canadian Journal of Law and Jurisprudence* 19, no. 2 (2006): 255–78.

—— *Justice Beyond Borders: A Global Political Theory*. Oxford: Oxford University Press, 2005.

Cohen, G. A. "Where the Action Is: On the Site of Distributive Justice." *Philosophy and Public Affairs* 26, no. 1 (1997): 3–30.

Falk, R. *Human Rights Horizons: The Pursuit of Justice in a Globalizing World*. London: Routledge, 2000.

Goodin, Robert E. "Globalizing Justice." In *Taming Globalization: Frontiers of Governance*, ed. David Held and M. Koenig-Archibugi. Cambridge: Polity Press, 2003.

—— *Protecting the Vulnerable: A Reanalysis of Our Social Responsibilities*. Chicago: University of Chicago Press, 1985.

—— "What is So Special about Our Fellow Countrymen?" *Ethics* 98 (1988): 663–87.

Jones, Charles. *Global Justice: Defending Cosmopolitanism*. Oxford: Oxford University Press, 1999.

Kokaz, Nancy. "Theorizing International Fairness." In *Global Institutions and Responsibilities: Achieving Global Justice*, ed. Christian Barry and Thomas W. Pogge, 65–89. Malden, MA: Blackwell, 2005.

Moellendorf, Darrel. *Cosmopolitan Justice*. Boulder, CA: Westview Press, 2002.

—— *Global Inequality Matters*. Basingstoke: Palgrave Macmillan, 2009.

—— "Equal Respect and Global Egalitarianism." *Social Theory and Practice* 32, no. 4 (2006): 601–16.

O'Neill, Onora. "Bounded and Cosmopolitan Justice." In *How Might We Live? Global Ethics in a New Century*, ed. Ken Booth, Timothy Dunne, and Michael Cox, 45–60. Cambridge: Cambridge University Press, 2001.

—— *Bounds of Justice*. Cambridge: Cambridge University Press, 2000.

—— *Faces of Hunger: An Essay on Poverty, Justice and Development*. London: Allen & Unwin, 1986.

—— "Transnational Justice." In *Political Theory Today*, ed. David Held. Cambridge: Polity Press, 1995.

Pogge, Thomas W. "Cosmopolitanism and Sovereignty." *Ethics* 103 (1992): 48–75.

—— ed. *Freedom from Poverty as a Human Right: Who Owes What to the Very Poor?* New York: Oxford University Press, 2007.

—— "Moral Universalism and Global Economic Justice." *Politics, Philosophy & Economics* 1, no. 1 (2002): 29–58.

—— "Priorities of Global Justice." In *Global Justice*, ed. Thomas W. Pogge. Oxford: Blackwell, 2001.

—— *World Poverty and Human Rights*. Malden, MA: Blackwell, 2002.

Richards, David A. "International Distributive Justice." In *Ethics, Economics and the Law*, ed. J. Roland Pennock and John W. Chapman. New York: New York University Press, 1982.

Scheffler, Samuel. *Boundaries and Allegiances: Problems of Justice and Responsibility in Liberal Thought*. Oxford: Oxford University Press, 2001.

Shapcott, Richard. "Cosmopolitan Conversations: Justice, Dialogue and the Cosmopolitan Project." *Global Society* 6, no. 3 (2002): 221–43.

Shue, Henry. *Basic Rights: Subsistence, Affluence, and U.S. Foreign Policy*. 2nd edn. Princeton, NJ: Princeton University Press, 1996.

Tan, Kok-Chor. "Boundary Making and Equal Concern." In *Global Institutions and Responsibilities: Achieving Global Justice*, ed. Christian Barry and Thomas W. Pogge, 48–64. Malden, MA: Blackwell, 2005.

—— "The Boundary of Justice and the Justice of Boundaries: Defending Global Egalitarianism." *Canadian Journal of Law and Jurisprudence* 19, no. 2 (2006): 319–44.

——*Justice without Borders: Cosmopolitanism, Nationalism, and Patriotism*. Cambridge: Cambridge University Press, 2004.

Tasioulas, John. "Global Justice without End?" In *Global Institutions and Responsibilities: Achieving Global Justice*, ed. Christian Barry and Thomas W. Pogge, 3–28. Malden, MA: Blackwell, 2005.

Wenar, Leif. "Contractualism and Global Economic Justice." In *Global Justice*, ed. Thomas W. Pogge. Oxford: Blackwell, 2001.

Ypi, Lea L. "Statist Cosmopolitanism." *Journal of Political Philosophy* 16, no. 1 (2008): 48–71.

Criticism of cosmopolitan justice

Critics of cosmopolitan justice tend to defend nationalist and statist views, according to which individuals are not necessarily the primary units of moral concern.

Nationalist/communitarian

Nationalists and communitarians criticize liberal theories of justice for failing to recognize the fundamental ethical significance of national and cultural communities.

Cheah, Pheng, and Bruce Robbins, eds. *Cosmopolitics: Thinking and Feeling Beyond the Nation*. Minneapolis: University of Minnesota Press, 1998.

Gellner, Ernest. *Nations and Nationalism*. Oxford: Blackwell, 1983.

Kymlicka, Will. "Liberal Nationalism and Cosmopolitan Justice." In *Another Cosmopolitanism*, ed. Robert Post. Oxford: Oxford University Press, 2006.

MacIntyre, Alasdair. "Is Patriotism a Virtue?" In *Theorizing Citizenship*, ed. Ronald Beiner. Albany, NY: State University of New York Press, 1995.

Margalit, Avishai, and Joseph Raz. "National Self-Determination." *Journal of Philosophy* 87 (1990): 439–61.

McKim, Robert, and Jeff McMahan, eds. *The Morality of Nationalism*. Oxford: Oxford University Press, 1997.

Miller, David. *Citizenship and National Identity*. Cambridge: Polity Press, 2000.

—— "Justice and Boundaries." *Politics, Philosophy & Economics* 8, no. 3 (2009): 291–309.

—— "The Limits of Cosmopolitan Justice." In *International Society: Diverse Ethical Perspectives*, ed. D. Mapel and T. Nardin. Princeton, NJ: Princeton University Press, 1998.

—— *National Responsibility and Global Justice*. Oxford: Oxford University Press, 2007.

—— *On Nationality*. Oxford: Oxford University Press, 1995.

Miller, Richard W. "Cosmopolitan Respect and Patriotic Concern." *Philosophy and Public Affairs* 27 (1998): 202–24.

Sandel, Michael. *Liberalism and the Limits of Justice*. Cambridge: Cambridge University Press, 1982.

Tamir, Yael. *Liberal Nationalism*. Princeton, NJ: Princeton University Press, 1993.

Walzer, Michael. *Spheres of Justice*. New York: Basic Books, 1983.

Statist

In recent years many statist critics of cosmopolitan justice have argued that equality is only a relevant concern within certain kinds of political community, which place people in a particular type of relationship with each other.

Blake, Michael. "Distributive Justice, State Coercion, and Autonomy." *Philosophy and Public Affairs* 30, no. 3 (2001): 257–96.

Freeman, Samuel. "The Law of Peoples, Social Cooperation, Human Rights, and Distributive Justice." *Social Philosophy and Policy* 23 (2006): 29–68.

Meckled-Garcia, Saladin. "International Justice, Human Rights and Neutrality." *Res Publica* 10, no. 2 (2004): 153–74.

—— "On the Very Idea of Cosmopolitan Justice: Constructivism and International Agency." *Journal of Political Philosophy* 16, no. 3 (2008): 245–71.

Nagel, Thomas. "The Problem of Global Justice." *Philosophy and Public Affairs* 33 (2005): 113–47.

Sangiovanni, Andrea. "Global Justice, Reciprocity, and the State." *Philosophy and Public Affairs* 35 (2007): 2–39.

—— "Justice and the Priority of Politics to Morality." *Journal of Political Philosophy* 16, no. 2 (2008): 137–64.

Special obligations

One key area of dispute about justice between cosmopolitans and their critics has been the issue of special obligations to co-nationals and fellow citizens.

Abizadeh, Arash, and Paolo Gilabert. "Is There a Genuine Tension between Cosmopolitan Egalitarianism and Special Responsibilities?" *Philosophical Studies* 138, no. 3 (2008): 349–65.

Arneson, Richard. "Do Patriotic Ties Limit Global Justice Duties?" *Journal of Ethics* 9, nos. 1–2 (2005): 127–50.

Cohen, Joshua, ed. *For Love of Country: Debating the Limits of Patriotism – Martha Nussbaum and Respondents.* Cambridge: Beacon Press, 1996.

Goodin, Robert E. *Protecting the Vulnerable: A Reanalysis of Our Social Responsibilities.* Chicago: University of Chicago Press, 1985.

—— "What is So Special about Our Fellow Countrymen?" *Ethics* 98 (1988): 663–87.

Lenard, Patti Tamara. "Motivating Cosmopolitanism? A Skeptical View." *Journal of Moral Philosophy*, forthcoming.

Lenard, Patti Tamara, Christine Straehle, and Lea Ypi. "Global Solidarity." *Contemporary Political Theory* 9 (2010): 99–130.

Mason, Andrew. "Special Obligations to Compatriots." *Ethics* 107 (1997): 427–47.

Miller, David. *National Responsibility and Global Justice.* Oxford: Oxford University Press, 2007.

Scheffler, Samuel. *Boundaries and Allegiances: Problems of Justice and Responsibility in Liberal Thought.* Oxford: Oxford University Press, 2001.

Shapcott, Richard. "On Universal and Particular Obligations." *The Responsive Community* 142, no. 3 (2004): 129–31.

Waldron, Jeremy. "Special Ties and Natural Duties." *Philosophy and Public Affairs* 22 (1993): 3–30.

Rawls and Rawlsian cosmopolitanism

Rawls himself denied the claim that his theory of justice implied cosmopolitan conclusions, but many cosmopolitans have disagreed and attempted to develop a theory of cosmopolitan justice from Rawlsian premises.

Beitz, Charles R. *Political Theory and International Relations.* Princeton, NJ: Princeton University Press, 1979.

—— "Rawls's Law of Peoples." *Ethics* 110, no. 4 (2000): 669–96.

Brown, Chris. "The Construction of a Realistic Utopia: John Rawls and International Political Theory." *Review of International Studies* 28, no. 1 (2002): 5–21.

—— "John Rawls, 'The Law of Peoples,' and International Political Theory." *Ethics and International Affairs* 14 (2000): 125–32.

Buchanan, Allen. "Rawls's Law of Peoples: Rules for a Vanished Westphalian World." *Ethics* 110, no. 4 (2000): 697–721.

Cabrera, Luis. "Toleration and Tyranny in Rawls's 'Law of Peoples.'" *Polity* 34, no. 2 (2001): 163–79.

Caney, Simon. "Cosmopolitanism and the Law of Peoples." *Journal of Political Philosophy* 10, no. 1 (2002): 95–123.

—— "Survey Article: Cosmopolitanism and the Law of Peoples." *Journal of Political Philosophy* 9 (2001).

Freeman, Samuel. "The Law of Peoples, Social Cooperation, Human Rights, and Distributive Justice." *Social Philosophy and Policy* 23 (2006): 29–68.

Hayden, Patrick. *John Rawls: Toward a Just World Order.* Cardiff: University of Wales Press, 2002.

James, Aaron. "Constructing Justice for Existing Practice: Rawls and the Status Quo." *Philosophy and Public Affairs* 33 (2005): 281–316.

Kuper, Andrew. "Rawlsian Global Justice." *Political Theory* 28, no. 1 (2000): 1–10.

Martin, Rex, and David Reidy, eds. *Rawls's Law of Peoples: A Realistic Utopia?* Oxford: Blackwell, 2006.

Meckled-Garcia, Saladin. "International Justice, Human Rights and Neutrality." *Res Publica* 10, no. 2 (2004): 153–74.

Pogge, Thomas W. "Rawls and Global Justice." *Canadian Journal of Philosophy* 18, no. 2 (1988): 227–56.

—— "An Egalitarian Law of Peoples." *Philosophy and Public Affairs* 23, no. 3 (1994): 195–224.

—— *Realizing Rawls*. Ithaca: Cornell University Press, 1989.

—— *World Poverty and Human Rights*. Malden, MA: Blackwell, 2002.

Rawls, John. "Kantian Constructivism in Moral Theory: The Dewey Lectures 1980." *Journal of Philosophy* 77 (1980).

—— *The Law of Peoples*. Cambridge, MA: Harvard University Press, 1999.

—— *A Theory of Justice*. Cambridge, MA: Harvard University Press, 1971.

Reidy, David. "Rawls on International Justice: A Defence." *Political Theory* 32, no. 3 (2004): 291–319.

Wenar, Leif. "Why Rawls is Not a Cosmopolitan Egalitarian." In *Rawls's Law of Peoples: A Realistic Utopia?* ed. Rex Martin and David Reidy. Oxford: Blackwell, 2006.

Capabilities approach

As an alternative to traditional liberal theories of justice, which generally focus exclusively on the distribution of political rights and economic resources, Amartya Sen and Martha Nussbaum have placed greater emphasis on providing "functioning" background conditions that enhance the capabilities of individuals. By doing so, the capability approach claims to provide greater normative clarity and direction for liberal and cosmopolitan schemes of distributive justice.

Alexander, John. "Capability Egalitarianism and Moral Selfhood." *Ethical Perspectives* 10, no. 1 (2003): 3–21.

Nussbaum, Martha C. "Beyond the Social Contract: Capabilities and Global Justice." In *The Political Philosophy of Cosmopolitanism*, ed. Gillian Brock and Harry Brighouse. Cambridge: Cambridge University Press, 2005.

—— *Women and Human Development: The Capabilities Approach*. Cambridge: Cambridge University Press, 2000.

Nussbaum, Martha C., and J. Glover, eds. *Women, Culture and Development: A Study of Human Capabilities*. Oxford: Oxford University Press, 1995.

O'Neill, Onora. "Justice, Capabilities, and Vulnerabilities." In *Women, Culture and Development: A Study of Human Capabilities*, ed. Martha C. Nussbaum and J. Glover. Oxford: Oxford University Press, 1995.

Robeyns, Ingrid. "Assessing Global Poverty and Inequality: Income, Resources, and Capabilities." In *Global Institutions and Responsibilities: Achieving Global Justice*, ed. Christian Barry and Thomas W. Pogge, 29–47. Malden, MA: Blackwell, 2005.

Sen, Amartya. *Development as Freedom*. Oxford: Oxford University Press, 1999.

—— *The Idea of Justice*. Cambridge, MA: Harvard University Press, 2009.

—— *Inequality Re-examined*. 3rd edn. Oxford: Oxford University Press, 1995.

Feminist approaches to global justice

Unfortunately cosmopolitans have so far tended to neglect specifically feminist issues, but some feminists have begun to consider the issue of global justice from the perspective of women, paying specific attention to the question of women's human rights.

Brown Thompson, Karen. "Women's Rights are Human Rights." In *Restructuring World Politics: Transnational Social Movements, Networks, and Norms*, ed. Sanjeev Khagram, James V. Riker, and Kathryn Sikkink. Minneapolis: University of Minnesota Press, 2002.

Bunch, Charlotte. "Women's Rights as Human Rights: Towards a Re-vision of Human Rights." *Human Rights Quarterly* 12 (1990): 486–98.

Held, Virginia. *The Ethics of Care: Personal, Political, and Global*. Oxford: Oxford University Press, 2006.

Hutchings, Kimberley. "Towards a Feminist International Ethics." In *How Might We Live? Global Ethics in a New Century*, ed. Ken Booth, Timothy Dunne, and Michael Cox. Cambridge: Cambridge University Press, 2001.

Jagger, Alison M. "Globalizing Feminist Ethics." In *Decentering the Center: Philosophy for a Multicultural, Postcolonial, and Feminist World*. Bloomington, IN: Indiana University Press, 2000.

Nussbaum, Martha C. "Beyond the Social Contract: Capabilities and Global Justice." In *The Political Philosophy of Cosmopolitanism*, ed. Gillian Brock and Harry Brighouse. Cambridge: Cambridge University Press, 2005.

—— *Women and Human Development: The Capabilities Approach*. Cambridge: Cambridge University Press, 2000.

Nussbaum, Martha C., and J. Glover, eds. *Women, Culture and Development: A Study of Human Capabilities*. Oxford: Oxford University Press, 1995.

Okin, Susan Moller. "Feminism, Women's Human Rights, and Cultural Differences." In *Decentering the Center: Philosophy for a Multicultural, Postcolonial, and Feminist World*. Bloomington, IN: Indiana University Press, 2000.

Reilly, Niamh. "Cosmopolitan Feminism and Human Rights." *Hypatia* 22, no. 4 (2007): 180–98.

Robinson, Fiona. *Globalizing Care: Ethics, Feminist Theory, and International Relations*. Boulder, CO: Westview Press, 1999.

Environmental justice

Another issue that has been paid little attention is the question of environmental justice, particularly in relation to the problem of anthropogenic climate change. However, some cosmopolitans have recently begun to consider this issue.

Caney, Simon. "Cosmopolitan Justice, Responsibility and Global Climate Change." *Leiden Journal of International Law* 18, no. 4 (2005): 747–75.

—— "Global Justice, Rights and Climate Change." *Canadian Journal of Law and Jurisprudence* 19, no. 2 (2006): 255–78.

Gardiner, Stephen. "Ethics and Global Climate Change." *Ethics* 114 (2004): 555–600.

—— "The Real Tragedy of the Commons." *Philosophy & Public Affairs* 30 (2001): 387–416.

Hayden, Patrick. *Cosmopolitan Global Politics*. Aldershot: Ashgate, 2005.

Hayward, Tim. "Human Rights vs. Emissions Rights." *Ethics and International Affairs* 21, no. 4 (2007): 431–50.

Linklater, Andrew. "Cosmopolitanism." In *Political Theory and the Ecological Challenge*, ed. Andrew Dobson and Robyn Eckersley. Cambridge: Cambridge University Press, 2006.

Young, Oran. *International Governance: Protecting the Environment in a Stateless Society*. Ithaca: Cornell University Press, 1994.

Political and Institutional Cosmopolitanism

Cosmopolitanism has both a moral and an institutional dimension. Whereas moral cosmopolitanism tends to explore what moral obligations we have toward all humanity, institutional approaches tend to deal more directly with questions about political and institutional structures. These questions generally concern debates about what political structures we should have and seek to explore questions about whether we should move toward a world state, a minimal federation of cosmopolitan states, or a more middle-ground system of global governance.

Barry, Christian, and Thomas W. Pogge, eds. *Global Institutions and Responsibilities: Achieving Social Justice*. Malden, MA: Blackwell, 2005.

Beardsworth, Richard. *Cosmopolitanism and International Relations*. Cambridge: Polity Press, 2010.

—— "The Future of Critical Philosophy and World Politics." In *Derrida: Negotiating the Legacy*, ed. M. Fagan et al. Edinburgh: Edinburgh University Press, 2007.

—— "Tragedy, World Politics and Ethical Community." In *Tragedy and International Relations*, ed. N. Lebow and T. Erskine. London: Macmillan, 2010.

Beck, Ulrich. *Power in the Global Age*. Cambridge: Polity Press, 2006.

Beitz, Charles R. "Cosmopolitan Liberalism and the States System." In *Political Restructuring in Europe: Ethical Perspectives*, ed. Chris Brown. London: Routledge, 1994.

Bohman, James. "Cosmopolitan Republicanism." *The Monist* 84 (2001): 3–22.

Brennan, T. "Cosmopolitanism and Internationalism." *New Left Review* 7 (2001): 75–84.

Brown, Chris. "Justice and International Order." In *International Justice*, ed. Tony Coates, 27–45. Aldershot: Ashgate, 2000.

Cabrera, Luis. *Political Theory of Global Justice: A Cosmopolitan Case for the World State.* London: Routledge, 2004.

Caney, Simon. "Cosmopolitan Justice and Institutional Design: An Egalitarian Liberal Conception of Global Governance." *Social Theory and Practice* 32, no. 4 (2006): 725–56.

Copp, David. "International Justice and the Basic Needs Principle." In *The Political Philosophy of Cosmopolitanism*, ed. Gillian Brock and Harry Brighouse, 39–54. Cambridge: Cambridge University Press, 2005.

Falk, R. *On Humane Governance: Towards a New Global Politics.* University Park: Pennsylvania University Press, 1995.

Franceschet, Antonio. "Justice and International Organization: Two Models of Global Governance." *Global Governance* 8, no. 1 (2002): 19–34.

Franck, Thomas M. *The Power of Legitimacy among Nations.* Oxford: Oxford University Press, 1990.

Habermas, Jurgen. *The Post-National Constellation.* Cambridge: Polity Press, 2001.

Harvey, David. *Cosmopolitanism and the Geographies of Freedom.* New York: Columbia University Press, 2009.

Hayden, Patrick. *Cosmopolitan Global Politics.* Aldershot: Ashgate, 2005.

Held, David, and M. Koenig-Archibugi, eds. *Global Governance and Public Accountability.* Oxford: Blackwell, 2005.

MacDonald, Terry, and Raffaele Marchetti, eds. "Symposium on Global Political Representation." *Ethics and International Affairs* 24, no. 1 (2010).

Pogge, Thomas W. "Cosmopolitanism and Sovereignty." *Ethics* 103 (1992): 48–75.

Santos, Boaventura de Sousa, and Jane Jensen, eds. *Globalizing Institutions.* Aldershot: Ashgate, 2000.

Shaw, M. *Theory of the Global State: Globality as Unfinished Revolution.* Cambridge: Cambridge University Press, 2000.

Tinnevelt, Ronald, and Gert Verschraegen, eds. *Between Cosmopolitan Ideals and State Sovereignty.* Basingstoke: Palgrave, 2006.

Weinstock, Daniel M., ed. *Global Justice, Global Institutions.* Calgary, Alta.: University of Calgary Press, 2007.

Zurn, M. "Democratic Governance Beyond the Nation-State." *European Journal of International Relations* 62 (2000): 183–221.

—— "Political Systems in the Post-National Constellation: Societal Denationalization and Multilevel Governance." In *Global Governance and the United Nations System*, ed. V. Rittberger. New York: United Nations University Press, 2002.

—— "Societal Denationalization and Positive Governance." In *Towards a Global Polity*, ed. R. Higgot and M. Ougaard. London: Routledge, 2002.

Cosmopolitan citizenship

Cabrera, Luis. *The Practice of Global Citizenship.* Cambridge: Cambridge University Press, 2010.

Delanty, Gerard. *Citizenship in a Global Age.* Buckingham: Open University Press, 2000.

Dower, Nigel. *An Introduction to Global Citizenship.* Edinburgh: Edinburgh University Press, 2003.

—— "The Idea of Global Citizenship – A Sympathetic Assessment." *Global Society* 14, no. 4 (2000): 553–67.

Dower, Nigel, and J. Williams, eds. *Global Citizenship: A Critical Reader.* Edinburgh: Edinburgh University Press, 2002.

Falk, R. "The Making of Global Citizenship." In *The Condition of Citizenship*, ed. B. v. Steenbergen. London: Sage, 1994.

Heater, Derek. *World Citizenship: Cosmopolitan Thinking and its Opponents.* London: Continuum, 2004.

Hutchings, Kimberley, and R. Dannreuther. *Cosmopolitan Citizenship.* London: Macmillan, 1999.

Linklater, Andrew. "Cosmopolitan Citizenship." *Citizenship Studies* 21 (1998): 113–37.

MacCunn, John. "Cosmopolitan Duties." *International Journal of Ethics* 9, no. 2 (1899): 152–68.

O'Byrne, Darren. *The Dimensions of Global Citizenship: Political Identity Beyond the Nation-State.* London: Frank Cass, 2003.

Rotblat, J., ed. *World Citizenship*. London: Macmillan, 1995.

Smith, William. "Cosmopolitan Citizenship: Virtue, Irony, and Worldliness." *European Journal of Social Theory* 10, no. 1 (2007): 37–52.

Soysal, Y. S. "Towards a Postnational Model of Citizenship." In *The Citizenship Debates: A Reader*, ed. G. Shafir. Minneapolis: University of Minnesota Press, 1998.

Thompson, Janna. "Planetary Citizenship: The Definition and Defence of an Ideal." In *Governing for the Environment: Global Problems, Ethics and Democracy*, ed. Brenda Gleeson and Nicholas Low. Houndmills: Palgrave, 2001.

Turner, B. S. "The Erosion of Citizenship." *British Journal of Sociology* 52, no. 2 (2001): 189–209.

—— "National Identities and Cosmopolitan Virtues: Citizenship in a Global Age." In *Beyond Nationalism? Sovereignty and Citizenship*, ed. F. Dallmayr and J. M. Rosales. Lanham, MD: Lexington Books, 2001.

Criticism of cosmopolitan citizenship

Chandler, David. "Critiquing Liberal Cosmopolitanism? The Limits of the Biopolitical Approach." *International Political Sociology*, 3, no. 1 (2009): 53–70.

Kymlicka, Will. "Citizenship in an Era of Globalization." In *Democracy's Edges*, ed. I. Shapiro and C. Hacker-Cordon. Cambridge: Cambridge University Press, 1999.

Miller, David. "Bounded Citizenship." In *Cosmopolitan Citizenship*, ed. Kimberley Hutchings and Roland Dannreuther. London: Macmillan, 1999.

Parekh, Bhikhu. "Cosmopolitanism and Global Citizenship." *Review of International Studies* 29, no. 1 (2003): 3–17.

Young, Iris Marion. "Polity and Group Difference: A Critique of the Ideal of Universal Citizenship." *Ethics* 99 (1989): 253–74.

Cosmopolitan democracy

Archibugi, Daniele, ed. "Global Democracy: A Symposium on a New Political Hope." *New Political Science* 32, no. 1 (2010): 83–121.

—— *The Global Commonwealth of Citizens: Towards Cosmopolitan Democracy*. Princeton, NJ: Princeton University Press, 2008.

Archibugi, Daniele, Mathias Koenig-Archibugi, and Raffaele Marchetti, eds. *Global Democracy: Normative and Empirical Perspectives*. Cambridge: Cambridge University Press, forthcoming 2010.

Archibugi, Daniele, and David Held, eds. *Cosmopolitan Democracy: An Agenda for a New World Order*. Cambridge: Polity Press, 1995.

Archibugi, Daniele, David Held, and M. Kohler, eds. *Re-Imagining Political Community. Studies in Cosmopolitan Democracy*. Cambridge: Polity Press, 1998.

Benhabib, Seyla. "Democratic Iterations: The Local, the National, and the Global." In *Another Cosmopolitanism*, ed. Robert Post. Oxford: Oxford University Press, 2006.

Bohman, James. *Democracy across Borders*. Cambridge, MA: MIT Press, 2007.

Cavallero, Eric. "Federative Global Democracy." *Metaphilosophy* 40, no. 1 (2009): 42–64.

Chatterjee, Deen. "The Conflicting Loyalties of Statism and Globalism: Can Global Democracy Resolve the Liberal Conundrum?" *Metaphilosophy* 40, no. 1 (2009): 65–76.

De Schutter, Helder, and Ronald Tinnevelt. "Is Liberal Nationalism Incompatible with Global Democracy?" *Metaphilosophy* 40, no. 1 (2009): 109–30.

Delanty, G. "The Idea of a Cosmopolitan Europe." *International Review of Sociology* 15, no. 3 (2005): 405–21.

Dryzek, John. *Deliberative Democracy and Beyond*. Oxford: Oxford University Press, 2000.

—— *Deliberative Global Politics: Discourse and Democracy in a Divided World*. Cambridge: Polity Press, 2006.

—— "Transnational Democracy." *Journal of Political Philosophy* 7, no. 1 (1999).

Gagnon, Alain-G., and James Tully, eds. *Multinational Democracies*. Cambridge: Cambridge University Press, 2001.

Gould, Carol C. *Globalizing Democracy and Human Rights*. Cambridge: Cambridge University Press, 2004.

—— "Structuring Global Democracy: Political Communities, Universal Human Rights, and Transnational Representation." *Metaphilosophy* 40, no. 1 (2009): 24–41.

Held, David. *Cosmopolitanism: A Defence*. Cambridge: Polity Press, 2003.

—— *Democracy and the Global Order: From the Modern State to Cosmopolitan Governance*. Stanford: Stanford University Press, 1995.

—— *Global Covenant: The Social Democratic Alternative to the Washington Consensus.* Malden, MA: Polity Press, 2004.

Holden, B., ed. *Global Democracy: Key Debates.* London: Routledge, 2000.

Koenig-Archibugi, Mathias. "Is Global Democracy Possible?" *European Journal of International Relations* (forthcoming 2010).

Kuper, Andrew. *Democracy Beyond Borders: Justice and Representation in Global Institutions.* New York: Oxford University Press, 2006.

List, Christian, and Mathias Koenig-Archibugi. "Can There Be a Global Demos? An Agency Based Approach." *Philosophy and Public Affairs* 38, no. 1 (2010): 76–110.

MacDonald, Terry. *Global Stakeholder Democracy: Power and Representation Beyond Liberal States.* Oxford: Oxford University Press, 2008.

Marchetti, Raffaele. "EU as a Cosmopolitan Model for Global Democracy?" In *EU and Global Democracy,* ed. Raffaele Marchetti and D. Vidovic. Zagreb: CPI, 2010.

—— *Global Democracy: For and Against: Ethical Theory, Institutional Design and Social Struggles.* New York: Routledge, 2008.

McGrew, Anthony. "Transnational Democracy." In *Democratic Theory Today,* ed. A. Carter and G. Stokes. Cambridge: Polity Press, 2002.

Monbiot, George. *The Age of Consent: A Manifesto for a New World Order.* New York: The New Press, 2004.

Shapcott, Richard. "Global Justice and Cosmopolitan Democracy." In *An Introduction to International Relations: Australian Perspectives,* ed. A. Burke and J. George. Cambridge: Cambridge University Press, 2007.

Stevenson, N. "Cosmopolitanism and the Future of Democracy." *New Political Economy* 7 (2002): 251–67.

Thompson, Dennis F. "Democratic Theory and Global Society." *Journal of Political Philosophy* 7, no. 2 (1999).

Warren, Mark. "Deliberative Democracy." In *Democratic Theory Today,* ed. A. Carter and G. Stokes. Cambridge: Polity Press, 2002.

Weinstock, Daniel. "Motivating the Global Demos." *Metaphilosophy* 40, no. 1 (2009): 92–108.

Young, Iris Marion. "Self-Determination and Global Democracy: A Critique of Liberal Nationalism." In *Designing Democratic Institutions,* ed. Ian Shapiro and Stephen Macedo. New York: New York University Press, 2000.

Zurn, M. "Democratic Governance Beyond the Nation-State." *European Journal of International Relations* 62 (2000): 183–221.

Criticism of cosmopolitan democracy

Bohman, James. "International Regimes and Democratic Governance: Political Equality and Influence in Global Institutions." *International Affairs* 75, no. 3 (1999): 499–513.

Dahl, Robert. "Can International Organizations Be Democratic? A Skeptical View." In *Democracy's Edges,* ed. Ian Shapiro and Casiano Hacker-Cordon. Cambridge: Cambridge University Press, 1999.

Gorg, C., and G. Hirsch. "Is International Democracy Possible?" *Review of International Political Economy* 5, no. 4 (1998): 458–615.

Schmitter, P. "The Future of Democracy: Could It Be a Matter of Scale?" *Social Research* 66, no. 3 (1999): 933–58.

Thaa, Winfred. "Lean Citizenship: The Fading Away of the Political in Transnational Democracy." *European Journal of International Relations* 7, no. 4 (2001): 503–24.

Urbanati, Nadia. "Can Cosmopolitan Democracy Be Democratic?" In *Debating Cosmopolitics,* ed. Daniele Archibugi. London: Verso, 2003.

Wendt, A. "A Comment on Held's Cosmopolitanism." In *Democracy's Edges,* ed. Ian Shapiro and Casiano Hacker-Cordon. Cambridge: Cambridge University Press, 1999.

Zolo, D. *Cosmopolis: Prospects for World Government,* trans. David McKie. Cambridge: Polity Press, 1997.

Cosmopolitan law

Archibugi, D. "Immanuel Kant, Cosmopolitan Law, and Peace." *European Journal of International Relations* 1, no. 4 (1995): 429–56.

Brown, Garrett Wallace. *Grounding Cosmopolitanism: From Kant to the Idea of a Cosmopolitan Constitution.* Edinburgh: Edinburgh University Press, 2009.

—— "Moving from Cosmopolitan Legal Theory to Legal Practice: Models of Cosmopolitan Law." *Legal Studies* 28, no. 3 (2008): 430–51.

Buchanan, Allen. *Justice, Legitimacy, and Self-Determination: Moral Foundations for International Law*. New York: Oxford University Press, 2004.

Capps, Patrick. *Human Dignity and the Foundations of International Law*. Oxford: Hart Publishing, 2009.

Falk, R. *Law in an Emerging Global Village: A Post-Westphalian Perspective*. Ardsley: Transnational Publishers, 1998.

de Sousa Santos, Boaventura, and Cesar A. Rodriguez-Garavito, eds. *Law and Globalization from Below: Towards a Cosmopolitan Legality*. Cambridge: Cambridge University Press, 2005.

Franceschet, Antonio. "Cosmopolitan Ethics and Global Legalism." *Journal of Global Ethics*, 1, no. 2 (2005).

—— "Four Cosmopolitan Projects: The International Criminal Court in Context." In *Governance, Order and the International Criminal Court: Between Realpolitik and a Cosmopolitan Court*, ed. Steven Roach. Oxford: Oxford University Press, 2009.

—— "Global(izing) Justice?: The International Criminal Court." In *Bringing Power to Justice? The Prospects for the International Criminal Court*, ed. J. Harrington, M. Milde, and R. Vernon. McGill: Queens University Press, 2006.

Hayden, Patrick. "Political Evil, Cosmopolitan Realism, and the Normative Ambivalence of the International Criminal Court." In *Governance, Order, and the International Criminal Court: Between Realpolitik and a Cosmopolitan Court*, ed. Steven Roach. Oxford: Oxford University Press, 2009.

Held, David. "The Changing Structure of International Law: Sovereignty Transformed?" In *The Global Transformations Reader: An Introduction to the Globalization Debate*, ed. David Held and A. McGrew. Cambridge: Polity Press, 2003.

Hirsh, D. *Law against Genocide: Cosmopolitan Trials*. London: The Glasshouse Press, 2003.

Kleingeld, Pauline. "Kant's Cosmopolitan Law: World Citizenship for a Global Order." *Kantian Review* 2 (1998): 72–90.

Teson, Fernando. *A Philosophy of International Law*. Boulder, CO: Westview Press, 1998.

Waldron, Jeremy. "Cosmopolitan Norms." In *Another Cosmopolitanism*, ed. Robert Post. Oxford: Oxford University Press, 2006.

Zurn, M., and C. Joerges, eds. *Law and Governance in Postnational Europe: Compliance Beyond the Nation-State*. Cambridge: Cambridge University Press, 2006.

Global governance

Cox, Robert W., and Timothy J. Sinclair. *Approaches to World Order*. Cambridge: Cambridge University Press, 1996.

Czempiel, E., and J. Rosenau, eds. *Governance without Government: Order and Change in World Politics*. Cambridge: Cambridge University Press, 1992.

Franceschet, Antonio. "Justice and International Organization: Two Models of Global Governance." *Global Governance* 8, no. 1 (2002): 19–34.

—— ed. *The Ethics of Global Governance*. Boulder, CO: Lynne Rienner Publishing, 2009.

Glossop, Ronald J. *World Federation? A Critical Analysis of Federal World Government*. Durham, NC: McFarland & Company, 1993.

Held, David, and A. McGrew, eds. *Governing Globalization: Power, Authority and Global Governance*. Cambridge: Polity Press, 2002.

Koenig-Archibugi, M., and David Held, eds. *Taming Globalization: Frontiers of Governance*. Cambridge: Polity Press, 2003.

Marchetti, Raffaele. "Global Governance or World Federalism? A Cosmopolitan Dispute on Institutional Models." *Global Society* 20, no. 3 (2006): 287–305.

Nye, S., and J. D. Donahue, eds. *Governance in a Globalizing World*. Washington, DC: Brookings Institution Press, 2000.

O'Brien, Robert, Anne Marie Goetz, Jan Aart Scholte, and Marc Williams. *Contesting Global Governance: Multilateral Economic Institutions and Global Social Movements*. Cambridge: Cambridge University Press, 2000.

Reinicke, Wolfgang H. *Global Public Policy: Governing without Government?* Washington, DC: Brookings Institution Press, 1998.

Rosenau, James N. *Along the Domestic–Foreign Frontier: Exploring Governance in a Turbulent World*. Cambridge: Cambridge University Press, 1997.

Shapcott, Richard. "Solidarism and After: Global Governance, International Society and the Normative Turn in International Relations." *Pacifica Review* 12, no. 3 (2000): 309–20.

Smith, William, and James Brassett. "Deliberation and Global Governance: Liberal, Cosmopolitan and Critical Perspectives." *Ethics and International Affairs* 22, no. 1 (2008): 69–92.

Taylor, Charles. *Toward World Sovereignty*. Lanham, MD: University Press of America, 2002.

Security

Deudney, Daniel H. *Bounding Power: Security Theory from the Polis to the Global Village*. Princeton, NJ: Princeton University Press, 2007.

Cultural Cosmopolitanism

Abizadeh, Arash. "Does Collective Identity Presuppose an Other? On the Alleged Incoherence of Global Solidarity." *American Political Science Review* 99, no. 1 (2005): 45–60.

Bartelson, Jens. *Visions of World Community*. Cambridge: Cambridge University Press, 2009.

Benhabib, Seyla. *The Claims of Culture: Equality and Diversity in the Global Era*. Princeton, NJ: Princeton University Press, 2002.

Breckenridge, Carol, ed. *Cosmopolitanism*. Durham: Duke University Press, 2002.

Brennan, T. *At Home in the World: Cosmopolitanism Now*. Cambridge, MA: Harvard University Press, 1997.

Connolly, W. E. "Speed, Concentric Cultures, and Cosmopolitanism." *Political Theory* 285 (2000): 596–618.

Fabre, Cecile, and David Miller. "Justice and Culture: Rawls, Sen, Nussbaum and O'Neill." *Political Studies Review* 1 (2003): 1–17.

Geertz, Charles. *The Interpretation of Cultures*. New York: Basic Books, 1973.

Lyotard, Jean François. *The Postmodern Condition: A Report of Human Knowledge*, trans. G. Bennington. Minneapolis: University of Minnesota Press, 1984.

Nava, M. "Cosmopolitan Modernity: Everyday Imaginaries and the Register of Difference." *Theory, Culture, and Society* 191, no. 2 (2002): 81–99.

Nowicka, Magdalena, and Maria Rovisco, eds. *Cosmopolitanism in Practice*. Farnham: Ashgate, 2009.

Post, Robert, ed. *Another Cosmopolitanism*. Oxford: Oxford University Press, 2006.

Szerszynski, B., and J. Urry. "Cultures of Cosmopolitanism." *The Sociological Review* 504 (2000): 461–81.

Waldron, Jeremy. "Minority Cultures and the Cosmopolitan Alternative." In *The Rights of Minority Cultures*, ed. Will Kymlicka. Oxford: Oxford University Press, 1995.

—— "What is Cosmopolitan?" *Journal of Political Philosophy* 8, no 2 (1999): 227–43.

Multiculturalism, communitarianism, and the limits of universalism

Avineri, S., and Avner de-Shalit, eds. *Communitarianism and Individualism*. Oxford: Oxford University Press, 1992.

Barry, Brian. *Culture and Equality*. Cambridge, MA: Harvard University Press, 2002.

Chandler, David. "Critiquing Liberal Cosmopolitanism? The Limits of the Biopolitical Approach." *International Political Sociology*, 3, no. 1 (2009): 53–70.

Cook, John. *Morality and Cultural Differences*. Oxford: Oxford University Press, 1999.

Grillo, R. *Pluralism and the Politics of Difference: State, Culture and Ethnicity in Comparative Perspective*. Oxford: Clarendon Press, 1998.

Habermas, Jurgen. "A Political Constitution for the Pluralist World Society." In J. Habermas, *Between Naturalism and Religion*. Cambridge: Polity Press, 2008.

Kelly, Paul, ed. *Multiculturalism Revisited*. Cambridge: Polity Press, 2002.

Kukathas, Chandran. *The Liberal Archipelago: A Theory of Diversity and Freedom*. Oxford: Oxford University Press, 2003.

Kymlicka, Will. *Politics in the Vernacular: Nationalism, Multiculturalism and Citizenship*. Oxford: Oxford University Press, 2001.

—— *The Rights of Minority Cultures*. Oxford: Oxford University Press, 1995.

Lenard, Patti Tamara, Christine Straehle, and Lea Ypi. "Global Solidarity." *Contemporary Political Theory* 9 (2010): 99–130.

Muthu, Sankar. *Enlightenment Against Empire*. Princeton, NJ: Princeton University Press, 2003.

Parekh, Bhiku. "Non-Ethnocentric Universalism." In *Human Rights in Global Politics*, ed. T. Dunn and N. Wheeler. Cambridge: Cambridge University Press, 1999.

—— *Rethinking Multiculturalism*. Basingstoke: Palgrave, 2000.

Pogge, Thomas W. "Moral Universalism and Global Economic Justice." *Politics, Philosophy & Economics* 1, no. 1 (2002): 29–58.

Sen, Amartya. *Human Rights and Asian Values*. New York: Carnegie Council on Ethics and International Affairs, 1997.

Shapcott, Richard. "Anti-Cosmopolitanism, Pluralism and the Cosmopolitan Harm Principle." *Review of International Studies*, 34, no. 2 (2008): 185–205.

—— "Dialogue and International Ethics: Religion, Cultural Diversity and Universalism." In *The Ashgate Research Companion to Ethics and International Relations*, ed. Patrick Hayden. Surrey: Ashgate, 2009.

Taylor, Charles. "Atomism." In *Communitarianism and Individualism*, ed. S. Avineri and Avner de-Shalit, 29–50. Oxford: Oxford University Press, 1992.

—— *Philosophical Arguments*. Cambridge, MA: Harvard University Press, 1995.

Tully, James. *Strange Multiplicity*. Cambridge: Cambridge University Press, 1995.

Turner, Terence. "Anthropology and Multiculturalism: What is Anthropology and What Multiculturalists Should Be Mindful Of?" *Cultural Anthropology* 8, no. 4 (1993): 411–29.

Waldron, Jeremy. "Minority Cultures and the Cosmopolitan Alternative." *University of Michigan Journal of Law Reform* 25 (1992): 751–93.

Walzer, Michael. "Pluralism: A Political Perspective." In *The Rights of Minority Cultures*, ed. Will Kymlicka. Oxford: Oxford University Press, 1995.

Young, Iris Marion. *Justice and Politics of Difference*. Princeton, NJ: Princeton University Press, 1990.

Cosmopolitan sociology

Anker, C. v. d. "Introduction: The Need for an Integrated Cosmopolitan Agenda." *Global Society* 144 (2000): 479–85.

Beck, Ulrich. "The Cosmopolitan Perspective: Sociology in the Second Age of Modernity." *British Journal of Sociology* 151 (2000): 79–106.

—— "The Cosmopolitan Society and Its Enemies." *Theory, Culture, and Society* 191–2 (2002): 17–44.

—— *The Cosmopolitan Vision*, trans. and ed. Ciaran Cronin. Cambridge: Polity Press, 2006.

—— "The Truth of Others: A Cosmopolitan Approach." *Common Knowledge* 10 (2004): 430–49.

—— *World Risk Society*. Cambridge: Polity Press, 1999.

Chandler, David. "Critiquing Liberal Cosmopolitanism? The Limits of the Biopolitical Approach." *International Political Sociology*, 3, no. 1 (2009): 53–70.

Fine, Robert. *Cosmopolitanism*. Abingdon: Routledge, 2007.

Kurasawa, Fuyuki. *The Work of Global Justice: Human Rights as Practices*. Cambridge: Cambridge University Press, 2007.

Touraine, A. "Sociology without Societies." *Current Sociology* 512 (2003): 123–31.

Urry, J. *Sociology Beyond Societies*. London: Routledge, 2000.

Cosmopolitan education

Harris, L. "The Cosmopolitan Illusion." *Policy Review* 118 (2003).

Nussbaum, Martha C. *Cultivating Humanity*. Cambridge: Cambridge University Press, 1998.

—— "Patriotism and Cosmopolitanism." In *For Love of Country: Debating the Limits of Patriotism*, ed. Joshua Cohen. Boston: Beacon Press, 1996.

—— "Toward a Globally Sensitive Patriotism." *Daedalus* 137, no. 3 (2008): 78–93.

Habermas

Fine, Robert, and William Smith. "Jürgen Habermas' Theory of Cosmopolitanism." *Constellations* 10, no. 4 (2003): 469–87.

Habermas, Jurgen. *Between Facts and Norms*, trans. W. Rehg. Cambridge: Polity Press, 1996.

—— *Between Naturalism and Religion*, trans. Ciaran Cronin. Cambridge: Cambridge University Press, 2008.

—— *The Divided West*, trans. and ed. Ciaran Cronin. Cambridge: Cambridge University Press, 2006.

—— "Kant's Idea of Perpetual Peace, with the Benefit of Two Hundred Years' Hindsight." In *Perpetual Peace: Essays on Kant's Cosmopolitan Ideal*, ed. James Bohman and Matthias Lutz-Bachmann. Cambridge, MA: MIT Press, 1997.

—— *The Post-National Constellation*. Cambridge: Polity Press, 2001.

Mertens, T. "Cosmopolitanism and Citizenship: Kant against Habermas." *European Journal of Philosophy* 4 (1996): 328–47.

Scheurman, W. "Global Governance without Global Government?" *Political Theory* 36, no. 1 (2008): 133–51.

Immigration

Barry, Brian, and Robert E. Goodin, eds. *Free Movement: Ethical Issues in the Transnational Migration of People and Money*. University Park, PA: Pennsylvania State University Press, 1992.

Benhabib, Seyla. *The Rights of Others: Aliens, Residents and Citizens*. Cambridge: Cambridge University Press, 2004.

Cabrera, Luis. "An Archaeology of Borders: Qualitative Political Theory as a Tool in Addressing Moral Distance." *Journal of Global Ethics* 5, no. 2 (2008): 109–23.

Carens, Joseph. "Aliens and Citizens: The Case for Open Borders." In *The Rights of Minority Cultures*, ed. Will Kymlicka. Oxford: Oxford University Press, 1995.

—— "Realistic and Idealistic Approaches to the Ethics of Migration." *International Migration Review* 30, no. 1 (1996).

—— "Refugees and the Limits of Obligations." *Public Affairs Quarterly* 63, no. 1 (1992).

—— "The Rights of Immigrants." In *Group Rights*, ed. Judith Baker. Toronto: University of Toronto Press, 1993.

—— "States and Refugees: A Normative Analysis." In *Refugee Policy in Canada and the United States*, ed. Howard Adelman. Toronto: York University Press, 1991.

Exdell, John. "Immigration, Nationalism, and Human Rights." *Metaphilosophy* 40, no. 1 (2009): 131–46.

Global civil society

Anheier, H., M. Glasius, and M. Kaldor, eds. *Global Civil Society*. Oxford: Oxford University Press, 2005.

Baker, Gideon. "Saying Global Civil Society with Rights." In *Human Rights: Critical Concepts in Political Science*, ed. R. Falk, H. Elver, and L. Hajjar. London: Routledge, 2007.

—— "Problems in the Theorisation of Global Civil Society." *Political Studies* 50, no. 5 (2002): 928–43.

Baker, Gideon, and David Chandler, eds. *Global Civil Society: Contested Futures*. London: Routledge, 2005.

Brown, Chris. "Cosmopolitanism, World Citizenship and Global Civil Society." *Critical Review of International Social and Political Philosophy* 31 (2000): 7–26.

Cohen, R., and S. Rai, eds. *Global Social Movements*. London: Athlone, 2000.

Delanty, Gerard. "Cosmopolitanism and Violence: The Limits of Global Civil Society." *European Journal of Social Theory* 41 (2001): 41–52.

Kaldor, Mary. *Global Civil Society: An Answer to War*. Cambridge: Polity Press, 2003.

Keck, M. E., and K. Sikkink. *Activists Beyond Borders: Advocacy Networks in International Politics*. Ithaca: Cornell University Press, 1998.

Smith, J., C. Chatfield, and R. Pagnucco, eds. *Transnational Social Movements and Global Politics: Solidarity Beyond the State*. Syracuse: Syracuse University Press, 1997.

Cosmopolitan hospitality

Baker, Gideon. "Cosmopolitanism as Hospitality: Revisiting Identity and Difference in Cosmopolitanism." *Alternatives* 34, no. 2 (2009): 107–28.

—— "The Double Law of Hospitality: Rethinking Cosmopolitan Ethics in Humanitarian Intervention." *International Relations* 24, no. 1 (2010).

—— "The Politics of Hospitality: Sovereignty and Ethics in Political Community." In *The Future of Political Community*, ed. G. Baker and J. Bartelson, 51–69. London: Routledge, 2008.

—— "The Spectre of Montezuma: Hospitality and Haunting." *Millennium: Journal of International Relations* 39, no. 1 (2010).

Benhabib, Seyla. *The Rights of Others*. Cambridge: Cambridge University Press, 2004.

Brown, Garrett Wallace. "The Laws of Hospitality, Asylum Seekers and Cosmopolitan Right: A Kantian Response to Jacques Derrida." *European Journal of Political Theory*, 9, no. 3 (2010): 1–20.

Cavallar, Georg. *The Rights of Strangers*. Aldershot: Ashgate, 2002.

Derrida, Jacques. "Foreign Question." In *Of Hospitality*. Stanford: Stanford University Press, 2000.

—— "On Cosmopolitanism." In *On Cosmopolitanism and Forgiveness*. London: Routledge, 2002.

—— "The Principle of Hospitality." *Parallax* 11, no. 1 (2005): 6–9.

Dikec, M. "Pera Peras Poros: Longings for Spaces of Hospitality." *Theory, Culture, and Society* 19, nos. 1–2 (2002): 227–47.

Doty, R. "Fronteras Compasivas and the Ethics of Unconditional Hospitality." *Millennium: Journal of International Relations* 35, no. 1 (2006): 53–74.

Onuf, N. "Friendship and Hospitality: Some Conceptual Preliminaries." *Journal of International Political Theory* 5, no. 1 (2009): 1–21.

Shapiro, M. "The Events of Discourse and the Ethics of Global Hospitality." *Millennium: Journal of International Relations* 27 (1998): 696–713.

Background

The following is a list of important contributions to fields related to, and influential upon, cosmopolitan thought.

Global justice

There is a quickly growing literature on the topic of global justice, much of which is taken up with the debate about justice between cosmopolitans and their statist and nationalist critics. Below is a list of important collections and survey articles from the field.

Amstutz, Mark. *International Ethics: Concepts, Theories, and Cases in Global Politics*. Lanham, MD: Rowman & Littlefield, 2008.

Beitz, Charles R. "Recent International Thought." *International Journal* 43 (1988): 183–204.

—— "International Liberalism and Distributive Justice: A Survey of Recent Thought." *World Politics* 52, no. 2 (1999): 269–96.

Booth, Ken, Timothy Dunne, and Michael Cox, eds. *How Might We Live? Global Ethics in a New Century?* Cambridge: Cambridge University Press, 2001.

Brock, Gillian, and Darrel Moellendorf, eds. *Current Debates in Global Justice*. Berlin: Springer, 2005.

Brown, Chris. *International Relations Theory: New Normative Approaches*. Hemel Hempstead: Harvester Wheatsheaf, 1992.

—— "Review Article: Theories of International Justice." *British Journal of Political Science* 27 (1997): 273–97.

Campbell, D., and M. Shapiro, eds. *Moral Spaces: Rethinking Ethics and World Politics*. Minneapolis: University of Minnesota Press, 1999.

Caney, Simon. "International Distributive Justice: A Review." *Political Studies Journal* 49 (2001): 974–89.

De Greiff, Pablo, and Ciaran Cronin, eds. *Global Justice and Transnational Politics: Essays on the Moral and Political Challenges of Globalization*. Cambridge, MA: MIT Press, 2002.

Dower, Nigel. *World Ethics: The New Agenda*. Edinburgh: Edinburgh University Press, 2006.

Horton, Keith, and Haig Patapan, eds. *Globalisation and Equality*. London: Routledge, 2004.

Jordaan, Eduard. "Dialogic Cosmopolitanism and Global Justice." *International Studies Review*, 11, no. 4 (2009): 736–48.

Mandle, Jon. *Global Justice*. Cambridge: Polity Press, 2006.

Mapel, David R., and Terry Nardin, eds. *International Society: Diverse Ethical Perspectives*. Princeton, NJ: Princeton University Press, 1998.

—— , eds. *Traditions of International Ethics*. Cambridge: Cambridge University Press, 1992.

Pogge, Thomas W., ed. *Global Justice*. Malden, MA: Blackwell, 2001.

Pogge, Thomas W., and Darrel Moellendorf, eds. *Global Justice: Seminal Essays*. St. Paul: Paragon House, 2008.

Shapcott, Richard. *International Ethics: A Critical Introduction*. Cambridge: Polity Press, 2010.

Shapiro, Ian, and Lea Brilmayer, eds. *Global Justice*. New York: New York University Press, 1999.

Tonnevelt, R., and G. Verschraegen, eds. *Between Cosmopolitan Ideals and State Sovereignty: Studies in Global Justice*. Basingstoke: Palgrave, 2006.

International relations

International Relations as a discipline in political science has a long pedigree. However, IR theorists have only recently turned their attention to the broadly normative questions addressed by cosmopolitanism.

Beardsworth, Richard. *Cosmopolitanism and International Relations*. Cambridge: Polity Press, 2010.

—— "Cosmopolitanism and Realism: Towards a Theoretical Convergence." *Millennium: Journal of International Relations* 38, no. 1 (2008).

Bull, Hedley. *The Anarchical Society*. London: Macmillan, 1977.

Clarks, I., and I. Neumann, eds. *Classical Theories of International Relations*. Houndsmill: Macmillan, 1996.

Frost, Mervyn. *Towards a Normative Theory of International Relations*. Cambridge: Cambridge University Press, 1986.

Harrison, Ewan. "Waltz, Kant and Systematic Approaches to International Relations." *Review of International Studies* 28 (2002): 143–62.

Hinsley, F. H. *Power and the Pursuit of Peace: Theory and Practice in the History of Relations between States*. Cambridge: Cambridge University Press, 1963.

Holsti, Kalvei. *Peace and War: Armed Conflicts and International Order*. Cambridge: Cambridge University Press, 1992.

Huntingdon, Samuel. *The Clash of Civilizations and the Remaking of the World Order*. New York: Simon and Schuster, 1996.

Hurrell, Andrew. *On Global Order: Power, Values and the Constitution of International Society*. Oxford: Oxford University Press, 2007.

Jackson, Robert. *The Global Covenant: Human Conduct in a World of States*. Oxford: Oxford University Press, 2000.

Linklater, Andrew. *Men and Citizens in the Theory of International Relations*. 2nd edn. Basingstoke: Macmillan, 1990.

Shapcott, Richard. "IR as Practical Philosophy: Defining a Classical Approach." *British Journal of Politics and International Relations* 6, no. 3 (2004): 271–91.

—— *Justice: Community and Dialogue in International Relations*. Cambridge: Cambridge University Press, 2001.

Thomas, Scott. *The Global Resurgence of Religion and the Transformation of International Relations*. New York: Palgrave, 2005.

Weber, Martin. "Keeping It Real? Kant and Systematic Approaches to IR – a Response to Harrison." *Review of International Studies* 29 (2003): 145–50.

Wight, Martin. "An Anatomy of International Thought." *Review of International Studies* 13 (1987).

—— *International Theory: The Three Traditions*, ed. G. Wight and A. Roberts. Leicester: Leicester University Press, 1991.

Globalization

There is a huge debate about the historical and contemporary extent of globalization and what it means for politics, economics, culture, and so on. Below is only a small selection of the contributions to this debate which relate to cosmopolitanism.

Albrow, M. *The Global Age*. Stanford: Stanford University Press, 1997.

Beck, Ulrich. *World Risk Society*. Cambridge: Polity Press, 1999.

Brown, Garrett Wallace. "Globalization is What We Make of It: Contemporary Globalization Theory and the Future Construction of Global Interconnection." *Political Studies Review* 6, no. 1 (2007): 42–53.

Held, David, "Cosmopolitanism: Globalization Tamed?" *Review of International Studies* 29 (2003): 465–80.

Held, David, and A. McGrew. *Globalization/Anti-Globalization*. Cambridge: Polity Press, 2002.

Held, David, and A. McGrew, eds. *Globalization Theory: Approaches and Controversies*. Cambridge: Polity Press, 2007.

Held, David, A. McGrew, D. Goldblatt, and J. Perraton. *Global Transformations: Politics, Economics, and Culture*. Cambridge: Polity Press, 1999.

Giddins, Anthony. *Consequences of Modernity*. Cambridge: Polity Press, 1990.

Yunker, James. *Political Globalization: A New Vision of Federal World Government*. Plymouth: University Press of America, 2007.

Index